International Handbooks on Information Systems

Series Editors

Peter Bernus, Jacek Błażewicz, Günter J. Schmidt, Michael J. Shaw

For further volumes:
http://www.springer.com/series/3795

Titles in the Series

M. Shaw, R. Blanning, T. Strader and A. Whinston (Eds.)
Handbook on Electronic Commerce
ISBN 978-3-540-65882-1

J. Błażewicz, K. Ecker, B. Plateau and D. Trystram (Eds.)
Handbook on Parallel and Distributed Processing
ISBN 978-3-540-66441-3

H.H. Adelsberger, Kinshuk, J.M. Pawlowski and D. Sampson (Eds.)
Handbook on Information Technologies for Education and Training
ISBN 978-3-540-74154-1, 2nd Edition

C.W. Holsapple (Ed.)
Handbook on Knowledge Management 1 Knowledge Matters
ISBN 978-3-540-43527-3
Handbook on Knowledge Management 2 Knowledge Directions
ISBN 978-3-540-43848-9

J. Błażewicz, W. Kubiak, I. Morzy and M. Rusinkiewicz (Eds.)
Handbook on Data Management in Information Systems
ISBN 978-3-540-43893-9

P. Bernus, P. Nemes and G. Schmidt (Eds.)
Handbook on Enterprise Architecture
ISBN 978-3-540-00343-4

S. Staab and R. Studer (Eds.)
Handbook on Ontologies
ISBN 978-3-540-70999-2, 2nd Edition

S.O. Kimbrough and D.J. Wu (Eds.)
Formal Modelling in Electronic Commerce
ISBN 978-3-540-21431-1

P. Bernus, K. Merlins and G. Schmidt (Eds.)
Handbook on Architectures of Information Systems
ISBN 978-3-540-25472-0, 2nd Edition

S. Kirn, O. Herzog, P. Lockemann and O. Spaniol (Eds.)
Multiagent Engineering
ISBN 978-3-540-31406-6

J. Błażewicz, K. Ecker, E. Pesch, G. Schmidt and J. Weglarz (Eds.)
Handbook on Scheduling
ISBN 978-3-540-28046-0

F. Burstein and C.W. Holsapple (Eds.)
Handbook on Decision Support Systems 1
ISBN 978-3-540-48712-8

F. Burstein and C.W. Holsapple (Eds.)
Handbook on Decision Support Systems 2
ISBN 978-3-540-48715-9

D. Seese, Ch. Weinhardt and F. Schlottmann (Eds.)
Handbook on Information Technology in Finance
ISBN 978-3-540-49486-7

T.C. Edwin Cheng and Tsan-Ming Choi (Eds.)
Innovative Quick Response Programs in Logistics and Supply Chain Management
ISBN 978-3-642-04312-3

J. vom Brocke and M. Rosemann (Eds.)
Handbook on Business Process Management 1
ISBN 978-3-642-00415-5

J. vom Brocke and M. Rosemann (Eds.)
Handbook on Business Process Management 2
ISBN 978-3-642-01981-4

Jan vom Brocke • Michael Rosemann
Editors

Handbook on Business Process Management 1

Introduction, Methods, and Information Systems

Springer

Editors

Prof. Dr. Jan vom Brocke
University of Liechtenstein
Institute of Information Systems
Fürst-Franz-Josef-Strasse 21
9420 Vaduz
Principality of Liechtenstein
jan.vom.brocke@uni.li

Prof. Dr. Michael Rosemann
Queensland University of Technology
Faculty of Science and Technology
126 Margaret Street
Brisbane Qld 4000
Australia
m.rosemann@qut.edu.au

ISBN 978-3-642-26455-9 ISBN 978-3-642-00416-2 (eBook)
DOI 10.1007/978-3-642-00416-2
Springer Heidelberg Dordrecht London New York

Cover design: WMXDesign GmbH, Heidelberg, Germany

Printed on acid-free paper

Springer is part of Springer Science+Business Media (www.springer.com)

to my wonderful wife Christina

from Jan

to Louise, Noah and Sophie – with love

from Michael

Foreword

Business Process Management (BPM) has emerged as a comprehensive consolidation of disciplines sharing the belief that a process-centered approach leads to substantial improvements in both performance and compliance of a system. Apart from productivity gains, BPM has the power to innovate and continuously transform businesses and entire cross-organizational value chains. The paradigm of "process thinking" is by no means an invention of the last two decades but had already been postulated by early economists such as Adam Smith or engineers such as Frederick Taylor.

A wide uptake of the process paradigm began at an early stage in the manufacturing sector, either as a central principle in planning approaches such as MRP II or as a factory layout principle. Yet, it took an amazingly long period of time before the service industries actually recognized the significance of processes as an important organizational variable. The ever increasing pressure in the ultimate journey for corporate excellence and innovation went along with the conception of a "process" as a unit of analysis and increasingly appeared in various disciplines.

As part of quality management, the critical role of process quality led to a plethora of process analysis techniques that culminated in the rigorous set of Six Sigma methods. In the information technology discipline, the process became an integral part of Enterprise Architectures and conceptual modeling frameworks. Processes became a "first class citizen" in process-aware software solutions and, in particular, in dedicated BPM-systems, formerly known as workflow management systems. Reference models such as ITIL or SCOR postulated the idea of best (process) practices, and the accounting discipline started to consider processes as a controlling object (Activity-based Costing). Universities are now slowly starting to build Business Process Management courses into their curricula, while positions such as business process analysts or chief process officers are increasingly appearing in organizational charts.

However, while the role of processes has been widely recognized, an all-encompassing discipline promoting the importance of process and providing integrated BPM methodologies has been lacking for a long time. This may be a major reason why process thinking is still not as common as cost awareness, employee focus, or ethical considerations.

BPM is now proposed as the spanning discipline that largely integrates and completes what previous disciplines have achieved. As such, it consolidates how to best manage the (re-)design of individual business processes and how to develop a foundational Business Process Management capability in organizations catering for a variety of purposes and contexts.

The high demand for BPM has encouraged a number of authors to contribute and capture different facets in the form of textbooks. Despite a substantial list of references, the BPM community is still short of a publication that provides a consolidated understanding of the true scope and contents of a comprehensively defined Business Process Management.

It has been our motivation to fill the gap for a point of reference that reflects the holistic nature of BPM without compromising the detail. In order to structure this Handbook, we defined BPM as consisting of six core factors, i.e., Strategic Alignment, Governance, Methods, Information Systems, People, and Culture. These six factors had been derived as part of a multiyear global research study on the essential factors of BPM maturity.

We now present a Handbook that covers these six factors in two volumes comprising more than 1,500 pages from over 100 authors including the world's leading experts in the field. Different approaches of BPM are presented reflecting the diversity of the field. At the same time, we tried to provide some guidance, i.e., by means of the six core elements, to make it easy to open up the various facets of BPM according to individual preferences. We give further comment on that in the "how to read this book" section.

Both volumes together reflect the scope of BPM. Each volume has been organized to have its own focus. The first volume includes the introduction to BPM and concentrates on its Methods and Process-aware Information Systems. The second volume captures in three sections: Strategic Alignment, Governance, and People, and Culture. Both volumes combine the latest outcomes of high standing BPM research with the practical experiences gained in global BPM projects.

This first volume is clustered in three sections.

1. A set of five introductory chapters provides an overview about the current understanding of the aims, boundaries, and essence of BPM. We are particularly proud that we were able to secure the contributions of the global BPM thought leaders for this critical section.
2. The second section is dedicated to the heavily researched area of BPM Methods covering, in particular, process lifecycle methods such as Six Sigma and the essential role of process modeling in 12 chapters. Further, complementary chapters discuss process simulation, process variant management, and BPM tool selection.
3. The third section covers Process-aware Information Systems and elaborates in nine chapters on the foundational role of workflow management, the agility that

results from service-enabled business processes and the new potential related to the uptake of recommender systems or collaborative networking tools.

We are very grateful to the outstanding, carefully crafted, and responsibly revised contributions of the authors of this Handbook. All contributions have undergone a rigorous review process, involving two independent experts in two to three rounds of review. The unconditional commitment to a high quality Handbook required, unfortunately, in some cases, rejections or substantial revisions. In any case, all authors have been very responsive in the way they addressed the requested changes. We are very much aware of the sum of the work that went into this book and cannot appropriately express our gratitude in the brevity of such a foreword.

While producing this Handbook, the authors' enthusiasm was truly interrupted as we in the community were confronted with and saddened by the tragic loss of two of the most inspirational BPM thought leaders the world has seen. Michael Hammer, founder of the Business Process Reengineering discipline and maybe the most successful promoter of the process paradigm passed away in September 2008. Shortly after, Geary A. Rummler, a pioneer in terms of the role of business process as part of the corporate search for organizational performance died in October 2008. We are honored that this Handbook features some of the last inspirations of these two admirable individuals; we also recognize that the BPM community will be a poorer place without them.

A special expression of our gratefulness goes to Karin-Theresia Federl and Christian Sonnenberg, Institute of Information Systems, University Liechtenstein, who brought order and discipline to the myriad of activities that were required as part of the compilation of this Handbook. We hope that this Handbook on Business Process Management will provide a much appreciated, sustainable summary of the state-of-the-art of this truly exciting discipline and that it will have the much desired positive impact for its future development and uptake.

Jan vom Brocke & Michael Rosemann, June 2010
Vaduz, Liechtenstein, and Brisbane, Australia

How to Read this Handbook

This book brings together contributions from BPM experts worldwide. It incorporates a rich set of viewpoints all leading towards an holistic picture of BPM. Compiling this Handbook, we did not intend to force all authors to go under one unique doctrine. On the contrary, we felt that it is rather the richness of approaches and viewpoints covered that makes this book a unique contribution. While keeping the original nature of each piece we provide support in navigating through the various chapters.

- *BPM Core Elements:* We identified six core elements of BPM that all authors are using as a frame to position their contribution. You will find an introductory chapter in volume 1 of this Handbook explaining these elements in detail.
- *BPM Cross-References:* We asked each author to thoroughly read corresponding chapters and to include cross-references to related sections of the BPM Handbook. In addition, further cross-references have been included by the editors.
- *BPM Index*: Both volumes have a detailed index. In order to support a maximum of integration in each volume, also the keywords of the other volume are incorporated.
- *BPM Who-is-Who:* We added an extended author index to each volume serving as a who-is-who. This section illustrates the individual background of each author that might be helpful in contextualizing the various contributions to the BPM Handbook.

We very much hope these mechanisms might help you in choosing the very contributions of the BPM Handbook most suitable for your individual interest.

Contents

Contributors

Gustav Aagesen Trondheim, Norway, gustav.aagesen@idi.ntnu.no

Wil M.P. van der Aalst Eindhoven, The Netherlands, w.p.v.d.aalst@tue.nl

Michael Adams Brisbane, Australia, mj.adams@qut.edu.au

Alistair Barros Brisbane, Australia, alistair.barros@sap.com

Thomas Bauer Ulm, Germany, tb.bauer@daimler.com

Jörg Becker Münster, Germany, becker@ercis.uni-muenster.de

Jim Champy Boston, MA, USA, Jim.Champy@ps.net

Sue Conger Irving, TX, USA, sconger@gsm.udallas.edu

Fred A. Cummins Pinckney, MI, USA, fred.cummins@hp.com

Thomas H. Davenport Wellesley, MA, USA, tdavenport@babson.edu

Islay Davies Brisbane, Australia, Islay.davies@ssa.qld.gov.au

Alexander Dreiling Brisbane, Australia, alexander.dreiling@sap.com

Marlon Dumas Tartu, Estonia, marlon.dumas@ut.ee

Thorsten Falk Münster, Germany, falk@picture-gmbh.de

Christian Flender Brisbane, Australia, christian.flender@qut.edu.au

Thomas Gulledge Alexandria, VA, USA, gulledge@eiisolutions.net

Alena Hallerbach Ulm, Germany, alena.hallerbach@daimler.com

Michael Hammer Cambridge, MA, USA

Paul Harmon San Francisco, CA, USA, pharmon@bptrends.com

Thomas Hettel Brisbane, Australia, thomas.hettel@qut.edu.au

Birgit Hofreiter Vaduz, Principality of Liechtenstein, birgit.hofreiter@uni.li

Christian Huemer Vienna, Austria, huemer@big.tuwien.ac.at

Florian Johannsen Regensburg, Germany, florian.johannsen@wiwi.uni-regensburg.de

Dimka Karastoyanova Stuttgart, Germany, dimka.karastoyanova@iaas.uni-stuttgart.de

Sandy Kemsley Toronto, Canada, sandy@kemsleydesign.com

Thomas Kohlborn Brisbane, Australia, t.kohlborn@qut.edu.au

Agnes Koschmider Karlsruhe, Germany, agnes.koschmider@kit.edu

John Krogstie Trondheim, Norway, krogstie@idi.ntnu.no

Akhil Kumar University Park, PA, USA, akhilkumar@psu.edu

Susanne Leist Regensburg, Germany, susanne.leist@wiwi.uni-regensburg.de

Frank Leymann Stuttgart, Germany, eymann@iaas.uni-stuttgart.de

Philipp Liegl Vienna, Austria, liegl@big.tuwien.ac.at

Mikael Lind Gothenburg, Sweden, Mikael.Lind@hb.se

Jan Mendling Berlin, Germany, jan.mendling@wiwi.hu-berlin.de

Joyce Nakatumba Eindhoven, The Netherlands, jnakatum@tue.nl

Andreas Oberweis Karlsruhe, Germany, andreas.oberweis@kit.edu

Chun Ouyang Brisbane, Australia, c.ouyang@qut.edu.au

Michael P. Papazoglou Tilburg, The Netherlands, mikep@uvt.nl

Daniel Pfeiffer Münster, Germany, mail@daniel-pfeiffer.de

Artem Polyvyanyy Potsdam, Germany, artem.polyvyanyy@hpi.uni-potsdam.de

Michael Räckers Münster, Germany, michael.raeckers@ercis.uni-muenster.de

Alan J. Ramias Chandler, AZ, USA, Aramias@ThePDLab.com

Jan Recker Brisbane, Australia, j.recker@qut.edu.au

Micheal Reeves Brisbane, Australia, Micheal.Reeves@justice.qld.gov.au

Manfred Reichert Ulm, Germany, manfred.reichert@uni-ulm.de

Hajo A. Reijers Eindhoven, The Netherlands, h.a.reijers@tue.nl

Michael Rosemann Brisbane, Australia, m.rosemann@qut.edu.au

Anne Rozinat Eindhoven, The Netherlands, a.rozinat@tue.nl

Geary A. Rummler Eindhoven Tucson, AZ, USA

Nick Russell Eindhoven, The Netherlands, n.c.russell@tue.nl

Rainer Schuster Vienna, Austria, Schuster@ec.tuwien.ac.at

Ulf Seigerroth Gothenburg, Sweden, ulf.seigerroth@jth.hj.se

Sergey Smirnov Potsdam, Germany, sergey.smirnov@hpi.uni-potsdam.de

Arthur H.M. ter Hofstede Brisbane, Australia, arthur@yawlfoundation.org

Moe ThandarWynn Brisbane, Australia, m.wynn@qut.edu.au

Jan vom Brocke Vaduz, Principality of Liechtenstein, jan.vom.brocke@uni.li

Jianrui Wang University Park, PA, USA, JerryWang@psu.edu

Mathias Weske Potsdam, Germany, mathias.weske@hpi.uni-potsdam.de

Marco Zapletal Vienna, Austria, marco@ec.tuwien.ac.at

Gregor Zellner Regensburg, Germany, gregor.zellner@wiwi.uni-regensburg.de

Part I
Introduction

The past 20 years have witnessed an increasing interest in the domain of Business Process Management (BPM) by an ever-growing community of managers, end users, analysts, consultants, vendors, and academics. This is visible in a substantial body of knowledge, a plethora of methodologies, tools, techniques, and an expanding scope of its boundaries. While the high demand for BPM and the maturing BPM capabilities unfold, the challenge develops fast to provide concise and widely accepted definitions, taxonomies, and overall frameworks for Business Process Management.

It has been one of the great honors for us that – as part of the production of this Handbook – we were able to attract the world's leading minds from within the BPM community. This introductory section features the contemporary views of global thought leaders who have shaped the understanding, development, and uptake of Business Process Management like no others.

In the opening chapter, Michael Hammer seeks to answer the essential question, "What is Business Process Management"? In his unique style, he characterizes BPM as the first fundamental set of new ideas on organizational performance since the Industrial Revolution. He briefly discusses the origins of BPM, the process management cycle, benefits, enablers, and necessary capabilities. All these lead to an extended set of BPM principles and the role of Enterprise Process Models.

In the following chapter, Thomas Davenport correlates Business Process Management and Knowledge Management to explore the challenges of process design for knowledge-intensive processes. In this context, he discusses the creation, distribution, and application of knowledge. Davenport contrasts the processes and the practice in knowledge work and lists different process interventions. In summary, the chapter raises the awareness for the challenges of BPM that emerge once the transactional processes are covered.

Critics often picture BPM as a hyped concept with a limited lifespan. However, Paul Harmon argues convincingly in the third chapter that BPM is in fact the culmination of a series of mature concepts that all share a passion for process. Harmon outlines three process traditions including Quality Management, Business Management, and Information Technology. Briefly, he discusses the key concepts and outcomes, and reflects on the thought leaders for each of the three traditions before expressing his views on the "today and tomorrow" of BPM. His differentiation in enterprise level and process level is picked up in a number of contributions in this Handbook.

One of the earliest contributors to the field of process-based management, Geary Rummler, provides his thoughts on the structure of work. This chapter, co-authored with Alan Ramias, focuses on the business layer within an Enterprise Architecture. The authors discuss the importance of a sound understanding of value creation and a corresponding management system. Rummler and Ramias stress that Business (Process) Architectures cannot stand in isolation but have to be linked to other architectural frameworks in order to form a complete Value Creation Architecture.

The fifth and final chapter by Michael Rosemann and Jan vom Brocke introduces the underlying structure for both volumes of this BPM Handbook. In order to provide a framework for a joint understanding of Business Process Management, six complementary core factors of Business Process Management are presented. These six factors need to be addressed as part of enterprise-wide, sustainable BPM initiatives. This chapter briefly describes the core essence of these factors that are explored in much more detail in the different sections of this Handbook.

What is Business Process Management?

Michael Hammer†

Abstract Googling the term "Business Process Management" in May 2008 yields some 6.4 million hits, the great majority of which (based on sampling) seem to concern the so-called BPM software systems. This is ironic and unfortunate, because in fact IT in general, and such BPM systems in particular, is at most a peripheral aspect of Business Process Management. In fact, Business Process Management (BPM) is a comprehensive system for managing and transforming organizational operations, based on what is arguably the first set of new ideas about organizational performance since the Industrial Revolution.

1 The Origins of BPM

BPM has two primary intellectual antecedents. The first is the work of Shewhart and Deming (Shewhart 1986; Deming 1953) on statistical process control, which led to the modern quality movement and its contemporary avatar, Six Sigma. This work sought to reduce variation in the performance of work by carefully measuring outcomes and using statistical techniques to isolate the "root causes" of performance problems – causes that could then be addressed. Much more important than the details of upper and lower control limits or the myriad of other analytic tools that are part of quality's armamentarium are the conceptual principles that underlie this work: the core assumption that operations are of critical importance and deserve serious attention and management; the use of performance metrics to determine whether work is being performed satisfactorily or not; the focus on hard data rather than opinion to isolate the root causes of performance difficulties; the concept of blaming the process not the people, that performance shortcomings are rooted in objective problems that can be identified and dealt with; and the notion

M. Hammer
Hammer and Company, Inc., One Cambridge Center, Cambridge, MA 02141, USA

J. vom Brocke and M. Rosemann (eds.), *Handbook on Business Process Management 1*,
International Handbooks on Information Systems,
DOI 10.1007/978-3-642-00416-2_1, © Springer-Verlag Berlin Heidelberg 2010

of never-ending improvement, that solving one set of problems merely buys an organization a ticket to solve the next round.

The quality approach suffered from two limitations, however. The first was its definition of process as essentially any sequence of work activities. With this perspective, an organization would have hundreds or even thousands of processes, from putting a parts box on a shelf to checking customer credit status, and the machinery of quality improvement could be applied to any and all of these. Focusing on such narrow-bore processes, however, is unlikely to have strategic significance for the enterprise as a whole; on the other hand, it is likely to result in a massive number of small-scale projects that can be difficult to manage in a coherent fashion. Even more seriously, the quality school took as its goal the elimination of variation and the achievement of consistent performance. However, consistent is not a synonym for good. A process can operate consistently, without execution flaws, and still not achieve the level of performance required by customers and the enterprise.

The other primary antecedent of BPM, my own work on Business Process Reengineering (Hammer 1990; Hammer and Champy 1993), had complementary strengths and weaknesses. On the one hand, at least in its early days, reengineering was positioned as an episodic rather than an ongoing effort; it lacked the continuous dimension of quality improvement. It also did not have as disciplined an approach to metrics. On the other hand, it brought two new wrinkles to the process world. The first was its refined definition of process: end-to-end work across an enterprise that creates customer value. Here, putting a box on a shelf would not qualify as a meaningful process; it would merely be a small part of an enterprise process such as order fulfillment or procurement. Addressing large-scale, truly end-to-end processes means focusing on high-leverage aspects of the organization's operations and so leads to far greater results and impacts. In particular, by dealing with processes that cross functional boundaries, reengineering was able to attack the evils of fragmentation: the delays, nonvalue-adding overhead, errors, and complexity that inevitably result when work transcends different organizations that have different priorities, different information sources, and different metrics. The other new theme introduced by reengineering was a focus on process design as opposed to process execution. The design of a process, the way in which its constituent tasks are woven together into a whole, was not of much concern to the founders of the quality school; they made a tacit assumption that process designs were sound, and that performance difficulties resulted from defects in execution. Reengineering recognized that the design of a process in fact created an envelope for its performance, that a process could not perform on a sustained basis better than its design would allow. Should performance requirements exceed what the design was capable of, the old design would have to be discarded and a new one substituted in its place.

2 The Process Management Cycle

Over the last decade, these two approaches to process performance improvement have gradually merged, yielding modern Business Process Management – an integrated system for managing business performance by managing end-to-end

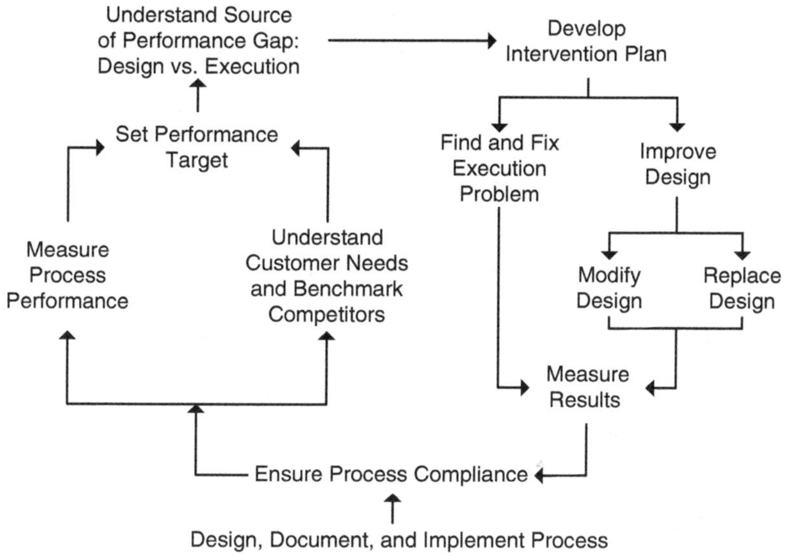

Fig. 1 The essential process management cycle

business processes. Figure 1 depicts the essential process management cycle. It begins at the bottom, with the creation of a formal process. This is not a minor, purely formal step. Many organizations find that certain aspects of their operations are characterized by wild variation, because they lack any well-defined end-to-end process whatsoever. This is particularly true of low-volume, creative processes such as product development or customer relationship management. In essence, they treat each situation as a one-off, with heroics and improvisation substituting for the discipline of a well-defined process. Such heroics are of course unreliable and unsustainable.

Once a process is in place, it needs to be managed on an ongoing basis. Its performance, in terms of critical metrics that relate to customer needs and company requirements, needs to be compared to the targets for these metrics. Such targets can be based on customer expectations, competitor benchmarks, enterprise needs, and other sources. If performance does not meet targets, the reason for this shortcoming must be determined. Broadly speaking, processes fail to meet performance requirements either because of faulty *design* or faulty *execution*; which one is the culprit can generally be determined by examining the pattern of performance inadequacy. (Pervasive performance shortcomings generally indicate a design flaw; occasional ones are usually the result of execution difficulties.) If the fault lies in execution, then the particular root cause (such as inadequate training, or insufficient resources, or faulty equipment, or any of a host of other possibilities) must be determined. Doing so is a challenging undertaking, because of the large number of possible root causes; as a rule, however, once the root cause has been found, it is easy to fix. The opposite is true of design problems: they are easy to find (being indicated by consistently inadequate performance) but hard to fix (requiring a wholesale rethinking of the structure of the process). Once the appropriate intervention has been chosen and implemented, the results are assessed, and the entire cycle begins again.

This cycle is derived from Deming's PDCA cycle (Plan Do Check Act) (Deming 1986), with the addition of the attention to process design. Although this picture is quite simple, it represents a revolutionary departure for how enterprises are managed. It is based on the premise that the way to manage an organization's performance is not by trial and error, not by pushing people harder, and not through financial manipulation, but through the deliberate management of the end-to-end business processes through which all customer value is created. Indeed, BPM is a customer-centered approach to organizational management. Customers neither know nor care about the many issues that typically are at the center of most executives' attention: strategies, organizational designs, capital structures, succession plans, and all the rest. Customers care about one thing and one thing only: results. Such results are not acts of God or the consequence of managerial genius; they are the outputs of business processes, of sequences of activities working together. Customers, results, and processes form an iron triangle; an organization cannot be serious about anyone without being equally serious about the other two.

To illustrate the process management cycle in action, consider the claims handling process at an auto insurance company. The old process consisted of the claimant reporting an accident to an agent, who passed it on to a customer service representative at the insurer, who passed it on to a claims manager, who assigned it with a batch of other claims to an adjustor, who then contacted the claimant and scheduled a time to inspect the vehicle. Because of the handoffs in this process, and the associated inevitable misunderstandings, it typically took 7–10 days before the adjustor arrived to see the vehicle. While this was no worse than others in the industry, the insurer's CEO recognized that this represented an opportunity to improve customer satisfaction at a "moment of truth," and insisted that this cycle time be reduced to 9 hours. No amount of productivity improvement in the individual activities would have approached this target, since the total actual work time was very little – the problem was in the process, not in the tasks. Accordingly, the company created a completely new process, in which claimants called a toll-free phone number and were connected directly to an adjustor, who took responsibility for the case and dispatched a teammate driving a mobile claims van in the field to the vehicle; upon arriving, the teammate would not only estimate the amount of damage but try to settle the claim on the spot. This new process was both much more convenient for customers and less expensive for the company, and was key to the company increasing revenue by 130% while increasing headcount by only 5%.

However, this was the beginning, not the end, for the process. Just having a good design does not guarantee continued good results, because problems are inevitable in the real world. Computers break, people do not absorb their training, data gets corrupted, and so on and so forth, and as a result a process does not achieve the performance of which it is capable. The company used process management to monitor the performance of the process and recognize and correct such performance problems. It also stayed alert to opportunities to modify the process design to make it perform even better. At one point, the company realized that the process as designed was not necessarily sending the most appropriate adjustor to the scene of the accident but just the next available one; a change to the design was made to address this. Of late, the company's management has gone further. They recognized flaws in the process design – for instance, that it required adjustors to make damage estimates "at midnight in the rain". Accordingly, they have come up with an even newer process, in which the claimant brings the damaged car to a company facility and picks up a loaner car; the adjustor estimates the damage at this facility and then arranges for the repair to be done by a garage. When the car is fixed, the claimant comes back and exchanges the loaner for his own car. This is much easier for the customer, and much more accurate and less costly for the company.

3 The Payoffs of Process Management

Through process management, an enterprise can create high-performance processes, which operate with much lower costs, faster speeds, greater accuracy, reduced assets, and enhanced flexibility. By focusing on and designing end-to-end processes that transcend organizational boundaries, companies can drive out the nonvalue-adding overhead that accumulates at these boundaries. Through process management, an enterprise can assure that its processes deliver on their promise and operate consistently at the level of which they are capable. Through process management, an enterprise can determine when a process no longer meets its needs and those of its customers and so needs to be replaced.

These operational benefits of consistency, cost, speed, quality, and service translate into lower operating costs and improved customer satisfaction, which in turn drive improved enterprise performance. Process management also offers a variety of strategic benefits. For one, process management enables companies to respond better to periods of rapid change (such as ours). Conventional organizations often do not even recognize that change is happening until it is reflected in financial performance, by which time it is too late; even should they recognize that change has occurred, they have no mechanism for responding to it in a disciplined fashion. Under a process management regime, by contrast, change is reflected in the decline of operational performance metrics, which are noted by the process management system; the design of the process is then the tool through which the organization can respond to this change. Process management also provides an umbrella for a wide range of other performance improvement initiatives, from globalization and merger integration to ERP implementation and e-business. Too many enterprises treat each of these phenomena as independent, which leads to a proliferation of uncoordinated and conflicting change initiatives. In fact, they are all either mechanisms for supporting high-performance processes or goals that can be achieved through them. Linking all of a company's improvement efforts under the common umbrella of process management, and managing them in an integrated fashion, leverages a wide range of tools and deploys the right tool to the right problem.

Thousands of organizations, large and small, private and public, are reaping extraordinary benefits by managing their end-to-end business processes. A handful of recent examples:

- A consumer goods manufacturer redesigned its product deployment process, by means of which it manufactures goods and delivers them to its distribution centers; inventory was reduced by 25% while out-of-stock situations declined 50%.
- A computer maker created a new product development process, which reduced time to market by 75%, reduced development costs by 45%, and increased customer satisfaction with new products by 25%.
- A capital goods manufacturer increased by 500% the accuracy of the availability dates on new products that it gave customers and reduced its supply chain costs by up to 50%.
- A health insurer created a new process for engaging with its customers and reduced costs by hundreds of millions of dollars while improving customer satisfaction.

Something to note in these and many other cases is the simultaneous achievement of apparently incompatible goals: reducing inventory, say, while also reducing out-of-stocks. Traditional organizations view these as conflicting goals and trade one off against another; process-managed organizations recognize that they can be improved by creating a new process design.

4 The Enablers of Process

Despite its elegance and power, many organizations have experienced difficulties implementing processes and process management. For instance, an electronics company designed a new product development process that was based on cross-functional product teams, but they were unable to successfully install it and get it operating. The reason, as they put it, is that "you can't overlay high performance processes on a functional organization". Traditional organizations and their systems are unfriendly to processes, and unless these are realigned to support processes, the effort will fail.

There are five critical enablers for a high-performance process; without them, a process will be unable to operate on a sustained basis (Hammer 2007).

Process design. This is the most fundamental aspect of a process: the specification of what tasks are to be performed, by whom, when, in what locations, under what circumstances, to what degree of precision, with what information, and the like. The design is the specification of the process; without a design, there is only uncoordinated individual activity and organizational chaos.

Process metrics. Most enterprises use functional performance metrics, which create misalignment, suboptimization, and confusion. Processes need end-to-end metrics that are derived from customer needs and enterprise goals. Targets need to be set in terms of these metrics and performance monitored against them. A balanced set of process metrics (such as cost, speed, and quality) must be deployed, so that improvements in one area do not mask declines in another.

Process performers. People who work in processes need a different set of skills and behaviors from those who work in conventional functions and departments. They need an understanding of the overall process and its goals, the ability to work in teams, and the capacity to manage themselves. Without these characteristics, they will be unable to realize the potential of end-to-end work.

Process infrastructure. Performers need to be supported by IT and HR systems if they are to discharge process responsibilities. Functionally fragmented information systems do not support integrated processes, and conventional HR systems (training, compensation, and career, etc.) reinforce fragmented job perspectives. Integrated systems (such as ERP systems and results-based compensation systems) are needed for integrated processes.

Process owner. In a conventional organization, no one is responsible for an end-to-end process, and so no one will be in a position to manage it on an end-to-end basis (i.e., carry out the process management cycle). An organization serious about its processes must have process owners: senior managers with authority and responsibility for a process across the organization as a whole. They are the ones who perform the work illustrated in Fig. 1.

Having some but not all of these enablers for a process is of little or no value. For instance, a well-designed process targeted at the right metrics will not succeed if performers are not capable of carrying it out or if the systems do not support them in doing so. Implementing a process in effect means putting in place these five enablers. Without them, a process may be able to operate successfully for a short term but will certainly fail in the long run.

5 Organizational Capabilities for Process

The experiences of hundreds of companies show that not all are equally able to install these enablers and so succeed with processes and process management. Some do so effectively, while others do not. The root cause of this discrepancy lies in whether or not an enterprise possesses four critical capabilities that are prerequisites to its summoning the resources, determination, and skills needed to succeed with processes (Hammer 2007).

Leadership. The absolute sine qua non for effective deployment of process management is engaged, knowledgeable, and passionate senior executive leadership of the effort. Introducing processes means introducing enormous change – realigning systems, authority, modes of operation, and more. There is no change that most organizations have experienced that can compare to the disruption that the transition to process brings. Unless a very senior executive makes it his or her personal mission, process will run aground on the shoals of inertia and resistance. Moreover, only a topmost executive can authorize the significant resources and changes that process implementation requires. Without such leadership, the effort is doomed; with it, all other problems can be overcome.

Culture. A Chief Operating Officer once remarked to me, "When one of my people says he doesn't like process, he really means that he doesn't want to share power". Process, with its focus on customers, outcomes, and transcending boundaries is anathema to those who are focused on defending their narrow bit of turf. Process demands that people at all levels of the organization put the customer first, be comfortable working in teams, accept personal responsibility for outcomes, and be willing to accept change. Unless the organization's culture values these principles, processes will just roll off people's backs. If the enterprise culture is not aligned with these values, leadership must change the culture so that it does.

Governance. Moving to process management, and institutionalizing it over the long run, requires a set of governance mechanisms that assign appropriate responsibilities and ensure that processes integrate with one another (and do not turn into a new generation of horizontal silos). In addition to process owners, enterprises need a process office (headed by a Chief Process Officer) that plans and oversees the program as a whole and coordinates process efforts, as well as a Process Council. This is a body consisting of the process owners, the executive leader, and other senior managers, which serves as a strategic oversight body, setting direction and priorities, addressing cross-process issues, and translating enterprise concerns into process issues. These mechanisms need to be put in place to manage the transition to process, but continue on as the essential management superstructure for a process-managed enterprise.

Expertise. Implementing and managing processes is a complex and high stakes endeavor, not for the inexperienced or the amateur. Companies need cadres of people with deep expertise in process design and implementation, metrics, change management, program management, process improvement, and other relevant techniques. These people must have formal methodologies to follow and must be sustained with appropriate career paths and management support. While not an insuperable barrier, many organizations fail to develop and institutionalize this capability, and then unsurprisingly find themselves unable to carry out their ambitious programs.

Organizations without these four capabilities will be unable to make process management work, and must undertake urgent efforts to put them in place. Developing leadership is the most challenging of these; it typically requires the intervention of a catalyst, a passionate advocate of process with the ear of a potential leader, who must patiently familiarize the candidate with the concepts of process and their payoffs. Reshaping culture is not, despite myths to the contrary, impossible, but it does take time and energy. The other two are less difficult, but are often overlooked.

6 The Principles of Process Management

It can be helpful to summarize the concepts of process management in terms of a handful of axiomatic principles, some obvious, some not, that together express its key themes.

All work is process work. Sometimes the assumption is made that the concepts of process and process management only apply to highly structured, transactional work, such as order fulfillment, procurement, customer service, and the like. Nothing could be further from the truth. The virtues of process also adhere to developmental processes, which center on highly creative tasks, such as product development, demand creation, and so on. Process should not be misinterpreted as a synonym for routinization or automation, reducing creative work to simplistic procedures. Process means positioning individual work activities – routine or creative – in the larger context of the other activities with which it combines to create results. Both transactional and development processes are what is known as *core* processes – processes that create value for external customers and so are essential to the business. Organizations also have *enabling* (or support) processes, which create value for internal customers; these include hire to retire, information systems development, and financial reporting. Such processes have customers and create value for them (as must any process, by definition), but those customers are internal. The third category is *governing* processes, the management processes by means of which the company is run (such as strategic planning, risk management, and performance management). (Process management is itself a governing process!) All processes need to be managed as such and so benefit from the power of process management.

Any process is better than no process. Absent a well-defined process design, chaos reigns. Individual heroics, capriciousness, and improvisation rule the day – and results are inconsistent and unsustainable. A well-defined process will at the least deliver predictable, repeatable results, and can serve as the staging ground for improvement.

A good process is better than a bad process. This statement is not as tautological as it seems. It expresses the criticality of process design, that the caliber of a process design is a critical determinant of its performance, and that some processes are better designed than others. If a company is burdened a bad process design, it needs to replace it with a better one.

One process version is better than many. Standardizing processes across all parts of an enterprise presents a single face to customers and suppliers, yields profound economies in support services such as training and IT systems, allows the redeployment of people from one business unit to another, and yields a host of other benefits. These payoffs must be balanced against the intrinsically different needs of different units and their customers, but our bias should be in favor of standardization.

Even a good process must be performed effectively. A good process design is a necessary but insufficient prerequisite for high performance; it needs to be combined with carefully managed execution, so that the capabilities of the design are realized in practice.

Even a good process can be made better. The process owner needs to stay constantly vigilant, looking for opportunities to make modifications to the process design in order to further enhance its performance.

Every good process eventually becomes a bad process. No process stays effective forever in the face of change. Customer needs change, technologies change, competition changes, and what used to be a high level of performance becomes a poor one – and it is time to replace the formerly good process with a new one.

7 The EPM as a Management Tool and BPMS

The foundation of process management is the Enterprise Process Model (EPM). This is a graphical representation of the enterprise's processes (core, enabling, and governing), showing their interconnections and inputs and outputs. Figure 1 is an example of such an EPM, from a large distributor of industrial products. An effective EPM should be simple and clear, fitting on one page, and typically including no more than 5–10 core processes. Such a high-level representation is then decomposed to provide additional detail, breaking each top-level process into a number of subprocesses, which are further decomposed into activities. There is as yet no standard (nor even near-standard) notation or architecture for process representation or for how many levels of detail are appropriate.

The EPM does more than just provide a vocabulary for a process program. It offers something few companies have, a coherent and comprehensible description of the company's operations. It is remarkable to note that conventional representations of an enterprise – the organization chart, the P&L and the balance sheet, the mission and value statements, the product catalog and customer list – say nothing about the actual work of the company and what people do on a regular basis. The EPM provides such an operational perspective on the enterprise and as such should be used as the basis for managing those operations.

In particular, the EPM offers a way of dealing with the projects and programs that constantly changing times raise, since ultimately every business issue must be translated into its impacts on and implications for operating processes. The following is a representative set of such issues that companies have recently needed to address:

- A risk management group has identified areas of high risk to the company. The processes that impact these risks need to be identified and redesigned in ways to help mitigate them.
- A new company has been acquired and there is a need to perform comparisons between the processes of the acquiring company and those of the acquired one, to help produce a roadmap for integrating the two companies by moving from the old processes to the new ones (Fig. 2).

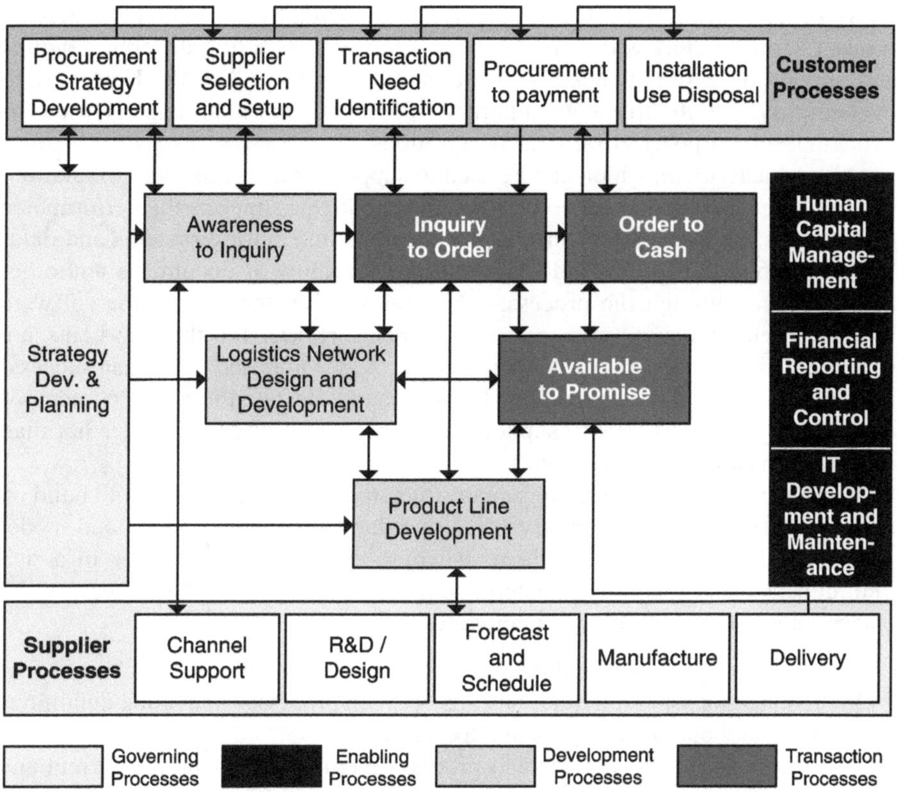

Fig. 2 Example of an enterprise process model (EPM)

- A new corporate strategy or initiative is announced, which entails changing the definitions of some of the company's key performance indicators (KPIs). The company needs to determine those process metrics that are drivers of these KPIs and update them appropriately.
- A change is made to some modules of an enterprise software system, and managers of different processes need to be made aware of the impact of the change on them.
- An activity that is used in several processes is modified in one of them, and these changes need to be reflected in all other occurrences of that activity.
- When a change is made to a business policy, it is necessary to make appropriate corresponding changes to all those processes in which it is embedded.

The EPM needs to be used as an active management tool for situations like these. More than that, companies focused on their processes need automated tools to help them actively manage their processes, for purposes like these and others. Such tools could legitimately be called Business Process Management Systems (BPMS), a term used at the opening of this chapter.

As of this writing, BPMS is a notoriously, broadly, and vaguely defined product area. Vendors with very different offerings, providing different features and supporting different needs, all claim the mantle of BPMS. However, to oversimplify, but slightly, contemporary BPMS software is principally used for two kinds of purposes: to create descriptions of processes (in terms of their constituent activities), which can be used to support process analysis, simulation, and design efforts; and to generate executable code that supports the performance of a process, by automating certain process steps, integrating systems and databases used by the process, and managing the workflow of documents and other forms passing through the process. While (as is often the case in the software industry) vendor claims and market research forecasts for these systems are somewhat exaggerated, they nonetheless do provide value and have been successfully deployed by many companies. Unfortunately, despite the name, contemporary BPM systems do little to support the management of processes (rather than their analysis and implementation).

A software system designed to support true process management would build on the capabilities that contemporary BPMS products provide (to define and model processes), but go far beyond them. It would embed these processes in a rich multidimensional model of the enterprise that captures at least these facets of the enterprise and the relationships among them:

- Definitions of processes and their activities, and their designs
- Interconnections and interrelationships between processes, including definitions of inputs and outputs and mutual expectations
- Metrics, both enterprise KPIs and process-level metrics, including current and target performance levels
- Projects and activities associated with process implementation and improvement
- Business organizations that are engaged in implementing and executing processes
- Process versions and variations
- Information systems that support processes
- Data elements created by, used by, and owned by processes
- Enterprise programs and initiatives and their connections to processes
- Control points and risk factors
- Roles in the organization involved in performing the process, including their organizational position, skill requirements, and decision-making authorities
- Management personnel associated with the process (such as the process owner)
- Enterprise strategies and programs that are impacted by processes.

Such a system would need to know the "semantics" of organizations and of these facets, so that instead of operating as merely a passive repository, it could act as an intelligent model of an enterprise and its processes. As such, it could serve as a powerful tool to support management decision-making and action in a complex, fast-changing environment. Such a model would not be populated by data created by operational systems but by a rich representation of the enterprise. It would be a tool for managing processes and not for executing them.

Some companies are using existing BPMS systems for these purposes, but they report that these tools offer little or no active support for these purposes, other than providing a relational database and a graphical front-end. There are no built-in semantics in contemporary systems that capture the characteristics of organizations and their many dimensions, nor do they have an embedded model of process management.

8 The Frontiers of BPM

Despite its widespread adoption and impressive results, BPM is still in its infancy. Even companies that have implemented it are far from finished and many companies – indeed many industries – have yet really to begin. Unsurprisingly, there are a host of issues with which we have yet to come to grips, issues that relate to truly managing an enterprise around its processes and to the impacts of Business Process Management on people, organizations, and economies. The following is a sampler of such issues, some of which are being actively investigated, some of which define challenges for the future.

Management structure and responsibility. As more power and authority get vested in process owners, other management roles and responsibilities change dramatically. Functional managers become managers of resource pools; business unit heads become agents of customers, representing their needs to process owners. These are radical shifts, and are still being worked out. Some companies are experimenting with moving many standard processes (not just support ones) from multiple business units into what amounts to shared service organizations. Others are outsourcing whole processes. The shape of the process-managed enterprise is still emerging.

IT support. How do developments in new information technologies impact processes and process management? ERP systems (somewhat belatedly) have come to be recognized as process software systems, since their cross-functional architecture enables them to address work on an end-to-end basis. What implications will SOA (service-oriented architecture) have on process design and implementation? How will process management impact data management? For instance, some companies are starting to give process owners responsibilities for master data management.

Interenterprise processes. Most organizations focus on processes that run end-to-end within their companies; however, in many cases, the real ends of these processes reside in different companies altogether. Supply chain processes, for instance, typically begin in the raw material supplier's operations and end with the final customer; product development processes are collaborative and must encompass suppliers' efforts. Some companies have been working on these processes, but we lack models for their governance and management. Who is the process owner? How should benefits be allocated? What are the right metrics?

Standards. Are there standard EPMs for companies in the same industry? Are there standard sets of enabling and governing processes that all companies should deploy? Will we see the emergence of best-in-class process designs for certain widely occurring processes, which many different companies will implement? What would these developments imply for enterprise differentiation?

Processes and strategy. Processes are, on the one hand, the means by which enterprise strategies are realized. On the other, they can also be determinants of such strategies. A company that has a world-class process can deploy it in new markets and in support of new products and services. At the same time, companies may decide that processes that do not offer competitive advantage should conform to industry standards or be outsourced.

Industry structure. How will process management affect the structure of industries? As companies recognize that certain processes represent their core capabilities, while others are peripheral, will we see greater outsourcing of the latter – perhaps to organizations that will provide processes on a service basis? Will customer and supplier organizations intertwine their processes to create what are in effect operational (rather than financial) *keiretsus*?

Beyond these macro questions, even the basic aspects of process management – designing processes, developing metrics, training performers, and all the rest – are far from settled issues. There is much work to be done. But even absent solutions to these challenges, it is clear that process management has moved from the wave of the future to the wave of the present, and that we are indeed in the Age of Process.

References

Deming WE (1953) Statistical techniques in industry. Adv Manage 18(11):8–12
Deming WE (1986) Out of the crisis. MIT Center for Advanced Engineering
Hammer M, Champy J (1993) Reengineering the corporation: A manifesto for business revolution. Harper Collins Publishers
Hammer M (1990) Reengineering work: Don't automate, obliterate. Harv Bus Rev 68:104–112
Hammer M (2007) The process audit. Harv Bus Rev 85:111–123
Shewhart W (1986) Statistical method from the viewpoint of quality control. Dover Publications, NY

Process Management for Knowledge Work

Thomas H. Davenport

Abstract In this chapter, the topic of using process improvement approaches to improve knowledge work is addressed. The effective performance of knowledge work is critical to contemporary sophisticated economies. It is suggested that traditional, engineering-based approaches to knowledge work are incompatible with the autonomy and work approaches of many knowledge workers. Therefore, a variety of alternative process-oriented approaches to knowledge work are described. Emphasis is placed on differentiating among different types of knowledge work and applying process interventions that are more behaviorally sensitive.

1 Introduction

Knowledge workers are the key to innovation and growth in today's organization.[1] They invent products and services, design marketing programs, and create strategies. In sophisticated economies, they are the horses that pull the plow of economic progress. If our companies are going to be more profitable, if our strategies are going to be successful, if our societies and economies are going to become more advanced – it will be because knowledge workers did their work in a more productive and effective manner.

In the early twenty-first century, it is likely that a quarter to a half of the workers in advanced economies are knowledge workers whose primary tasks involve the manipulation of knowledge and information. Even if they are not a majority of all workers, they have the most influence on their companies and economies. They are paid the most, they add the most economic value, and they are the greatest

T.H. Davenport
Babson College, Wellesley, MA, USA
e-mail: tdavenport@babson.edu

[1]This chapter draws from several published sources, including Chaps. 1–3 of Davenport (2005) and Davenport and Iyer (2009).

J. vom Brocke and M. Rosemann (eds.), *Handbook on Business Process Management 1*, International Handbooks on Information Systems,
DOI 10.1007/978-3-642-00416-2_2,

determinant of the worth of their companies. Companies with a high proportion of knowledge workers – let's call them knowledge-intensive – are the fastest-growing and most successful in the US and other leading economies, and have generated most of their growth in the past couple of decades. The market values of many knowledge-intensive companies – which include the market's perception of the value of knowledge and knowledge workers – dwarf their book values, which include only tangible assets (and the ratio of market to book value in US companies has doubled over the past 20 years, suggesting a great acceleration of knowledge asset value). Even in the so-called "industrial" companies, knowledge is increasingly used to differentiate physical goods and to diversify them into product-related services. As James Brian Quinn has pointed out, high proportions of workers in manufacturing firms (roughly 90% in semiconductors, for example) never touch the manufacturing process, but instead provide knowledge-based services such as marketing, distribution, or customer service (Quinn 1992).

It is already apparent that the firms with the highest degree and quality of knowledge work tend to be the fastest-growing and the most profitable ones. Leading IT firms, which are almost exclusively knowledge-based, are among the most profitable organizations in the history of the planet. Pharmaceutical firms not only save peoples' lives with their drug treatments but also tend to have high profit margins. "Growth industries" generally tend to be those with a high proportion of knowledge workers.

Within organizations, knowledge workers tend to be closely aligned with the organization's growth prospects. Knowledge workers in management roles come up with new strategies. Knowledge workers in R&D and engineering create new products. Knowledge workers in marketing package up products and services in ways that appeal to customers. Without knowledge workers, there would be no new products and services, and no growth.

Yet, despite the importance of knowledge workers to the economic success of countries, companies, and other groups, they have not received sufficient attention. We know little about how to improve knowledge workers' performances, which is very unfortunate, because no less an authority than Peter Drucker has said that improving knowledge worker performance is the most important economic issue of the age (Drucker 1968). In this chapter, I will describe how business process management – not in its traditional formulation, but using several modified variants of the idea – can contribute to better performance of knowledge work.

2 Improving Knowledge Work Through Process Management

A time-honored way of improving any form of work is to treat it as a process. To treat something as a process is to impose a formal structure on it – to identify its beginning, end, and intermediate steps, to clarify who the customer is for it, to measure it, to take stock of how well it is currently being performed, and ultimately to improve it. This process-based approach to improving performance is very familiar (and is described in various forms in the rest of this Handbook) and is an obvious candidate for improving knowledge work activities.

But knowledge work and knowledge workers have not often been subject to this sort of analysis. In some cases, they have actively avoided it, and in others, it is just slid by them. Knowledge workers often have the power to resist being told what to do, and process analysis is usually a sophisticated approach to having someone else tell you how to do your job. It is not easy to view knowledge work in terms of processes, because much of it involves thinking, and it is often collaborative and iterative, which makes it difficult to structure.

When I had interviewed knowledge workers about their jobs, they had often said that they did not think that their workdays were consistent and repeatable enough to be viewed as processes. This does not mean, of course, that a process perspective could not be applied, or that there could not be more structure to knowledge work jobs – only that there has not been thus far.

Given the historical antipathy of knowledge workers to formalized processes, it is an obvious question to ask how a process orientation is in their interest. Many knowledge workers will view a formal process approach as a bureaucratic, procedural annoyance. A much more appealing possibility is that a process orientation is beneficial to knowledge workers – that they would benefit from the discipline and structure that a process brings, while remaining free to be creative and improvisational when necessary and desirable. In other words, a process can be viewed as art rather than science (Hall and Johnson 2009). Whether this is true, of course, varies by the process involved, by the way a process is implemented and managed, and by the particular individuals involved.

There is some case for optimism in this regard, however. Several researchers studied the issue of what happens to one type of knowledge workers – software developers – as a process orientation increases (Adler et al. 2003). In that particular process domain, there is a widely used measure of process orientation, the Software Engineering Institute's Capability Maturity Model (CMM), which allows analysis of different levels of process maturity. The researchers looked at two groups within a company that were at CMM Level 5, the highest level of process maturity, and two other groups in the same firm at Level 3.

They found that, for the most part, software developers experienced the increased process orientation as positive. He noted, for example, that

> "...the more routine tasks in software development were rendered more efficient by standardization and formalization, leaving the non-routine tasks relatively unstructured to allow more creativity in their performance."

> "...process maturity was experienced by many developers as enabling and empowering rather than coercive and alienating."

> "The key to ensuring a positive response to process discipline was extensive participation..." "People support what they help create."

This is good news for anyone interested in taking a process perspective on knowledge work. Of course, the findings do not necessarily generalize to all knowledge work, and much more research is needed. But it is a signal that a process orientation can make knowledge work more productive as well as "enabling and empowering" if managed correctly, i.e., with extensive participation.

There will probably also be cases in which knowledge workers will actively resist or ignore a process orientation. In these cases, imposing it becomes a power struggle. The outcome of such struggles will vary across situations, but adopting more effective and productive processes in many industries may sometimes conflict with knowledge worker autonomy. As one expert in the health care industry, for example, puts it, "Less discretion for doctors would improve public safety." (Swidey 2004). Other industries are likely to face similar tradeoffs.

3 Processes and Knowledge Work Segments

Of course, all knowledge workers are not alike, and there are some key differences in process orientations among different types of knowledge work and workers. In the matrix shown in Fig. 1, there are four key types of knowledge work based on the degree of expertise and the level of coordination in the work. "Transaction" work is generally more easily structured in process terms than any other, because the work is normally repeatable, and because the people who do the work have less discretion to do it the way they like. At the opposite extreme are "Collaboration" workers, who present a challenge for process-oriented managers. These workers typically have a more iterative, collaborative approach to work for which patterns are more difficult to discern. They may deny that their work has any structure at all – "every day is different," they have often said to me. And if a process analyst should figure out a process to recommend to these workers, they have the power and the independence to be able to successfully resist it.

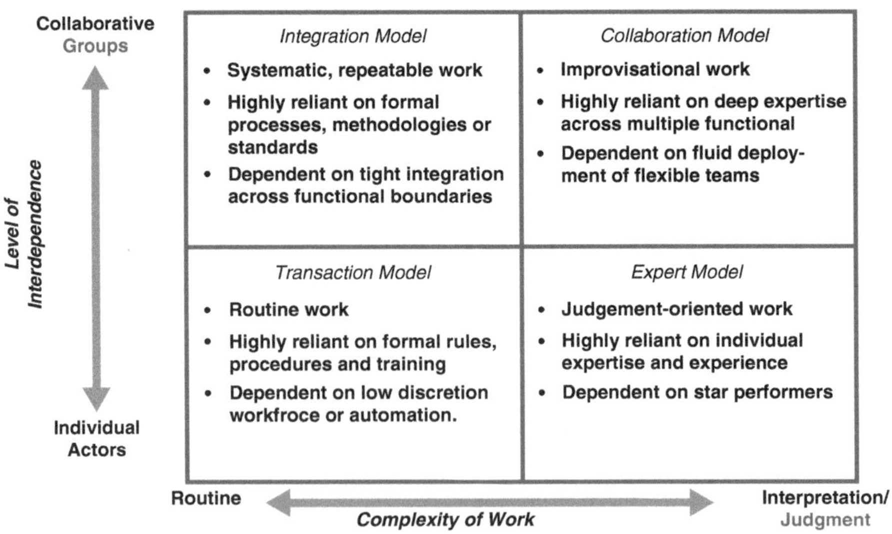

Fig. 1 Four approaches to knowledge work

"Integration" and "Expert" workers are somewhere in the middle in this process-orientation continuum. Integration work is often fairly structured, although higher levels of collaboration often lead to more process complexity. Integration-oriented workers are relatively likely to adopt process interventions. Expert work can be made more process-oriented, but experts themselves often resist an imposed process. Typically, one has to give them the ability to override or step out of the process, and they are often wary of "cookbook" approaches to their work.

Of course, it is not a binary question whether a process orientation is relevant to a particular type of knowledge work. For each of these types, there are rules of thumb about how best to move in a more process-oriented direction:

Transaction workers. These workers need to understand the flow of their work and the knowledge needed to perform it, but they rarely have time to consult external guidelines or knowledge sources. Fortunately, it is often relatively easy to embed a process flow into some form of computer-based application. These typically involve structured workflows or scripts. Such systems usually bring the work – and all information and knowledge required to perform it – to the worker, and they measure the process and worker productivity at the same time.

Integration workers. With this type of work, it is possible to articulate the process to be followed in documents, and workers typically have enough time and discretion to consult the documents. There is nothing new about describing a process, but the practice continues across many industries. Medical technicians, for example, often follow health care protocols in administering tests and treatments. Salespeople at the electronics retailer Best Buy follow a series of "standard operating procedures" for working with customers and making a sale. Even the US Army describes in detail its "doctrine" for how work is done – and with new technologies and war fighting methods, that work is increasingly knowledge-oriented.

Expert workers. These workers have high autonomy and discretion in their work, but there are some examples of organizations, such as several leading health care providers, which have applied technology to key aspects of the process (in their cases, ordering medications, tests, referrals, and other medical actions) (Davenport and Glaser 2002). But unless there is a way to embed a computer into the middle of the work process, experts will be a challenge from the standpoint of structuring work. Instead of specifying detailed aspects of the workflow, those who attempt to improve expert knowledge work should provide templates, sample outputs, and high-level guidelines. It is unlikely that expert workers will pay much attention to detailed process flows anyway.

Collaboration workers. As I have noted, this is the most difficult category to address in traditional process terms. The cautions above for experts also apply to collaborators – a gentle process touch is desirable. Rather than issuing process flow charts, specifying and measuring outputs, instilling a customer orientation, and fostering a sense of urgency are likely intervention approaches. If external knowledge and information are necessary to do the job, they must generally be made available through repositories and documents – it is very unusual for work in this category to be fully mediated and structured by a computer. Of course, this means that it is relatively less likely that the knowledge and information will be used.

4 Knowledge Creation, Distribution, and Application

But the four types of knowledge work I have discussed above are not the only way to segment it in terms of processes. Perhaps a more obvious segmentation approach is to think about processes in terms of the knowledge activity involved. That is, the process orientation differs by whether workers create knowledge, distribute it, or apply it.[2] This simple three-step model – a process in itself – is a useful way to think about how different knowledge activities require different process interventions.

4.1 Creation

The bugaboo of process management is knowledge *creation*. This is widely viewed as a creative, idiosyncratic, "black box" activity that is difficult to manage as a process but not impossible. Perhaps there are circumstances in which knowledge creation is totally unstructured, unmeasured, and unrepeatable – but in most situations, progress can still be made in this direction.

One common approach to knowledge creation processes is simply to decompose them into several pieces or stages. Many companies in the 1980s and 1990s, for example, divided their new product development processes into a series of stages or phases. The objective was to allow evaluation of the new knowledge created at the transition from one stage to another – stage gates. A new drug compound, a new car design, or a new toy model would move through a stage gate if it met the criteria for moving ahead – typically a combination of technical and market feasibility factors. If this approach is employed in a disciplined fashion, it has the virtue of freeing up resources from unproductive projects without imposing too heavy a process burden on new product developers. However, this approach does not really address the activities within the stages, or treat the new product development activity as an end-to-end process (Holmes and Campbell 2003).

Another challenge to the use of process thinking in new product development is that the early stages of the process are often called the "fuzzy front end." At this stage it is not clear what the customer requirements are, what the new product should do, or how it will work. There are things that can be done to make the fuzzy front end somewhat less fuzzy (Quality Function Deployment, for example, is a method for clearly articulating customer requirements; Conjoint Analysis is a statistical technique used to calculate the relative value of different product attributes to customers). However, no amount of technique or process management is going to make the fuzzy front end as clear and well-structured as the final stages of new product development, e.g., manufacturing or market testing. A process orientation may be less relevant to the beginning of the process than to the end based on the inherent degree of structure in each stage.

---

[2]I first employed this distinction in an article with Sirkka Jarvenpaa and Michael Beers, "Improving Knowledge Work Processes" (Davenport et al. 1996).

Other knowledge creation processes have been the subject of alternative approaches, but still with a relatively low degree of process orientation. Scientific research, for example, is the prototypical example of an unstructured knowledge creation process. While there are valid aspects of scientific research that are difficult to structure, there are plenty of approaches and tactics for bringing more process discipline to research. One is simply to measure outputs – number of patents or compounds or published papers per researcher per year, for example. Another is to assess quality – the number of citations a researcher receives per year, for example, is a widely used measure of scientific influence. A third approach is to involve customers of the research (either internal or external to the organization) in the creation process so that their influence is more directly felt. A number of corporate research laboratories – including IBM's Watson Labs and GE's Corporate Research organization – have adopted this approach over the past several years as they attempt to become more productive and profitable. If an organization is creative – and does not automatically resort to process flowcharts – there are a number of ways to make knowledge creation processes more effective and efficient.

Another knowledge creation process is oil exploration. Geologists and geological engineers create seismological knowledge of a targeted drilling area and try to progressively lower the risk of a dry hole with more knowledge over time. At Amerada Hess, a medium-sized oil firm with many exploration projects scattered around the globe, an attempt was made to document the process of oil exploration – the "Exploration Decision-Making Process." This was a cultural stretch for Hess, in that exploration had historically been a highly unstructured and iterative activity, and the people who did it enjoyed a free-thinking, "maverick" culture. Certainly, there were benefits from the exercise; depicting the Exploration Decision-Making Process in a visual format greatly enhanced the ability of participants to understand their roles, responsibilities, and interactions throughout the process. But the creation of a document was perhaps of greater value than the process map, which had strong support from some exploration managers and less from others. A "Prospect Evaluation Sheet" reviewed the story and history of how the lead progressed to its current prospect level. This documentation served to encourage open discussions among peers of alternative interpretations and enabled them to make sense of ambiguities. Even more important was the insistence that peer Reviews and peer Assists (carried out by peers within other parts of the Hess organization) take place prior to prospects qualifying to pass through decision gates. The Prospect Evaluation Sheet was just a way of recording how the prospect field was maturing through the process.

In general, it seems that workers engaged in knowledge creation should be given some structure, but not too much. IDEO, the highly successful new product design firm, for example, provides its employees with a structured brainstorming process, but few other processes have much if any structure or formality. Corning's R&D lab, like many scientific research organizations, employs a "stage gate" model of the innovation process, but there is substantial freedom within stages. Alessi, the Italian design studio, allows considerable creativity and intuition from designers in the early stages, and imposes more structure and evaluation on designs later in the process. More structure than these organizations provide would begin to seem heavy-handed, and indeed some organizations have had difficulty in applying process-oriented disciplines such as Six Sigma to innovation (Hindo 2007; 'Conger 2010). Some observers feel that Six Sigma enforces too much structure and process-based discipline for traditionally creative activities such as innovation.

4.2 Distribution

As for knowledge *distribution* – sharing or transfer are other words for this activity – it is also difficult to structure. Some professions, such as customer service, journalism, and library workers, are only about distribution. For most knowledge workers, however, this is a part of the job, but not all of it. The lawyer or consultant is primarily responsible for generating solutions for clients, but also for sharing that solution with colleagues, and for searching out whether existing knowledge is already available that would help the client. This sharing is difficult to enforce, since we do not know what any person knows, or how diligently they have searched for available knowledge. Yet, there is a substantial body of research suggesting that knowledge worker groups that share knowledge perform better than those that do not.[3]

The most viable approach to managing knowledge distribution or sharing is not to manage the process itself, but rather the external circumstances in which knowledge distribution is undertaken. This typically involves changing where and with whom people work. Chrysler, for example, formed "platform teams" to improve the circulation of new car development knowledge across all the functions involved in building a car. Managers specified a process for the platform teams to follow, but they got much more knowledge sharing from the fact that platform teams were put together in the same sections of the Auburn Hills, MI Technical Center than from a process that instructed them to share at various points.

4.3 Application

Then there is the application of knowledge, which is filtered through the human brain and applied to job tasks. Examples of this type of work include sales, computer programming, accounting, medicine, engineering, and most professions. All of these jobs involve a degree of knowledge creation, but that is not the primary objective. In such cases, we generally want these knowledge workers not to invent new knowledge but to apply existing knowledge to familiar or unfamiliar situations. We do not want computer programmers to create new programming languages, but rather use existing ones to program applications. At best we want "small ideas" from these individuals – not reinvention of their jobs and companies.

[3]For an example of the relationship between knowledge sharing and performance, see Cummings (2004).

How do we make knowledge application better? In many cases, the goal is to reuse knowledge more effectively. We can greatly improve performance by having a lawyer reuse knowledge created in another case, or having a programmer employ a subroutine that someone else created.

Knowledge asset reuse is a frequently stated objective for organizations, but it is hard to achieve. Many organizational and professional cultures reward – sometimes unconsciously – knowledge creation over knowledge reuse. Furthermore, effective knowledge asset reuse requires investment in making knowledge reusable: documentation, libraries, catalogs, modular structures for knowledge objects. Many organizations and managers just do not take a sufficiently long view of reuse processes to make those investments.

When some colleagues and I researched knowledge asset reuse processes across several types of organizations (Davenport et al. 2003), there were several factors explaining whether organizations were successful with reuse. Leadership was one of the factors – having an executive in charge who understood the value of reuse and was willing to manage so as to make reuse a reality. Another factor was asset visibility, or the ability to easily find and employ the knowledge asset when there was a desire to do so. The third and final factor was asset control, or the activities designed to ensure that the quality of knowledge assets was maintained over time. Therefore, if you are interested in knowledge reuse as a means of improving knowledge use processes, you should try to put these three factors in place.

There are other factors that can be employed to improve use. Computers, of course, can oversee the process of reuse. At General Motors, for example, the Vehicle Engineering Centers want new car designers to reuse knowledge and engineering designs when possible, rather than create new ones. So they ensure that the desirable dimensions of new vehicles, and the parameters of existing component designs, are programmed into the computer-aided design systems that the engineers use, and it becomes difficult not to use them. One GM executive told me that you cannot force the engineers to reuse designs and components – you just have to make it much easier for them to do that than to create new ones.

Today, in most organizations, reuse is only addressed at the institutional level if at all. But it stands to reason that the most effective knowledge workers reuse their own knowledge all the time. A productive lawyer, for example, would index and rapidly find all the opinions and briefs he has ever written and reuse them all the time for new clients. But while we know this is true, organizations have yet to help knowledge workers do this sort of reuse. If they were smart, they would make it easier – and provide taxonomies, training, role models, and encouragement.

5 Process Versus Practice in Knowledge Work

In addition to taking a process perspective on knowledge work, it is important to remember that there is also a *practice* side to this type of work, which has to be balanced with the process perspective. This balance, first defined by Brown and

Duguid (1991), is an important consideration for anyone attempting to address knowledge work.[4]

Every effort to change how work is done needs a dose of both *process* – the design for how work is to be done – and *practice*, an understanding of how individual workers respond to the real world of work and accomplish their assigned tasks. Process work is a designing, modeling, and engineering activity, sometimes created by teams of analysts or consultants who do not actually do the work in question and often have only a dim understanding of how it is being done today. A process design is fundamentally an abstraction of how work should be done in the future. Process analysts may superficially address the "as is" process, but generally only as a quick preamble to the "to be" environment.

Practice analysis is a well-informed description of how work is done today by those who actually do it. Some analyses of work practice are done by anthropologists (ethnographers), who observe workers carefully over months, either through participant observation or through video. To really understand work practice, it requires detailed observation and a philosophical acceptance that there are usually good reasons for why work gets done by workers in a particular way. Just the acceptance of the practice idea suggests a respect for workers and their work, and an acknowledgement that they know what they are doing much of the time.

A pure focus on process in knowledge work means that a new design is unlikely to be implemented successfully; it probably would not be realistic. On the other hand, a pure focus on practice is not very helpful either – it leads to a detailed description of today's work activities, but it may not improve them much. Some anthropologists go just as far in the practice direction as some consultants go in the process direction. They argue that you have to observe work for a year or so in order to have any chance of understanding it at all, which is clearly unrealistic in a business context.

It is certainly true that some processes can be designed by others and implemented successfully – because they are relatively straightforward to begin with or because it is easy to use people or systems to structure and monitor their performance. Other jobs – particularly those involving knowledge and experts – are very difficult for outsiders to understand and design, and require a high proportion of practice orientation.

What does it mean to combine a process and practice orientation? Here are some obvious implications:

- Involve the knowledge workers in the design of the new process. Ask them what they would like to see changed and what is stopping them from being more effective and efficient.
- Watch them do their work (not for a year, but a few weeks is not unreasonable). Talk to them about why they do the things they do. Do not automatically assume that you know a better way.

[4]Brown and Duguid have elaborated on the process–practice distinction in their book "The Social Life of Information" (Brown and Duguid 2000, p. 91–116).

- Enlist analysts who have actually done the work in question before. If you are trying to improve health care processes, for example, use doctors and nurses to design the new process.
- Take your time. Devote as much attention to the "as is" as the "to be." Knowledge work is invisible, and it takes a while to understand the flow, rationale, and variations for the work process.
- Exercise some deference. Treat experienced workers as real experts (they probably are!). Get them on your side with credible assurances that your goal is to make their lives better.
- Use the Golden Rule of Process Management. Ask yourself, "Would I want to have my job analyzed and redesigned in the fashion that I'm doing it to others?"

6 Types of Process Interventions

There are many different types of process-oriented interventions that we can make with knowledge work. Some, such as process improvement, measurement, and outsourcing, have long been used with other types of business processes. Others, such as agile methods and positive deviance, are only present in particular knowledge work domains, but could be generalized.

6.1 Process Improvement Approaches for Knowledge Work

There are many ways to improve processes. Which work best with knowledge work? Process improvement can be radical or incremental, participative or top-down, one-time or continuous, focused on large, cross-functional processes or small ones at the work group level, and oriented to process flows or other attributes of processes. There is no single right answer to the question of which variant makes sense – it obviously depends on the organization's strategy, the degree of improvement necessary, and the type of work.

However, as I have noted, with knowledge work it is a good idea to make the improvement process as participative as possible. Knowledge workers are much more likely to agree with and adopt any process changes if they have been a party to designing them. This begins to restrict the change options some what. It is very difficult to have thousands of people participate in a highly participative change approach, so that largely dictates a focus on small processes. Participative change also typically yields more incremental change results, in that it is somewhat difficult for large numbers of people who are highly conversant with a process to develop a radical new approach to performing it. Participative, incremental change processes are often also continuous in their orientation, as opposed to one-time. It does not make sense to make one-time incremental changes if the organization is not going to follow them up with more improvements over time.

Based on this logic, the most desirable forms of process improvement for knowledge work are participative, incremental, and continuous. An example of this type of approach would be Six Sigma, which has been adapted and adopted for knowledge work by a variety of firms (although, as I noted above, some firms have found it burdensome for innovation-oriented processes). General Electric, for example, has employed the approach extensively within its Global Research organization. It applies Six Sigma in research and design processes using its "Design for Six Sigma" (DFSS) methodology, which is about understanding the effects of variation on product performance before it is manufactured. Many of its researchers and engineers have Six Sigma green or black belts, and are experts in the application of statistical analysis to research and engineering processes. GE is perhaps the most advanced of all organizations in applying process management techniques to research. Even at GE, however, managers I have recently interviewed have suggested that the influence of Six Sigma over innovation-oriented processes is waning.[5]

The other key aspect of selecting a process-oriented intervention is the particular attribute of process management an organization addresses. As I have mentioned, it is all too common for organizations to interpret "process" as "flow diagram." It specifies "first you do this, and then you do this..." Such an engineering orientation to processes breaks down work into a series of sequential steps, and it is the aspect of process management that knowledge workers like least. Similar forms of this orientation are found when organizations attempt to create detailed methodologies for knowledge work, such as a system development methodology. It may be necessary in some cases to engineer the process flow, but it should not be the centerpiece of a knowledge work improvement initiative.

A simpler form of a highly detailed process flow is a straightforward checklist of what activities a knowledge worker needs to perform. This may seem obvious and simplistic, but there are some industries in which knowledge workers are benefitting from it. Medical workers such as doctors and nurses, for example, are increasingly using checklists to ensure that all major steps in a surgical operation are performed. One study found that a 19-item surgery checklist improved communication between surgical team members and reduced death rates by almost half (Haynes et al. 2009).

6.2 Agile Methods

Another alternative to highly engineered processes might be called "agile" methods. They are less focused on the specific steps to be followed in a process, and more oriented to the managerial and cultural context surrounding the process. Instead of detailed process flows, for example, agile methods might emphasize the size and composition of process teams, a highly iterative workflow, and a culture of urgency. This is the case, for example, in the agile method known as "extreme programming."

[5]For more on the relationship between Six Sigma and process management in general, see Conger (2010).

Martin Fowler, an expert on agile methods, describes the contrast between engineered methodologies and agile approaches in common-sense language on his web site:

- *Agile methods are adaptive rather than predictive.* Engineering methods tend to try to plan out a large part of the software process in great detail for a long span of time, this works well until things change. So their nature is to resist change. The agile methods, however, welcome change. They try to be processes that adapt and thrive on change, even to the point of changing themselves.
- *Agile methods are people-oriented rather than process-oriented.* The goal of engineering methods is to define a process that will work well whoever happens to be using it. Agile methods assert that no process will ever make up for the skill of the development team, so the role of a process is to support the development team in their work (Fowler 2005).[6]

As of now, agile methods are only established within software development, but over time they may migrate to other knowledge work processes.

It is not hard to imagine that before long we will see, for example, "extreme product development" or "extreme marketing."

6.3 Measurement

A key component of process management has always been to measure the performance of workers. In the industrial age, this was a relatively easy task; an individual worker's performance could be assessed through outputs – work actually produced – or visible inputs, including hours worked or apparent effort expended. Output measures over input measures, of course, are typically described as "productivity." The appeal of measuring productivity for knowledge workers is that it is a universal measure. Productivity-oriented approaches convert the value of outputs to currency. It is very appealing to look across an entire corporation or even a country and argue that we have increased productivity by an exact percentage – and economists often do so.

In the world of knowledge work, evaluating productivity and performance is much more difficult. How can a manager determine whether enough of a knowledge worker's brain cells are being devoted to a task? What is the formula for assessing the creativity and innovation of an idea? Given the difficulty of such evaluations, managers of knowledge workers have traditionally fallen back on measuring visible inputs, e.g., hours worked. Hence the long hours put in by attorneys, investment bankers, and consultants. However, the increasing movement of knowledge work out of the office and into homes, airplanes, and client sites makes it difficult to use hours worked as a measure, and that criterion never had much to do with the quality of knowledge produced.

[6]The use of Business Process Management approaches in collaborative work settings is explored in Kemsley (2010).

Quality is perhaps the greatest problem in measuring knowledge work. Why is one research paper, one advertising slogan, or one new chemical compound better than another? If you cannot easily measure the quality of knowledge work, it makes it difficult to determine who does it well, and to what degree interventions have improved it. Many organizations tend to fall back on measuring the volume of knowledge outputs produced – lines of programming code, for example – simply because it is possible to measure them. But without some measure of quality, the improvement of knowledge work is unlikely to succeed.

It is possible to measure the quality of knowledge work, albeit with a subjective method. It involves determining who is a relevant peer group for the particular work involved, and asking them what they think of it. This technique has often been used, for example, in evaluating professors for promotion and tenure. A jury of peers – usually from within and outside the professor's school – is consulted, and the quality of their published work assessed. Similarly, student evaluations are used to assess the quality of teaching. Any problems with lack of objectivity are remedied in the volume and diversity of responses. In the same fashion, a few organizations ask for multiple peer evaluations in annual performance reviews and promotion decisions. Some knowledge management applications ask each user of the system to rate the quality of the knowledge found. Thus, there are means of assessing quality, although the peer group and the assessment approach will vary by the context.

There does not seem to be, however, a universal measure for the quality or quantity of knowledge work outputs. What matters is high-quality outputs per unit of time and cost, and the specific outputs vary widely across knowledge worker types. A computer programmer produces lines of code; a physician produces well people; a scientist produces discoveries and research. The only way we can determine whether a particular intervention improves knowledge work performance is to assess the quantity and quality of the outputs produced by those workers. Universal measures are pretty much useless for this purpose.

Therefore, the appropriate output (and sometimes input) measures for knowledge work will vary by the industry, process, and job. In improving knowledge worker performance, it is important to determine what measures make sense for the particular type of work being addressed. Organizations need to begin to employ a broad array of inputs and outputs, some of which are internal to the knowledge worker's mind. One input might involve the information and knowledge that a knowledge worker consulted in making a decision or taking an action (a particularly important criterion for managers). ABB, the global electrical and engineering firm, uses this factor as one of many in assessing managerial performance. Another input could be the process that a knowledge worker follows in producing knowledge work. The self-reported allocation of the knowledge worker's time and attention is a third possible input.[7]

---

[7]For an example of how to assess self-reported attention allocation, see Davenport and Beck (2002).

Outputs could include the volume of knowledge produced, the quality of the decisions or actions taken on the basis of knowledge, and the impact of the knowledge produced (as judged by others). In the consulting industry, some consultants are already evaluated in part on the knowledge they bring to the firm and the impact it has on clients – in addition to the usual measures of chargeability and consulting projects sold.

Some knowledge work processes already employ well-defined measures. IT is certainly one of the more measured knowledge work domains. IT measurement is relatively advanced in both programming and in IT processes and capabilities. In programming, some organizations have measured for decades the production of either lines of code or function points, and various researchers have analyzed the considerable variance in productivity. These measures are not perfect, but they have allowed IT organizations to begin to understand differences across groups and individuals – something that lawyers, doctors, and managers cannot measure nearly as well.

The other primary domain of measurement is the assessment of IT processes, particularly software engineering (but also software acquisition, people management, and the development of software-intensive products). Thanks to the Software Engineering Institute and researcher Watts Humphrey, we have an international standard for the quality of software engineering: the Capability Maturity Models (Software Engineering Institute 1995). Thousands of organizations have been assessed along these five-level models. The Software Engineering Institute has developed a more general approach to assessing capability maturity (called CMMI – Capability Maturity Model Integration), but thus far it has largely been applied to software-related processes only (Crissis et al. 2003). Unfortunately, there is no similar global standard for other forms of knowledge work, other than perhaps the ISO 9000 family of standards for manufacturing quality.

6.4 Positive Deviance

Once measures have been developed for knowledge work, there are other approaches that can take advantage of them. One is called positive deviance, defined by Wikipedia as:

> Positive Deviance (PD) is an approach to personal, organizational and cultural change based on the idea that every community or group of people performing a similar function has certain individuals (the "Positive Deviants") whose special attitudes, practices/strategies/behaviors enable them to function more effectively than others with the exact same resources and conditions. Because Positive Deviants derive their extraordinary capabilities from the identical environmental conditions as those around them, but are not constrained by conventional wisdoms, Positive Deviants standards for attitudes, thinking and behavior are readily accepted as the foundation for profound organizational and cultural change (Wikipedia 2009).

Positive deviance-based approaches have been employed in health care (for example, to reduce infection from antibiotic-resistant bacteria) and international development. To use it for knowledge work improvement, different knowledge workers within an organization would be measured on key metrics. Those individuals or groups that score relatively well are publicized, and their approaches investigated. They would become examples for less successful knowledge workers. Because humans are often competitive and want to improve, they often adopt the approaches used by their most successful peers.

6.5 Knowledge Management-Based Interventions

Since knowledge workers employ knowledge as a primary aspect of their jobs, it is natural that organizations would try to improve the work with knowledge management, or systematic attempts to improve the distribution and utilization of knowledge. However, most implementations of knowledge management within organizations do not employ a process-based approach. Instead, they typically involve adding knowledge management activities on top of existing work activity.

In a few cases, however, organizations have attempted to use knowledge management approaches to make knowledge available at the time of need in the context of the work process. This is similar to the idea of "performance support," which specified that learning would be delivered in real time as task performance required it (Gery 1991). One successful example of applying knowledge to the work process is at healthcare provider Partners HealthCare, where knowledge of appropriate therapies is made available to physicians as they input online orders for patients (Davenport and Glaser 2002). The system and the process have led to many benefits, including a 55% reduction in adverse drug events.

In such situations knowledge management can be a very effective way to improve knowledge work processes, but it is more difficult to implement than "traditional" knowledge management. It requires focusing on and supporting a particular work process, as opposed to an entire organization. It also may require considerable customization and integration of information technology tools. This is presumably the reason why more organizations do not implement knowledge management in a process context.

6.6 Outsourcing Knowledge Work

Outsourcing of business processes began for most organizations with structured, repetitive activities with high labor content, such as routine IT development, a call center, or an accounting back office. But today, many more intellectual and less structured activities are being outsourced. Back-office work is being supplanted by "knowledge process outsourcing" (KPO) of various types.

This transition began quietly more than a decade ago at GE's captive offshore center in India. GE Capital set up the center to do back-office work. But managers began to notice that they could get help with decision algorithms from their Indian employees. Soon the Indian operation was the primary provider of analytical tools for credit and risk analysis. When GE spun out its captive offshore group in 2005, the resulting company, Genpact, began to take on KPO work for other clients in addition to GE. And GE eventually established a captive (offshore but not outsourced) R&D center in India that takes on the thorniest problems it encounters in its global operations.

Today, several offshore firms in addition to Genpact specialize in various forms of decision analysis. Organizations such as E-Valueserve, Mu Sigma, and MarketRX (now owned by Cognizant) are helping some of the largest US-based firms with their knowledge-based processes. They are helping a major retailer, for example, determine where to build their next stores. They are helping a major pharmaceutical firm decide which salespeople are most effective, and which drugs are passing their clinical trials. They are helping a major insurance company decide what price to charge different customers for automobile insurance. They are helping a major office products firm decide which promotions and products to offer to which customers. They are taking on a wide variety of product development activities for IT and other firms. Even larger offshore outsourcers that previously specialized in IT – such as Wipro, Infosys, and Satyam – have decided that KPO is a future growth area. With their scale and marketing budgets, as well as their orientation to process improvement, we will undoubtedly see substantial offshore KPO in the future.

Companies working with offshore decision outsourcers report great success in improving their decision processes and results, but they warn that the structure of the projects is critical. The result of a decision analysis is not useful unless it is implemented, and offshore analysts cannot easily influence executives to adopt the results. Therefore, the clients say, it is important to have at least one of their own employees on the analysis team. It is that person's job to ensure that the analysis is consistent with the decisions the organization wants to make, and to communicate the results to responsible executives. They also report that it is valuable to have at least one representative of the offshore firm working onshore at the client site. That person typically has responsibility for communicating and coordinating between the offshore team and the client.

With the shortage of knowledge workers in the US and Western Europe, and the ready supply of them in India, Eastern Europe, and China, it is perhaps not surprising that organizations are now outsourcing not only hands, but also brains. Outsourcing knowledge work can be just as effective an intervention as improving a process internally, for example.

7 Summary

This chapter has addressed process-oriented approaches to improving knowledge work. The different process techniques include:

- Segmentation of knowledge work into its more and less structured components;
- Differentiation by types of knowledge workers by level of integration and expertise, with different process-oriented interventions for each type;

- Different process interventions for knowledge creation, distribution, and application;
- Distinction between a process orientation and a practice orientation;
- The application of participative, incremental, and continuous process management approaches;
- The use of "agile" process methods;
- Process measurement as a tool for improvement;
- "Positive deviance" approaches to improvement;
- Knowledge management applied in a process context;
- Outsourcing of knowledge work processes.

The breadth of potential approaches to knowledge work improvement confirms that taking a traditional, engineering-oriented process approach is not the only or even the best way to improve a knowledge worker's performance. Any engineering perspective on processes has to be balanced against the day-to-day practice of knowledge workers, and the "softer" means of intervening into knowledge work.

In an ideal situation, knowledge work processes can create a climate in which innovation and discipline coexist. Knowledge workers are often passionate about their ideas, and would not abandon them easily. Yet, it is sometimes necessary to kill some knowledge work initiatives in order to free up resources for new ones. Managers in pharmaceutical firms, for example, have noted that a key aspect of a strong drug development program is the ability to cancel projects that do not meet success criteria. But cancellation should be the result of a process, not a matter of an individual's taste.

Kao Corporation, Japan's largest consumer products firm, is an example of an organization with both a strong orientation to knowledge and learning, and a sense of process-oriented discipline when necessary. Kao's CEO describes the company as an "educational institution," and it was one of the earliest adopters of knowledge management in Japan. Kao's researchers have a high degree of autonomy in the research they pursue, at least for Japanese firms. But Kao also has discipline. It has well-structured continuous process improvement programs, even in the R&D function. It also kills undesirable products and projects when necessary. The company had entered the floppy disk business and had become the world's second largest producer, but by the late 1990s it became clear that the business was fully commoditized. Most large Japanese firms are slow to restructure, but Kao first closed down half and then all of the business. 1998 was the first year in seventeen that Kao had not grown profits, but it was already back on the profit growth track by 1999 – and it is continued on that track since then.

Organizations like Kao take a process approach to knowledge work because it is one of the most successful and time-honored approaches to business improvement – dating back at least as far as Frederick Taylor at the dawn of the twentieth century. But a process orientation would not be successful without modifications and supplementary approaches that equip it for the unique attributes of knowledge work and workers.

References

Adler PS, McGarry FE, Talbot WB, Binney DJ (2003) Enabling process discipline: lessons from Computer Sciences Corporation on Capability Maturity Model Level 5, working paper, University of Southern California, May 26, 2003

Brown JS, Duguid P (1991) Organizational learning and communities-of-practice: toward a unified view of working, learning, and innovation. Organisation Science 2:40–57

Brown JS, Duguid P (2000) The social life of information. Harvard Business School Press, Boston

Conger S (2010) Six sigma and business process management. In: vom Brocke J, Rosemann M (eds) Handbook on business management, vol 1. Springer, Heidelberg

Crissis MB, Conrad M, Shrum S (2003) CMMI: guidelines for process integration and product improvement. Reading, MA, USA

Cummings JN (2004) Work groups, structural diversity, and knowledge sharing in a global organization. Manage Sci 50(3):352–364

Davenport TH (2005) Thinking for a living: how to get better performance and results from knowledge workers. Harvard Business School Publishing, Boston

Davenport TH, Beck JC (2002) The attention economy. Harvard Business School Press, Boston

Davenport TH, Glaser J (2002) Just in time delivery comes to knowledge management. Harvard Business Review 80:107–111

Davenport TH, Iyer B (2009) Should you outsource your brain? Harv Bus Rev, Feb 2009

Davenport TH, Jarvenpaa SL, Beers MC (1996) Improving knowledge work processes. In: Sloan Management Review, pp 53–65

Davenport TH, Thomas RI, Desouza KC (2003) Reusing intellectual assets. Industrial Management, 45(3):12–18

Drucker PF (1968) The age of discontinuity. Harper & Row, New York

Fowler M (2005) The new methodology. http://www.martinfowler.com/articles/newMethodology.html#N400058

Gery G (1991) Electronic performance support systems. Ziff Institute, Cambridge, MA

Hall JM, Johnson ME (2009) When should a process be art, not science? Harv Bus Rev, March 2009

Haynes AB, Weiser TG, Berry WR et al. (2009) A surgical safety checklist to reduce morbidity and mortality in a global population. N Engl J Med 360(5):491–499

Hindo B (2007) At 3M, a struggle between efficiency and creativity. Bus Week. http://www.businessweek.com/magazine/content/07_24/b4038406.htm

Holmes MF, Campbell Jr. RB (2003) Product Development processes: three vectors of improvement. MIT Center for Innovation in Product Development working paper. http://hdl.handle.net/1721.1/3819

Kemsley S (2010) Enterprise 2.0 meets business process management. In: vom Brocke J, Rosemann M (eds) Handbook on business process management, vol 1. Springer, Heidelberg

Quinn JB (1992) Intelligent enterprise: a knowledge and service-based paradigm for industry. Free Press, New York

Software Engineering Institute (1995) The capability maturity model: guidelines for improving the software process. Reading, MA, USA

Swidey (2004) The Revolutionary, The Boston Globe, http://www.boston.com/news/globe/reprints/010404_the_revolutionary/, Mai 1, 2010

Wikipedia (2009) Positive deviance. http://en.wikipedia.org/wiki/Positive_Deviance. Accessed 22 Feb 2009

The Scope and Evolution of Business Process Management

Paul Harmon

Abstract Business Process Management or BPM, broadly speaking, is part of a tradition that is now several decades old that aims at improving the way business people think about and manage their businesses. Its particular manifestations, whether they are termed "Work Simplification," "Six Sigma," "Business Process Reengineering," or "Business Process Management," may come and go, but the underlying impulse, to shift the way managers and employees think about the organization of business, will continue to grow and prosper. This chapter will provide a very broad survey of the business process movement. Anyone who tries to promote business process change in an actual organization will soon realize that there are many different business process traditions and that individuals from the different traditions propose different approaches to business process change. If we are to move beyond a narrow focus on one tradition or technology, we need a comprehensive understanding of where we have been and where we are today, and we need a vision of how we might move forward. We will begin with a brief overview of the past and of the three business process traditions that have created the context for today's interest in BPM. Then we will turn to a brief survey of some of the major concerns that process practitioners are focused on today and that will probably impact most corporate BPM efforts in the near future.

1 The Three Business Process Traditions

The place to begin is with an overview of the world of business process change technologies and methodologies. In essence, there are three major process traditions: the management tradition, the quality control tradition, and the IT tradition.

P. Harmon
Business Process Trends, San Francisco, CA, USA
e-mail: pharmon@bptrends.com

J. vom Brocke and M. Rosemann (eds.), *Handbook on Business Process Management 1*, International Handbooks on Information Systems,
DOI 10.1007/978-3-642-00416-2_3, © Springer-Verlag Berlin Heidelberg 2010

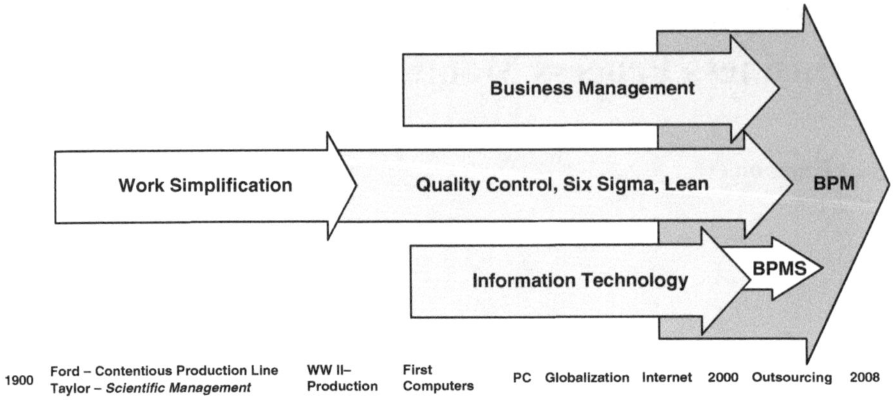

Fig. 1 An overview of approaches to business process change

Too often, individuals who come from one tradition are inclined to ignore or depreciate the other approaches, feeling that their approach is sufficient or superior. Today, however, the tendency is for three traditions to merge into a more comprehensive BPM tradition.

One could easily argue that each of the three traditions has roots that go right back to ancient times. Managers have always tried to make workers more productive, there have always been efforts to simplify processes and to control the quality of outputs, and, if IT is regarded as an instance of technology, then people have been trying to use technologies of one kind or another ever since the first human picked up a stick to use as a spear or a lever. All three traditions got a huge boost from the Industrial Revolution, which started to change manufacturing at the end of the eighteenth century. Our concern here, however, is not with the ancient roots of these traditions but the recent developments in each field and the fact that practitioners in one field often choose to ignore the efforts of those working in other traditions.

We will begin by considering each of the traditions pictured in Fig. 1 in isolation, and then consider how companies are using and integrating the various business process change technologies today.

2 The Work Simplification/Quality Control Tradition

In Fig. 1, we pictured the Quality Control tradition as a continuation of the Work Simplification tradition. The modern roots of quality control and process improvement in the United States, at least, date from the publication by Frederick Winslow Taylor of *Principles of Scientific Management* in 1911 (Taylor 1911). Taylor described a set of key ideas he believed that good managers should use to improve their businesses. He argued for work simplification, for time studies, for systematic experimentation to identify the best way of performing a task, and for control systems that measured and rewarded output. Taylor's book became an international best-seller and has influenced many in the process movement. Shigeo Shingo, one of the co-developers of the Toyota Production System, describes how he first read a Japanese translation of Taylor in 1924 and the book itself in 1931 and credits it for setting the course of his work life (Shingo 1983).

One must keep in mind, of course, that Taylor wrote immediately after Henry Ford introduced his moving production line and revolutionized how managers thought about production. The first internal-combustion automobiles were produced by Karl Benz and Gottlieb Daimler in Germany in 1885. In the decades that followed, some 50 entrepreneurs in Europe and North America set up companies to build cars. In each case, the companies built cars by hand, incorporating improvements with each model. Henry Ford was one among many who tried his hand at building cars in this manner (McGraw 1997).

In 1903, however, Henry Ford started his third company, the Ford Motor Company, and tried a new approach to automobile manufacturing. First, he designed a car that would be of high quality, not too expensive, and easy to manufacture. Next, he organized a moving production line. In essence, workmen began assembling a new automobile at one end of the factory building and completed the assembly as it reached the far end of the plant. Workers at each point along the production line had one specific task to do. One group moved the chassis into place, another welded on the side panels, and still another group lowered the engine into place when each car reached their station. In other words, Henry Ford conceptualized the development of an automobile as a single process and designed and sequenced each activity in the process to assure that the entire process ran smoothly and efficiently. Clearly, Ford had thought deeply about the way cars were assembled in his earlier plants and had a very clear idea of how he could improve the process.

By organizing the process as he did, Henry Ford was able to significantly reduce the price of building automobiles. As a result, he was able to sell cars for such a modest price that he made it possible for every middle-class American to own a car. At the same time, as a direct result of the increased productivity of the assembly process, Ford was able to pay his workers more than any other auto assembly workers. Within a few years, Ford's new approach had revolutionized the auto industry, and it soon led to changes in almost every other manufacturing process as well. This success had managers throughout the world scrambling to learn about Ford's innovations and set the stage for the tremendous popularity of Taylor's book, which seemed to explain what lay behind Ford's achievement.

Throughout the first half of the twentieth century, engineers worked to apply Taylor's ideas, analyzing processes, measuring and applying statistical checks whenever they could. Ben Graham, in his book on *Detail Process Charting*, describes the Work Simplification movement during those years, and the annual Work Simplification conferences, sponsored by the American Society of Mechanical Engineers (ASME), which were held in Lake Placid, New York (Graham 2004). These conferences, which lasted into 1960s, were initially stimulated by a 1911 conference at on Scientific Management, held at Dartmouth College, and attended by Taylor and the various individuals who were to dominate process work in North America during the first half of the twentieth Century.

The American Society for Quality (ASQ) was established in 1946, and the Work Simplification movement gradually transitioned into the Quality Control movement. In 1951, *Juran's Quality Control Handbook* appeared for the first time and this magisterial book has become established at the encyclopedic source of information about the quality control movement (Juran 1951).

In 1980s, when US auto companies began to lose significant market share to the Japanese, many began to ask what the Japanese were doing better. The popular answer was that the Japanese had embraced an emphasis on Quality Control that they learned, ironically, from Edwards Deming, a quality guru sent to Japan by the US government in the aftermath of World War II. (Deming's classic book is *Out of the Crisis,* published in 1982.) (Deming 1982) In fact, of course the story is more complex, and it includes the work of native Japanese quality experts, such as Shigeo Shingo and Taiichi Ohno, who were working to improve production quality well before World War II, and who joined in the postwar period to create the *Toyota Production System*, and thereby became the fathers of Lean (Shingo 1983; Ohno 1978). (The work of Shingo and Ohno was popularized in the US by James Womack, Daniel Jones and Daniel Roos in their book *The Machine That Changed the World: The Story of Lean Production*, 1991 (Womack et al. 1991). This book was a commissioned study of what the Japanese auto manufacturing companies were doing and introduced "lean" into the process vocabulary.)

2.1 TQM, Lean and Six Sigma

In 1970s, the most popular quality control methodology was termed Total Quality Management (TQM), but in the late-1980s, it began to be superseded by Six Sigma – an approach developed at Motorola (Ramias 2005; Barney 2003) (see also Conger 2010). Six Sigma combined process analysis with statistical quality control techniques and a program of organizational rewards and emerged as a popular approach to continuous process improvement. In 2001, the ASQ established a SIG for Six Sigma and began training black belts. Since then the quality movement has gradually been superseded, at least in the US, by the current focus on Lean and Six Sigma.

Many readers may associate Six Sigma and Lean with specific techniques, such as DMAIC, Just-In-Time (JIT) delivery, or the Seven Types of Waste, but, in fact, they are just as well-known for their emphasis on company-wide training efforts designed to make every employee responsible for process quality. One of the most popular executives in the US, Jack Welsh, who was CEO of General Electric when his company embraced Six Sigma, not only mandated a company-wide Six Sigma effort but also made 40% of every executive's bonus dependent on Six Sigma results. Welch went on to claim that it was the most important thing he did while he

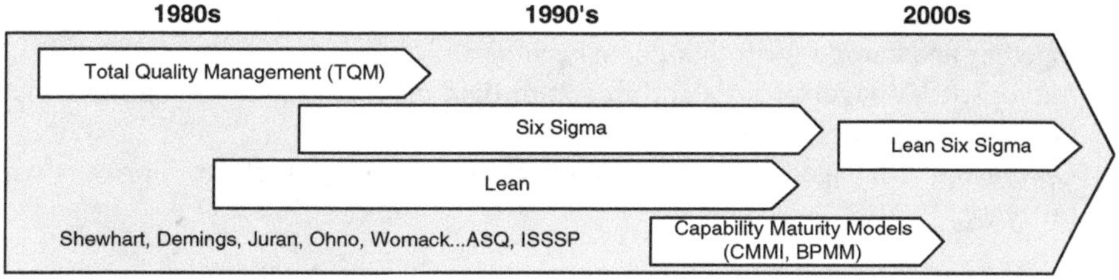

Fig. 2 The quality control tradition

was CEO of GE. In a similar way, Lean, in its original implementation as the Toyota Production System, is a company-wide program embraced with an almost religious zeal by the CEO and by all Toyota's managers and employees. Of all the approaches to process improvement, Lean and Six Sigma come closest, at their best, in implementing an organizational transformation that embraces process throughout the organization.

An overview of the recent history of the quality control tradition is illustrated in Fig. 2. Throughout most of 1990s, Lean and Six Sigma were offered as independent methodologies, but starting in this decade, companies have begun to combine the two methodologies and tend to increasingly refer to the approach as Lean Six Sigma.

2.2 Capability Maturity Model

An interesting example of a more specialized development in the Quality Control tradition is the development of the Capability Maturity Model (CMM) at the Software Engineering Institute (SEI) at Carnegie Mellon University. In the early 1990s, the US Defense of Department (DoD) was concerned about the quality of the software applications being delivered, and the fact that, in many cases, the software applications were incomplete and way over budget. In essence, the DoD asked Watts Humphrey and SEI to develop a way of evaluating software organizations to determine which were likely to deliver what they promised on time and within budget. Humphrey and his colleagues at SEI developed a model, which assumed that organizations that did not understand their processes and that had no data about what succeeded or failed were unlikely to deliver as promised (Paulk et al. 1995). They studied software shops and defined a series of steps organizations went through as they become more sophisticated in managing the software process. In essence, the five steps or levels are:

1. *Initial*: Processes are not defined.
2. *Repeatable*: Basic departmental processes are defined and are repeated more or less consistently

3. *Defined*: The organization, as a whole, knows how all their processes work together and can perform them consistently
4. *Managed*: Managers consistently capture data on their processes and use that data to keep processes on track
5. *Optimizing*: Managers and team members continuously work to improve their processes

Level 5, as described by CMM, is nothing less that the company-wide embrace of process quality that we see at Toyota and at GE.

Once CMM was established, SEI proceeded to gather large amounts of information on software organizations and began to certify organizations as being level 1, 2, etc., and the DoD began to require level 3, 4, or 5 for their software contracts. The fact that several Indian software firms were able to establish themselves as CMM Level 5 organizations is often credited with the recent, widespread movement to outsource software development to Indian companies.

Since the original SEI CMM approach was defined in 1995, it has gone through many changes. At some point, there were several different models, and, recently, SEI has made an effort to pull all of the different approaches back together and have called the new version CMMI – Capability Maturity Model Integrated. At the same time, SEI has generalized the model so that CMMI extends beyond software development and can be used to describe entire companies and their overall process maturity (Chrissis et al. 2007). We will consider some new developments in this approach, later, but suffice to say here that CMMI is very much in the Quality Control tradition with emphasis on output standards and statistical measures of quality.

If one considers all of the individuals working in companies who are focused on quality control, in all its variations like Lean and Six Sigma, they surely constitute the largest body of practitioners working for process improvement today.

3 The Management Tradition

At this point, we will leave the Quality Control tradition, whose practitioners have mostly been engineers and quality control specialists, and turn to the management tradition. As with the quality control tradition, it would be easy to trace the Management Tradition to Ford and Taylor. And, as we have already suggested, there have always been executives who have been concerned with improving how their organizations functioned. By the mid-twentieth century, however, most US managers were trained at business schools that did not emphasize a process approach. Most business schools are organized along functional lines, and consider Marketing, Strategy, Finance, and Operations as separate disciplines. More important, operations have not enjoyed as much attention at business schools in the past decade.

Joseph M. Juran, in an article on the United States in his *Quality Control Handbook*, argues that the US emerged from World War II with its production capacity in good condition while the rest of the world was in dire need of manufactured goods of all kinds (Juran 1951). Thus, during the 50s and 60s, US companies focused on producing large quantities of goods to fulfill the demand of consumers who were not very concerned about quality. Having a CEO who knew about finance or marketing was often considered more important than having a CEO who knew about operations. It was only in 1980s, when the rest of the world had caught up with the US and began to offer superior products for less cost that things began to change. As the US automakers began to lose market share to quality European and Japanese cars in 1980s, US mangers began to refocus on operations and began to search for ways to reduce prices and improve production quality. At that point, they rediscovered, in Japan, the emphasis on process and quality that had been created in the US in the first half of the twentieth century.

Unlike the quality control tradition, however, which focuses on the quality and the production of products, the management tradition has focused on the overall performance of the firm. The emphasis is on aligning strategy, with the means of realizing that strategy, and on organizing and managing employees to achieve corporate goals.

3.1 Geary Rummler

The most important figure in the management tradition in the years since World War II has been Geary Rummler, who began his career at the University of Michigan, at the very center of the US auto industry. Rummler derives his methodology from both a concern with organizations as systems and combines that with a focus on how we train, manage, and motivate employee performance (see also Rummler and Ramias 2010). He began teaching courses at the University of Michigan in 1960s where he emphasized the use of organization diagrams, process flowcharts to model business processes, and task analysis of jobs to determine why some employees perform better than others. Later, Rummler joined with Alan Brache to create Rummler–Brache, a company that trained large numbers of process practitioners in 1980s and early 1990s and co-authored, with Alan Brache, one of the real classics of our field – *Improving Performance: How to Manage the White Space on the Organization Chart* (Rummler 1990). Rummler always emphasized the need to improve corporate performance, and argued that process redesign was the best way to do that. He then proceeded to argue that improving managerial and employee job performance was the key to improved processes.

Figure 3 illustrates Rummler's approach, which integrates three levels of analysis and concerns with measures, design and implementation and management. This diagram suggests the broader concerns that the management tradition in process has always embraced. The focus is on process and on all the elements in the business environment that support or impede good process performance.

	Goals & Measures	Design & Implementation	Management
Organizational Level	Organizational Goals and Measures of Organizational Success	Organizational Design and Implementation	Organizational Management
Process Level	Process Goals and Measures of Process Success	Process Design and Implementation	Process Management
Activity or Performance Level	Activity Goals and Measures of Activity Success	Activity Design and Implementation	Activity Management

Fig. 3 A performance framework (modified after a figure in Rummler and Brache (1990))

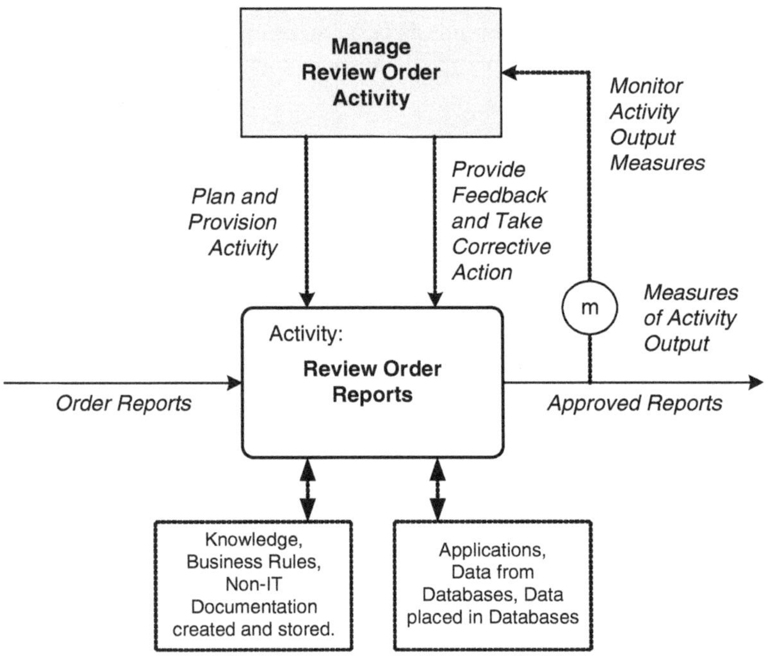

Fig. 4 Each process or activity must be managed (modified after a figure in Rummler and Brache (1990))

A good example of this is illustrated in Fig. 4, another diagram that Rummler frequently uses, which shows the role of the process manager. Where someone in the work simplification tradition might be inclined to look at the steps in a procedure and at how employees perform, Rummler is just as likely to examine the performance of the process manager and ask if the manager has provided the needed resources, if he is monitoring the process, and if he is providing the feedback and incentives needed to motivate superior employee performance.

Unlike the work simplification and quality control literature that was primarily read by engineers and quality control experts, Rummler's work has always been read by business managers and human resource experts.

3.2 Michael Porter

The second important guru in the Management tradition is Harvard Business School Professor Michael Porter. Porter was already established as a leading business strategy theorist, but in his 1985 book, *Competitive Advantage*, he moved beyond strategic concepts, as they had been described until then, and argued that strategy was intimately linked with how companies organized their activities into value chains, which were, in turn, the basis for a company's competitive advantage (Porter 1985).

Figure 5 provides an overview of a value chain as described by Porter (1985). A value chain supports a product line, a market, and its customers. If your company produces jeeps, then you have a value chain for jeeps. If you company makes loans, then you have a value chain for loans. A single company can have more than one value chain. Large international organizations typically have from 5–10 value chains. In essence, value chains are the ultimate processes that define a company. All other processes are defined by relating them to the value chain. Put another way,

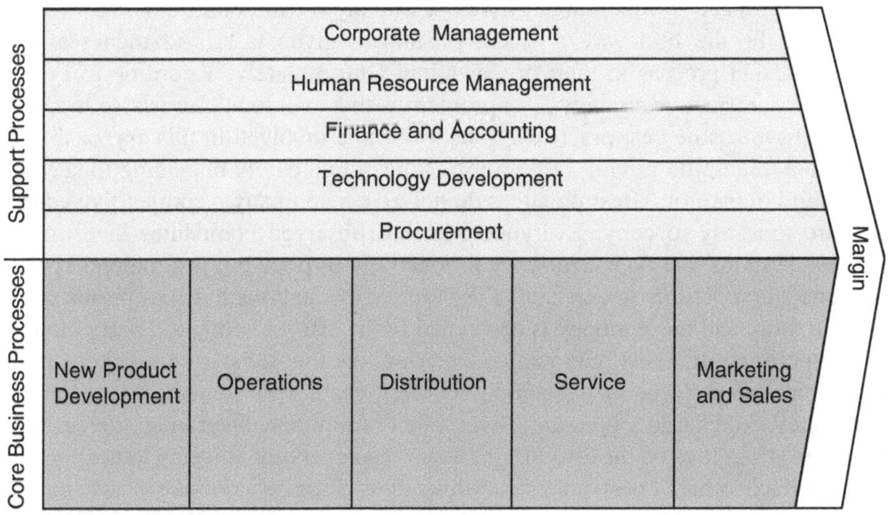

Fig. 5 Michael Porter's value chain

a single value chain can be decomposed into major operational process like Market, Sell, Produce, and Deliver and associated management support processes such as Plan, Finance, HR, and IT. In fact, it was Porter's value chain concept that emphasized the distinction between core and support processes. The value chain has been the organizing principle that has let organizations define and arrange their processes and structure their process change efforts during the past two decades.

As Porter defines it, a competitive advantage refers to a situation in which one company manages to dominate an industry for a sustained period of time. An obvious example, in our time, is Wal-Mart, a company that completely dominates retail sales in the US and seems likely to continue to do so for the foreseeable future. "Ultimately," Porter concludes, "all differences between companies in cost or price derive from the hundreds of activities required to create, produce, sell, and deliver their products or services such as calling on customers, assembling final products, and training employees..." In other words, "activities... are the basic units of competitive advantage." This conclusion is closely related to Porter's analysis of a value chain. A value chain consists of all the activities necessary to produce and sell a product or service. Today, we would probably use the word "processes" rather than "activity," but the point remains the same. Companies succeed because they understand what their customers will buy and proceed to generate the product or service their customers want by means of a set of activities that create, produce, sell, and deliver the product or service.

So far, the conclusion seems like a rather obvious conclusion, but Porter goes further. He suggests that companies rely on one of two approaches when they seek to organize and improve their activities or processes. They either rely on an approach that Porter terms "operational effectiveness" or they rely on "strategic positioning." "Operational effectiveness," as Porter uses the term, means performing similar activities better than rivals perform them. In essence, this is the "best practices" approach we hear so much about. Every company looks about, determines what appears to be the best way of accomplishing a given task, and then seeks to implement that process in their organization. Unfortunately, according to Porter, this is not an effective strategy. The problem is that everyone else is also trying to implement the same best practices. Thus, everyone involved in this approach gets stuck on a treadmill, moving faster all the time, while barely managing to keep up with their competitors. Best practices do not give a company a competitive edge – they are too easy to copy. Everyone who has observed companies investing in software systems that do not improve productivity or price but just maintain parity with one's competitors understands this. Worse, this approach drives profits down because more and more money is consumed in the effort to copy the best practices of competitors. If every company is relying on the same processes, then no individual company is in a position to offer customers something special for which they can charge a premium. Everyone is simply engaged in an increasingly desperate struggle to be the low cost producer, and everyone is trying to get there by copying each others' best practices while their margins continue to shrink. As Porter sums it up: "Few companies have competed successfully on the basis of operational effectiveness over an extended period, and staying ahead of rivals gets harder every day".

The alternative is to focus on evolving a unique strategic position and then tailoring the company's value chain to execute that unique strategy. "Strategic positioning," Porter explains, "means performing different activities from rivals' or performing similar activities in different ways." He goes on to say that "While operational effectiveness is about achieving excellence in individual activities, or functions, strategy is about combining activities." Indeed, Porter insists that those who take strategy seriously need to have lots of discipline, because they have to reject all kinds of options to stay focused on their strategy.

Rounding out his argument, Porter concludes "Competitive advantage grows out of the entire system of activities. The fit among activities substantially reduces cost or increases differentiation." He goes on to warn that "Achieving fit is difficult because it requires the integration of decisions and actions across many independent subunits." Obviously, we are just providing the barest summary of Porter's argument. In essence, however, it is a very strong argument for defining a goal and then shaping and integrating a value chain to assure that all the processes in the value chain work together to achieve the goal.

The importance of this approach, according to Porter, is derived from the fact that "Positions built on systems of activities are far more sustainable than those built on individual activities." In other words, while rivals can usually see when you have improved a specific activity, and duplicate it, they will have a much harder time figuring out exactly how you have integrated all your processes. They will have an even harder time duplicating the management discipline required to keep the integrated whole functioning smoothly.

Porter's work on strategy and value chains assured that most modern discussion of business strategy are also discussions of how value chains or processes will be organized. This, in turn, has led to a major concern with how a company aligns its strategic goals with its specific processes, and many of the current concerns we discuss in the following pages represent efforts to address this issue.

Figure 6 pictures Rummler, Porter, and some of the other major trends in the management tradition.

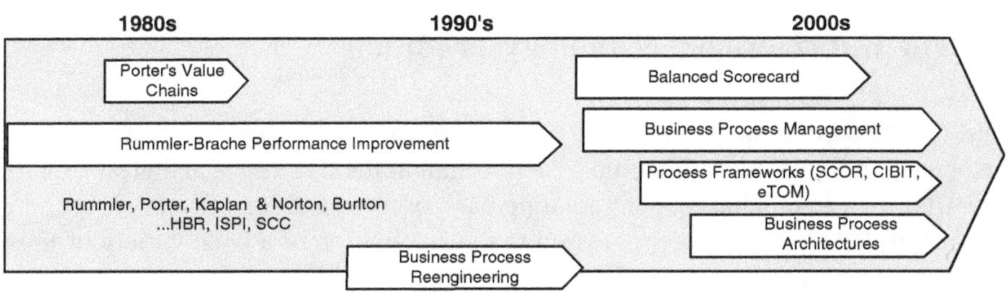

Fig. 6 The management tradition

3.3 Balanced Scorecard

One methodology very much in the management tradition is the Balanced Scorecard methodology developed by Robert S. Kaplan and David P. Norton (Kaplan and Norton 1996). Kaplan and Norton began by developing an approach to performance measurement that emphasized a scorecard that considers a variety of different metrics of success. At the same time, the Scorecard methodology proposed a way of aligning departmental measures and managerial performance evaluations in hierarchies that could systemize all of the measures undertaken in an organization. Later, they linked the scorecard with a model of the firm that stressed that people make processes work, that processes generated happy customers, and that happy customers generated financial results (Kaplan and Norton 2004). In other words, Kaplan and Norton have created a model that begins with strategy, links that to process and people, and then, in turn, links that to measures that determine if the operations are successfully implementing the strategy.

In its initial use, the Balanced Scorecard methodology was often used by functional organizations, but there are now a number of new approaches that tie the scorecard measures directly to value chains and business processes, and process people are increasingly finding the scorecard approach a systematic way to align process measures from specific activities to strategic goals.

3.4 Business Process Reengineering

One can argue about where the Business Process Reengineering (BPR) movement should be placed. Some would place it in the management tradition because it motivated lots of senior executives to rethink their business strategies. The emphasis in BPR on value chains certainly derives from Porter. Others would place it in the IT tradition because it emphasized using IT to redefine work processes and automate them wherever possible. It probably sits on line between the two traditions, and we will consider in more detail under the IT tradition.

4 The Information Technology Tradition

The third tradition involves the use of computers and software applications to automate work processes. This movement began in the late 1960s and grew rapidly in 1970s with an emphasis on automating back office operations like book keeping and record keeping and has progressed to the automation of a wide variety of jobs, either by doing the work with computers, or by providing desktop computers to assist humans in performing their work.

When your author began to work on process redesign with Geary Rummler, in the late 1960s, we never considered automation. It was simply too specialized. Instead, all of our engagements involved straightening out the flow of the process and then working to improve how the managers and employees actually implemented the process. That continued to be the case through the early part of 1970s, but began to change in the late 1970s as more and more core processes, at production facilities and in document processing operations, began to be automated. By the early 1980s, we were working nearly full time on expert system problems and focused on how we could automate the decision making tasks of human experts, and had realized that, eventually, nearly every process in every organization would either be automated, or performed by humans who relied on access to computers and information systems.

We will not attempt to review the rapid evolution of IT systems, from mainframes to minis to PCs, or the way IT moved from the back office to the front office. Suffice to say that, for those of us who lived through it, computers seemed to come from nowhere, and within two short decades they completely changed the way we think about the work and the nature of business. Today, it is hard to remember what the world was like without computer systems. And that it all happened in about 40 years. Perhaps the most important change, to date, occurred in 1995 when the Internet and the Web began to radically alter the way customers interacted with companies. In about 2 years, we transitioned from thinking about computers as tools for automating internal business processes to thinking of them as a communication media that facilitated radically new business models. The Internet spread computer literacy throughout the entire population of developed countries and has forced every company to reconsider how its business works. And it is now driving the rapid and extensive outsourcing of processes and the worldwide integration of business activities.

Figure 7 provides an overview of the IT Tradition. It is the youngest, and also the most complex tradition to describe in a brief way. Prior to the beginning of 1990s, there was lots of work that focused on automating processes, but it was rarely described as process work and was instead referred to as software automation. As it proceeded, jobs were changed or eliminated and companies became more dependent on processes, but in spite of lots of arguments about how IT supported business, IT largely operated independently of the main business and conceptualized itself as a service.

4.1 *Business Process Reengineering*

That changed at the beginning of 1990s with Business Process Reengineering (BPR), which was kicked off, more or less simultaneously, in 1990, by two articles: Michael Hammer's "Reengineering Work: Don't Automate, Obliterate" (*Harvard Business Review*, July/August 1990) (Hammer 1990) and Thomas Davenport and

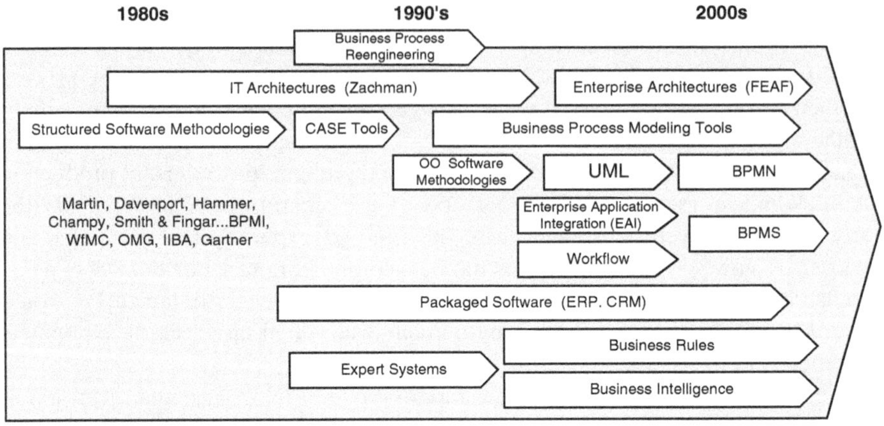

Fig. 7 The information technology tradition

James Short's "The New Industrial Engineering: Information Technology and Business Process Redesign" (*Sloan Management Review*, Summer 1990) (Davenport and Short 1990). Later, in 1993, Davenport wrote a book, *Process Innovation: Reengineering Work through Information Technology*, and Michael Hammer joined with James Champy to write *Reengineering the Corporation: A Manifesto for Business Revolution* (Hammer and Champy 1993) (Hammer 2010; Davenport 2010).

Champy, Davenport, and Hammer insisted that companies must think in terms of comprehensive processes, similar to Porter's value chains and Rummler's Organization Level. If a company focused only on new product development, for example, the company might improve the new product development subprocess, but it might not improve the overall value chain. Worse, one might improve new product development process at the expense of the overall value chain. If, for example, new process development instituted a system of checks to assure higher-quality documents, it might produce superior reports, but take longer to produce them, delaying marketing and manufacturing ability to respond to sudden changes in the marketplace. Or the new reports might be organized in such a way that they made better sense to the new process development engineers, but became much harder for marketing or manufacturing readers to understand. In this sense, Champy, Davenport, and Hammer were very much in the Management Tradition.

At the same time, however, these BPR gurus argued that the major force driving changes in business was IT. They provided numerous examples of companies that had changing business processes in an incremental manner, adding automation to a process in a way that only contributed an insignificant improvement. Then they considered examples in which companies had entirely re-conceptualized their processes, using the latest IT techniques to allow the process to function in a radically new way. In hindsight, BPR began our current era, and starting at that point, business people began to accept that IT was not simply a support process that managed data, but a radical way of transforming the way processes were done, and henceforth, an integral part of every business process.

BPR has received mixed reviews. Hammer, especially, often urged companies to attempt more than they reasonably could. Thus, for example, several companies tried to use existing technologies to pass information about their organizations and ended up with costly failures. Keep in mind that these experiments were taking place in 1990–1995, before most people knew anything about the Internet. Applications that were costly and unlikely to succeed in that period, when infrastructures and communication networks were all proprietary, became simple to install once companies adopted the Internet and learned to use email and web browsers. Today, even though many might suggest that BPR was a failure, its prescriptions have largely been implemented. Whole industries, like book and music retailers and newspapers, are rapidly going out of business while customers now use online services to identify and acquire books, download music, and provide the daily news. Many organizations have eliminated sales organizations and retail stores and interface with their customers online. And processes that were formerly organized separately are now all available online, allowing customers to rapidly move from information gathering, to pricing, to purchasing.

Much more important, for our purposes, is the change in attitude on the part of today's business executives. Almost every executive today uses a computer and is familiar with the rapidity with which software is changing what can be done. Video stores have been largely replaced by services that deliver movies via mail, directly to customers. But the very companies that have been created to deliver movies by mail are aware that in only a few years movies will be downloaded from servers, and their existing business model will be obsolete. In other words, today's executives realize that there is no sharp line between the company's business model and what the latest information technology will facilitate. IT is no longer a service – it has become the essence of the company's strategy. Companies no longer worry about reengineering major processes and are more likely to consider getting out of an entire line of business and jumping into an entirely new line of business to take advantage of an emerging development in information or communication technology.

4.2 *Enterprise Resource Planning Applications*

By the late 1990s, most process practitioners would have claimed to have abandoned BPR and were focusing instead on more modest process redesign projects. Davenport wrote *Mission Critical*, a book that suggested that Enterprise Resource Planning (ERP) applications could solve lots of process problems, and by the end of the decade, most large companies had major ERP installation projects underway (Davenport 2000). ERP solved some problems and created others. Meanwhile, workflow applications also came into the own in the late 1990s, helping to automate lots of document processing operations (van der Aalst and van Hee 2000).

4.3 CASE and Process Modeling Tools

The interest in Computer Aided Software Engineering (CASE) tools, originally created in 1980s to help software engineers create software from the diagrams created by software developers using structured methodologies, declined rapidly in the early 1990s as companies embraced minis, PCs, and a variety on non-COBOL development languages and new object-oriented development methodologies (McClure 1989). The CASE vendors survived, however, by redesigning their tools and repositioning themselves as business process modeling tools. Thus, as companies embraced BPR in the mid-1990s, they did it, in part, by teaching business people to use modeling tools to better understand their processes (Scheer 1994).

4.4 Expert Systems and Business Rules

In a similar way, software developed to support Expert Systems development in 1980s morphed into business rule tools in 1990s. The expert systems movement failed, not because it was impossible to capture the rules that human experts used to analyze and solve complex problems, but because it was impossible to maintain the expert systems once they were developed. To capture the rules used by a physician to diagnose a complex problem required tens of thousands of rules. Moreover, the knowledge kept changing and physicians needed to keep reading and attending conferences to stay up-to-date (Harmon and King 1985; Harmon and Hall 1993). As the interest in expert systems faded, however, others noticed that small systems designed to help mid-level employees perform tasks were much more successful. Even more successful were systems designed to see that policies were accurately implemented throughout the organizations (Ross 2003). Gradually, companies in industries like insurance and banking established business rule groups to develop and maintain systems that enforced policies implemented in their business processes. Processes analysis and business rule analysis have not yet fully merged, but everyone now realizes that they are two sides of the same coin. As a process is executed, decisions are made. Many of those decisions can be described in terms of business rules. By the same token, no one wants to deal with huge rule bases, and process models provide an ideal way to structure where and how business rules will be used.

4.5 Process and the Interface Between Business and IT

Stepping back from all the specific software initiatives, there is a new spirit in IT. Executives are more aware than ever of the strategic value of computer and software technologies and seek to create ways to assure that their organizations remain current. IT is aware that business executives often perceive that IT is focused on technologies rather than on business solutions. Both executives and IT managers hope that a focus on process will provide a common meeting ground. Business executives can focus on creating business models and processes that take advantage of the emerging opportunities in the market. At the same time, IT architects can focus on business processes and explain their new initiatives in terms of improvements they can make in specific processes. If Business Process Management platforms can be created to facilitate this discussion, that will be very useful. But even without software platforms, process seems destined to play a growing role in future discussions between business and IT managers.

One key to assuring that the process-focused discussions that business and IT managers engage in are useful is to assure that both business and IT managers begin with a common, comprehensive understanding of process. A discussion of only those processes that can be automated with today's techniques is too limited to facilitate discussions that can help business executives. Business executives are just as concerned with customer and employee issues as they are with automation issues. While it is impossible today to think of undertaking a major business process redesign project without considering what information technology can do to improve the process, it is equally impossible to think about a major redesign that does not call for major changes in how employees perform their jobs. Employees and the management of employees are just as important as information technology, and business managers need, more than ever, an integrated, holistic approach to the management of process change.

5 Business Process Change Today and Tomorrow

While many individuals continue to work largely within one of the three traditions we just described, a growing number are struggling to create a new synthesis, which is increasingly referred to as Business Process Management (BPM) and which, at its best, embraces all three traditions.

To organize our discussion of some of the more important efforts under way today, it is useful to have some general framework. The one we are most familiar with describes corporate business process change efforts in terms of levels. Some organizations are only focused on one level. Organizations with a CMM maturity of 2.5 are focused mainly on the Business Process Level. Increasingly, however, as organizations become more mature in managing their processes, they are working on all levels, simultaneously. At the Enterprise Level, organizations seek to organize their processes across the entire enterprise, aligning processes with strategies and defining process governance and measurement systems for the entire organization. At the Process Level, organizations are exploring a wide variety of new approaches to process analysis and redesign, and at the Implementation level, new technologies are evolving to support process work. Some of the initiatives at

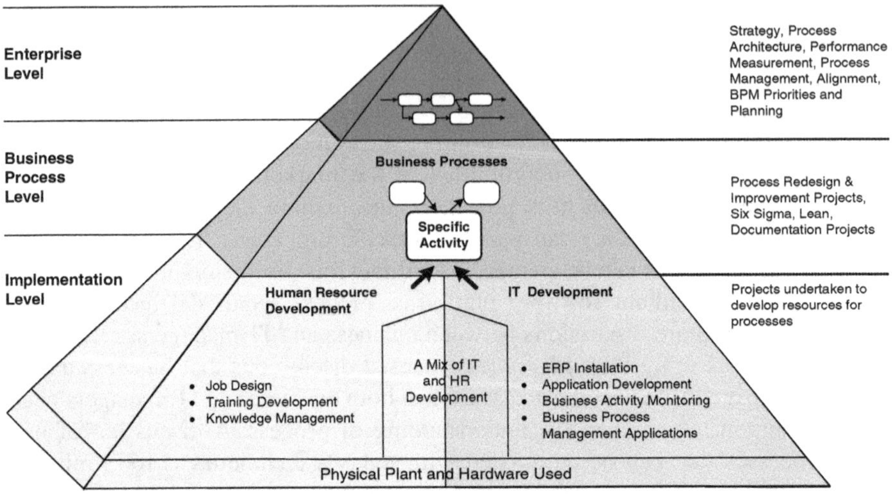

Fig. 8 The business process trends pyramid

each level can be associated with specific traditions, but, increasingly, as companies seek an integrated approach to process, we are witnessing the evolution of approaches at each level that combine elements of more than one tradition. We will organize the discussion that follows around the current initiatives on these three levels (see Fig. 8).

6 Enterprise Level Initiatives

Enterprise Level initiatives are focused on strategy, architecture, process governance, and on process measurement systems. As companies become more mature in their use of processes and increasingly try to integrate around business processes, they continue to place more emphasis on enterprise level initiatives.

6.1 Enterprise Architecture

Enterprise Architecture has always been a concern of those in IT. The focus has traditionally been on identifying how all of the software technologies, applications, and infrastructure elements fit together. The leading IT approach to enterprise architecture development was defined by John Zachman, (Zachman 1987), and is usually termed the Zachman Framework. It is an approach that is very oriented towards classifying elements and storing them in a database. The Zachman Framework mentions processes, but process concerns are simply not a major focus of the Zachman Framework.

Beginning in the early years of this decade, however, Enterprise Architecture began to take on a different meaning, and was increasingly used not only to define IT elements but also to show how the IT elements supported business processes. In effect, senior IT managers have begun to redefine their jobs and consider that they are not so much service providers as business managers who are responsible for using new technology to improve the company's business processes. IT managers who used to try to sell new technologies are now more likely to work with other business managers to see how business processes can be improved. This reflects the fact that IT no longer consists of applications running on mainframes in a special location, but with the advent of the PC, the Internet, and email, it is now integrated throughout every process in the organization. This, in turn, has led those involved in architectural efforts to embrace a broader, more process-oriented view of an enterprise architecture. Increasingly, the Business Process Architecture is the heart of enterprise architecture, and IT elements, policies, and jobs are seen as supporting components that are important as they support processes. At the same time, processes are increasingly aligned with corporate strategies and performance measures to generate architectural models that emphasize alignment and facilitate the rapid identification of related elements when strategic and process change is required (Harmon 2007).

In the US, Enterprise Architecture work has been strongly influenced by recent government laws that require government departments to have and use Enterprise Architectures to justify new initiatives. Although some of these architectures are more traditional IT architectures, they are modeled increasingly on the US government's Federal Enterprise Architecture Framework (FEAF) and rely on a layered, hierarchical model that emphasizes the alignment of strategy, missions, and customer results, and business processes with human and IT resources (see Fig. 9) (www.gov.cio/Documents/fedarch1.pdf).

The emphasis on process-focused ways of conceptualizing an enterprise architecture have, in turn, led architects to explore ways of representing value chains and high level processes. Today, there is a lot of emphasis on creating a Business Process Architecture and not too much agreement on exactly how to do it.

6.2 Value Chains and Value Networks

For the last 20 years, the organizing principle that most business process architects have relied upon has been the Value Chain. Michael Hammer relied heavily on the concept in *Reengineering the Corporation*, which he published in 1993. He urged companies to begin their process work by identifying their value chains and then, as needed, to reengineer each value chain (Hammer 2010).

In the last decade, however, the value chain has come under attack in academic circles. Those who dislike the value chain approach argue that it is too rigid; that is was developed when most companies emphasized manufacturing operations and

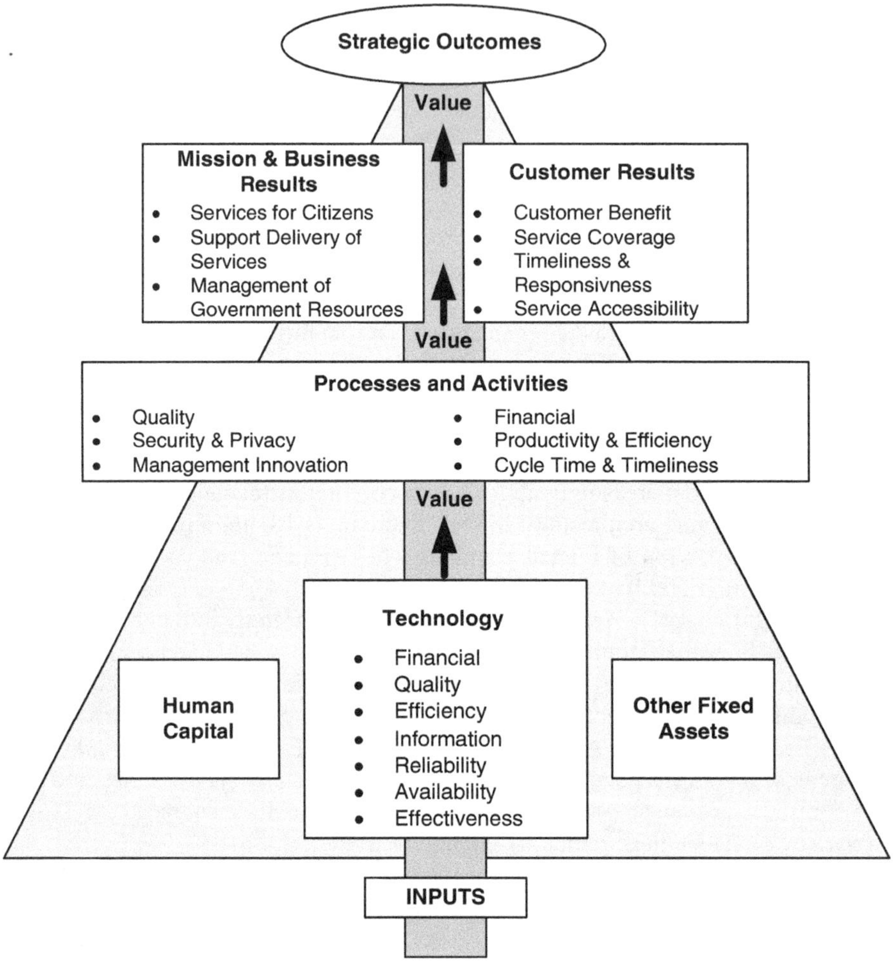

Fig. 9 An overview of the US government's Federal Enterprise Architecture Framework

focused on making large-scale processes as efficient as possible. In other words, they argue that the idea of the value chain is another artifact of the over emphasis on mass production. As companies become more agile and respond to customers in more creative ways, they argue, companies need a more flexible way of representing the relationships among their business processes.

6.2.1 Value Nets

Most of those who oppose the Value Chain approach support an alternative model that is usually termed a Value Net. There have been several books published on

Value Nets. The book that is most cited is David Bovet and Joseph Martha's *Value Nets: Breaking the Supply Chain to Unlock Hidden Profits* (Bovet and Martha 2000). Recently, IBM's Global Services group has begun to suggest that companies develop Component Business Models (CBM), which IBM claims that it derives from a Value Nets approach. IBM's Component Business Models offer a very specific and practical approach to organizing a Business Process Architecture, and thus they move the discussion of whether one should emphasize a Value Chain or a Value Net out of the academic arena and make it an issue that business process architects and practitioners will need to consider.

Clearly, IBM has thought quite a bit about its Component Business Model approach. Two IBM publications trace the evolution of CBM. The first is a paper by Luba Cherbakov, George Galambos, Ray Harishankar, Shankar Kalyana, and Guy Rockham entitled "Impact of Service Orientation at the Business Level." This appeared in the *IBM Systems Journal* in April 2005 (Cherbakov et al. 2005). It clearly lays out the Component Business Model, but seems to suggest that the CBM can be derived from the Value Chain, which seems to come first. The method has apparently evolved since then. In a white paper, *Component Business Models: Making Specialization Real*, issued by IBM Institute for Business Value in August 2005 (Pohle et al. 2005), and authored by George Pohle, Peter Korsten and Shanker Ramamurthy, IBM suggests that a CBM can be developed without reference to a value chain. Recent practice seems to rely grouping similar processes based on interviews and statistics. In either case, the result on an IBM CBM effort is a diagram, such as the one pictured in Fig. 10.

An IBM CBM architecture starts by grouping processes into broad categories, which it terms Business Competency Domains. The domains vary from company to company and seem to be an informal way to organize the specific company's large-scale processes. Typical domains include Managing Customers, Supply Chain, and Administration. IBM subdivides those categories into three fixed Accountability Levels: Strategy, Tactics, and Operations to form the basic CBM matrix. Both Strategy and Tactics level processes tend to be management processes. Operations level processes include both core and support processes.

No explicit relationships between the Business Components placed within the matrix are indicated. In other words, if we imagine a company with two value chains, each of which had an inventory process, both inventory processes would be merged here into a single generic Inventory process. Thus, an IBM CBM classifies a set of business processes (i.e., components) but does not suggest how they combine to provide specific value to particular customers. The whole point of the IBM CBM is to avoid showing specific chains of business processes in order to emphasize common, standard processes that are independent of any specific chain.

Reading the Value Net literature, one could easily conclude that Value Nets are primarily being used by consulting companies that are primarily focused on how to assemble unique processes to support one-of-a-kind engagements. The Value Net is just the shelf they keep their skill and knowledge on before they will assemble it in any way necessary to satisfy a given client.

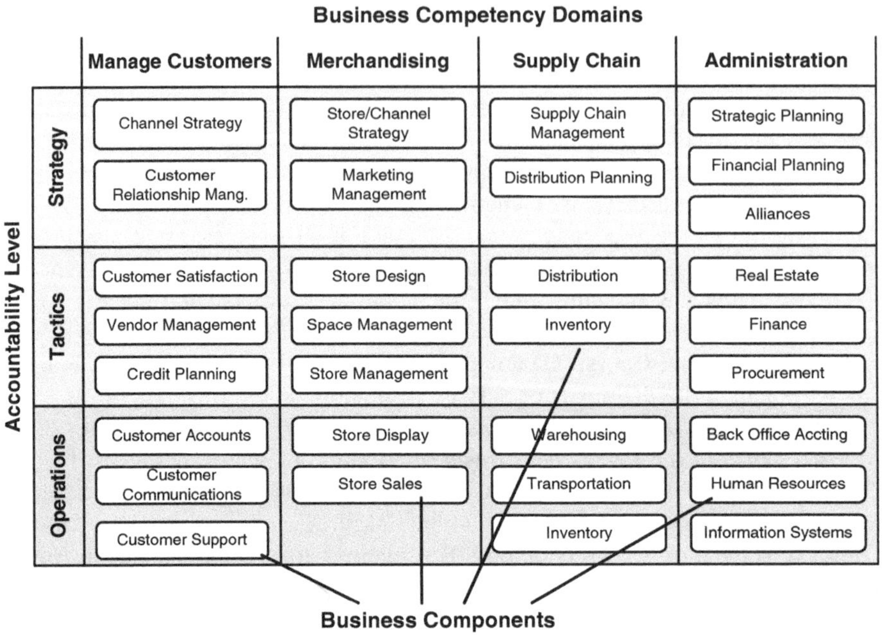

Fig. 10 IBM's component business model

On the other hand, we have encountered clients who increasingly focus on their management competencies and put less emphasis on their core or operational processes. This is often the case when companies outsource manufacturing to China and rely on distributors to market to customers. The traditional core capabilities of these companies have become commodities. Increasingly, their new core competencies consist of designing new products and assembling the capital and organizing the overall supply chain needed to bring new products or services to market. In other words, the core competencies of virtual companies are tactical and strategic management processes. For these companies, value nets seem to place more emphasis on the management processes and less on the traditional operational processes.

In a similar way, many companies are focused on building Service-Oriented Architectures and want to have a way of thinking of alternative services that can be used in any given process. Other companies are interested in simplifying their ERP systems, and want to standardize similar processes throughout the company to facilitate shifting to a single instance of ERP. Finally, value net approaches often seem to provide a better way of describing business process frameworks like SCOR and VRM. Suffice to say there are lots of groups that are deemphasizing value chains and focusing, instead, on sets of business processes that can be integrated on an ad hoc basis.

6.2.2 Tight Integration and Efficiency Versus Flexibility

Recall that Michael Porter argued that a company should work hard to integrate a value chain (Porter 1996). His primary concern was not efficiency as such, but the fact that a tightly integrated value chain that focused on executing a specific strategy was much more difficult for a competitor to copy. In other words, you optimize a value chain not only to assure efficiency but also to implement a strategy in a manner that gives you a competitive advantage that competitors find it difficult to duplicate. The alternative, which Porter terms "operational effectiveness," tries to make each individual process as efficient as possible, while ignoring the integration of the processes.

The Value Net theorists and IBM's CBM approach argue that few companies, today, have the time to integrate and refine their value chains. New technologies and new customer demands keep coming faster, and product lifecycles keep getting shorter. Thus, they argue that companies should conceptualize their organizations as a set of competencies, and to refine the business processes that embody each of the competencies. Then, as specific and unique challenges arise, the companies are well positioned to combine these competency-based processes, as needed, to create the large-scale processes they need to satisfy ad hoc customer needs. Obviously, IBM's approach is very much in the spirit of the Service-Oriented Architecture (SOA) that increasingly thinks of processes as assemblages created as needed. It is also very much in line with efforts underway at companies that seek to standardize business processes throughout the company in order to support a single instance (or at least a few instances) of ERP throughout the company.

A tightly integrated value chain can usually produce outputs for the minimum price in the fastest possible time. A flexible value net, assembled quickly, probably cannot produce outputs as efficiently or as cheaply. On the other hand, it can be hard to change a tightly integrated value chain, although it can be done if one design's variation is from the start. In either case, efficiency and success will depend on anticipating the right scope and size of the business components one creates. Too large and they would not snap together to handle the various and changing demands one faces. Too small and one faces too many hassles when one seeks to assemble them for a specific purpose.

Table 1 pictures the two approaches and compares some of the obvious advantages and disadvantages of the two approaches.

The authors who have written about Value Nets have tended to be both defensive and over enthusiastic. They suggest that there is a sharp either–or difference between the two approaches and that everyone will want to shift to the "more modern" value net approach. In reality, we suspect, most large companies will want both. Most large companies have at least some large-scale processes that are done over-and-over. Success in these operations requires efficiency and tight integration. It makes sense to model those processes as value chains and to work hard to make those processes as efficient as possible. In these cases, competitive advantage will clearly reside with tightly integrated processes that support a high quality, low cost strategy. At the same time, most large companies also have large-scale processes

Table 1 Advantages and disadvantages of value chains and value nets

Value chain	Value net (CBM)
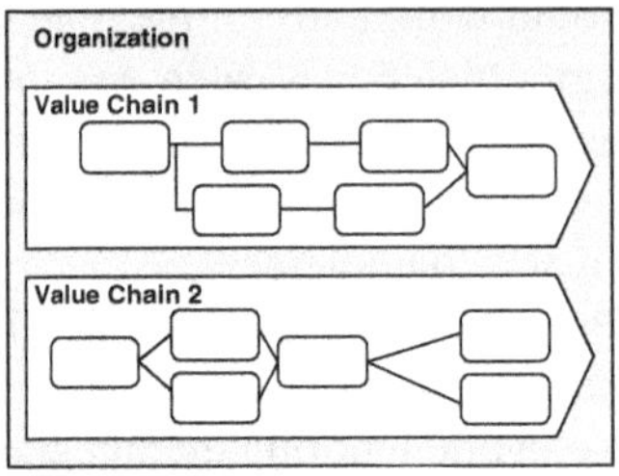	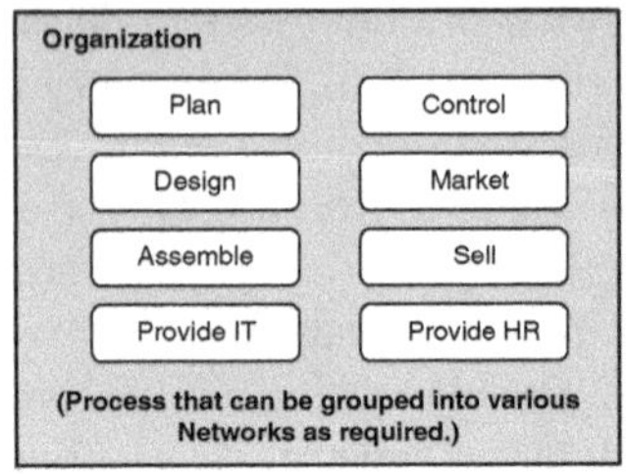
Advantages • Defines an actual process undertaken by the organization • Identifies customer • Shows specific relationships between internal sub-processes • Allows you to measure results of chain and use that measure to evaluate the results of the internal processes that make up the value chain	*Advantages* • Defines all processes company has that could be used to assemble a new value chain • Identifies all processes that company supports that have competencies and that take similar inputs and make similar outputs
Disadvantages • Defines a specific way in which processes fit together • May use similar processes in more than one value chain without identifying that fact	*Disadvantages* • Does not identify specific process • Does not identify customer • Does now show relationships between business processes

that change rapidly and that generate highly tailored outputs. It may not make sense to model those processes as value chains, or to spend too much time trying to integrate all the subprocesses. In this case, competitive advantage will lie with a strategy that emphasizes on flexibility.

Overall, however, the business process architects job is not becoming easier. Companies will increasingly need to rely on a variety of different approaches to organize their business process architectures.

6.3 *Business Process Frameworks*

Business Process Frameworks (also called Operation Reference Frameworks) are one of the most exciting developments in process work in the past decade. Frameworks provide a quick way for a company to establish a high-level process architecture, complete with core, management, and support processes, and with measures to use in evaluating performance. The use of process frameworks were driven, initially, by the growing interdependency of company supply chains, by outsourcing, and by a heightened need for a standard vocabulary to facilitate communication between companies that are trying to coordinate how their respective processes can work together. As more companies have decided to create formal business process architectures, however, frameworks have become popular as templates that can be used to help a company quickly create a business architecture.

6.3.1 The Supply Chain Council's SCOR Framework

The Supply Chain Council's SCOR Framework is undoubtedly the best known example of a business process framework. The Supply Chain Council (SCC) was established as a nonprofit consortium in 1996. Today, it is a worldwide organization with over 700 members. The Council conducts meetings that allow companies to gather together to discuss supply chain problems and opportunities. In addition, it has been working on a standard supply chain framework or reference model (Bolstorff and Rosenbaum 2007; Poluha 2007).

SCOR is comprised of three levels, as illustrated in Fig. 11. The SCOR Reference Manual defines each level 2 and level 3 subprocess and also indicates what

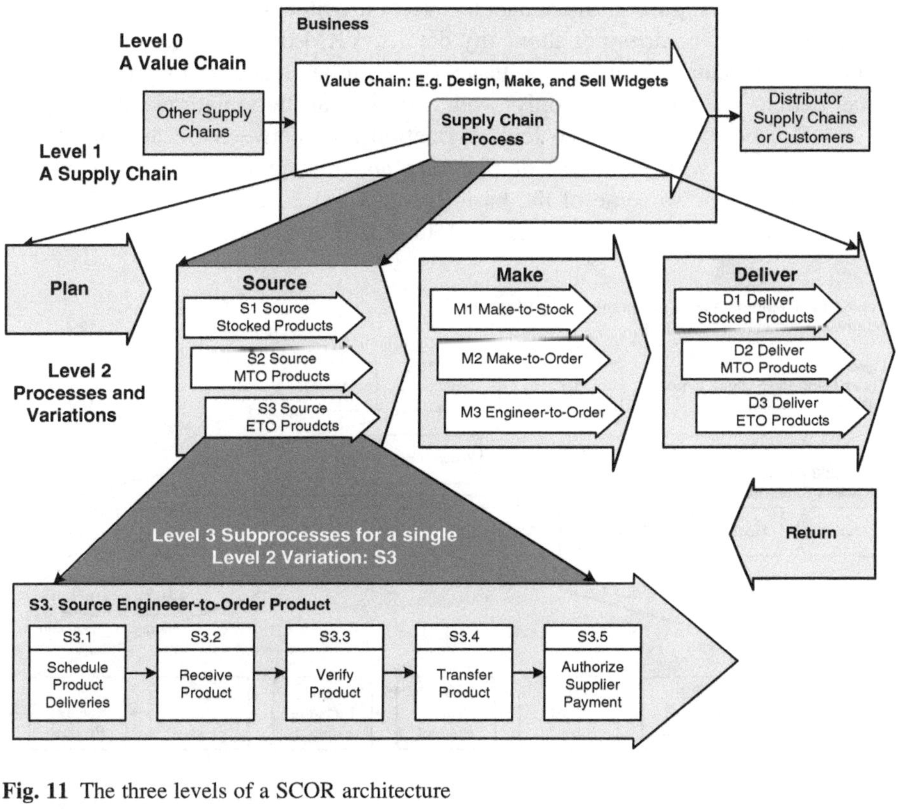

Fig. 11 The three levels of a SCOR architecture

planning and support processes are typically linked to each of process or subprocess. The SCC does not define a fourth level, leaving the specification of level four activities to individual companies. In other words, SCOR defines a supply chain architecture and all of the high-level processes and leaves the technical implementation of the level 3 processes to the individual members.

In a similar way, the SCOR Reference Manual defines metrics for each of the processes in the SCOR framework. Thus, using SCOR a company can quickly characterize its supply chain architecture and choose metrics appropriate to their industry and strategy. Several organizations that track benchmarks are working with the Supply Chain Council and can provide generic benchmarks for SCOR measures for specific industries. Thus, a company can not only create architecture but also obtain information to determine where their existing processes are superior or deficient.

6.3.2 Other Business Frameworks

The Value-Chain Group has created its own model, the Value Reference Model or VRM, which is similar to SCOR, but more comprehensive and, in some ways, better integrated. Figure 12 illustrates the VRM architecture.

Although Fig. 12 does not show any details, VRM defines an extensive set of Planning and Managing processes. If we wanted to analyze *B4: Verify Product* in some detail, we would not only want to look at the relationships between B3–B4–B5, but we would also look at relationships between B4 and other core processes along with a variety of planning and managing processes. Consider Fig. 13, which shows some of the basic Level 3 processes that link to B4. Then imagine that each of those processes had four or five inputs and four or five outputs.

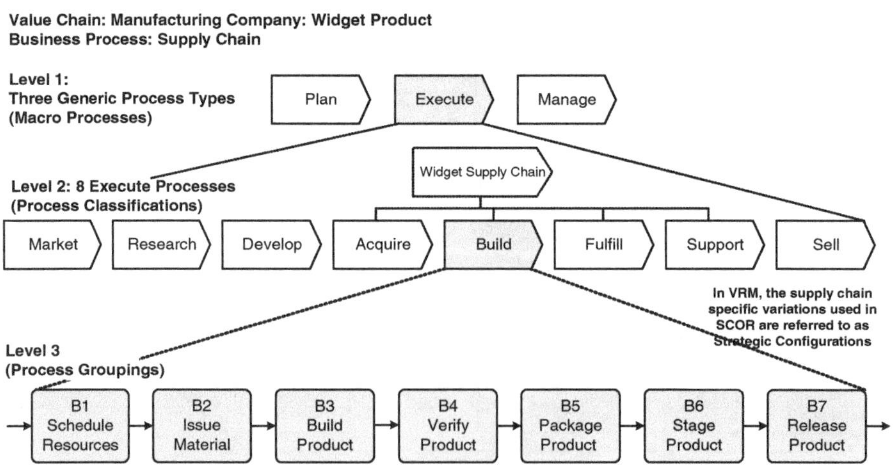

Fig. 12 The Value-Chain Group's VRM framework

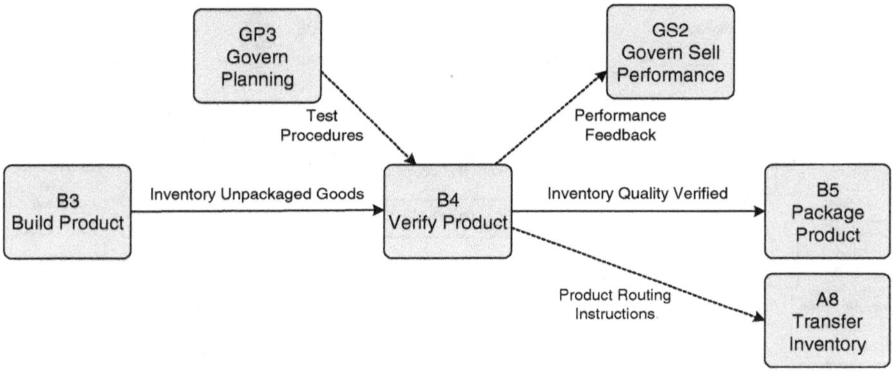

Fig. 13 Processes linked to B4 in the VRM framework

Thus, the high level processes we find in Frameworks and Business Process Architectures, in general, are often simply nodes in a complex network of relationships and hard to represent in traditional flow diagrams. We will consider the implementations of this in a moment.

Another effort to define a complete value chain framework was undertaken by the TeleManagement Forum, a consortium of telecom companies. Their framework is highly tailored to the needs of telecom companies. Thus, it cannot be used by nontelecoms, but it does provide a comprehensive approach for telecom companies.

In addition to SCOR, VRM, and eTOM, there are a number of other initiatives underway to create business process frameworks. AQPC offers a framework that incorporates elements of SCOR. ITIL and COBIT are more specialized frameworks that can be used by IT departments. The insurance industry consortium, ACORD, is working on a framework for the insurance industry, the OMG's Finance Task Force is working on a framework for finance companies, and there are probably others we have not heard of yet.

All of these framework efforts not only provide companies with an easy way to create a process architecture, but they focus everyone on the various issues involved in the creation and maintenance of a process architecture. There is already talk about how to best model frameworks, and there are software tools being developed to help companies use the various frameworks. ISSSP has a SIG focused on how to integrate SCOR models with Six Sigma development efforts, and similar initiatives will undoubtedly appear in the next few years. Once companies accept the idea that they do not need to create their own process architecture from scratch, many different aspects of process work will gradually change.

6.3.3 Roger Burlton, Process Scope, and Value Chain Diagrams

Roger Burlton, a well-known process consultant, is also very much in the management tradition, and his book, *Business Process Management*, which was published

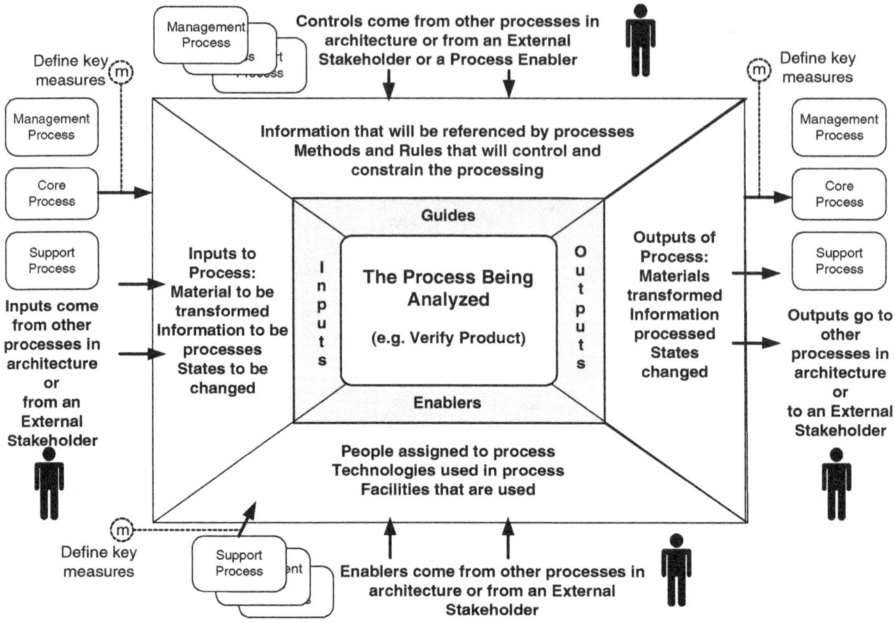

Fig. 14 Burlton's process scope diagram

in 2001, is, as far as we know, the first book to use the term *BPM* in its modern sense (Burlton 2001) (Burlton 2010). As with all those working in the management tradition, Burlton emphasizes the need to align organizations from the top, down, to assure that processes are measured and can be shown to support customers and strategic goals. Similarly, he puts as much emphasis on the management and the way employees implement the processes as on the formal organization of the processes themselves.

Just as Rummler is associated with process flow diagrams (Rummler–Brache Diagrams) that include swimlanes and a top line for the customers of the process, Burlton is associated with Process Scope Diagrams or IGOEs (Inputs, Guides, Outputs and Enablers) (see Fig. 14).

Scope diagrams represent an extension of an earlier type of diagram found in a US Air Force methodology – IDEF – but extended by Burlton and others to support high-level process analysis work. IGOE diagrams are particularly useful for analyzing the problems associated with the types of processes you find in process architectures and in frameworks like SCOR and VRM – processes that linked, in complex ways, to a variety of other core, management, and support processes. They are also useful for emphasizing the role of policies and rules and management and employee issues that are largely ignored in traditional flow diagrams.

The process-in-scope is placed in the middle box. Inputs and outputs are then examined. The sources of the inputs and those who receive the outputs are also identified. Then, in addition, one looks at Guides – information that controls the execution of the process, including business rules and management policies – and we look at what Enables the process, including employees, data from IT applications, and the physical layout of the work environment. As we define the flows into and out of the process-in-scope, we look for problems and we also begin to define how we will measure the effectiveness of the process and where the problems seem to reside.

As companies begin to work with process architectures, they will need ways to focus on specific processes and examine all of the relationships between a given high level process and all of the other processes associated with it. Rummler–Brache process flow diagrams have evolved into BPMN diagrams. We would not be surprised to find that Burlton's IGOE diagrams, or something very similar, will evolve into a new standard type of diagram that those interested in process architectures sand frameworks will use to document, analyze, and model high level business processes. Some authors have begun to refer to this type of diagram as a value chain diagram.

6.4 Process Maturity Models

CMM and CMMI remain the most popular descriptions of process maturity, but they are increasingly seen as too oriented towards the concerns of groups like the US Department of Defense, which uses this approach to evaluate contractors. In the past few years, we have seen several efforts aimed at producing maturity models that are more aligned with the concerns of business process architects.

One effort, the Business Process Maturity Model, was developed by Bill Curtis and Charles Weber, researchers who had formerly worked with SEI. Their effort resulted in a process-oriented maturity standard, BPMM, which has been adopted by the OMG (www.bpmn.org).

Another effort has been led by Dr. Michael Rosemann and Tonia de Bruin at the Business Process Management Research Group at Queensland University of Technology, Australia, and has been undertaken in conjunction with a related effort, which is being led by Tom Davenport and Brad Power at Babson College (Rosemann et al. 2006). This group has been developing a Holistic Model for BPM Maturity (Rosemann and vom Brocke 2010). In essence, this work has extended the CMM model to three dimensions and seeks to coordinate a wider range of variables in their characterizations of maturity. This model has been derived from a comprehensive study of related literature in the areas of maturity models and critical success factors of Business Process Management. The model has been applied in a number of case studies, and the findings from these case studies motivated further revisions. Rather than simply analyzing existing process efforts, the maturity model developed by Rosemann and others has proven useful in helping companies develop their BPM strategies and create roadmaps to guide their ongoing process efforts.

All of these efforts, and undoubtedly others we do not know about, seek to provide tools that companies can use to characterize how they currently manage processes and suggestions about what steps companies can take to improve their performance. The costs for the user range from a few thousand dollars for a "quickie" evaluation by an individual consultant, to over $100,000 for a very detailed assessment by a certified team. Maturity modeling is not the right approach for everyone, but many companies have found these assessments can serve as a way to rally their organization and focus everyone's attention on a specific process management improvement effort. Others use assessments to establish milestones and then reevaluate in subsequent years to determine their improvement and maintain their focus. It is a tool that many companies have found very useful, and we will undoubtedly witness more work in this domain in the near future.

6.5 Integrated Process Measurement Systems

Most business process practitioners have struggled to define systematic process measurement systems. It is relatively easy to define measures that can be used to determine if a specific process is functioning efficiently. It is much harder to determine if a given process is contributed to customer happiness or company success. What is needed is a way of systematically aligning company goals with process goals. At the moment, the approach that is attracting the most attention is a variation on the Balanced Scorecard system popularized by Kaplan and Norton. Today, there are a variety of scorecards, including Six Sigma Scorecards and SCORcards (Gupta 2006; Bolstorff and Rosenbaum 2007; Poluha 2007). The real challenge, however, is not to come up with a scorecard on which to record a variety of measures, but to create a system that aligns the measures from the top to the bottom of the organization.

Most scorecards developed by those working in the Balanced Scorecard tradition have tended to align functional or departmental measures rather than process measures. Using such a system, one begins by creating an Organization Scorecard. Then each division or department creates its own variation on the Organization Scorecard, showing how the division or department will measure its contribution the organizational effort. Similarly, each department or group in each division creates its own scorecard to show how it will support the divisional effort. Once the scorecards are complete and aligned, the scorecards are used to evaluate the divisional, departmental, and group managers responsible for the respective business units. A wide variety of organizations currently use some slight variation on this approach.

Imagine tailoring the scorecard approach for a company that is serious about measuring the performance of its processes. In effect, we begin with an organizational scorecard, then create scorecards for each value chain, and then for each major process and each subprocess, etc. A few organizations have experimented with this approach.

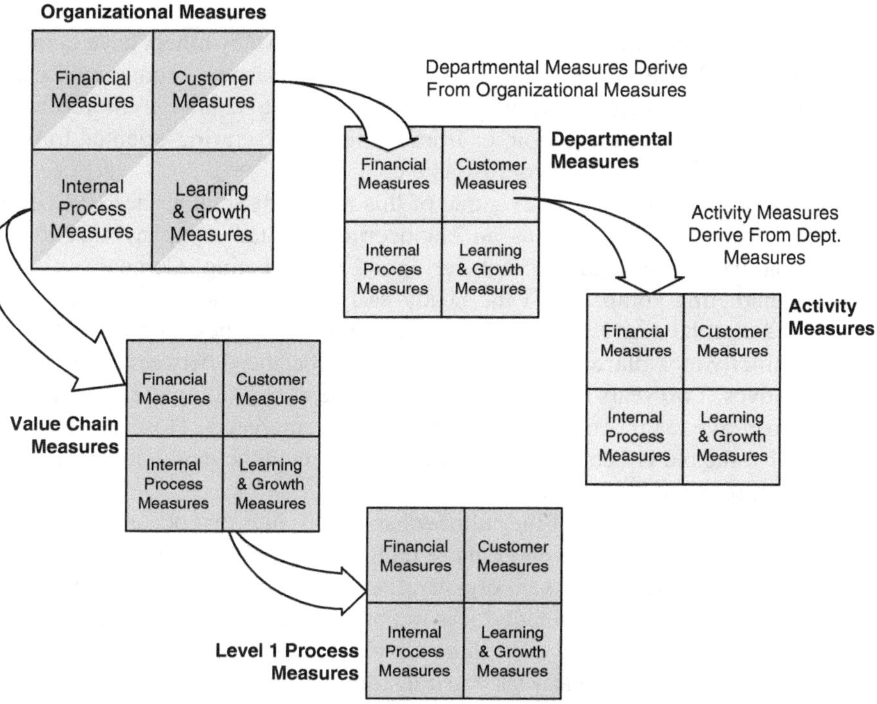

Fig. 15 Dual scorecard system for a company with both functional and process managers

Most organizations that embrace process management in a significant way, however, also maintain a functional structure and end up with a matrix pattern, with some managers responsible for processes and others for functional units. This requires a dual set of scorecards, as illustrated in Fig. 15. In this case, one divides the organizational goals between goals that will be the responsibility of a functional manager and others that will be the responsibility of a value chain manager and then proceed to decompose each independently. Done with care, this can provide an organization with interesting insights into which of its goals are really dependent on processes and which are independent of process considerations.

Aligning process measurement systems via scorecard hierarchies is relatively new and there is a lot of experimentation going on to determine the most efficient ways to create and manage these systems (Gupta 2006; Smith 2007).

6.6 Managing Culture Change and Organizational Transformations

In additional to the more or less technical concerns, companies are very interested in tools and techniques that facilitate large scale changes in their organizations.

Many companies have launched programs to make managers and employees more conscious of the importance of quality or of processes. Many others have launched programs to achieve some more strategic culture change – sometimes called organization transformation – as when a company tries to change from a technical to a customer-focused orientation, or from being manufacturing-oriented to being service-oriented (Hilti case in vom Brocke et al. 2010).

Anyone who wants a trivial example of this need only look at the HP-Compaq merger. HP was well known as an engineering-oriented company that toward operational excellence and was not very good at marketing. Compaq was very much a marketing company. In the heady early days of the merger, executives speculated that the new HP would be able to combine the best of both. When the merger initially took place, the executive team was balanced between Compaq and HP executives. Two years later, there were only one or two Compaq executives still on the executive team. To those who observed the merger at close range, it was obvious that the old HP engineering culture had rejected the marketing positioning that was represented by Compaq.

Figure 16 suggests some of the culture change activities that occur and contrasts culture change with concerns about more traditional process methodologies, tools, and techniques. Popular books on organizational transformation or culture change often offer platitudes. Undoubtedly, it is important to communicate with everyone and meet together and maybe even share a rock climbing experience. Beyond that, however, anyone who has really tried to transform a company knows that it requires a major top-down effort and a very forceful senior executive to drive the changes and a well-structured plan to drive the effort. Organization transformation is about politics and motivation, as well as communication.

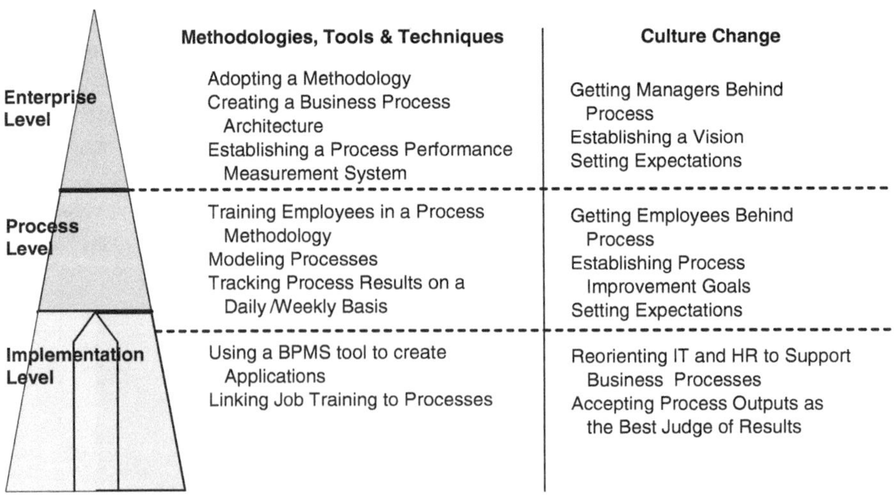

Fig. 16 Tools and techniques versus culture change activities

We have visited several companies and have been told by senior executives that they intend to reorient their companies, to make them more process centric. If all they mean is that they intend to analyze their processes more effectively and begin to gather data on their processes that will support better decisions, then we are usually reasonably confident they can succeed. If, on the other hand, they are really talking about a major organizational transformation and they want to create a company, like Toyota's automotive business, in which every manager and employee obsesses about process and quality, then we are usually much less sanguine about their prospects. Put a little differently, organizational transformation is very hard.

The best cultural change stories we know of come from the Six Sigma community. Six Sigma has often been introduced and strongly supported by the CEO of the company. One thinks of Jack Welsh, at GE, who made a significant portion of every senior executive's bonus dependent on getting results with Six Sigma. Under those circumstances organizational transformation is much more likely.

Consider, however, the situation discussed by *Business Week* in its June 11, 2007 issue. The cover story was on 3M and described how 3M hired James McNerney as CEO in 2000. McNerney had previously worked for Jack Welch at GE and promised, when hired, to use Six Sigma at 3M to make the organization for process focused. 3M's stock was down – it had stayed nearly flat during the hyperactive late 1990s – and most outside analysts thought that 3M was overstaffed. McNerney introduced Six Sigma after laying off 11% of the workforce (8,000 people). Thousands of 3M staffers were trained as Black Belts and many more received Green Belt training. The company embraced both DMAIC and Design for Six Sigma and began to improve its processes with a vengeance.

McNerney slashed capital expenditures by 22% from $980 million to $763 million in his first year and was down to $677 by 2003. Operating margins went from 17% in 2001 to 23% in 2005. As a percentage of sales, capital expenditures dropped from 6.1% in 2001 to 3.7% in 2003. Profits under McNerney grew by 22% a year.

After four and a half years, McNerney left 3M to become the new CEO of Boeing. Given the training and the good results, one might have thought that 3M, a company previously famous for its product innovation focus, might have transitioned to a more process or operationally oriented culture. In fact, according to *Business Week,* McNerney's successor at 3M, George Buckley, immediately began to dial back the Six Sigma effort. The major complaint among the 3M people was that "innovation" was down. 3M had always been a company that promoted innovation. It is where Thinsulate and Post-Its were invented. The company had historically prided itself on the fact that, at any one time, at least 33% of its products sales came from products released in the past 5 years. By the time McNerney left, the percentage of sales from products released during the past 5 years was down to 25%. Those who complained argued that Six Sigma is somehow incompatible with innovation. Given growth of 22% a year and operating margins that grew from 17% to 23%, one might have thought that 3M had made a reasonable transition to be better balanced culture. At this point, however, it seems likely that 3M will reject the effort at organizational transformation and shift back to the norms of its earlier product-focused, innovation-oriented culture.

As we suggested: culture change is hard. It takes a massive, sustained effort, and even then it often fails. Clearly, anyone interested in process change is going to want to pay close attention to developments in this area in the years ahead.

7 Process Level Initiatives

Process Level Initiatives focus on projects that seek to create, redesign, or improve specific business processes. At this level, companies are interested in methodologies and tools that they can use to undertake business change projects.

7.1 The Emphasis on Innovation

Suddenly, *Innovation* is a very hot term. It is recently replaced *Agile* and *Excellence* as the accolade of choice in the business press. It might even replace *BPM* as a popular way to describe process initiatives. *Merriam Webster's Collegiate Dictionary* suggests that *Innovation* involves: (1) introducing something new, which can be (2) an idea, a method, or a device. The *Oxford English Dictionary* suggests the word is derived from Latin, where it referred to the introduction of novelty and that it was first used in English, in something like its current meaning, in 1297. Clearly, we are not talking about a new concept here. Equally clearly, businesses have always tried to be innovative. An entrepreneur creates something new when he starts a new business and a manager is innovative when he introduces a new process. Marketing is innovative when they introduce a new ad campaign that gets a lot of attention, and New Product Development innovates when they use new technology to create a new product or service.

If we focus more narrowly on innovation in the context of process change, we can divide the recent literature, very roughly, into three broad piles. One school stresses creativity and focuses on brainstorming and a variety of related techniques that can help teams of people think of alternative ways of accomplishing a task. This school might be summed up as the creative thinking school.

A second school derives from the work of Genrich Altshuller, a Russian theorist who has created a systematic or "engineering" approach – called TRIZ – which can be used to examine problems and generate new possibilities. TRIZ is a Russian acronym that means something like the theory of inventive problem solving, and it was originally developed in conjunction with work on patent analysis (Altshuller 1984). Most of the early interest in TRIZ, in the US, was generated by Six Sigma practitioners who adopted TRIZ for use with Six Sigma improvement efforts (Silverstein et al. 2005). Recently, Howard Smith has written a wonderful series of columns for BPTrends in which he has shown how TRIZ can be used in conjunction with process redesign (Smith 2007).

The third major use of the term *Innovation* is being driven by Michael Hammer, who has written on the importance of innovation (Hammer 2004). Hammer contrasts *Innovation* with *Improvement* and suggests that there are times when you simply want to improve existing processes and then there are other times when you want to innovate and completely change the way you do business. In other words, Hammer is simply using *Innovation* as a synonym for *reengineering*.

We have heard people argue that innovation distinguishes between process improvement and process redesign. Hammer seems to suggest that innovation distinguishes between reengineering and either redesign or improvement. We do not think either distinction is very useful. Let's face it: almost everyone is engaged in introducing new ideas, new methods, and new devices. Some are "newer" than others, no doubt, but everyone is looking for new ways to get things done. Clearly, if we are going to make sense out of *Innovation*, we are going to need a continuum. The best continuum that we have found is provided by Charles A. O'Reilly III and Michael L. Tushman. O'Reilly and Tushman (2004) review a wide variety of different examples of innovation and end up proposing the continuum pictured in Fig. 17.

In the area above the bold arrow in Fig. 17, we describe the three categories that O'Reilly and Tushman use to map the various examples of innovation they studied. Below the bold arrow, we have listed the three general approaches to process change. Obviously, Fig. 17 is a continuum and there are all kinds of instances that would lie on the line between Incremental Innovations and Discontinuous Innovations, but at least this figure suggests why all kinds of people will be using the term *Innovation* to mean different things. Once you realize that innovation is usually just a synonym for process or product change and accept that there is a whole continuum of possibilities, then the trick, for a given company, becomes a matter of getting the mix right.

Everyone is going to hear a lot more about innovation in the years ahead (Seidel and Rosemann 2008) (Seidel et al. 2010). Getting a good idea of what is involved,

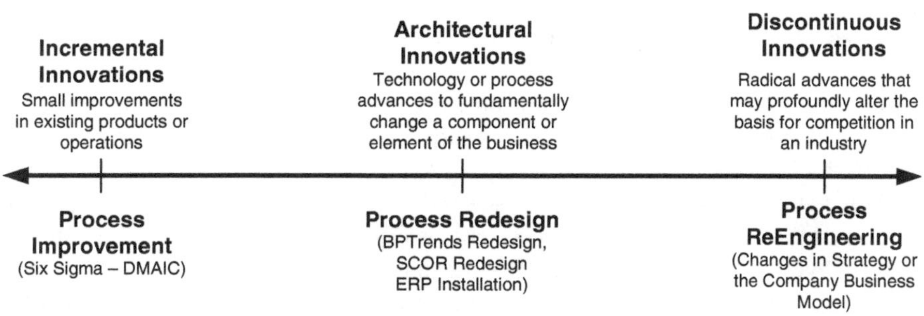

Fig. 17 The O'Reilly–Tushman innovation continuum

and focusing on what is important, and what can be used at your company today, are important. Similarly, every reader should understand that there will be a lot of nonsense peddled in the name of innovation and should try to avoid getting carried away by either narrow definitions or by the spurious correlations that always seem to accompany any hot new business jargon. The bottomline, however, is that if management wants to talk about innovation, then processes practitioners should be prepared to say, we can make innovation happen.

7.2 *Analyzing and Modeling Complex Processes*

Another area of process work that is receiving a lot of attention involves the analysis and modeling of complex processes. There are different ways of describing complex processes. Some emphasize that they are unique – as when an engineering firm creates a process to create a unique product. Some industries refer to them as Cases. Keith Harrison-Broninski has written extensively about them and has emphasized that collaborative processes that require people to network to find unique solutions (Harrison-Broninski 2005) (Harrison-Broninski 2010). We sometimes think of them as expert systems – processes that would require tens of thousands of rules if one were to try to describe the decision processes involved. The OMG has recently issued a request for information about what it terms Dynamic Business Processes. However you describe them, we all recognize that there are processes and activities that are very difficult to analyze or describe.

It is easy enough to describe complex processes a very high level; of course, you simply create a box called "Design Software Architecture," "Manage Marketing," or "Write Business Plan." As you begin to drill down, however, you realize just how little we know about how these activities are actually done. These are processes that – given current technologies – are impossible to automate in a cost-effective manner. In other words, complex processes challenge our ability to define the specific procedures involved.

Figure 18 suggests a continuum from simple to very complex processes. Manufacturing production line processes were easy because they involved watching what people do. Many service processes are more complex, but can still be defined without too much difficulty. At the other extreme from procedures, however, there are complex or dynamic processes. Most companies do not focus on defining the jobs, but concentrate, instead, on hiring people who have already proven they can perform the activities.

As we already suggested, expert systems developers were focused on this type of process in the late 1980s. The expert systems effort failed to create useful applications, in even narrowly prescribed domains (e.g., Meningitis Analysis), not because they could not capture the thousands of rules a human expert used, but because they could not maintain the rule bases. A human expert is always learning and changing

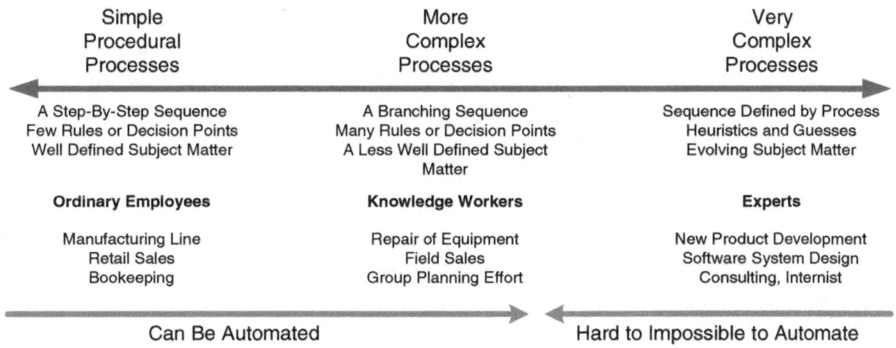

Fig. 18 A process complexity continuum

his or her rules as the environment changes and knowledge evolves. Using existing techniques, an expert system is out of date the day after it is completed.

We recently looked at a BPMS tool, the EMC Documentum BPM Suite that has introduced a way of dealing, indirectly, with some of the more complex collaborative activities process modelers encounter. In essence, a developer creates a special type of activity, which the EMC product calls an "e-room." When an input is made to an instance of the activity when the process is being executed, several employees associated with the activity are notified and can create a web dialog that focuses on creating the desired output. If we were to define some of the activities that make up an e-room process, we would find activities like: Name project, identify who should be involved, send emails inviting people to e-meeting, define steps in project, define roles for team members in project, etc. In effect, the BPMS product avoids the problem of analyzing the activity and simply recognizes that people will need to collaborate to arrive at a solution, and then provides groupware to facilitate their collaboration.

Another approach to complex process analysis is termed Cognitive Task Analysis (Crandall et al. 2006). When we first started analyzing human performance problems, in the late 1960s, the techniques we used were generally termed "behavioral task analysis." This term reflected the dominant trend in psychology in the late 1960s – behaviorism – which stressed observation of overt activity. By the late 1970s, however, most academic psychologists had returned to the study of cognition. Using new techniques, derived primarily from work with computers, psychologists began to conceptualize human performers as information processing systems, and ask questions about the nature of human cognitive processing. The new cognitive psychology put its emphasis on observation and was at least as rigorous as behaviorism. An early classic of cognitive task analysis was Allen Newell and Herbert A. Simon's *Human Problem Solving*. In *Human Problem Solving*, Newell and Simon (1972) analyzed a variety of human cognitive tasks, including cryptarithmetic, logic, and chess playing and reached a variety of interesting conclusions that formed the basis for several decades of work in both cognitive psychology and artificial intelligence. Indeed, it could be argued that their work led directly to expert systems and, more recently to Cognitive Task Analysis. The key point to make here, however, is that psychologists and computer scientists spent several years, in the early 1980s developing techniques to capture human expertise and embed expert knowledge in software systems.

The work in cognitive psychology led to the development of expert systems. They have not provided to be very useful, but the same techniques are now being used in business rules analysis efforts and in cognitive task analysis, which rely on many of the techniques used in expert systems design. Object models are constructed to describe the concepts and knowledge structures used by the human decision makers and rules are written to describe specific decisions.

The emphasis today, however, is on avoiding expert activities and focusing on the tasks undertaken by knowledge workers. While a true expert, an engineer who could design an M1 Battle Tank, might have models with many hundreds of objects and use ten or twenty thousand rules, the soldiers who diagnose M1 Battle Tank problems in the field might only require a hundred objects and a thousand rules.

The trend, in other words, is to ignore true expertise, which is too hard to analyze or maintain – given our current techniques – and to focus on analyzing the knowledge that knowledge workers bring to bear on their more circumscribed but still demanding tasks. The work of knowledge workers is, of course, very important and valuable, and if we can capture significant portions of it, we can share it, and use it to design processes that can contribute significantly to the value of our organizations. To date, cognitive task analysis has proven very expensive, and is largely confined to complex tasks required by institutions, like military organizations, which need to train large numbers of new recruits to operate very complex equipment in a very short period of time. As more is learned, however, we can hope that new tools and techniques will make it easier to analyze and then automate the more complex tasks in most organizations.

The line between what can be analyzed and automated will keep moving in the decade ahead. The successful process practitioner will want to stay abreast of where the line is at any point in time to assure that the processes he or she chooses to analyze and automate are within the means available at that point in time.

8 Implementation Level Initiatives

The development of specific solutions to business process problems usually occurs on the implementation level. If a process is changed, it usually implies that software will have to be developed or changed. Similarly, job descriptions and training programs require changes. In extreme cases, offices will need to be changed to different locations in different countries to support the new processes. Just as there are challenges, methodologies, and techniques that are used at the process level, there are other methodologies and techniques that are appropriate to the implementation level.

8.1 Business Process Management Systems (BPMS)

A major change has occurred in this decade. Business people have realized that IT is no longer a support service but an integral element in the company's strategy. IT managers, for their part, have decided to stop focusing on technology and support, as such, and to focus, instead, on how they help implement business processes. In essence, the description of the goals and workings of business processes has emerged as the common language that both business executives and IT managers speak. This reorientation, has, in turn, led to a sweeping reconsideration of how IT supports business managers and to the development of integrated packages of Business Process Management software suites. Software tools that, a decade ago, would have been described as workflow, business intelligence, rules engines, or enterprise application integration tools are now being integrated together and spoken of as BPMS products (Khan 2004).

No one, today, is exactly sure what BPMS means or how BPMS products will evolve. It is a complex software market, made up, as it is of vendors who would formerly have said they were in different niches (BI, EAI, Rules, Modeling, CASE), and who are now trying to determine exactly how they work with others to generate a common Business Process Management Software platform. Many users do not discriminate between modeling tools, such as ARIS and Casewise, and BPMS suites such as webMethods or webSphere, and applications suites with some BPMS capabilities, like BizTalk and NetWeaver. Perhaps it is not important to do so at this time, as all are rapidly evolving and each will change as the functionality desired by users, after they have had a change to experiment with the various products, becomes clearer.

In 2003, Howard Smith and Peter Fingar wrote *Business Process Management* as a clarion call for companies to develop and use BPMS products to automate and manage their business processes. Smith and Fingar envisioned a world in which business managers would be able to glance at computer screens and see how their business processes were performing, and then, as needed, modify their processes to respond better to the evolving business situation. In other words, BPMS was to be a new type of software – a layer of software that sat on top of other software and managed all the people and software elements required to control major business processes. It is worth stepping back and asking to what degree that vision has been realized.

With a few exceptions, the BPMS software market has not evolved from scratch. Instead, the BPMS vendors were already in existence, offering workflow, documentation, rules engines, enterprise application integration (EAI), business intelligence (BI), or even ERP applications. Vendors from each of these older software domains have rushed to modify and expand their software products to incorporate capabilities associated with an evolving idea of what a BPMS product might include. Thus, workflow vendors have added EAI and vice versa. Most vendors have added a rule capability and incorporated BI (zur Mühlen 2004).

There has been a lot of consolidation as the various vendors have acquired each other to assemble the right set of capabilities. For all that effort, there is still, as of

2008, a very vigorous BPMS market with at least 15 vendors fighting for market share. At this point, the platform vendors – like IBM, Oracle, SAP, and Software AG – seem to be doing best with process automation projects that are essentially EAI projects. The smaller vendors who are more focused on workflow, however, taken together, still constitute about half the market. And this, in turn, suggests the current immaturity of the 2008 BPMS market. In part, vendors have focused on what they know best. Vendors from an EAI background have focused on automating processes that primarily involve software systems. Vendors from a workflow background have focused on automating processes with lots of human interaction. And that, in turn, means that both are working on relatively small scale processes, or only working on one part of larger business processes.

We are still looking for good case studies that describe large-scale business processes whose managers now monitor and control those processes using BPMS suites. Most "BPMS" products, to date, are, in fact, workflow or EAI projects that could have been done in 2000. They are done by IT and IT manages them. This is not to say that they are not important automation projects and that business managers are not happy to have them in place, but we are only beginning to realize the goal proposed by Smith and Fingar – to create overarching process management systems that business managers can own and control (Smith and Fingar 2003).

If there is a major difference between today's "BPMS" applications and EAI or workflow applications that would have been built in 2000, it lays in the fact that today's EAI and workflow systems are built to take advantage of the Internet and, increasingly, a Service-Oriented Architecture (SOA) (Dumas and Kohlborn 2010; Cummins 2010). Elementary SOA projects can be done without reference to BPM, but sophisticated SOA projects, to be of value to the company, must be integrated with a deep understanding of the organization's business processes. Indeed, it is the emphasis on SOA, and the role that SOA infrastructure plays in the thinking of the leading platform vendors, which explains their growing support for BPM and BPMS.

The new emphasis on BPMS and SOA, as the two sides of the same coin, is a mixed blessing for the BPM community. It has attracted the interest of the platform vendors and driven their commitment. At the same time, it has led them to emphasize the more technical aspects of BPMS and make discussions of BPMS sound more and more like discussions of enterprise integration. BPM and BPMS need not get lost when the discussion turns to SOA, but they often do (Inaganti 2007). Or, more correctly, they get relegated to a very secondary role. Like too many IT discussions in the past, SOA developers are inclined to simply ask the business people for "their requirements" and then move on to the serious and complex work involved in creating the infrastructure environment.

None of this is final, of course. We are at an early stage in the development of the BPMS market. Some vendors will go off track and focus too much on SOA and thereby confine themselves to selling products to IT developers. Others, however, still have the vision that motivated Smith and Fingar and others of us and will continue to work on BPMS products that subsume technology to an interface that can support business managers as they interact with the business processes that do the work in their organizations. Large-scale business processes invariably involve a mix of software systems and people, and true BPMS products must evolve to support both if they are to really help business managers to manage the processes and their companies.

8.2 Standards and Certification

Because BPMS is dependent on the Internet and various Internet protocols (e.g., UDDI, XML), there have been a variety of efforts to generate software standards that would support BPMS development. BPEL, being standardized by Oasis and BPMN, and OMG standard are good examples (Leymann et al. 2010).

At the same time, a variety of different organizations are working to formalize the knowledge and the competencies needed by business process professionals. There is a certification program at ASQ. The ABPMP has just released a draft Body of Knowledge (BOK) for BPM. The OMG is working on a set of certification exams for the various process standards it supports, and the IIBA has just released an updated BOK for Process Analysts that incorporates more business process ideas.

Certification and standards always take time to develop and are hard to do when a body of practice is evolving as rapidly as BPM is today, but these efforts will undoubtedly bear fruit at some point in the future.

8.3 Other Implementation Concerns

The other major area of implementation activity concerns techniques for redesign jobs and training and motivating employees and managers to implement and support changing processes. We would not consider human performance change further at this point, having already discussed Haskett's work when we considered the process level. Suffice to say that automation and employee empowerment continue to evolve together and each needs the attention of anyone seeking to change processes within an organization.

9 Towards a Comprehensive BPM

We have tried to give readers a feel for the breadth and scope of today's Business Process Management efforts. In reviewing so many different domains and techniques, we have undoubtedly misrepresented some of the details. Our goal, however, was not a definitive history, but, instead, a survey that would suggest how much needs to be integrated and coordinated by any company that would organize and manage a comprehensive BPM effort.

This survey has undoubtedly missed a number of important concerns. We have, however, highlighted some of the key issues that we think will increasingly concern business process practitioners in the near future. These concerns include:

Enterprise Level Concerns

- Enterprise Architecture
- Value Chains and Value Networks
- Business Process Frameworks
- Value Chain Diagrams
- Process Maturity Models
- Integrated Process Measurement Systems
- Managing Culture Chan

Process Level Concerns

- Innovation
- Analyzing and Modeling Service Processes
- Analyzing and Modeling Complex Processes

Implementation Level Concerns

- Business Process Management Systems (BPMS)
- Standards and Certification

One could easily argue that any one of these topics could be repositioned at a different level. Similarly, though some topics seem more the concern of one tradition than another, all are being discussed by practitioners from each tradition and some already benefit from efforts that draw on practitioners from each of the major process traditions. In other words, they are emerging as the common concerns of Business Process Management.

While our list may be incomplete and while the names may change, we are confident that the idea of process, technologies and methodologies to manage and improve processes, will continue to grow in importance. We even expect to see process courses showing up at the better business schools in the course of the next decade.

What we want to urge, here, is the creation of a Business Process Management discipline that embraces all of the various approaches we have discussed. The world is changing very fast and will change even faster in the near future. The very nature of business models and processes will continue to change rapidly as outsourcing and information systems continue to change the way we organize to create value for customers. Change and business process are two sides of the same coin. Process concepts and technologies are the best way to organize businesses to adopt to change. But the use of process concepts and techniques would not be nearly as effective if different groups continue to approach process problems from their respective silos. We need an integrated, comprehensive process discipline and process mangers and practitioners who can integrate all of the concepts we have considered, and others besides. It is not sufficient to provide process monitoring technology and not concern yourself with what employees must do to help the organization succeed. It is not sufficient to focus on managing day-to-day processes without concerning yourself with technologies that will soon render your current approach inadequate. It is not sufficient to improve specific processes without a clear idea of how the specific process contributes to other processes, or supports the goals of the value chain, or results in a great customer experience.

Ultimately, process practitioners must not be so concerned with decomposing and analyzing, although those skills are very important, but the process practitioner must be a holist who works to synthesize and assure that the performance of the whole organization is optimized to achieve its strategic goals.

There are too many common place organizations in the world today. There is an oversupply of productive capacity. And, at the same time there are people who are not being served well, or at all. We need to create the next generation of global organizations that will draw on resources and people from throughout the world to produce products they can tailor and deliver anywhere in the world at prices everyone can afford. At the same time, we need to create the techniques and technologies that will allow individuals and small companies to flourish in the niches in between the corporate giants. These are the challenges we face and they will call for a new generation of more sophisticated process practitioners who can integrate everything we know to accomplish these tasks.

References

Altshuller G (1984) Creativity as an exact science. Gordon & Breach, New York

ASQ – American Society of Quality. www.asq.org

Baldrige National Quality Award. www.quality.rist.gov

Barney M, McCarty T (2003) The new Six Sigma. Prentice Hall, Upper Saddle River, NJ

Bolstorff P, Rosenbaum R (2007) Supply chain excellence: a handbook for dramatic improvement using the SCOR model, 2nd edn. Amacom, New York

Bovet D, Martha J (2000) Value nets: breaking the supply chain to unlock hidden profits. Wiley, New York

Burlton R (2001) Business process management. Profiting from process. Sams, Indianapolis

Burlton R (2010) Delivering business strategy through process management. In: vom Brocke J, Rosemann M (eds) Handbook on business process management, vol 2. Springer, Heidelberg

Cherbakov L, Galambos G, Harishankar R, Kalyana S, Rockham G (2005) Impact of service orientation at the business level. IBM Syst J 44(1):81–107

Chrissis MB, Konrad M, Shrum S (2007) CMMI second edition: guidelines for process integration and product improvement. Person Education, Addison-Wesley, New York

Conger S (2010) Six sigma and business process management. In: vom Brocke J, Rosemann M (eds) Handbook on business process management, vol 1. Springer, Heidelberg

Crandall B, Klein G, Hoffman RR (2006) Working minds: a practitioner's guide to cognitive task analysis. MIT Press, Cambridge, MA

Cummins F (2010) BPM meets SoA. In: vom Brocke J, Rosemann M (eds) Handbook on business process management, vol 1. Springer, Heidelberg

Davenport TH, Short JE (1990) The new industrial engineering: information technology and business process redesign. Sloan Manage Rev 31(4):11–27

Davenport TH (1993) Process innovation: reengineering work through information technology. Harvard Business School Press, Boston, MA
Davenport TH (2000) Mission critical. Harvard Business School Press, Boston, MA
Davenport TH (2010) Process management for knowledge work. In: vom Brocke J, Rosemann M (eds) Handbook on business process management, vol 1. Springer, Heidelberg
Deming WE (1982) Out of the crisis. MIT Press, Cambridge, MA
Dumas M, Kohlborn T (2010) Service-enabled process management. In: vom Brocke J, Rosemann M (eds) Handbook on business management, vol 1. Springer, Heidelberg
Federal Enterprise Architecture Framework (FEAF), US Government. www.gov.cio/Documents/fedarch1.pdf
Graham B (2004) Detail process charting. Wiley, New York
Gupta P (2006) Six Sigma business scorecard, 2nd edn. McGraw-Hill, New York, NY
Hammer M (1990) Reengineering work: don't automate, obliterate. Harv Bus Rev 68(4):104–113
Hammer M, Champy J (1993) Reengineering the corporation: a manifesto for business revolution. Harper Business, New York, NY
Hammer M (2004) Deep change: how operational innovation can transform your company. Harv Bus Rev 82(4):84–96
Hammer M (2010) What is business process management? In: vom Brocke J, Rosemann M (eds) Handbook on business process management, vol 1. Springer, Heidelberg
Harmon P, King D (1985) Expert systems: artificial intelligence in business. Wiley, New York, NY
Harmon P, Hall C (1993) Intelligent systems. Wiley, New York, NY
Harmon P (2007) Business process change. A guide for business managers and BPM and Six Sigma professionals, 2nd edn. Morghan Kaufman, San Francisco, CA
Harrison-Broninski K (2005) Human interactions. Meghan-Kiffer, Tampa, FL
Harrison-Broninski K (2010) Dealing with human-driven processes. In: vom Brocke J, Rosemann M (eds) Handbook on business process management, vol 2. Springer, Heidelberg
Inaganti S (2007) SOA maturity model scenarios. BPTrends www.bptrends.com, New York
ISSSP – International Society for Six Sigma Professionals. www.isssp.org
ISPI – International Society for Performance Improvement. www.ispi.org
Juran JM (1951) Quality control handbook. McGraw-Hill, New York, NY
Khan RN (2004) Business process management: a practical guide. Meghan-Kiffer, Tampa, FL
Kaplan RS, Norton DP (1996) The balanced scorecard: translating strategy into action. Harvard Business School Press, Boston, MA
Kaplan RS, Norton DP (2004) Strategy maps. Harvard Business School Press, Boston, MA
Leymann F et al. (2010) Bussiness process management standards. In: vom Brocke J, Rosemann M (eds) Handbook on business process management, vol 1. Springer, Heidelberg
McClure C (1989) CASE is software automation. Prentice Hall, Englewood Cliffs, NJ
McGraw T (1997) Creating modern capitalism: how entrepreneurs, companies, and countries triumphed in three industrial revolutions. Harvard University Press, Cambridge, MA
Newell A, Simon HA (1972) Human problem solving. Prentice-Hall, Englewood Cliffs, NJ
Ohno T (1978) Toyota production system: beyond large-scale production. Productivity Press, Portland, OR
O'Reilly CA, Tushman ML (2004) The ambidextrous organization. Harv Bus Rev 82(4):74–82
Paulk MC et al. (1995) The capability maturity model: guidelines for improving the software process. Addison-Wesley, Boston, MA
Pohle G, Korsten P, Ramamurthy S (2005) Component business models: making specialization real. Whitepaper issued by IBM institute for business value. IBM Global Services, New York
Poluha RG (2007) Application of the SCOR model in supply chain management. Cambria Press, Amherst, NY
Porter ME (1985) Competitive advantage. Free Press, New York, NY
Porter ME (1996) What is strategy? Harv Bus Rev 74(6):61–78
Ramias A (2005) The mists of Six Sigma. BPTrends, New York

Rosemann M, de Bruin T, Power B (2006) BPM maturity. In: Jeston J, Nelis J (eds) Business process management. Practical guidelines to successful implementations. Elsevier, NY, pp 299–315
Rosemann M, vom Brocke J (2010) The six core elements of business process management. In: vom Brocke J, Rosemann M (eds) Handbook on business process management, vol 1. Springer, Heidelberg
Ross RG (2003) Principles of the business rule approach. Addison-Wesley, Boston, MA
Rummler GA, Brache A (1990) Improving performance. How to improve the white space in the organization chart. Jossey-Bass, San Francisco, CA
Rummler GA, Ramias AJ (2010) A framework for defining and designing the structure of work. In: vom Brocke J, Rosemann M (eds) Handbook on business process management, vol 1. Springer, Heidelberg
Scheer AW (1994) Business process reengineering, 2nd edn. Springer, New York
Seidel S, Rosemann M (2008) Creativity management – the new challenge for BPM. BPTrends, New York
Seidel S, Shortland K, Court D, Elzinga D (2010) Managing creativity-intensive processes: learning from film and visual effects production. In: vom Brocke J, Rosemann M (eds) Handbook on business process management, vol 2. Springer, Heidelberg
Shingo S (1983) A revolution in manufacturing. The SMED system. Productivity Press, Portland, OR
Silverstein D, DeCarlo N, Slocum M (2005) INsourcing innovation. How to achieve competitive excellence using TRIZ. Auerbach Publications, New York, NY
Smith H, Fingar P (2003) Business process management. Meghan-Kiffer Press, Tampa, FL
Smith RF (2007) Business process management and the balanced scorecard. Using processes as strategic drivers. Wiley, New York, NY
Supply Chain Council. www.supply-chain.org
Taylor FW (1911) Principles of scientific management. Harper & Brothers, New York
TeleManagement Forum. www.tmforum.org
Value Chain Group. www.value-chain.org
van der Aalst W, van Hee K (2000) Workflow management. Models, methods and systems. MIT Press, Cambridge, MA
vom Brocke J, Petry M, Sinnl T, Østerberg Kristensen B, Sonnenberg C (2010) Global processes and data: the cultural process journey at the Hilti Corporation. In: vom Brocke J, Rosemann M (eds) Handbook on business process management, vol 2. Springer, Heidelberg
Womack JP, Jones DT, Roos D (1991) The machine that changed the world: the story of lean production. Simon & Schuster, New York, NY
Zachman JA (1987) A framework for information systems architecture. IBM Syst J 26(3):276–292
zur Mühlen M (2004) Workflow-based process controlling. Foundation, design, and application of workflow-driven process information systems. Logos, Berlin

A Framework for Defining and Designing the Structure of Work

Geary A. Rummler† and Alan J. Ramias

Abstract This chapter describes a framework for modeling the business architecture layer of enterprise architecture. We subscribe to the definition of enterprise architecture provided by Ken Orr, who identifies business architecture as the top layer of four linked architectures in an enterprise architecture. This chapter describes a value creation architecture consisting of the business architecture, the management system architecture, the technology performance architecture, and the human performance architecture.

1 Introduction

We do not need to belabor the potential value to an organization of modeling its business and technologies in an enterprise architecture (EA) framework (see Fig. 1 for typical EA framework layers), but here are a couple of expert opinions on the subject.

Paul Harmon, founder and executive editor of BPTrends, has written, "Most people who use the term 'enterprise architecture' today, are probably from the IT world, and they tend to use the term as (an overview of how all the various IT models and resources in the organization work together). Depending on the individual, they might insist that their concept of an enterprise architecture includes business process elements and even strategy elements, but if you look at their actual models and their practices, you will see that they chiefly look at processes as a source of system requirements that can drive software development" (Harmon 2004) (Harmon 2010).

Dave Ritter, co-founder and vice president of Proforma, said, "Enterprise Architecture is often touted as one of the tools needed to bridge the gap between the business and IT [...]. Successful alignment of business and IT will maximize enterprise performance. This will only be achieved by organizations that understand

G.A. Rummler
Performance Design Lab, Tucson, AZ, USA

J. vom Brocke and M. Rosemann (eds.), *Handbook on Business Process Management 1*, International Handbooks on Information Systems,
DOI 10.1007/978-3-642-00416-2_4,

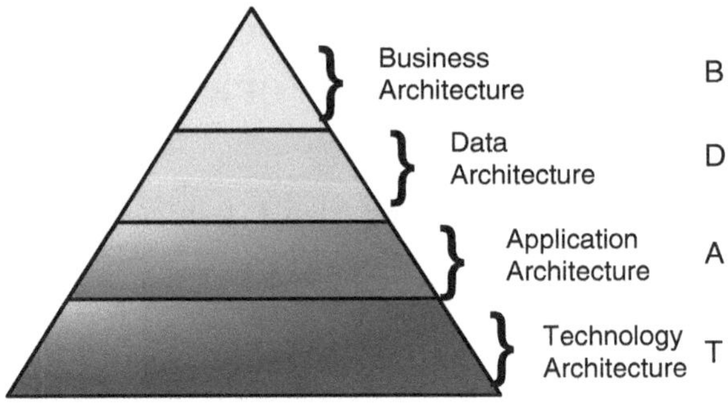

Fig. 1 Typical layers of an enterprise architecture

how to develop and maintain an accurate model of their companies' business and strategy architectures and provide value to the business through their introduction of automation solutions." (Ritter 2004).

However, even though there is value to organizations in having a complete, accurate EA, problems abound. Ritter points out, "Despite the fact that Enterprise Architecture concepts have been around since the early 1980s, their critical mission of defining and linking Business, Systems, and Technology Architectures is rarely achieved. Enterprise Architecture projects are all too often reduced to nothing more than elaborate exercises to inventory systems and technologies, with little or no effort put into documenting and analyzing their companies' strategic direction and business processes – the very strategic direction and business processes which should be the driving force for IT initiatives".

In our view, these problems with EA exist for several reasons:

First, EAs are typically built by IT people. IT is disadvantaged in its efforts to depict the business aspects of an EA without the participation of other members of the organization. The result is inevitably an EA model skewed to IT interests.

Second, there is not enough structure available in any of the models of EA we have seen that would aid someone interested in building a sufficiently complete picture of the BA layer. While business processes are typically identified as the contents of the BA layer, the labeling, organizing, and relating of the processes are done in a rudimentary fashion, leading some business people to say, "So what?" Besides, there is more to the BA view than processes.

Third, there is insufficient recognition in the EA models we have reviewed that the purpose of all this modeling is to show how work is (or should be) performed. The emphasis is on linkages between systems and applications, and sometimes to processes, but without enough clarity about who does the work, and how the work is actually being performed. The critical focus of an EA should be on how work gets done, who (both human and technology) is performing the work, and how performance is managed. If an EA does not make accomplishment and management of work quite clear, it ends up being little more than, in Harmon's words, "processes as a source of system requirements that can drive software development".

Fourth, EA models need to (but generally do not) recognize the basic premises of the organization as a system, namely that:

- All organizations are systems that exist to produce valued outputs (desired products or services to customers and economic returns to stakeholders);
- All organizations need to be adaptive systems existing inside a larger Super-System, and in order to succeed over the long term, organizations need to continuously adapt to the changes in their Super-System. The Super-System is the ultimate reality and performance context for every organization. Bluntly put, any organization must adapt to its Super-System or die.

Any EA model that does not recognize or provide clarity about the organization as a system will fall short in providing clarity or direction. So our approach is based upon the concept of the organization as a system, starting from the outside (i.e., the Super-System) and then drilling into the organization level by level.

2 The Value Creation Hierarchy

Our view starts via a view we call the Value Creation Hierarchy (VCH). Every organization exists in order to create something (goods, services) of value to a market, and in order to create and deliver that value, it needs an internal system of processes and resources to make good on its promises.

Fig. 2 shows a Hierarchy consisting of five levels. The VCH is a top-to-bottom framework for organizing work in a way that meets the following criteria:

- Value is created and delivered to the market
- The work of value creation and delivery can be effectively and efficiently performed
- The work can be effectively managed
- Whenever practical, the work is organized in a way that gives the business a competitive advantage

2.1 Enterprise Level

At the top level is the entire organization as a system, with the organization's business units operating as the engines that create, sell, and deliver value, and generate revenue for the enterprise. The enterprise is depicted in the context of its marketplace, its resources and competitors, and the general environment in which the organization must operate. Most of the time, people are not referring to this topmost level when they talk about processes, but what this model suggests is that every organization is in fact a giant processing system, and all of its individual processes are contained somewhere in this system.

2.2 Value Creation Level

The next level is a depiction of the organization's Value Creation System (VCS), which is the means by which the organization creates, sells, and delivers products

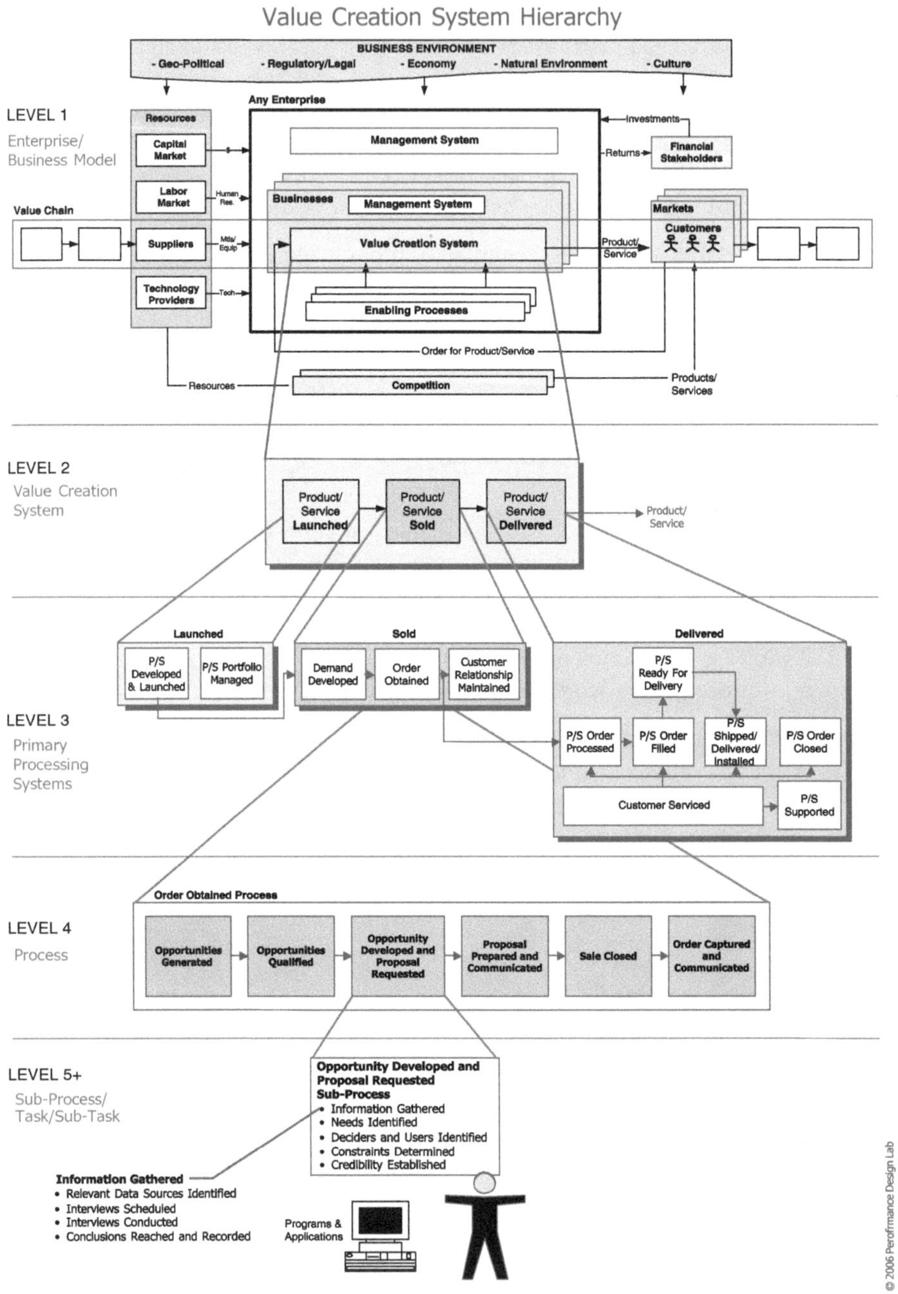

Fig. 2 Value creation hierarchy

and services of value to the marketplace. The value-creation level is kind of a mega-process view, and in a large, complex company, there may be a different VCS for different products and services. Sometimes people who talk about process do mean the entire Value Creation System, and quite often, improvement is needed at this level, when parts of the VCS are misaligned or missing.

2.3 Primary Processing Systems Level

The third level then divides the components of the VCS into three general types of processes, what we call the Launched, Sold, and Delivered processes. Launched includes those processes – such as research, product development, and product extensions – whose purpose is to create new products and services. Sold includes those processes that are aimed at marketing and selling the goods and services. Delivered includes those many processes that get the products and services to customers and provide ongoing support. At this level, we are still talking about multiple sets, or bundles, of processes, which we call Primary Processing Systems.

2.4 Process Level

It is at the fourth level that we reach the individual process level, and it may be one of those processes contained inside Launched, Sold, or Delivered. Often, this is the level of process that people mean when they talk about "end-to-end" processes, because these processes typically begin with a market or customer input (e.g., an order, a product idea) and end with an output that either goes to the customer or becomes an input to another stage of the value chain. For example, the output of the product development process in Launched is a new product that now can be marketed and sold by those employees who participate in the Sold processes. The other processes to be found at this level are management processes and supporting processes (for example, the hiring process or the information system development process).

2.5 Subprocess/Task/Subtask Level

The fifth level then decomposes a given process into subprocesses and tasks. It is at this level that the performer (whether human or technology or a combination) becomes visible. The final level goes into even greater detail, delving into substeps and procedures. Sometimes, people who use the word "process" are actually talking about this level, because from their vantage point, what they do is a whole process, although from the VCH view, they are well down in the weeds within a single subprocess or even a single task.

3 Business Architecture

The VCH can be used to derive the Business Architecture (BA) for a given organization. Corresponding to each level of the Hierarchy are one or more diagrams that depict elements of that level and their interrelationships. Fig. 3 depicts a generic BA.

3.1 Super-System Map

Corresponding to the super-system level of the VCH is a Super-System Map (Fig. 4), which displays specific information about a given organization. There is information about the external variables that affect the organization (i.e., the markets and customers, competitors, resources, and general environmental factors). Inside the organizational box is a high-level depiction of the organization's lines and major organizational units. Outputs from the organization (i.e., its products and services) are depicted.

3.2 Cross-Functional Value Creation System Map

Corresponding to the value chain level of the VCH is a Cross-Functional Value Creation System Map (Fig. 5), which depicts the organization's value-creation processes and the organizational players who participate in those processes. This level is a very high-level view of the organization way of doing business (i.e., its business model) and delivering value to its customers.

3.3 Business Process Architecture Framework

The tool for displaying the Primary Processing Systems of an organization is called a Business Process Architecture (BPA) framework (Fig. 6). This diagram shows all of the significant processes (i.e., value creation processes, management processes, and supporting processes) of the organization and their systematic interrelationships.

The BPA Framework provides executives and employees with a common view of all the major processes of the business – on one page. The document is a concise summary of the value-adding work that must be performed and managed to provide value to customers – the operative word being *work*. The picture is a work-centric picture and does not reflect who does the work – so the primary focus of dialog, troubleshooting, and decision making stays on the work and on the creation and delivery of value.

3.4 BPA Detail Chart

The BPA Detail Chart (Fig. 7) is a tool that bridges the multiple processes shown in a BPA and the details required to depict a single cross-functional process.

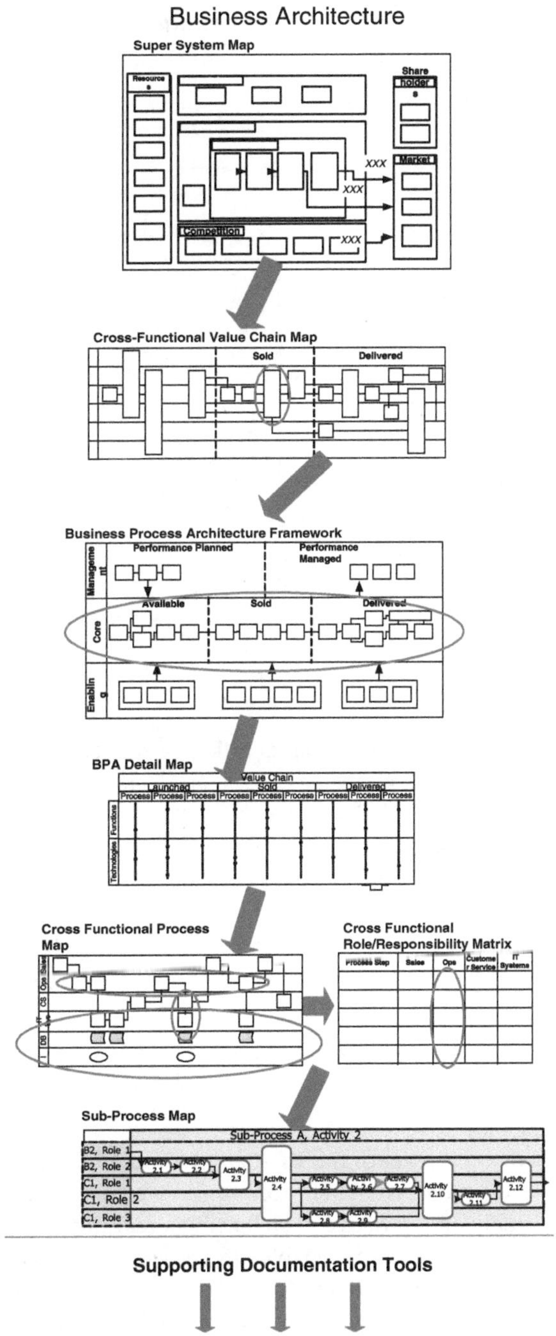

Fig. 3 Business architecture

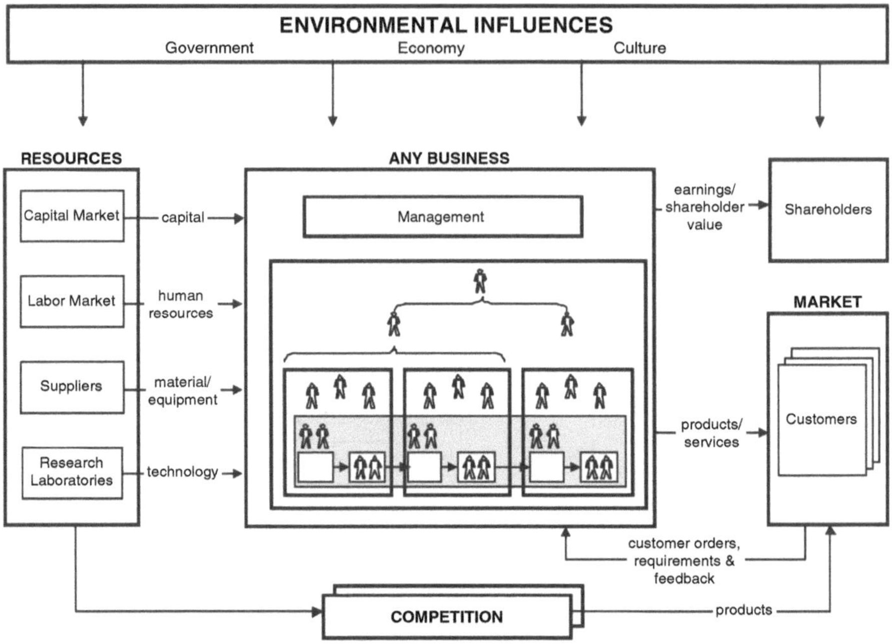

Fig. 4 Super-system map template

The BPA Detail Map is a device for identifying all processes in a given VCS, participants in those processes, and enabling technologies in a given section of an organization's BPA (such as in its Launched processes) or it may be applied to identify only certain processes (and corresponding participants and technologies) relevant to a given business issue or proposed change (for example, a new way to go to market, which would affect multiple processes in the Sold area of the BPA. The processes included in a given BPA Detail Chart can include not only primary, value-adding processes but also support and management processes.

3.5 Cross-Functional Business Process Map

Below the level of the BPA are the individual processes, which are captured using the classic "swimlane" format pioneered by Geary Rummler and used today by virtually all process flowcharting practitioners and imbedded in BPM software (Fig. 8). The format enables the process map to provide rich detail about the tasks performed in a given process and who participates in the process. The map can also show how technology is employed in executing the tasks, and may show how various systems and applications interact with each other in performing various subtasks. In addition, maps may contain other information such as time consumption, metrics, resources, etc.

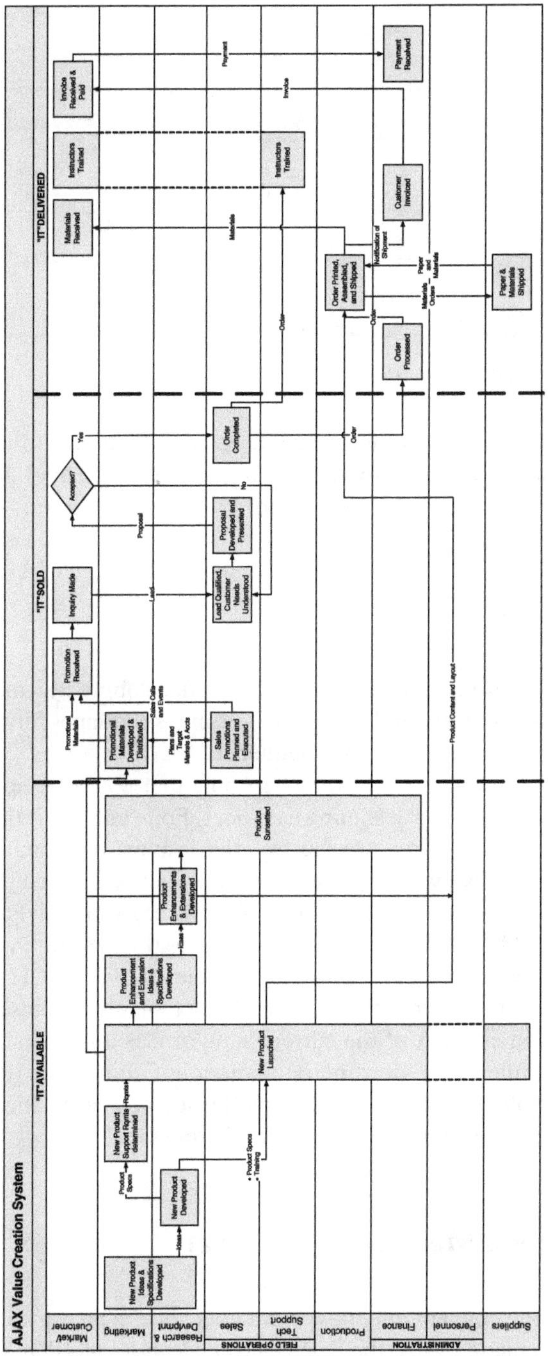

Fig. 5 Cross-functional value creation system map

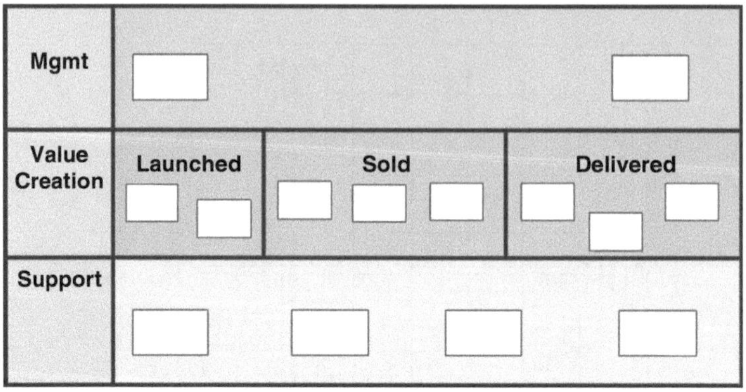

Fig. 6 Business process architecture framework

Corresponding to the cross-functional process map is a cross-functional Role-Responsibility Matrix, which provides even more detail about how the tasks contained in the process are being performed.

3.6 Subprocess Maps

If it is useful to delve into even greater process detail, a subprocess map can be used to decompose a single task and, using the same swimlane format, show the subtasks, performers, technologies, and sequence.

Below this level are any number of other tools that could be applied in either analyzing existing processes or designing new ones. For example, if the purpose is to identify where controls exist in a process in order to meet the compliance requirements of the Sarbanes–Oxley Act, subprocess maps can be applied to this purpose, providing a picture of exactly where various controls exist in a given process.

In summary, the BA is derived from the Value Creation Hierarchy. As shown in Fig. 9, each component of the BA corresponds to a level of the VCH. In our view, a complete BA constitutes a completely mapped set of all of these components, whether it is intended as a BA of the current state or it is a future-state BA.

This then constitutes our view of one important dimension that should be contained in a complete BA: a vertical depiction of how a business creates and delivers value through its complex hierarchy of processes.

4 Value Creation Management System

An EA model should show not only how work gets done in an organization but also how performance is managed. At the Performance Design Lab (PDL), we have long argued that to be effective any organization needs to have a well-designed

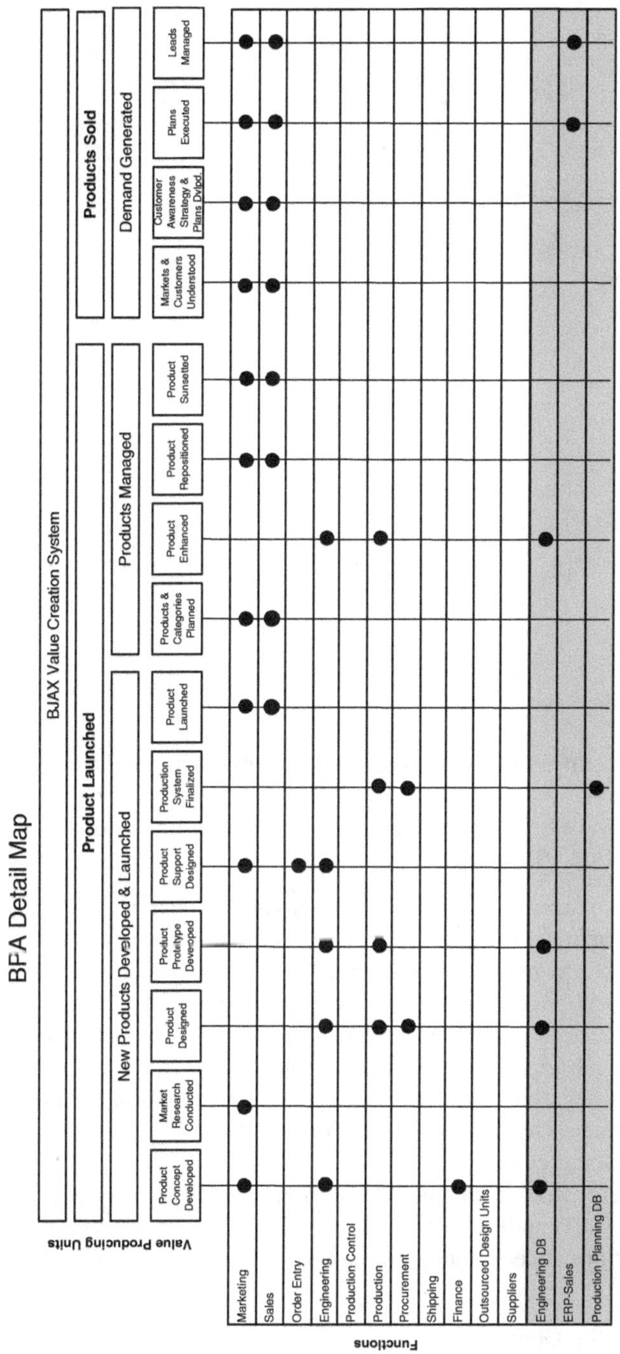

Fig. 7 BPA detail chart

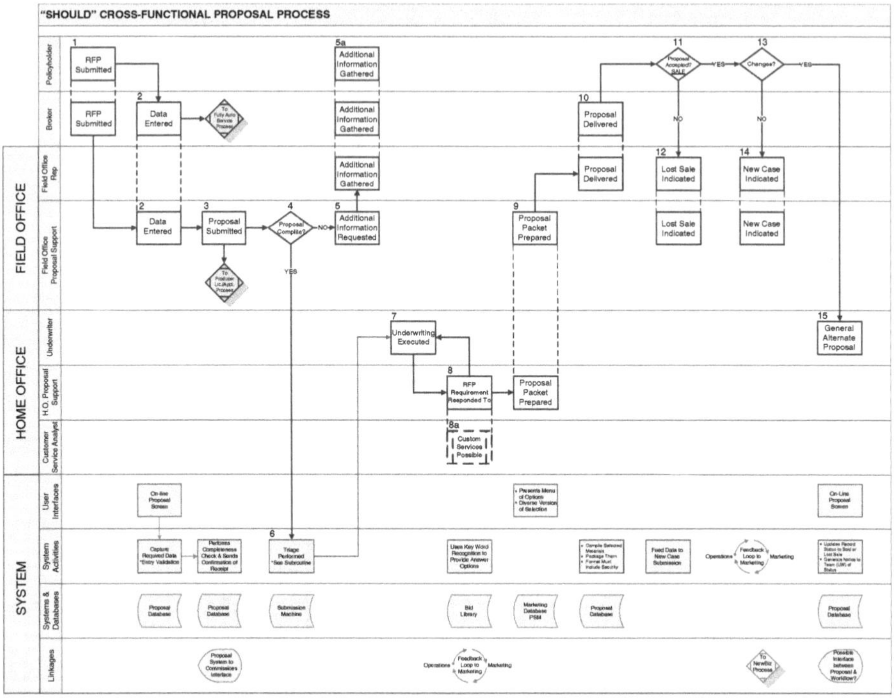

Fig. 8 Cross functional process map

management system. We have a framework for reviewing the management system of an organization.

We know that desired performance/results are a function of the three components shown in Fig. 10:

1. *Performance planned* – goals and plans (including necessary resources and processes to achieve the goals) are set and communicated to the "performer".
2. *Performance executed* – the "performer" (which can be an individual, a process, or an organization entity – e.g., a company division, plant, or department) delivers the desired performance/results prescribed in the goals and plans.
3. *Performance managed* – actual performance is monitored against the goals and plans and if a negative deviation is detected, there may be a "change" signal sent to the performer. The bottom-line of Performance Managed is closing any gaps between Plan and actual.
   (a) The "performer" to change their execution in some way (e.g., better scheduling of staff) and/or
   (b) The Performance Planned component to do some combination of the following:
      – Alter the Goals
      – Modify the Strategy to achieve those Goals

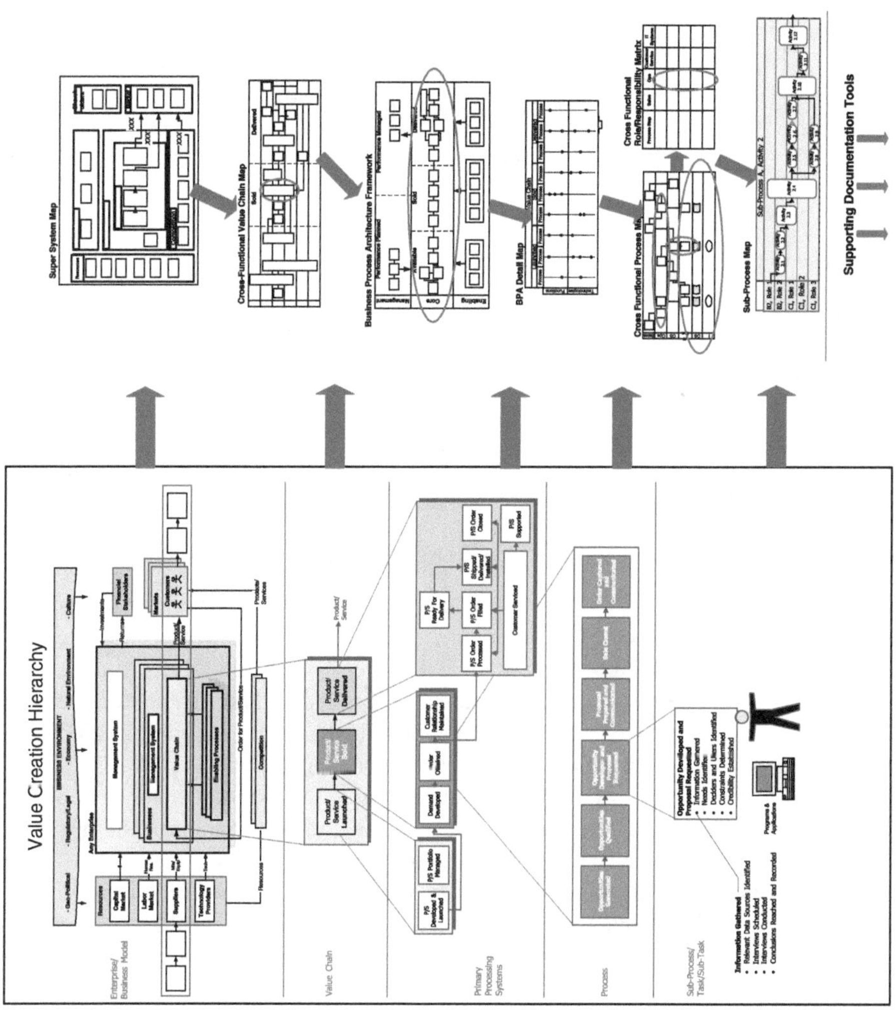

Fig. 9 Value creation hierarchy and corresponding business architecture

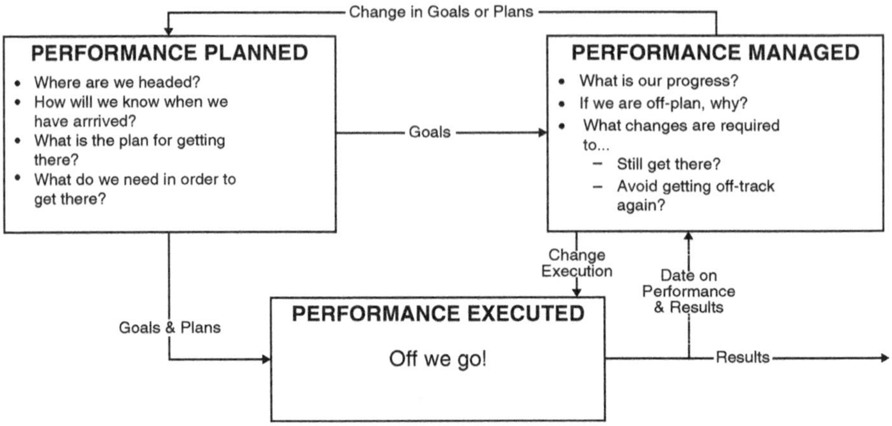

Fig. 10 Management model

- Modify the Operating Plan and Budget to better support the Strategy including: (a) The allocation of resources, (b) The Organization design, (c) Process requirements, and (d) Policies

Put another way,

- Performance Planned = (equals) "Plan"
- Performance Executed = "Actual"
- Performance Managed = Action to close the gap between "plan" and "actual".

"Performance Executed" (PE), the individual, process, or entity that performs the work, is always a very visible component of this fundamental performance system. On the other hand, the "Performance Planned" (PP) and "Performance Managed" (PM) components, which constitute the "brains" or intelligence of the performance system tend to be invisible and flawed. This PP/PM combination (which we refer to as the Performance Planned and Managed System [PPMS]) is what makes it possible for the performance system to adapt to external changes and react to execution failures. It is the mechanism whereby the performance system is both an effective processing system and an adaptive (learning) system.

Figure 11 provides more details about the functioning of the Performance Planned and Performance Managed components. An extra detail from the earlier diagram to point out is that in addition to providing Goals (direction) and Plans to Performance Executed, the Performance Planned component also makes available the necessary structure, processes, policies, and resources (financial and other) to achieve said goals.

You might think of the PPMS as a sophisticated guidance/control mechanism – a "management chip," if you will – whose goal it is to optimize the Performance Executed component and produce the desired results. A *management system* for an organization is a collection of these "management chips," inserted at key junctures in the organization, and *linked* as shown in Fig. 12.

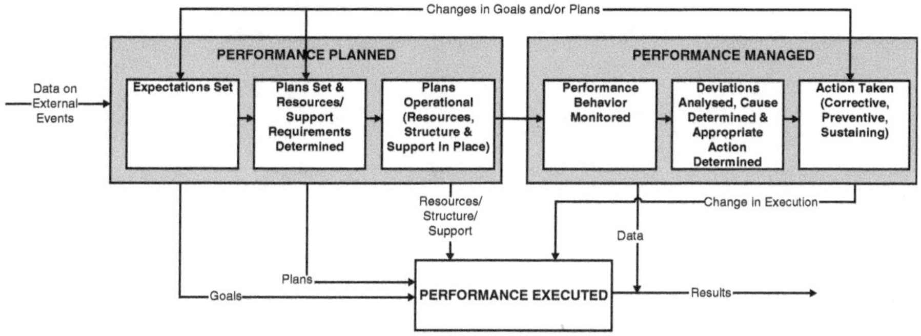

Fig. 11 Management model details

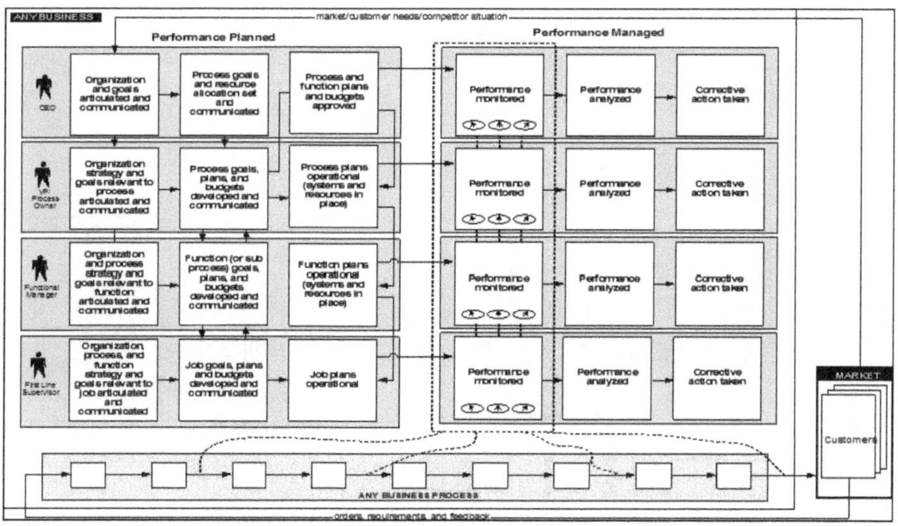

Fig. 12 Performance planned and managed hierarchy

The diagram in Fig. 12 (a variation of Fig. 11, the preceding diagram) is a powerful template for both "troubleshooting" an existing management system and designing a new management system.

5 Management System Architecture

Corresponding to the Management System Hierarchy is a set of tools that collectively can be used to design and organize the management system (see Fig. 13). Just as with the BA, these tools can be used to define and analyze an organization's

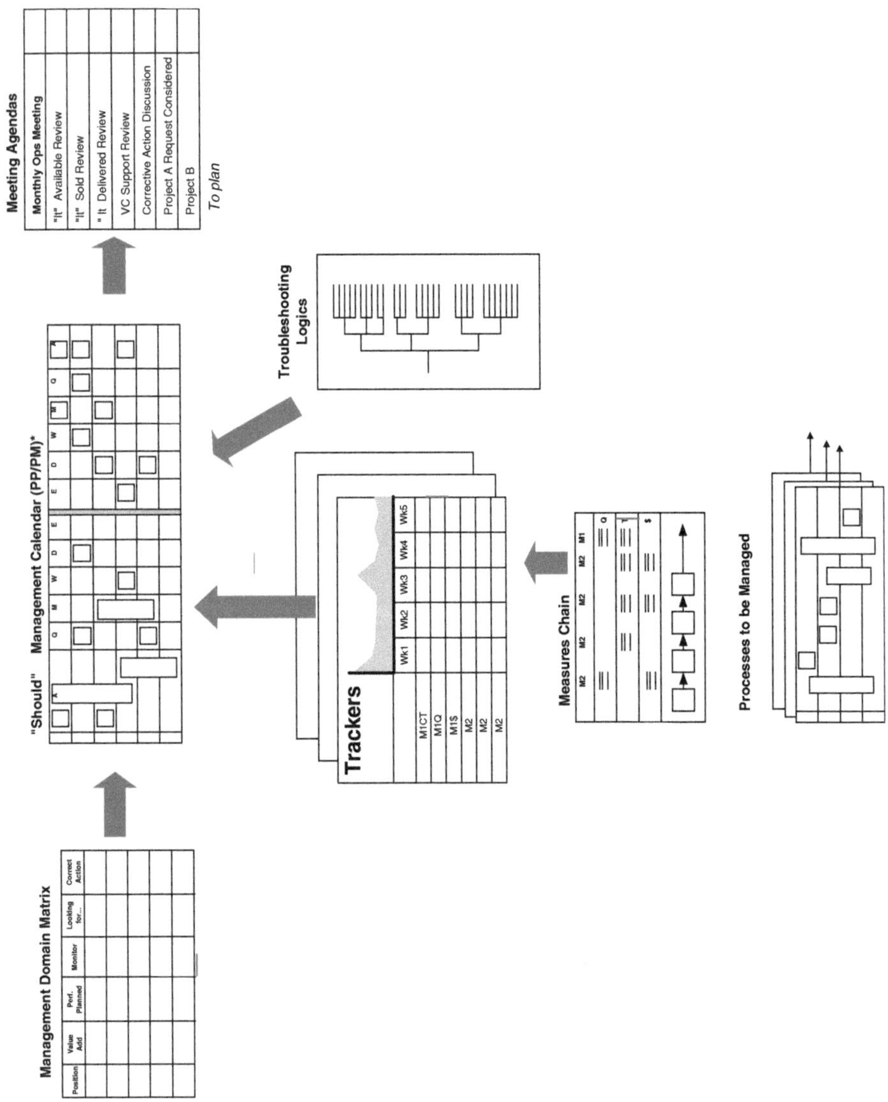

Fig. 13 Management system architecture

current state ("is") or future state ("should"). The Management System components are anchored by the processes to be managed. Starting from the bottom, the components are arranged in rough order of their development when building a management system.

5.1 *Measures Chain*

For each process in the BA, a Measures Chain identifies what critical dimensions of performance and measures are applicable, and where in the process the performance data should be monitored. The way a Measures Chain is developed is to start at the right, with the requirements of customers and stakeholders and translate them into dimensions of performance such as timeliness, quality, and price, and applied to the process. For example, if the timeliness requirement is to deliver a product within 30 days, the requirements on the whole process might be 25 days (assuming 5 days for shipping), and then those 25 days are allocated appropriately to the subprocesses based on the worked required. The result is a set of measures for a given process. When Measures Chains are created for all the key processes in an organization's BPA, the management team has a powerful means of monitoring and controlling process performance across the organization.

5.2 *Performance Trackers*

Performance Trackers are tools for collecting and displaying performance data. The trackers are derived from the performance measures required by the Measures Chains. Typically, a tracker shows the trends in performance for a given measure, such as cost, timeliness, or quality. A hierarchy of trackers corresponding to the management levels contained in the Management Domain Matrix and covering all the key processes in the BPA results in a comprehensive "dashboard" for viewing and management organization-wide performance.

5.3 *Troubleshooting Logic Diagrams*

Much of the management work required to manage the organization as a system is diagnosing and acting upon performance feedback with the appropriate corrective action, which might be to provide coaching, better training or feedback, different tools or methods, etc. Troubleshooting tools are intended to help managers assess data, make the right conclusions, and choose the right actions.

5.4 Management Calendar

The central tool is the Management Calendar, which provides a road map and timeline for a total Performance Planned and Managed System (PPMS) for any organization. It prescribes the key points of interaction between key management roles (the vertical axis) at specific points in time (across the top of the chart, from Annual to Weekly/Daily). As the Management Architecture shows, the metrics used by management are derived from Measures Chains for each key process, and the levels of management are defined in the Management Domain Matrix.

5.5 Management Domain Matrix

This tool identifies each level of management, specifies the mission and value of each role, and the responsibilities for performance management of each role. How these responsibilities are carried out can be seen in the Management Calendar, where each manager participates in planning and management activities appropriate to their level.

5.6 Meeting Agendas

In most organizations, the best arena for managing the organization as a system are in those regular meetings where management teams plan and make decisions. The Management Calendar is typically built according to the schedule of management meetings. This final tool is a set of meeting agendas that aid management teams in optimizing and leading the organization.

For example, the Management Calendar for our fictitious organization includes a monthly Performance Managed meeting to emphasize that Functions exist to support Primary processes, which in turn meet customer and organization requirements. It works like this.

The executive team of the president and all vice-presidents meets every month for a review of operations and performance against goals. It is usually a 4-h meeting, chaired by the president. The first 30 min of the meeting is a quick briefing on performance against corporate goals for the month and year-to-date, including financials, sales performance, and customer satisfaction data. The next segment of the meeting, usually an hour and a half, is a review of Process performance against goals. The Process Management Team Chair (also a functional VP on the executive team) for each Primary Process reports on how their Process has performed against the goals for the period. The Chair/VP is also expected to comment on any issues regarding "suboptimization" of their process by any function. On a rotational basis, each month the performance of one of the Support Processes is reviewed in a similar manner. The president is a big advocate of "functions exist to support processes" and listens carefully during this segment of the meeting for indications that this is not the case.

In the final hour-and-a-half segment of the meeting, the focus shifts to a review of each major function in the company. Each VP gives a brief summary of their function's performance against their monthly goals and raises any issues they are having or anticipate having supporting any of the Primary Processes. The president is quick to ask questions if he senses a function is failing to support one of the Processes as required. If such a problem is identified, the president leads a positive "problem-solving" discussion of "why" the problem exists and what must be done (by all VP's, not just that function VP) to correct the problem, prevent the problem happening again, and recover from the problem.

The whole idea of the Management System is to make complex organizations more manageable. A company has hundreds of individuals in hundreds of jobs performing thousands of more or less related activities aimed at meeting ever changing customer requirements or expectations. It is a major management challenge to provide direction for such a complex organism. The alternative is to view the company as a processing system that delivers valued products to customers through a handful of critical processes – basically three Primary Processes and several Support Processes. With this processing system view of organizations, the primary management task for executives and managers becomes twofold:

- First, assure that the internal processing system is aligned with the external "Super-System" requirements and reality. For example, if customers expect to receive their orders in 5 days (because that is what your competition does), then you need to be sure that "5 days" is the standard for delivery of the Order Fulfillment Process. Likewise with expectations for new product development, customer service, etc.
- Secondly, assure that the internal processing system is efficient and effective in meeting organization goals and customer requirements. That is, if you set an order fulfillment standard of 5 days, your job as a management team is to see that the Order Fulfillment Process can meet that standard. You must see that the process is appropriately designed and resourced to consistently meet that customer-driven performance goal.

6 Bridge to Enabling Architectures

Now we are in position to bridge between the BA and other architectures. We want to specify performance and performers. We will define the "performer" as:

- A human being executing tasks with no use of an enabling information technology (i.e., the human performer performs a manual task without any use of a computer);
- Or a human using a supporting technology (e.g., the human performer uses a computer to process information, access data, perform analysis, etc.);

- Or a technology acting as a performer (e.g., a system sends information to another system)

Each of the above options describes a performance situation in which the task is executed in a particular manner, and our process maps should make clear which performance situations are required in the process. In turn the maps become the basis for defining what kinds of technologies are needed and what knowledge and skills the human performers must possess in order to perform the processes as they have been designed.

6.1 *Technology Performance Architecture*

The jumping off point for defining the enabling technologies are the process maps described earlier in the BA. Taken together, the maps for all the affected processes contain the specifications for what technologies are going to be needed. Figure 14 shows the elements of the Technology Performance Architecture.

One key element of the Technology Performance Architecture is the Use Case. A Use Case is developed for each instance in each process where a human performer uses technology to execute a task. For a change of significant magnitude, affecting multiple processes, there may be dozens of Use Cases developed. Each Use Case is a specific requirement for a specific item of technology to be designed, purchased, or modified to meet process needs.

At times, the use of a technology may be so complex that it cannot be adequately captured in a process map or use case document. What may be more revealing are "drilldowns" that show how the performance will happen. For example, a process may require very different actions depending on whether a customer is new; existing; existing but with a late-payment history; existing but with no credit, etc. Such complicated algorithms might be diagramed using tools such as if-then scenarios or other techniques that work better than process maps.

Another element of the Technology Performance Architecture is the Technology Enabler Chart, which is a compilation of all the technologies embedded in the various processes identified in the BA. When developed in the context of an improvement effort, the Technology Enabler Chart also specifies the current state of each required technology, some of which may be existing and others brand-new. This list amounts to "marching orders" for the IT organization, as it lists all of the requirements of all the processes needed to support the business.

From the Technology Enabler Chart, all of the requirements can be and appropriately distributed into three categories of IT technologies that link to the three classic IT architectures (data architecture, applications architecture, and technical architecture) listed in most EA models.

In addition, the Technology Performance Architecture contains some other elements not generally found in EA models:

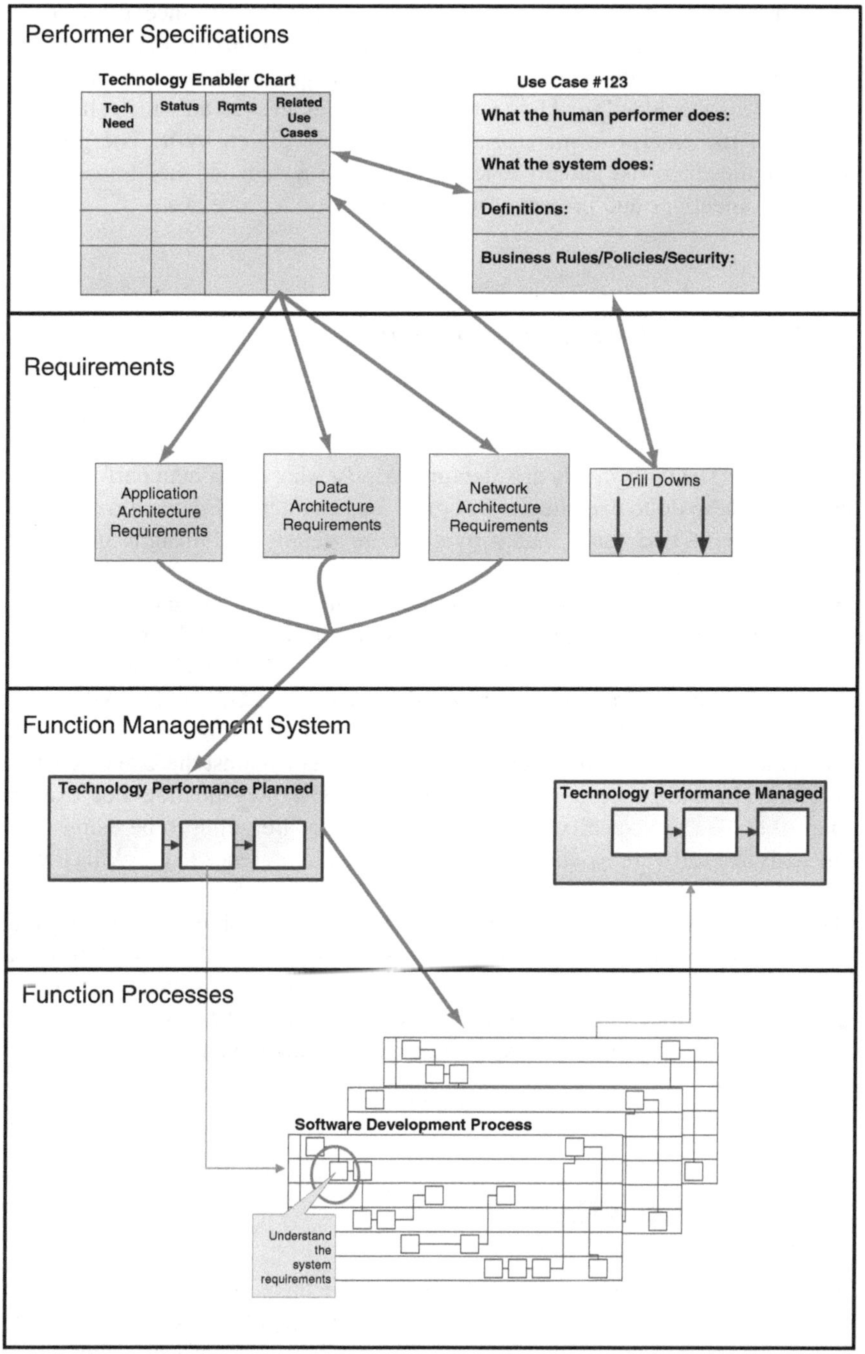

Fig. 14 The technology performance architecture

- We have included the IT organization's own processes, since these are the processes that produce the technologies needed by the business. How well these processes are designed, executed, and managed are key to success.
- We have also included the IT function's management system, which should be a mirror of the enterprise management system and driven by it. The goals and needs of the enterprise should be received by this system and then translated into specific objectives and projects for the IT function's processes.

6.2 *Human Performance Architecture*

This architecture is derived from the BA as well, with a focus on the human performers who execute the processes (see Fig. 15 for the Human Performance Architecture). The tools in this architecture specify what the human performers will have to be able to do to execute the BA processes as intended. The path down from the BA leads to two tools that provide more details and insight into human performance of the targeted processes.

The function role–responsibility matrices identify each job that participates in the affected processes and how the performers in those jobs will do their work.

Then for each affected job we develop a complete Job Model that specifies the job accomplishments, measures, performance goals, and knowledge/skill requirements.

With the Job Models completed, we can check them against the Use Cases to see if they match, and make appropriate adjustments if they do not. For example, perhaps the use cases specify that order entry clerks are going to be using supply chain analytics software, yet the Job Models make no reference to the skills it would take to use such software.

Then, as we did with the Technology Performance Architecture, we now distribute the requirements into several buckets (knowledge and skills, staffing, and performance management) and link them to the HR function's processes that deal with those areas. For example, in order to execute some of the processes in the BA, we may have to train people, or maybe we will hire from outside, which impacts the staffing process.

7 The Complete VCA

Now, with these enabling architectures defined, we have produced what we would consider to be a complete EA, or what we prefer to call a Value Creation Architecture (VCA). It consists of the Business Architecture, the Management System Architecture, the Technology Performance Architecture, and the Human Performance Architecture.

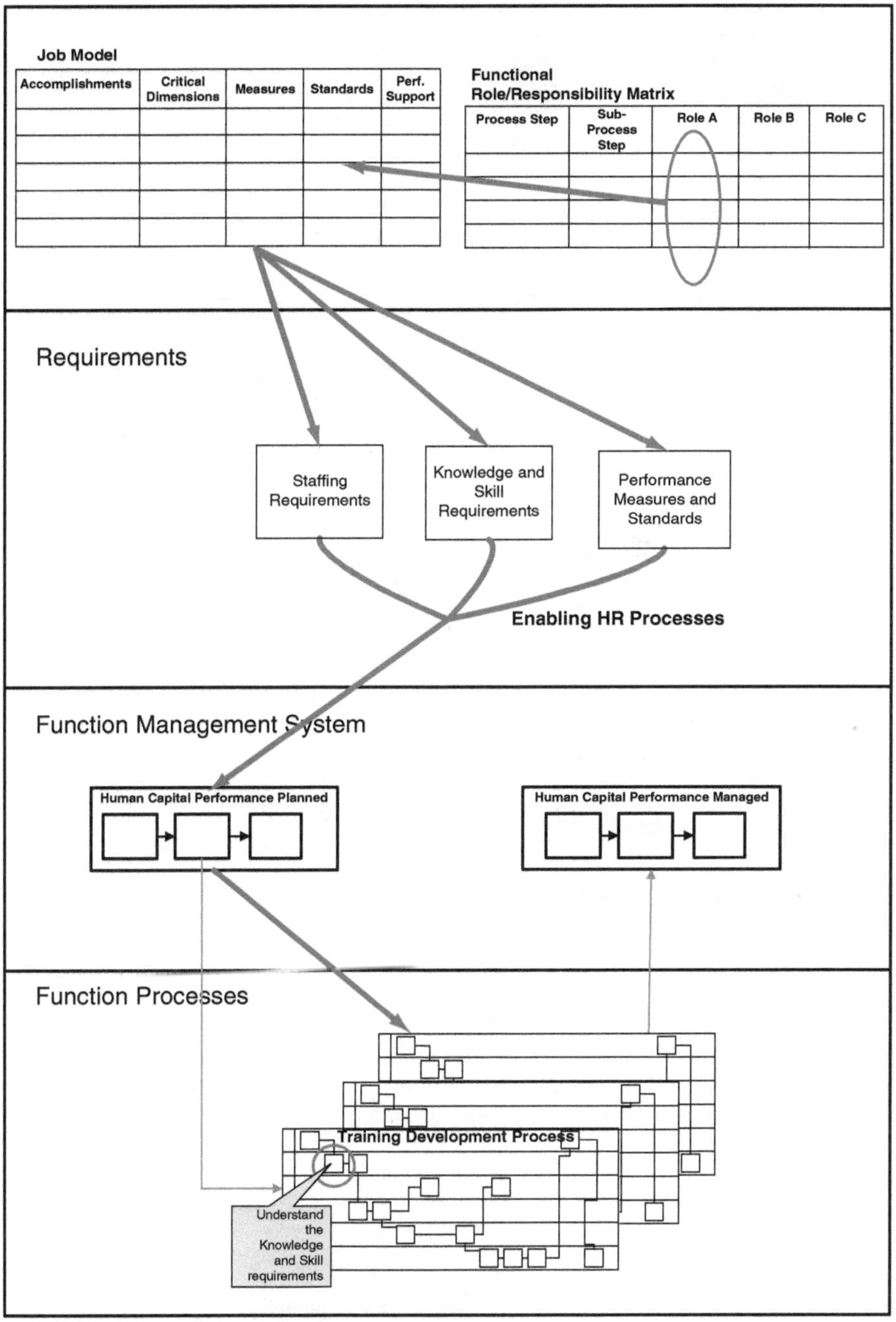

Fig. 15 The human performance architecture

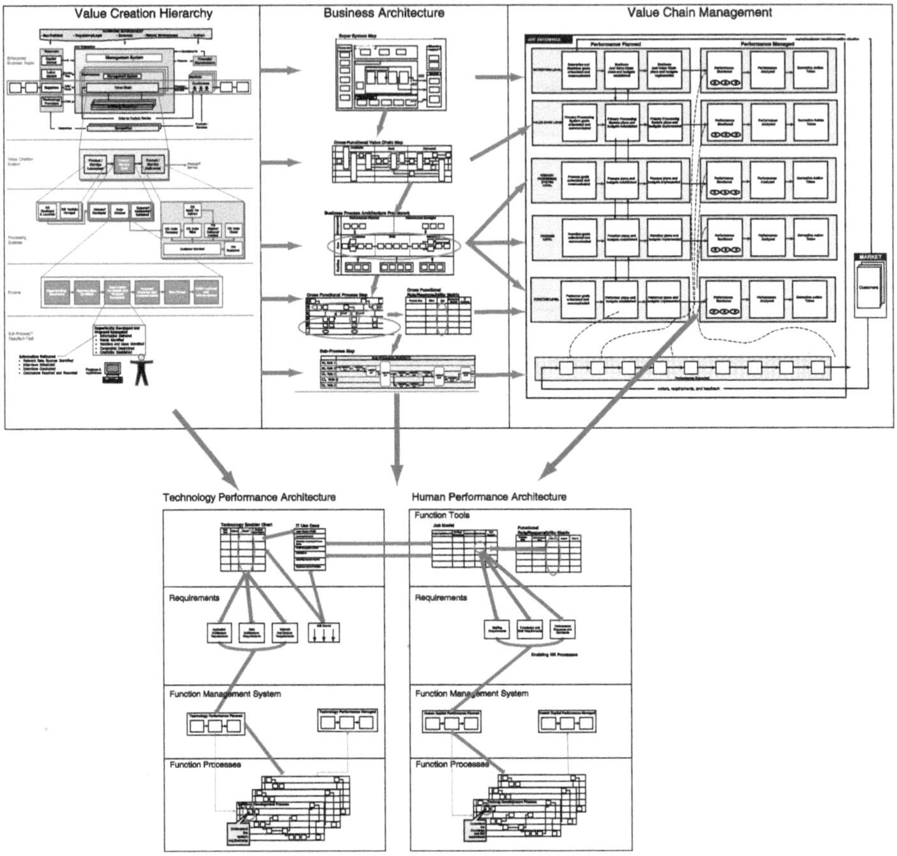

Fig. 16 Whole value creation architecture

This unifying architecture (see Fig. 16) will be constantly affected by changes large and small, but an organization that has developed a complete and accurate VCA like this one is capable of accommodating even large changes much more rapidly than an organization that has not defined its VCA.

References

Harmon P (2004) Enterprise architectures. BPTrends: www.bptrends.com, Jan 2004
Harmon P (2010) The scope and evolution of business process management. In: vom Brocke J, Rosemann M (eds) Handbook on business process management, vol 1. Springer, Heidelberg
Ritter D (2004) Successful enterprise architecture: aligning business and IT to maximize performance. Proforma White Paper

The Six Core Elements of Business Process Management

Michael Rosemann and Jan vom Brocke

Abstract The previous chapters gave an insightful introduction into the various facets of Business Process Management. We now share a rich understanding of the essential ideas behind designing and managing processes for organizational purposes. We have also learned about the various streams of research and development that have influenced contemporary BPM. As a matter of fact, BPM has become a holistic management discipline. As such, it requires that a plethora of facets needs to be addressed for its successful und sustainable application. This chapter provides a framework that consolidates and structures the essential factors that constitute BPM as a whole. Drawing from research in the field of maturity models, we suggest six core elements of BPM: strategic alignment, governance, methods, information technology, people, and culture. These six elements serve as the structure for this BPM Handbook.

1 Why Looking for BPM Core Elements?

A recent global study by Gartner confirmed the significance of BPM with the top issue for CIOs identified for the sixth year in a row being the improvement of business processes (Gartner 2010). While such an interest in BPM is beneficial for professionals in this field, it also increases the expectations and the pressure to deliver on the promises of the process-centered organization.

This context demands a sound understanding of how to approach BPM and a framework that decomposes the complexity of a holistic approach such as Business Process Management. A framework highlighting essential building blocks of BPM can particularly serve the following purposes:

M. Rosemann (✉)
Information Systems Discipline, Faculty of Science and Technology, Queensland University of Technology, Brisbane, Australia
e-mail: m.rosemann@qut.edu.au

J. vom Brocke and M. Rosemann (eds.), *Handbook on Business Process Management 1*, International Handbooks on Information Systems,
DOI 10.1007/978-3-642-00416-2_5,

- *Project and Program Management*: How can all relevant issues within a BPM approach be safeguarded? When implementing a BPM initiative, either as a project or as a program, is it essential to individually adjust the scope and have different BPM flavors in different areas of the organization? What competencies are relevant? What approach fits best with the culture and BPM history of the organization? What is it that needs to be taken into account "beyond modeling"? People for one thing play an important role like Hammer has pointed out in his chapter (Hammer 2010), but what might be further elements of relevance? In order to find answers to these questions, a framework articulating the core elements of BPM provides invaluable advice.
- *Vendor Management*: How can service and product offerings in the field of BPM be evaluated in terms of their overall contribution to successful BPM? What portfolio of solutions is required to address the key issues of BPM, and to what extent do these solutions need to be sourced from outside the organization? There is, for example, a large list of providers of process-aware information systems, change experts, BPM training providers, and a variety of BPM consulting services. How can it be guaranteed that these offerings cover the required capabilities? In fact, the vast number of BPM offerings does not meet the requirements as distilled in this Handbook; see for example, Hammer (2010), Davenport (2010), Harmon (2010), and Rummler and Ramias (2010). It is also for the purpose of BPM make-or-buy decisions and the overall vendor management, that a framework structuring core elements of BPM is highly needed.
- *Complexity Management*: How can the complexity that results from the holistic and comprehensive nature of BPM be decomposed so that it becomes manageable? How can a number of coexisting BPM initiatives within one organization be synchronized? An overarching picture of BPM is needed in order to provide orientation for these initiatives. Following a "divide-and-conquer" approach, a shared understanding of the core elements can help to focus on special factors of BPM. For each element, a specific analysis could be carried out involving experts from the various fields. Such an assessment should be conducted by experts with the required technical, business-oriented, and socio-cultural know-how.
- *Standards Management*: What elements of BPM need to be standardized across the organization? What BPM elements need to be mandated for every BPM initiative? What BPM elements can be configured individually within each initiative? A comprehensive framework allows an element-by-element decision for the degrees of standardization that are required. For example, it might be decided that a company-wide process model repository will be "enforced" on all BPM initiatives, while performance management and cultural change will be decentralized activities.
- *Strategy Management*: What is the BPM strategy of the organization? How does this strategy materialize in a BPM roadmap? How will the naturally limited attention of all involved stakeholders be distributed across the various BPM elements? How do we measure progression in a BPM initiative ("BPM audit")?

A BPM framework that clearly outlines the different elements of BPM has the potential to become an essential tool for such strategy and road-mapping exercises as it facilitates the task of allocating priorities and timeframes to the progression of the various BPM elements.

Based on this demand for a BPM framework that can be used for project and program management, vendor management, complexity management, standards management, and strategy management, we propose a framework that can guide BPM decision makers in all of these challenges. In the following section, we outline how we identified these elements. We then introduce the six core elements by first giving an overview and second presenting each element and its subcomponents in more detail.

2 How to Identify Core Elements of BPM?

The framework to be identified has to comprehensively structure those elements of BPM that need to be addressed when following a holistic understanding of BPM, i.e., BPM as an organizational capability and not just as the execution of the tasks along a process lifecycle (identify, model, analyze, improve, implement, execute, monitor, and change). This standpoint requires an organization-wide perspective and the identification of the core capability areas that are relevant for successful BPM. We, thus, base our work on BPM maturity models that have been subject to former research.

Recently, a number of models to decompose and measure the maturity of Business Process Management have been proposed as shown in Fig. 1.

The basis for the greater part of these maturity models has been the *Capability Maturity Model* (CMM) developed by the Software Engineering Institute at Carnegie Mellon University, Pittsburgh, PA. This model was originally developed in order to assess the maturity of software development processes and is based on the concept of immature and mature software organizations. The basis for applying the model is confirmed by Paulk et al. (1993) who stated that improved maturity results "*in an increase in the process capability of the organization*". CMM introduces the concept of five maturity levels defined by special requirements that are cumulative.

Among others, Harmon (2004) developed a BPM maturity model based on the CMM (Harmon 2003). In a similar way, Fisher (2004) combines five "levels of change" with fives states of maturity. Smith and Fingar (2004) argue that a CMM-based maturity model, which postulates well-organized and repeatable processes, cannot capture the need for business process innovation. Further, BPM maturity models have been designed by the Business Process Management Group (BPMG) and the TeraQuest/Borland Software (Curtis et al. 2004) that is now supported by the OMG (OMG 2008).

Model	Subject	Source
Process Condition Model	Effectiveness and efficiency measurement to rate a process' condition	DeToro and McCabe (1997)
Strategic Alignment Maturity Model	Maturity of strategic alignment	Luftman (2003)
BPR Maturity Model	Business Process Re-engineering Programmes	Maull et al. (2003)
Harmon's BPM Maturity Model	BPM maturity model based on the CMM	Harmon (2003, 2004)
Rummler-Brache Group's Process Maturity Model	Success factors for managing key business processes	Rummler-Brache (2004)
OMG's BPM Maturity Model	Practices applied to the management of discrete processes	Curtis et al. (2004); OMG (2008)
Rosemann and de Bruin's BPM Maturity Model	Maturity of Business Process Management capabilities	Rosemann; de Bruin (2005); de Bruin (2009)
Capability Maturity Model Integration (CMMI)	Maturity of software development processes	SEI (2006a, 2006b)
Hammer's BPM Maturity Model (Process Audit)	Defining process and enterprise competencies	Hammer (2007)

Fig. 1 Selected maturity models in BPM

Curtis and Alden (2006) take a prescriptive approach to process management. This model combines a number of process areas by either applying a staged or a continuous approach. Progress through the stages is dependent on all requirements of preceding and completed stages. Some discretion is allowed at lower stages using the continuous approach but it largely evolves around the order in which the process areas are addressed. Hammer (2007), likewise, adopts a prescriptive approach (the "Process Audit") defining a number of process and enterprise competencies. Hammer also demands that all aspects of a stage are to be completed before progressing to higher stages of maturity.

A recognized shortcoming of the universalistic approaches adopted by Curtis and Alden (2006) and Hammer (2007) is that they seem to be more appropriate for relatively narrow domains and do not capture various aspects of an organization sufficiently (Sabherwal et al. 2001). A further critique of these BPM maturity models has been the simplifying focus, the limited reliability in the assessment, and the lack of actual (and documented) applications of these models leading to limited empirical validations.

A proposal to divide organizations into groups with regard to their grade and progression of BPM implementation was made by Pritchard and Armistead (1999). The Rummler–Brache Group commissioned a study, which used ten success factors gaging how well an organization manages its key business processes (Rummler–Brache 2004). The results have been consolidated in a Process Performance Index. Pritchard and Armistead (1999) provide a proposal for how to divide organizations into groups depending on their grade and progression of BPM implementation.

In an attempt to define maturity of BPR programs, Maull et al. (2003) encountered problems in that they could not use objective measures. They define BPM by using two dimensions, an objective measure (time, team size, etc.) and a "weighting for readiness to change" (Maull et al. 2003). This approach, however, turned out to be too complex for measurement. Therefore, they chose a phenomenological approach assessing the organization's perception of their maturity, using objective measures as a guideline. Another example of how to define maturity (or in their case "process condition") is provided by DeToro and McCabe (1997), who used two dimensions (effectiveness and efficiency) to rate a process' condition. These models show that a clear distinction should be made between process maturity models and Business Process Management maturity models.

In addition to these dedicated process and BPM maturity models, a number of models have been proposed that study and structure the maturity of single elements of BPM in a more general way. An example is Luftman's (2003) maturity model for strategic alignment.

As our base for identifying the core elements of BPM, we have used Rosemann and de Bruin's (2005) BPM maturity model (de Bruin 2009). This BPM maturity model was selected for a number of reasons:

- First, it was developed on the contemporary understanding of BPM as a holistic management approach.
- Second, it is based on a sound academic development process. Starting with an in-depth and comprehensive literature review, the experiences and preliminary versions of three previous BPM maturity models have been consolidated. The model has been validated, refined, and specified through a series of international Delphi studies involving global BPM thought leaders (de Bruin and Rosemann 2007). A number of detailed case studies in various industries further contributed to the validation and deeper understanding of the model (de Bruin 2009).
- Third, the model distinguishes factors and capability areas on two levels of abstraction. This hierarchical structure allows different types of granularity in the analysis. As a result, definitions of the factors and capability areas are available and provide a basis for consistent interpretation (Rosemann et al. 2006; de Bruin 2009).
- Fourth and finally, the model has been applied within a number of organizations by means of documented case studies including embedded surveys and workshops (Rosemann and de Bruin 2004; Rosemann et al. 2004; de Bruin and Rosemann 2006; de Bruin 2009). Hence, the core elements have been validated and proven to be of practical relevance in real life projects.

For all these reasons, we are using this maturity model to identify the six core elements of BPM. That said, we use the model in a slightly modified way: We do not explicitly elaborate on the maturity assessment process and the various maturity stages of this model. Rather we take a static view and simply discuss the factors and corresponding capability areas of this BPM framework.

3 Introducing the Six Core Elements of BPM

3.1 Overview

The consolidation of related literature, the merger of three existing BPM maturity models, the subsequent international Delphi studies and the case studies led to a set of well-defined factors that together constitute a holistic understanding of BPM (de Bruin 2009). Each of the six core elements represents a critical success factor for Business Process Management. Therefore, each element, sooner or later, needs to be considered by organizations striving for success with BPM. For each of these six factors, the consensus finding Delphi studies (de Bruin and Rosemann 2007) provided a further level of detail, the so called *Capability Areas*. Both factors and capability areas are displayed in Fig. 2.

Our model distinguishes six core elements critical to BPM. These are strategic alignment, governance, methods, information technology, people, and culture.

- *Strategic Alignment*: BPM needs to be aligned with the overall strategy of an organization. Strategic alignment (or synchronization) is defined as the tight linkage of organizational priorities and enterprise processes enabling continual and effective action to improve business performance. Processes have to be

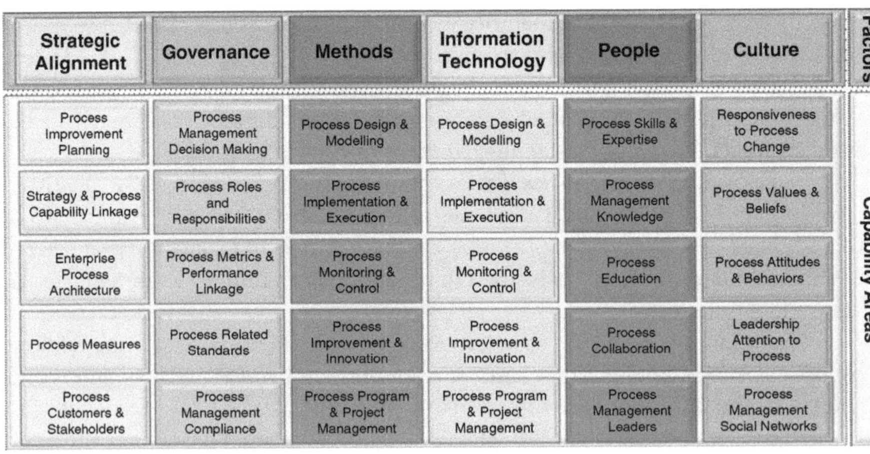

Fig. 2 The six core elements of BPM

designed, executed, managed, and measured according to strategic priorities and specific strategic situations (e.g., stage of a product lifecycle, position in a strategic portfolio; Burlton 2010). In return, specific process capabilities (e.g., competitive advantage in terms of time to execute or change a process) may offer opportunities to inform the strategy design leading to process-enabled strategies.

- *Governance*: BPM governance establishes appropriate and transparent accountability in terms of roles and responsibilities for different levels of BPM (portfolio, program, project, and operations). A further focus is on the design of decision-making and reward processes to guide process-related actions.
- *Methods*: Methods in the context of BPM are defined as the set of tools and techniques that support and enable activities along the process lifecycle and within enterprise-wide BPM initiatives. Examples are methods that facilitate process modeling or process analysis and process improvement techniques. Six Sigma is an example for a BPM approach that has at its core a set of integrated BPM methods (Conger 2010).
- *Information Technology*: IT-based solutions are of significance for BPM initiatives. With a traditional focus on process analysis (e.g., statistical process control) and process modeling support, BPM-related IT solutions increasingly manifest themselves in the form of process-aware information systems (PAIS) (Dumas et al. 2005). Process-awareness means that the software has an explicit understanding of the process that needs to be executed. Such process awareness could be the result of input in the form of process models or could be more implicitly embedded in the form of hard-coded processes (like in traditional banking or insurance applications).
- *People*: People as a core element of BPM is defined as individuals and groups who continually enhance and apply their process and process management skills and knowledge in order to improve business performance. Consequently, this factor captures the BPM capabilities that are reflected in the human capital of an organization and its ecosystem.
- *Culture*: BPM culture incorporates the collective values and beliefs in regards to the process-centered organization. Although commonly considered a "soft-factor," comparative case studies clearly demonstrate the strong impact of culture on the success of BPM (de Bruin 2009). Culture is about creating a facilitating environment that complements the various BPM initiatives. However, it needs to be recognized that the impact of culture-related activities tends to have a much longer time horizon than activities related to any of the other five factors.

The six identified factors in this BPM maturity model are heavily grounded in literature. A sample summary of literature supporting these factors is shown in Fig. 3.

In the following, we will elaborate on the capability areas that further decompose each of these six factors. Here, we particularly draw from the results of a set of international Delphi Studies that involved BPM experts from the US, Australasia, and Europe (de Bruin and Rosemann 2007). We can only provide a brief overview

Factor	Source
Strategic Alignment	Elzinga et al. 1995; Hammer, 2001; Hung, 2006; Jarrar et al. 2000; Pritchard and Armistead, 1999; Puah K.Y. and Tang K.H, 2000; Zairi, 1997; Zairi and Sinclair, 1995
Government	Braganza and Lambert, 2000; Gulledge and Sommer, 2002; Harmon, 2005; Jarrar et al. 2000; Pritchard and Armistead, 1999
Methods	Adesola and Baines, 2005; Harrington, 1991; Kettinger et al. 1997; Pritchard and Armistead, 1999; Zairi, 1997
Information Technology	Gulledge and Sommer, 2002; Hammer and Champy, 1993; McDaniel, 2001
People	Elzinga et al. 1995; Hung, 2006; Llewellyn and Armistead, 2000; Pritchard and Armistead, 1999; Zairi and Sinclair, 1995; Zairi, 1997
Culture	Elzinga et al. 1995; Llewellyn and Armistead, 2000; Pritchard and Armistead, 1999; Spanyi, 2003, Zairi, 1997; Zairi and Sinclair, 1995

Fig. 3 The six BPM core elements in the literature

about each of the six factors in the following sections and refer to the chapters in this Handbook for deeper insights per factor.

3.2 Strategic Alignment

Strategic alignment is defined as the tight linkage of organizational priorities and enterprise processes enabling continual and effective action to improve business performance. Five distinct capability areas have been identified as part of an assessment of strategic alignment in BPM.

- A strategy-driven *process improvement plan* captures the organization's overall approach towards BPM. The process improvement plan should be directly derived from the organization's strategy, and outline how process improvement initiatives are going to meet strategically prioritized goals. This allows a clear articulation of the corporate benefits of BPM initiatives. The process improvement plan also provides information related to how the BPM initiative relates to underlying projects such as the implementation of an Enterprise System.
- A core element of strategic alignment, in the context of BPM, is the bidirectional *linkage between strategy and business processes*. Do the business processes directly contribute to the strategy? Do organizational strategies explicitly incorporate process capabilities? By way of example, do we know which processes

are impacted by a change of the strategy? Which processes could become a bottleneck in the execution of the strategy? Is the strategy designed and continually reviewed in light of current and emerging process capabilities? How should scarce resources be allocated to competing processes? Which processes are core to the organization and should be executed in-house (core competency)? Which processes are candidates for process outsourcing or off-shoring (Bhat et al. 2010)? Common methodologies such as Strategy Maps (Kaplan and Norton 2004) play an important role in linking strategy and process design.

- *An enterprise process architecture* is the highest level abstraction of the actual hierarchy of value-driven and enabling business processes (Aitken et al. 2010; Spanyi 2010). A well-defined enterprise process architecture clearly depicts which major business processes exist, describes the industry-/company-specific value chain, and captures the enabling processes that support this value chain, for example, finance, human capital management, or IT services. A well-designed process architecture provides a high level visualization from a process view and complements, and not replicates, organizational structures. In addition, it serves as the main process landscape and provides a starting point for more detailed process analyses and models.
- In order to be able to evaluate actual process performance, it is important to have a clear and shared understanding of *process outputs* and related key performance indicators (KPIs). A hierarchy of cascading, process-oriented, and cost-effectively measured KPIs provides a valuable source for the translation of strategic objectives to process-specific goals and facilitates effective process control. Relevant KPIs can differ in their nature, including financial, quantitative, qualitative, or time-based data, and will be dependent on the strategic drivers for the specific enterprise process (vom Brocke et al. 2010). As far as possible, such KPIs should be standardized across the various processes and in particular across the different process variants (e.g., in different countries). Only such a process performance standardization allows consistent cross-process performance analysis (e.g., what processes can explain a drop in the overall customer satisfaction?). Often equally important, but more difficult to measure, are those KPIs related to characteristics of an entire process, such as flexibility, reliability or compliance.
- Strategies are typically closely linked to individuals and influential stakeholder groups. Thus, a strategic assessment of BPM has to evaluate the actual priorities of *key customers and other stakeholders such as senior management, shareholders, government bodies, etc*. For example, it can be observed that a change of a CEO often will have significant impact on the popularity (or not) of BPM even if the official strategy remains the same. The consideration of stakeholders also includes an investigation of how well processes with touch-points ("moments of truth") to external parties are managed, how well external viewpoints have been considered in the process design, and what influence external stakeholders have on the process design. Such a view can go so far that organizations consciously design processes the way they are perceived by their business partners, and then start to position their services in these processes.

3.3 Governance

BPM governance is dedicated to appropriate and transparent accountability in terms of roles and responsibilities for different levels of BPM (portfolio, program, project, and operations). Furthermore, it is tasked with the design of decision-making and reward processes to guide process-related actions.

- The clear definition and consistent execution of related BPM *decision-making processes* that guide actions in both anticipated and unanticipated circumstances is a critical challenge for BPM governance. In addition to *who* can make *which* decision, the speed of decision-making and the ability to influence resource allocation and organizational responses to process change is important. This requires alignment with related governance processes such as IT change management or Business Continuity Management.
- A core element of BPM governance is the definition of *process roles and responsibilities*. This covers the entire range of BPM-related roles, from business process analysts to process owners up to potential chief process officers (CPO). It also encompasses all related committees and involved decision boards, such as Process Councils and Process Steering Committees. The duties and responsibilities of each role need to be clearly specified, and precise reporting structures must be defined.
- Processes must exist to ensure the direct linkage of process performance with strategic goals. While the actual process output is measured and evaluated as part of the factor strategic alignment, accountabilities and the process for *collecting the required metrics* and linking them to performance criteria is regarded as being a part of BPM governance.
- *Process management standards* must be well-defined and documented. This includes among others the coordination of process management initiatives across the organization, and guidelines for the establishment and management process measures, issue resolution, reward, and remuneration structures.
- *Process management controls* as part of BPM governance cover regular review cycles to maintain the quality and currency of process management principles (e.g., "process reuse before process development"). Appropriate compliance management forms another key component of process management controls (Spanyi 2010).

3.4 Methods

Methods, in the context of BPM, have been defined as the tools and techniques that support and enable consistent activities on all levels of BPM (portfolio, program, project, and operations). Distinct methods can be applied to major, discrete stages of the process lifecycle. This characteristic, which is unique to the "methods" and "information technology" factors, has resulted in capability areas that reflect the process lifecycle stages rather than specific capabilities of BPM methods or information technology. An advantage of associating the method capability with a specific process lifecycle stage is that a method can be assessed with regards to a specific purpose. For example, it is possible to assess the specific methods used for designing processes as distinct from those used for improving processes. Therefore, the methods dimension focuses on the specific needs of each process lifecycle, and considers elements such as the integration of process lifecycle methods with each other and with other management methods, the support for methods provided by information technology, and the sophistication, suitability, accessibility, and actual usage of methods within each stage.

- *Process design and modeling* is related to the methods used to identify and conceptualize current (as-is) business processes and future (to-be) processes. The core of such methods is not only to process modeling techniques but also to process analysis methods.
- *Process implementation and execution* covers the next stages in the lifecycle. Related methods help to transform process models into executable business process specifications. Methods related to the communication of these models and escalation methods facilitate the process execution.
- The *process control and measurement* stage of the process lifecycle is related to methods that provide guidance for the collection and consolidation of process-related data. These data can be related to process control (e.g., risks), or could be process performance measures (e.g., time, cost, and quality).
- The *process improvement and innovation* stage includes all methods which facilitate the development of improved business processes. This includes approaches that support the activities of process enhancement (e.g., resequencing steps in a process), process innovation (e.g., creative thinking techniques), process utilization (better use of existing resources such as people, data, or systems), and process derivation (reference models, benchmarking, etc.).
- The assessment component *process project management and program management* evaluates the methods that are used for the overall enterprise-wide management of BPM and for specific BPM projects. The latter requires a sound integration of BPM methods with specific project management approaches (e.g., PMBOK, PRINCE 2).

3.5 Information Technology

Information technology (IT) refers to the software, hardware, and information systems that enable and support process activities. As indicated, the assessment of IT as one of the BPM core elements is structured in a similar way to that of BPM methods, and also refers to the process lifecycle stages. Similar to the methods dimension, the IT components focus on the specific needs of each process lifecycle stage and are evaluated from viewpoints such as customizability, appropriateness of automation, and integration with related IT solutions (e.g., data warehousing, enterprise systems, reporting). Further evaluation criteria capture the sophistication, suitability, accessibility, and usage of such IT within each stage.

- *IT solutions for process design and modeling* cover the (semi-)automated support that enables derivation of process models from log files (process mining), and tool-support for business process modeling and analysis (e.g., process animation, process simulation) (van der Aalst et al. 2010).
- *IT-enabled process implementation and execution* focuses on the automated transformation of process models into executable specifications and the subsequent workflow-based process execution, (Ouyang et al. 2010). This also includes related solutions such as document management systems or service-enabled processes. This entire category of software is often labeled "process-aware information systems" (Dumas et al. 2005).
- *Process control and measurement* solutions facilitate (semi-)automated process escalation management, exception handling, performance visualization (e.g., dashboards), and process controlling. There is a high demand for these type of solutions to be integrated in the corporate landscape (e.g., via Balanced Scorecard systems).
- Tools for *process improvement and innovation* provide (semi-)automated support for the generation of improved business processes. These could be solutions that provide agile (i.e., self-learning) tools that continuously adjust business processes based on contextual changes.
- *Process project management and program management* tools facilitate the overall management of different types of BPM initiatives. They provide among others decision support systems for process owners.

3.6 People

While the information technology factor covered IT-related resources, the factor "people" comprises human resources. This factor is defined as the individuals and groups who continually enhance and apply their process and process management skills and knowledge to improve business performance.

- *Process skills and expertise* is concentrated on the comprehensiveness and depth of the capabilities of the involved stakeholders in light of the specific requirements of a process. This is an important capability area for process owners and all stakeholders involved in the management and operations of a process.
- *Process management knowledge* consolidates the explicit and tacit knowledge about BPM principles and practices. It evaluates the level of understanding of BPM, including the knowledge of process management methods and information technology, and the impact these have on business process outcomes (Karagiannis and Woitsch 2010). In particular, business process analysts and

the extent to which they can apply their process management knowledge to a variety of processes are assessed within this capability area.

- *Process education and learning* measures the commitment of the organization to the ongoing development and maintenance of the relevant process and process management skills and knowledge. The assessment covers the existence, extent, appropriateness, scope of roll-out, and actual success (as measured by the level of learning) of BPM education programs. Further items are devoted to the qualification of the BPM educators and BPM certification programs.
- *Process collaboration and communication* considers the ways in which individuals and groups work together in order to achieve desired process outcomes. This includes the related evaluation of the communication patterns between process stakeholders, and the manner in which related process knowledge is discovered, explored, and disseminated.
- The final "people" capability area is dedicated to *process management leaders.* The assessment according to this element evaluates the willingness to lead, take responsibility, and be accountable for business processes. Among others, this capability area also captures the degree to which desired process leadership skills and management styles are actually practiced.

3.7 Culture

Culture, the sixth and final BPM core element, refers to the collective values and beliefs that shape process-related attitudes and behavior to improve business performance.

- *Responsiveness to process change* is about the overall receptiveness of the organization to process change, the propensity of the organization to accept process change, and adaptation. It also includes the ability for process change to cross functional boundaries seamlessly and for people to act in the best interest of the process.
- *Process values and beliefs* investigates the broad process thinking within the organization. For example, do members of the organization naturally see processes as the way things get done? Do "processes" play a prominent role in the corporate vision, mission, value statements? (vom Brocke et al. 2010). Furthermore, this capability area concentrates on the commonly held beliefs and values of the key BPM stakeholders. Among them is the longevity of BPM, expressed by the depth and breadth of the ongoing commitment to BPM.
- The *process attitudes and behavior* of those who are involved in and those who are affected by BPM form a further assessment item in the "culture" factor. This includes, among others, the willingness to question existing BPM practices in the light of potential process improvements. It also captures actual process-related behavior (e.g., willingness to comply with the process design or extent to which processes get priority over resources).

- *Leadership attention to process management* covers the level of commitment and attention to processes and process management shown by senior executives, the degree of attention paid to process on all levels, and the quality of process leadership. For example, do "processes" regularly appear as a term in presentations of the senior executives of the organization?
- Finally, *process management social networks* comprise the existence and influence of BPM communities of practice, the usage of social network techniques, and the recognition and use of informal BPM networks.

4 Conclusion and Outlook

This chapter aimed at providing a brief overview of a framework for BPM comprising of six core elements. Each element represents a key success factor for implementing BPM in practice. We referred to a well-established and empirically validated BPM maturity model in order to identify the six core elements of BPM: strategic alignment, governance, methods, information technology, people, and culture.

These grounded elements provide the primary structure of the BPM Handbook at hand. The following chapters present contributions to each of these elements and have been provided by the most recognized thought leaders in these areas. While focussing on a specific element each contribution also considers relations to the other elements. We are presenting contributions from academics as well as case studies from practitioners. Some are more technical in nature, some more business oriented. Some look more at the soft side of BPM while others study the conceptual details of advanced methodologies. By proposing this sixfold structure, the reader may grasp what they consider most appropriate for their individual background. In any case, we trust that the discussion of these six core elements and the corresponding capability areas helps to make the holistic view on Business Process Management more tangible.

References

Aitken C, Stephenson C, Brinkworth R (2010) Process classification frameworks. In: vom Brocke J, Rosemann M (eds) Handbook on business process management, vol 2. Springer, Heidelberg

Bhat JM, Fernandez J, Kumar M, Goel S (2010) Business process outsourcing. In: vom Brocke J, Rosemann M (eds) Handbook on business process management, vol 2. Springer, Heidelberg

Burlton R (2010) Delivering business strategy through process management. In: vom Brocke J, Rosemann M (eds) Handbook on business process management, vol 2. Springer, Heidelberg

Conger S (2010) Six sigma and business process management. In: vom Brocke J, Rosemann M (eds) Handbook on business process management, vol 1. Springer, Heidelberg

Curtis B, Alden J, Weber CV (2004) The use of process maturity models in business process management. Borland Software Corporation, Austin, TX, White Paper

Curtis B, Alden J (2006) BPM and Organizational Maturity. BPTrends, November 2006
Davenport TH (2010) Process management for knowledge work. In: vom Brocke J, Rosemann M (eds) Handbook on business process management, vol 1. Springer, Heidelberg
de Bruin T, Rosemann M (2006) Towards understanding strategic alignment of business process management. In: Proceedings of the 17th Australasian conference on information systems, Adelaide, Australia, 6–8 Dec 2006
de Bruin T, Rosemann M (2007) Using the Delphi technique to identify BPM capability areas. In: Proceedings of the 18th Australasian conference on information systems, Toowoomba, Australia, 5–7 Dec 2007
de Bruin T (2009) Business process management: theory on progression and maturity. PhD Thesis, Queensland University of Technology, Brisbane, Australia
DeToro I, McCabe T (1997) How to stay flexible and elude fads. Qual Progr 30(3):55–60
Dumas M, van der Aalst WM, ter Hofstede AH (2005) Process-aware information systems: bridging people and software through process technology. Wiley, New York
Fisher DM (2004) The business process maturity model. A practical approach for identifying opportunities for optimization. (Online). http://www.bptrends.com/resources_publications.cfm. Accessed 26 Aug 2009
Gartner (2010) Leading in times of transition. The 2010 CIO Agenda. Stamford, CA, USA
Hammer M (2007) The process audit. Harv Bus Rev 85:111–143
Hammer M (2010) What is business process management? In: vom Brocke J, Rosemann M (eds) Handbook on business process management, vol 1. Springer, Heidelberg
Harmon P (2003) Business process change: a manager's guide to improving, redesigning, and automating processes. Morgan Kaufmann, Amsterdam, Boston
Harmon P (2004) Evaluating an organization's business process maturity. http://www.bptrends.com/resources_publications.cfm. Accessed 26 Aug 2009
Harmon P (2010) The scope and evolution of business process management. In: vom Brocke J, Rosemann M (eds) Handbook on business process management, vol 1. Springer, Heidelberg
Kaplan RS, Norton DP (2004) Strategy maps: converting intangible assets into tangible outcomes. Harvard Business Press, Boston, MA, USA
Karagiannis D, Woitsch R (2010) Knowledge engineering in business process management. In: vom Brocke J, Rosemann M (eds) Handbook on business process management, vol 2. Springer, Heidelberg
Luftman JN (2003) Assessing strategic alignment maturity. In: Luftman JN (ed) Competing in the information age: align in the sand, 2nd edn. Oxford University Press, Oxford, pp 15–48
Maull RS, Tranfield DR, Maull W (2003) Factors characterising the maturity of BPR programmes. Int J Oper Prod Manage 23(6):596–624
OMG (2008) Business process maturity model (BPMM), Version 1.0, Standard document. http://www.omg.org/spec/BPMM/1.0/PDF. Accessed 26 Aug 2009
Ouyang C, Adams M, Wynn MT, ter Hofstede AHM (2010) Workflow management. In: vom Brocke J, Rosemann M (eds) Handbook on business process management, vol 1. Springer, Heidelberg
Paulk MC, Curtis B, Chrissis MB, Weber CV (1993) The capability maturity model for software, Version 1.1 (No. CMU/SEI-93-TR-24). Software engineering institute, Pittsburgh, PA
Pritchard J-P, Armistead C (1999) Business process management – lessons from European business. Bus Process Manage J 5(1):10–32
Rosemann M, de Bruin T (2005) Towards a business process management maturity model. In: Proceedings of the 13th European conference on information systems, Regensburg, Germany, May 2005
Rosemann M, de Bruin T (2004) Application of a holistic model for determining BPM maturity. In: Akoka J, Comyn-Wattiau I, Favier M (eds) Proceedings of the AIM Pre-ICIS workshop on process management and information systems, 46–60. (Actes du 3e colloque Pre-ICIS de l'AIM), Washington, DC, 12 Dec 2004
Rosemann M, de Bruin T, Hueffner T (2004) Testing a model for business process management maturity with two case studies. In: Proceedings of the 15th Australasian conference on information systems, Hobart, Australia, 1–3 Dec 2004

Rosemann M, de Bruin T, Power B (2006) A model to measure business process management and improve performance. In: Jeston J, Nelis J (eds) Business process management. Butterworth-Heinemann, London, Chapter 27

Rummler GA, Ramias AJ (2010) A framework for defining and designing the structure of work. In: vom Brocke J, Rosemann M (eds) Handbook on business process management, vol 1. Springer, Heidelberg

Rummler-Brache Group (2004) Business process management in US firms today. A study commissioned by Rummler-Brache Group, Mar 2004

Sabherwal R, Hirschheim R, & Goles T (2001) The dynamics of alignment: Insights from a punctuated equilibrium model. Org Sci, 12(2):179–197

Smith H, Fingar P (2004) Process management maturity models. (Online) http://www.bptrends.com/resources_publications.cfm. Accessed 26 Aug 2009

Spanyi A (2010) Business process management governance. In: vom Brocke J, Rosemann M (eds) Handbook on business process management, vol 2. Springer, Heidelberg

van der Aalst WMP, Nakatumba J, Rozinat A, Russell N (2010) Business process simulation. In: vom Brocke J, Rosemann M (eds) Handbook on business process management, vol 1. Springer, Heidelberg

vom Brocke J, Petry M, Sinnl T, Østerberg Kristensen B, Sonnenberg C (2010) Global process and data: the cultural journey at the Hilti Corporation. In: vom Brocke J, Rosemann M (eds) Handbook on business process management, vol 2. Springer, Heidelberg

vom Brocke J, Recker J, Mendling J (2010) Value-oriented Process Modeling: Integrating Financial Perspectives into Business Process Re-design. Business Process Management Journal (BPMJ), 16(2):333–356

Part II
Methods

In the tradition of BPM, the design of methods, tools, and process modeling methodologies has attracted a substantial amount of interest within the BPM community. This section covers the comprehensive set of methods, essentially including rules and guidelines on how to proceed in the various stages of BPM. Very often, these methods form the most tangible knowledge asset within BPM.

At least three levels of methods can be differentiated. First, there are process-specific individual techniques that provide guidance for modeling, analyzing, animating, simulating, improving, or automating a process. Second, there is a class of methods that covers the entire business process lifecycle though often with different emphasis on the single lifecycle phases. Six Sigma and Lean Management are prominent representatives of this class of methodologies. Third, and most comprehensive in their scope, there are methods that guide the enterprise-wide roll-out of Business Process Management as a corporate capability. It is characteristic of the current status of BPM that the body of knowledge on type 1 methods is very rich and a number of type 2 methods are widely used, though in most cases, they are still incomplete. However, type 3 BPM methodologies are still in their infancy. The comprehensiveness of this section is a clear indicator not only for the high interest in this area but also for the requirement to further develop a BPM methodology.

In the first chapter, Sue Conger describes Six Sigma as one of the most popular business process lifecycle management methodologies. Key techniques within Six Sigma are explained and an overall positioning of Six Sigma is provided. A core capability in the analysis and redesign of business processes is abstraction. In the second chapter in this section, Artem Polyvyanyy, Sergey Smirnov, and Mathias Weske feature a process model abstraction methodology including process transformation rules that help to focus on the significant parts of a process model.

While there is no shortage on recommendations for modeling business processes, the discipline of process model assessment has not yet matured to the same extent. Hajo Reijers, Jan Mendling, and Jan Recker tackle this challenge in the third chapter by proposing a framework for the holistic evaluation of the quality of business process models. One way to improve the quality of process models, and subsequent process analyses, is to use semantic building blocks. In the fourth chapter, Jörg Becker, Daniel Pfeiffer, Thorsten Falk, and Michael Räckers propose and evaluate PICTURE, a complexity-reduced way for cost-effective process modeling.

As part of the plethora of process modeling techniques, first attempts towards standardization have emerged, and the most prominent candidate for such a process modeling standard is the Business Process Modeling Notation (BPMN). The fifth chapter by Gustav Aagesen and John Krogstie provides an overview about research that has been conducted on the analysis and design of processes using BPMN. A particular challenge in process modeling across all modeling techniques is the management of business process variants, an issue that especially emerges in large-scale distributed modeling initiatives. The sixth chapter by Alena Hallerbach, Thomas Bauer, and Manfred Reichert discusses how such process variants can be configured and managed using practical examples from the automotive industry.

While an intraorganizational approach towards process modeling is still dominating, we are witnessing an increasing demand for interorganizational modeling activities to appropriately conceptualize entire value networks. Two chapters are dedicated to this domain. The seventh chapter by Alistair Barros, Thomas Hettel, and Christian Flender is an introduction to a process choreography modeling technique for different levels of abstraction including the required refinement steps. A comprehensive case study, Intersport, is used in the subsequent eighth chapter in order to sensitize for the real word requirements of interorganizational process design. With a focus on strategic alignment, Mikael Lind and Ulf Seigerroth describe the collaborative process modeling in this specific case.

Two chapters are concentrated on advanced solutions that facilitate the design and analysis of business processes. In the ninth chapter, Agnes Koschmider and Andreas Oberweis propose a recommendation-based editor for process modeling. Already widely used in many web-based applications, recommender systems only start making an entry into the world of business process modeling. In the tenth chapter, process simulation as one of the key quantitative process analysis techniques is discussed. Wil van der Aalst, Joyce Nakatumba, Anne Rozinat, and Nick Russell investigate three typical pitfalls of process simulation and provide specific advice for the improved modeling of resource availability.

This section closes with two case studies: Islay Davies and Micheal Reeves report on the experiences of the Queensland Court of Justice as part of their process management tool selection process in the eleventh chapter. In the twelfth and final chapter of this section, Florian Johannsen, Susanne Leist, and Gregor Zellner elaborate on the development of a Six Sigma prototype that facilitated the selection and combination of techniques within an automotive bank.

1. Six Sigma and Business Process Management
   by Sue Conger
2. Business Process Model Abstraction
   by Artem Polyvyanyy, Sergey Smirnov, and Mathias Weske

3. Business Process Quality Management
   by Hajo A. Reijers, Jan Mendling, and Jan Recker
4. Semantic Business Process Management
   by Jörg Becker, Daniel Pfeiffer, Thorsten Falk, and Michael Räckers
5. Analysis and Design of Business Processes using BPMN
   by Gustav Aagesen and John Krogstie
6. Configuration and Management of Process Variants
   by Alena Hallerbach, Thomas Bauer, and Manfred Reichert
7. Process Choreography Modeling
   by Alistair Barros, Thomas Hettel, and Christian Flender
8. Collaborative Process Modeling: The Intersport Case Study
   by Mikael Lind and Ulf Seigerroth
9. Designing Business Processes with a Recommendation-based Editor
   by Agnes Koschmider and Andreas Oberweis
10. Business Process Simulation
    by Wil M.P. van der Aalst, Joyce Nakatumba, Anne Rozinat, and Nick Russell
11. BPM Tool Selection. The Case of the Queensland Court of Justice
    by Islay Davies and Micheal Reeves
12. Implementing Six Sigma for Improving Business Processes
    at an Automotive Bank
    by Florian Johannsen, Susanne Leist, and Gregor Zellner

Six Sigma and Business Process Management

Sue Conger

Abstract Business Process Management has no set methods of analysis for removing unneeded process steps, identifying inefficient or ineffective process steps, or simply determining which process steps to focus on for improvement. Often, tools and techniques from Six Sigma, an orientation to error-proofing that originated in the quality movement of the 1980s, are borrowed for those tasks. This chapter defines several Six Sigma techniques and shows how they can be used to improve deficient processes. The application of Six Sigma techniques is illustrated through a case study. Six Sigma can add to BPM efforts, however, it has few guidelines on how to choose techniques or redesign processes, thus requiring special skills and experience to add value to a process improvement project.

1 Introduction

Organizations should constantly improve their functioning to remain competitive. Yet, problems develop in the translation of strategy to actual business process, that is, the series of steps that accomplish some work (Kaplan and Norton 2001). Further, by improving business processes, the intellectual capital of the workers increases through added understanding of their role in the organization and through removal of resource gaps (Herremans and Isaac 2004; Harrison-Broninski 2010).

Business organizations are comprised of people who conduct thousands of processes in their daily business conduct. Organizations that do not manage their processes are less effective than those that do (Kaplan and Norton 2001). Further, organizations that allocate information technologies to processes, but do not manage the process, are mostly wasting their money.

S. Conger
IT and IT Service Management Programs, University of Dallas, Graduate School of Management, Irving, TX, USA
e-mail: sconger@gsm.udallas.edu

J. vom Brocke and M. Rosemann (eds.), *Handbook on Business Process Management 1*, International Handbooks on Information Systems,
DOI 10.1007/978-3-642-00416-2_6,

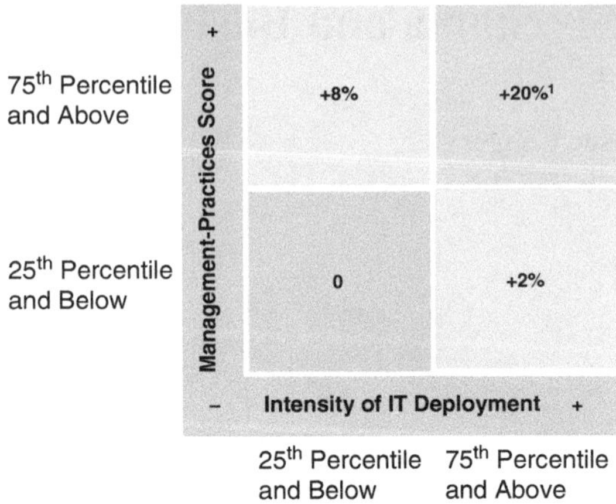

Fig. 1 Gains from managing both IT and business (Dorgan and Dowdy 2004)

As Dorgan and Dowdy (2004) show in Fig. 1, companies that actively manage their business processes but have a low intensity of technology for supporting work experienced an 8% gain from their investment. This shows that by simply doing no other changes than managing business processes can lead to higher return on investment. Companies that both actively managed business processes and had a high intensity of technology support for work experienced a 20% average gain from their investment. This result argues both for intelligent process management and strategic, intelligent technology deployment to support business processes.

Thus, in their search for survival capabilities, organizations have come to understand that excess of any sort is costly and should be removed. The first step to removing excess is to understand business processes, the work those processes accomplish, and how that work relates to the organization strategy (vom Brocke et al. 2010). Any process, process step, or process product (e.g., document, email, data, or other product of a process step) that does not contribute to the organization strategy or its ability to meet its mission is waste. Process value accrues to the extent that it fulfills some aspect of the organization's customer value proposition (Kaplan and Norton 2001). Thus, the overall goal of Business Process Management (BPM) is to improve processes to optimize fulfillment of customer value (see also Hammer 2010).

BPM uses techniques to measure, analyze, and improve processes; however, there is no single body of knowledge or techniques that apply to BPM. Six Sigma provides useful techniques for BPM (Harmon 2010).

1.1 Six Sigma

Modern quality programs have their roots in the 1950s in the U.S. and in Japan where Walter Shewhart and W. Edwards Deming popularized continuous process improvement as leading to quality production. Six Sigma is the practice of continuous improvement that follows methods developed at Motorola and is based on the notion that no more than 3.4 defects per million are acceptable (Motorola 2009). This means that a company fulfilling one million orders per year, and having only one error opportunity per order with 3-sigma correctness (99.95%) will experience 66,738 errors versus a 6-sigma (99.9997%) company, which would experience 3.4 errors. As engineered product complexity has increased (in telecommunications, for instance, the potential for over 50,000 errors per product are possible), without the type of quality management provided through Six Sigma tenets, virtually every product would experience some type of defect.

Six Sigma borrows from the lean manufacturing practice *genba kanri*, which loosely translates from Japanese as "workshop management," to error-proof and remove waste from processes (genba-kanri.com 2009). The guiding principles of lean are not to make defects, accept defects, create variation, repeat mistakes, or build in defects (genba-kanri.com 2009).

A sigma is a standard deviation from some population mean. Six Sigma practice strives for 99.9997% accuracy in the process. Lean Six Sigma combines lean manufacturing waste removal discipline with Six Sigma's defect prevention goal.

Six Sigma and lean are compatible families of techniques. Where lean removes waste, Six Sigma removes errors from processes. The purpose of Six Sigma is to improve predictable quality of developed products and services through the removal of normally distributed errors (see Fig. 2). If outcomes of a process are normally distributed, errors vary from the mean, or average, which is marked as the vertical line in the center of the diagram. The standard deviation, or sigma, is a measure of variance from the mean with equal areas on either side of the mean line. The tolerances for sigma levels one through six are listed in Fig. 3 (σ is the Greek symbol for sigma).

To set up a statistical process measurement system, the normal distribution is hypothetically turned 90° and compared to process control charts containing measures of product characteristics to determine which measures are outside accepted tolerance limits. The diagram in Fig. 4 shows a normal distribution on the right and a control chart on the left. The lines approximate 3-sigma tolerances, which is the industry norm for companies that do not practice Six Sigma. As can be seen in the diagram, there are many measures outside of the 3-sigma tolerance limits that would need investigation.

When applied to business processes, Six Sigma is useful for eliminating unnecessary or inefficient steps from a process through the application of techniques such as check sheets, Pareto analysis, cause and effect diagrams, root cause analysis, and value added analysis. These are only a few of the hundreds of techniques useful for identifying, prioritizing, analyzing, and fixing errors or inefficiencies in processes.

Six Sigma's organizing concepts are DMAIC and DMADV, which translate to define – measure – analyze – improve – control and define – measure – analyze – design – verify, respectively. In general, DMAIC is the approach recommended for improving an existing process and DMADV is the approach recommended for new process design. But, these sets of methods are more similar than different and all activities tend to be done for all projects.

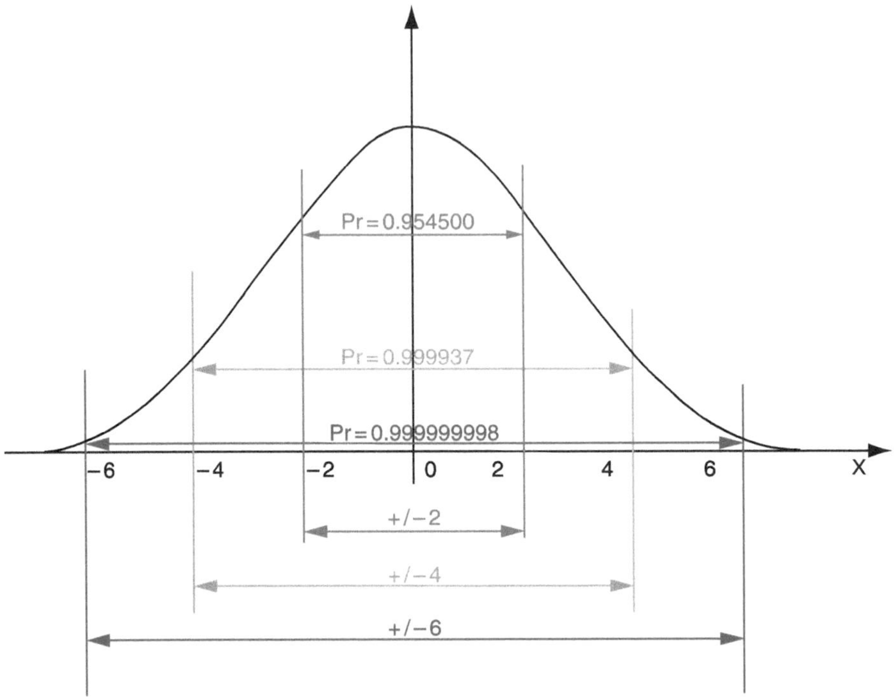

Fig. 2 Normal distribution with 2, 4, and 6 Sigma shown

1σ	690,000 per million opportunities (69% error rate)
2σ	308,000 per million opportunities (30.8%)
3σ	66,800 per million opportunities (6.7%)
4σ	6,210 per million opportunities (.62%)
5σ	230 per million opportunities (.02%)
6σ	3.4 per million opportunities (.00003%)

Fig. 3 Six Sigma errors and error rates

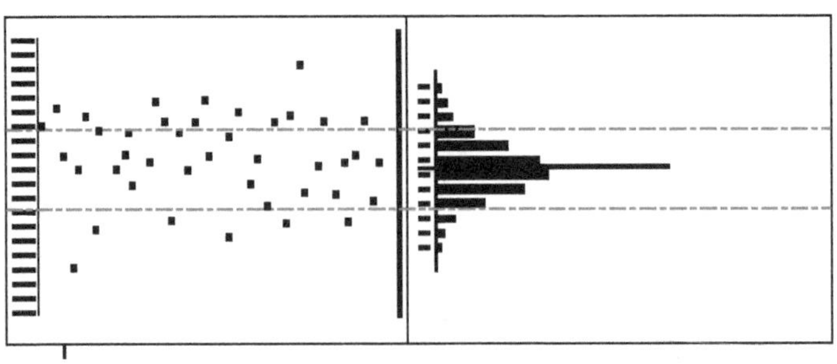

Fig. 4 Setup of SPC control charts

1.2 Process Management

Process management and improvement requires leaning – that is removal of unneeded steps for improvement, cleaning – that is the simplification and step-level leaning of remaining steps, and greening – that is the potential use of outsourcing, coproduction, or automation. The application of several techniques to each process improvement step is demonstrated through the analysis of a help desk.

Within these three areas of analysis, a set of basic Six Sigma techniques are applied.

- Business Process Mapping
- Cause and Effect Diagram
- Check Sheets and other manual forms of problem identification
- Pareto Diagrams and other Graphic
- Quality Function Deployment
- Root Cause Analysis

These techniques are commonly applied to a wide range of problems and are representative of the reasoning used for process improvement. Each of these methods is demonstrated in the following Help Desk process.

2 Help Desk Process and Problem Analysis

The purpose of a Help Desk is to take requests that may be problems, service, or access requests, and satisfy them according to type and priority. Help Desks can be formalized following the IT Infrastructure Library, (ITIL®, Rudd and Loyd 2007). In this particular case, the current process is known to be error prone with lost requests, many open requests that are known to be closed, and other issues. The current process in Fig. 5 works as follows. A client calls the help desk and makes a request. The Help Desk is manned by Level-1 support staff who, typically, are more junior than the other levels, but are capable of resolving known issues and simple requests and perform all client interface activities. When the Level-1 person does not know the resolution to a request, it is sent to a Level-2 person who evaluates and prioritizes the request for completion. After some delay, the request is researched and a resolution is developed and sent to the Level-1 support person. Upon receipt, the resolution is sent after a delay to the client who, after some delay, tests the resolution. The client sends the outcome of the test to the Level-1 support person. If the request is correct or is fixed, it is marked as complete and the process ends. If the request is not correct or is not fixed, it is resent to Level-2 support for further action and goes through their process again.

There are some fairly obvious problems with this method of Help Desk process management. For instance, the use of Excel requires coordination. How is one to know what the most current version of the spreadsheet is? Level-1 and Level-2

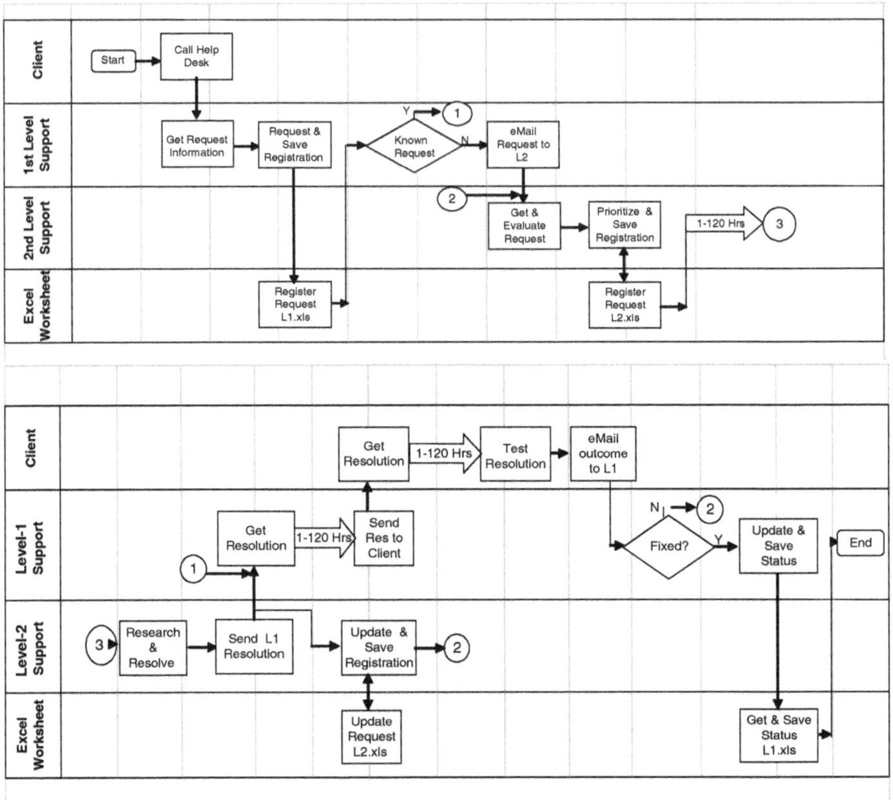

Fig. 5 Help desk current process map

appear to use different spreadsheets. Status is only updated at the end of the process; therefore, significant delays beyond the 120 h identified are possible. There is no reminder system and no method of automatic escalation. Therefore, loss of requests and unclosed requests are to be expected.

2.1 Process Map

To enable an analysis of the process, a process map is first developed. Process maps depict the roles, activities, and interactions of all participants in a process. Participants might include people, roles, departments, computer applications, and external organizations. If the focus is the information technology support for a process, the applications might also show individual databases that are accessed and/or updated by a process.

Suppliers	Inputs	Process	Outputs	Customer
Customer	Problem, issue, or request	Call Help Desk	Open Request Information	Help Desk Level-1 Support Staff
Customer	Request Information	Get Request Information	Request Information	Customer
Level-1 Support	Request Information	Request & Save Information	Register Requester L1.xls	Customer
Level-1 Support	If known	eMail Request to Level-2	Known request	Customer
Level-2 Support	If unknown to Level-1, Request	Get & Evaluate Request	Evaluation	Level-1 Support
Level-2 Support		Prioritize & Save Registration	Register Request L2.xls	Level-1 Support

Fig. 6 Help desk SIPOC diagram

Complex processes may require more elaborate information. One such Six Sigma technique is process *S*uppliers, *I*nputs, *P*rocess, *O*utputs, *C*ustomers analysis (SIPOC). A SIPOC analysis is a tabular summary of all related information to each process step (see Fig. 6). Suppliers and Customers are shown on the process map as roles with interactions, but the SIPOC details the actual documents, files, databases, and actual data affected by or used in the process (Rasmusson 2006).

Obvious as the problems may be, formal review and analysis is needed to determine all possible root causes for mitigation. The first course of action is to determine the frequency of the known problems. For this, a combination of check sheets and Pareto analysis can be used.

2.2 Check Sheets

A check sheet is a customized form used to collect data about the frequency of error occurrence. The data can be input to other analysis tools such as Pareto diagrams. While the format of a check sheet is usually a simple table with room for tick marks for the counts, more complex diagrams might be used to both locate and find errors that recur. Check sheets can be used to count errors, identify defect locations or causes, or to confirm presence or absence of an attribute.

A check sheet with the errors identified by tick marks is shown in Fig. 7. The most common error is lost requests but request not updated is also fairly common. It is likely that all errors would be addressed in priority order by the frequency of their occurrence. Therefore, to determine which should be the priority for immediate resolution, a Pareto analysis might be used.

Error	Count
Spreadsheet version	卌 卌 卌
Request entry not made	卌 卌
Request not updated upon resolution	卌 卌 卌 卌
Lost request	卌 卌 卌 卌 卌 卌 卌

Fig. 7 Example of check sheet for error counts

2.3 Pareto Analysis

A Pareto distribution is a special form of distribution named for Vilfredo Pareto who discovered its 80–20 rule properties. The Pareto distribution has since been recognized to apply to a wide range of social, geophysical, and scientific situations such as sales revenue from number of customers, error rates in software modules, and manufacturing defects in a process.

A Pareto diagram, in this case, is a graphical representation of problems to be prioritized for further action. Items to be compared are sorted from highest to lowest frequency and placed across the X-axis of a histogram. Item frequencies are on the Y-axis. A cumulative percentage line shows where the 80% point is found.

According to classic Pareto analysis, the breakdown is 80–20. However, in reality, many problems show a clear break point at some other distribution, such as 60–40 or 70–30. Variations of Pareto analysis – ABC and XYZ – look at different distributions for errors or management. ABC concentrates on consumption value of raw materials in different combinations while XYZ analysis evaluates classes of finished goods in terms of their demand qualities as high, medium, low, or sporadic (Bhattacharya et al. 2007; Canen and Galvio 1980; Katz 2007; Kumar et al. 2007).

The Pareto diagram for the Help Desk (Fig. 8) can be interpreted in two ways. The first two categories represent 69% of the total problems counted; however, by adding the third category, 87% of the problems are presented. Either analysis could be defended, but the highest priorities would be the focus of immediate work. The other items would be considered at a future date. One would not redesign the process without analyzing all of the problems in any case.

Next, the analysis would focus on the reason requests are lost since it is the most frequent issue. A cause and effect diagram is often used for this type of analysis.

2.4 Cause and Effect Diagram

Cause and effect diagrams were developed by Kaoru Ishikawa in 1982 to support systematic identification and classification of different types of causes that might

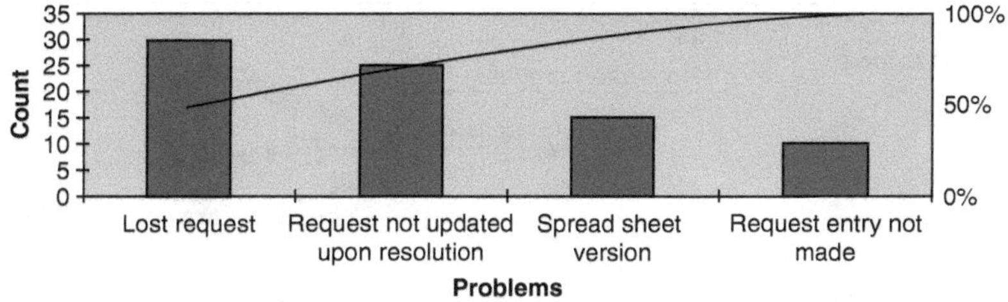

Fig. 8 Pareto analysis help desk problems

contribute to a problem. The graphic, also called an Ishikawa or fishbone diagram, facilitates identification of errors and the relationships between them.

Development of cause–effect diagrams uses brainstorming activity to combine the expertise of subject matter experts with the probing capabilities of a process improvement team. The group meets and identifies as many sources of errors as possible in the time allotted, categorizing them by type.

The backbone of the diagram is a right-facing arrow for which the problem being analyzed is listed near the arrowhead. Lines creating the fishbone effect, "bones," branch off of the backbone and each are named with a type of cause, such as the 4-Ms: Methods, man, machines, materials, the 4-Ps: Policy, procedure, people or plant/equipment (Brassard et al. 2000). Alternatively, the main bones can be customized to fit the context. For instance, when analyzing a process map, the bones could be the steps of the process. As the group discusses possible causes for the error, it identifies subcauses relating each to cause type. This, in effect, sorts the subcauses by type and allows discussion by cause type or by general cause. One drawback to Cause and Effect Diagrams is that they can quickly become so complex that understandability decreases. Therefore, they are best used with problems that have no more than six main "bones" each with fewer than six related problems.

The Ishikawa analysis (see Fig. 9) shows that lack of process, inadequate backup and learning, personnel who are not up to date, and use of Excel, without standards or security and lack of regular backups are key issues.

2.5 *Root Cause Analysis*

The purpose of root cause analysis (RCA) is to find all potential causes for some problem then ensure that sufficient changes are made to prevent the problem from recurrence (Wilson et al. 1993). Root cause analysis starts with a problem identified from, for instance, a Cause and Effect Diagram, to probe further into the root causes of problems to ensure that all aspects are evaluated and mitigated.

The RCA process is used to identify the true root (most fundamental) cause and the ways to prevent recurrence for significant issues for which outcomes can be

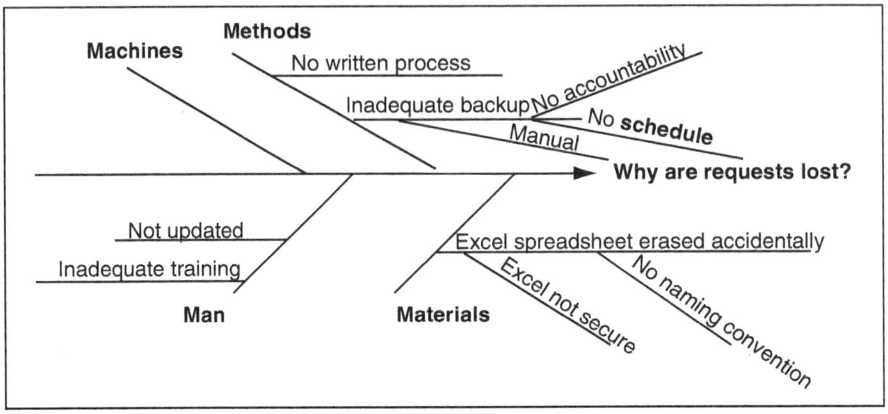

Fig. 9 Cause and effect diagram for lost requests

affected. This technique is also called "why – why chart" or "five whys". Attention in each level of analysis is drawn to all possible contributing factors through repeatedly asking questions that build on answers to prior questions. The steps to RCA are:

1. *Immediate action:* If the problem is still active, it should be resolved so that a normal operational state is achieved before anything is done.
2. *Identify the problem:* At this stage the problem should be completely, clearly articulated. The author should attempt to answer questions Who? What? Why? When? How? and How many? each relating to the problem to be analyzed.
3. *Identify the RCA team:* The team should include 4–10 subject matter specialists and experts in the RCA method to ensure analysis addresses all issues. The team should be given authority to correct the problems and empowered to define process changes as required.
4. *Root Cause analysis:* The method is applied to ask progressively more detailed levels of probing to determine the root cause. Although called the 5-whys, there is no number of levels that is correct; rather, the probing continues until one or more root causes for each problem are found.
5. *Action Plan:* The corrective action plan should eliminate the problem while maintaining or improving customer satisfaction. In addition to the plan, metrics to determine the effectiveness of the change are also developed. Once complete, the action plan is implemented.
6. *Follow Up Plan:* The follow-up plan determines who will take and who will evaluate the measures of the revised process, how often the metrics will be taken, and the criteria that will be applied to determine that the problem is resolved. The follow-up plan can be created while the action plan is being implemented; it goes into effect immediately upon the action plan implementation.

Root Cause Analysis: Why is there no Help Desk training?
A. There have never been processes for the Help Desk
  Q. Why has there never been a Help Desk process?
  A. **Supervisor turnover** and supervisor lack of training; when the Help Desk was established, the staff were knowledgeable and did not need training
    Q. Why is there supervisor turnover?
    A. ...
A. Supervisor turnover and **supervisor lack of training**; when the Help Desk was established, the staff were knowledgeable and did not need training
  Q. Why is there no supervisor training?
...
A. Supervisor turnover and supervisor lack of training; when the Help Desk was established, the **staff were knowledgeable and did not need training**
  Q. Why were staff knowledgeable and now they are not?
  A. Because of **staff turnover, which is about every six months** and because new people, rather than existing staff, are now taking the Help Desk jobs.
    Q. Why is staff turnover so high?
    A. Help Desk has been viewed as a way to train new staff. The best Help Desk staff are moved as soon as possible to other IT positions.

Fig. 10 Partial root cause analysis

The RCA for the "Inadequate Training" problem that caused requests to be lost is evaluated here. The RCA would be conducted for each of the problems with appropriate mitigations developed.

1. *Identify the problem:* On December 15, 2009, when numerous internal customers complained to the CIO about lost and unsatisfied requests, the Help Desk in Dallas, TX was found to be operating with no written process. The problem was highlighted by the short tenure of most of the Help Desk staff; 10 of the 15 staff members had been on the job for less than 6 months. No one took ownership for the lost requests problem, so the cause was unknown. No one on the Help desk had attended any formal job training. Help Desk staff learned problem resolutions on the job from each other. All 15 Help Desk staff members were affected by this problem.
2. *Identify the team:* The team consisted of two RCA specialists, two Level-1 Help Desk members and two Level-2 support people – one each from operations and application support.
3. *Immediate action:* The immediate action was to identify and resolve the lost problems. The Help Desk Manager sent an email to all users identifying the loss of several problems and asking anyone with outstanding requests to call, verifying all requests. Two Help Desk staff manned phones for 3 days to verify requests and add them to the Excel spreadsheet, as needed. As a result of this action, 400 requests were identified as outstanding; 100 of those requests had not been in the Excel spreadsheet.
4. Training, turnover, and lack of multiuser software were key issues. A partial *root cause analysis* of training issues is shown in Fig. 10.

5. *Action Plan:*

   - Provide a plan for the Help Desk Manager to remain in the position for a minimum of 1 year.
   - Create a career path for someone to stay in the Help Desk area if desired to reduce constant staff change.
   - Provide for senior Level-1 staff to mentor junior staff.
   - Change job descriptions of the Manager and Help Desk staff to provide merit pay for single-call request completion, short times from open to close of requests, etc.
   - Create a process for the Help Desk so that there is accountability for all requests with metrics to verify that all requests are logged as received and monitored for daily completion.
   - Develop in-house training for Help Desk staff that the Manager also attends. In the development of training, use the Help Desk process as the basis for the training.
   - Create measures to monitor Help Desk operation that become the responsibility of the Help Desk Manager.

6. *Follow Up Plan:*

   - The Manager of the Help Desk is to be tasked with monitoring training effectiveness as evidenced through measures to be defined. Metrics and an analysis of them should be in the monthly report to the CIO and Manager of Operations.

As can be seen from the analysis of the Help Desk problems, each of the techniques is useful but they require significant analysis and take time. Each technique assumes that skilled staff is conducting the analysis to minimize opinion and maximize the potential for complete mitigation of problems. Plus, each technique focuses on only one aspect of a problem, rather than a whole problem. Thus, many such analyses are required to fully analyze all issues relating to a complex process, and all recommendations must be integrated.

2.6 Value Added Analysis (VAA)

Where RCA seeks to prevent incidents from recurring in a process, value-added analysis seeks to remove nonessential process steps. VAA is not strictly part of the Six Sigma training but is a useful complementary technique nonetheless. There are four types of event-driven processes: Management, customer affecting, primary (relate to customer affecting, e.g., design engineering), and support (e.g., HR, legal, IT). A single process can have elements of more than one process type within it and, when conducting analysis, part of the task is to tease out the each step's process type.

To conduct value added analysis, the following steps are conducted:

1. Map the process.
2. List all process steps and place them in a table with four other columns for duration, value adding activities (VA), nonvalue-adding activities that are required (NVA), and nonvalue adding activities that are unnecessary (NVAU).
3. Review each process step, asking the questions:
   (a) Does an end Customer require this activity, and will that Customer pay for this activity? If yes, then it is value adding (VA).
   (b) Could a customer-facing activity be eliminated if another activity were done differently or correctly? Is this activity required to support or manage the value adding activities, e.g., legal, HR, etc.? If yes to either, then it is nonvalue-adding (NVA).
   (c) Could this activity be eliminated without impacting the form, fit, or function of the Customer's "product?" If yes, then it is nonvalue adding and unnecessary (NVAU).
4. Evaluate all NVAU activities for elimination.
5. Evaluate remaining activities for automation, outsourcing, or coproduction.

NVA and NVAU activities that do not appear able to be automated or eliminated are marked for further analysis for streamlining, outsourcing, or some other replacement with VA activities.

Figure 11 indicates a significant number of NVAU, unneeded activities. The goal of analyzing this information is to completely eliminate as many of the NVAU activities as possible. The times associated with each step are added to establish a baseline against which to measure changes for improvement. Figure 12 shows the time for a single request to provide a basis for evaluating potential savings that might be gained by changing the method of performing Help Desk activities.

Figure 12 analysis indicates that significant time can be saved from using a different method of performing Help Desk request monitoring. The NVA and NVAU steps should be further evaluated to simplify the process and reduce the amount of human interaction. Plus, wait times should be completely eliminated if possible; they are simple waste, exacerbating the loss of Help requests.

Automation can streamline the VA times and remove much of the NVA time. For instance, by using an online data entry method for entering Help requests, approximately 3 min per request can be eliminated since only the user is involved in that activity. By letting the user select priority, 5 min per request of Level-2 support time can be saved. Because Excel is not multiuser software, every time an update is needed, the Help Desk Representative finds the current file, opens the file, and waits while it opens. With multiuser software that can stay open on all Help Desk PCs throughout the day that time is eliminated. Additionally, because the software would be running nonstop on all Help Desk PCs during work hours, there should be fewer delays in saving files, thus saving another several minutes per request.

Use of multiuser software for all levels of staff provides a single file that is updated with one record per Help request, thus mitigating the likelihood of request losses both from the single instance and from the single file with multiuser

	Evaluation		
Process Step	**VA**	**NAV**	**NVAU**
Call help desk		NVA	
Get request information		NVA	
Request registration		NVA	
Save registration		NVA	
Register request L1.xls			NVAU
Check if known request	VA		
EMail request to L2			NVAU
Get request			NVAU
Evaluate request	VA		
Prioritize registration		NVA	
Save registration		NVA	
Register request L2.xls			NVAU
Wait 1-120 Hours			NVAU
Research and resolve request	VA		
Update and save resolution		NVA	
Update resolution L2.xls			NVAU
Send L1 resolution			NVAU
Get resolution	VA		
Wait 1-120 Hours			NVAU
Send resolution to client			NVAU
Update resolution		NVA	
Save resolution		NVA	
Update request L2.xls			NVAU
Get resolution	VA		
Wait 1-120 Hours			NVAU
Test resolution	VA		
eMail test results to l1		NVA	
Test if resolution fixes the problem		NVA	
Update and save status		NVA	
Get and save status		NVA	

Fig. 11 Value added analysis

protections. In addition, by selecting software with automatic escalation, no request should ever go unresolved.

Evaluating the NVAU time affords savings as well. By automating with a multiuser Help desk tool, much of the NVA and NVAU work can be automated. With a selectable problem type, the software can determine that the problem is novel or not by user selection from a drop-down problem type or entry of a new problem. Then, routing to Level-1 is bypassed and the problem could go immediately to Level-2. There are two "send-get resolution emails" in the current system that take significant time. By automating the workflow, the emails are produced automatically when the status of the software is updated, thus saving 1,500 h/month.

Figure 13 below shows the proposed changed process that would use multiuser Help Desk software.

By eliminating any steps not needed as a result of automation and by streamlining those that remain, plus by forcing lower wait times of all types by building into

	Evaluation		
Process Steps	**VA**	**NVA**	**NAVU**
Call help desk		1 Min	
Get request information		1-4 Min, $\bar{X}$=2 Min	
Register request		1 Min	
Save request		10 Sec	
Register request L1.xls			10 Sec
Check if known request	5-15 Min, $\bar{X}$=10 Min		
EMail request to L2			2-5 Min, $\bar{X}$=3 Min
Get request			2-5 Min, $\bar{X}$=3 Min
Evaluate request	5-60 Min, $\bar{X}$=20 Min		
Prioritize request		5 Min	
Save registration		3 Min	
Register request L2.xls			10 Sec
Wait 1-120 Hours			1-120 Hrs $\bar{X}$= 20 Hrs
Research and resolve request	20 Min – 40 Hr $\bar{X}$= 2 Hrs		
Update and save resolution		5-60 Min, $\bar{X}$=20 Min	
Update resolution L2.xls			10 Sec
Send L1 resolution			5-60 Min $\bar{X}$=20 Min
Get resolution	5-60 Min, $\bar{X}$=20 Min		
Wait 1-120 Hours			1-120 Hrs $\bar{X}$= 20 Hrs
Send resolution to client			5-60 Min $\bar{X}$=10 Min
Wait			1-120 Hrs $\bar{X}$= 20 Hrs
Get resolution	5-60 Min, $\bar{X}$-20 Min		
Wait 1-120 Hours			1-120 Hrs $\bar{X}$= 20 Hrs
Test resolution	20 Min – 40 Hr		
	$\bar{X}$= 2 Hrs		
eMail test results to l1		5-60 Min, $\bar{X}$=10 Min	
Test if resolution fixes the problem		1 Min	
Update and save status		3 Min	
Get and save status		10 Sec	
Cumulative Individual Step Time	82.16 Hours	20.4 Hours	36 Min + 80 Hrs Wait

Fig. 12 Value added analysis – potential time savings

	Evaluation		
Process Step	**VA**	**NVA**	**NVAU**
Enter request information		1-4 Min, $\bar{X}$=2 Min	
Save registration		10 Sec	
Check if known request (2,000/mo)	0-15 Min, $\bar{X}$=2 Min		
Forward request to L2			0-5 Min, $\bar{X}$=2 Min
Evaluate request	5-60 Min, $\bar{X}$=20 Min		
Prioritize request (500)	5 Min 25Hr/Mo		
Wait 1-120 Hours			1-40 Hrs $\bar{X}$=8 Hrs
Research and resolve request	20Min – 40 Hr $\bar{X}$= 2 Hrs		
Update and save resolution		5-60 Min, $\bar{X}$=20 Min	
Update resolution L2.xls			10 Sec
Get resolution	5-60 Min, $\bar{X}$=20 Min		
Wait 1-120 Hours			1-40 Hrs $\bar{X}$=8 Hrs
Wait			1-40 Hrs $\bar{X}$=8 Hrs
Get resolution	5-60 Min, $\bar{X}$=20 Min		
Wait 1-120 Hours			1-40 Hrs $\bar{X}$=8 Hrs
Test resolution	20 Min – 40 Hr, $\bar{X}$=2 Hr		
Update and save status		10 Sec	
Get and save status		10 Sec	
Cumulative Individual Step Time	5.3 Hours	22.5 Min	2.2 Min with 32 Hrs wait time

Fig. 13 Proposed automated process

the software an automatic escalation of notices of noncompletion, makes the results dramatic (see Fig. 14, summary). The value-added time is reduced from 82 to 5.3 h, nonvalue added time is reduced from 20.4 h to 22.5 min, and the nonvalue added, unneeded time drops from 36 min with 40+ h of wait time to 2 min plus wait time.

Thus, the problems of lost and uncompleted requests could be reduced or eliminated completely by the use of software specifically for Help Desks. Plus, the movement of the request from Level-1 to Level-2 and the decision process could potentially also be automated so that Level-1 staff receive only problems for which a known solution exists; this implies that all calls to Level-1 should be resolvable in a single phone call. In addition to automated movement of problems to Level-2 staff for resolution, automated escalation would ensure that no problem went unnoticed for any period of time and the 120-h waits could be eliminated.

BEFORE			
	VA	NVA	NVAU
Cumulative Individual Step Time	82.16 Hours	20.4 Hours	36 min + 40 Hrs Wait time
AFTER			
Cumulative Individual Step Time	5.3 Hours	22.5 Min	2 Min + 32 Hrs wait time

Fig. 14 Improvement from automation and elimination of unneeded actions

2.7 *Quality Function Deployment (QFD)*

Quality Function Deployment supports both design and redesign of processes, and can be modified for different types of analyses. QFD is a technique to translate customer needs, requirements, and expectations into detailed product and process specifications. Therefore, while it can be used to analyze existing products, QFD is often applied to analyzing new needs and requirements that determine the nature of a new product. QFD is very good for summarizing complex thought processes and competing analyses of the same situation (Cohen 1995). One disadvantage is that the data can be very complex to interpret because the diagram can actually present too much information. Another disadvantage is that many items require subjective judgments that can alter the outcome. By attending to possible disadvantages, they can be managed.

QFD builds a "house of quality" matrix (Fig. 15) with project goals or needs in rows (what information), alternative means to reach the goals in columns (how), and the priority or quantity of each in each cell (how much), using simple symbols to rate the means on their ability to meet requirements (Cohen 1995).

To complete the "house," each need is prioritized and/or weighted in the "importance" column (Fig. 16). Priorities can be expressed in many ways; one simple method is to allocate a portion of 100% to each with the total allocations adding to 100. The method of assigning importance should be defined and provided in any reports so the reading audience understands its rationale; simple is better because it is more defensible and understandable.

A row is added below the "roof" to indicate the type of eventual metric or amount of the means that is desired. These entries are informational in the QFD but are used later when metrics for determining process success are developed.

The cells of the triangular "roof" of the house compare means of meeting needs when competing methods are defined. A positive relationship indicates synergy between two means while a negative relationship indicates a conflict or choice required between two means.

The right side of a QFD diagram seeks to answer "why" questions about the entries. This area also can be used for several types of information. Two common uses are benchmarks and rationale for rankings. In developing marketing plans or products, the right side can provide columns for benchmark information of this company versus its competition, industry average, and/or best practice. The use of

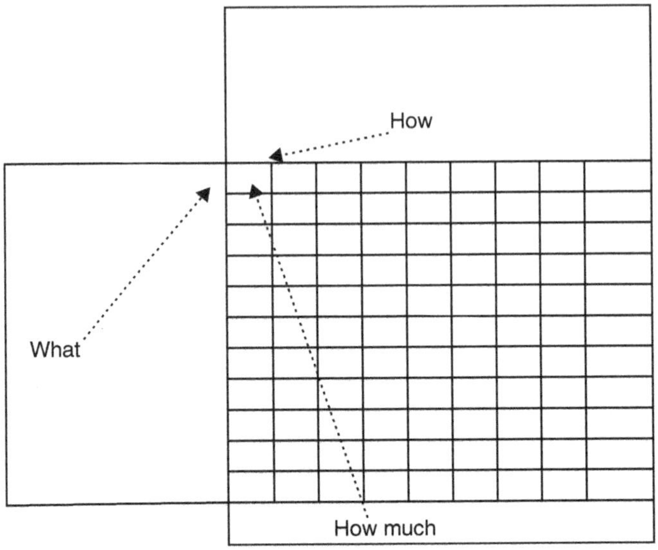

Fig. 15 Basic QFD matrix

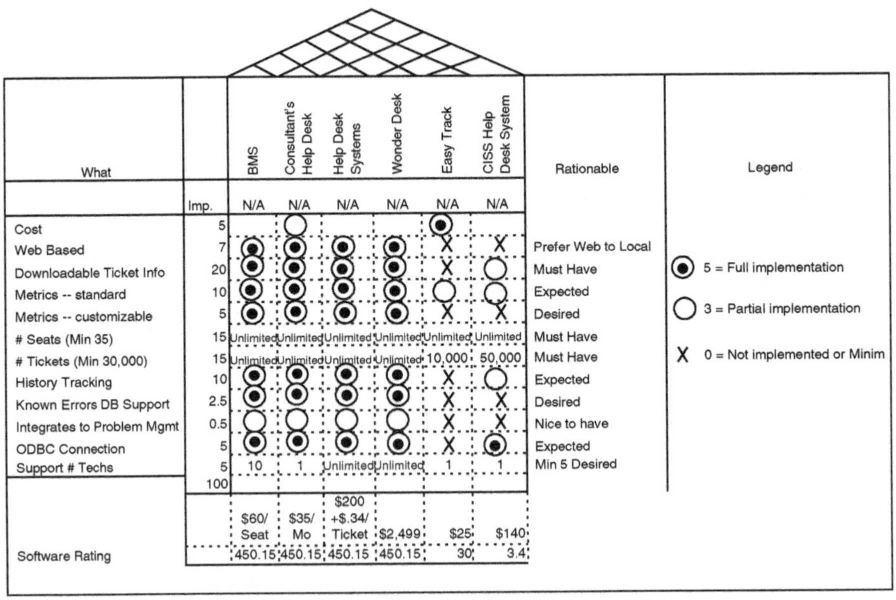

Fig. 16 QFD software evaluation

benchmark data provides an instant check on the importance of each need. Second, the area is also used in product development QFDs to identify the rational for priority definition, with a rationale provided on each row's need entry. This is useful for deflecting any political discussion that might relate to how needs are prioritized.

The last area is the "basement" of the house, which seeks to answer "how much" questions about the means entries. The basement can contain several types of information: raw materials costs or amounts, financial contribution or margin for a product feature, or other supply chain or financial information.

Figure 16 is a modified QFD for selecting software. In this modification, the "means" or alternatives for raw materials is replaced with potential product choices. These are evaluated according to the requirements down the left margin, and a score for each product is developed from the analysis. There are no synergies from combining products so the roof of the QFD is empty. The diagram shows that the Consultant's Help Desk option at $35 per month is the most cost-beneficial option of those evaluated.

Some advantages of QFD are that features and functions or products and processes analyzed using QFD tie directly to customer requirements. By providing benchmark, supply chain, financial, and trade-off information in a single place, analysis of the overall QFD outcomes is simplified. Further, QFD supports the thinking required to develop a complete summary of decisions relating to product concept definition, product design, process design, engineering design, and production documentation. Some disadvantages of QFD are that it is time-consuming and can be an expensive activity; the technique requires expertise to develop a solid analysis; the subjective evaluations can skew results; and the outcome can be difficult to interpret.

2.8 Process Redesign

While the Help Desk case somewhat oversimplifies real life problems, it is a useful example of the issues and complexities that arise during a process improvement project. The redesigned process increases individual contribution to organizational success by removing resource gaps by the use of software to provide a single point of storage and contact for all parties involved in entering or resolving a request. The redesigned process uses coproduction to have the users enter their own requests, which are served automatically to the next available support person. Help Desk Level-1 support evaluates whether or not the request has a known solution and applies the known solution. If this evaluation can be automated, its time is removed from the process. If no Level-1 solution exists, the escalation to Level-2 support is automatic. An automated process can provide reminders of outstanding requests, escalate the reminders as the request ages, and provide detailed metrics of performance.

3 Discussion

This chapter presents only a few of hundreds of techniques available for problem analysis and, while they provide adequate expert guidance to obtain an efficient process redesign, often such simple tools are not adequate.

BPM is critical to organizational success. Six Sigma is a proven, globally accepted technique that facilitates the analysis and improvement of processes (Antony 2006). As demonstrated through the Help Desk case, application of numerous techniques is needed to fully analyze a process and determine the importance, priority, causes, and possible solutions to the problems of a process. As process areas are more complex, the tools likewise become more robust and complex. QFD and SPC are defined briefly in this chapter and are two robust and scalable techniques. Another is failure mode effects analysis (FMEA). FMEA is a technique through which all possible errors for every possible eventuality and stage of a process, usually manufacturing, are analyzed for breadth and depth of impact, expected frequency, and cost (Casey 2008). Thus, many RCAs might be performed to define all possible problems for a single product or process. Then, FMEA analysis would design mitigations on the basis of prioritizing based on potential damage to the organization. Thus, the more complex the problem, the more elaborate the tools and techniques to remove and manage the process and its risks.

There are two main drawbacks to Six Sigma practice. The first drawback is organizational and the second relates to the techniques. Six Sigma can develop its own bureaucracy that risks overpowering the importance of "getting product out the door". This is not unique to Six Sigma; the tendency of organizations is to grow or wither. However, companies need to guard against becoming cultist about following Six Sigma and remember that producing products or services for their customers must always come first in importance.

The second issue relates to the techniques. Without Six Sigma, Business Process Management is a set of concepts without an organizing core. However, even with Six Sigma as an organizing theme, there are hundreds of Six Sigma techniques that can be applied to aspects of areas under study. There is little organization of techniques into a cohesive body of knowledge. The various Six Sigma certification levels – yellow, green, brown, black – discuss toolkits from which technique selection is made at the discretion of the user (Andersen 1999). Yet, there is no fixed set of techniques with variation of what is taught from one person to another (Antony 2008).

Within a process improvement project, there are about four key thought processes relating to problem recognition, analysis, redesign, and metrics definition, yet Six Sigma is unclear about which methods are best in any given phase or situation. And, occasionally, a method that might be used, such as cause and effect diagrams, is overwhelmed by the complexity of the situation and proves unusable (Conger and Landry 2009). Six Sigma also offers little guidance on how to customize or improvise tools to make them usable in such situations. Finally, while Lean Six Sigma is useful for removing errors and waste from a process, the techniques do not assist in developing recommendations for change or for designing new processes. Recommendations and design still rely on the skill and insight of the people conducting the analysis. Thus, Six Sigma is not only a useful way of focusing attention on elimination of waste and the reduction of errors but it can also be an overwhelming toolkit without much guidance for developing project outcomes.

4 Conclusion

Process management is a management imperative that is not done once. Either ongoing or periodic assessment of processes with improvement analysis is required for businesses to stay competitive. Analysis techniques from Six Sigma complement process management by introducing rigor to waste reduction and quality improvement. This chapter demonstrates how Six Sigma techniques can be applied to process analysis to improve its operation (Johannsen et al. 2010).

Acknowledgments I thank the reviewers, my students, colleagues, and process clients at University of Dallas.

References

Andersen B (1999) Business process improvement toolbox. ASQ Quality Press, New York

Antony J (2006) Six Sigma for service processes. Bus Process Manage J 12(2):234–248

Antony J (2008) What is the role of academic institutions for the future development of Six Sigma? Int J Prod Perform Manage 57(1):107–110

Brassard M, Field C, Oddo F, Page B, Ritter D, Smith L (2000) The problem solving memory jogger. GOAL/QPC, Salem, NH

Bhattacharya A, Bijan S, Sanat M (2007) Distance-based consensus method for ABC analysis. Int J Prod Res 45(15):3405–3420

Canen A, Galvio RD (1980) An application of ABC analysis to control imported material. Interfaces 10(4):22–24

Casey JJ (2008) Strategic error-proofing: achieving success every time with smarter FMEAs. Florence, Ky: Productivity Press

Cohen L (1995) Quality function deployment: how to make QFD work for you. Prentice Hall PTP Reading, MA: Addison-Wesley Publishing Company

Conger S, Landry B (2009) Problem analysis: when established techniques don't work. In: Proceedings of the 2nd annual conf-IRM conference, Dubai, May 19–24, 2009

Dorgan SJ, Dowdy JJ (2004) When IT lifts productivity, The McKinsey Quarterly, Boston, MA: Mckinsey Company 4, pp 9–11

genba-kanri.com (2009) Genba-Kanri introduction. http://www.genba-kanri.com/gkweb/Briefweb.htm

Hammer M (2010) What is business process management? In: vom Brocke J, Rosemann M (eds) Handbook on business process management, vol 1. Springer, Heidelberg

Harmon P (2010) The scope and evolution of business process management. In: vom Brocke J, Rosemann M (eds) Handbook on business process management, vol 1. Springer, Heidelberg

Harrison-Broninski K (2010) Dealing with human-driven process. In: vom Brocke J, Rosemann M (eds) Handbook on business process management, vol 2. Springer, Heidelberg

Herremans IM, Isaac RG (2004) The intellectual capital realization process (ICRP): an application of the resource-based view of the firm. J Manag Issues 16(2):217–231

iSixSigma staff, Sigma performance levels – One to Six Sigma. iSixSigma.com. http://www.isixsigma.com/library/content/c020813a.asp. Accessed 16 Aug 2002

Johannsen F, Leist S, Zellner G (2010) Implementing six sigma for improving business processes at an automotive bank. In: vom Brocke J, Rosemann M (eds) Handbook on business process management, vol 1. Springer, Heidelberg

Kaplan RS, Norton DP (2001) The strategy focused organization. Harvard Business School Press, Boston
Katz N (2007) The weakest link: understanding and detecting supply-chain fraud. Fraud Magazine
Kumar S, Nottestad DA, Macklin JF (2007) A profit and loss analysis for make-to-order versus make-to-stock policy – a supply chain case study. Eng Econ 52(2), pp 141–156
Motorola (2009) About Motorola University: the inventors of Six Sigma, Motorola Corporation. http://www.motorola.com/content.jsp?globalObjectId=3079
Rasmusson D (2006) The SIPOC picture book: a visual guide to the SIPOC/DMAIC relationship. Oriel Incorporated, Madison, WI
Rudd C, Loyd V (2007) ITIL v3 book 2: service design. The Stationery Office of the Office of General Commerce, London, UK
vom Brocke J, Recker J, Mendling J (2010) Value-oriented Process Modeling: Integrating Financial Perspectives into Business Process Re-design. Business Process Management Journal (BPMJ), 16(2):333–356
Wilson PF, Dell LD, Anderson GF (1993) Root cause analysis: a tool for total quality management. ASQ Quality Press, New York

Business Process Model Abstraction

Artem Polyvyanyy, Sergey Smirnov, and Mathias Weske

Abstract In order to execute, study, or improve operating procedures, companies document them as business process models. Often, business process analysts capture every single exception handling or alternative task handling scenario within a model. Such a tendency results in large process specifications. The core process logic becomes hidden in numerous modeling constructs. To fulfill different tasks, companies develop several model variants of the same business process at different abstraction levels. Afterwards, maintenance of such model groups involves a lot of synchronization effort and is erroneous.

We propose an abstraction technique that allows generalization of process models. Business process model abstraction assumes a detailed model of a process to be available and derives coarse-grained models from it. The task of abstraction is to tell significant model elements from insignificant ones and to reduce the latter. We propose to learn insignificant process elements from supplementary model information, e.g., task execution time or frequency of task occurrence. Finally, we discuss a mechanism for user control of the model abstraction level – an abstraction slider.

1 Introduction

Business process modeling is crucial when it comes to design of how companies provide services and products to customers or how they organize internal operational processes. To improve the understanding of processes and to enable their analysis, business processes are represented by models (Davenport 1993; Hammer and Champy 1994; Weske 2007). Process models are used for different purposes: to

A. Polyvyanyy (✉)
Business Process Technology Group, Hasso Plattner Institute of IT Systems Engineering, University of Potsdam, Potsdam, Germany
e-mail: artem.polyvyanyy@hpi.uni-potsdam.de

J. vom Brocke and M. Rosemann (eds.), *Handbook on Business Process Management 1*, International Handbooks on Information Systems,
DOI 10.1007/978-3-642-00416-2_7,

communicate a message, to share knowledge or vision, as a starting point for redesigning or optimizing processes, or as precise instructions for executing business tasks. In such conditions, the goal of a process model is to capture working procedures at a level of detail appropriate to fulfill its envisioned tasks. Often, achievement of such a goal results in complex, "wallpaper-like" models, which tend to capture every minor detail and exceptional case that might occur during process execution.

The desired level of model granularity also depends on a stakeholder working with a model and a current task. Top level company management appreciates coarse-grained process descriptions that allow fast and correct business decisions. At the same time, employees who directly execute processes value fine granular specifications of their daily job. Thus, it might be often the case that a company ends up with maintaining several models of one business process.

Abstraction is generalization that reduces undesired details in order to retain only essential information about an entity or a phenomenon. Business process model abstraction goal is to produce a model containing significant information based on the detailed model specification. Significant information is the information required by a certain stakeholder to fulfill his/her tasks.

We propose a business process model abstraction methodology that can be summarized as follows. As input, we assume to possess a complex process model (a detailed process specification). Afterwards, a number of abstractions are performed on the initial model. Conceptually, each abstraction is a function that takes a process model as input and produces a process model as output. In the resulting model, initial process fragment gets replaced with its generalized version. Thus, each individual abstraction hides process details and brings a model to a higher abstraction level.

When applied separately, process model abstractions do not provide much value to an end user. Rather, it is of interest to study how individual abstractions can be combined together and afterwards controlled in order to deliver the desired abstraction level. As a solution, we propose an abstraction slider – a mechanism providing a user control over process model abstraction.

The rest of the chapter is organized as follows. In the next section, we discuss several application scenarios of process model abstraction. Section 3 introduces a slider and explains how it is employed for the control of process model abstraction. Transformation rules and their composition aimed to allow process model graph generalization are discussed in Section 4. Section 5 presents results of a case study on abstraction efficiency and usefulness conducted together with an industry partner. The chapter concludes with a survey on related work and summarizing remarks.

2 Process Model Abstraction Scenarios

Abstraction generalizes insignificant model elements. Abstraction scenarios have direct implication on the identification of insignificant elements. In this section we clarify the concept of process model abstraction and discuss its common use cases. We then extract abstraction criteria from the proposed use cases. Abstraction criteria are properties of process model elements that enable their partial ordering. Afterwards, obtained partial ordering is used when differentiating significant model elements from the insignificant ones. It is not claimed for the proposed list of scenarios to be complete. It should be extended once there is a demand for new abstraction scenarios.

Essentially, business process model abstraction deals with finding answers to two questions of *what* and *how*:

- What parts of a process model are of low significance?
- How to transform a process model so that insignificant parts are removed?

Answers to both questions should address the current abstraction use case. The choice of an abstraction criterion helps in answering the *what* question. Whereas, an answer to the *how* question allows deriving models where insignificant elements get generalized.

Considering aforesaid, business process model abstraction is a function for which holds:

- A detailed process model and an *abstraction criterion* are the input of this function; an abstraction criterion helps to differentiate significant model elements from the insignificant.
- The function output is an abstracted process model.
- From the structural perspective abstraction reduces the number of model elements.
- From the semantic perspective abstraction generalizes initial model.

When studying a business process model, analysts might be interested in tasks which are executed frequently in a process. One can presume that frequent tasks capture main process logic while nonfrequent ones constitute seldom alternative scenarios or exceptional flow. Preservation of only frequent process tasks might allow faster understanding of the core process logic by an end user. In order to fulfill the described use case, one might classify significant process elements as those that have a high occurrence number. Thus, the abstraction criterion is the mean occurrence number of a process task.

Mean occurrence number of a process task (m_i) is the mean number that the process task i occurs in a process instance.

Alternatively, analysts might be interested in process tasks that consume most of the process execution time (execution *effort*). These tasks are natural candidates for being studied during the task of process improvement. Once such tasks are optimized, the overall process execution time might drop considerably. Also, in many cases, cost required to execute process tasks is proportional to the execution time. Process task effort is another process model abstraction criterion.

Relative effort of a process task (e_r) is the time required to execute the task.

Absolute effort of a process task (e_a) is the mean effort contributed to the execution of the process task in a process instance. Absolute effort can be obtained as the product of the relative effort and the mean occurrence number of the process task.

As proposed, the effort of a process task is measured in time units (e.g., minutes or hours) and quantitatively coincides with the duration. However, semantically the effort concept resembles the concept of cost. For instance, if two process tasks run in parallel, their total effort is the sum of efforts of each task.

The cost of process tasks and the overall process execution cost are important properties of business processes. Similar to *process task effort* one might define a process model abstraction criterion of *process task cost*.

Process model abstraction criteria can also be defined on process fragments. For example, one might be interested in "typical" executions of a business process model. A typical business process execution means that among all possible ways of a process completion, it is the one that is executed most often. Applying such an abstraction to a process model should result in a new model that reflects only most common process scenarios. A process scenario is a minimal part of a process model that covers certain instance execution.

Probability of a process scenario (P_i) is the probability of a process scenario i to happen when executing the process.

Similarly, process scenarios with the highest duration or cost may be in the focus of process abstraction. As a result of the abstraction, one should obtain a model representing either the most time consuming or the most "expensive" process execution paths.

Effort of a process scenario (E_i) is the effort to be invested in the execution of a process scenario i and can be found as the sum of efforts of all the tasks executed within this scenario.

Figure 1 shows the process model fragment, modeled using EPC notation (Keller et al. 1992; Scheer et al. 2005), and illustrates presented concepts. Here, all the outgoing connections of the exclusive or split are supplied with transition probabilities that sum up to one. All the other connections are assumed to have the transition probability of one. Each function is enriched with relative and absolute (visualized in italic type) efforts given by the time interval in minutes that a worker needs to perform a function. For instance, the function "Contact a representative" has the relative effort of one minute, meaning that it is expected to take one minute of worker's time once reached in a process instance. On average, this function requires $1 \times 0.92 = 0.92$ min in every process instance, which constitutes the absolute effort of the function. The absolute effort is obtained under the assumption that the process fragment is reached only once in a process instance with the probability of one.

Often, abstraction criteria require models to be annotated with additional information like statistical data on average time required in order to perform process tasks, probabilities of reaching tasks in a process, etc. In many cases, incorporation of such information requires extension of modeling notation.

3 Abstraction Slider

In this section, we focus on the *what* question of process abstraction. We propose a *slider metaphor* (Polyvyanyy et al. 2008a) as a tool for enabling flexible control over the process model abstraction level. We explain how the slider can be

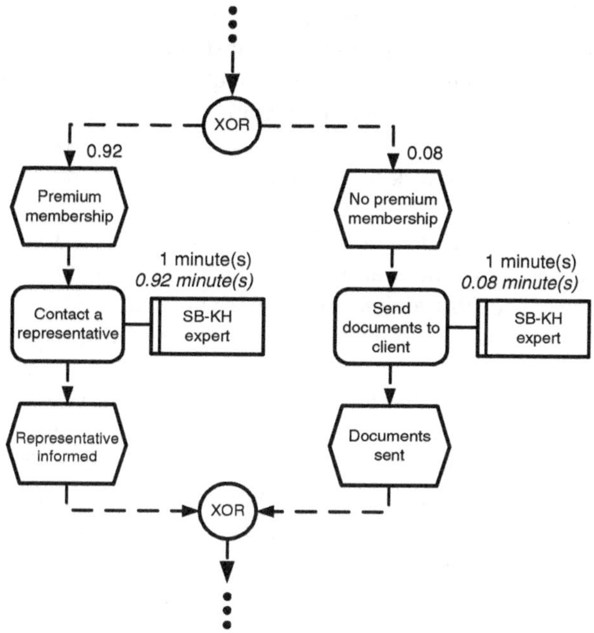

Fig. 1 Example of the EPC fragment enriched with probabilities and efforts

employed for distinguishing significant process model elements from insignificant ones. We provide an example of applying the abstraction slider.

When a user selects suitable abstraction criterion, the desired level of abstraction should be specified. Abstraction level cannot be predicted without a priori knowledge about the abstraction context. In the best case, the user should be able to change abstraction level smoothly from an initial detailed process model to a process model containing only one task. In this example, the single abstracted process task semantically corresponds to the abstraction of the whole original process model.

A slider is an object that operates on a slider interval $[S_{min}, S_{max}]$. The interval is constrained by the minimum and maximum values of the abstraction criterion. The slider specifies criterion value as a slider state $s \in [S_{min}, S_{max}]$ and allows operation of a state change within this interval.

All of the discussed abstraction criteria (see Sect. 2) have quantitative measurement. Therefore, criterion values for a particular criterion type are in a partial order relation. Correspondingly, the partial order relation can be transferred on process model elements by arranging them according to the values of some particular criterion. For example, if a criterion is *task relative effort*, then a 2 min task precedes a 4 min task. The partial order relation enables element classification. It is possible to split model elements into two classes: those with criterion value less than and those with criterion value greater than some designed separation point. Elements that are the members of the first class are assumed to be insignificant and have to be omitted in the abstracted model. Members of the other class are significant and should be preserved in the abstracted model. We refer to the separation point according to which the element classes are constructed as *abstraction threshold*. Assuming an abstraction threshold of three minutes in the example discussed above, the 2 min task is insignificant and has to be reduced. On the opposite, the four minutes task is significant and should be preserved in the abstracted model.

Thus, a *process model abstraction slider* is a slider, which, for a given process model fragment and a specified abstraction threshold, classifies the fragment as significant or not. The abstraction slider interval is defined on an interval of abstraction criterion values, and the slider state is associated with the abstraction threshold.

A slider control regulates the amount of elements preserved in an abstracted process model. In the simplest case, a user specifies an arbitrary value used as a threshold (which means that the slider interval is $[-\infty, +\infty]$). The challenge for a user in this approach is to inspect a process model in order to choose a meaningful threshold value. A threshold value which is too low makes all the process model elements to be treated as significant, i.e., no nodes or edges are reduced. On the other hand, a threshold that is too high may result in a one task process model. To avoid such confusing situations, the user should be supported by suggesting an interval in which all the "useful" values of abstraction criterion lie. Alternatively, the abstraction slider can control a share of nodes to be preserved in a model. In this case, abstraction mechanism has to estimate the threshold value which results in the reduction of the specified share of the process model.

Figure 2 exemplifies the work of process model abstraction slider. It provides a comparison of the initial process model (a) and its two abstracted models. The business process is captured in EPC notation. In the example, we have used the abstraction criterion of absolute effort of a process function. Functions with a higher absolute effort are considered to be more significant. (a) shows the business process model that corresponds to the abstraction slider state of 0.00 – the original process model. The model visualized in (b) is obtained by changing the abstraction threshold to 0.37. In the proposed example, more than 50% of the model nodes get reduced. The process model shrinks to one function when the slider state is set to 1.00.

4 Process Model Transformation

In this section, we address the *how* question of the process model abstraction task. We base our solution on process model transformation rules. In this section, two classes of abstraction rules are introduced: elimination and aggregation. Afterwards, requirements for abstraction and their influence on the transformation

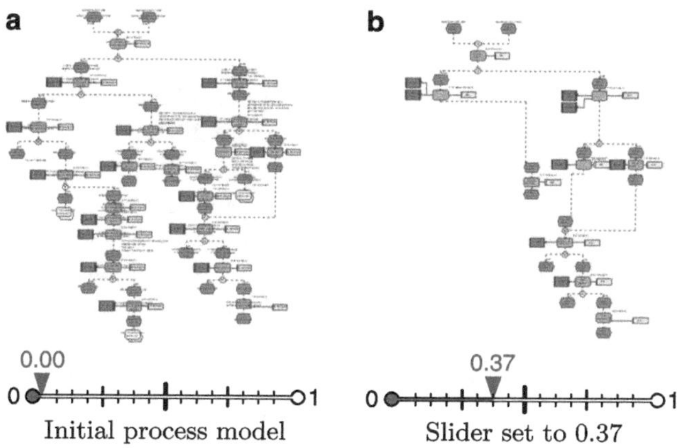

Fig. 2 Process model abstraction slider (function names unreadability intended). (**a**) Initial process model (**b**) Slider set to 0.37

rules are discussed. We argue when each of the techniques is appropriate. Finally, an example of transformation rules is presented.

4.1 Elimination Versus Aggregation

When the insignificant process model elements are identified, they have to be abstracted. Several techniques can be proposed for reduction, we distinguish two: elimination and aggregation.

Elimination means that a process model element is omitted in the abstracted process model. The main feature of elimination is that the resulting model does not contain any information about the eliminated element. Elimination has to assure that the resulting process model is well-formed and that the ordering constraints of the initial model are preserved.

Aggregation implies that insignificant elements of a process model are grouped with other elements. Aggregation preserves information about the abstracted element in the resulting model. When two sequential tasks are aggregated into one, properties of the aggregating task are derived from the properties of the aggregated tasks, e.g., the execution cost of an aggregating task is the sum of execution costs of aggregated tasks.

In general case, the rules of elimination are simpler than the aggregation rules. Aggregation requires more sophisticated specification of how the properties of the aggregated elements influence properties of aggregating elements. In many cases, elimination is insufficient, since it leads to the loss of important information. If an abstraction cannot tolerate information loss, aggregation should be used.

4.2 Transformation Requirements

Preservation of the process execution logic is an essential abstraction requirement. This means that process model abstraction should neither introduce new ordering constraints, nor change the existing ones. For instance, if an original process model specifies to execute either activity *A* or *B*, it should not be the case that in the abstracted model these activities appear in a sequence. Another essential abstraction requirement is that well-formed process models should be produced. Thus, used transformation rules should take into account features of modeling notations. Consequently, we can expect different rules to be used, e.g., for EPC and for BPMN.

Further, extra requirements on abstraction rules can be imposed. For instance, a company may use process models for estimation of the workforce required to execute business processes. In this case, information about the overall effort of process execution should be preserved. Process model abstractions preserving process properties are called *property preserving abstractions*. Elimination can be used in a property preserving abstraction with restrictions, since once a model element is omitted, all the information about its properties is lost. Therefore, elimination can be applied only to those elements that do not influence the property being preserved.

Every new requirement imposed on an abstraction restricts transformation rules and makes the design of these rules more complex. It is important to learn which class of process models can be abstracted to one task by a given set of rules and abstraction requirements. An abstraction that is not capable of reducing a process model to one function is called *best effort abstraction*. Such an abstraction *tries* to assure that a given process model is abstracted to the requested level using the given set of rules.

4.3 Transformation Rules

A process model abstraction approach is presented in Polyvyanyy et al. (2008b). Its cornerstone is a set of abstraction rules. We would like to use these rules as an illustration of the concepts discussed earlier and demonstrate how these rules can function together with the abstraction slider and task absolute effort abstraction criterion.

The approach presented in Polyvyanyy et al. (2008b) is capable of abstracting process models captured in EPC notation. Two requirements are imposed on abstraction:

1. Ordering constraints of a process model should be preserved.
2. Absolute process effort should be preserved.

The approach is based on the set of transformation rules called *elementary abstractions*. Four elementary abstractions are proposed: sequential, block, loop, and dead end abstraction. Every elementary abstraction defines how a certain type of a process fragment is generalized. The order of elementary abstractions can vary. Application of an elementary abstraction may succeed once there is a suitable process fragment in a process model. This also means that any function can be the result of a prior abstraction.

4.3.1 Sequential Abstraction

Business process models of high fidelity often contain sequences of tasks. In EPCs, such sequences turn into sequences of functions. *Sequential abstraction* replaces a sequence of functions and events by one aggregating function. This function is more coarse-grained and brings a process model to a higher abstraction level.

Definition 1: An EPC process fragment is a *sequence* if it is formed by a function, followed by an event, followed by a function.

The mechanism of sequential abstraction is sketched in Fig. 3. Functions f_1, f_2, and event e_1 constitute a sequence. Aggregating function f_s replaces this sequence. Semantically, the aggregating function corresponds to execution of functions f_1 and f_2.

4.3.2 Block Abstraction

To model parallelism or a decision point in a process, modelers use split connectors with outgoing branches. Depending on the desired semantics, an appropriate connector type is selected: AND, OR, or XOR. In the subsequent parts of a process model, these branches are synchronized with the corresponding join connectors. A process fragment enclosed between connectors usually has a self-contained business semantics. Therefore, the fragment can be replaced by one function of coarse granularity. *Block abstraction* enables this generalization. To define block

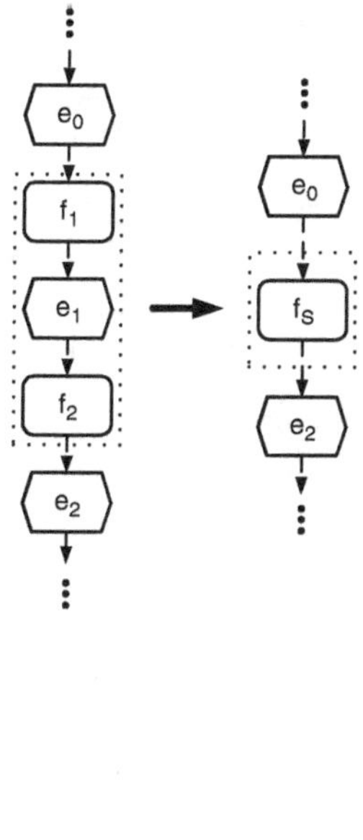

Fig. 3 Sequential abstraction

abstraction, we use a notion of a path in EPC – a sequence of nodes such that for each node there exists a connection to the next node in the sequence.

Definition 2: An EPC process fragment is a *block* if:

- It starts with a split and ends with a join connector of the same type.
- All paths from the split connector lead to the join connector.
- There is at most one function on each path.
- Each path between the split and the join contains only events and functions.
- The number of the outgoing connections of the split connector equals the number of the incoming connections of the join connector.
- The split connector has one incoming connection and the join connector – one outgoing.

Figure 4 describes the mechanism of block abstraction. Block abstraction replaces an initial process fragment by a sequence of event, aggregating function, and another event. Events assure that a new EPC is well-formed. Semantics of the aggregating function corresponds to the semantics of the abstracted block and conforms to the block type. For instance, if a XOR block is considered, the aggregating function states that only one function of the abstracted fragment is executed.

4.3.3 Loop Abstraction

Often, tasks (or sets of tasks) are iterated for successful process completion. In a process model, the fragment to be repeated is enclosed into a loop construct. In EPC notation, control flow enables loop modeling. Wide application of loops by

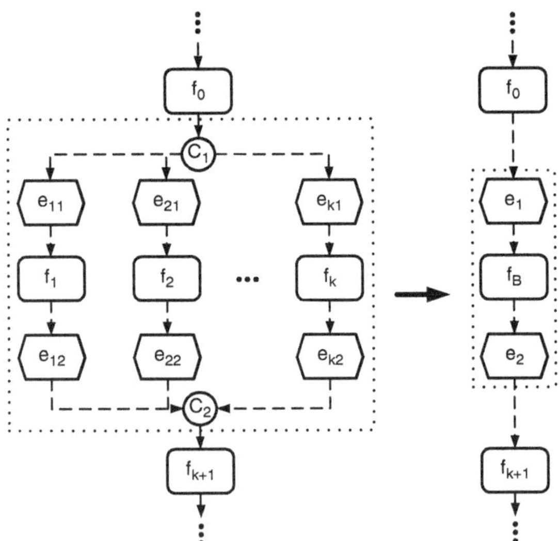

Fig. 4 Block abstraction

modelers makes support of loop abstraction an essential part of the abstraction approach. Therefore, one more elementary abstraction – *loop abstraction* – is introduced. Following, we define the process fragment considered to be a loop.

Definition 3: An EPC process fragment is a *loop* if:

- It starts with a XOR join connector and ends with a XOR split connector.
- The process fragment does not contain any other connectors.
- The XOR join has exactly one outgoing and two incoming connections.
- The XOR split has exactly one incoming and two outgoing connections.
- There is exactly one path from the split to the join and exactly one path from the join to the split.
- There is at least one function in the process fragment.

As shown in Fig. 5, aggregating function f_L replaces the whole process fragment corresponding to a loop. Event e_0 is inserted between functions f_0 and f_L in order to obtain a well-formed EPC model. An aggregating function states that functions f_1 and f_2 are executed iteratively.

4.3.4 Dead End Abstraction

Exceptional and alternative control flows result in "spaghetti-like" process models with lots of control flow branches leading to multiple end events. Abstraction aims to reduce excessive process details. Thus, abstraction mechanism should be capable of eliminating these flows. *Dead end abstraction* addresses this problem. First, the term *dead end* should be specified.

Definition 4: An EPC process fragment is a *dead end* if it consists of a function, followed by a XOR split connector, followed by an event, followed by a function,

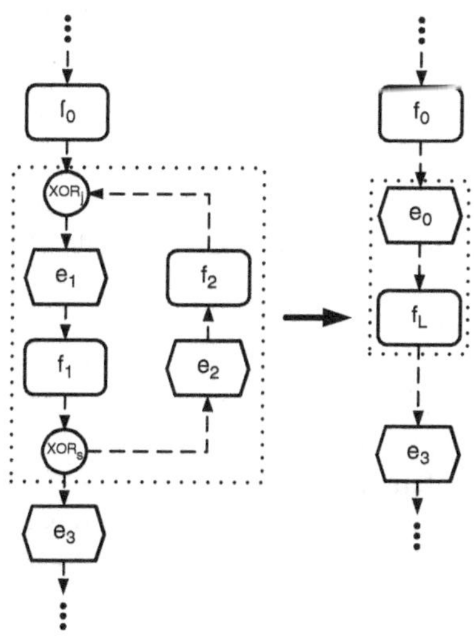

Fig. 5 Loop abstraction

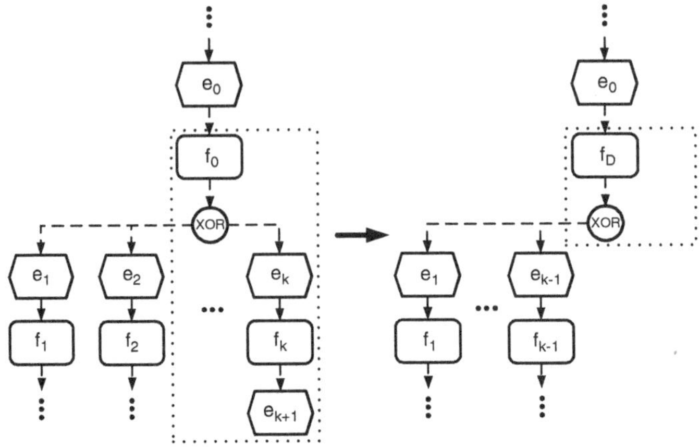

Fig. 6 Dead end abstraction

followed by an end event. The XOR split connector has only one incoming connection.

Figure 6 visualizes the dead end abstraction mechanism. The initial process fragment is provided on the left side of the figure. The dead end is formed by functions f_0 and f_k, events e_k and e_{k+1}, and the XOR split connector. The XOR split has k outgoing branches, and abstraction removes the k-th branch. The abstracted process is presented on the right side of Fig. 6. Rectangles with dotted borders enclose the dead end fragment and its replacement.

Dead end abstraction completely removes a XOR split branch that belongs to a dead end. Aggregating function f_D replaces function f_0. An aggregating function in dead end abstraction has the following semantics: upon an occurrence of function f_D in a process, function f_0 is executed. Afterwards, function f_k may be executed. Upon execution of function f_k, the branch is terminated and f_D is not left. Otherwise, the execution of the branch is continued. When an XOR split has two outgoing connections in the initial process model, the XOR split in the abstracted process model can be omitted. A new connection from the aggregating function to the event, following the omitted XOR split, should be added to the EPC.

4.3.5 Abstraction Strategy

A single application of an elementary abstraction is not of great value for the task of process abstraction. Therefore, elementary abstractions can be invoked according to an *abstraction strategy* – a rule of composition of elementary abstractions. An abstraction strategy is a sequence of elementary abstraction steps. Every step aims to simplify a process model. At each abstraction step, one elementary abstraction is applied. Since elementary abstractions are atomic, i.e., they do not depend on the previous ones, one might come up with various abstraction strategies. In general case, different strategies lead to different resulting process models.

We propose to organize the abstraction strategy in compliance with the slider concept. Hence, first we aim to abstract from functions of low significance. Once the function with the lowest significance is identified, it is tested to which type of process fragment it belongs. If a process fragment is recognized, appropriate abstraction transformation rules are applied. Otherwise, another elementary abstraction is tested. The next elementary abstraction to test is selected according to the predefined priority. Abstraction is continued until either no more elementary abstraction process fragments are recognized, or the lowest element significance in the process has reached the preset threshold.

An abstraction strategy using only one type of elementary abstraction can be seen as a basic abstraction strategy. Basic abstraction strategy result in process models where only sequential, dead end, block, or loop process fragments are reduced. For instance, in case of the basic sequential abstraction strategy, sequences of an arbitrary length are reduced.

Advanced abstraction strategies combine several elementary abstractions and define their priority. The priority dictates the application order of elementary abstractions. One possible strategy is the precedence of sequential, dead end, block, and then loop abstraction. Application of one elementary abstraction might enable further application of another one.

5 Case Study

In this section, we conduct an in-depth analysis of the proposed mechanisms. We evaluate the results of process model abstractions conducted in a joint project with an industry partner. The project objective was to derive process model abstraction mechanisms and to apply them on a process model repository composed of around 4,000 models captured in EPC notation. The additional requirement for abstraction was to preserve overall process effort, i.e., the overall process effort before and after abstraction should stay unchanged. We evaluate the developed abstraction mechanisms in terms of efficiency and usefulness. An estimation of abstraction efficiency is based on the analysis of the number of model nodes reduced by abstractions. Obviously, this measure does not witness the usefulness of the abstraction. In order to learn the usefulness of abstractions, we appeal to the project partner's expertise.

Following, we provide the results of performing abstraction on a subset of models from the repository composed of 1,195 models. Each model consists of 10 or more nodes. Models with less than 10 nodes are not considered. Three abstraction strategies take part in the case study. Each strategy uses one or several elementary abstractions and applies them iteratively (see Sect. 4.3). The following abstraction strategies are used:

Table 1 Comparison of node reduction caused by various abstraction strategies

Number of nodes	Original	Strategy 1	Strategy 2	Strategy 3
1–10	0	274	511	871
11–20	464	359	306	156
21–30	225	182	137	82
31–40	130	150	81	54
41–50	118	69	56	20
51–60	65	36	38	2
61–70	47	33	29	4
71–80	31	29	18	4
81–90	22	15	5	0
91–100	22	14	2	0
>100	71	34	12	2

1. Basic sequential abstraction (strategy 1)
2. Sequential then block abstraction (strategy 2)
3. Sequential, dead end, block, and then loop abstraction (strategy 3)

Abstraction strategies are applied with a threshold level equal to the overall process effort. This guarantees that an abstraction tries to reduce all the nodes in a model to the point when no more abstractions are applicable.

Table 1 presents results of applying abstraction strategies, i.e., correspondence between intervals of number of nodes in a model and the number of models that fall into the interval, provided for original as well as abstracted models. The table illustrates how different abstraction strategies reduce the amount of nodes in models.

Additionally, we use the notion of abstraction compression coefficient – a ratio between the number of nodes in abstracted and original models. Each line in Fig. 7 corresponds to the probability density function of the compression coefficient for a certain abstraction strategy. The line for strategy 1 hints on the fact that most of the models were reduced by 40% or less. Whereas in the case of strategy 3, the number of nodes in most models were reduced by 70% or more. This clearly witnesses that strategy 3 excels its evaluated competitors.

In order to evaluate the usefulness of the abstraction approach, we refer to project partner's experts. Abstractions capable of aggregating more model elements are considered as most valuable. Thus in general case, strategy 3 can be seen as more useful strategy. The project partners argued that the choice of an abstraction method depends on the structure of a particular process model. For instance, strategy 1 can be seen as useful for some particular process model if it allows same generalization as in the case of strategy 3.

6 Related Work

The problem of managing large complex process models emerges as BPM technologies penetrate modern enterprises. This challenging situation is addressed by various approaches. The authors of several process modeling notations, like

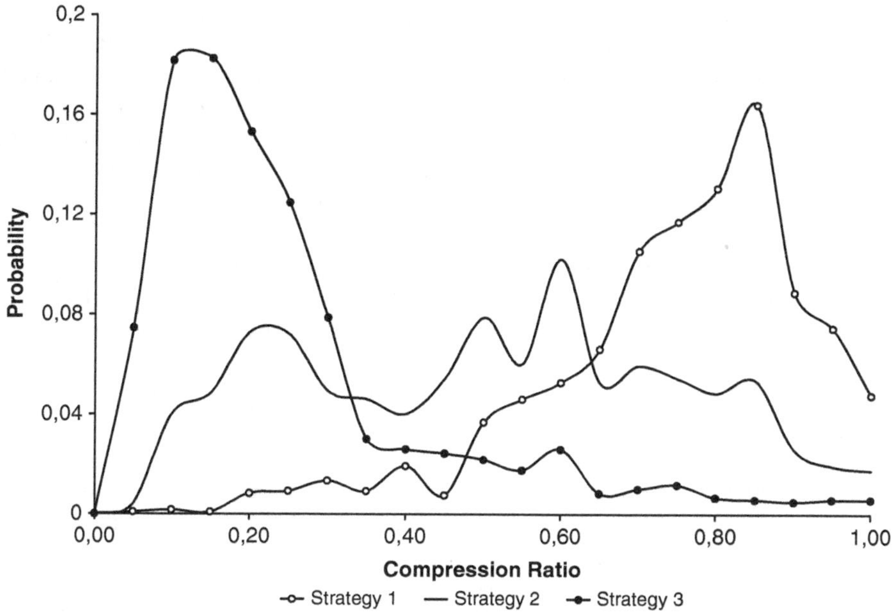

Fig. 7 Comparison of compression ratios for three discussed abstraction strategies

Business Process Modeling Notation (BPMN) (OMG 2008) or Yet Another Workflow Language (YAWL) (van der Aalst and ter Hofstede 2003) envisioned this problem. These notations allow hierarchical structuring of models. The goal of the hierarchical model organization is to distribute information describing a process among several levels with the general process flow on the highest level of hierarchy and the process details on the lowest one. Unfortunately, such a mechanism is not sufficient to cope with the problem, since it assumes that the hierarchy is designed and maintained manually. Zerguini (2004) proposed an algorithm for identifying special kind of regions called *reducible subflows* in workflow nets. Once such regions are found, a process model can be decomposed into their hierarchy.

A number of studies focused on creation of process views from available process models. The purpose of a process view is to hide certain fragments of a process model. For instance, one can imagine an actor-specific process view or a process view reflecting parts of a process instance to be executed (the last case corresponds to a process view on an instance level). Therefore, the goal of a process view creation differs from the goal of process model abstraction and can be seen as a more generic task. On the other hand, process view creation focuses on the *how* question, but does not discuss the *what* of abstraction, i.e., it does not say how to identify significant model elements. Bobrik et al. (2007) propose an approach capable of creating customized process views on model level and on instance level. The approach relies on graph reduction rules. Eshuis and Grefen (2008) propose a method for constructing views aiming to ease communication between partners by adapting internal process descriptions into ones suitable for external usage. As an input, the approach takes a process model captured in UML activity diagram notation and a user requirement to hide certain process elements. Liu and Shen (2003) propose an order preserving approach for creation of process views. An important issue is that the mentioned approaches do not incorporate the notion of nonfunctional properties of a process and, thus, do not define how nonfunctional properties of a process (e.g., execution effort and execution cost) can be preserved during transformations.

Günther and van der Aalst (2007) proposed a framework allowing to judge about significance of model elements basing on their nonfunctional properties. The framework bases on various metrics evaluating significance of process model nodes and edges. The proposed technique can be employed to answer the *what* question of abstraction, i.e., to derive reasonable significance values for process model elements.

The abstraction mechanism proposed in this chapter makes use of the set of elementary abstraction rules. Each rule has the goal of model simplification and defines how a process model fragment is transformed. Polyvyanyy et al. (2008b) have shown how these rules can be extended for evaluation of nonfunctional properties of model elements. In particular, it is described how properties of aggregating elements are derived from the properties of aggregated. Graph transformation rules are widely used for analysis of process model soundness and are well studied in literature (van Dongen et al. 2007; Liu and Shen 2003; Mendling et al. 2008; Sadiq and Orlowska 2000; Vanhatalo et al. 2007). An approach proposed by Sadiq and Orlowska (2000) presents rules facilitating soundness analysis of process models captured in the notation proposed by Workflow Management Coalition. van Dongen et al. (2007) and Mendling et al. (2008) focus on the rules facilitating analysis of EPC models soundness. Cardoso et al. (2002) propose a method for the evaluation of workflow properties (e.g., execution cost, execution time, and reliability) based on the properties of workflow tasks. However, the approach is restricted to block-structured process models free of OR blocks.

The presented outlook of the related work witnesses: there is no comprehensive approach, which addresses all the aspects of the business process model abstraction task. Several approaches provide a solid basis of reduction rules, capable of handling sophisticated graph-structured processes. However, these approaches do not allow estimating process properties, such as effort or cost. On the other hand, there is an approach (cf. Cardoso et al. 2002) supporting process properties estimation, but it is limited to block-structured processes excluding OR block constructs. Finally, to the best of our knowledge, there is no means for controlling process abstraction. Therefore, in this chapter, we have shown how process model abstraction can be conceptually realized. We have introduced the slider concept – a mean for the user to control the abstraction. The approach uses transformation rules proposed by Polyvyanyy et al. (2008b). The rules prescribe how the process nonfunctional properties can be estimated.

7 Conclusions

In this chapter, we presented a business process model abstraction technique – an approach to derive process models of high abstraction level from the detailed ones. We argued that the abstraction task can be decomposed into two independent subtasks: learning process model elements, which are insignificant (abstraction *what*), and abstracting from those elements (abstraction *how*). The proposed technique can be applied for abstraction of an arbitrary graph-structured process model.

Several abstraction scenarios were provided to motivate the task of business process model abstraction. These scenarios were used to extract abstraction criteria. Afterwards, we proposed to adopt a slider concept in order to achieve control over abstraction process. Finally, we discussed process model transformation rules, which can be employed together with the slider for abstraction of insignificant model elements.

We proposed a concrete scenario of applying graph transformation rules for the purpose of model abstraction. Elementary abstractions: sequential, block, loop, and dead end abstraction were presented. For every elementary abstraction, it was defined to which type of process fragment it can be applied and in which model transformation it results. It was explained how these individual abstractions can be combined into abstraction strategies. Derived abstraction methodology preserves function ordering constraints of the initial model. To the limitation of the approach, one can count the fact that not an arbitrary model can be abstracted to one function, if such a behavior is desired. We conducted a case study on abstraction efficiency and usefulness with the industry project partner and presented obtained statistical results. The technique of process model abstraction can be extended by other transformation rules that assume process graph generalization, e.g., rules proposed by Liu and Shen (2003) and Sadiq and Orlowska (2000).

References

Bobrik R, Reichert M, Bauer T (2007) View-based process visualization. In: BPM, volume 4714 of LNCS. Springer Berlin / Heidelberg, pp 88–95

Cardoso J, Miller J, Sheth A, Arnold J (2002) Modeling quality of service for workflows and web service processes. Technical report, University of Georgia, Web Services.

Davenport T (1993) Process innovation: reengineering work through information technology. Harvard Business School Press, Boston, MA

Eshuis R, Grefen P (2008) Constructing customized process views. Data Knowl Eng 64 (2):419–438

Günther C, van der Aalst WMP (2007) Fuzzy mining – adaptive process simplification based on multi-perspective metrics. In: BPM 2007, volume 4714 of LNCS. Springer Berlin / Heidelberg, pp 328–343

Hammer M, Champy J (1994) Reengineering the corporation: a manifesto for business revolution. HarperBusiness, New York

Keller G, Nüttgens M, Scheer A (1992) Semantische Prozessmodellierung auf der Grundlage "Ereignisgesteuerter Prozessketten (EPK)". Technical Report Heft 89, Veröffentlichungen des Instituts für Wirtschaftsinformatik University of Saarland

Liu D, Shen M (2003) Workflow modeling for virtual processes: an order-preserving process-view approach. Inf Syst 28(6):505–532

Mendling J, Verbeek H, van Dongen B, van der Aalst WMP, Neumann G (2008) Detection and prediction of errors in EPCs of the SAP reference model. Data Knowl Eng 64(1):312–329

OMG (2008), Business Process Model and Notation (BPMN) 1.1

Polyvyanyy A, Smirnov S, Weske M (2008) Process model abstraction: a slider approach. In: EDOC '08: proceedings of the 12th IEEE international enterprise distributed object computing conference, IEEE Computer Society, München, Germany, 9 2008

Polyvyanyy A, Smirnov S, Weske M (2008) Reducing complexity of large EPCs. In: EPK'08 GI-Workshop, Saarbrücken, Germany, 11 2008

Sadiq W, Orlowska M (2000) Analyzing process models using graph reduction techniques. Inf Syst 25(2):117–134

Scheer A, Thomas O, Adam O (2005) Process aware information systems: bridging people and software through process technology, chapter process modeling using event-driven process chains. Wiley, Hoboken, pp 119–145

van der Aalst WMP, ter Hofstede AHM (2003) YAWL: yet another workflow language (Revised version). Technical report FIT-TR-2003-04. Queensland University of Technology, Brisbane

van Dongen B, Jansen-Vullers M, Verbeek H, van der Aalst WMP (2007) Verification of the SAP reference models using EPC reduction, state-space analysis, and invariants. Comput Ind 58 (6):578–601

Vanhatalo J, Völzer H, Leymann F (2007) Faster and more focused control-flow analysis for business process models through SESE decomposition. In: ICSOC 2007, volume 4749 of LNCS. Springer Berlin / Heidelberg, pp 43–55

Weske M (2007) Business process management: concepts, languages, architectures. Springer Berlin / Heidelberg

Zerguini L (2004) A novel hierarchical method for decomposition and design of workflow models, vol 8. IOS Press, Amsterdam, The Netherlands, pp 65–74.

Business Process Quality Management

Hajo A. Reijers, Jan Mendling, and Jan Recker

Abstract Process modeling is a central element in any approach to Business Process Management (BPM). However, what hinders both practitioners and academics is the lack of support for *assessing* the quality of process models – let alone *realizing* high quality process models. Existing frameworks are highly conceptual or too general. At the same time, various techniques, tools, and research results are available that cover fragments of the issue at hand. This chapter presents the SIQ framework that on the one hand integrates concepts and guidelines from existing ones and on the other links these concepts to current research in the BPM domain. Three different types of quality are distinguished and for each of these levels concrete metrics, available tools, and guidelines will be provided. While the basis of the SIQ framework is thought to be rather robust, its external pointers can be updated with newer insights as they emerge.

1 Introduction

Just now, you started to read a chapter about another "framework" with a funny name. It did not deter you so far and we are glad it did not. If you have an interest in process modeling and agree with us that process modeling is an important activity in many contexts, keep on reading. What we want to present to you is an integrated view on many concepts and ideas – most of which, admittedly, are *not* our own – that are related in some way to the *quality* of process models. However, hardly anybody outside a small community of researchers really knows about these notions, how they are related to one another or how they are helpful in any way.

H.A. Reijers (✉)
Eindhoven University of Technology, Eindhoven, The Netherlands
e-mail: h.a.reijers@tue.nl

J. vom Brocke and M. Rosemann (eds.), *Handbook on Business Process Management 1*, International Handbooks on Information Systems,
DOI 10.1007/978-3-642-00416-2_8,

That is exactly what the SIQ framework is about. Its aim is to help you make *better process models*, using the methods, techniques, and tools that are already available.

Quality is an issue due to a combination of three facts. First of all, Rosemann (2006a) illustrates that large modeling projects can hardly assume that all participating modelers know modeling well. Many of them have only run a brief starter training and have little or no experience. Beyond that, they often model as a side activity to their usual tasks and duties. Second, and as a consequence of that, the quality of process models is often poor. As indicated in Mendling (2008), there are quite significant error rates in process model collections for practice of 10–20%. Thirdly, this has detrimental consequences of the usage and application of business process models in later design phases. It is a common insight of software engineering, (Boehm et al. 1978; Moody 2005), that flaws can be easily corrected in early design stages while they become increasingly expensive with the progression of a project. Due to these three issues, it is of considerable importance to understand how process model quality can be achieved.

Having said this, the chapter is structured as follows. First, we will reflect on the use of process modeling and the need for a framework as the one we propose. After that, we will explain the framework, which consists of just a small set of quality aspects. If you like, you can go on reading about the various sources we draw from and a methodological justification for the framework. But if you are already convinced and want to start using the framework at that point, that is really fine with us too. The chapter ends with a summary and some final reflections on process modeling.

2 The Power of Process Modeling

Imagine that you are asked to lead a project in your organization to improve the service delivery to customers. Chances are that you will embark on it by focusing on the *business processes* that flow through your organization. Since Thomas Davenport (1993) and Michael Hammer (Hammer and Champy 1993) produced their breakthrough views on the drivers behind organizational performance, the power of *process-thinking* has become deeply entrenched in management practice. By:

1. Understanding all actions in a process, from the first interaction with a customer until the final delivery of a service or product to that customer,
2. Questioning and rethinking the various parts of the process and their mutual relations, and
3. Implementing a thoroughly new process that exploits the benefits of the latest available technologies,

you have taken the most effective path towards organizational improvement. Ask any management consultancy firm: This is the recipe they will give you, simply because it works so well.

For a process-oriented improvement project to be successful – whether its goal is to improve customer satisfaction, introduce an ERP system, implement yet another regime of checks and balances, etc. – a deep understanding will be required of the process as it currently *exists*. Not only do you need to understand it: But also all stakeholders should do so. (Do not suppose for a minute that there is agreement between people on what any particular process does, how it works, or even who is involved.) Similarly, the *changed* vision on that process will need to be communicated too, widely and vigorously. This is to ensure that (1) those who are responsible for bringing about the process change will know what to change and (2) those whose work will be affected will know what to expect. Clearly, *communication* is the central word here, both in *as-is* and *to-be* process models.

By far the best way to support communication in process improvement projects is to use *process models*. A process model helps to visualize what the important steps are in a process, how they are related to each other, which actors and systems are involved in carrying out the various steps, and at what points communication takes place with customers and external parties. All this is usually described in a visual way, using icon-like figures that are connected to each other and which are supported with textual annotations. An example can be seen in Fig. 1, where a complaint handling procedure is modeled.[1]

In part, the use of process models is the answer to a lot of the hassle associated with process improvement projects. At the same time, it brings hassle of its own. To start with: Which process modeling technique or tool should you use? In a small country like the Netherlands alone, a stock-taking in March 2008 arrives at *24* different tools available in the marketplace for process modeling, each with its own modeling paradigm. Some vendors will hit you with the intuitive user-interface their tool is equipped with, while others will point out their compliance with a standard you never heard of. So, what is it going to be?

Let us suppose here that you have selected your process modeling tool. That is good: Any choice for a dedicated tool is an infinitely better one than the use of PowerPoint or Visio for process modeling. A next question may well be: Who will make the models for you? Can business professionals be trained to map their own processes or are you better off hiring experts to do this with their input? The different alternatives have their own pros and cons. For example, the right experts will make such models faster, but when they leave your organization again you are left with models nobody cares for or is capable of updating.

The list of issues does not stop here. You will also need to make a decision on which specialists will be involved in the modeling exercise – either active or passive – to provide the content of the process models, how you want to deal with the inevitable updates to your models, where and how you will store process models, how you can allow for reuse of parts of the models you already made, how process models can link up with the working instructions you are using in your organization, how you can keep your process models in line with the compliance

[1]Note that the particular technique being used here is not so relevant.

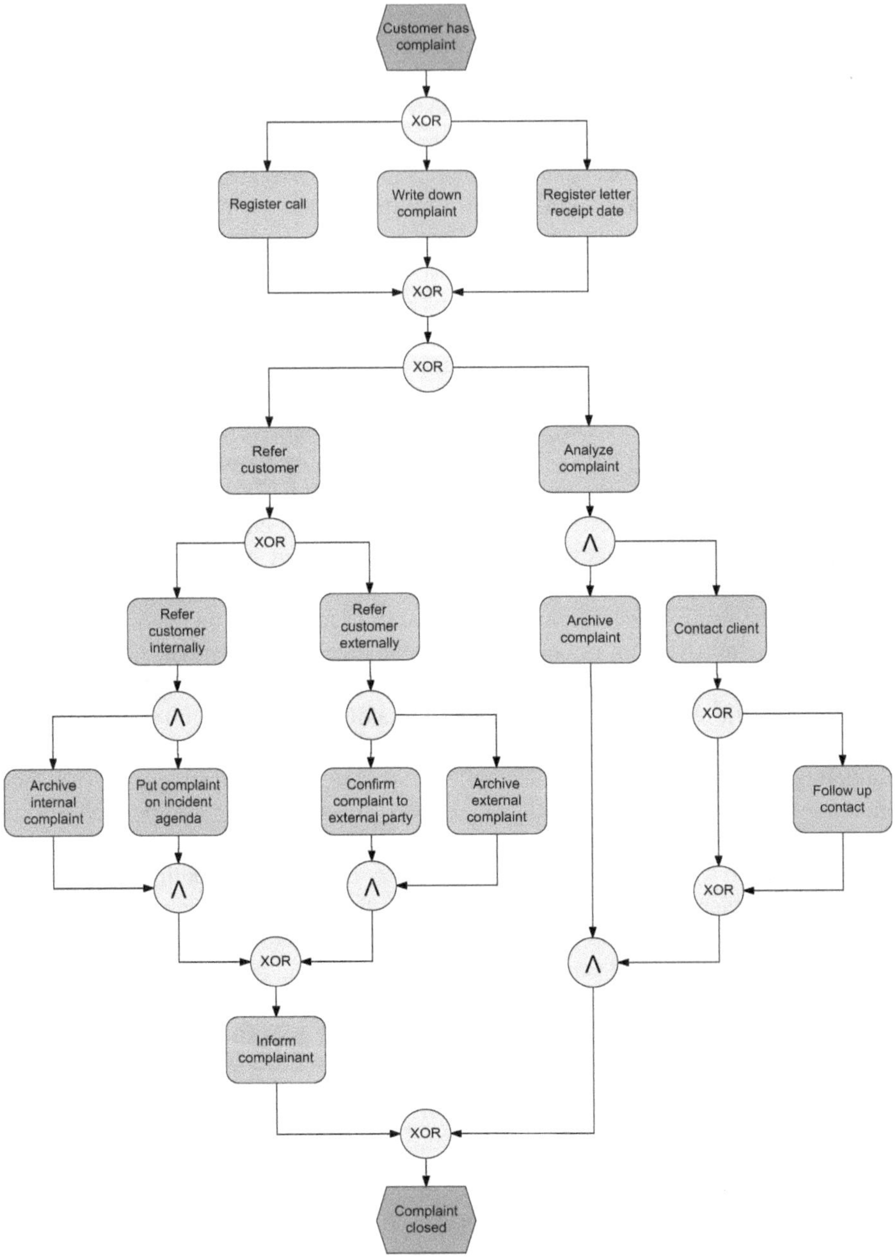

Fig. 1 An example process model

documentation you must generate periodically, and how you will distribute the models to interested parties.

Researchers in the BPM field, all over the world, are working very hard on finding answers to these questions and related ones. A very nice and extensive discussion of the issues we mentioned and some others too is, for example, reported in Rosemann (2006a, b). Process modeling is an art with a history of only 15 years[2] and there is not enough evidence to clearly tell the best way to undertake all things. Moreover, the field is in movement: New process modeling techniques and tools, for instance, are constantly being proposed.

This chapter will not – nor could it – provide you with all the answers to the issues you will encounter in the use of process models to achieve organizational benefits. It will just single out one issue, but an important one at that. The issue is: *What is a good process model*? In other words, how can you tell that a process model that you have created over a period of weeks or months, with the input of perhaps dozens of individuals, actually incorporates the quality to help you communicate about your improvement project? Or better still, how can you ensure *during* your modeling efforts that what comes out of it is a high-quality model? The goal of the framework that we will describe is to help you with these questions.

3 The Purpose of a Framework

Is it really important whether a process model is a good model? Actually, we cannot think of a more important issue. What good is it to invest in process modeling at all if you cannot distinguish between a bad model and a good model? At the universities we work, we tell our freshmen the joke that you can model any business process as a box with one incoming and one outgoing arc: Just remember to label the box correctly with the name of the business process you are interested in. (Students hardly ever laugh.) Clearly, such an approach results in a correct model, but is it a good model? Will it be of help to anyone? Probably not, but why is this?

Let us turn our attention to the framework proper to deal with this question. It will be referred to as the SIQ framework for process models, because it is *S*imple enough to be practically applicable, yet *I*ntegrates the most relevant insights from the BPM field, while it deals with *Q*uality – a notoriously intangible concept. While the acronym accurately reflects our intentions with the framework, it has a deliberate connotation. The main entrance to the ancient city of Petra in southern Jordan, once used by trade caravans to enter the strategically located city, is called the Siq.[3] It is a natural geological vault produced by tectonic forces and worn smooth by

[2]The publication of Curtis et al. (1992) is used as rough birth date of the modern business process modeling discipline. The specific focus of the paper, however, was on software processes.

[3]http://en.wikipedia.org/wiki/Siq.

Fig. 2 The Siq into Petra, with a view on the treasury

water erosion. A visitor that passes through the Siq will eventually stand face-to-face with the beautiful facade of the treasury of Petra (see Fig. 2). Similarly, our SIQ framework is the result of a lengthy, organic evolvement of insights on process models, which – if you allow it to guide you through your process modeling efforts – will result in something really worthwhile: a good process model.

We should make a disclaimer right here and now. The SIQ framework is not the final answer. But it seems unlikely that process improvement projects around the world will be put on halt until that answer has arrived. Therefore, the SIQ framework is built on a basis of three basic types of quality. We propose these as the fundament of process model quality. For each of the three types of quality, we will provide links with the current state of the start to measure these for specific models, which tools are available to establish the metric values, and which guidelines are available to do it right the first time. By the latter we mean that much of the current approaches are *retrospective* in nature: "Give me a complete model and I tell you what is wrong about it". However, a proactive approach to process modeling seems much more useful: "Follow this guideline and the resulting model will be good". Both of these views are supported by the SIQ framework.

Does it matter which modeling approach you are using to profit from the SIQ framework? Yes and no. We cannot rule out that you have encountered someone that will convince you of writing process models in Sanskrit.[4] In that case, the SIQ

[4]The use of *speech-acts* would be a good example of a modeling concept not particularly well supported by the SIQ framework.

framework will be of limited use beyond just providing a conceptual basis to reason about quality. But if you stick with activity-oriented modeling approaches, as found in EPCs, UML Activity diagrams, BPMN, etc., – in other words, the industry standards – it is not so important which particular flavor you use.

Another issue that concerns the applicability of the SIQ framework is the process modeling *purpose*. As we argued, in many contexts, the goal is to support interhuman communication. This is not the only purpose there is. Process models can also be used for a wide variety of modeling purposes, look for discussions on this in (Becker et al. 2003; Reijers 2003). If you make a process model that will only need to be interpreted by a computer system – as in some scenario's of workflow management support or simulation experiments – only parts of the SIQ framework will be relevant. The SIQ framework as a whole is relevant for "models-for-people." All other decisions do not affect the applicability of the SIQ framework at all, such as which process is modeled, who will make the model for you, how big the particular model is, etc. The SIQ framework is a one-size-fits-all approach: If you use an industry-like standard modeling approach and it is relevant that people should take a look at the process models, the SIQ framework is for you.

4 The SIQ Framework

The SIQ framework is about process model quality. In line with the ISO 9000 guideline and definitions on model quality from Moody (2005), we could try to become more specific by expressing this as "the totality of features and characteristics of a process model that bear on its ability to satisfy stated or implied needs." Its is questionable whether this will help you much. Therefore, take a look at Fig. 3, where you will see a visualization of the SIQ framework. We will discuss the framework, working inside-out.

4.1 The Center

At the center of the model, in the bright area, you see the three subcategories of process model quality that are distinguished within the SIQ framework. These categories are the *syntactic*, *semantic*, and *pragmatic* quality of the process model under consideration. Before dealing with the "walls" that surround the center, we will first describe these categories in more detail: They represent the main quality goals a process model should satisfy.

4.1.1 Syntactic Quality

This category relates to the goal of producing models that conform to the rules of the technique they are modeled with. In other words, all statements in the model are

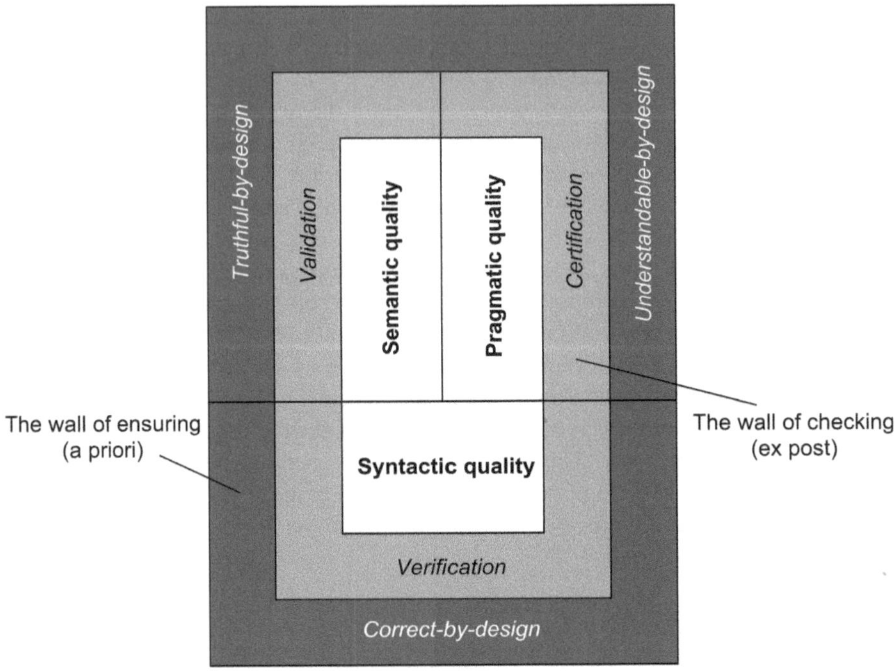

Fig. 3 The SIQ framework

according to the syntax and vocabulary of the modeling language (Lindland et al. 1994). If a process model is captured as an EPC (Keller et al. 1992; Scheer 2000), it would be syntactically incorrect to connect one event directly to another. Therefore, the model in Fig. 1 would not be a good EPC; the rounded boxes blocks are often used to visualize functions and many are connected in this model. Similarly, a Workflow Net (van der Aalst 1997) is not correct if does not contain a source and a sink place, i.e., a proper start and end of the process model. For most popular modeling techniques, it not really hard to find the rules that determine the syntactical quality, but usually there are hard and soft rules/conventions.

Syntactic quality is the *basis* for each of the other categories. This explains why it is shown as the lower part of the inner passage in Fig. 3, supporting the other categories. It is not sensible to consider the semantic or pragmatic quality of a process model if it contains syntactical errors. Think of it like this: Although you may be able to understand the meaning of a word that is not spelled correctly, you may be in doubt sometimes whether it is the actual word the writer intended. But there should be *no* room for any misunderstanding of the modeler's intent with a process model.[5] As such there is a hierarchical relation between the

[5]Note that a process model may certainly contain parts of which the modeler is not completely sure of. The point is that a modeler should model and identify such uncertainty in no uncertain terms that are syntactically correct.

categories: Both semantic and pragmatic quality assessments *suppose* syntactical correctness.

4.1.2 Semantic Quality

This category relates to the goal of producing models that make true statements on the real world they aim to capture, either for existing processes (*as is*) or future processes (*to be*). This goal can be further decomposed in the subgoals of *validity* and *completeness*. Validity means that all statements in the model are correct and are relevant to the problem; Completeness means that the model contains all relevant statements that *would be* correct (Lindland et al. 1994). So, if a particular process model expresses that any clerk may carry out the task of checking an invoice while in truth this requires a specific financial qualification, then the model suffers from a low semantic quality. Similarly, if this particular task is omitted from the process model while its purpose is to identify all checks in the process, then it also suffers from a low semantic quality. It should be noted that the requirements on *as-is* models may differ from those on *to-be* models. For example, the validity of a model describing an existing situation may obviously be checked more stringently than that of a hypothetical situation.

Semantic quality is a relative measure. In that sense, it is not so different from syntactic quality, which must be established against a set of rules. However, the baseline to determine the semantic quality is normally less explicit than that for syntactic quality. To evaluate a model's validity, we must first be certain about the *meaning* of the model elements that are used, i.e., what does an arrow express?[6] Next, we should compare the meaning of a process model with the *real world* it is trying to capture. In other words, you cannot say much about the semantic quality of a model if you do not understand how things actually take place. Finally, it is the modeling *goal* that needs to be known. In particular, if you want to assess whether a model is complete, you will need to know what insight you hope to derive from that model. So, checking a model's semantic quality can only be done by knowing the *meaning* of the modeling constructs, understanding the *domain* in question, and knowing the exact *purpose* of the process model (beyond that, it must support human communication).

4.1.3 Pragmatic Quality

This category relates to the goal of arriving at a process model that can be understood by people. This notion is a different one from semantic quality. You

[6]In an interview, the famous computer scientist Edsger W. Dijkstra said: "Diagrams are usually of an undefined semantics. The standard approach to burn down any presentation is to ask the speaker, after you have seen his third diagram, for the meaning of his arrows."

can probably imagine a process model where big parts from the real world are not captured, which will lead to a low semantic quality. But the same model can be perfectly understood in terms of the relations that are being expressed between its elements, which indicate a high pragmatic quality. But the inverse case – which seems much more frequent if you will browse through some realistic models – could also be true. Therefore, semantic quality and pragmatic quality are not hierarchically related.

Pragmatic quality is the least understood aspect of process model quality at this point. Although practitioners have developed experience over the years of what works well and what does not, few scientific explorations of this aspect have taken place. Evidence is growing, however, that small details of a model may have a big effect on its pragmatic quality.

4.2 The Wall of Checking

Let us now turn to the first "wall" surrounding the heart of the SIQ framework (see again Fig. 3). Process modeling, as much as programming, is essentially a problem-solving task. This implies that the validity of the solution must be established (Adrion et al. 1982). The three dimensions of quality require different approaches for checking the degree of validity. In particular, in this wall of checking of the SIQ framework, we distinguish between verification, validation, and certification.

4.2.1 Verification (Syntactic Quality Checking)

Verification essentially addresses formal properties of a model that can be checked without knowing the real-world process. In the context of process model verification, static and behavioral properties can be distinguished.

Static properties relate to the types of elements that are used in the model, and how they are connected. For instance, a transition cannot be connected to another transition in a Petri net; in a BPMN model, it is not allowed to have a message flow within a lane; or in EPCs, an organizational unit cannot be associated with a connector routing element. Typically, such static properties can easily be checked by considering all edges and their source and target elements.

Behavioral properties relate to termination of process models. It is a general assumption that a process should never be able to reach a deadlock and that a proper completion should always to be guaranteed. Different correctness criteria formalize these notions. Most prominently, the *soundness* property requires that (1) it has in any state the option to complete; (2) every completion is a proper completion with no branches being still active; and (3) that there are no tasks in the model that can never be executed (van der Aalst 1997). Other notions of correctness have been derived from soundness for various modeling languages (van der Aalst 1997; Dehnert and van der Aalst 2004; Wynn et al. 2006; Puhlmann and Weske 2006;

Mendling and van der Aalst 2007). The appeal of behavioral properties is that they can be checked by computer programs in an automatic fashion. For Petri nets, the open source tool Woflan[7] can be used to perform such a check (Verbeek et al. 2001). Indeed, there is a good reason to use verification in the design of process models. Different studies have shown that violations of soundness are included in about 10–20% of process models from practice (van Dongen et al. 2007; Mendling et al. 2007a, 2008c; Vanhatalo et al. 2007; Gruhn and Laue 2007).

4.2.2 Validation (Semantic Quality Checking)

There are different techniques that support the validation of a process model. Most of them are discussed in requirements engineering (Gemino 2004; Nuseibeh and Easterbrook 2000). A problem in this context is that, as indicated by the high error rates, users hardly understand the behavioral implications of their models. Here, we aim to emphasize two particular techniques: simulation and paraphrazation.

In essence, *simulation* refers to presenting the formal behavior of the model to the user in an intuitive way. It is closely related to animation as a visualization of dynamics (Philippi and Hill 2007). A simulation shows the user which paths he can use to navigate through the process, and which decisions have to be made. This way, it is easier to assess the completeness and the correctness of a model with respect to the real-world process. In D'Atri et al. (2001), we describe an even more advanced approach to validation: A to-be process model is animated and extended with user-interaction facilities to give end-users a good feeling of how a particular process will behave.

Simulation also provides valuable insights into the performance characteristics of a process, but for this application, the arrival pattern of new cases, the routing probabilities through a process, the involved resources, their maximum workload, and their execution times need to be specified. A good introduction into business process simulation can be found in the chapter Business Process Simulation in the Handbook volume 1 (van der Aalst et al. 2010), while a treatment of this subject in the specific context of process optimization can be found in ter Hofstede et al. (2008). Open source software packages available for business process simulation are CPN Tools[8] and ExSpect.[9]

Paraphrazation is an alternative technique to make a process model understandable to somebody who is not familiar with modeling. The key idea is that the model can be translated back to natural language (Frederiks and van der Weide 2006; Halpin and Curland 2006). The derived text can be easily discussed with a business expert, and potential shortcomings can be identified.

---

[7]http://is.tm.tue.nl/research/woflan.htm.

[8]http://wiki.daimi.au.dk/cpntools/.

[9]http://www.exspect.com/.

Validation and verification are meant to complement each other. Accordingly, approaches like van Hee et al. (2006) include them as consecutive steps of quality assurance in the overall design cycle.

4.2.3 Certification (Pragmatic Quality Checking)

The pragmatic quality of a model has its foundations in the psychological theory of dual coding, (e.g. Brooks 1967; Paivio 1991). It suggests that humans have two distinct and complementary channels for information processing: visual and auditory. While text activates the auditory channel, a process model stimulates the visual understanding. Accordingly, the Cognitive Theory of Multimedia Learning (CTML) (Mayer 1989, 2001) recommends that learning material intended to be received, understood, and retained by its recipients should be presented using *both* words (activity labels) and pictures (process graph). Furthermore, this theory offers a way to check the learning effect of a model. Gemino and others have identified an experimental design to quantify this learning effect (Bodart et al. 2001; Gemino and Wand 2005; Recker and Dreiling 2007).

In practice, you often find a less systematic approach to pragmatic quality. In this setting, the process owner is responsible for a sign-off of the process model, in the sense that he or she is satisfied with the clarity and readability of the model. In essence, this certifies that the model is adequate to be used by the intended stakeholders. The sign-off usually follows up on extensive validation and verification to guarantee that the model is also valid and correct.

4.3 The Wall of Ensuring

Given these different threats to correctness, there have been concepts developed to prevent them right from the start. These concepts constrain the design space. In particular, we distinguish correctness-by-design, truthful-by-design, and understandable-by-design. These are all part of the second "wall" of the SIQ framework, the wall of ensuring (see again Fig. 3).

4.3.1 Correctness-by-Design (Syntactic Quality Ensuring)

There are two essential ideas that contribute to correctness-by-design. The first one is that *static correctness directly guarantees behavioral correctness*. This principle is embodied in the Business Process Execution Language for Web Services (BPEL) (Alves et al. 2007). It imposes a block structure of nested control primitives. Due to this restriction, there are particular challenges of transforming graph-structured languages like BPMN or EPCs to BPEL, (van der Aalst and Lassen 2008; Mendling et al. 2008a; Ouyang et al. 2006). The second concept builds on *change operations that preserve correctness* (Weber et al. 2007). In this way, the modeler is able to add, modify, or delete activities in a process model by using primitives like *add parallel activity*. A criticism on both of these concepts is that not all correct graph-based process models can be expressed as block structure or constructed using change operations. Therefore, correctness-by-design comes along with a restriction on expressiveness. At the same time, it seems reasonable to say that the vast majority of process models can be captured in this way. For example, in an investigation in the Netherlands of a dozen companies that carried out workflow implementations (Reijers and van der Aalst 2005), it would have been possible to capture all encountered business processes using block structures of nested control primitives.

4.3.2 Truthful-by-Design (Semantic Quality Ensuring)

This aspect relates to the ways of constructing process models in such a way that they accurately capture reality. We focus on *process mining* and *natural language processing* as important techniques in this area.

Process mining is an approach to infer what a business process looks like from traces that are left behind in all kinds of information systems when executing that process (van der Aalst et al. 2003). Unlike the traditional approach to ask people who are active in a particular approach to describe that process (cf. Sharp and McDermott (2001) for example), process mining is a much less subjective means to discover that process. For example, if the event log of a specific information system always shows that payment by a client precedes delivery of the goods, process mining algorithms will order these events in the process model in this way – there is no need for interviewing anybody about this. ProM is a state of the art software platform that supports the execution of such algorithms, along with various additional analysis features. In a recent industrial application of the ProM framework (van der Aalst et al. 2007), it was found that, for example, an invoice handling process was characterized by many more points of iteration than the involved business people themselves thought. Process mining, therefore, seems a promising approach to truthfully outline a business process as it actually happens.

Beyond this rather recent development, the relationship between process models and natural language has been discussed and utilized in various works. Fliedl et al. (2005) define a three-step process of building a process model. Based on linguistic analysis, component mapping, and schema construction, they construct the model automatically from natural language text. Just as correctness-by-design, this approach is limited to a subset of natural language.

4.3.3 Understandable-by-Design (Pragmatic Quality Ensuring)

The empirical connection between understanding, errors, and model metrics, for instance (Mendling et al. 2007a, b, 2008c; Mendling and Reijers 2008), has led to

Table 1 Seven process modeling guidelines (Mendling et al. 2008b)

G1	Use as few elements in the model as possible
G2	Minimize the routing paths per element
G3	Use one start and one end event
G4	Model as structured as possible
G5	Avoid OR routing elements
G6	Use verb-object activity labels
G7	Decompose a model with more than 50 elements

the definition of a set of seven process modeling guidelines (7PMG) that are supposed to direct the modeler to creating understandable models that are less prone to errors (Mendling et al. 2008b). Table 1 summarizes the 7PMG guidelines. Each of them is supported by empirical insight into the connection of structural metrics and errors or understanding, which makes it standout in comparison to personal modeling preferences. The size of the model has undesirable effects on understandability and likelihood of errors (Mendling et al. 2007a, b, 2008c). Therefore, G1 recommends to use as few elements as possible. G2 suggests to minimize the routing paths per element. The higher the degree of elements in the process model the harder it becomes to understand the model (Mendling et al. 2007a, b). G3 demands to use one start and one end event, since the number of start and end events is positively connected with an increase in error probability (Mendling et al. 2007a). Following G4, models should be structured as much as possible. Unstructured models tend to have more errors and are understood less well (Mendling et al. 2007a, b; Gruhn and Laue 2007; Laue and Mendling 2008). G5 suggests to avoid OR routing elements, since models that have only AND and XOR connectors are less error-prone (Mendling et al. 2007a). G6 recommends using the verb-object labeling style because it is less ambiguous compared to other styles (Mendling and Reijers 2008). Finally, according to G7, models should be decomposed if they have more than 50 elements.

The model that is shown in 1 is, in fact, developed in conformance with these guidelines.

5 Related Work

By now, the SIQ framework has been outlined for you. In case you are wondering about that, it is not the first framework for process model quality. On the contrary, it owes heritage to some notable predecessors. To give the reader a better feeling of the SIQ framework's resemblances to and differences with these earlier frameworks, we will describe the most important ones.

First of all, there are the Guidelines of Modeling (GoM) (Becker et al. 2000, 2003). The inspiration for GoM comes from the observation that many professional disciplines cherish a commonly shared set of principles to which their work must adhere. GoM is intended to be that set for the process modeling community.

The guidelines include the six principles of correctness, clarity, relevance, comparability, economic efficiency, and systematic design. These principles partly overlap with the three main quality aspects that are distinguished in the SIQ framework:

- GoM's correctness refers to both the syntactic and the semantic quality in the SIQ framework,
- GoM's clarity relates to the pragmatic quality in the SIQ framework, and
- GoM's relevance is connected to the semantic quality in the SIQ framework.

In comparison, it is fair to say that the GoM framework covers a broader array of quality issues than the SIQ framework. For example, systematic design is not considered in the SIQ framework, but this may be a highly relevant to consider in certain situations. So in that sense, the SIQ framework is truly a simple framework. At the same time, the SIQ framework is more geared towards integrating a wide variety of existing notions, techniques, and tools from the BPM domain. In that sense, it is a more integrative approach to process modeling quality. What both frameworks share is the intent of their developers: To advocate the development of widely shared and usable guidelines for establishing process model quality.

The second important framework that we should mention here is the SEQUAL framework. It builds on semiotic theory and defines several quality aspects based on relationships between a model, a body of knowledge, a domain, a modeling language, and the activities of learning, taking action, and modeling. It was originally proposed in Lindland et al. (1994), after which a revision was presented in Krogstie et al. (2006). The notions of a syntactic, semantic, and pragmatic quality in the SIQ framework can be immediately traced back to that first version of the SEQUAL framework. But these criteria aspects are not the only SEQUAL notions by far. The most striking characteristic of the SEQUAL framework is that it is so complex. It seems hard to explain to anybody – in particular practitioners – what its various components are and what they mean. Its *raison d'être* seems to be to feed philosophical discussion than practical application: There is nothing close to concrete guidelines, as in GoM or in the SIQ framework, let alone any links to empirical work or tools. Finally, the revision of the original pillars of the SEQUAL framework cast doubts on its robustness. In contrast, the SIQ framework is proposed as an extensible framework, rather than a revisable one.

Finally, Moody has made various contributions on the subject of conceptual model quality (Moody 2003, 2005). Most relevant for our purpose, he investigated the proliferation of various model quality frameworks, discusses many of them, and dryly observes that none of them have succeeded in receiving any acceptance. The most important link between Moody's work and the SIQ framework is that the latter tries to live up to the principles for structuring conceptual model quality frameworks as proposed in the former:

- We decomposed the overall quality notion into the subcharacteristics of syntactic, semantic, and pragmatic quality, described their relations, and – if available – described the metrics for these.

- We used commonly understood terms to distinguish and describe the various quality aspects; descriptions were commonly given in one sentence.
- We provided the links to tools, procedures, guidelines, and related work to clarify how quality evaluations can take place.

Admittedly, we did not provide concrete metrics for each of the characteristics and subcharacteristics we discussed, as is also suggested by Moody. This is a clear avenue for further improving the SIQ framework, so that its chances will be increased of becoming widely adopted and making an impact on modeling practice.

6 Conclusion

In this chapter, we introduced the SIQ framework for the quality of business process models. Its core consists of the three dimensions of syntactic, semantic, and pragmatic quality. These have been discussed in conceptual modeling before, but the SIQ framework has some distinct features of its own. It is much *simpler* than other frameworks, in the sense that only three subcategories of quality are distinguished. You can see from this that it is not so much that *truth* was the dominant principle in developing the SIQ framework, but *utility*. Also, the SIQ framework is a sincere effort to link up with the most powerful and relevant notions, techniques, and tools that already exist but provide part of the picture. In that sense, the SIQ framework is *integrative*: It identifies mechanisms and techniques that can be applied complementarily. What is completely new in the framework is the identification of both *ex post* checking of quality and *a priori* ensuring of quality. In this regard, we have organized existing work on verification and correctness-by-design on the syntax level, validation, and truthfulness-by-design on the semantic level, and certification and understandable-by-design on the pragmatic level.

In the end, frameworks do not become popular by themselves. Readers like you determine whether the SIQ framework meets their purposes or not. But in our mind, there are more important issues than whether you will use the SIQ framework as we described it. We hope that you will remember our claim that process model quality is much more than simply adhering to a particular modeling notation. We also hope that reading this chapter will help you to focus your energies more effectively. Rather than joining "process model battles" – technique X is much better than Y! – focus on creating models that stick to the rules of the technique you are using, rightfully describe what you need, and do so in a way that is comprehensible to the people using it.

We will spend our time and energy on extending the SIQ framework, linking it with the latest insights and tools. Besides time being an eroding factor in this, we expect that it will make the SIQ framework even stronger and more effective – just like time has made the Siq into Petra all the more beautiful. We aim for a close cooperation with our industry and academic partners to further populate the white spaces in the SIQ framework, validate its applicability, and develop even more concrete guidelines on how to create process models. In the mean time, we hope you will try the SIQ framework out. Process modeling is simply too important to carry out poorly.

References

Adrion WR, Branstad MA, Cherniavsky JC (1982) Validation, verification, and testing of computer software. ACM Comput Surv 14(2):159–192

Alves A, Arkin A, Askary S, Barreto C, Bloch B, Curbera F, Ford M, Goland Y, Guizar A, Kartha N, Liu CK, Khalaf R, Koenig D, Marin M, Mehta V, Thatte S, van der Rijn D, Yendluri P, Yiu A (2007) Web services business process execution language version version 2.0. Committee specification 31 January 2007

Becker J, Kugeler M, Rosemann M (eds) (2003) Process management, a guide for the design of business processes, Springer, Berlin, pp 41–78

Becker J, Rosemann M, von Uthmann C (2000) Guidelines of business process modeling. In: van der Aalst WMP, Desel J, Oberweis A (eds) Business process management. Models, techniques, and empirical studies. Springer, Berlin, pp 30–49

Bodart F, Patel A, Sim M, Weber R (2001) Should optional properties be used in conceptual modelling? A theory and three empirical tests. Inf Syst Res 12(4):384–405

Boehm BW, Brown JR, Kaspar JR et al. (1978) Characteristics of software quality. TRW Series of Software Technology, Amsterdam

Brooks LR (1967) The suppression of visualization by reading. Q J Exp Psychol 19(4):289–299

Curtis B, Kellner MI, Over J (1992) Process modeling. Commun ACM 35(9):75–90

D'Atri A, Solvberg A, Willcocks L (eds) (2001) Using prototyping in a product-driven design of business processes, proceedings of the open enterprise solutions: systems, experiences, and organizations conference. Luiss Edizioni

Davenport TH (1993) Process innovation: reengineering work through information technology. Harvard Business School Press, Boston

Dehnert J, van der Aalst WMP (2004) Bridging the gap between business models and workflow specifications. Int J Coop Inf Syst 13(3):289–332

Fliedl G, Kop C, Mayr HC (2005) From textual scenarios to a conceptual schema. Data Knowl Eng 55(1):20–37

Frederiks PJM, van der Weide TP (2006) Information modeling: the process and the required competencies of its participants. Data Knowl Eng 58(1):4–20

Gemino A (2004) Empirical comparisons of animation and narration in requirements validation. Requir Eng 9(3):153–168

Gemino A, Wand Y (2005) Complexity and clarity in conceptual modeling: comparison of mandatory and optional properties. Data Knowl Eng 55(3):301–326

Gruhn V, Laue R (2007) What business process modelers can learn from programmers. Sci Comput Program 65(1):4–13

Halpin TA, Curland M (2006) Automated verbalization for orm 2. In: Meersman R, Tari Z, Herrero P (eds) On the move to meaningful internet systems 2006: OTM 2006 workshops, Montpellier, France, October 29–November 3. Proceedings, part II, vol 4278, Lecture notes in computer science. Springer, Heidelberg, pp 1181–1190

Hammer M, Champy J (1993) Reengineering the corporation: a manifesto for business revolution. Harpercollins, New York

Keller G, Nüttgens M, Scheer AW (1992) Semantische Prozessmodellierung auf der Grundlage "Ereignisgesteuerter Prozessketten (EPK)", Heft 89. Institut für Wirtschaftsinformatik, Saarbrücken, Germany

Krogstie J, Sindre G, Jørgensen HD (2006) Process models representing knowledge for action: a revised quality framework. Eur J Inform Syst 15(1):91–102

Laue R, Mendling J (2008) The impact of structuredness on error probability of process models. In: Kaschek R, Kop C, Steinberger C, Fliedl G (eds) Information systems and e-business technologies: 2nd international united information systems conference. Lectures notes in business information processing, vol 5. Springer, Heidelberg

Lindland OI, Sindre G, Sølvberg A (1994) Understanding quality in conceptual modeling. IEEE Software 11(2):42–49

Mayer RE (1989) Models for understanding. Rev Educ Res 59(1):43–64

Mayer RE (2001) Multimedia learning. Cambridge University Press, Cambridge, MA

Mendling J (2008) Metrics for process models: empirical foundations of verification, error prediction, and guidelines for correctness, vol 6, Lecture notes in business information processing. Springer, Berlin

Mendling J, Reijers HA (2008) How to define activity labels for business process models? In: Oberweis A, Hesse W (eds) Proceedings of the Third AIS SIGSAND European Symposium on Analysis, Design, Use and Societal Impact of Information Systems (SIGSAND Europe 2008), Marburg, Germany. Lecture notes in informatics

Mendling J, van der Aalst WMP (2007) Formalization and verification of EPCs with OR-joins based on state and context. In: Krogstie J, Opdahl AL, Sindre G (eds) Proceedings of the 19th conference on advanced information systems engineering (CAiSE 2007), vol 4495, Lecture notes in computer science. Springer-Verlag, Trondheim, Norway, pp 439–453

Mendling J, Neumann G, van der Aalst WMP (2007a) Understanding the occurrence of errors in process models based on metrics. In: Meersman R, Tari Z (eds) OTM conference 2007, proceedings, part I, vol 4803, Lecture notes in computer science. Springer, Heidelberg, pp 113–130

Mendling J, Reijers HA, Cardoso J (2007b) What makes process models understandable? In: Alonso G, Dadam P, Rosemann M (eds) Business process management, 5th international conference, BPM 2007, Brisbane, Australia, September 24–28, 2007, proceedings, vol 4714, Lecture notes in computer science. Springer, Berlin, pp 48–63

Mendling J, Lassen KB, Zdun U (2008) Transformation strategies between block-oriented and graph-oriented process modelling languages. Int J Bus Process Integrat Manage 3(2):297–312

Mendling J, Reijers HA, van der Aalst WMP (2008b) Seven process modeling guidelines (7PMG). Qut eprint, Queensland University of Technology, Brisbane

Mendling J, Verbeek HMW, van Dongen BF, van der Aalst WMP, Neumann G (2008c) Detection and prediction of errors in EPCs of the SAP reference model. Data Knowl Eng 64(1):312–329

Moody DL (2003) Measuring the quality of data models: an empirical evaluation of the use of quality metrics in practice. In: Proceedings of the 11th European conference on information systems, ECIS 2003, Naples, Italy 16–21 June 2003

Moody DL (2005) Theoretical and practical issues in evaluating the quality of conceptual models: current state and future directions. Data Knowl Eng 55(3):243–276

Nuseibeh B, Easterbrook SM (2000) Requirements engineering: a roadmap. In: Proceedings of the Conference on Software Engineering on The Future of Software Engineering, ACM: New York, pp 35–46, 2000

Ouyang C, Dumas M, Breutel S, ter Hofstede AHM (2006) Translating standard process models to bpel. In: Dubois E, Pohl K (eds) Advanced information systems engineering, 18th international conference, CAiSE 2006, Luxembourg, Luxembourg, June 5–9, 2006, proceedings, vol 4001, Lecture notes in computer science. Springer, Heidelberg, pp 417–432

Paivio A (1991) Dual coding theory: retrospect and current status. Can J Psychol 45(3):255–287

Philippi S, Hill HJ (2007) Communication support for systems engineering – process modelling and animation with april. J Syst Software 80(8):1305–1316

Puhlmann F, Weske M (2006) Investigations on soundness regarding lazy activities. In: Dustdar S, Fiadeiro JL, Sheth A (eds) Business process management, 4th international conference, BPM 2006, vol 4102, Lecture notes in computer science. Springer, Heidelberg, pp 145–160

Recker J, Dreiling A (2007) Does it matter which process modelling language we teach or use? An experimental study on understanding process modelling languages without formal education.

In: Toleman M, Cater-Steel A, Roberts D (eds) 18th Australasian conference on information systems. The University of Southern Queensland, Toowoomba, Australia, pp 356–366
Reijers HA (2003) Design and control of workflow processes: business process management for the service industry. Springer, Berlin
Reijers HA, van der Aalst WMP (2005) The effectiveness of workflow management systems: predictions and lessons learned. Int J Inf Manage 25(5):458–472
Rosemann M (2006a) Potential pitfalls of process modeling: part A. Bus Process Manage J 12 (2):249–254
Rosemann M (2006b) Potential pitfalls of process modeling: part B. Bus Process Manage J 12 (3):377–384
Scheer A-W (2000) ARIS business process modelling. Springer Verlag, Berlin
Sharp A, McDermott P (2001) Workflow modeling: tools for process improvement and application development. Artech House Publishers, Norwood, MA
ter Hofstede AHM, Benatallah B, Paik H-Y (eds) (2008) Trade-offs in the performance of workflows–quantifying the impact of best practices. Lecture notes in computer science, vol 4928. Springer, Berlin
van der Aalst WMP (1997) Verification of workflow nets. In: Azéma P, Balbo G (eds) Application and theory of petri nets 1997, vol 1248, Lecture notes in computer science. Springer, Heidelberg, pp 407–426
van der Aalst WMP, Lassen KB (2008) Translating unstructured workflow processes to readable BPEL: theory and implementation. Inform Softw Tech 50(3):131–159
van der Aalst WMP, van Dongen BF, Herbst J, Maruster L, Schimm G, Weijters AJMM (2003) Workflow mining: a survey of issues and approaches. Data Knowl Eng 47(2):237–267
van der Aalst WMP, Reijers HA, Weijters AJMM, van Dongen BF, Alves de Medeiros AK, Song M, Verbeek HMW (2007) Business process mining: an industrial application. Inf Syst 32(5):713–732
van der Aalst WMP, Nakatumba J, Rozinat A, Russell N (2010) Business process simulation. In: vom Brocke J, Rosemann M (eds) Handbook on business process management, vol 1. Springer, Heidelberg
van Dongen BF, Vullers-Jansen MH, Verbeek HMW, van der Aalst WMP (2007) Verification of the sap reference models using epc reduction, state-space analysis, and invariants. Comput Ind 58(6):578–601
van Hee K, Sidorova N, Somers L, Voorhoeve M (2006) Consistency in model integration. Data Knowl Eng 56:4–22
Vanhatalo J, Völzer H, Leymann F (2007) Faster and more focused control-flow analysis for business process models through sese decomposition. In: Krämer BJ, Lin K-J, Narasimhan P (eds) Service-oriented computing – ICSOC 2007, fifth international conference, Vienna, Austria, September 17–20, 2007, proceedings, vol 4749, Lecture notes in computer science. Springer, Berlin, pp 43–55
Verbeek HMW, Basten T, van der Aalst WMP (2001) Diagnosing workflow processes using Woflan. Comput J 44(4):246–279
Weber B, Rinderle S, Reichert M (2007) Change patterns and change support features in process-aware information systems. In: Krogstie J, Opdahl AL, Sindre G (eds) Advanced information systems engineering, 19th international conference, CAiSE 2007, Trondheim, Norway, June 11–15, 2007, proceedings, vol 4495, Lecture notes in computer science. Springer, Heidelberg, pp 574–588
Wynn MT, Verbeek HMW, van der Aalst WMP, ter Hofstede AHM, Edmond D (2006) Reduction rules for yawl workflow nets with cancellation regions and or-joins. BPMCenter Report BPM-06-24, BPMcenter.org

Semantic Business Process Management

Jörg Becker, Daniel Pfeiffer, Thorsten Falk, and Michael Räckers

Abstract The objective of this chapter is to describe and evaluate an approach for the automated analysis of business process models. It is described why an automated way of process analysis is necessary and why it is beneficial to use our approach. As business process models are moving in the center of decision making, it is important for the corresponding decision makers to get transparent, fast, and comprehensive results of process analysis. Dealing with huge amount of data this is only possible with automated support. Based on a comprehensive literature study, we identified different deviations and conflicts that usually arise in business process modeling projects. The class of semantic building block-based languages which combines structural modeling elements with corresponding domain semantics can help avoiding these conflicts. Beside the conceptual development of the language class we conducted an empirical evaluation of PICTURE, a business process modeling language that is an instantiation of semantic building block-based languages. Our results show that (a) our derived language class is applicable, (b) modeling conflicts significantly can be reduced, and (c) modeled data can be analyzed automatically.

1 Introduction

Business Process Management is moving more and more in the center of organizational staff. Business process models (BPMos) enable them to get a transparent overview over the relevant extracts of the organization. BPMos are used to create clarity about the logical sequence of activities in an organization. They are also applied to describe the resulting products and services, the required resources and data, as well as the involved organizational units. They have been discussed in

J. Becker (✉)
European Research Center for Information Systems, University of Münster, Münster, Germany
e-mail: becker@ercis.uni-muenster.de

J. vom Brocke and M. Rosemann (eds.), *Handbook on Business Process Management 1*, 187
International Handbooks on Information Systems,
DOI 10.1007/978-3-642-00416-2_9,

Information Systems (IS) literature as a tool to evaluate security issues (Herrmann and Herrmann 2006), potential risks (Jallow et al. 2006), or the overall performance of an organization (Kueng 2000). These findings show that the analysis of BPMos exhibits great potential to systematically inform and guide managerial actions. However, a semantic analysis of BPMo is necessary for the identification of relevant information for managerial decision making (Dalal et al. 2004; Davenport and Beers 1995). Furthermore, dealing with BPMo of the whole organization means often dealing with a huge amount of data.

Currently, in companies and public administrations business process models are mainly analyzed manually. Especially in smaller organizations the methodical knowledge of how to collect data about the business processes is often not available (Benamou 2005). Therefore, external consultants are hired to construct the models (Davenport and Short 1990; Rosemann 2007). These consultants coming from outside of the organization use their methodical skills to acquire the relevant domain knowledge. By modeling the processes, they gain an understanding of the structures, products, and services of the company or public administration. Subsequently, they manually analyze the process models with the objective to identify potential weaknesses (Becker et al. 2006; Kusiak et al. 1994), to evaluate the compliance with corporate rules (Namiri and Stojanovic) (Sadiq and Governatori 2010), to find possible risks (Herrmann and Herrmann 2006; Jallow et al. 2006), to assess the overall performance of an organization (Kueng 2000), or to reorganize processes, e.g., through implementing ICT-concepts (Arendsen et al. 2008; Becker et al. 2008). Assessing this way of business process analysis, it can be stated that this approach is expensive, time consuming and, as the explorative examination only is done by consultants, not in every case comprehensible to the decision makers. Due to these reasons a common, transparent, and fast way of semantic process analysis, an automated support is desirable.

So far, process modeling has mainly been performed with generic (general-purpose) languages (Algermissen et al. 2005; Janssen 2005). These modeling languages, such as Activity Diagrams (AD) (Object Management Group 2004), Business Process Modeling Notation (BPMN) (Object Management Group 2006), or Event-driven Process Chains (EPC) (Scheer 2000), are flexible instruments to describe diverse processes in many different domains. However, they usually cannot answer in particular specific questions like: (a) how can a very large number of processes be acquired efficiently, (b) what changes have what impact on the process efficiency, or (c) what processes, activities, or products depend on which legal regulations (Fraser et al. 2003; Seltsikas and Palkovits 2006) in an automated way. This result in the conclusion that these generic approaches are not suitable for an automated semantic process analysis as a direct combination of modeling elements and analysis algorithms is not possible as an inherent domain ontology is missing.

In recent years four different approaches for the automated analysis of BPMos have emerged (Pfeiffer 2008). The formal structural, the formal behavioral, the semantic annotation-based, and the modeling language-based approach have been suggested:

- In the *formal structural approach* to analyze BPMs, the models are considered as graphs. Similarity metrics for graphs have been suggested based on the maximal common subgraph (Bunke and Shearer 1998) or the graph edit distance (Bunke 1997). In the structural approach two BPMos are equivalent when they have the same formal structure.
- The *formal behavioral approach* is concerned with the dynamic aspects of process models. The approach comprises multiple, varyingly strong equivalence notions which rely on the formal execution semantics of the underlying models (e.g., Arnold 1993; de Medeiros et al. 2008; Hidders et al. 2005; Hirshfeld 1993; Pomello et al. 1992). In general, two BPMos are considered equivalent in this approach when both models show an identical behavior during a simulation.
- The *semantic annotation-based* approach has its roots in the ontological research on the foundations of conceptual modeling (Guizzardi et al. 2002a; Wand and Weber 1990). It addresses the analysis of BPMos by offering a common terminological reference point in the form of a domain ontology (Höfferer 2007; Thomas and Fellmann 2007). Two model elements are identical when they refer to the same ontology element.
- The *modeling language-based* approach is concerned with specifically designed business process modeling grammars that avoid semantic conflicts in the first place (Pfeiffer 2007). It addresses the problem of deviations by offering language constructs that limit the choices of the model creator. For this purpose, the set of constructs is carefully selected, and restrictive meta-models or grammars are defined. In this approach, two model elements are the same when they have been constructed from the same real-world fact.

In order to automatically analyze BPMos a holistic approach is needed. A detailed examination of the existing approaches shows that they only partially solve the semantic analysis conflicts (Pfeiffer 2008). Therefore, an integrated approach is required that handles all conflicts which can occur while modeling and comparing different BPMo in an automated form.

The objective of this chapter is to describe an approach for the automated analysis of BPMos. We call this the *semantic building block-based approach*, which is an integration of the semantic annotation-based and modeling language-based approach. To reach this aim the semantic building block-based approach is conceptually introduced and empirically evaluated.

This chapter proceeds as follows: in the next section issues and conflicts of a semantic analysis of BPMos are discussed. It is explained what factors hamper their automated semantic analysis. In the subsequent section, the semantic building block-based approach is described. Its main characteristics are presented and it is illustrated how the approach avoids the semantic analysis conflicts. In the following section, the semantic building block-based approach is evaluated with respect to its practical usefulness, its ability to resolve the conflicts, and its support of an automated analysis. The chapter closes with a short discussion of our contribution and an outlook to further research.

2 Semantic Analysis of Business Process Models

2.1 Semantic Issues in Automated Business Process Analysis

With an analysis, a BPMo is examined for specific structural or behavioral properties. As the analysis is a read-only operation, the BPMo is not modified during that process. An analysis operation takes BPMos as input. As output, it provides specific facts about the BPMo based on the given data. The semantic analysis of BPMos is concerned with providing relevant facts for human actors. It leads to answers to decision-relevant issues from the perspective of a managerial audience. These can, for example, be questions such as: does a process comply with the quality regulations of an organization (Namiri and Stojanovic 2007), are there any substantial weaknesses in the process (Becker et al. 2007c), is a service in two different organizations performed by the same process (Pfeiffer and Gehlert 2005), or how much money could be saved through the introduction of a Document Management System (Baacke et al. 2007a)?

A BPMo is constructed based on two different languages, a modeling language and a domain language. On the one hand, the modeling language provides the categories and distinctions, so called *constructs*, to give the world a structure. Modeling language constructs are for example "events," "functions," "organizational units," or "documents." On the other hand, a domain language is used to make *statements* about the world. For instance, a statement could be "Application arrives," "Application has arrived," or "Application is checked". To create a BPMo means to apply a modeling language together with a domain language. A modeling language construct is employed to more precisely characterize a domain statement. The results are model elements such as the *event* "Application arrives" or the *function* "Application is checked". The role of these the two languages is explained in Fig. 1.

The semantics of the modeling language constructs and the domain language statements are defined in a different way. The semantics of a modeling language is

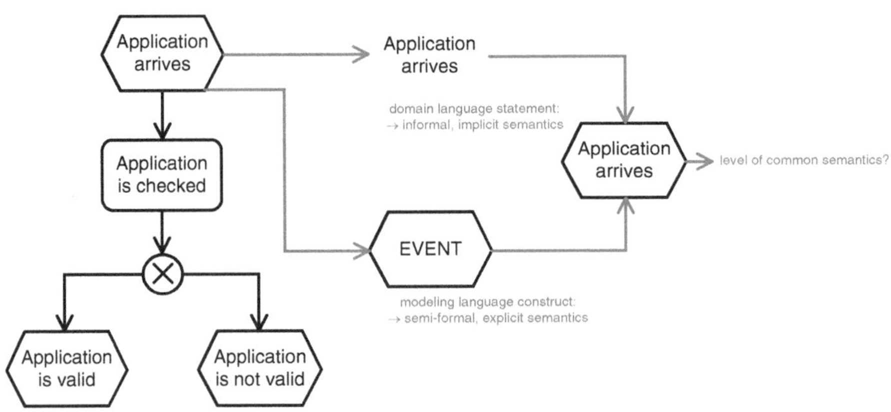

Fig. 1 Influence of the modeling and domain language on the semantics of a BPM

at least semiformally specified. This means the language has a precisely defined syntax and an explicitly stated semantics. Therefore, the modeling language constructs can be automatically examined as their meaning is precisely known. In contrast, a domain language has an informal, partially implicit semantics. It is in possession of a linguistic community that decides on the meaning of the corresponding language statements by shared conventions. These shared conventions have been established implicitly by using the language. Consequently, only the linguistic community can decide on the correctness of a domain language statement. The behavior of a linguistic community can only be partially simulated by a computer. Therefore, it is difficult to analyze the semantics of a domain language statement in an automated form as complex natural language processing is necessary. Furthermore, automated natural language processing is still an active research field that has not yet provided a final solution to automate the understanding of natural languages.

2.2 *Semantic Analysis Conflicts*

From the findings of the last section it can be concluded that the equivalence of two domain statements cannot be precisely identified in an automated way. However, the semantics of BPMos is significantly influenced by domain statements. Therefore, it is most likely that due to the current limitations of natural language processing manual involvement is needed to enable a computer to analyze BPMos. Thus, an examination of possible conflicts which may be arose while analyzing BPMos is necessary to discuss the feasibility of a fully automated semantic analysis. Disregarding the natural language part only allows for an automated syntactical analysis of BPMos which will not deliver a sufficient result set for later on decision making of, e.g., process reorganization. If these conflicts can be avoided in the first place, i.e., during the construction of a BPMo, an automated analysis is possible.

A *conflict* is a semantic or syntactic deviation between different models that refer to the same or a similar real-world phenomenon. Conflicts can be due to two different reasons (Soffer and Hadar 2007). First, they can be caused by a varying mental representation of the world. Second, different decisions during the explication of the mental representation can lead to the conflicts.

- *Conflicts due to varying mental representations.* The mental representations of two model creators are most likely not exactly the same. This means the model creators perceive or structure real-world phenomena differently. Likewise, they can, consciously or unconsciously, consider deviating aspects of the phenomenon as relevant. This can lead to BPMos at diverse levels of abstraction (Polyvyanyy et al. 2010). Likewise, in these models the sequence of activities can vary or the model elements can be annotated with a different number of details.
- *Conflicts due to the explication.* Even when the model creators share "the same" mental representation conflicts can arise. These conflicts result from a different

explication of the mental representations. Domain and modeling languages offer certain degrees of freedom to express a given fact. Model creators can utilize this freedom in diverse ways. For example, different domain statements can be chosen to express a specific aspect of the mental representation. Similarly, a model creator may have the choice between multiple constructs to describe a given fact. Thus, even with equivalent mental representation, different BPMos with corresponding conflicts can emerge.

It is important to stress that conflicts are not necessarily unwanted. In large modeling projects it is often helpful to start with an abstract model, to gradually decompose it, and, subsequently, to refine the emerging parts (Soffer et al. 2003). This leads to BPMos with different levels of abstraction. Likewise, it can be reasonable to avoid presenting the same aspects of a model to all target groups (Becker et al. 2007b). Consequently, BPMos with a varying number of elements can emerge. However, although the conflicts may serve a specific purpose, they become problematic when multiple BPMos have to be analyzed in automated form. While analyzing BPMos with such conflicts similar processes will not be found. If decision makers are searching, e.g., for similar weaknesses within BPMos it is much more difficult to find sufficient potentials for process improvement as many similarities remain undetected. If process improvement is contemplated, e.g., through ICT-investments the case could arose that not enough saving potentials can be found although an introduction of ICT should be worthwhile.

Deviations between models have been investigated especially in the context of structural models. UML Class Diagrams have been analyzed in multiple modeling experiments (Hadar and Soffer 2006; Lange and Chaudron 2006; Soffer and Hadar 2007). Other studies have focused mainly on the advantages of specific constructs in comparison to alternative forms of representation, such as entity types and attributes (Shanks et al. 2003), properties of relations (Burton-Jones and Meso 2002; Burton-Jones and Weber 1999), optional properties (Bodart et al. 2001), or whole–part relations (Shanks et al. 2002). There are only a very few empirical studies that refer to variations in process models. Mendling et al. (2006), for example, have analyzed the SAP Reference Model to identify errors and inconsistencies. Gruhn and Laue (2007) have investigated the role of OR-connectors in EPC models, Recker (2008) has analyzed BPMN notation and has identified several shortcomings in usage, e.g., regarding lack of comparability. Beneath these studies, conflicts between models have theoretically been discussed in the database schema matching and integration literature (e.g., Batini et al. 1986; Kashyap and Sheth 1996; Lawrence and Barker 2001; Parent and Spaccapietra 1998), in publications about meta-modeling (e.g., Rosemann and zur Mühlen 1998), and ontology engineering (Davis et al. 2003). In this chapter, we draw upon Pfeiffer (2008) (Breuker et al. 2009) who has derived an extensive theoretical analysis of the conflicts in the context of business process modeling. The different semantic analysis conflicts are described in Table 1 as well as exemplified in Figs. 2 and 3. In order to automate the semantic analysis of BPMos these conflicts have to be avoided or resolved.

Table 1 Description of the semantic analysis conflicts

Conflict name	Conflict description
Type conflict	Two model elements have the same meaning but a different construct (type) assigned. The model elements "drawing is delivered" and "drawing has been delivered' in Fig. 2 have an equivalent semantics but different types "function" and "event" assigned.
Synonym conflict	Two model elements have the same meaning but different labels. Consider for example the model elements "accept payment" and "receive payment" in Fig. 2.
Homonym conflict	Two model elements have the same label but a different meaning. Consider for instance the two model elements in Fig. 2 that are annotated by the domain statement "contact drawer." The model element "contact drawer" in the first model stands for getting in touch with an artist. The same model element in the second BPMo, however, refers to contacting the drawer of a promissory note.
Abstraction conflict	Model elements in two different models have a deviating level of abstraction. The model element "ship drawing" in the first BPMo in Fig. 2 is for instance more general than two or more model elements in the second BPMo. The model elements "package drawing" and "commit package to logistics provider" in the second model are more specific than "ship drawing".
Control flow conflict	The number of outgoing or incoming control flows of two corresponding model elements differs. An example for a control flow conflict is described in Fig. 3.
Annotation conflict	A model element in the first model is annotated with a different number of model elements or different types of model elements than a model element with a similar meaning in the second model. For instance, in Fig. 2 the model element "accept payment" is not annotated by a document. In contrast, the model element "receive payment" is annotated with the document "promissory note".
Order conflict	The order of the two model elements is permuted between two BPMs. For instance the model element "pay artist" in the first model in Fig. 2 has a different predecessor and successor than the same element in the second model.
Separation conflict	There is a model element that has no corresponding model element in the second model with the same, a more general, or a more specific meaning. The model element "book transaction" in the first BPMo (Fig. 2) has no corresponding counterpart in the second BPMo.

In the next section, an approach is described that avoids most of these conflicts by offering a specifically designed business process modeling language.

3 The Semantic Building Block-Based Approach

3.1 Characteristics of the Semantic Building Block-Based Approach

As stated in the introduction the *semantic building block-based approach* is based upon integration work of the semantic annotation-based and modeling language-based approach.

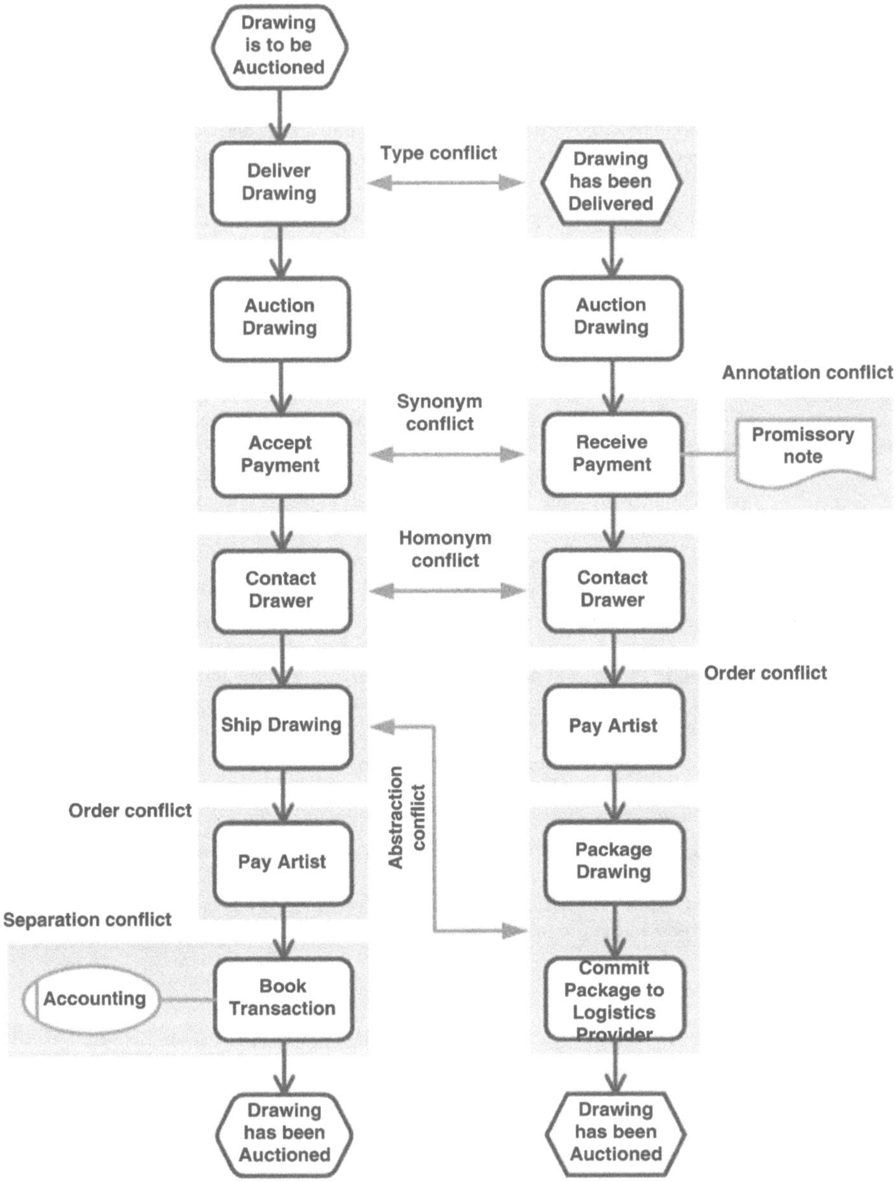

Fig. 2 Examples of major semantic analysis conflicts

The *semantic annotation-based approach* has its roots in the ontological research on the foundations of conceptual modeling (Brinkkemper et al. 1999; Guizzardi et al. 2002a; Milton and Kazmierczak 2004; Wand 1996; Wand and Weber 1990; Wimmer and Wimmer 1992). In this context, the value of ontologies for the construction and interpretation of conceptual models has been investigated

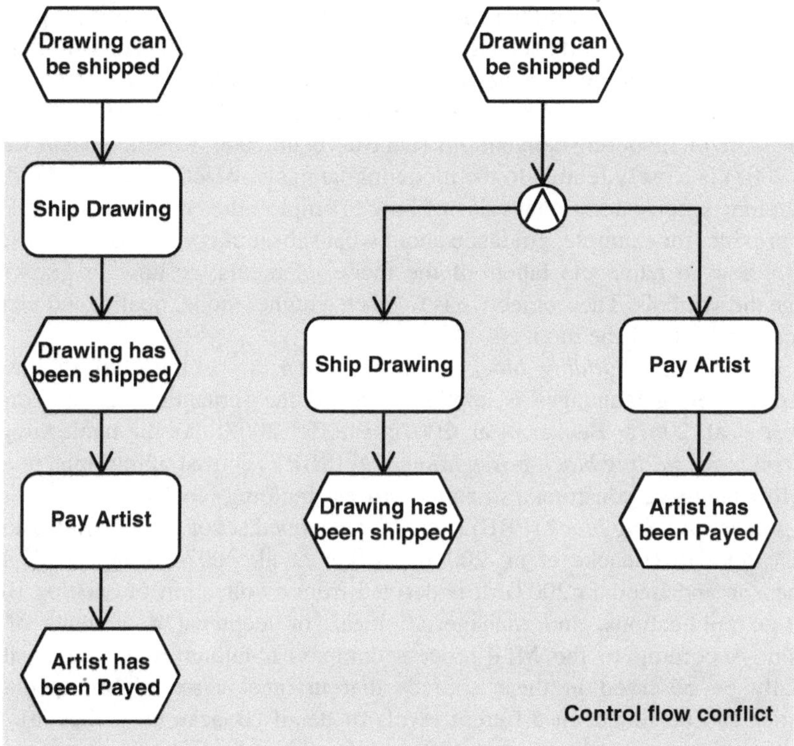

Fig. 3 Examples of a control flow conflict

and explained. Recently, the ontological description of conceptual models has been further advanced by the Semantic Business Process Management Community (SBPM) (Betz et al. 2006; Brockmans et al. 2006; Ehrig et al. 2007; Hepp and Dumitri 2007; Hepp et al. 2005). The objective of SBPM is to utilize semantic web technology in the context of Business Process Management.

The semantic annotation-based approach addresses the conflicts between BPMos by offering a common terminological reference point in the form of a domain ontology. Domain ontologies are an intensively discussed measure in IS to capture the common knowledge of a certain part of reality (Chandrasekaran et al. 1999; Wimmer and Wimmer 1992). They provide a set of shared concepts that describe what exists in this specific domain and formalizes the relevant vocabulary (Evermann 2005). Therefore, they have been suggested as a mechanism to systematically guide the construction of BPMos and conceptual models in general (Guizzardi et al. 2002a, b; Mylopoulos 1998). Through a semantic annotation with elements from an ontology, BPMos are underpinned with the shared conceptual vocabulary of a specific domain (Höfferer 2007; Thomas and Fellmann 2007).

The *modeling language-based approach* is concerned with a specifically designed Business Process Modeling Grammar (BPMG) that avoids semantic conflicts in the first place. It addresses the problem of deviations by offering language constructs that limit the choices of the model creator. For this purpose, the set of constructs is carefully selected, and restrictive meta-models or grammars are defined. This can mainly be done with the help of the well-formedness conditions and a comprehensive and unambiguous definition for each construct.

The work on modeling conventions (Du Bois et al. 2006; Rosemann and van der Aalst 2007) is closely related to the modeling language-based approach. Modeling conventions specify additional rules of how to employ the constructs of a BPMG. They provide, for example, guidance about what subset of constructs to choose in a BPMG, how to name the labels of the model elements, or how to graphically arrange the symbols. Their objective is to reach a higher model quality and increase the comparability of the models.

In the *semantic building block-based approach*, a specific class of business process modeling languages is applied to avoid the semantic analysis conflicts (Becker et al. 2007a; Becker et al. 2007c; Pfeiffer 2007). As the name suggests, such *semantic building block-based languages* (SBBL) consist of multiple, reusable modeling language constructs, so-called process building blocks.

A *process building block* (PBB) stands for a defined set of reoccurring tasks in a specific domain (Baacke et al. 2007b; Becker et al. 2007c; Lang et al. 1997; Stephenson and Bandara 2007). It is derived from a collection of existing BPMs, scientific publications, and managerial, legal, or technical documents of that domain. According to the MIT process compass (Malone et al. 2003), it can normally be observed in these sources that in most cases highly specialized activities can be found on different levels of detail (Baacke et al. 2007a). Next work to do is to generalize these results while taking the occurring activities and consolidate them. Furthermore, this has to be separated from the processed information of the examined processes. All of this information can be used to create to domain ontology. The resulting PBBs have a defined level of abstraction and, most importantly, they are semantically specified by a domain statement (Rupprecht et al. 2000). Generally, a PBB has to be deemed as an atomic model element and not as a container which can be refined. They only can be further described with the help of predefined attributes (ATT). Each PBB comprises a specific set of such attributes. An example for a PBB is given in Fig. 4.

From the perspective of other modeling languages such as BPMN, EPC, or UML AD PBBs correspond to constructs such as activity, function, or sometimes also event. The difference is, however, that PBBs represent particular activities, functions, and events in a given domain. Due to this, sufficient domain ontology is necessary for the application of our approach. If there is nothing available our approach would not work. PBBs can be instantiated as any other construct and these instantiations are model elements of BPMs.

To specify the constructs of an instantiation of the class of SBBL a domain ontology is employed. Suitable, i.e., semantically disjoint, ontology elements are chosen and translated into PBBs. In Fig. 4, for example, the ontology element "encash/receive a payment" has been incorporated into an instance of a SBBL as PBB. Also the corresponding attributes of a PBB are taken from the domain ontology. In the example, the attribute "information system" has been constructed

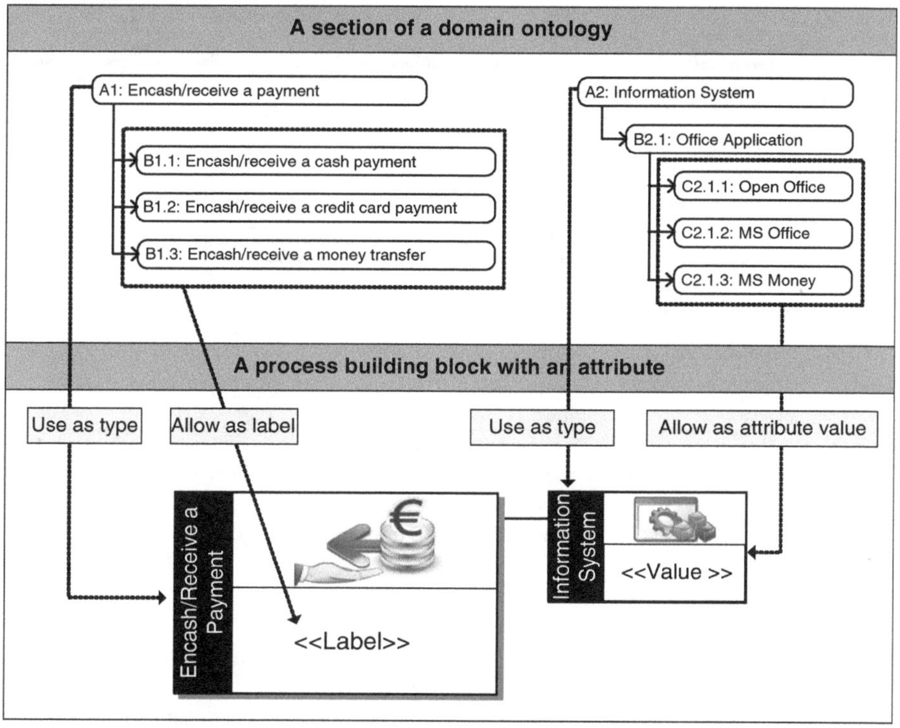

Fig. 4 A process building block and a section from a domain ontology

based on an ontology element. In the optimal case, a language can be designed which complete set of constructs is part of the domain ontology. However, from a practical perspective it is often necessary to include also at least some constructs from other modeling languages that are not part of the domain ontology. It can, for example, be necessary to add constructs to split up and join the control flow.

Not only is the type of the PBBs specified based on a domain ontology, also the range of values allowed for labels and attribute values is fixed by using the ontology. In the example of the PBB "encash/receive a payment," all kinds of subordinate tasks with specific business objects can be chosen as a label. For example, "encash/receive a cash payment," "encash/receive a credit card payment," or "encash/receive a money transfer" are allowed. Likewise, the values of the attributes can also be controlled by using the ontology. In the example of the attribute "information system" only specific office applications are permitted, such as "open office," "ms office," and "ms money". The resulting domain ontology is important for an applicable instantiation of SBBL as mentioned before. At least it is hard to decide on when the domain ontology is suitable. At least it is necessary to evaluate the results of modeling efforts and see how they are accepted by domain experts. We will come to this in our evaluation section. The meta-model of the language class SBBL is described in Fig. 5. In Table 2, the characteristics of the language class SBBL are summarized.

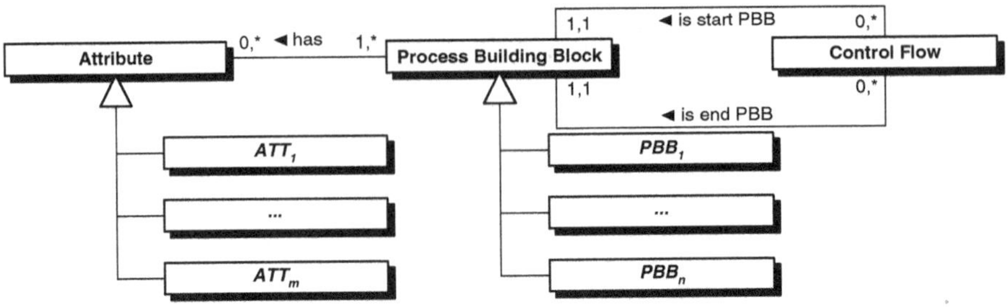

Fig. 5 Meta-model of the language class SBBL

Table 2 Characteristics of the language class SBBL

No.	Characteristic	Description
C1	Ontology-based constructs	The semantics of the constructs in SBBL is defined based on a domain statement from the domain ontology. By mapping the constructs to the ontology they are kept free of homonyms.
C2	Disjoint constructs	The constructs are chosen from the ontology such that they do not contain synonyms and have a comparable level of abstraction.
C3	Ontology-based values	All domain statements in the resulting BPMos, i.e., labels and attribute values, are also chosen from the domain ontology.
C4	Control flow rules	The number of outgoing and incoming control flows of each PBB is restricted by well-formedness conditions.
C5	Annotation rules	For each PBB it is specified how many attributes can be annotated and whether they are mandatory or optional.
C6	Order free areas	In SBBL a construct is included that defines what model elements in a BPMo have an arbitrary order. The construct is implemented in the form of an attribute.
C7	Semantic modeling rules	The combination of model elements in the BPMos is guided by semantic rules. These rules suggest certain orders of PBBs. Furthermore, they can indicate missing or redundant PBBs in the BPMos.

3.2 Conflict Handling with Semantic Building Blocks

By using the language class SBBL, with the *process building block-based approach* BPMos can be created that are tailored to the purposes of semantic process analysis. In the following, the coverage of the analysis conflicts within the semantic PBB-based approach is discussed.

- *Type conflicts.* All PBBs and attributes that are included in a SBBL have to be semantically disjoint (cf. C2). In Pfeiffer (2007), it has been proven that type conflicts can be completely avoided if this condition is fulfilled. Hence, when there are no constructs that overlap semantically, then different model creators are urged to pick the same PBB and attributes to represent a given phenomenon. In this way, type conflicts cannot emerge.

- *Synonym conflicts.* The language class SBBL avoids synonym conflicts because it offers a controlled vocabulary in the form of domain ontology (cf. C1, C3). All labels and attribute values can only be chosen from the domain ontology. Within the domain ontology synonyms can be made explicit. Alternatively, they can be eliminated in the first place if only one of the synonym domain statements is included in the domain ontology. Consequently, different model creators have no alternative statement available to express a given phenomenon. Therefore, synonym conflicts cannot arise.
- *Homonym conflicts.* Homonym conflicts are avoided based on the domain ontology due to three different reasons (cf. C1, C3). First, during the construction of the domain ontology, ambiguous statements that may have multiple distinct meanings are not included. Second, for each domain statement within the ontology, an explicit definition is provided. However, this definition describes only one meaning of a domain statement. Model creators are guided by these definitions when they select a label or attribute value. Consequently, they are encouraged to employ a domain statement in the sense it is suggested by its definition. Third, the type of a PBB and the type of an attribute constrain the selection of corresponding labels and attribute values. Since the domain statements must be more specific than their types, a model creator is substantially restricted in choosing a domain statement. Thus, there is only a very limited probability that one of the remaining choices has multiple meanings in this particular context. By taking the three measures together homonym conflicts can be ruled out.
- *Abstraction conflicts.* In a SBBL all PBBs and attributes have the same level of abstraction (cf. C1, C2). The type of a PBB covers a significant part of the semantics of a model element. In parallel, it can be enforced that the domain statement of a model element is more specific than its type. Thus, since these two aspects restrict the selection of domain statements, abstraction conflicts are significantly reduced. In order to completely avoid abstraction conflicts it is possible to define a specific area in the ontology from where all labels and attribute values have to be chosen (cf. C3). Assume, for example, that in Fig. 4 only domain statements from the B-level of the ontology can be selected. Thus, the abstraction level is fixed to the ontology elements B1.1–B1.3 and B2.1. If this measure is considered too restrictive, alternatively, abstraction conflicts can be resolved during a semantic analysis. This can be achieved when only the type of the PBB is taken into account but not its domain statement. Since both, type and domain statement, have a closely related semantics, this is an acceptable simplification. Thus, abstraction conflicts can either be avoided or resolved within the language class SBBL.
- *Control flow conflicts and annotation conflicts.* The control flow conflicts can be reduced when rules for the number of outgoing and incoming control flows are specified (cf. C4). In the case of sequential modeling, they can be completely avoided since uncontrolled split ups of control flow are not supported. Furthermore, to eliminate the annotation conflicts the attributes of each PBB can be

classified as mandatory or optional (cf. C5). For semantic modeling languages such as SBBL it is comparatively easy to specify the number of control flows and to divide the attributes into the two groups. In contrast, for a modeling language such as BPMN or EPC it is hard to decide how many control flows or attributes, in general, are relevant for an activity or function. In the case of a SBBL, however, this choice is much simpler because its constructs are more specific and related to a given domain. Let us consider the case of the PBB "perform a formal verification". Based on the knowledge about its material semantics it is unproblematic to come to a decision about what attributes should be allowed or required to be annotated. For instance, it could only be permitted to specify a single mandatory attribute in the form of a document that is verified. Likewise, it is straightforward to determine whether it makes sense to split up the control flow after a particular PBB. It could, for example, be specified that after "perform a formal verification" exactly two *control flows* must always be modeled since it implies a binary yes/no decision. Thus, control flow and *annotation conflicts* can be fully handled by SBBL.

- *Order conflicts*. Order conflicts can be partially addressed by using a construct that indicates an arbitrary order of model elements (cf. C6). In a SBBL such a construct can, for example, be added in the form of an attribute of selected PBBs. Furthermore, semantic modeling languages like SBBL allow for defining heuristic order rules for its elements (cf. C7). In contrast, in a modeling language such as BPMN or EPC it is hardly feasible to make any general statements about the order of the constructs. For instance, no viable information about an order can be drawn from the fact that a statement is typed as an activity. However, in a SBBL such semantic rules can be defined. Suppose, for example, the two PBBs "perform a formal verification" and "approve". It seems reasonable that the verification step always precedes the approval. Therefore, a corresponding rule can be specified. Consequently, the order of the PBBs can be monitored and guided by a SBBL. Thus, this language class allows for a further reduction of the order conflicts.
- *Separation conflicts*. The language class SBBL is based on a domain ontology and uses it during modeling. A model creator is supported by choosing appropriate constructs, labels, and attribute values. Thus, based on the domain statements in the ontology the scope of the modeling activities is restricted. Consequently, separation conflicts are reduced. Additionally, the domain ontology can be extended by a process catalog where the interfaces and the objectives of the processes are specified for a material domain. This catalog can guide multiple model creators to construct their BPMos with similar boundaries and contents in mind. Furthermore, semantic rules can be defined to evaluate a model for completeness (cf. C7). Assume, for example, a BPMo with "perform a formal verification" as its last PBB. It is probable that this PBB does not represent the intended end of this process since neither a decision is made nor a document created. This is an indication for a separation conflict. Hence, "approve" or "archive" could be suggested as potentially following PBBs (Betz et al. 2006). With such plausibility checks missing model elements can be identified and,

thus, variations with respect to their number can be harmonized. Therefore, SBBL also partially addresses separation conflicts.

Based on these results it can be concluded that the semantic building block-based approach allows avoiding most semantic analysis conflicts. Thus, it offers the basis for an automated analysis of BPMos. In the next section, empirical evidence is provided that the semantic building block-based approach as one instantiation of the class of SBBL enables an automated analysis of BPMos in practice.

4 Evaluation of the Semantic Building Block-Based Approach

The semantic building block-based approach has been derived with respect to avoiding the analysis conflicts. Based on these theoretical properties of the semantic building block-based approach empirically testable propositions can be derived. The first proposition refers to the question of whether the class SBBL allows for deriving a nonempty set of practically useful languages:

PR1. Based on the language class SBBL practically relevant business process modeling languages can be instantiated.

The answer to proposition PR1 is crucial to decide on two important questions. First, PR1 addresses the issue of whether the language class SBBL has a sufficiently large scope of application such that a practical adoption is possible. Second, it refers to the problem of whether an analysis based on the models of SBBL can cover practically relevant cases. Both aspects are directly related to the general usefulness of the semantic building block-based approach.

A second proposition is concerned with the adequacy of the analysis result. It refers to the elimination of conflicts by applying the language class SBBL:

PR2. All BPMos of a given (real world) business process described with the language class SBBL exhibit significantly fewer semantic analysis conflicts than models that are formulated with a traditional business process modeling language.

The answer to proposition PR2 has important implications on the quality of the analysis results. In the semantic building block-based approach, syntactic operations are employed to perform a semantic analysis. This presupposes that two BPMos that refer to the same (real world) process have to share an identical structure and must consist of corresponding pairs of syntactically equivalent domain statements. It is evident that this assumption only holds when all of the eight conflicts have been eliminated. However, if empirical results show that not all of these conflicts are avoided or, alternatively, so far unknown conflicts are found, this precondition is violated. Consequently, a semantic analysis will return wrong results. However, to empirically support the viability of the semantic building block-based approach it is sufficient to find evidence that it performs better than the established analysis approaches.

A third proposition is connected with the theoretical result that the semantic analysis can be automated based on SBBL. It addresses the issue if a software-based analysis is feasible from an empirical perspective:

PR3. For BPMos of SBBL the semantic analysis operations can be automated.

The straightforward way to demonstrate that such automation is feasible is to provide software that implements semantic analysis operations.

4.1 Applicability of Semantic Building Block-Based Languages

In the IS literature, the PICTURE-language is a well documented example for a SBBL (Becker et al. 2007a; Becker et al. 2007c). The PICTURE-language has been specifically designed for the public administration domain. It consists of 24 PBBs and more than 50 attributes that can be used to further describe the PBBs. The PICTURE-language is supported by a procedure model and has been implemented in a corresponding process modeling tool. Examples of PBBs in PICTURE are "document/information comes in," "perform a formal verification," "enter data into IT," "print," or "scan". A complete overview of the 24 PBBs is given in Becker et al. (2007a). Typical attributes of the PBB "document/information comes in" are, for instance, "document received," "information system," or "sending organizational unit". The values of these attributes are chosen from predefined lists of business documents and IT components. For the organizational units a corresponding hierarchy is also provided. With the PICTURE-language business processes are modeled only in a sequential form. Concurrent or alternative process flows are either represented by attributes or in the form of process variants.

Figure 6 shows the process "Update Citizen Register" as an example of a PICTURE-model. The process is triggered when a citizen moves to a new address. By law a citizen is required to inform the government by handing in a change request. This fact is visualized by using the PBB "Incoming Document." Within the following four columns additional information is given regarding attributes, the organization responsible, the business object, and the resources used to process the building block. This information is relevant for an analysis of the process model. The next step within the process depicted by the next PBB is "Formal Assessment." In this PBB, the completeness of the change request is verified. Afterwards the citizen register database is updated and the change request is archived for at least 1 year.

Up to now the PICTURE-language has been applied in 12 public administrations in two different federal states in Germany (cf. Table 3). Altogether, 1,056 processes of different size and complexity have been modeled with this approach within these projects. As described in Becker et al. (2007a), the resulting BPMos have been used for process analysis and to derive reorganization proposals. For instance, in the project at the University of Münster more than 40 suggestions for process improvements could be made based on the BPMos.

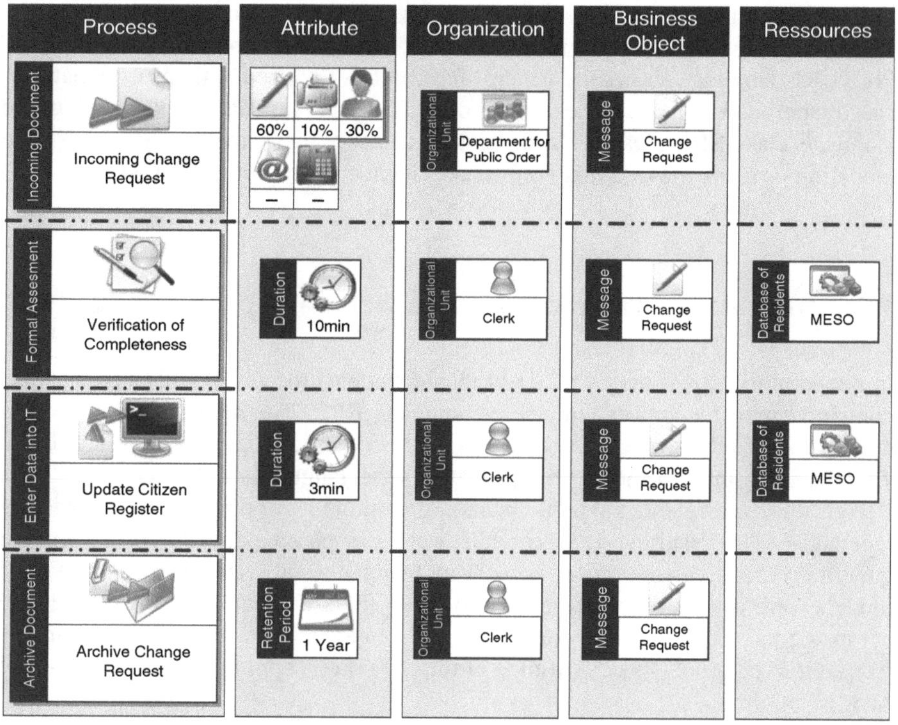

Fig. 6 Example process "Update Citizen Register" in PICTURE-Notation

Table 3 Overview of the processes modeled in PICTURE-projects

Year	PICTURE-project	Number of processes
2005	Administration of the University of Münster (PICTURE@UNI)	209
2006	Examination offices at the University of Münster (PICTURE TE@M)	28
2006	Municipality of the city of Hagen	162
2006	Municipality of the city of Münster (PICTURE@MS)	172
2007	Ministry of the Interior Baden-Württemberg	2
2007	Municipality of Altenberge (ProWiKom)	379
2007	Municipality of the city of Datteln	12
2007	Regional board of Freiburg	9
2007	Regional board of Karlsruhe	12
2007	Regional board of Stuttgart	27
2007	Regional board of Tübingen	9
2008	District of Ortenau in Offenburg	35
	Total number	1,056

This high amount of successfully created BPMos demonstrates that the PICTURE-language is applicable in the public administration domain. In parallel, the PICTURE-language shows the general feasibility of the semantic process pattern-based approach. Thus, the example of PICTURE-language confirms that the language class SBBL can be instantiated. Consequently, the results from these modeling projects provide first empirical evidence that proposition PR1 holds.

4.2 Adequacy of the Analysis

In a laboratory experiment with 13 graduate students the PICTURE-language was compared with the process modeling language EPC. The students were given a description of the business processes "issue resident parking permit" in text form. They had the task to model this process in the languages EPC and PICTURE. Before the experiment, all participants were trained in applying both modeling languages. The resulting EPC models were compared pair-wise based on the quantitative equivalence criterion of van Dongen et al. (2008). The PICTURE models were manually transformed into EPCs first. Subsequently, they were also compared pair-wise with the metric of van Dongen et al. (2008). For the comparisons, the ProM-tool (Process Mining Group 2007) was applied that implements the metric.

While the PICTURE models have achieved an average similarity of 47.45%, the EPCs could only reach a value of 0.43%. It can be concluded then, that for the process "issue resident parking permit," PICTURE avoids more conflicts than the language EPC. An additional manual analysis revealed that the deviations that can still be found in the PICTURE models are mainly due to separation and order conflicts. In contrast, in the EPC models all kinds of conflicts could be identified. In particular, synonym and control flow conflicts emerged very frequently. The low average similarity value of the EPC models can be explained by the high number of conflicts that could not be resolved by the ProM-tool. This finding provides support for proposition PR2 that models of the PICTURE-language, in general, exhibit fewer conflicts (Breuker et al. 2009).

4.3 Automation of the Analysis

Proposition PR3 states that the semantic analysis of BPMos can be automated if the language class SBBL is applied. This means for PICTURE that its corresponding modeling tool should be able to implement semantic analysis operations. Currently, the PICTURE modeling tool comprises a comparison and a pattern search module. These modules allow for a quantitative as well as qualitative analysis of the PICTURE-BPMos.

In the qualitative part of the comparison module two given BPMos can be matched and their differences visualized. This feature is helpful for an in-depth analysis of BPMos. However, from a practical perspective, it is not only interesting to get a mapping between model elements but also to identify similar BPMos in a large set of processes. Thus, within the quantitative part of the module, it is possible to compare a specific BPMo with a set of other models. The results of this operation are the most similar process models with respect to a given BPMo.

With the pattern search module PICTURE-BPMos can be analyzed for specific reoccurring sequences of model elements. In the PICTURE-tool, a pattern consists of a sequence of PBBs that can exhibit specific corresponding attribute values. A pattern can contain required and/or unwanted PBBs as well as placeholders for arbitrary PBBs. In order to quantify the specific effect of a match, a pattern can be connected to key figures. A key figure is a formula that is defined based on the attributes of a PBB. Examples of key figures are “processing time of the process,” “printed pages per year,” or “number of cases per year”. The data to calculate the key figure is derived from the attribute values of the BPMos where the pattern is found. Based on patterns and key figures, reports can be compiled. When a report is accessed, a pattern search is executed. All available BPMos are analyzed to see whether they match. For the BPMos that fit to the pattern the key figures are computed and displayed in the report. Process patterns of this relatively simple form have proven to be sufficient to search the BPMos in the PICTURE-tool. The experiences from the implementation of the pattern search module demonstrate that the elimination of conflicts within the PICTURE-language significantly simplifies the matching algorithm.

Figure 7 shows the screenshot of the specification of a *pattern* in the PICTURE-tool. The pattern is called “processing time for scanning documents.” It consists of

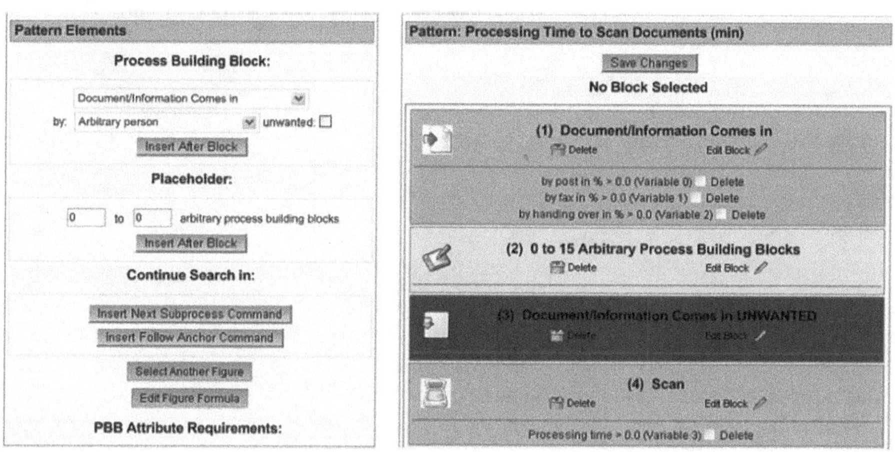

Fig. 7 Specification of a process pattern in the PICTURE-tool (Becker et al. 2008)

the PBB "document/information comes in," up to 15 arbitrary intermediate steps where other documents must not arrive, and the PBB "scan". Thus, this pattern matches a situation where a document is received in paper form and is the implementation of C7 *Semantic modeling rules* of the definition of SBBL. Subsequently, some process steps are performed before it is scanned. This pattern is an indicator for a media break. A technology that addresses media breaks is a Document Management System (DMS). In Fig. 8, a report is shown that calculates the expected savings potential of the introduction of a DMS. The saving potentials are calculated based on different assumptions. On the one side through the introduction of a DMS, some activities (represented through PBB) can be canceled; other activities can be sped up through the support of a DMS. Within the calculation formula these assumptions are integrated and linked to occurring activities. This allows us to calculate the potentials based on the given quantitative numbers like process cases per year or handling times. The key figures in the screenshot have corresponding patterns too, similar to "processing time for scanning documents".

The implementation of the operations comparison and pattern search in the PICTURE-tool shows that the semantic analysis of process models can be realized based on the PICTURE-language. This finding is a strong argument in favor of proposition PR3 and the conclusion that semantic operations can in general be automated for the language class SBBL.

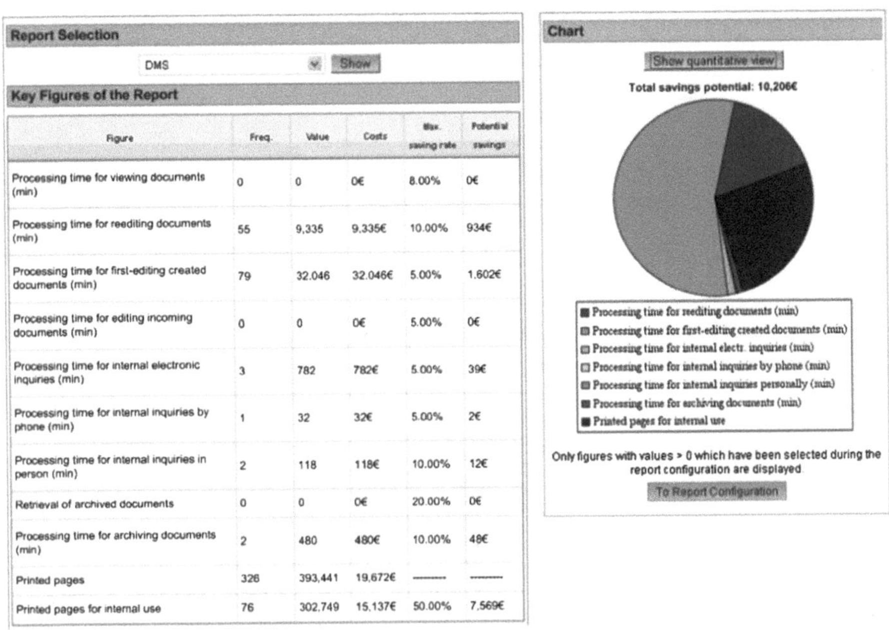

Figure	Freq.	Value	Costs	Max. saving rate	Potential savings
Processing time for viewing documents (min)	0	0	0€	8.00%	0€
Processing time for reediting documents (min)	55	9,335	9,335€	10.00%	934€
Processing time for first-editing created documents (min)	79	32,046	32,046€	5.00%	1,602€
Processing time for editing incoming documents (min)	0	0	0€	5.00%	0€
Processing time for internal electronic inquiries (min)	3	782	782€	5.00%	39€
Processing time for internal inquiries by phone (min)	1	32	32€	5.00%	2€
Processing time for internal inquiries in person (min)	2	118	118€	10.00%	12€
Retrieval of archived documents	0	0	0€	20.00%	0€
Processing time for archiving documents (min)	2	480	480€	10.00%	48€
Printed pages	326	393,441	19,672€	--------	--------
Printed pages for internal use	76	302,749	15,137€	50.00%	7,569€

Fig. 8 Report in the PICTURE-tool regarding a DMS (Becker et al. 2008)

5 Summary and Outlook

The starting point of this chapter has been the observation that BPMos are mainly analyzed manually in practice leading to an expensive and complex analysis. Based on the insight that a holistic approach for the automated analysis of BPMos is missing, the semantic building block-based approach has been proposed. It has been described that this approach solves the majority of the semantic analysis conflicts. Subsequently, the semantic building block-based approach has been evaluated from a theoretical and an empirical perspective. Based on the PICTURE-language an implementation of the language class SBBL has been described.

For the PICTURE-language there exists a modeling tool that implements the operations comparison and pattern search. In order to practically apply a pattern search, a set of appropriate process patterns is required. Currently, only a few proposals for process patterns exist in the IS literature (e.g., Baacke et al. 2007a; Becker et al. 2006; Namiri and Stojanovic 2007). Therefore, it is a subject for further research to identify process patterns for different purposes and subject areas.

Future research can also focus on the transfer of SBBL to other domains. With PICTURE, the language class SBBL has been implemented for process modeling in public administrations. Some of the PBBs in PICTURE, however, stand for activities that can also be found in private organizations. Thus, the general approach may also be helpful in other domains. Promising areas seem to be, for example, the financial sector, the insurance industry, or health care systems. Currently, there is an ongoing project that strives for deriving a SBBL for the banking domain. Additional implementations of SBBL are necessary to further evaluate the semantic building block-based approach.

References

Algermissen L, Delfmann P, Niehaves, B (2005) Experiences in process-oriented reorganization through reference modelling in public administrations – the case study Regio@KomM. In: Proceedings of the 13th European conference on information systems (ECIS 2005), Regensburg

Arendsen R, van Engers T, Schurink W (2008) Adoption of high impact governmental eServices: seduce or enforce? In: Wimmer MA, Scholl HJ, Ferro E (eds) Proceedings of the 7th international conference on electronic government (EGOV 2008) at the 19th international conference on database and expert systems applications (DEXA 2008), Turin, Italy, pp 73–84

Arnold A (1993) Verification and comparison of transition systems. In: Gaudel M-C, Jouannaud J-P (eds) Proceedings of the 4th international joint conference on theory and practice of software development (TAPSOFT 1993), Orsay, France, pp 121–135

Baacke L, Fitterer R, Rohner P (2007a) Measuring impacts of ICT on the process landscape of public administrations. In: Remenyi D (ed) Proceedings of the 3rd international conference on e-government (ICEG 2007), Montreal, Canada, 2007, pp 21–30

Baacke L, Rohner P, Winter R (2007b) Aggregation of reference process building blocks to improve modeling in public administrations. In: Grönlund A, Scholl HJ, Wimmer MA (eds) Electronic government: 6th international EGOV conference, proceedings of ongoing research, project contributions and workshops, Trauner Druck, Linz, 2007, pp 149–156

Batini C, Lenzerini M, Navathe SB (1986) A comparative analysis of methodologies for database schema integration. ACM Comput Surv 18(4):323–364

Becker J, Algermissen L, Falk T, Pfeiffer D, Fuchs P (2006) Model based identification and measurement of reorganization potential in public administrations: the PICTURE-approach. In: Proceedings of the 10th pacific Asia conference on information systems (PACIS 2006), Kuala Lumpur, Malaysia, 2006, pp 860–875

Becker J, Algermissen L, Pfeiffer D, Räckers M (2007a) Bausteinbasierte Modellierung von Prozesslandschaften mit der PICTURE-Methode am Beispiel der Universitätsverwaltung Münster. Wirtschaftsinformatik 49(4):267–279

Becker J, Bergener P, Kleist S, Pfeiffer D, Räckers M (2008) Evaluation of ICT investments in public administrations based on business process models. In: Proceedings of the 14th Americas conference on information systems (AMCIS 2008), Toronto, Canada, 2008, pp 1–12

Becker J, Delfmann P, Knackstedt R (2007b) Adaptive reference modeling: integrating configurative and generic adaptation techniques for information models. In: Becker J, Delfmann P (eds) Reference modeling: efficient information systems design through reuse of information models. Physica, Heidelberg, pp 23–49

Becker J, Pfeiffer D, Räckers M (2007c) Domain specific process modelling in public administrations: the PICTURE-approach. In: Wimmer MA, Scholl HJ, Grönlund A (eds) Proceedings of the 6th international conference on electronic government (EGOV 2007) at the 18th international conference on database and expert systems applications (DEXA 2007), Regensburg, Germany, 2007, pp 68–79

Benamou N (2005) Bringing eGovernment interoperability to local governments in Europe. Eur Rev Polit Technol 3(1):1–9

Betz S, Klink S, Koschmider A, Oberweis A (2006) Automatic user support for business process modeling. In: Hinkelmann K, Karagiannis D, Stojanovic N, Wagner G (eds) Proceedings of the workshop on semantics for business process management at the 3rd European semantic web conference (ESWC 2006), Budva, Montenegro, 2006, pp 1–12

Bodart F, Patel A, Sim M, Weber R (2001) Should optional properties be used in conceptual modelling: a theory and three empirical tests. Inform Syst Res 12(4):384–405

Breuker D, Pfeiffer D, Becker J (2009) Reducing the variations in intra- and interorganizational business process modeling – an empirical evaluation. In: Proceedings of the internationale tagung wirtschaftsinformatik, Wien, Austria, 2009

Brinkkemper S, Saeki M, Harmsen F (1999) Meta-modelling based assembly techniques for situational method engineering. Inform Syst 24(3):209–228

Brockmans S, Ehrig M, Koschmider A, Oberweis A, Studer R (2006) Semantic alignment of business processes. In: Manolopoulos Y, Filipe J, Constantopoulos P, Cordeiro J (eds) Proceedings of the 8th international conference on enterprise information systems (ICEIS 2006), Paphos, Cyprus, 2006, pp 191–196

Bunke H (1997) On a relation between graph edit distance and maximum common subgraph. Pattern Recognit Lett 18(8):689–694

Bunke H, Shearer K (1998) A graph distance metric based on the maximal common subgraph. Pattern Recognit Lett 19(3):255–259

Burton-Jones A, Meso P (2002) How good are these UML diagrams: an empirical test of the Wand and Weber good decomposition model. In: Applegate L, Galliers R, DeGross J (eds) Proceedings of the 23rd international conference on information systems (ICIS 2002), Barcelona, Spain, 2002, pp 101–114

Burton-Jones A, Weber R (1999) Understanding relationships with attributes in entity-relationship diagrams. In: De P, De Gross JI (eds) Proceedings of the 20th international conference on information systems (ICIS 1999), Charlotte, NC, 1999, pp 214–228

Chandrasekaran B, Joesephson J, Benjamins R (1999) What are ontologies and why do we need them? IEEE Intell Syst 14(1):20–26

Dalal NP, Kamath M, Kolarik WJ, Sivaraman E (2004) Toward an integrated framework for modeling enterprise processes. Commun ACM 47(3):83–87

Davenport TH, Beers M (1995) Managing information about processes. J Manage Inform Syst 12(1):57–80

Davenport TH, Short JE (1990) The new industrial engineering: information technology and business process redesign. Sloan Manage Rev 31(4):11–27
Davis I, Green P, Milton S, Rosemann M (2003) Using meta models for the comparison of ontologies. In: Siau K, Krogstie J, Halpin T (eds) Proceedings of the 8th international workshop on evaluation of modeling methods in systems analysis and design (EMMSAD 2003) at the 15th international conference on advanced information systems engineering (CAiSE 2003), Velden, Austria, 2003, pp 1–10
de Medeiros AKA, van der Aalst WMP, Weijters AJMM (2008) Quantifying process equivalence based on observed behavior. Data Knowl Eng 64(1):55–74
Du Bois B, Lange CFJ, Demeyer S, Chaudron MRV (2006) A qualitative investigation of UML modeling conventions. In: Kühne T (ed) Proceedings of the 1st workshop on quality in modeling at the 9th international conference on model driven engineering languages and systems (MoDELS 2006), Genoa, Italy, 2006, pp 91–100
Ehrig M, Koschmider A, Oberweis A (2007) Measuring similarity between semantic business process models. In: Roddick JF, Hinze A (eds) Proceedings of the 4th Asia-pacific conference on conceptual modelling (APCCM 2007), Ballarat, Australia, 2007, pp 71–80
Evermann J (2005) Towards cognitive foundation for knowledge representation. Inform Syst J 15(2):147–178
Fraser J, Adams N, Macintosh A, McKay-Hubbard A, Lobo TP, Pardo PF, Martínez RC, Vallecillo JS (2003) Knowledge management applied to E-government services: the use of an ontology. In: Proceedings of the knowledge management in electronic government (KMGov 2003), Rhodes, Greece, 2003, pp 116–126
Gruhn V, Laue R (2007) What business process modelers can learn from programmers. Sci Comput Program 65(1):4–13
Guizzardi G, Herre H, Wagner G (2002a) On the general ontological foundations of conceptual modeling. In: Spaccapietra S, March ST, Kambayashi Y (eds) Proceedings of the 21st international conference on conceptual modeling (ER 2002), Tampere, Finland, 2002, pp 65–78
Guizzardi G, Pires LF, van Sinderen MJ (2002b) On the role of domain ontologies in the design of domain-specific visual modeling languages. In: Tolvanen J-P, Gray J, Rossi M (eds) Proceedings of the 2nd workshop on domain-specific visual languages at the 17th annual ACM conference on object-oriented programming, systems, languages and applications (OOPSLA 2002), Seattle, WA, 2002, pp 1–14
Hadar I, Soffer P (2006) Variations in conceptual modeling: classification and ontological analysis. J Assoc Inform Syst 7(8):568–592
Hepp M, Dumitri R (2007) An ontology framework for semantic business process management. In: Oberweis A, Weinhardt C, Gimpel H, Koschmider A, Pankratius V, Schnizler B (eds) Proceedings of the 8th international conference Wirtschaftsinformatik (WI 2007), Karlsruhe, Germany, 2007, pp 423–440
Hepp M, Leymann F, Domingue J, Wahler A, Fensel D (2005) Semantic business process management: a vision towards using semantic web services for business process management. In: Proceedings of the 3rd IEEE international conference on e-Business Engineering (ICEBE 2005), Beijing, China, 2005, pp 535–540
Herrmann P, Herrmann G (2006) Security requirement analysis of business processes. Electron Commerce Res 5(3–4):305–335
Hidders J, Dumas M, van der Aalst WMP, ter Hofstede AHM, Verelst J (2005) When are two workflows the same? In: Atkinson M, Dehne F (eds) Proceedings of the 11th Australasian symposium on theory of computing (CATS 2005), Newcastle, Australia, 2005, pp 3–11
Hirshfeld Y (1993) Petri nets and the equivalence problem. In: Börger E, Gurevich Y, Meinke K (eds) Proceedings of the 7th workshop on computer science logic (CSL 1993), Swansea, United Kingdom, 1993, pp 165–174
Höfferer P (2007) Achieving business process model interoperability using metamodels and ontologies. In: Österle H, Schelp J, Winter R (eds) Proceedings of the 15th European conference on information systems (ECIS 2007), St. Gallen, Switzerland, 2007, pp 1620–1631
Jallow AK, Majeed B, Vergidis K, Tiwari A, Roy R (2006) Operational risk analysis in business processes. BT Technol J 25(1):168–177

Janssen M (2005) Modeling for accountability: the case of the virtual business counter. In: Proceedings of the 11th Americas conference on information systems (AMCIS 2005), Omaha, NE, 2005, pp 2021–2029

Kashyap V, Sheth A (1996) Semantic and schematic similarities between database objects a context-based approach. VLDB J 5(4):276–304

Kueng P (2000) Process performance measurement system: a tool to support process-based organizations. Total Qual Manage 11(1):67–85

Kusiak A, Larson TN, Wang JR (1994) Reengineering of design and manufacturing processes. Comput Ind Eng 26(3):521–536

Lang K, Glunde J, Bodendorf F (1997) A framework for reusable reference process building blocks. ACM SIGGROUP Bulletin 18(1):68–70

Lange CFJ, Chaudron MRV (2006) Effects of defects in UML models: an experimental investigation. In: Osterweil LJ, Rombach D, Soffa ML (eds) Proceedings of the 28th international conference on software engineering (ICSE 2006), Shanghai, China, 2006, pp 401–411

Lawrence R, Barker K (2001) Integrating relational database schemas using a standardized dictionary. In: Proceedings of the 16th ACM symposium on applied computing (SAC 2001), Las Vegas, NV, 2001, pp 225–230

Malone TW, Bernstein A, Carr NG, Crowston K, Dellarocas C, Grunniger M, Herman GA, Jin Y, Klein M, Lee J, O'Donnell E, Orlikowski W, Osborn CS, Quimby J, Pentland BT, Tate A, Wyner GM, Yates J, Yoshioka T, Yost G (2003) Organizing business knowledge – MIT process handbook. The MIT Press, Cambridge, Massachusetts, London, England

Mendling J, Moser M, Neumann G, Verbeek HMW, van Dongen BF, van der Aalst WMP (2006) Faulty EPCs in the SAP reference model. In: Dustdar S, Fiadeiro JL, Sheth A (eds) Proceedings of the 4th international conference business process management (BPM 2006), Vienna, Austria, 2006, pp 451–457

Milton SK, Kazmierczak E (2004) An ontology of data modelling languages: a study using a common-sense realistic ontology. J Database Manage 15(2):19–38

Mylopoulos J (1998) Information modeling in the time of the revolution. Inform Syst 23(3–4):127–155

Namiri K, Stojanovic N (2007) Pattern-based design and validation of business process compliance. In: Meersman R, Tari Z (eds) Proceedings of the 15th international conference on cooperative information systems (CoopIS 2007), Vilamoura, Portugal, 2007, pp 59–76

Object Management Group (2004) UML 2.0 Superstructure Specification. http://www.omg.org/cgi-bin/doc?formal/05-07-04, Accessed on 30 Apr 2006

Object Management Group (2006) BPMN final adopted specification 1.0 http://www.bpmn.org/Documents/OMG%20Final%20Adopted%20BPMN%201-0%20Spec%2006-02-01.pdf. Accessed on 30 Apr 2006

Parent C, Spaccapietra S (1998) Issues and approaches of database integration. Commun ACM 41(5):166–178

Pfeiffer D (2007) Constructing comparable conceptual models with domain specific languages. In: Österle H, Schelp J, Winter R (eds) Proceedings of the 15th European conference on information systems (ECIS 2007), St. Gallen, Switzerland, 2007, pp 876–888

Pfeiffer D (2008) Semantic business process analysis: building block-based construction of automatically analyzable business process models. Dissertation, Westfälische Wilhelms-Universität Münster, Münster, Germany

Pfeiffer D, Gehlert A (2005) A framework for comparing conceptual models. In: Desel J, Frank U (eds) Proceedings of the 1st international workshop on enterprise modelling and information systems architectures (EMISA 2005) at the 24th international conference on conceptual modeling (ER 2005), Klagenfurt, Austria, 2005, pp 108–122

Polyvyanyy A, Smirnov S, Weske M (2010) Business process model abstraction. In: vom Brocke J, Rosemann M (eds) Handbook on business process management, vol 1. Springer, Heidelberg

Pomello L, Rozenberg G, Simone C (1992) A survey of equivalence notions for net based systems. In: Rozenberg G (ed) Advances in Petri nets: the DEMON project. Springer, London, pp 410–472

Process mining group the ProM framework (2007) http://is.tm.tue.nl/~cgunther/dev/prom/. Accessed on 01 May 2008

Recker J (2008) Understanding process modelling grammar continuance – a study of the consequences of representational capabilities. PhD Thesis, Queensland University of Technology, Brisbane, Australia

Rosemann M (2007) Preparation of process modeling. In: Becker J, Kugeler M, Rosemann M (eds) Process management: a guide for the design of business processes, 2nd edn. Springer, Berlin, pp 41–78

Rosemann M, van der Aalst WMP (2007) A configurable reference modelling language. Inform Syst 32(1):1–23

Rosemann M, zur Mühlen M (1998) Evaluation of workflow management systems: a meta model approach. Aust J Inform Syst 6(1):103–116

Rupprecht C, Funffinger M, Knublauch H, Rose T (2000) Capture and dissemination of experience about the construction of engineering processes. In: Wangler B, Bergman L (eds) Proceedings of the 12th international conference on advanced information systems engineering (CAiSE 2000), Stockholm, Sweden, 2000, pp 294–308

Sadiq S, Governatori G (2010) Managing regulatory compliance in business processes. In: vom Brocke J, Rosemann M (eds) Handbook on business process management, vol 2. Springer, Heidelberg

Scheer A-W (2000) ARIS – business process modeling, 3rd edn. Springer, Heidelberg

Seltsikas P, Palkovits S (2006) Process modeling notations for eGovernment: an assessment of modeling notations for identity management and GUIDE's methodology in practice. In: Proceedings of the eGo-vInterop'06 conference, Bordeaux, France

Shanks G, Nuredini J, Tobin D, Moody DL, Weber R (2003) Representing things and properties in conceptual modelling: an empirical evaluation. In: Ciborra CU, Mercurio R, de Marco M, Martinez M, Carignani A (eds) Proceedings of the 11th European conference on information systems (ECIS 2003), Naples, Italy, 2003, pp 1–17

Shanks G, Tansley E, Nuredini J, Tobin D, Weber R (2002) Representing part-whole relationships in conceptual modeling: an empirical evaluation. In: Applegate L, Galliers R, DeGross J (eds) Proceedings of the 23rd international conference on information systems (ICIS 2002), Barcelona, Spain, 2002, pp 89–100

Soffer P, Golany B, Dori D (2003) ERP modeling: a comprehensive approach. Inform Syst 28(6):673–690

Soffer P, Hadar I (2007) Applying ontology-based rules to conceptual modeling: a reflection on modeling decision making. Eur J Inform Syst 16(5):599–611

Stephenson CP, Bandara W (2007) Enhancing best practices in public health: using process patterns for business process management. In: Österle H, Schelp J, Winter R (eds) Proceedings of the 15th European conference on information systems (ECIS 2007), St. Gallen, Switzerland, 2007, pp 2123–2134

Thomas O, Fellmann M (2007) Semantic EPC: enhancing process modeling using ontology languages. In: Hepp M, Hinkelmann K, Karagiannis D, Klein R, Stojanovic N (eds) Proceedings of the workshop on semantic business process and product lifecycle management (SBPM 2007) at the 3rd European semantic web conference (ESWC 2007), Innsbruck, Austria, 2007, pp 64–75

van Dongen BF, Dijkman R, Mendling J (2008) Measuring similarity between business process models. In: Proceedings of the 20th international conference on advanced information systems engineering (CAiSE 2008), Montpellier, France, 2008

Wand Y (1996) Ontology as a foundation for meta-modelling and method engineering. Inf Softw Technol 38(4):281–287

Wand Y, Weber R (1990) An ontological model of an information system. IEEE Trans Softw Eng 16(11):1282–1292

Wimmer K, Wimmer N (1992) Conceptual modeling based on ontological principles. Knowl Acquis 4(4):387–406

Analysis and Design of Business Processes Using BPMN

Gustav Aagesen and John Krogstie

Abstract In 2004, the Business Process Modeling Notation (BPMN) was presented as a standard business process modeling language. Its development was considered to be an important step in reducing the fragmentation that was witnessed between the existing process modeling tools and notations. Since then BPMN has been evaluated in different ways by the academic community and has become widely supported by the industry. After completing the first major revisions of BPMN, the Object Management Group (OMG) is working toward a new BPMN standard, BPMN 2.0. This chapter summarizes some of the evaluations of BPMN and presents these together with reported experiences as well as some examples of proposed extensions and future expectations based on these.

1 Introduction

Models of business and work processes have for a long time been utilized to learn about, guide, and support practice in a number of areas. In software process improvement (Derniame 1998), enterprise modeling (Fox and Gruninger 2000), active knowledge modeling (Lillehagen and Krogstie 2008), and quality management, process models describe methods and working procedures. Simulation and quantitative analyses are also performed to improve efficiency (Kuntz et al. 1998) (van der Aalst et al. 2010). In process-centric software engineering environments (Ambriola et al. 1997) and workflow systems (WfMC 2000), model execution is automated. Thus, process modeling is not done for one specific objective only, which partly explains the great diversity of approaches found in literature and

G. Aagesen (✉)
Norwegian University of Science and Technology, Trondheim, Norway
e-mail: gustav.aagesen@idi.ntnu.no

J. vom Brocke and M. Rosemann (eds.), *Handbook on Business Process Management 1*, International Handbooks on Information Systems,
DOI 10.1007/978-3-642-00416-2_10,

practice. Five main categories of usage of process modeling can be distinguished (Krogstie et al. 2008):

1. Human sense-making and communication to make sense of aspects of an enterprise and to support communication between different stakeholders. Sense-making models are used within an activity to make sense of something in an ad hoc manner, and will usually not be maintained afterwards.
2. Computer-assisted analysis to gain knowledge about the enterprise through simulation or deduction based on the contents of the model.
3. Quality management, following up the adherence of the work process to standards and regulations. Here the model is meant to act as part of a corporate memory meant to exist as a reference point over time and as input to and basis for process improvement.
4. Model deployment and activation to integrate the model in an information system. Deployment can be manual, automatic (in automated workflow systems), or interactive (Krogstie and Jørgensen 2004).
5. Using the model as a context for a system development project, without being directly implemented (as it is in category 4).

Business Process Management (BPM) is a structured, coherent, and consistent way of understanding, documenting, modeling, analyzing, simulating, executing, and continuously changing end-to-end business process and all involved resources in light of their contribution to business performance (Recker et al. 2006). We see that the potential usage of modeling in BPM covers all the areas of use for process modeling in general as outlined above.

Traditionally, a wide variety of approaches and notations have been used for BPM and workflow. Inspired by a number of previous languages, BPMN has over the last years been promoted and suggested as a standard and has been met with the same kind of diverse needs; i.e., to create models to be understandable both for humans and machines, for sense-making, quality management, simulation, and execution. The main approach for execution is the mapping of BPMN models to BPEL.

This chapter aims to identify and report on the main efforts to evaluate BPMN, both analytical and empirical, and by this providing a current state of the art on this area.

The following section will introduce BPMN and the remaining sections will focus on the evaluation of the language. We will introduce the methods used in evaluating BPMN briefly. The trends of the outcome of the evaluations will be presented. Some of the proposed extensions of BPMN will then be described.

2 Business Process Modeling and BPMN

The wide range of applications of process modeling described in the introduction is reflected in current modeling notations, which emphasize different aspects of work. Ten years ago, Carlsen (1998) identified five categories of process modeling languages: transformational, conversational (speech-act-based), role-oriented, constraint-based, and systemic. The increased interest in modeling processes with UML indicates that object-oriented process modeling can be looked upon as a sixth category. On the other hand, most process modeling languages take a transformational approach (input–process–output). Processes are divided into activities, which may be divided further into subactivities. Each activity takes inputs, which it transforms to outputs. Input and output relations thus define the sequence of work. This perspective is chosen for the standards of the Workflow Management Coalition (WfMC 2000), the Internet Engineering Task Force (IETF) (Bolcer and Kaiser 1999), and the Object Management Group (OMG 2000) as well as most commercial systems for the last 10–15 years (Abbot and Sarin 1994; Fischer 2000). IDEF (1993), Data Flow Diagram (Gane and Sarson 1979), Activity Diagrams (Booch et al. 2005), Event-driven Process Chains (Scheer 2000), BPMN (BPMI.org and OMG 2008) and Petri nets (van der Aalst et al. 2000) are well-known transformational languages. We focus here on this type of process modeling, with the emphasis on BPMN.

2.1 BPMN

In 2004, the Business Process Modeling Notation (BPMN) was presented as the standard business process modeling notation (White 2004). Since then BPMN has been evaluated in different ways by the academic community and has become widely supported in industry.

There are currently 50 current and 4 planned implementation of (BPMN).[1] The tool support in industry has increased with the awareness of the potential benefits of BPM. Analytical evaluations showing weaknesses in BPMN have been available for some time, but the first reports on the experiences and perceived use of BPMN have however been published just recently.

The Business Process Modeling Notation (BPMN version 1.0) was proposed in May 2004 and adopted by OMG for ratification in February 2006. The current version is BPMN 1.1 (OMG 2008) and the following version BPMN 2.0 is in development. BPMN is based on the revision of other notations and methodologies, especially UML Activity Diagram, UML EDOC Business Process, IDEF, ebXML BPSS, Activity-Decision Flow (ADF) Diagram, RosettaNet, LOVeM, and Event-driven Process Chains.

The primary goal of BPMN was to provide a notation that is readily understandable by all business users, from the business analysts who create the initial draft of the processes, to the technical developers responsible for implementing the technology that will support the performance of those processes, and, finally, to the business people who will manage and monitor those processes (White 2004).

[1]http://www.bpmn.org/.

Another factor that drove the development of BPMN is that, historically, business process models developed by business people have been technically separated from the process representations required by systems designed to implement and execute those processes. Thus, it was a need to manually translate the original process models to execution models. Such translations are subject to errors and make it difficult for the process owners to understand the evolution and the performance of the processes they have developed. To address this, a key goal in the development of BPMN was to create a bridge from notation to execution languages. As indicated above BPMN models can be activated through the mapping to BPEL.

BPMN allows the creation of end-to-end business processes and is designed to cover many types of modeling tasks constrained to business processes. The structuring elements of BPMN will allow the viewer to be able to differentiate between sections of a BPMN Diagram using groups, pools, or lanes. Basic types of submodels found within a BPMN model can be *private business processes* (internal), *abstract processes* (public), and *collaboration processes* (global).

Private business processes are those internal to a specific organization and are the types of processes that have been generally called workflow or BPM processes.

Abstract processes represent the interactions between a private business process and another process or participant. Abstract processes are contained within a Pool and can be modeled separately or within a larger BPMN Diagram to show the Message Flow between the abstract process activities and other entities.

Collaboration processes depict the interactions between two or more business entities. These interactions are defined as a sequence of activities that represent the message exchange patterns between the entities involved.

2.1.1 Language Constructs and Properties

The Business Process Diagram is the graphical representation of the BPMN. Its language constructs are grouped in four basic categories of elements, viz., Flow Objects, Connecting Objects, Swimlanes, and Artifacts. The notation is further divided into a core element set and an extended element set. The intention of the core element set is to support the requirements of simple notations and most business processes should be modeled adequately with the core set. The extended set provides additional graphical notations for the modeling of more complex processes.

Flow objects (Fig. 1) contain events, activities, and gateways. *Events* are either start events, intermediate events, or end events. *Activities* are divided into process, subprocess, and tasks and denote the work that is done within a company. *Gateways* are used for determining branching, forking, merging, or joining of paths within the process. Markers can be placed within the gateway to indicate behavior of the given construct.

Connecting objects (Fig. 2) are used for connecting the flow objects. *Sequence Flow* defines the execution order of the activities within a process while *Message*

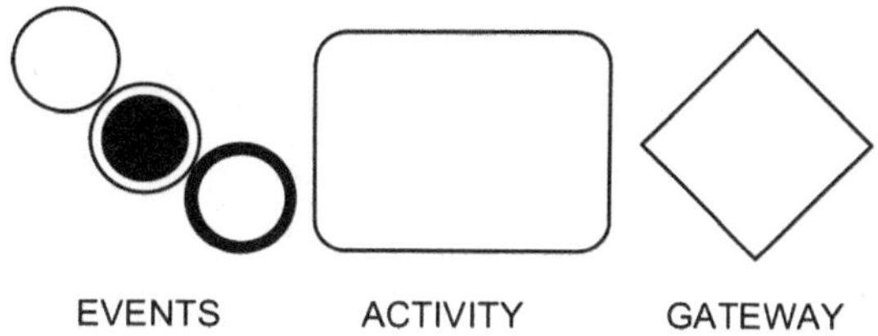

Fig. 1 BPD elements events (start, intermediate, and end), activity, and gateway

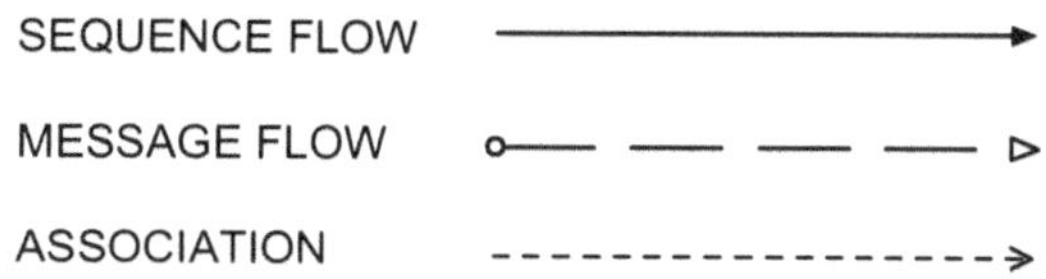

Fig. 2 BPD connection objects: Sequence flow, message flow, and association

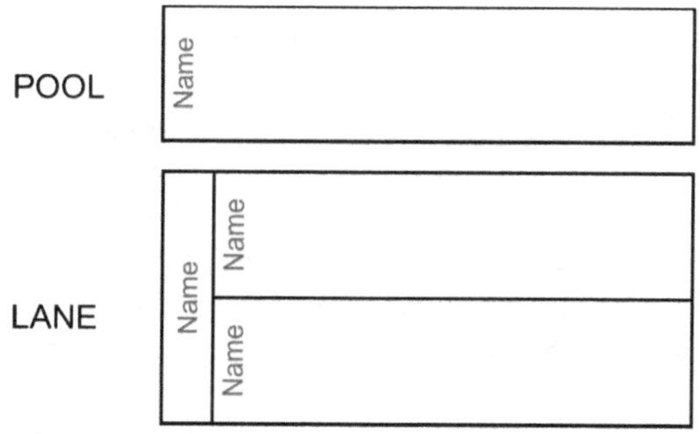

Fig. 3 BPD pool and lanes

Flow indicates a flow of messages between business entities or roles prepared to send and receive them. *Association* is used to associate both text and graphical nonflow objects with flow objects.

Swimlanes (Fig. 3) are used to denote a participant in a process and acts as a graphical container for a set of activities taken on by that participant. By dividing *Pools* into *Lanes* (thus creating subpartitioning), activities can be organized and categorized.

Artifacts (not illustrated) are data objects, groups, and annotations. *Data Objects* are not considered as having any other effect on the process than information on resources required or produced by activities. The *Group* construct is a visual aid used for documentation or analysis purposes while the *Text Annotation* is used to add additional information about certain aspects of the model.

Figure 4 shows an example BPMN process summoning participants for a workshop. The workshop organizer sends out the invitations, which are received by the potential participants. The participants evaluate the relevance of the workshop and decide whether they will participate or not. Those who want to participate, sign up for the workshop by informing the organizer.

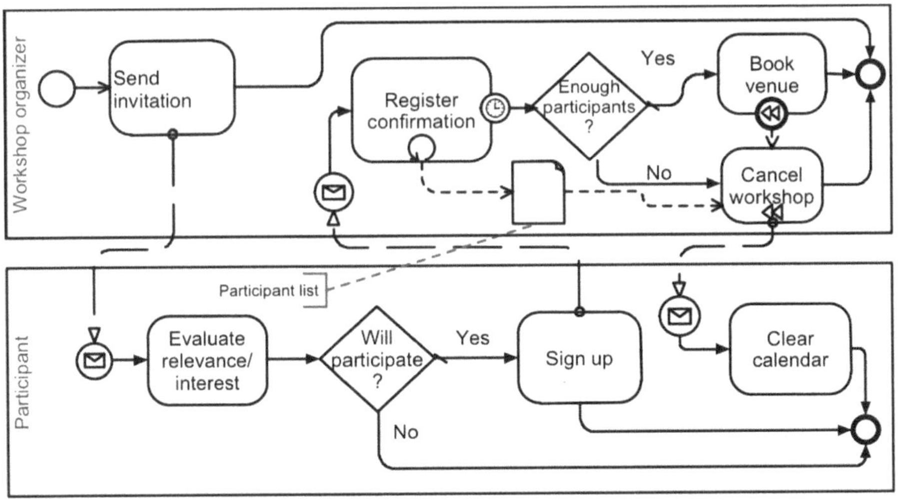

Fig. 4 BPMN model showing the summons for a workshop

The organizer registers the confirmations from the participants until the deadline for registering, making a list of participants. When the deadline is reached (indicated by the timer event on the looping register confirmation activity), the organizer will see if there are enough participants to conduct the workshop. If there are too few participants, the organizer will inform those participants who signed up that the workshop is canceled, and the registered participants will clear their calendar for the day.

If there are sufficient participants registered for the workshop, the organizer will try to book a venue. But if there is no venue available, the workshop will have to be canceled by informing registered participants. This is shown using the compensation and undo activity.

3 Evaluations of BPMN

The importance of evaluating available methods for modeling increases as the amount of available methods grow, since the results will guide the users in selecting the most fit method for the task at hand. Traditionally the research community has focused on creating new modeling languages rather than evaluating those that already exist (Wahl and Sindre 2005).

By evaluating existing methods one will not only be able to compare their suitability for solving the problem at hand, but it will also help determine the skills required of the user and model audience, before taking on the modeling task. By using formalized frameworks in the assessment of newly arrived methods and comparing the data with results from earlier studies it would be possible to determine whether the overall rating of the new method is higher than its predecessors.

Different approaches to evaluating modeling languages include analytical and empirical methods, and both single-language and comparative evaluations exist. Empirical methods should investigate both the possibility for modelers to use the language, comprehension of models developed in the language, and the ability to learn from and act according to the knowledge provided in the models (Gemino and Wand 2003; Krogstie et al. 2006). While analytical evaluations can be conducted as soon as the specification of the language is made available, empirical evaluations would in most cases require the users of the new method to have some experience with its use, and for that the method would need some time with the user community before evaluations can take place. Empirical studies might involve the investigation of whether the results from the analytical studies are supported and to what extent they have impact in practice. It would also involve performing case studies and surveys to discover if the method is as appropriate as expected and if it is used according to expectation.

BPMN is no longer considered to be new and it has been evaluated both analytically and empirically. The following section introduces the evaluation approaches followed by their outcomes. The evaluation results will be summarized in Sect. 4. For details about the evaluations please refer to their original reporting.

3.1 Ontological Analysis Using the Bunge–Wand–Weber Framework

As computerized information systems are representations of real-world systems, Wand and Weber suggest that a theory of representation based on philosophical *ontology* can be used to help define and build information systems that contain the necessary representations of real world constructs including their properties and interactions (Rosemann et al. 2006). The Bunge–Wand–Weber framework defines a set of models based on an ontology defined by Bunge in 1977 (Wand and Weber 1993; Recker et al. 2006). The BWW *representation model* is one of these models, and it is suggested that it can be used to analyze a particular modeling technique so as to make predictions on the modeling strengths and weaknesses of the technique, in particular its capabilities to provide *complete* and *clear* description of the domain being modeled. The current key constructs of the BWW model can be grouped into the following clusters: things including properties and types of things; states assumed by things; events and transformations occurring on things; and systems structured around things.

Two main evaluation criteria may be studied according to *Ontological Completeness* and *Ontological Clarity*.

Ontological Completeness is decided by the degree of *construct deficit*, indicating to what level the modeling language maps to the constructs of the BWW representation model.

Ontological Clarity is decided by *construct overload*, where the modeling language constructs represent several BWW constructs, *construct redundancy*, where one BWW construct can be expressed by several language constructs and *construct excess*, having language constructs not represented in the BWW model.

Three reasons for selecting the BWW framework for evaluating BPMN is stated by Recker et al. (2005): It has, unlike other ontologies, been derived with the Information Systems discipline in mind. It is an upper ontology, with a comprehensive scope that allows wide applicability. Further, there is an established track record and demonstrated usefulness of ontological analyses of modeling techniques using BWW.

BWW based evaluations are presented in Recker et al. (2005), Rosemann et al. (2006), and Recker et al. (2007) and their findings include:

Representation of state. The BPMN specification provides a relatively high degree of ontological completeness (Rosemann et al. 2006), but BPMN is not ontologically complete. For example, states assumed by things cannot be modeled with the BPMN notation. This situation can result in a lack of focus in terms of state and transformation law foundations for capturing business rules.

System structure. Systems structured around things are under-represented, and as a result of this problems will arise when information needs to be obtained about the dependencies within a modeled system.

Representational capabilities compared with other approaches. A representational analysis was done in Rosemann et al. (2006) on different approaches that show that BPMN appears to be quite mature in terms of representation capabilities. This can perhaps be partly explained by the fact that the previous approaches like EPC and Petri nets influence the development of BPMN. It is interesting that only BPMN of the process modeling notations is able to cover all aspects of things, including properties and types of things. From this it is possible to note that BPMN appears to denote a considerable improvement compared with other techniques. The combination of ebXML and BPMN would provide maximum ontological completeness (MOC) with minimum ontological overlap (MOO) (Recker et al. 2005).

3.2 The Workflow Patterns Framework

The Workflow Patterns Framework[2] (van der Aalst et al. 2003; Russell et al. 2006) provides a taxonomy of generic, recurring concepts, and constructs relevant in the context of process-aware information systems (Wohed et al. 2005) (see also Ouyang et al. 2010).

The workflow patterns describe a core of foundational structures that one could expect workflow systems to support. Defining these patterns made it possible to

[2]http://www.workflowpatterns.com.

compare the expressive power of available commercial tools for business process modeling. Later, the patterns have been found applicable in a much broader sense and they have been used to examine the capabilities of business process modeling languages such as BPMN, UML Activity Diagrams, and EPCs; web service composition languages such as WCSI; and business process execution languages such as BPML, XPDL, and BPEL (Russell et al. 2006).

The available patterns are divided into the *control-flow perspective*, the *data perspective*, and the *resource perspective*. The original patterns were comprised of 20, 40, and 43 patterns, respectively. A revision of the control-flow patterns conducted in 2006 resulted in additional 23 patterns.

Three reasons for selecting the Workflow Patterns Framework are stated by Recker et al. (2007). It is a well accepted framework that has been widely used both for the selection of workflow management systems as well as vendor's self-evaluations of process modeling products; The framework has proven impact in the industry and it has triggering extensions to process modeling systems and inspired their development.

Workflow pattern-based evaluations are presented in Recker et al. (2007) and Wohed et al. (2005, 2006). The outcomes of the evaluations include:

Representation of state. Due to the lack of representation of state in BPMN there are difficulties in representing certain control-flow patterns (Wohed et al. 2006). There are further inherent difficulties in applying the Workflow Patterns Framework for assessing a language that does not have a commonly agreed-upon formal semantic or an execution environment. The BPEL mapping provided in the BPMN specification is only partial, leaving aside models with unstructured topologies. There are several ambiguities that can be found in the BPMN specification due to the lack of formalization (Wohed et al. 2006).

Multiple representations of the same pattern. The simple workflow patterns have multiple BPMN representations while capturing the most advanced patterns required deep knowledge of the attributes associated to BPMN's modeling constructs that do not have a graphical representation.

Support for instances. Workflow and environment data patterns are not supported due to the lack of support for instance-specific data for a task or subprocess with a "multiple instance" marker cannot be specified.

Resource modeling. Support for the resource perspective in BPMN is minimal, but the modeling of organizational structures and resources is regarded to be outside the scope of BPMN. The authors state that the lane and pool constructs are in contradiction to this.

3.3 SEQUAL

SEQUAL (Semiotic Quality Framework) (Krogstie et al. 2006; Lillehagen and Krogstie 2008) is used for evaluating different quality aspects of models, and for evaluating the potential of the language to build models having high quality based on the appropriateness of the domain in which the language is applied. The framework is based on linguistic and semiotic concepts (Reijers et al. 2010).

The dimensions in which model quality is determined are as follows. *Physical quality*: The basic quality goal is that the model is available for the audience. This includes aspects related to digital distribution and file formats. *Empirical quality* deals with predictable error frequencies when a model is read or written by different users, coding (e.g., shapes of boxes) and HCI-ergonomics for documentation and modeling-tools. *Syntactic quality* is the correspondence between the model and the modeling language extension. *Semantic quality* is the correspondence between the model and the domain, including validity and completeness. *Perceived semantic quality* is the similar correspondence between the audience interpretation of a mode l and his or hers current knowledge of the domain. *Pragmatic quality* is the correspondence between the model and the audience's interpretation and application of it. SEQUAL differentiates between social pragmatic quality (to what extent people understand and are able to use the models) and technical pragmatic quality (to what extent tools can be made that interpret the models, e.g., for execution purposes). Pragmatic quality also includes in what extent the participants and audience after interpreting the model are able to learn based on the model and are able to act based on that knowledge to interact with or change the domain (preferably in a positive direction relative to the goal of modeling). *Social quality* is determined based on agreement among audience members' interpretations of the model while the *organizational quality* of the model relates to that all statements in the model contribute to fulfilling the goals of modeling (organizational goal validity), and that all the goals of modeling are addressed through the model (organizational goal completeness).

Language quality is a mean to achieve model quality and relates the modeling language used, and its appropriateness for the modeling task based on six quality areas. *Domain appropriateness* relates the language and the domain. Ideally, the language must be powerful enough to express anything in the domain, not having what Wand and Weber (1993) terms construct deficit. On the other hand, you should not be able to express things that are not in the domain, i.e., what Wand and Weber (1993) terms construct excess. Domain appropriateness is primarily a mean to achieve semantic quality. *Participant appropriateness* relates the social actors' explicit knowledge to the language. Participant appropriateness is primarily a mean to achieve pragmatic quality both for comprehension, learning, and action. *Modeler appropriateness* relates the language to the knowledge of the modeler. Modeler appropriateness is primarily a mean to achieve semantic quality. *Comprehensibility appropriateness* relates the language to the social actor interpretation. The goal is that the participants in the modeling effort using the language understand all the possible statements of the language. Comprehensibility appropriateness is primarily a mean to achieve empirical and pragmatic quality. *Tool appropriateness* relates the language to the technical audience interpretations. For tool interpretation, it is especially important that the language lend itself to automatic reasoning. This requires formality (i.e., both formal syntax and semantics being operational and/or logical), but formality is not necessarily enough, since the reasoning must also be efficient to be of practical use. This is covered by what we term analyzability (to exploit any mathematical semantics of the language) and executability (to exploit any operational semantics of the language). Different aspects of tool appropriateness are means to achieve syntactic, semantic, and pragmatic quality (through formal syntax, mathematical semantics, and operational semantics, respectively). *Organizational appropriateness* relates the language to standards and other organizational needs within the organizational context of modeling. These are means to support organizational quality.

For more information on SEQUAL, please refer to Krogstie et al. (2006) and Lillehagen and Krogstie (2008).

3.3.1 Evaluating BPMN Using the Semiotic Framework

Semiotic evaluations of BPMN are performed by Nysetvold and Krogstie (2006), Wahl and Sindre (2005) and discussed in Recker et al. (2007). The approach has also been used for the evaluation and comparison of a number of other modeling notations. In relation to BPMN the following findings can be mentioned:

Support for business-specific terms. Wahl and Sindre (2005) confirm that the constructs of the language do not contain any business-specific terms even though the purpose of the language is the modeling of business processes. Because of this, it would be applicable to model nonbusiness-related processes using BPMN, but only to a certain extent.

Understanding and use of constructs. The language notation is similar to that of other available languages with the same purpose, which would be helpful with users familiar with different approaches. The goal of BPMN is, however, to be understandable not only for users with previous experience and the complexity of the most advanced aspects of BPMN is, according to the authors, unrealistic to grasp without extensive training. This is somewhat confirmed by the case study reported by zur Mühlen and Ho (2008) (see Sect. 3.7).

Diagram layout. The authors also argue that it would be hard to externalize relevant knowledge using only BPDs if the knowledge in question goes beyond the domain of business processes. There are few strict guidelines in the BPMN specification on how to layout diagram constructs in relation to each other, which proposes a potential for creating BPDs with poor empirical quality.

3.3.2 Empirical Evaluation of BPMN, EEML, and UML Activity Diagrams

Nysetvold and Krogstie (2006) conducted an empirical evaluation of BPMN relative to EEML (Krogstie 2008) and UML Activity Diagrams using the SEQUAL framework. The usage area to be supported was process modeling in relation to implementation of Service-Oriented Architecture (SOA) in an insurance company. The evaluation rank BPMN highest in all categories except domain appropriateness (expressiveness), in which EEML came out best. However, EEML lost to BPMN on both tool and modeler appropriateness. The evaluation on domain appropriateness partly overlapped the evaluations above, e.g., by including an evaluation relative to control patterns. Other parts of this evaluation were adapted particularly to the expressed needs in the organization based on existing experience.

Comprehensibility appropriateness is the category that was appointed the second highest importance (based on number of criteria), since the organization regarded it to be very important that it was possible to use the language across the different areas of the organization and to improve communication between the IT-department and the business departments. In this category, BPMN and Activity Diagrams ranked equally high, which is not surprising given that they use the same swimlane-metaphor as a basic structuring mechanism. The reason why EEML came out behind is primarily due to the graphical complexity of some of the concepts, combined with the fact that EEML has a larger number of concepts in total, not surprising given that is a general enterprise modeling notation also useful for data, resource, and goal modeling.

Participant appropriateness and tool appropriateness were given equal importance, and BPMN ranked somewhat surprisingly high on both areas. When looking at the evaluation not taking tool appropriateness into account, the three languages ranked almost equal. Thus, it was in this case the focus toward the relevant implementation platforms (BPEL and web services) that ranked BPMN highest. On the other hand, the focus on tool appropriateness did not appear to get in the way for the language as a communication tool between people, at least not in this case.

In the category organizational appropriateness, BPMN and Activity Diagrams ranked almost equal. The organization had used UML and Activity Diagrams for some time, but it also appeared that tools supporting BPMN were available for the relevant parts of the organization.

3.4 Combined Semiotic, Ontological, and Workflow Patterns Evaluation

Recker et al. (2007) propose a generic framework for language evaluation based on the combination of ontological, semiotic, and pattern-based evaluation. They report on the first attempt to classify existing theoretical frameworks for process modeling language evaluation by using this framework. Their work provides an evaluation of existing frameworks as well as an evaluation of BPMN. For more information on the framework, consult Recker et al. (2007).

Some general statements on BPMN can be summarized from the analysis based on the study of Recker et al. (2007), which partly confirms the findings of the studies performed by the standalone approaches:

Representation of state. BPMN lacks the capabilities to model state-related aspects of business processes and is limited, if not incapable of modeling states assumed by things and state-based patterns.

Specialization of constructs. BPMN lacks attributes in the specification of the language constructs.

Weak support for resource modeling. There is lacking support for representing resource patterns and the evaluation comment the same as Wohed et al. (2006) when regarding the lane and pool constructs that are additionally criticized for being overloaded.

Redundant constructs. There is a relatively high degree of construct redundancy, which might explain why there are as many as three different BPMN representations for the same basic workflow patterns (Wohed et al. 2006).

3.5 Formal Analysis Using Petri Nets

Dijkman et al. map BPMN models to Petri Nets to be able to use efficient analysis techniques already available for Petri Net models. In doing this, they are able to evaluate the semantic correctness of BPMN models as well as disambiguating the core constructs of BPMN. The approach is used for empirical analysis with BPMN models found online. For more information on their work, consult Dijkman et al. (2007).

In converting BPMN diagrams to Petri Nets, Dijkman et al. (2007) discovered some issues in the BPMN specification and discuss possible solutions for these.

Process models with multiple start events. This is a situation where the BPMN specification indicates that each start event should generate a process instance. In situations where there are multiple start events without wait, there has to be some correlation mechanism to link the occurrence of a start event to an appropriate process instance.

Process instance completion. This is a situation where there are multiple end events and no clear indication in the specification when a process model is considered to be "completed". When the first end is reached, or when all tasks have met their end.

Exception handling for concurrent subprocess instances. There are unaddressed issues in the specification regarding the interrupt caused by subprocesses experiencing exceptions in a parallel multi-instance activity. The unclarity is related to whether the exception caused would only affect the subprocess in question or all subprocess instances spawned by the invocation activity.

OR-join gateway. The semantics of OR-join gateways is argued to be unclear regarding the relative definition of "upstream". It is advised that the BPMN specification adopt existing semantics with a formal foundation rather than attempting to define a new one.

3.6 Semistructured Interviews of BPMN Users

One effort to seek empirical evidence of theoretical propositions is done by following up a BWW representational analysis (see Sect. 3.1) with semistructured interviews with BPMN users. The research questions for this study were initially to discover the representational shortcomings of BPMN in light of the BWW-framework and to discover which of these were perceived as actual shortcomings by the BPMN users. This study involved 19 participants from six organizations distributed over four Australian states. The results are reported in Recker et al. (2005, 2006).

A follow-up of this study is the latest reported empirical evaluation of BPMN. A web-based survey performed between May and August 2007 including 590 BPMN users from different parts of the world. A presentation of the results is available in Recker (2008).

Interviews based on weaknesses discovered by representational analysis uncover how this affects the users (Recker et al. 2006).

Workarounds to fit local needs. The general impression regarding construct deficit is that even though the participants claim that they do not need to model state changes, business rules, or system structure they in fact find workarounds and represent this information outside the BPD itself. In modeling events, as many as 74% did not experience any limitation in using BPMN for this, and the problem declined for users using the expanded set compared with interviewees using the core set of elements. This is in contradiction to the theoretical proposition claiming that there would be confusion connected to using the expanded set.

Construct overload. The analytical evaluation proposed that there would be ambiguities regarding the lane and pool constructs. This was supported by the interviews and is mainly based on the fact that these constructs are used to represent a whole range of different real-world constructs as discussed in Recker et al. (2007).

In reporting the web-based quantitative survey (Recker 2008), the following issues were identified:

Support for business rule specification. Rule specification is an essential task in understanding business processes, and it would be good to see that process modeling solutions acknowledge this a bit better and provide support for this. This is suggested by one of the participants to be as simple as an additional graphical symbol implying that there is a business rule at work.

Weak support for resource modeling. The ambiguity that comes with the flexible semantics of lanes and pools is contradictory to their ease of use in modeling. One advice here is to provide better support for differentiating the multiple purposes for which lanes and pools can be used.

Understanding and use of constructs. The survey show that there is some doubt related to the use of gateways, off-page connectors, and groups. Basically, there is confusion on when to use these concepts and why. This might stem from the fact that they are constructs of the model and not the process modeled. When it comes to events, it is a question of frustration related to selecting the right kind of event.

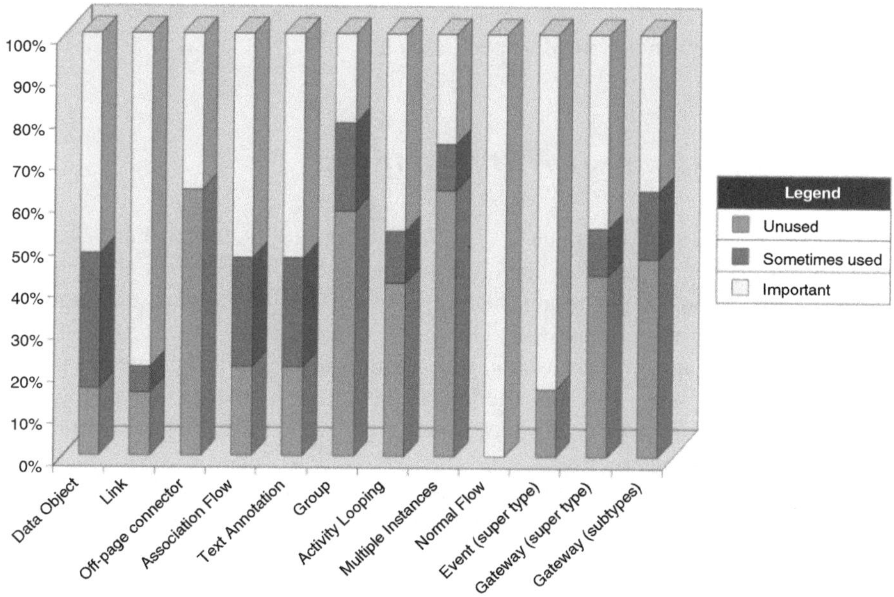

Fig. 5 Reported need for BPMN constructs (Adapted from Recker 2008)

Figure 5 shows results from the survey for the expressed need for the different BPMN constructs.

3.7 *Case Study of BPMN in Practice*

zur Mühlen and Ho (2008) followed the redesign of a service management process in a truck dealership in USA using action research. The study included reports on experiences from using BPMN with participatory modeling of the AS_IS and TO_BE process and the activation of the models for simulation purposes, providing the following results:

Understanding and use of constructs. Experience from the case study shows that the core set is used and understood. In cases where the entire set of BPMN constructs is used, the audience tends to disregard the richer meaning provided by the extended set (zur Mühlen and Ho 2008). The applied notation is primarily limited to the core constructs.

Workarounds to fit local needs. Use of constructs different from what suggested in the specification has been observed. Modelers purposely create syntactically wrong models to improve readability and to simplify the modeling task. One example of this is placing activity constructs across lanes to indicate that there are several organizational units participating in completing a task.

Tool dialects. The tool used had its own BPMN dialect that was not fully compliant with the official BPMN specification.

3.8 Statistical Analysis of BPMN Models

Similar to the work of Dijkman et al. (2007) mapping models to Petri Nets for analysis, zur Mühlen and Recker (2008) have coded BPMN models to Excel spreadsheets and used the representation with different mathematical tools for statistical analysis and comparison. The models investigated were collected from three different groups: models used in consulting project, models created as part of BPMN education seminars, and models found online. Investigated phenomena include the general use of constructs, their frequency of use, and the correlation of use of different constructs.

Modeling constructs use similar to that of natural language. By arranging constructs by frequency, the study revealed a distribution similar to the distribution previously observed for natural languages. This suggests that the use of BPMN constructs for expressing business processes mirrors the use of natural language. This would further suggest that expressiveness is based on the modelers existing vocabulary and that one will use whatever constructs one has knowingly available. The study found further support for this through observing that precise semantics is used by the consultant group and for models created in seminars, thus suggesting that this is based on formal training increasing construct vocabulary. Like many natural languages, BPMN has a few essential constructs, a wide range of constructs commonly used, and an abundance of constructs virtually unused (zur Mühlen and Recker 2008).

Precise constructs replace the need for text annotations. Another issue discovered by mapping the correlation of constructs is based on the negative correlation between the extended set gateways and text annotations. Text annotations seem to act as a substitute for formal event and gateway types by describing their behavior informally.

Practical language complexity does not equal theoretical complexity. Based on the result, the study also made an attempt to measure the practical complexity of BPMN based on the number of semantically different constructs used in each model. On average this resulted in the number of different constructs used as 9 (consulting), 8.87 (web), and 8.7 (seminars). There is, however, variation in what constructs are used, but nevertheless this has provided an image of a far less practical complex language compared with its theoretical complexity opening for as many as 50 different constructs in one model. Altogether, there was found six pairs of models out of 120 models examined that shared the same constructs, but there were several models sharing the same construct combinations or subsets.

Models focus on choreography or orchestration, not both. By organizing the model subsets using Venn diagrams showing what subsets were used in combination, the study revealed that modelers either focus on process orchestration by refining models by means of extended gateways or they focus on process choreography by adding organizational constructs, such as pools and lanes (zur Mühlen and Recker 2008).

4 Reported Results of the Evaluations

Even if there were criticism of a modeling approach based on analytical evidence, the potential weaknesses would have to be backed up or confirmed empirically to determine its real impact. A weakness based on analytical proof found in some remote part of a specification might not even be apparent to the user not aware of its existence, or in the opposite case the user might end up designing erroneous or ambiguous models due to poor formalism or tool support.

In this section, we will look at both the analytical and empirical evaluations together to identify similarities and difference. We will see that the consequences of the findings to a large extent depend on the goal of the modeling task, and that the goal of the language itself also must be taken into consideration when assigning the final score. BPMN seeks to serve both a broad audience in the business segment on the one hand, and on the other hand it reaches out to the technical community. In doing so, it is of potential use within all five categories of process modeling, as suggested by Krogstie et al. (2008), and further it has several groups of users whose requirements for use and modeling goals are quite different.

We will use the six language quality areas of SEQUAL (Krogstie et al. 2006) to classify the findings in the different evaluations. This is both out of convenience and based on the fact that it is a readily available framework for classifying quality, and thus it should be able to cover the findings.

4.1 Domain Appropriateness

Weak support for resource modeling is discovered using the Workflow Patterns Framework and the generic framework. This is confirmed also by the semistructured interviews and web-based surveys. In addition the BWW framework finds BPMN to have weak support for modeling system structure. The statistical analysis shows that BPMN models focus on choreography or orchestration, not both.

The BWW and Workflow Patterns Framework also find the representation of state to be weak. The generic framework confirms this, which does not come as a surprise since it is based on the first two.

4.2 Modeler Appropriateness

Missing support for business rule specification is one weakness mentioned in the web-based survey, whereas the semiotic and generic evaluation framework is missing the support for business-specific terms or specialized constructs. One workaround for these issues is observed in the semistructured interviews where there are cases where own constructs are used to fit the modeling needs. There is also an observed difference in the use of text annotations, particularly they tend to be used less for models designed by using more precise constructs from the extended set and in the opposite case act as a surrogate for the expressiveness of rich constructs in less precise models.

4.3 Participant Appropriateness

Several evaluations discuss the understanding and use of constructs and the key findings include the fact that some form of training is needed to use BPMN properly. Constructs like the off-page connectors support modeling and not the process which can be confusing for some users.

4.4 Comprehensibility Appropriateness

There are redundant constructs in BPMN and there are cases of multiple representations of the same patterns. In addition the lane and pool constructs are considered to be overloaded. The practical language complexity does not, however, equal the theoretical complexity and in understanding models, there is a tendency to disregard the richer meaning of the extended set. This is probably the only area in which the empirical evaluations do not directly support the analytical.

4.5 Tool Appropriateness

Workflow patterns report the lack of support for representation of multiple instances.

The Petri net analysis reveals some issues regarding the use of BPMN for simulation in cases with multiple start or end events and concurrency of subprocesses. There are also indications of a need for a more formal definition of the semantics of the language.

4.6 Organizational Appropriateness

The case study of BPMN in practice discovered an issue related to the fact that there are several different tool dialects and these are not fully compliant with the BPMN specification.

5 BPMN Extensions

Results from the evaluations show that users are able to find workarounds for some of the weaknesses found in BPMN. In most of these cases, there is a gap between what is possible to achieve using BPMN and the desired goal of the user. One way to approach this problem is by building extension to close this gap, and by doing this, prototype different kinds of functionality possible to include in the BPMN specification. The following section presents four reported efforts to extend BPMN and by this show identified weaknesses discovered by means of practical use and proposed solutions for these weaknesses. The first three proposals address issues related to choreography, semantic correctness, and modeling of resources while the fourth discusses a topic not discussed in the evaluations but which is still important: Combining user-interface modeling with process modeling which is relevant in scenarios involving the reengineering of existing processes supported by information systems for the end user.

5.1 Using BPMN for Modeling Choreography

An assessment of BPMN using the Service Interaction Patterns (Barros et al. 2005) presented by Decker and Puhlmann (2007) shows weak support for modeling complex choreographies in BPMN. This weakness is connected to distinguishing between several instances of participants and using references to single participants for messaging. By adding participant sets, references, reference sets, and reference passing to BPMN this paper demonstrates that it would be possible to support most of the service integration patterns. The authors also point out an unclarity in the semantics of the BPMN data objects regarding their ability to buffer data similar to what is possible in UML Activity Diagrams. Based on this, a required distinction between data object and data object sets is introduced to their extension of BPMN. Aspects raised by the need of choreography modeling are discussed by Barros et al. (2009) in this Handbook.

5.2 Checking Semantic Correctness Using Petri Nets

By using the XML serialization created by a BPMN tool, Dijkman et al. (2007) have implemented a tool to translate BPMN models to Petri Nets via the Petri Net Markup Language (PNML). Once converted to a Petri Net, the BPMN model can be semantically analyzed using Petri net analysis toolset. This work is limited to the control-flow perspective of BPMN and the order in which activities and events are allowed to occur. Weaknesses found in this paper are discussed in Sect. 4, but the suggested extension allowing semantic validation of BPMN models is considered to be a potentially helpful tool for assisting the building of formal models.

5.3 *Modeling of Task-Based Authorization Constraints in BPMN*

An extension of BPMN is suggested by Wolter and Schaad (2007) to support resource allocation patterns. These patterns allow specifying authorization constraints, for instance role-task assignments, separation of duty, and binding of duty constraints. This is done by adding security relevant semantics to the group and lane elements of BPMN and deriving a new textual artifact from the textual annotation element. Extending BPMN with the support for describing security aspects of workflow can widen its scope and application and can be relevant also for modeling business scenarios.

5.4 *Combined User-Interface and Process Modeling*

The main approach for execution support of BPMN is mapping to BPEL. On the other hand, the focus of BPEL engines is on process executions and not on the user-interface of the applications, which in practice can result in good process support systems that is hampered by an inappropriate user-interface, thus meeting unnecessary implementation problems. Trætteberg (2008) presents an approach for combining model-based user-interface design (MBUID)-approaches with BPMN as a task modeling language to make it easier to develop appropriate user-interfaces and user-interfaces applicable for user tailoring for BPM-solutions.

6 Discussion and Conclusions

This chapter has identified and reported on the main efforts to evaluate BPMN, both analytical and empirical. From the findings it is possible to suggest that the analytical evaluations performed are at this point sufficient and self-confirming. Even though there is little evidence from the empirical investigations so far, it seems like most of the weaknesses uncovered by analytical evaluations are by the users treated lightly and through workarounds.

Local model interpretation and tool dialects might be problematic, as models will not be directly available for externalization and interoperability issues might arise when moving models between organizations or groups within organizations.

Two issues related to tool appropriateness not mentioned by the reported evaluations covered already, but which are apparent problems in BPMN, are that there is no explicit meta-model for BPMN and there is not specified any means for interchanging BPDs between the different modeling tools (Frankel 2008).

By limiting the evaluation of practical use of BPMN within one organization or group, some of the analytically identified weaknesses might not be problematic since the model has limited use and fit local (but not organizational) goals. When evolving the same model through different phases, from sense-making to analysis through simulation, and when integrating the model to the process by involving different tools for modeling, simulation, and execution, which also requires different levels of formalism and detail and user skill, this suggests that BPMN in fact does not scale up for the use across organizations unless there is formal training based on precise semantics and that the BPMN tools are built on a precise meta-model.

There is a level of freedom requested by the modelers not needing to express formal models and by restricting the creation of ad hoc models and process sketches one might discriminate against one of the key user groups. The question is whether formality and freedom are in conflict and if there are conflicts within the goal of the language of being readily available for both technical and nontechnical users.

The focus in most evaluations so far has been on BPMN in isolation and, except for two cases, little comparison between BPMN and other approaches has been done. The evaluations on which this report is based are primarily based on BPMN 1.0 and not the maintenance version (BPMN 1.1). As for the empirical studies these are partly reliant on the local implementation of BPMN and the dialect of the BPMN tool in question, rather than the specification.

On the account of BPMN 2.0 it might be that there are issues within BPMN that are more important to solve than others in order for the continued use and growth of BPMN. The overall goal for BPMN 2.0 (OMG 2007) is to integrate both notations, meta-model and interchange format within one language. Requested features include the following: Aligning BPMN with the Business Process Definition Meta-model (BPDM). Based on current proposals (Frankel 2008), it is not sure whether BPMN will be used as meta-model or if there will be a dedicated BPMN 2.0 meta-model mapping to BPDM; Enabling the exchange of business process models and their diagram layouts among process modeling tools to preserve semantic integrity; Expand BPMN to allow model orchestrations and choreographies as stand-alone or integrated models; Support the display and interchange of different perspectives on a model that allow a user to focus on specific concerns; Serialize BPMN and provide XML schemas for model transformation and to extend BPMN toward business modeling and executive decision support (Recker 2008). The RFP also rate consistency checks and model validation as important features.

From the empirical studies one can further see that there is a difference in the perceived use of BPMN regarding the use of the core or the expanded set. Few of the studies indicate whether they are based on the one or the other, which might impose a problem on the user-side. One might select BPMN for a task based on expressiveness, but planning to use the core set which at one point would go wrong.

There is room for more empirical work on the actual use of BPMN. It would be wise to perform replication studies on future BPMN work on the revision of the standard when it becomes available to determine eventual improvement.

Some other questions for future work are: How fast the tool support for a revised version of the standard will be available and what are the consequences of having two significantly different versions available? How will the different versions of BPMN map to each other? If the proposed weaknesses found impose actual problems or if the workarounds found among the users (extending BPMN with local support utilities of their choice) provide a better approach all together than trying to build an all-in-one language.

References

Abbot KR, Sarin SK (1994) Experiences with workflow management: issues for the next generation, In: ACM CSCW conference

Ambriola V, Conradi R, Fuggetta A (1997) Assessing process-centered software engineering environments. ACM Trans Softw Eng Meth 6(3):283–328

Barros A, Dumas M, ter Hofstede AHM (2005) Service interaction patterns. In: Proceedings of the 3rd international conference on business process management, Nancy, France, September 2005, Springer Verlag, pp 302–318

Barros A, Hettel T, Flender C (2009) Bridging the gap from process analysis to design through choreography modeling. In: Rosemann M, vom Brocke J (eds) Handbook on business process management. Berlin, Springer

Bolcer G, Kaiser G (1999) SWAP: leveraging the web to manage workflow. IEEE Internet Comput 3(1):85–88

Booch G, Rumbaugh J, Jacobson I (2005) The unified modeling language: user guide, 2nd edn. Addison-Wesley, Reading, MA

Carlsen S (1998) Action port model: a mixed paradigm conceptual workflow modeling language. In: Third IFCIS conference on cooperative information systems (CoopIS'98), New York

Decker G, Puhlmann F (2007) Extending BPMN for modeling complex choreographies. In: Proceedings of the 15th international conference on cooperative information systems (CoopIS), LNCS 4803

Derniame JC (ed) (1998) Software process: principles, methodology and technology. Lecture notes in computer science, vol 1500. Springer, Berlin, Heidelberg, New York

Dijkman RM, Dumas M, Ouyang C (2007) Formal semantics and analysis of BPMN process models. Queensland University of Technology, Brisbane

Fischer L (2000) Excellence in practice IV – innovation and excellence in workflow and knowledge management. Workflow Management Coalition, Future Strategies Inc., Florida, USA

Fox MS, Gruninger M (2000) Enterprise modeling, AI Magazine

Frankel DS (2008) Requirements for BPMN 2.0, MDA Journal. http://www.bptrends.com/. Accessed June 2008.

Gane C, Sarson T (1979) Structured systems analysis: tools and techniques. Prentice Hall, Englewood Cliffs, NJ

Gemino A, Wand Y (2003) Evaluating modeling techniques based on models of learning. Commun ACM 46:79–84

IDEF-3x (1993) Process modeling language specification, standard NA-94-1422B, Rockwell International

Krogstie J (2008) Integrated goal, data and process modeling: from TEMPORA to model-generated work-places. In: Johannesson P, Søderstrøm E (eds) Information systems engineering from data analysis to process networks. IGI Publishing, Hershey, PA, pp 43–65

Krogstie J, Jørgensen H (2004) Interactive models for supporting networked organizations. In: 16th conference on advanced information systems engineering. Springer, Riga, Latvia, Berlin, Heidelberg, New York

Krogstie J, Sindre G, Jørgensen HD (2006) Process models representing knowledge for action: a revised quality framework. Eur J Inform Syst 15(1):91–102

Krogstie J, Dalberg V, Jensen SM (2008) Process modeling value framework, Enterprise Information Systems In: Manolopoulos Y, Filipe J, Constantopoulos P, Cordeiro J (eds) Selected papers from 8th international conference, ICEIS 2006, Paphos, Cyprus, May 23–27, 2006. Lecture notes in business information processing, vol 3. Springer, Berlin

Kuntz JC, Christiansen TR, Cohen GP, Jin Y, Levitt RE (1998) The virtual design team: a computational simulation model of project organizations. Commun ACM 41(11):84–92

Lillehagen F, Krogstie J (2008) Active knowledge models of enterprises. Springer, Heidelberg

Nysetvold AG, Krogstie J (2006) Assessing business process modeling languages using a generic quality framework. In: Siau K (ed) Advanced topics in database research, vol 5. Idea Group. Hershey, Pennsylvania, pp 79–93

OMG (2000) Workflow management facility v. 1.2. Object Management Group
OMG (2007) Business process model and notation (BPMN) 2.0 request for proposal. Technical report, OMG. http://www.omg.org/. Accessed June 2007
OMG (2008) BPMN v1.1 specification. Technical report, OMG. http://www.omg.org/, http://www.omg.org/spec/BPMN/1.1/. Accessed January 2008.
Ouyang C et al. (2010) Workflow management. In: vom Brocke J, Rosemann M (eds) Handbook on business process management, vol 1. Springer, Heidelberg
Recker J (2008) BPMN modeling – who, where, how and why. BPTrends
Recker J, Indulska M, Rosemann M, Green P (2005) Do process modelling techniques get better? A comparative ontological analysis of BPMN. 16th Australasian conference on information systems, Sydney, Australia
Recker J, Indulska M, Rosemann M, Green P (2006) How good is BPMN really? Insights from theory and practice. 14th European conference on information system (ECIS 2006). Gothenburg, Sweden, 1–12
Recker J, Rosemann M, Krogstie J (2007) Ontology-versus pattern-based evaluation of process modeling languages: a comparison. Comm Assoc Inform Syst 20:774–799
Reijers HA et al. (2010) Business process quality management. In: vom Brocke J, Rosemann M (eds) Handbook on business process management, vol 1. Springer, Heidelberg
Rosemann M, Recker J, Indulska M, Green P (2006) A study of the evolution of the representational capabilities of process modeling grammars. Advanced Information Systems Engineering-CAiSE, vol 4001, 447–461
Russell N, ter Hofstede AHM, van der Aalst WMP, Mulyar N (2006) Workflow control-flow patterns: a revised view. BPM Center Report BPM-06-22, BPMcenter. org, 6–22
Scheer AW (2000) ARIS – business process modeling, 3rd edn. Springer, Berlin
Trætteberg H (2008) UI design without a task modeling language – using BPMN and Diamodl for task modeling and dialog design. To be published at Tamodia 2008
van der Aalst, WMP, Desel J, Oberweis A (eds) (2000) Business process management. Lecture notes in computer science, vol 1806. Springer, Berlin, Heidelberg, New York
van der Aalst WMP, ter Hofstede AHM, Kiepuszewski B, Barros AP (2003) Workflow patterns. Distrib Parallel Databases 14:5–51
van der Aalst WMP et al. (2010) Business process simulation. In: vom Brocke J, Rosemann M (eds) Handbook on business process management, vol 1. Springer, Heidelberg
Wahl T, Sindre G (2005) An analytical evaluation of BPMN using a semiotic quality framework. In: Proceedings of EMMSAD'2005, 533–544
Wand Y, Weber R (1993) On the ontological expressiveness of information systems analysis and design grammars. J Inform Syst 3(4):217–237
WfMC (2000) Workflow Handbook 2001. Workflow Management Coalition, Future Strategies Inc., Lighthouse Point, Florida, USA
White SA (2004) Introduction to BPMN. IBM Cooperation
Wohed P, van der Aalst WMP, Dumas M, ter Hofstede AHM (2005) Pattern-based analysis of BPMN – an extensive evaluation of the control-flow, the data and the resource perspectives (revised version), BPM Center Report BPM-06-17, BPMcenter.org
Wohed P, van der Aalst WMP, Dumas M, ter Hofstede AHM (2006) On the suitability of BPMN for business process modelling. Business Process Management – BPM 2006, Vienna, Austria. Lecture notes in computer science, vol 4102. pp 161–176
Wolter C, Schaad A (2007) Modeling of task-based authorization constraints in BPMN. BPM Conference. Springer, 64–79
zur Mühlen M, Ho DT (2008) Service process innovation: a case study of BPMN in practice. Hawaii international conference on system sciences, proceedings of the 41st annual, 2008
zur Mühlen M, Recker JC (2008) How much language is enough? Theoretical and practical use of the business process modeling notation, Proceedings CAiSE'08. Springer Verlag, Montpellier, France

Configuration and Management of Process Variants

Alena Hallerbach, Thomas Bauer, and Manfred Reichert

Abstract This chapter deals with advanced concepts for the configuration and management of business process variants. Typically, for a particular business process, different variants exist. Each of them constitutes an adjustment of a master process (e.g., a reference process) to specific requirements building the process context. Contemporary Business Process Management tools do not adequately support the modeling and management of such process variants. Either the variants have to be specified in separate process models or they are expressed in terms of conditional branches within the same process model. Both methods can result in high model redundancies, which make model adaptations a time-consuming and error-prone task. In this chapter, we discuss advanced concepts of our Provop approach, which provides a flexible and powerful solution for managing business process variants along their lifecycle. Such variant support will foster more systematic process configuration as well as process maintenance.

1 Introduction

Process support is required in almost all business domains (Mutschler et al. 2008). As examples, consider healthcare (Lenz and Reichert 2007), automotive engineering (Müller et al. 2006), and public administration (Becker et al. 2007). Characteristic process examples from the automotive industry, for instance, include product change management (VDA 2005), release management (Müller et al. 2006), and product creation (see below).

Usually, there exists a multitude of *variants* of a particular process model, whereby each of these variants is valid in a specific scenario; i.e., the *configuration*

A. Hallerbach (✉)
Group Research and Advanced Engineering, Daimler AG, Ulm, Germany
e-mail: alena.hallerbach@daimler.com

J. vom Brocke and M. Rosemann (eds.), *Handbook on Business Process Management 1*, International Handbooks on Information Systems,
DOI 10.1007/978-3-642-00416-2_11,

of a particular *process variant* depends on concrete requirements building the *process context* (Hallerbach et al. 2008b). Regarding release management, for example, we have identified more than twenty process variants depending on the considered product series, involved suppliers, or development phases. Similar observations can be made with respect to the product creation process in the automotive domain for which dozens of variants exist. Thereby, each variant is assigned to a particular product type (e.g., car, truck, or bus) with different organizational responsibilities and strategic goals, or varying in some other aspects.

In this chapter, we refer to the service process handling vehicle repair in a garage (cf. Fig. 1a). Basically, this process works as follows: It starts with the reception of a vehicle. After a diagnosis is made, the vehicle is repaired (if necessary). During diagnosis and repair, the vehicle is maintained; e.g., oil and wiping water may be checked and refilled. The process completes when handing the repaired and maintained vehicle back to the customer. Depending on the process context, different variants of this process are required, whereas the context is described by country-specific, garage-specific, and vehicle-type-specific variables. In our case studies, we have identified hundreds of such variants and we have learned that existing process modeling tools do not provide sophisticated support for modeling and maintaining such large number of process variants.

Figure 1b–d show three simplified examples of such variants of a vehicle repairs process. Variant 1, as depicted in Fig. 1b, assumes that the damaged vehicle requires a checklist of *Type 2* to perform the diagnosis. Therefore, activity *Diagnosis*

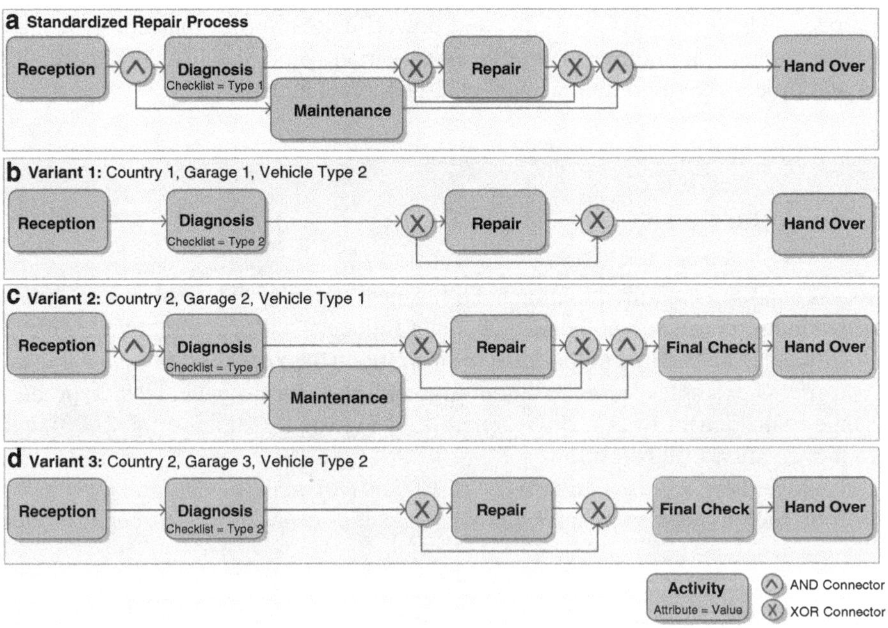

Fig. 1 Variants of a standardized vehicle repair process (*simplified view*)

is adapted by modifying its attribute *Checklist* to value "*Type 2*". Additionally, the garage omits maintenance of the vehicle as this is considered as a special service not offered conjointly with the repair process. At the model level, this is realized by skipping activity *Maintenance*. As another example, consider Variant 2 as depicted in Fig. 1c. Due to country-specific legal regulations, a final security check is required, before handing over the vehicle back to the customer. Regarding this variant, the new activity *Final Check* has to be added when compared to the standardized process from Fig. 1a. Finally, Variant 3 will become relevant if a checklist of *Type 2* is required for diagnosis, the garage does not link maintenance to the repair process, and there are legal regulations requiring a final check (cf. Fig. 1d).

As can be seen from these simple examples, variants exist for many processes, and thus have to be adequately managed. This chapter presents selected concepts of the Provop (*PROcess Variants by OPtions*) approach for managing large collections of process variants. More precisely, Provop allows to configure relevant process variants out of one basic process model (Hallerbach et al. 2008a; Hallerbach et al. 2008c) and to manage them along their lifecycle. This chapter focuses on the technical issues, which become relevant in this context. Also very important, but out of the scope of this chapter, are governance issues (e.g., Who selects or enforces configurations? What does variant management mean for process ownership?).

The chapter is structured as follows: First, we present problems, which will arise if we do not treat variants as first class objects and only model them conventionally. Second, we describe key requirements with respect to process variant management. Then, we introduce our Provop approach and selected concepts for process variant management. Finally, we discuss related approaches. The chapter concludes with a summary and an outlook.

2 Dealing with Process Variants in Existing BPM Tools

Solutions for managing variants in existing BPM tools can be divided into two approaches: the *multi-model* and the *single-model* approach.

Multi-Model Approach. In existing BPM tools, process variants often have to be defined and kept in separate process models as shown in Fig. 1. Typically, this results in highly redundant model data as the variant models are identical or similar for most parts. Furthermore, the variants cannot be strongly related to each other; i.e., their models are only loosely coupled (e.g., based on naming conventions). Furthermore, there is no support for (semi-) automatically combining existing variants to a new one; e.g., Variant 3 of our repair process (cf. Fig. 1d) combines the adjustments made by Variant 1 and Variant 2, and applies them to the standardized process. However, it cannot be created out of the existing models of these two variants as there is no indication which model parts are variant-specific and which are common for all models.

This multi-model approach will therefore be only feasible if few variants exist or the variants differ to a large degree from each other. Considering the large number of variants occurring in practice, however, the aforementioned drawbacks increase modeling and maintenance efforts significantly. Particularly, the efforts for maintaining and changing process variants become high since more fundamental process changes have to be accomplished for each variant separately (e.g., due to changed or new legal regulations). This is both time-consuming and error-prone. As another consequence, over time models representing the variants more and more differ from each other; e.g., when optimizations are only applied to single variants without considering their relations to other ones (Weber and Reichert 2008b). This, in turn, makes it a hard job for process designers to analyze, compare, and unify business processes and to implement the multiple variants within a common IT system. As conclusion, generally, modeling all process variants in separate models does not constitute an adequate solution for variant management.

Single-Model Approach. Another approach, frequently applied in practice, is to capture multiple variants in one single model using conditional branchings (i.e., XOR-/OR-Splits). Consider Fig. 2 as an example, which shows the repair process together with different variants (cf. Fig. 1a–d). Each execution path in the model represents a particular variant. Therefore, branching conditions indicate which path belongs to which variant.

Generally, specifying all variants in one process model can result in a large model, which is difficult to comprehend and expensive to maintain. (Note that in realistic scenarios there might be dozens to up to hundreds of variants of a particular process type.) As another drawback, variants are then mixed with "normal" process logic; i.e., branchings relevant for all process variants cannot be distinguished from the ones representing a variant selection. For example, our repair process includes a decision to only perform activity *Repair* if necessary. Therefore, on the model side, there is a conditional branching to either perform or skip the repair step. This branching is relevant for all discussed variants of the repair process; i.e., it is no variant-specific branching. However, the user cannot distinguish between normal and variant-specific branchings, unless there are special conventions to represent variant specific conditions or other model extensions used to mark a branching as normal or variant-specific. In summary, variants are neither transparent nor explicitly defined in this approach. As a consequence, the supporting IT system is unaware of the different process variants and only treats them as "normal" branchings within a single process model.

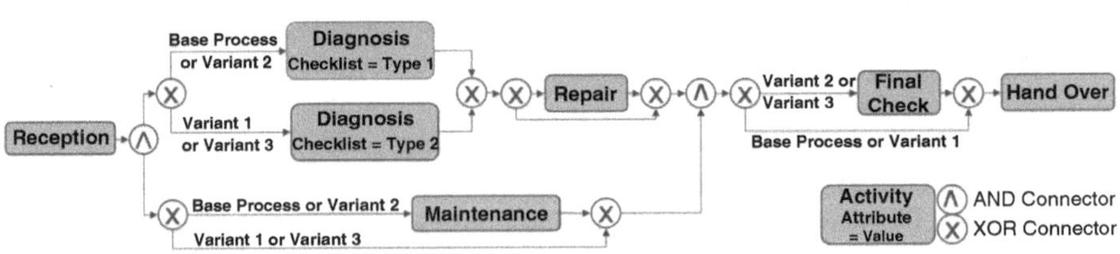

Fig. 2 Process variants realized by conditional branches

Discussion. Neither the use of separate models for capturing process variants nor their definition in one model based on conditional branchings constitutes adequate methods. Both approaches do not treat variants as first class objects; i.e., the variant-specific parts of a process are maintained and hidden either in separate models (multi-model approach) or in control flow logic (single-model approach). Another drawback of these approaches is the lack of context-awareness. Contextual knowledge might only be integrated and used in terms of process meta-data or branching conditions. As the process context mainly influences variant configuration, however, this fundamental aspect has to be considered more explicitly.

Note that these limitations also apply to popular business process modeling tools like ARIS Business Architect or WBI Modeler. ARIS Business Architect (IDS Scheer 2008), for example, allows to create a new process variant by copying the respective model directory and its objects, resulting in high redundancy of model data. Though the derived variant objects refer to the original objects (denoted as *master objects* in ARIS) afterwards, changes of the latter are not propagated to the variants. In principle, this corresponds to the multi-model approach as described above. However, through the explicit documentation of relation structures (between original and variant objects) some improvement is achieved.

3 Requirements

We conducted several case studies not only in the automotive industry (Müller et al. 2006, VDA 2005) but also in other domains like healthcare (Lenz and Reichert 2007), to elaborate key requirements for the configuration, adaptation, and management of process variants. This strong linkage to practice was needed in order to realize a complete and solid approach for process variant management. The requirements we identified are related to different aspects including the modeling of process variants, their linkage to process context and context-driven configuration, their execution in workflow management systems (WfMS), and their continuous optimization to deal with evolving needs; i.e., we have to deal with requirements related to the whole process life cycle (Hallerbach et al. 2008c, e, Weber et al. 2006, Weber et al. 2009). The standard process life cycle is depicted in Fig. 3. It consists of three phases, namely the design and modeling of the process, the creation of a particular process variant, and the deployment of this variant in a runtime environment. The process life cycle can be described as a (feedback) loop

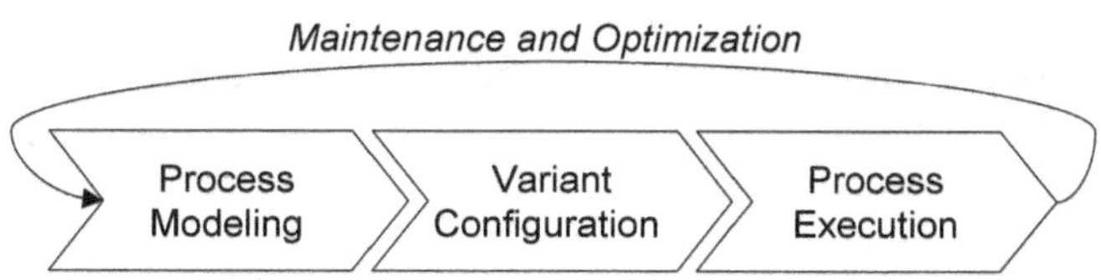

Fig. 3 Process life cycle

of these phases during which a process is continuously optimized and adapted (Weber et al. 2006, Weber et al. 2009). The major requirements to be met are described in the following.

Modeling. Efforts for modeling process variants should be kept as minimal as possible. Reuse of the variant models (or parts of them) has to be supported. In particular, it should be possible to create new variants by taking over properties from existing ones, but without creating redundant or inconsistent model data. Thus, the hierarchical structure of such "variants of variants" has to be adequately represented and should be easy to adapt.

Variant Configuration. The configuration of a process variant (i.e., its derivation from a given master or base process) should be done automatically if possible. Therefore, the specific circumstances (i.e., the *process context*) under which this configuration takes place have to be considered. In particular, an elaborated procedure for context-aware, automated variant configuration is required. At the same time, consistency and correctness of the configured process variants have to be ensured throughout the entire process life cycle.

Execution. To execute a process variant, its model has to be interpreted by a workflow engine. In this context, it is important to keep information about the configured process variant and its relation to a master or base process (and to other variants) in the runtime system. To deal with dynamic changes of the process context, the runtime system should additionally allow to dynamically switch process execution from one variant to another if required (i.e., to reconfigure the corresponding process variant on-the-fly). Finally, if context information is only available during runtime, the specific variant will have to be determined (i.e., configured) at runtime as well.

Maintenance and Optimization. To reduce maintenance efforts and cost of change, fundamental changes affecting multiple process variants should be conducted only once. As a consequence, all process variants concerned by the respective change should be adapted automatically and correctly.

There exist other requirements addressed by Provop, but not treated here. Examples include the consistency of configured variants, adequate visualization of the variants in all life cycle phases, and provision of intuitive user interfaces for variant configuration. In this chapter, we focus on the main requirements discussed above, covering the complete *process life cycle*.

4 The Provop Approach

In practice, process variants are often created by cloning and adjusting an existing process model of a particular type according to the given context. For example, regarding the three process models from Fig. 1b–d, we can see that they can be derived from the standardized process as depicted in Fig. 1a by adding, removing, or modifying activities. Generally, every process model can be derived out of another one by adjusting it accordingly, i.e., by applying a set of change operations and change patterns, respectively, to it (Weber et al., 2008). Starting from this observation, Provop provides an *operational approach* for managing process variants based on a single process model (see Fig. 4a). In particular, process variants can be configured by applying a set of high-level change operations to a given process model. We denote the latter as *base process.*

In the following, we provide an overview of our Provop approach and describe it along the different phases of the process lifecycle.

4.1 Modeling

In the modeling phase, first of all, a base process, from which the different process variants can be derived through configuration, has to be defined. Following this, high-level change operations, which can be applied to this base process, are specified (Hallerbach et al. 2008a; Hallerbach et al., 2008d).

Defining the Base Process: Basic to the configuration of process variants is a base process, which serves as reference for the high-level change operations. When considering typical use cases as well as the overall process landscape in an enterprise, different policies for defining such base process are relevant. Basically, Provop supports the following ones:

- *Policy 1 (Standard Process)*: Here, the base process represents a domain-specific standard or reference process. In the automotive domain, for example, such reference processes exist for Engineering Change Management. Usually, a standard process has to be adjusted to meet specific requirements; i.e., it must be possible to derive variants from it. Provop assists designers in correctly defining the necessary adjustments when configuring a process variant out of the reference process.
- *Policy 2 (Most Frequently Used Process)*: If one process variant is used more frequently than others, it can be chosen as base process. This reduces configuration efforts in terms of the number of processes for which adjustments become necessary. Provop maintains statistics on the use of process variants to enable

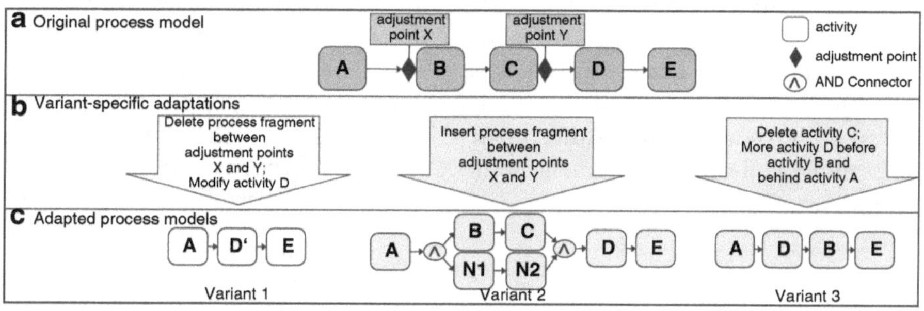

Fig. 4 Variant configuration by process model adaptation

Policy 2. Generally, Policy 2 does not ensure that the average number of change operations needed to configure the variants out of the base process becomes minimal.

- *Policy 3 (Minimal Average Distance)*: When applying change mining to a collection of variants, we can derive a base model such that average distance between this model and its variants (i.e., the number of high-level operations needed to transform the base process into the process variant) becomes minimal (Li et al. 2008a). Thus, configuration efforts can be reduced accordingly. For mining process variants, we utilize algorithms we developed in the MinAdept project (Li et al. 2008b).
- *Policy 4 (Superset of all Process Variants)*: The base process is created by merging all variants into one process model using conditional branchings; i.e., the base process realizes a "superset" of all relevant variants. Consequently, every element that is part of at least one variant belongs to the base process as well. When deriving process variants, therefore, only DELETE operations have to be applied.
- *Policy 5 (Intersection of all Process Variants)*: The base process comprises only those elements that are part of all variants; i.e., the base process realizes a kind of "intersection" of relevant variants. Therefore, the base process covers the identical elements of the process variants. When deriving process variants, no DELETE operations have to be performed, but elements may have to be moved, modified, or inserted.

Policies 1–5 differ in one fundamental aspect: When using Policy 1 or 2, the respective base process serves a specific use case; i.e., it represents one process variant valid in a specific context. Policies 3–5, in turn, have been especially designed for configuring variants and thus do not necessarily represent a semantically valid process model. Which policy to choose mainly depends on the modeling scenario and the present process landscape; e.g., if a standard process already exists, Policy 1 will be recommended.

Change Operations: A base process can be adjusted in different ways to configure a specific variant. Provop supports the following adaptation patterns: INSERT, DELETE, and MOVE process fragments, and MODIFY process element attributes. And fragments constitute connected process subgraphs (including single activity nodes and edges respectively), which not necessarily have a single entry and single exit. To refer to fragments and elements of the base process within such change operations, we use *adjustment points*, which correspond to the entry or exit of an activity or connector node (e.g., split and join nodes) of the base process.[1] Adjustment points are labeled with unique names. As an example consider "adjustment point X" in Fig. 4, which corresponds to the entry of activity B.

[1]If only single elements are affected by a particular change operation, their process element IDs may be used alternatively.

Table 1 Change operations (i.e., change patterns) supported by Provop

1. INSERT-Operation	
Symbol	
Purpose	Addition of process fragments (A process fragment consists of at least one process element, e.g., activity nodes or control edges).
Parameters	Process fragment to be added with entries and exits marked by adjustment points. Target position of the process fragment within the base process, marked by adjustment points for entries and exits. Mapping between entries and exits of the added fragment to the target position within the base process (i.e., mapping of the respective adjustment points).
2. DELETE-Operation	
Symbol	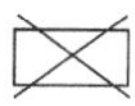
Purpose	Removal of process elements
Parameters	Process fragment to be deleted with entries and exits marked by adjustment points. Alternatively: deleting single elements by referring to their ID.
3. MOVE-Operation	
Symbol	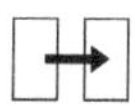
Purpose	Change execution order of activities
Parameters	Process fragment to be moved with entries and exits marked by adjustment points. Target position of the process fragment marked by adjustment points.
4. MODIFY-Operation	
Symbol	
Purpose	Change attributes of process elements
Parameters	Element ID Attribute name Value to be assigned

Table 1 gives an overview of the change operations currently supported by Provop. Each entry describes the purpose of the respective operation, its parameters, and the symbol representing it. The formal semantics of respective change patterns is described in Rinderle-Ma et al. (2008). Note that Provop covers only a subset of the change patterns presented in Weber et al. (2007, 2008), which have turned out to be the most relevant ones needed for variant configuration in practice; i.e., we were able to capture the different scenarios discussed in the introduction section based on these change patterns. It is also worth mentioning that Provop provides an extensible approach, to which other change patterns may be added later.

Grouping Change Operations into Options: As the number of change operations required to configure all relevant variants might become large, Provop allows to structure multiple change operations by grouping them into the so-called *options*. This is useful, for example, if the same change operations are always applied in conjunction with each other when configuring certain variants. Think of, for example, the handling of a medical examination in the radiology unit of a hospital. While for ambulant patients no transport between ward and radiology room is required, basic patients first have to be transferred from the ward to the radiology unit and later back to the ward. To capture the latter variant, we need to add two activities at different positions of the respective base process. This can be achieved by defining the two insert operations and grouping them in one option.

Constraint-based use of Options: Our case studies have revealed that options are often correlated in a structural or semantical manner. To capture this, Provop considers three types of relations between options, which can be explicitly defined by the user: dependency, mutual exclusion, and hierarchy.

- *Dependency*: When applying different options conjointly to the base process (e.g., due to semantical dependencies), the user can explicitly define a dependency relation between them. Dependency relations are directed; i.e., if relation "Option 1 depends on Option 2" holds, the inverse relation (i.e., "Option 2 depends on Option 1") is not true.
- *Mutual exclusion*, in turn, is helpful to describe which options must not be used in conjunction with each other when configuring variants.
- *Hierarchy*: The definition of option hierarchies allows for the inheritance of change operations. If an option is selected to configure a particular variant and has an ancestor in the option hierarchy, the change operations defined by the ancestor options will be applied as well. This reduces the amount of change operations defined in options and also structures the options landscape; i.e., maintenance is improved.

When defining relations between options, generally, the designer does not only use one relation type but may also apply them in combination with each other as well. Provop allows for the combined use of multiple relations and ensures consistency of a set of relations applied in a given context. For example, contradictory relations (e.g., a mutual exclusion between an option and its parental option) must not be applied. Due to lack of space, we omit further details on how such contradicting constraints can be identified.

The ability to define explicit relations between different options eases their use significantly. Additionally, Provop excludes semantic errors when configuring a process variant, as we will discuss in the sequel.

Context Model: Provop allows for context-aware process configurations; i.e., it allows for the configuration of a process variant by applying only those options relevant in the given *process context* (Hallerbach et al. 2008b). This, in turn, necessitates a model capturing the process context. In Provop, such context model comprises a set of *context variables*. Each context variable represents one specific dimension of the process context, and is defined by a name and value range.

Table 2 Context model of a vehicle repair process

Variable name	Range of values	Behavior
Vehicle type	Type 1, Type 2, Type 3, Type 4	Static
Maintenance	Yes, No	Static
Security level	low, medium, high	Static
Workload	low, medium, high	Dynamic

Table 2 shows an example of the context model defined for the vehicle repair process from Fig. 1. The depicted context variables do not only differ in their names and range of values but also in another important aspect. While some context variables are defined as *static*, others are classified as *dynamic*. For example, the value of the context variable *Workload* is raised or lowered from time to time according to the current workload of the garage (e.g., switching from "medium" to "high" if many new repair orders emerge at the same time). Thus, this variable is of dynamic nature, as its value may change during process execution. The context variable *Vehicle Type*, in turn, is static as the vehicle type is set once and does not change during the repair process.

4.2 Variant Configuration

In the configuration phase, the base process, the options defined for it, and the context model are used to configure the models of the different variants. More precisely, a particular variant is configured by applying a sequence of options and their corresponding change operations to the base process. We describe the steps needed for configuring a variant in Provop:

Step 1: Select relevant options. To configure a particular variant, usually, only a subset of the defined options is relevant. Therefore, as a first step in the configuration phase, the set of relevant options has to be identified. One possible approach is to ask users to manually select the relevant options. However, this would require sufficient knowledge about available options and their effects (i.e., change operations). In particular, if users have to choose among a large number of options, this approach will get error-prone (e.g., relevant options might be omitted or wrong ones chosen).

A more sophisticated approach is to select relevant options based on contextual knowledge. Rather than mapping already configured process variants to a context description, *context-aware process configuration* allows for the combination of the concepts provided by options and context models. In Provop, this linkage is realized by the use of *context rules*. Such rules, can be assigned to the options and make use of the defined *context model*. Regarding a given context, all options whose context rules evaluate to true, are applied to the base process and therefore determine the respective variant. As special case, the base process itself may serve as variant (i.e., no option is applied). In Step 3, we describe the order in which the selected options are applied to the base process.

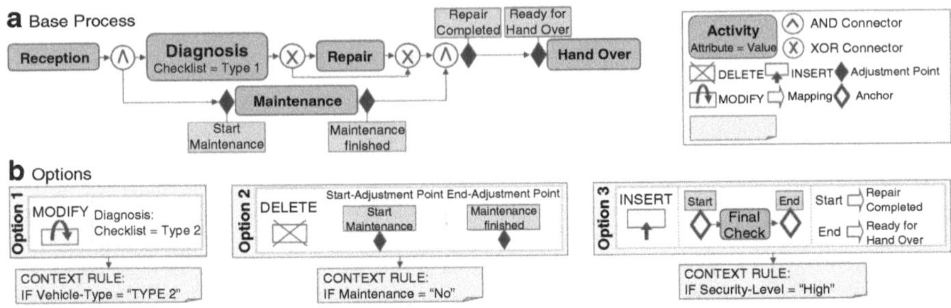

Fig. 5 Example of context dependent options

Figure 5 illustrates how the three variants of the repair process (cf. Fig. 1) are captured in Provop: The standardized process of Fig. 1a is defined as the base process out of which the variants are configured. This base process contains several adjustment points (e.g., "Start Maintenance" at the entry of activity *Maintenance*). As mentioned, adjustment points may be referred to by options and their change operations. Furthermore, Fig. 5b depicts three options: Option 1 performs a modification of activity *Diagnosis*. It will be applied if the type of the vehicle is of value *Type 2*. Option 2, in turn, will delete the maintenance activity if no maintenance of the vehicle is requested. Finally, Option 3 inserts a final security check activity in case of high security levels. The variants of Fig. 1b–d can now be configured by applying a subset of these options to the base process. For example, if the context of a process variant is defined by the expression "*Vehicle-Type* = *Type 2* AND *Maintenance* = *No* AND *Security-Level* = *Low*," Options 1 and 2 will be applied resulting in Variant 1 (cf. Fig. 1b).

Step 2: Evaluate relations between selected options. As aforementioned, options may be related. Generally, for a sequence of options to be applied to the base process, compliance with explicitly defined constraints has to be ensured. For example, if a selected option depends on another one, not yet contained in the set of selected options, this set will have to be adjusted accordingly. Generally, this can be achieved either by adding missing options to the selection list or by removing the ones that cause the constraint violation. Another constraint violation will occur if the selection set comprises mutually excluding options. In this case, one of the conflicting options has to be removed by the user in order to restore consistency. In summary, option constraints are considered to ensure semantical correctness and consistency of the selected set of options at configuration time.

Step 3: Determine the order in which options shall be applied. Generally, selected options have to be applied in sequence; i.e., their order has to be specified when configuring a variant. A naïve approach would be to sort these options in the order they were created; e.g., by making use of their creation time stamps. Obviously, this approach will only make sense if the options and their change operations are commutative. Otherwise, unintended and inconsistent variant models can result, particularly when applying options in the wrong order. Figure 6 shows an example: After applying Option 1 to the base process, an intermediate model is derived with

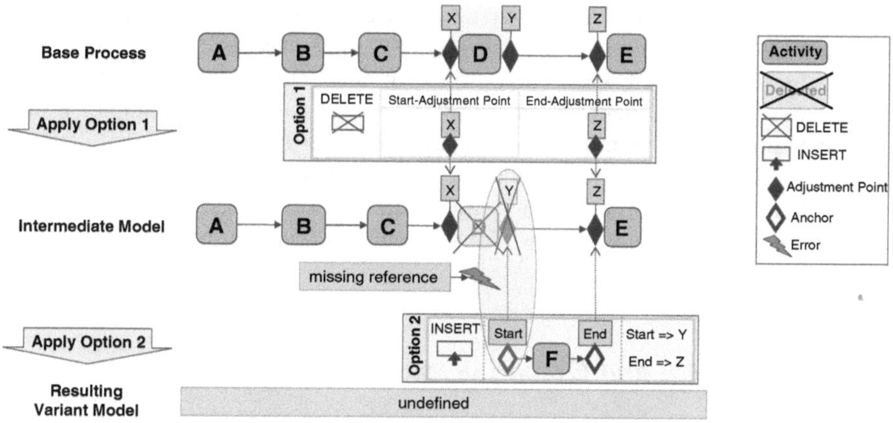

Fig. 6 Syntactical error after applying options in wrong order

activity D and adjustment point Y being deleted.[2] This model is now used as "reference model" for applying Option 2. In the present case, Option 2 cannot be applied as the adjustment point Y it refers to was deleted when applying Option 1. In order to avoid such inconsistencies, Provop allows defining the order in which selected options shall be applied. Furthermore, wrong option sequences, resulting in erroneous variant models afterwards, are excluded based on well-defined correctness criteria (see Step 5). Finally, by evaluating predefined sequencing constraints, a correct application order can be determined.

Step 4: Applying options and their change operations. After selecting the options and determining their order, their change operations are applied to the base process in order to configure the model of the respective variant. Generally, change operations have specific pre- and postconditions, which allow us to guarantee their correct application.[3] As one precondition, for example, process elements to which an operation refers have to be present in the respective model. Thus, the problem depicted in Fig. 6 would be recognized before applying the INSERT-operation of Option 2; i.e., Provop would disallow to apply the two options in the depicted order.

Step 5: Checking consistency. The variant models resulting from the sketched configuration procedure are supposed to be executed in the process enactment phase. Therefore, consistency and correctness of the models have to be guaranteed. In addition to the already described constraint-based selection approach (cf. Step 2), Provop validates the resulting models by checking the consistency and correctness

[2]Note that this example indicates that we need more advanced change support considering the special semantics of adjustment points. Generally, the user should be able to define whether adjustment points may be deleted when applying certain change operations or shall be kept in the intermediate model. In the latter case, the deleted activities and nodes respectively are replaced by silent activities without associated actions. Generally, silent activities and adjustment points are removed after application of all selected options.

[3]For a formal semantics of respective change patterns, we refer to (Rinderle-Ma et al. 2008).

of data and control flow. Unlike other variant configuration approaches (van der Aalst et al. 2008), Provop does not necessarily require a consistent and correct base process as starting point when configuring variants. This follows from the above described policies for defining the base process. Assume, for example, a base process being defined as intersection of its variants. If two variants have different activities to write a data object, read by a common activity, the base process would only contain the reading activity and thus be inconsistent in terms of data flow. Of course, Provop excludes such flaws for the configured variant models.

4.3 Deployment and Execution

After the configuration phase, the resulting variant model needs to be translated into an executable workflow model. Common tasks emerging in this context are to assign graphical user interfaces, to subdivide workflow activities into human and automated tasks, or to choose the right level of granularity for the workflow model. In Provop, we are focusing on problems arising in the context of variant management.

One major aspect concerns the *context-aware configuration* of the different variants. To also capture *context changes* during process instance execution, Provop supports *dynamic context variables*; i.e., variables whose values may change during process execution. When using dynamic context variables for defining a context rule of an option, the decision whether to apply the corresponding change operations or not has to be made at runtime. As a consequence, the respective process variant either cannot be completely configured when creating the process instance or it has to be reconfigured during runtime. To allow for the dynamic reconfiguration of a process instance of a variant model, Provop supports *variant branches*. Basic idea is to encapsulate the adjustments of single options within these variant branches. The split condition at a variant branching corresponds to the context rule of the option. Whenever process execution reaches a variant branch, the current context is evaluated. If the split condition evaluates to true, the variant branch will be executed, i.e., the change operations will be applied to the base process. Otherwise, the variant branch is skipped and therefore all adjustments of the option are ignored. Provop ensures the constraints regarding the use of options in the context of such dynamic reconfigurations as well. However, the handling of respective correctness issues is outside the scope of this chapter.

Figure 7 shows an example of a *variant branch definition* in conjunction with the INSERT operation.[4] If the workload of a garage is *high*, subcontractors will be commissioned to provide maintenance activities. Thus, Option 4 will be applied adding corresponding activities *Commissioning Sub-contractor* and *Support*

[4]Note that every change operation supported by Provop requires specific considerations here.

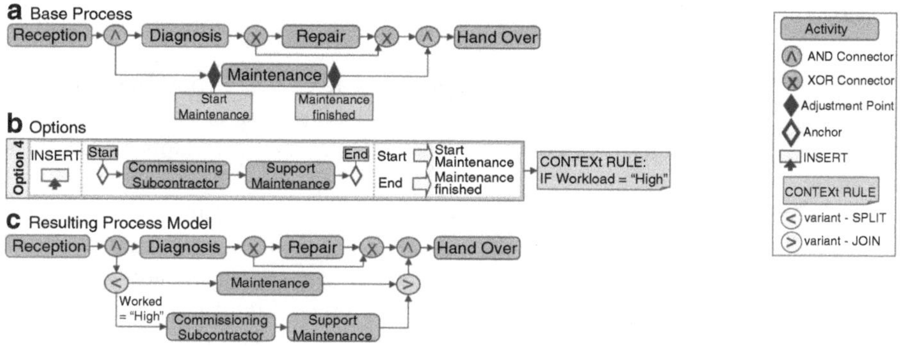

Fig. 7 Dynamic configuration of process variants

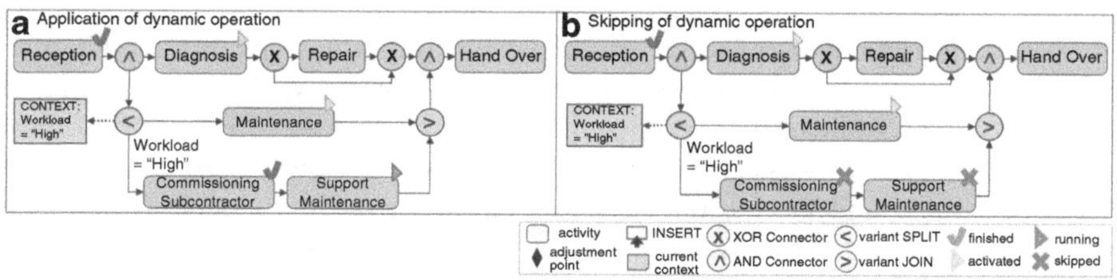

Fig. 8 Determine variant at runtime

Maintenance to the base process. As the context variable *Workload* is dynamic (cf. Table 2), these activities are encapsulated in a variant branch (indicated by the encircled "less than" and "greater than" symbols). Furthermore, context rule of Option 4 is used as split condition. Whenever a variant branch is reached during process execution, corresponding context rules are evaluated. If they evaluate to true (cf. Fig. 8a), the variant branch will be executed; otherwise, it will be skipped (cf. Fig. 8b).

4.4 *Maintenance and Optimization*

When evolving base processes in Provop (e.g., due to organizational optimization efforts), all related process variants (i.e., their models) are reconfigured automatically. Thus, maintenance efforts can be significantly reduced. However, evolving and optimizing the base process may affect existing options, for example, when referred adjustment points are moved to a new position or are even deleted. Such problems are detected in Provop; e.g., by checking whether the definitions of existing options are affected by the adaptations of the base process model. Furthermore, solving those conflicts is largely automated.

5 Related Work

Though the support of process variants is highly relevant for practice, only few approaches for variant management exist. In particular, there is no comprehensive solution for the adequate modeling of a large number of variants based on a common master process model.

There exist approaches that provide support for the management and retrieval of separately modeled process variants (i.e., optimizations of the multi-model approach). For example, Lu and Sadiq (2006) allow storing, managing, and querying large collections of process variants within a process repository. Graph-based search techniques are used in order to retrieve process variants that are similar to a user-defined process fragment (i.e., the query is represented as graph). Obviously, this approach requires profound knowledge about the structure of stored processes, an assumption that does not always hold in practice. Variant search based on process metadata (e.g., the process context) is not considered.

An important area related to variant management is reference process modeling. Usually, a reference process has recommending character, covers a family of process models, and can be customized in different ways to meet specific needs. Configurable event process chains (C-EPCs), for example, provide support for both the specification and the customization of reference process models (Rosemann and van der Aalst 2007; Rosa et al. 2007; vom Brocke 2007). When modeling a reference process, EPC functions (and decision nodes) can be annotated to indicate whether they are mandatory or optional. Respective information is considered when configuring the C-EPCs. A similar approach is presented in Gottschalk et al. (2007). Here, the concepts for configuring a reference process model (i.e., to enable, hide, or block a configurable workflow element) are transferred to workflow models. Similar to Provop, these approaches allow to define constraints (denoted as "requirements") regarding the application of different adjustments of the reference process (e.g., two activities either may have to be deleted together from the reference process or none of them).

In principle, respective approaches constitute optimizations of the *single model approach* introduced at the beginning of this chapter. As opposed to Provop, the suggested methods neither allow to move nor add model elements nor to adapt element attributes when configuring a variant out of a reference process model. Basically, the provided configuration support corresponds to the one of Policy 4 where the chosen base process (i.e., reference process) constitutes the superset of all process variants. Obviously, in this specific scenario, only delete or optional delete operations (i.e., dynamic delete operations in Provop) become necessary in order to configure a particular process variant out of a reference process model. However, Policy 4 is only one out of several configuration policies supported by Provop; i.e., a base process can be defined in a more flexible way.

Different work exits on how specialization can be applied to deal with process model variability taking advantage of the generative power of a specialization hierarchy (Wyner et al. 2003; van der Aalst and Basten 2002). In the context of the MIT Process Handbook, for example, Wyner and Lee (2003) show how specialization can be enabled for simple state diagrams and dataflow diagrams, respectively. For both kinds of diagrams, a corresponding set of transformation rules is provided that result in process specializations when being applied to a particular model. Similarly, van der Aalst (2002) discusses transformation rules to define specialization for process models based on Petri Nets. Finally, Wyner et al. (2003) show how specialization can be used to generate a taxonomy of processes to facilitate the exploration of design alternatives and the reuse of existing designs. Obviously, specialization and process taxonomies also allow to capture process variants to some degree. As opposed to the discussed approaches, Provop follows an operational approach, which is independent of the underlying process meta model. In addition, Provop provides comprehensive support for the context- and constraint-based configuration of process variants.

Variants are relevant in many other domains as well, including product line engineering and software engineering. For example, fundamental characteristics of software variability have been described in Bachmann and Bass (2001). In particular, software variants exist in software architectures and software product lines (Becker et al. 2001, Halmans and Pohl 2003). In many cases, feature diagrams are used for modeling software systems with varying features. A similar approach is offered by the so-called plus-minus-lists known from variant management in bill-of-materials. Correctness issues are not considered in both cases.

Another contribution stems from the PESOA project (Bayer et al. 2005, Puhlmann et al. 2005), which provides basic concepts for variant modeling based on UML. More precisely, different variability techniques like inheritance, parameterization, and extension points are provided and can be used when describing UML models. As opposed to PESOA, the operational approach enabled by Provop provides a more powerful instrument for describing variance in a uniform and easy manner; i.e., no distinction between different variability mechanisms is required.

Finally, La Rosa et al. (2008) present an approach, which goes beyond control flow and extends business process configuration to roles and objects.

6 Summary and Outlook

We have described the Provop approach for configuring and managing process variants. Provop considers the whole process life cycle and supports variants in all phases. This includes advanced techniques for modeling variants in a unified way and within a single process model, but without resulting in too complex or large model representations. Based on well-defined change operations, on the ability to group change operations into reusable options and on the possibility to combine options in a constrained way, necessary adjustments of the base process can be easily and consistently realized when creating and configuring a variant.

In future research, we will apply Provop in industrial context. One of the challenges we have to tackle concerns flexible execution of variants; i.e., to allow for dynamic switches between variants during runtime. Finally, a detailed case study based on a prototype implementing the Provop approach will be conducted. This prototype is based on the ARIS tool utilizing the programming interface provided by ARIS (IDS Scheer 2008).

References

Bachmann F, Bass L (2001) Managing variability in software architectures. In: Proceedings of symposium on software reusability, New York, ACM Press, pp 126–132

Bayer J, Buhl W, Giese C, Lehner T, Ocampo A, Puhlmann F, Richter E, Schnieders A, Weiland J, Weske M (2005) PESOA – process family engineering – modeling variant-rich processes. TR 18/2005, Hasso-Plattner-Institute, Potsdam, Germany

Becker M, Geyer L, Gilbert A, Becker K (2001) Comprehensive variability modeling to facilitate efficient variability treatment. In: Proceedings of 4th international workshop of product family engineering (PFE'01), LNCS 2290, Bilbao, Spain, pp 294–303

Becker J, Lis L, Pfeiffer D, Räckers M (2007) A process modeling language for the public sector – the PICTURE approach. In: Wybrane Problemy Elektronicznej Gospodarki, pp 271–281

Gottschalk F, van der Aalst WMP, Jansen-Vullers MH, la Rosa M (2007) Configurable workflow models. Int J Cooper Inform Syst 17(2):177–221

Hallerbach A, Bauer T, Reichert M (2008a) Modellierung und darstellung von prozessvarianten in provop. In: Proceedings of modellierung'08 (in German), Berlin, Germany, LNI P-127, pp 41–56

Hallerbach A, Bauer T, Reichert M (2008b) Context-based configuration of process variants. In: Proceedings 3rd international workshop on context-aware business process management (TCoB'08), Barcelona, Spain, pp 31–40

Hallerbach A, Bauer T, Reichert M (2008c) Managing process variants in the process life cycle. In: Proceedings of 10th international conference on enterprise information systems (ICEIS'08), Barcelona, Spain, pp 154–161

Hallerbach A, Bauer T, Reichert M (2008d) Issues in modeling process variants with provop. In: Proceedings of BPM'08 workshops, Milan, Italy

Hallerbach A, Bauer T, Reichert M (2008e) Anforderungen an die modellierung und ausführung von prozessvarianten. Datenbank Spektrum 24:48–58

Halmans G, Pohl K (2003) Communicating the variability of a software-product family to customers. Software Syst Model 2(1):15–36

IDS Scheer (2008) ARIS platform method 7.1

La Rosa M, Lux J, Seidel S, Dumas M, ter Hofstede AHM (2007) Questionnaire-driven configuration of reference process models. In: Proceedings of the 19th international conference on advanced information systems engineering, LNCS 4495, Trondheim, Norway, pp 424–438

La Rosa M, Dumas M, ter Hofstede AHM, Mendling J, Gottschalk F (2008) Beyond control-flow: extending business process configuration to roles and objects. In: Proceedings of ER'08, pp 199–215

Lenz R, Reichert M (2007) IT support for healthcare processes – premises, challenges, perspectives. Data Knowl Eng 61(1):39–58

Li C, Reichert M, Wombacher A (2008) Mining process variants: goals and issues. In: IEEE 5th international conference on services computing (SCC'08), pp 573–576

Li C, Reichert M, Wombacher A (2008a) Discovering reference process models by mining process variants. In: Proceedings of 6th international conference on web services (ICWS'08), Beijing, China, IEEE Computer Society Press, pp 45–53

Lu R, Sadiq S (2006) On managing process variants as an information resource. Technical report no. 464, University of Queensland, Australia

Müller D, Herbst J, Hammori M, Reichert M (2006) IT support for release management processes in the automotive industry. In: Proceedings of 4th international conference on business process management (BPM'06), LNCS 4102, Vienna, Austria, pp 368–377

Mutschler B, Reichert N, Bumiller J (2008) Unleashing the effectiveness of process-oriented information systems: problem analysis, critical success factors and implications. IEEE Trans Syst Man Cyberm C 38(3):280–291

Puhlmann F, Schnieders A, Weiland J, Weske M (2005) PESOA – variability mechanisms for process models. Hasso-Plattner-Institute, Potsdam, Germany

Rinderle-Ma S, Reichert M, Weber B (2008) On the formal semantics of change patterns in process-aware information systems. In: Proceedings 27th international conference on conceptual modeling (ER'08), LNCS 5231, Barcelona, Spain, pp 279–293

Rosemann M, van der Aalst W (2007) A configurable reference modeling language. Inform Syst 32:1–23

van der Aalst W, Basten T (2002) Inheritance of workflows: an approach to tackling problems related to change. Theor Comput Sci 270(1–2):125–203

van der Aalst W, Dumas M, Gottschalk F, ter Hofstede AHM, La Rosa M, Mendling J (2008) Correctness-preserving configuration of business process models. In: Proceedings of fundamental approaches to software engineering, LNCS 4961, Budapest, pp 46–61

VDA (2005) Engineering change management (ECM) – Part 1: engineering change request (ECR) Version 1.1, Recommendation 4965 T1

vom Brocke J (2007) Design principles for reference modelling. Reusing information models by means of aggregation, specialisation, instantiation, and analogy. In: Fettke P, Loos P (eds) Reference modelling for business systems analysis. Idea Group Publishing, Hershey, PA, USA, pp 47–75

Weber B, Reichert M (2008b): Refactoring process models in large process re-positories. In: Proceedings of the 20th international conference on advanced information systems engineering (CAiSE'08), LNCS 5074, Montpellier, France, pp 124–139

Weber B, Reichert M, Rinderle S, Wild W (2006) Towards a framework for the agile mining of business processes. In: Proceedings of BPM'05 Workshop, LNCS 3812, pp 191–202

Weber B, Rinderle S, Reichert M (2007) Change patterns and change support features in process-aware information systems. In: Proceedings of 11th international conference on advanced information systems engineering (CAiSE'07), LNCS 4495, Trondheim, Norway, pp 574–588

Weber B, Rinderle S, Reichert M (2008) Change patterns and change support features – enhancing flexibility in process-aware information systems. Data Knowl Eng 66(3):438–466

Weber B, Reichert M, Wild W, Rinderle-Ma S (2009) Providing integrated life-cycle support in process-aware information systems. Int J Cooper Inform Syst (IJCIS) 18(1):115–165

Wyner GM, Lee J (2003) Defining specialization for process models. In: Malone TW, Crowston K, Herman GA (eds) Organizing business knowledge – the MIT process handbook. MIT Press, Cambridge, MA, pp 131–174

Process Choreography Modeling

Alistair Barros, Thomas Hettel, and Christian Flender

Abstract A significant development in business process modeling over recent years has involved the B2B choreography perspective, where message exchanges between collaborating partners are explicitly captured. Most of the proposals to date have focused on how message exchanges can be captured through a shared, global perspective between collaborating partners and used to enforce the ordering of individual message send and receive tasks within the processes of the partners. In the wider setting of analysis and design, the B2B perspective represents an important context through which requirements for information systems and their business processes are elicited, as seen through numerous informal methods and techniques. In this chapter, we address the gap between high-level analysis and detailed design concerning the B2B context, proposing extensions for choreography languages to allow for modeling of this context to be seamless across the analysis and design phases. Based on an example taken from the supply chain management domain, we identify three important requirements for extensions: *functional scoping* of different areas concerning a domain, which can then be modeled and related to each other in isolation; *stepwise refinement* of choreography models, reminiscent of classical analysis techniques; and the introduction of *conversation semantics* expressing the intent of logically related message exchanges of choreographies. Accordingly, we propose extensions to choreography modeling and an improved analysis of requirements, such as breakdowns in negotiations that take place between collaborating partners, using an adaptation of BPMN.

A. Barros (✉)
SAP Research, Brisbane, Australia
e-mail: alistair.barros@sap.com

J. vom Brocke and M. Rosemann (eds.), *Handbook on Business Process Management 1*, International Handbooks on Information Systems,
DOI 10.1007/978-3-642-00416-2_12,

1 Introduction

Choreography, as originally coined through Web services standardization efforts, is a particular aspect of business processes, which relates to the way business partners coordinate their activities in a value-chain. The focus is not on full orchestrations of processes operating within these partners, but rather on the collaboration that takes place *between* partners (Hofreiter et al. 2008). Collaboration in value-chains entails messages (document) exchanges in an orderly fashion: e.g., first, a retailer sends a purchase order request to a supplier; next, the supplier either confirms or rejects intention to investigate the order; then supplier proceeds to investigate stock for line-items and seeks outside suppliers if necessary; accordingly, the supplier sends a confirmation or rejection back; during this period, the retailer can send requests to vary the order, etc.

The need for modeling choreographies, over and above conventional business process modeling, has become increasingly important as businesses shift their operations into wider value-chains featuring many collaborating partners and dynamic outsourcing and insourcing of services. Such a setting can involve not tens but hundreds of message exchanges. Interactions between partners can go beyond simple request–response interactions into more complex multicast, contingent requests, competing receives, streaming, and dynamic routing among different patterns (Barros et al. 2005). Moreover, message exchanges cluster around distinct scenarios, otherwise known as *conversations*, such as: creation of sales orders; assignment of carriers of shipments involving different sales orders; managing the "red tape" of crossing customs and quarantine; processing payment and investigating exceptions. Conversations as such entail a set of message exchanges that are correlated in different ways, e.g., Barros et al. (2005) provide a list of patterns for correlating message exchanges into conversations (e.g., key-based, function-based).

By abstracting away from internal processing details of processes, choreography models bring message exchanges and their logical grouping as conversations into view (Polyvyanyy et al. 2010). This allows partners to plan their business processes for interoperation without introducing conflicts. An example of a conflict could arise if a retailer was allowed to send a variation on a purchase order immediately after sending the initial request – because a supplier may not be able to efficiently confirm availability of stock. Once conversational sequences in choreography models are agreed upon, they can be mapped to each partner's orchestration models (Decker and Weske 2007).

In terms of developments in business process modeling, choreography languages, as introduced in recent years, are largely suitable at the detailed design and often implementation focused phase. This is because the details of message exchange and message correlation are seen as an extended consideration of interoperability, which is relevant once implementation choices have been made (e.g., using Web services and orchestration through WS-BPEL) (Leymann et al. 2010).

The concern of collaborations, however, is also of interest during higher levels of process analysis where interactions between partners establish the *context* upon which requirements are analyzed. Typical lines of enquiry involve determining the functional scope of the business domain being analyzed and the landscape of partners, their underlying business processes and the triggers that activate their execution, the business objectives advanced and the operational impediments that stand in the way, etc. This is the subject of the early stages of IS analysis and design in which informal, diagrammatic techniques are typically used to understand collaborations between partners, e.g., Structured Analysis and Design (Yourdon 1989).

The difference between classical techniques of analysis and contemporary techniques for choreography modeling – both of which concern process collaboration – is that former is informal, omitting detailed considerations of message exchange, and supporting business analysts to establish the broader organizational context through iterative and typically intensive "whiteboard" analysis.

This chapter provides insights into the way choreography modeling can be extended for the purposes of both high-level process analysis and detailed design. To this end, it first provides an insight into current state-of-the-art for choreography modeling, illustrating how message exchanges and conversations can be modeled by adapting the widely used Business Process Modeling Notation (BPMN) (Aagesen and Krogstie 2010). With this insight in place, it then discusses requirements for choreography languages that are pertinent for high-level process analysis. Three requirements for extending choreography modeling are proposed, namely: the way choreography models are scoped, detailed, and interrelated for large domains; the way they are refined in a stepwise manner from the highest context level to the detailed implementation-specific level; and the way intent of message exchanges qualify message exchanges in order to improve analysis of models from a semantic point of view. To illustrate how these requirements can be met, specific extensions are illustrated using the Semantic Object Modeling (SOM) framework. The result is that choreography modeling is carefully managed in complex domains and harmonized across high-level analysis and detailed design, with improved analysis of models possible, e.g., breakdown in the negotiations intended by message exchanges can be automatically detected.

2 Choreography Modeling at Detailed Process Design

A straightforward way of modeling choreographies is by connecting process models at points where messages are exchanged. In BPMN, this is done through the collaboration diagrams, as illustrated in Fig. 1[1]. For a detailed insight into BPMN, the reader is referred to Aagesen and Krogstie (2010), Kemsley (2010), and White et al. (2008).

Figure 1 shows a collaboration diagram where BPMN pools are expanded to reveal orchestration details per participant (for *Shipper*, *Retailer* etc). Message flows (dashed arrows) connect the elements in the different pools related to different participants and thus indicate message exchanges. For example, a *Planned*

[1]Zapletal et al. 2010 deal with choreography modeling using the UML profile UN/CEFACT's Modeling Methodology (UMM).

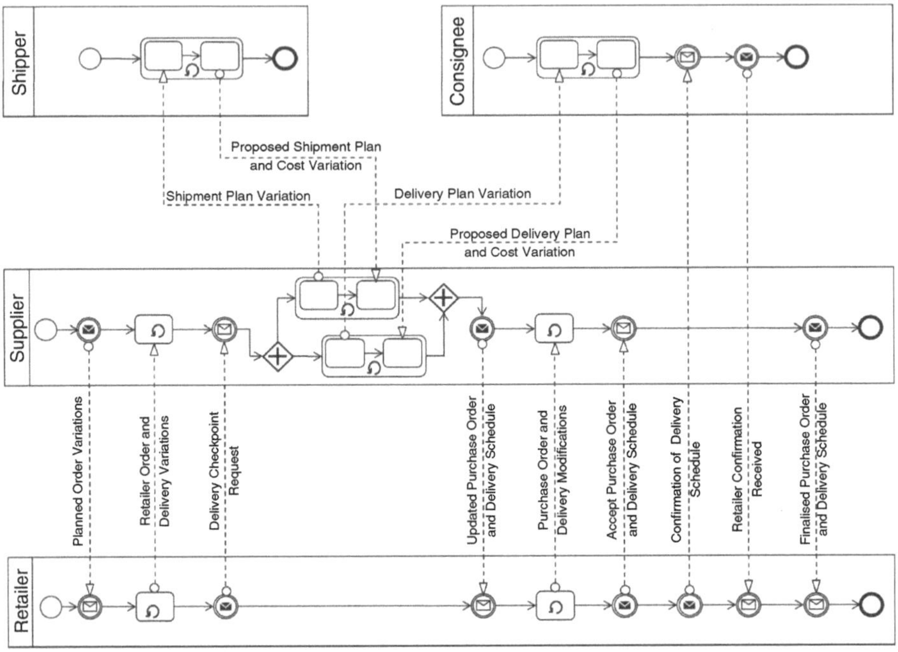

Fig. 1 Interconnecting process models

Order Variations message is sent by the *Supplier* to the *Retailer*; the corresponding send and receive have been modeled using regular BPMN messaging events. BPMN also lends itself to supporting a number of messages of the same type being sent. For example, a number of *Retailer Order* and *Delivery Variations* messages can be sent from the *Retailer* to the *Supplier*, indicated by respective multiple instances constructs (for brevity, the actual elements for sending/receiving inside the multiple instances construct have been omitted).

Taken as a whole, the scenario modeled in Fig. 1 entails shipment planning for the next supply replenishment variations: the *Supplier* confirms all previously accepted variations for delivery with the *Retailer*; the *Retailer* sends back a number of further possible variations; the *Supplier* requests to the *Shipper* and *Consignee* possible changes in delivery; accordingly, the *Retailer* interacts with the *Supplier* and *Consignee* for final confirmations.

It should be noted that in practice, interprocess connections would be made against process models, which serve as interfaces, since these allow hiding of actual internal processes and provide flexibility for internal processes to change without "breaking" interconnections. A major problem with model interconnections for complex choreographies is that they are vulnerable to errors – interconnections may not be sequenced correctly, since the logic of message exchanges is considered from each partner at a time. This in turn leads to deadlocks. For example, consider the role of *Retailer* in Fig. 1 and assume that here, by error, the order of *Confirmation Delivery Schedule* and *Retailer Confirmation received* (far right) were swapped.

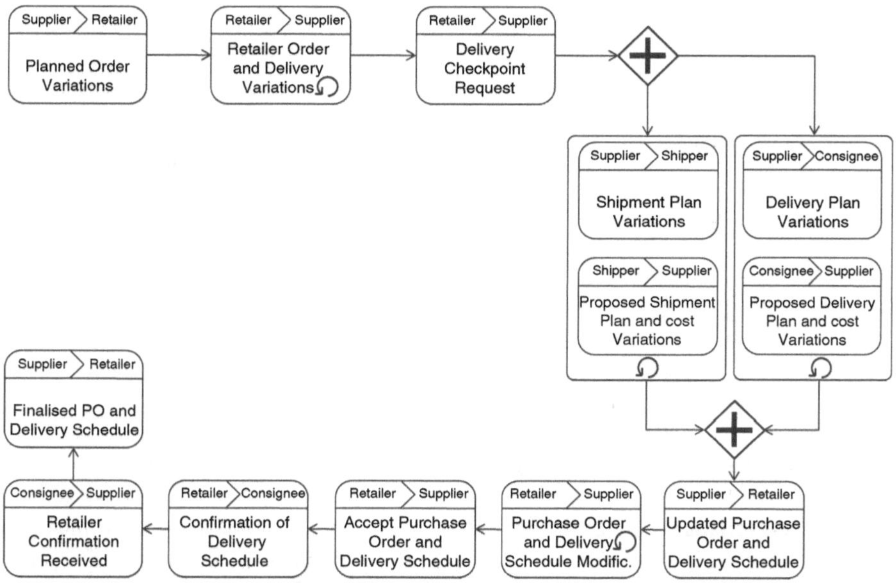

Fig. 2 Modeling of message exchanges as flow elements

This would result in a deadlock since both Retailer and Consignee would wait for the other to send a message. Deadlocks in general, however, are not that obvious and might be difficult to spot.

Accordingly, the need to model choreographies, independent of the perspective of individual partners – the so-called *global* perspective – was inspired through Web services standardization efforts. WS-CDL (Kavantzas et al. 2005), which has succeeded previous efforts, models messages exchanges as first-class constructs. WS-CDL is implementation-specific and, as it turned out, difficult to map into popular process execution languages like WS-BPEL. This has inspired efforts for developing *implementation independent* (conceptual) modeling languages, notably Let's Dance (cf. Zaha et al. 2006). Figure 2 reformulates the above example of Fig. 1 to show how the message construct in Let's Dance can be adapted to describe choreographies explicitly in BPMN.

As shown in Fig. 2, a choreography activity represents the message exchange as an activity-like construct. The sender and receiver, directionality of message exchange, and the message type are expressed. Multiple instances, looping, and subprocess from regular BPMN are adapted for choreography activities to model concurrent iterations and decomposition of message exchanges in choreography activities.

As can be seen, the logic of a conversation is relatively simple to follow. Process routing constructs are leveraged to model the sequencing of message exchanges – without any dependency on processes of the participants. Of course, the choreography model needs to be mapped to participant processes. A major problem in this regard is the *local enforceability* of the required sequencing. That is to say, the sequencing in the global choreography model should be reflected in the sequencing

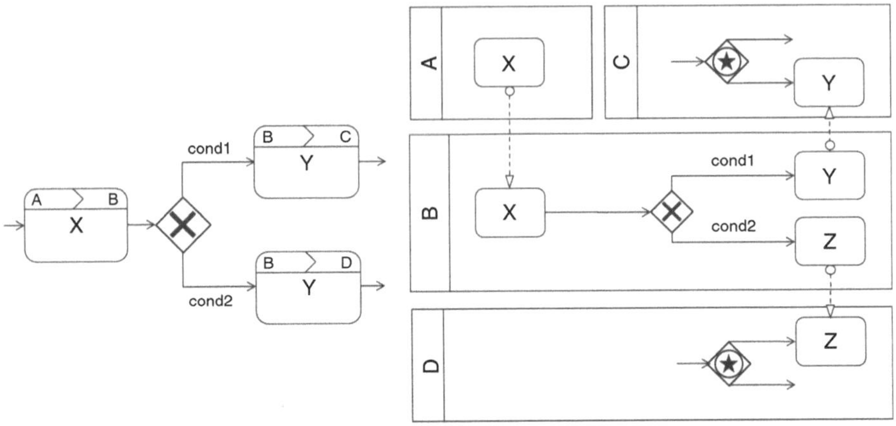

Fig. 3 Mapping an OR-split in a choreography model into partner process models

of message exchanges related within individual partner processes. An example of an unenforceable sequence would be if an exchange took place between a *Retailer* and a *Supplier*, which was followed by an exchange between *Shipper* and *Consignee*. How does *Shipper* know when *Supplier* received the message from *Retailer*?

Figure 3 provides an insight into how a choreography model containing an exclusive OR-split would be mapped into local models.

The choreography fragment on the left hand side in Fig. 3 specifies that there is an exclusive decision after message exchange *X* between actor roles *A* and *B*. The alternatives are sending message *Y* from *B* to *C* or message *Z* from *B* to *D*. This decision is reflected in the process model by an exclusive gateway in pool *B*, followed by two sending activities *Y* and *Z*. Pools *D* and *C* feature the corresponding receiving activities preceded by an event-based gateway, which not only waits for the potential interaction to happen but also for other events – indicating that interaction *Y* or *Z* may not happen. Such events could be further interactions or even a timer event to prevent the process from waiting indefinitely.

A problem with introducing additional behavioral logic in the choreography models is that it increases the complexity of the model, making it practically useful only for *individual* conversations to be modeled. In Let's Dance, there is a dedicated view depicting several conversations, as single logical groups (of message exchanges) in a separate diagram. This provides a "birdseye" perspective of the different conversations, which relate to a choreography domain (Barros et al. 2007a, b). Figure 4 illustrates an example of this. The different conversations once brought into view can then be detailed in separate choreography models, as shown in Fig. 3. Conversations that are closely related could be combined in the same choreography models – e.g., a message exchange in the Delivery Negotiation conversation leads to Shipment Schedule, Delivery Planning, and Delivery/ Dispatch conversations, and these could be modeled together.

This brief insight concludes with Fig. 5 showing how message exchanges can be expanded from the conversation view of Fig. 4. This essentially structural view

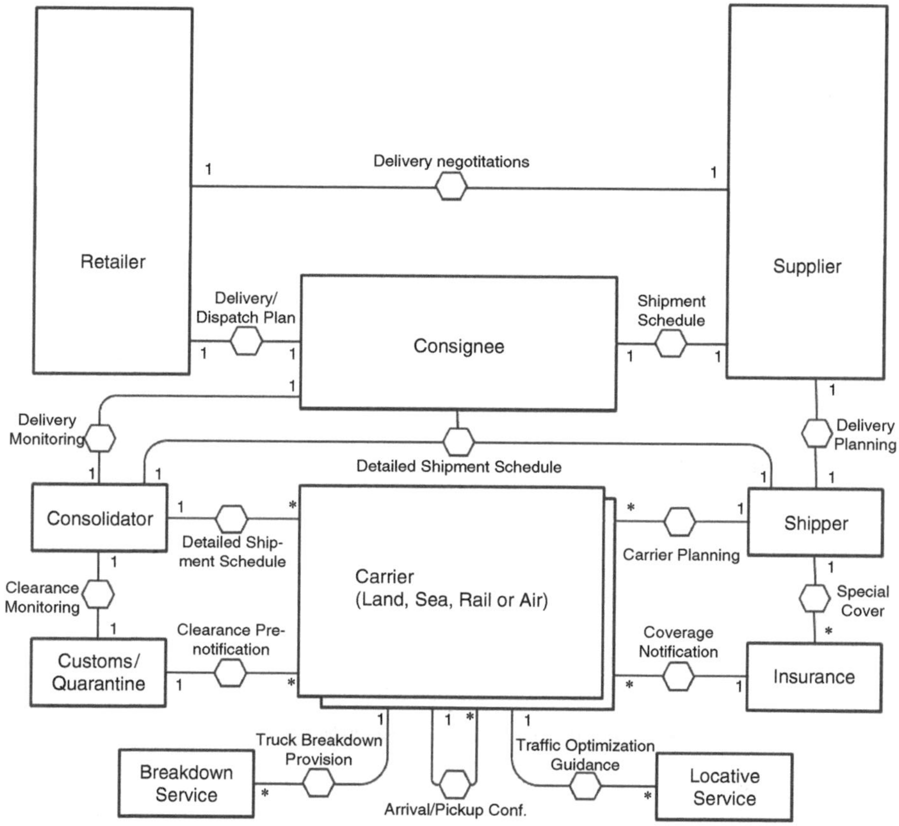

Fig. 4 View of a choreography domain summarizing the different conversations

shows the message exchanges without any behavioral ordering and can serve as a more detailed context for behaviorally focused choreography models. Similar to the use of UML Sequence Diagrams, they provide a "shorthand" insight into the message exchanges that take place. Figure 5 also indicates the correlation key type (e.g., *Order Id*) related to the conversation. This is required by message exchanges for association of messages with partner processes and their specific elements. Interestingly, a subconversation (keyed through *Variation Id*) is depicted, meaning that its message exchanges will include the parent and current conversation's correlation identifiers (*Order Id* and *Variation Id*).

3 Choreography Modeling at High-Level Process Analysis

To provide an impression of the complexity involved in B2B domains beyond the individual scenarios that are typically used to exemplify various choreography language proposals, consider the following:

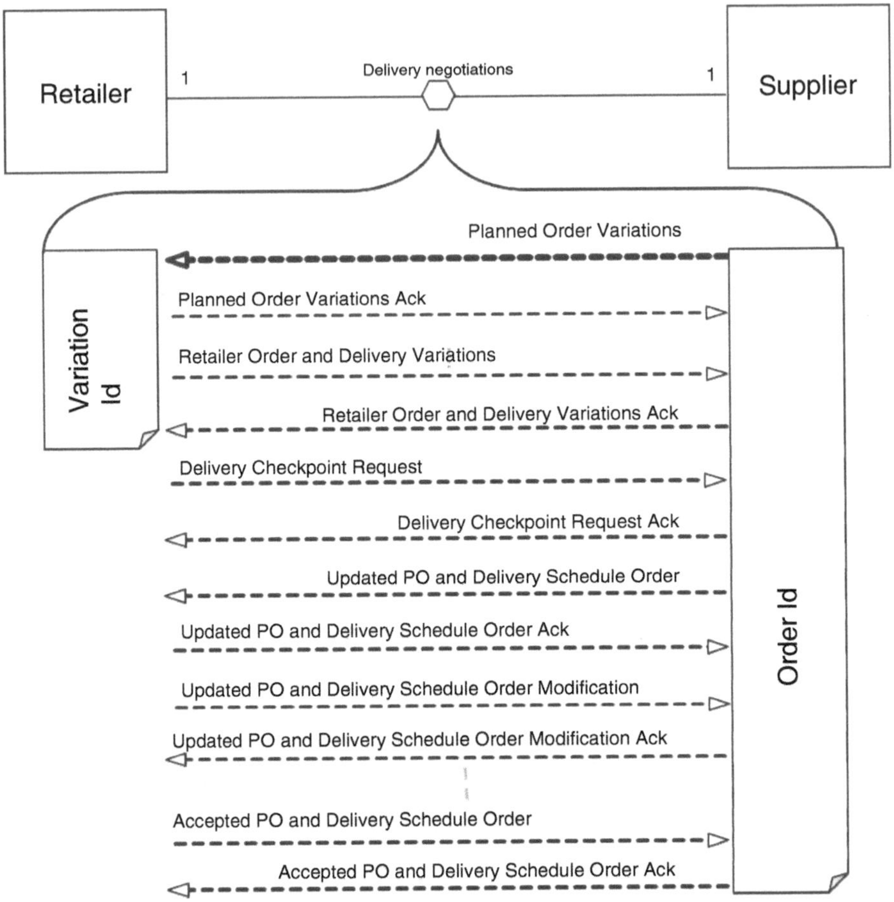

Fig. 5 Conversational view choreographies

Logistics, broadly understood, has the goal of fulfilling sales orders between buyers and suppliers, potentially spanning national boundaries. The process is triggered through a sales order and involves the management of shipments involving carriers and potentially different modalities (air, sea, and land). Different parts of the order can be shipped from different suppliers, and shipments starting from different origins can be consolidated at different warehouses whose capability (e.g., availability of freezing facilities) and capacity for different stock vary. Shipments that cross national boundaries need clearance from regulation authorities such as customs and quarantine. Payments for large or expensive shipments are made through letters of credit, whose monitoring and fulfillment need ongoing interactions with banks or payment intermediaries. Each one of these requirements entails different parties in different processes, leading to different conversations with a variety of start conditions, exceptional conditions, and object types.

Logistics concerns not only one-off sales orders but also sales contracts established over a certain period, e.g., a year, with replenishment quantities of line items subject to change over a rolling-wave (e.g., next 3 months). To sketch the organizational scenario:

The buyer (e.g., a supermarket) having determined supply requirements through market and relevant purchase patterns establishes a replenishment contract with each supplier (wholesalers of dairy, fruit and vegetable, meat, etc.) over a period. Contracts identify periodic delivery at specific times. Variations on replenishment can occur after contracts are established; however within rolling wave periods (e.g., next 3 months), strict obligations are required for replenishment. Any deviations in time and materials, which violate replenishment thresholds defined in the contract, lead to financial liability for the supplier. In addition, ad hoc orders can be requested during the rolling wave.

Since value chains in practice feature tens to hundreds of stakeholders, the process of capturing a choreography needs to be incremental, iterative, and detailed at the right level, to shed light on requirements in the first place, prior to detailed validation and implementation concerns. Some parties come to the fore through analysis of the operations of others. Other parties fade into the background as their operations are seen as ancillary. Only when the system landscape stabilizes around common functions can detailed modeling of collaborations proceed.

To support the choreography modeling for the wider spectrum of analysis and design, the requirements, discussed in the following sections, are considered crucial.

3.1 Functional Scoping

For choreographies to be comprehensively modeled across a wide variety of requirements related to different business operations, models need to be carefully scoped and freed of unnecessary requirements. This would focus analysis on a related set of business requirements. In the logistics example, procurement of sales, establishment of a sales order/contract, assignment of carriers, and payments and exceptions are distinct and considerable business concerns, each entailing significant requirements for collaboration across different partners. Before the details of message exchanges can be properly discerned, a firm understanding of the following sorts of contextual issues needs to be established:

- What partners are involved and, specifically, which of their functional areas are involved? What is the risk of their inclusion (or noninclusion) given their current and future strategic directions?
- What are the broad business operations from the functional areas that are involved? In what ways do they need to be transformed (e.g., outsourcing decisions)? What problems for integration do they present (e.g., information, service or resource redundancies, bottlenecks, and disconnections)?

- What scenarios are involved and do they cohere with the common functional areas? What would be the impact of broader restructuring of coordination?
- What are the different systems involved and, again, what problems of integration do they present (e.g. redundancies, bottlenecks, disconnections)?

Addressing these requires insights and consensus from different stakeholders with a variety of perspectives, be they: internal or external to an organization; strategic, tactical, or operational; marketing, sales, or delivery; regulatory or commercial; specific cases or concerned with overall analytics, etc. In diverse value-chains, analysis of the many and different parts should therefore be focused through carefully scoped functional areas.

Different models for different functional considerations can arise by decomposing them from a common, ancestor choreography model. However, in diverse value-chains featuring related yet distinct areas – like product merchandizing, sales, transportation, payment, and exception processing – starting from same process and refining models is unnatural. While these choreographies may relate to each other through shared interactions, it is not natural to think of such diverse processes as refinements of a common starting point. Indeed, this would lead to conceiving of an entire organization through a single high-level process.

Thus, we require dedicated mechanisms for supporting the scoping of choreography models. This would facilitate effective analysis of wide-spanning choreographies through common functional areas. Identifying common areas, indeed the basis for commonality, is not straightforward. Commonality could relate directly to existing organizational units, business activities, or services. Under modern practice of enterprises, however, processes should be expected to cut organizational boundaries, be utilized through different markets (e.g., a logistics company could support customers in health, manufacturing, and high-tech), and delivery channels (e.g. franchises, subsidiaries, and resellers of a company and its services).

3.2 Stepwise Refinement

In addition to the scoping of choreography models, refinement/decomposition is a well-known mechanism used to manage the modeling of nontrivial processes.

Choreography languages such as WS-CDL and Let's Dance use classical process decomposition through which an ordered set of interactions (e.g., purchase order validation) are contained in submodels. Choreography submodels, as such, are used to simplify their parent models, leaving certain details to lower level models. Submodels may also be reused in other models, allowing common functionality referenced in a variety of models.

However, a distinct feature of B2B value-chains is the number of different partners and the range of interactions that can take place for shared concerns. This can lead to cumbersome submodels that are hard to comprehend outside the explanation of those who created them. To address this problem, extensions have been proposed for a *structural* aspect of choreography modeling, as we saw in

Fig. 4, and also in Let's Dance's role-based choreography views. This allows a modeler to depict the presence of many conversations in a single choreography model diagram.

Role-based views have been introduced in Let's Dance and BPEL4Chor (Decker et al. 2008). A major limitation of these proposals, however, is that a *single* modeling level is used to abstract details of interactions. For choreographies with a large number of interactions, it limits the modeler's freedom to introduce as many levels of abstraction in order to describe a conversation with different levels of detail. Too many details of interactions are introduced at the same level, limiting the comprehensibility of individual conversations.

In contrast, classical analysis and design techniques such as Data Flow Diagrams and Structured Analysis Design Technique (Yourdon 1989) allow for *stepwise refinement* of models. Although quite general and lacking in a precise meaning, these techniques are typically applied in large-scale projects to capture interactions between functional entities (which include business processes). Once models are refined at detailed levels, a behavioral perspective is introduced to capture sequencing dependencies of actions being modeled. Being informal, these techniques require the modeler to form correspondence between structural and behavioral aspects.

Clearly, stepwise refinement of choreography models should be supported, incorporating a structural perspective depicting conversations and reciprocal message exchanges (the "Birdseye") and behavioral perspective providing message ordering details.

3.3 Conversation Semantics

Message exchanges in choreography models generally designate request–response patterns between collaborating partners. Message exchanges, as discussed above, are logically related to conversations, which are intended to achieve a particular outcome (e.g., creation of a sales order or the preparation of a shipping contract). This is the case for even complex conversations in which, for example, request–responses can become nested at different levels and cascaded to other partners (e.g., assignment of external carriers) not involved in the highest request–response directly related to an outcome (e.g., fulfillment of a shipment contract).

Understanding when message exchanges have been sufficiently captured is a problem of requirements validation that is peculiar to choreographies. For well-established business operations, the insights developed through requirements analysis can lead to an adequate capture of message exchanges, and present practice can drive the validation of the different scenarios. If, on the other hand, a system is being extended or an altogether new system is being embarked upon, that assumption is far less likely to hold. Modeling of choreographies at the *conceptual* level is aimed at minimizing as far as possible inadequacies of supporting requirements, which are determined at the more expensive phase of implementation. Since B2B value-chains encompass different partners, business processes, and applications, the problem of insufficiently capturing requirements has a wide impact and therefore cost.

Current choreography techniques do not offer ways of guiding modelers towards sufficiently captured and validated models. Apart from soundness checks for livelocks, deadlocks, and termination that has been the subject of a considerable research in workflow analysis techniques (van der Aalst 1997), choreography models remain susceptible to semantic discrepancies. This is, of course, true of business process modeling techniques in general. However, choreography language developments, having being steered mostly from the Web services community, have not engaged in techniques from conceptual modeling that have been specialized on collaboration.

In particular, action-oriented techniques (Agerfalk 2004; Dietz 2006) were proposed to explicitly model pragmatic aspects of human language in order to understand collaborations semantically – beyond the goal of achieving interoperability. Action-modeling techniques draw from Speech Act theory (Searle 1969) to explicate the *intent* of interactions between actors. The fundamental idea, determined from an understanding of how humans communicate, is that through a word or sentences, a *speech act* is performed. This is qualified by further components, most notably an illocutionary act, which expresses an actor's intention (e.g., make an offer, request a quote, etc.); and a propositional act that refers to some propositional content and identifies what it is being talked about (e.g., an offer referring to a product, a sequence of tasks to be conducted in the future).

Speech acts formalize the social meaning of collaborations, e.g., initial requests, promises, or obligations to act, and ensuing action. Consequently, they can be used to develop negotiation patterns so that message exchanges can be understood from the context of interactions that are taking place. A technique, DEMO (Dietz 2006), utilizes Speech Acts to model interactions and provides some insight. Based on the illocutionary act (the intention of what is being said), DEMO identifies three phases within an interaction:

- The *offer* phase is made up of two speech acts, namely request, where an initiator requests something from an executor, and promise, where the executer promises to fulfill the request.
- In the *execution* phase, the executer executes what has been promised and thereupon states the fulfillment of the promise to the initiator in the result phase.
- In the *result* phase, the initiator then accepts the execution as being what has been requested and promised.

DEMO uses the illocutionary act to express how a speech act is to be taken. This is especially useful as the social context is implicitly or explicitly constituted by the intentional network of coordinating actors. When it comes to implementation, representational concepts are derived from this context. In that sense, context is determined by the potential actions, e.g., usage (make, accept, reject) of an offer.

Other approaches based on speech acts are Coordinator (Winograd 1987), SAMPO (Auramäki et al. 1988), Action Workflow (Medina-Mora et al. 1992)

(Denning and Medina-Mora 1995), MILANO (De Michelis and Grasso 1994), BAT (Goldkuhl 1995), and Action Diagrams (Agerfalk 2004).

A major critique of traditional action-oriented modeling approaches is their usage of interactional patterns, which are too restrictive. For instance, consider Winograd's action for conversation patterns (Winograd 1987), Medina's workflow loop (Denning and Medina-Mora 1995), or DEMO's simple request, state, accept pattern (Dietz 2006). Here, a requirement for using individual speech-acts for compositions of conversational actions must strive for maximum flexibility. From an empirical point of view, this is quite obvious since anything (e.g., interruptions, requestionings, sudden withdrawals, etc.) can happen during conversations and thus it should be possible to refine actions towards arbitrary complex coordination between actors. A second critique is related to the refinement of conversational networks towards executable representations.

4 Illustrative Modeling Proposals

This section illustrates modeling proposals that address the following of the requirements for choreography modeling that have been identified in the previous section:

- Functional scoping
- Stepwise refinement
- Conversation semantics

4.1 Functional Scoping

The scoping of choreography models, as discussed in the previous section, is required to bring distinct areas of B2B value-chains into view, allowing detailed analysis to proceed from a wider perspective. To illustrate how model scoping applies to choreographies and some of the subtle issues of supporting what seems to be a rather simple requirement, consider Fig. 6. It depicts some of the different functional areas of the Sales and Logistics case study, hereafter referred to as *choreography domains*.

Choreography domains (depicted as ellipses) provide the highest level of scoping for choreography models. As indicated in Fig. 6, more detailed submodels of choreographies are associated with – indeed *contained* in – a given choreography domain model. For instance, Let's Dance provides role-based, milestone-based, and interaction-based submodel types, and each of these would be contained in a domain model. Domains could also be associated with other organizational artifacts (e.g., organizational units, resources, and policies) that are not explicitly used in

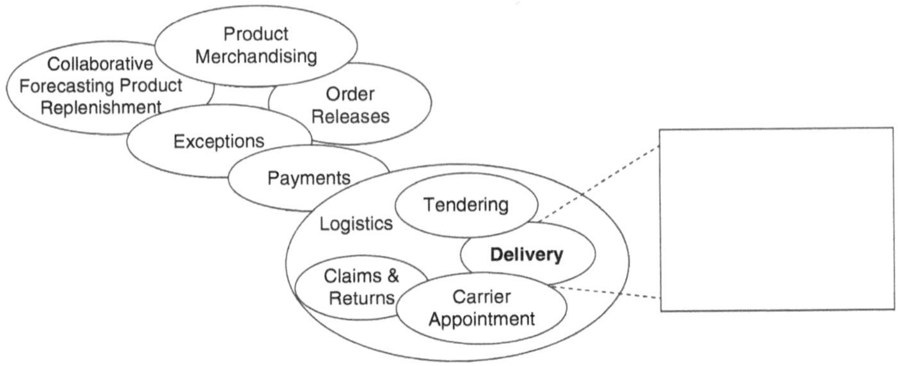

Fig. 6 Choreography domains

choreography modeling but which are supported through, say an enterprise modeling framework that a choreography modeling tool "plugs" into.

As with the functional areas in a value-chain, domain models have dependencies with other domain models (seen by the adjacencies of ellipses). In the context of choreographies, this means that they share message exchanges. As examples, Collaborative Forecasting Product Replenishment (out of which an order is produced) connects with Logistics (governing shipment of goods) and with Collaborative Forecasting, Planning, and Replenishment; Logistics connects with Payments and Exceptions. Dependencies between domains could be derived through the message exchanges of models that they contain, or the modeler may enforce dependencies at the domain level, thus constraining the scope of message exchanges in their contained models.

From Fig. 6, it can be seen that domains can be hierarchically structured: Logistics is decomposed into Carrier Appointment, Delivery, and Claims and Returns. Large and complex domains may be decomposed at an arbitrary number of levels. Thus, a given domain can be decomposed into leaf and nonleaf domains. However, only at leaf-levels do domains have models directly contained in them (nonleaf domains are purely used for abstracting domains).

Given that domain models are essentially containers and the concrete details of their choreography are captured in models that they contain, an issue for tooling is synchronizing a domain model. This is because different conversations modeled in different domains would be at different stages of development. Therefore, as different conversations are captured for domains, they need be synchronized and thus be made available for cross-domain interactions.

4.2 Stepwise Refinement and Conversation Semantics

As discussed in the previous section, stepwise refinement and conversation semantics play a part in the detailed analysis of choreography models. Current

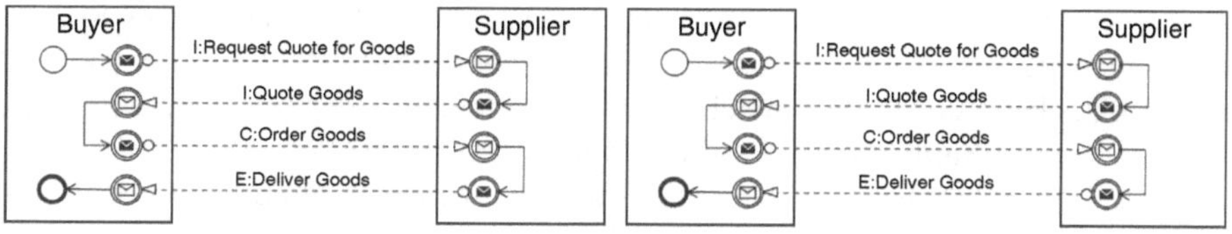

Fig. 7 Layer 1: Initial structural and behavioral view

choreography languages inadequately support these, limiting their suitability for modeling large and complex B2B value-chains. To show how they can be supported and are closely related, the extension of Semantic Object Model (Ferstl and Sinz 2006) for choreographies, as proposed in (Hettel et al. 2008), is presented.

Modeling of choreographies entail both structural and behavioral views of message exchanges between roles, as shown in left and right hand sides, respectively, of Fig. 7.

In the structural view, there are no routing constructs for expressing the ordering of message exchanges. Instead, Speech Acts are used to qualify the intent of a message exchange. The Speech Acts fit a negotiation pattern underpinning SOM's conversation semantics, as follows:

- Initializing (I) where both roles (actors in SOM) exchange information about the provided service
- Contracting (C) where both roles negotiate the terms of the service delivery/consumption
- Enforcing (E) where the negotiated services are provided/consumed.

I, C, and E identify the type of the illocutionary act (intention) of the Speech Act using a verb, e.g., order, request, confirm, and a noun identifying what is being talked about (propositional content), e.g., goods, delivery. In Fig. 7, a *Buyer* uses I act to request a quote from *Supplier* for a specific product he is interested in purchasing and the I act from the Supplier signifies the corresponding response. While a single request and response feature in the I phase of this negotiation, further message exchanges could take place. With the C act, the *Buyer* places an order, and thus a relationship between the quote and order is implied. In the next step, *Buyer* and *Supplier* commit to provide and consume a service, as such, with respect to the negotiated terms. This service, namely the delivery of the ordered goods, is signified using the *E:Deliver Goods* transaction. In a negotiation pattern, the I and C may be optional depending on whether both roles already know each other and whether a basic agreement has been established between both.

The behavioral view in SOM provides details about the sequence of acts beyond the broader negotiation protocol established in the structural view. Unlike other choreography languages, behavior is encapsulated within roles and not across roles (e.g., choreography activities in the between pools as has been proposed for BPMN 2.0). This arguably provides more flexibility for the way roles act and respond to speech acts. For detailing the behavior of partners, a BPMN-like notation was chosen with sending and receiving intermediate events linked by message flow edges. Sequence flow and gateways can be used to specify how one partner acts and reacts with respect to speech acts with others. When considered in isolation, none of the partners has a completely specified behavior. It is only in connection with other partners that a complete behavioral description can be derived.

In support of stepwise refinement, reminiscent of classical analysis and design techniques like Data Flow Diagrams that have been prevalent in commercial projects for value-chain analysis, roles can be decomposed in order to reveal further roles. Figure 8 provides some details of a refinement of the SOM model shown in Fig. 7 (layer 1).

As depicted in Fig. 9, a number of decompositions have been applied. *Buyer* was decomposed into *Procurement* and *Consignee* interacting according to the feedback-control principle: the management role *Procurement* acts as a management role regulating (R) the operational role *Consignee* by sending an advice to receive goods, whereupon *Consignee* replies (F for feedback) by confirming the receipt

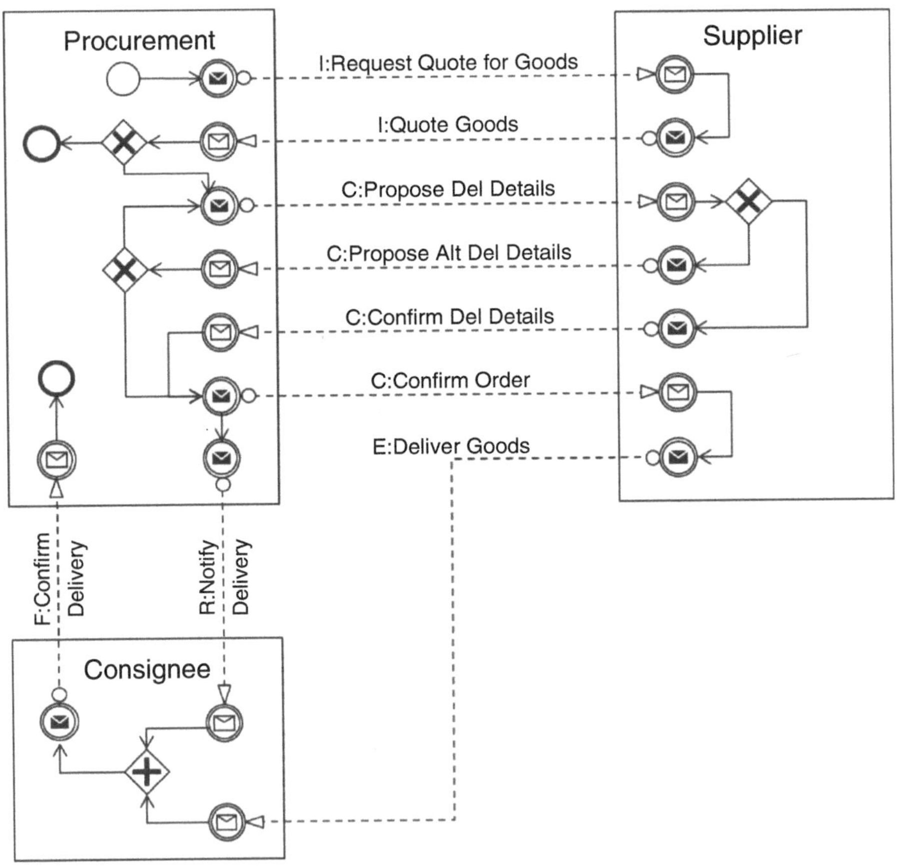

Fig. 8 Layer 2: Behavioral view showing the decomposition of Buyer into Procurement and Consignee

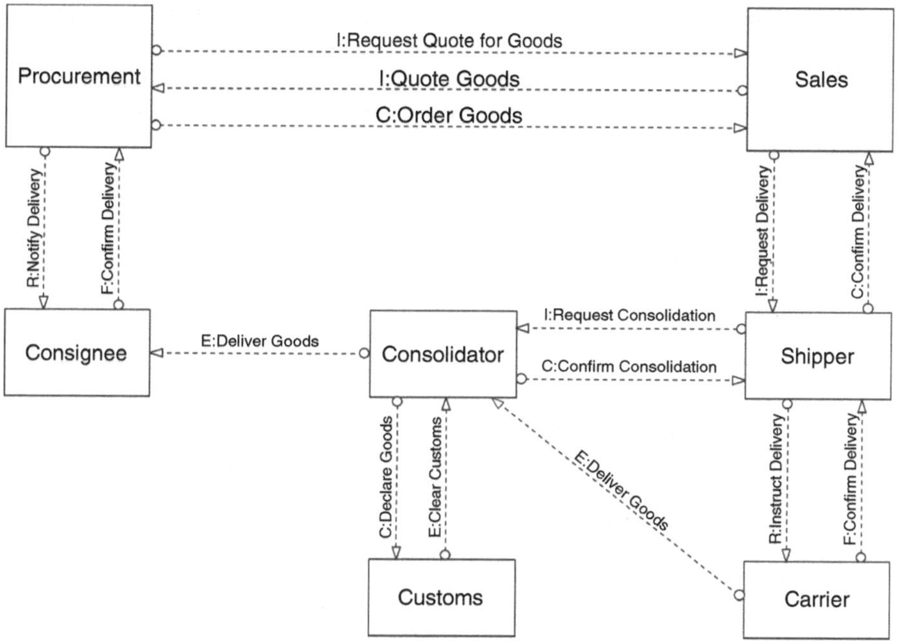

Fig. 9 Layer 1: Initial structural and behavioral view

of the delivery. On the right hand side, *Supplier* has been first decomposed into *Sales* and *Logistics*. Furthermore, Logistics was decomposed into Shipper, Carrier, Consolidator, and Customs.

The rule of role refinement requires that speech acts in the parent role be preserved. In Fig. 9, the acts between *Buyer* and *Supplier* have been preserved through *Procurement* and Sales as well as *Consolidator* and *Consignee*. Altogether, new acts can be introduced between subroles of the same super-role, as seen with *Sales* and *Shipper*.

In addition, speech acts and corresponding tasks may be decomposed. As shown in Fig. 8, *C:Order Goods* was decomposed to reveal a detailed negotiation: *C:Propose Delivery Details*, where *Procurement* proposes details (such as date, quantity, quality, and price); *C:Confirm Or Propose Alternative Details*, where *Supplier* confirms the details or proposes alternative details; and *C:Confirm Order*, where *Procurement* confirms the order with respect to the negotiated details. A further refinement sees *C:Confirm Or Propose Alternative Details* decomposed into the parallel subacts *C:Propose Alt Del Details* and *C:Confirm Del Details*. Here, *Supplier* has the choice between one of the aforementioned speech acts as reflected in XOR gateway. In turn, *Procurement* has a choice between either accepting the alternative details or proposing new details.

Taken together, the interplay of structural and behavioral views, and Speech Acts, provides improved manageability of the complexity and meaning of choreographies compared to that available in current choreography languages. The structural view provides simplified abstractions, holding the broad architecture of the choreography together. The behavioral view, with sequencing details of message exchanges (speech acts) localized in roles, can be developed in tandem with each level of the structural views or can be left to more detailed levels of modeling. Speech Acts on message exchanges provide the bridge between the two views.

4.3 Detecting Errors in Conversations

A major benefit of having conversational semantics, as described above, is the improved model checking that goes beyond detection of deadlocks, livelocks, and the like. In particular, it is possible to detect semantic discrepancies in conversations. An insight into these and their detection is now described. The reader is referred to (Hettel et al. 2008) where a formalization of SOM and model checking is presented.

Key to error detection in conversations is the precise description of a conversation in SOM models. So far, conversations have been intuited as a set of message exchanges, represented as speech acts between two roles. With Speech Acts, a conversation can be said to encompass all acts that are derived from an initial ICE or RF act between two roles. On a lower layer, a conversation may span several actors. By keeping track of all refinements that have been introduced for acts, different acts can be combined to one conversation. For instance, the Speech Act *E:Deliver Goods* between *Consolidator* and *Consignee* and the other acts between *Procurement* and *Sales* together form one conversation as they all originate from the same ICE.

4.3.1 Negotiation Breakdown

Requirements for successful negotiations may be other subsequent negotiations necessary to arrange additional services needed to provide the overall service. As choreographies model the collaboration of loosely coupled and autonomous roles, participants may withdraw from negotiations at any time, causing it to fail. Such failures may cascade through the model and cause encompassing negotiations to fail as well – leading to a so-called *negotiation breakdown*. A possible negotiation breakdown may be caused by *Shipper*, as an unsuccessful negotiation between *Sales* and *Shipper* may impact on the negotiation between *Procurement* and *Sales* and may cause it to fail, too (cf. Fig. 10 (left) and Fig. 9).

The negotiation breakdown analysis leverages SOM's typed Speech Acts to find subsequent negotiations between third parties that are encompassed in another negotiation. In order for a negotiation breakdown to occur, at least three actors, say X, Y, and Z, must be involved, connected via two ICE conversations C1 and C2. Assume X initiates the negotiation with Y. To be able to provide the requested service to X, Y needs to arrange for additional services provided by Z, which has to be negotiated as well. Only when these additional services are secured, the

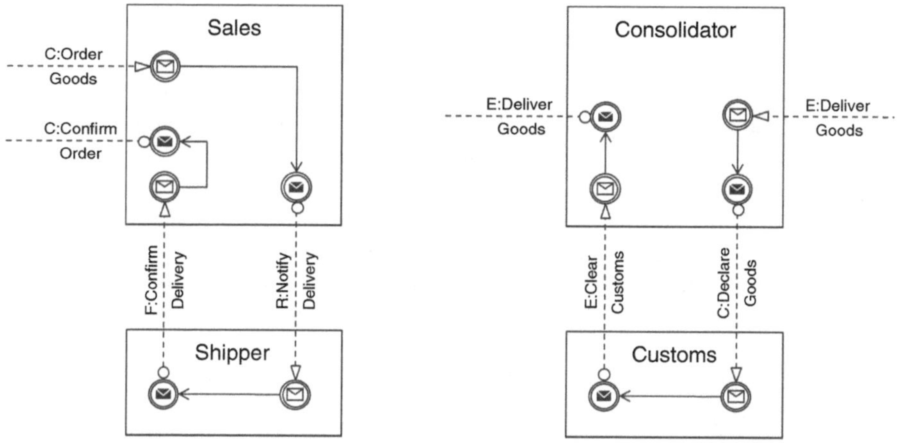

Fig. 10 *Left* relevant part of the behavior involving Sales and Shipper as shown in Fig. 8. *Right* relevant part of the behavior involving Consolidator and Customs as shown in Fig. 8

negotiation with X can be closed successfully. A negotiation breakdown can occur when the last negotiation act in C2 leads to the last negotiation act in C1.

4.3.2 Provision Breakdown

Once, two actors have agreed upon consumption and delivery, the service has to be provided and consumed. However, it may happen that after committing to a service provision, additional negotiations for supplementary services are required. If any of these negotiations fail, it may not be possible to provide the promised service, causing a *provision breakdown*. For instance, such a breakdown may be caused by *Consolidator* and *Customs* in the example depicted in.

For example, *Consolidator* talks to *Customs* after it received the goods from *Carrier*. If customs cannot be cleared for these goods, then the promised delivery cannot be made (cf. Fig. 10 (right) and Fig. 9.) This may pose a serious problem to other partners as they may be held liable to pay compensation for violating the contract. This scenario may be the result of erroneous modeling and therefore needs to be rectified by turning a possible provision breakdown into a possible negotiation breakdown. However, it may not always be possible to model the choreography differently to avoid such situations. Customs cannot be cleared upfront without having the actual delivery inspected. In this case, the affected actors may consider a risk mitigation strategy to counter such scenarios.

For a provision breakdown to occur, two ICE conversations C1 and C2 are necessary. The two conversations need to be intertwined in such a way that after the negotiation part in C1 is done, more negotiation speech acts follow in C2. Moreover, the service provision in C2 must lead to the service provision in C1. In such a constellation, failing to acquire the service provision in C2 causes a provision breakdown in C1.

5 Conclusion

The notion of choreography has its origins in Web standardization efforts, out of which dedicated modeling proposals have emerged for implementation-specific languages and platforms. Choreographies address collaborations between partners in B2B domains, and focus on message exchanges in particular. Hence, languages and techniques supporting choreography modeling are of relevance across high level analysis, where cross-organizational contexts are necessary to guide requirements acquisition, to detailed design, where cross-partner interaction dependencies need to come into view for detailed specifications of individual and interoperating processes.

In this chapter, we provided a background on choreography modeling and argued that the current capabilities are mostly suitable for detailed design. This creates a dichotomy for process specifications across modeling and design, despite situational differences in how modeling is applied. Based on insights from a logistics use case, we proposed three requirements for extending choreography modeling so that it could be equally suitable for high-level analysis. The requirement of scoping and stepwise refinement addresses the way models can be developed under the flux of requirements acquisition. In particular, we developed through SOM a structural view of message exchanges between collaborating partners, which simplify the context upon which the details of sequencing are introduced. For the requirement of conversational semantics, we introduced intent behind message exchanges through speech act theory. We discussed how analysis of conflicts in conversations, in the business sense, are possible, specifically breakdown in conversational negotiations and provisions.

Taken together, new insights are available for extending choreography modeling and the further challenges that lay ahead.

References

Aagesen G, Krogstie J (2010) Analysis and design of business processes using BPMN. In: vom Brocke J, Rosemann M (eds) Handbook on business process management, vol 1. Springer, Heidelberg

Agerfalk PE (2004) Action-oriented conceptual modelling. Eur J Inf Sys 13(1):80–92

Auramäki E, Lehtinen E, Lyytinen K (1988) A speech-act-based office modeling approach. ACM Trans Inf Sys 6(2):126–152

Barros AP, Dumas M, ter Hofstede AHM (2005) Service interaction patterns: towards a reference framework for service-based business process interconnection. Proceedings of the 3rd international conference on business process management 2005 (BPM 2005), Springer, Nancy, France

Barros AP, Decker G, Dumas M (2007a) Multi-staged and multi-viewpoint service choreography modelling. Workshop on software engineering methods for service-oriented architectures 2007 (SEMSOA 2007), Hannover, Germany

Barros AP, Decker G, Dumas M, Weber F (2007b) Correlations patterns in service-oriented architectures, fundamental approaches to software engineering, FASE'07. Braga, Portugal

De Michelis G, Grasso M (1994) Situating conversations within the language/action perspective: the Milan conversation model. In: Proceedings of the 1994 ACM conference on computer supported cooperative work. ACM Press, New York, NY, USA, pp 89–100
Decker G, Weske M (2007) Local enforceability in interaction petri nets. 5th international conference on business process management (BPM), LNCS vol 4714. Springer, Brisbane, Australia, pp 305–319
Decker G, Kopp O, Leymann F, Pfitzner K, Weske M (2008) Modeling service choreographies using BPMN and BPEL4Chor. 20th international conference on advanced information systems engineering (CAiSE), LNCS vol 5074. Springer, Montpellier, France, pp 79–93
Denning P, Medina-Mora R (1995) Completing the loops. Interfaces 25(3):42–57
Dietz J (2006) The deep structure of business processes. Commun ACM 49(5):58–64
Ferstl O, Sinz E (2006) Foundations of information systems (In German), 5th edn. Oldenbourg, Germany
Goldkuhl G (1995) Information as action and communication. In: Dahlblom B (ed) The infological equation, essays in the honour of B. Langefors. Gothenburg Studies in Information Systems, Gothenburg University, Sweden
Hettel T, Flender C, Barros AP (2008) Scaling choreography for B2B value-chain analysis. 6th international conference on business process management 2008 (BPM 2008), LNCS vol 5240. Springer, Milan, Italy, pp 294–309
Hofreiter B, Huemer C (2008) A model-driven top-down approach to inter-organizational systems: From global choreography models to executable BPEL. Paper presented at the Joint Conference on E-Commerce Technology (CEC'08) and Enterprise Computing, E-Commerce, and E-Services (EEE'008), Crystal City, Washington D.C., USA
Kavantzas N, Burdette D, Ritzinger G, Lafon Y (2005) Web services choreography description language version 1.0, W3C candidate recommendation, Technical report, 2005: http://www.w3c.org/TR/ws-cdl-10
Kemsley S (2010) Collaborative BPM: drivers and impacts. In: vom Brocke J, Rosemann M (eds) Handbook on business process management, vol 1. Springer, Heidelberg
Leymann F, Karastoyanova D, Papazoglov MP (2010) Business process management standards. In: vom Brocke J, Rosemann M (eds) Handbook on business process management, vol 1. Springer, Heidelberg
Medina-Mora R, Winograd T, Flores R, Flores F (1992) The action workflow approach to workflow management technology. 1992 ACM conference on computer-supported cooperative work. ACM, Toronto, ON, Canada, pp 281–288
Polyvyanyy A, Smitnov S, Weske M (2010) Business process model abstraction. In: vom Brocke J, Rosemann M (eds) Handbook on business process management, vol 1. Springer, Heidelberg
Searle J (1969) Speech acts. Cambridge University Press, Cambridge
van der Aalst W (1997) Verification of workflow nets. In: P. Azema and G. Balbo (eds), Application and Theory of Petri Nets, volume 1248 of Lecture Notes in Computer Science, pp. 407–426. Springer, Berlin
White SA, Miers D, Fischer L (2008) BPMN modeling and reference guide. Future Strategies Inc., Lighthouse Pt, FL
Winograd T (1987) A language/action perspective on the design of cooperative work. Hum Comput Interact 3(1):3–30
Yourdon E (1989): Modern structured analysis. Yourdon Computing Series Press, Upper Saddle River, NJ, USA
Zaha JM, Barros A, Dumas M, ter Hofstede A (2006) Let's dance: a language for service behaviour modelling. Proceedings of the 14th international conference on cooperative information systems 2006 (CoopIs 2006), Montpellier, France
Zapletal M, Schuster R, Liegl P, Huemer C, Hofreiter B (2010) Modelling inter-organisational business processes. In vom Brocke J, Rosemann M (eds) Handbook on business process management, vol 1. Springer, Heidelberg

Collaborative Process Modeling: The Intersport Case Study

Mikael Lind and Ulf Seigerroth

Abstract Business strategies need to be aligned with business process models. In this chapter, experiences from a collaborative process modeling effort performed at Intersport, Sweden, for the purpose of creating a solid base for taking a business into the future will be elaborated. In this effort, the new process design is aligned with strategic goals. By a codesign approach for deriving business process models, diverse stakeholders' knowledge and interests are captured in the development of tangible descriptions of the future. Business plans are given a meaning, and participating actors become committed to implement business strategies.

1 Introduction

The task of modeling and designing business processes has been acknowledged as critical for strategic development of business practices and appurtenant information systems (cf. Harmon 2009). Business processes have during the last decade won great attention in conceiving business practices due to its focus on the client as well as on other stakeholders (e.g., Davenport 1993; Davis 2001; vom Brocke and Thomas 2006). Business process modeling has been used for several purposes (cf. Bandara et al. 2006; Harmon 2009), such as reconstructing existing practice (AS-IS) and consequently using evolving process models for reflection, modeling the future (TO-BE), as well as determining historical chains of events. Practitioners within the IS-field tend to engage in conceptual modeling, focusing on business processes among other aspects, for the purpose of analysis, design, and evaluation of information systems (Davies et al. 2006). So far, little research has, however, been conducted on process modeling practices (cf. Bandara et al. 2006) and the

M. Lind (✉)
University of Borås, Viktoria Institute, Gothenburg, Sweden
Linköping University, Linköping, Sweden
e-mail: Mikael.Lind@hb.se

J. vom Brocke and M. Rosemann (eds.), *Handbook on Business Process Management 1*, International Handbooks on Information Systems,
DOI 10.1007/978-3-642-00416-2_13,

same consequently goes for procedures of collaboration in modeling. In related areas such as requirements engineering collaboration, workshops are pinpointed as an important success factor (cf. e.g., Gottesdiener 2002).

Business process models are also to be seen as tangible descriptions of patterns of actions performed by people, often supported by artifacts, within and between organizations (Goldkuhl and Lind 2008). This also means that such models could be used as a support in a transition process to take a business from one state to another. The aim of this chapter is to report experiences from an action research project where we have been involved in the transition process of Intersport, one of the largest sport retail chains in Sweden, in the task of designing business processes of the future in a collaborative modeling endeavor. The task of modeling TO-BE situations is often conceived as a design process that needs to be governed by clear and understandable guidelines. Many times, such governance has its foundation in business strategies where there is a need to create alignment between business strategies and different types of models and architectures (Ward and Peppard 2003; Pearlson and Saunders 2006; Lankhorst 2005). Using business process modeling for the management of processes has been acknowledged by several scholars (cf. e.g., Günther et al. 2008; van der Aalst et al. 2007). Having people engaged in the design of tangible process patterns based on strategic plans could be a way to create commitment and reveal flaws in strategic declarations. In this chapter, we address the process of designing Intersport's business processes for the purpose of creating a solid base for taking a business into the future where the new process design is aligned with the strategic goals.

We conceive this type of research as closely related to design science (e.g., Hevner et al. 2004) by regarding the creation of business process models as new and innovative artifacts. The process of deriving models is much about capturing different people's knowledge about diverse parts of business processes on different levels. Based on a social-constructivist view on knowledge creation, business process modeling becomes a design issue. Knowledge and commitment about the future are created by people interacting, i.e., acting socially in relation to each other. Throughout the process, different versions of models (solutions) coevolve with the understanding of the problem (cf. e.g., Dorst and Cross 2001). This means that different roles need to be involved in the process of modeling thereby constructing a joint view of the business processes that are the object of investigation. One way to conceive such process is to regard it as a codesign process (Lind et al. 2008) in which a number of views on reality coexist, in a setting of collaborative modeling, to be used for exploring solutions and the problem domain from different viewpoints. This coinnovative approach has been closely related to the streams of Web 2.0 (Lind and Forsgren 2008) in which clients are engaged in collaborative processes of design (cf. Albinsson et al. 2007; Lind et al. 2007).

This chapter also touches upon the area of enterprise modeling. As distinguished by Stirna and Kirikova (2008), this area could be divided into three parts; Modeling product (language and notation), Modeling Process (guidance), and Modeling Tool (support). We conceive process modeling as one subarea within enterprise modeling. Historically, a lot of emphasis has been put upon languages and notation for modeling. The notation is used for directing attendance during process modeling. The notation characteristics are however formed as ideals and an unresolved quest is how these should be applied in relation to situational characteristics in the modeling situation. Less research has thus been performed in relation to the modeling process, i.e., guidance for how the modeling should be performed.

The research reported in this chapter is driven from the question of *how to codesign business process models as a foundation for the implementation of business strategies*. The purpose of this chapter is to take important steps towards guidelines that elaborate on how to conduct collaborative process modeling in business process design. Following this section, instruments and theoretical insights related to business processes, process modeling, and strategic alignment will be presented. Following that, the case of Intersport will be described and then further reflected upon in a first strive towards guidelines for process design, collaboration, and alignment. The chapter will be concluded by some reflections related to performing business process design endeavors.

2 Process Modeling and Strategic Alignment

2.1 Collaborative Process Modeling for Strategic Alignment

In the domain of business process modeling, models being produced should be aligned with intended business plans and strategies. To meet this challenge, there is a need to understand and to be able to handle the complexity that exists in terms of different aspects or conceptual domains in the business (Lankhorst 2005; Vernadat 2002; cf. Langefors 1973). Lankhorst et al. (2005) exemplify these multiple enterprise aspects with five heterogeneous architectural domains (i.e., Information architecture, Process architecture, Product architecture, Application architecture, and Technical architecture) that are related to each other and the need for them to be integrated and aligned. The challenge is not to deal with isolated domains but to go beyond the individual models and to cope with how they are related to each other on different levels and how they, as parts, in the total picture, support different strategic goals (Lankhorst 2005). One way to achieve alignment between strategies, models, and in the end IS/IT-architectures is to adopt a codesign approach (Lind et al. 2007; Liu et al. 2002; Rittgen 2007). The aim with a codesign approach to process modeling is to simultaneously work with several different stakeholders in a collaborative way to avoid conceptual deviations between strategic plans and models on different levels. The necessity of such collaborative approach to process modeling has also been put forward by vom Brocke and Thomas (2006). They claim that relevant stakeholders in a certain modeling situation must be identified, and efficient ways of coordination between them need to be established.

Much of the discourse related to strategic alignment is based on the framework by Henderson and Venkatraman (1999) who put forward four dimensions and their strategic fit to each other (cf. e.g., Ward and Peppard 2003). Many of these dimensions are usually elaborated through modeling, and different models are used as an instrument to express how to achieve alignment and competitive advantage. Another more recent framework that also put forward alignment issues is the Strategic Triangle by Pearlson and Saunders (2006). In this chapter, our basic assumption is that different types of process models can serve as a vehicle for realization of strategic business plans.

2.2 Collaborative Process Modeling in Business Process Design

Process modeling requires the involvement and engagement of people. Design science as research approach has gained a lot of attention in IS and management research. In the design-science paradigm, knowledge and understanding of a problem domain and solutions are achieved through building and implementing designed artifacts (Hevner et al. 2004). As claimed by van Aaken (2007), a design science approach to management research makes this research more valid and reliable. The task of Business Process Management (BPM) is highly integrated with information systems development. "The design of organizational and interorganizational information systems plays a major role in enabling effective business processes..." (Hevner et al. 2004, pp 85). IS design research is concerned with an ongoing iterative exploratory creation and evaluation of IT artifacts where the artifact may be ranging from conceptual drawings to rigorously mathematically defined executables (Hevner et al. 2004).

In the context of this chapter, questions addressing the problem domain of how to codesign business processes, as formulated in the introduction, are *how can business principles in business strategies be transformed into business process models?, how could models be used as an essential transformational tool for successively reaching a desired state?, what kind of models should be used and in which stages of the process design?, which different versions of models do exist during a process design setting?, which patterns of cooperation should be emphasized during such endeavor?*, etc.

Within design science, the core concept is the artifact. Our conception is that an artifact, which does not exist without human involvement either by design or by interpretation, is created by human beings. In our perspective, an artifact can be instantiated as something with physical- and/or social properties. From this conception, some examples of artifacts are computers, softwares, methods, models, norms, attitudes, and values (cf. also March and Smith 1995). In social settings, several artifacts and several subjects often coexist (Lind et al. 2008).

In a conceptual framework proposed by Hevner et al. (2004), the understanding, the execution, and the evaluation of IS research combining behavioral-science and design-science paradigms are brought forward. In this framework, three integrated dimensions are depicted; *the environment* including people, organizations, and technology, the *IS research* pinpointing the creation and justification of artifacts, and *the knowledge base* bringing forward foundations and methodologies to be used in the creation and evaluation of artifacts. Further, by basing designs on existing theories and putting those into use through design science principles may also shed new light on these theories and their applicability in specific situations (cf. Markus et al. 2002). Hevner et al. (2004) continues by presenting seven design science guidelines for performing research.

For several reasons, the design-science framework with appurtenant guidelines provided by Hevner et al. (2004) is a good point of departure, towards a theory for performing business process design endeavors. The framework highlights a necessity to go into interaction with the environment relying on a defined knowledge base in the construction and evaluation of evolving business models. The guidelines prescribe important areas of concern to arrive at artifacts; in our case, business process models, which comply with validity claims, raised in the field of design science. As indicated in the introduction of this chapter, business process design is a task highly involving people's knowledge and commitment. In this task, the (different) models focusing business processes become core in the interplay of stating questions and giving answers by the people involved in the design.

In business process design settings, process models are continuously refined in a transformation process. These processes are highly characterized by people interacting with models as a point of reference and where the models can be seen as means for coordination of the modeling process. Business process models are built upon modeling languages (cf. e.g., Schuette and Rotthowe 1998), i.e., concepts and notation to be used for stating and answering questions. This means that the conception of business processes as well as the ways that people are interacting in a business process design becomes crucial in order to arrive at models for guiding people in the realization of business strategies (cf. vom Brocke and Thomas 2006). For the latter aspect, we rely on a codesign approach (Lind et al. 2008) as a way for adopting a line of thinking that business process models need to be part of, and the result of, people engaging in cocreation processes aligning business strategies and business process models. In this approach, an infinite number of views of reality are designed based on the intention of the participants of the process. As not stressed as much in the design science research proposed by Hevner et al. (2004), this approach means that people in the environment and researchers *jointly* create artifacts (business process models) and *collaboratively* develop an understanding of the problem to be solved.

2.3 Is a Business Process a Transformation or a Coordination?

Aspects to capture in business process models have been put forward by several scholars. Stemming from systems science (cf. e.g., Langefors 1973), a strive has for a long time been to distinguish aspects to conceive as essential constituting business processes (cf. Lind 2006). As advocated for by vom Brocke and Thomas (2006), the use of reference models can increase the efficiency and effectiveness of specific modeling processes. Reference models are conceived as a special information model that can be reused in the design process of other business process models (vom Brocke and Thomas 2006, pp 681). Reference models consist of generic aspects to focus upon and these need to be stated for the purpose of declaring views captured in business process models.

Traditionally, a view on organizations putting emphasis on the horizontal work in contrast to vertical division of labor has dominated the field of BPM. BPM has its origin from total quality management – TQM (Harrington 1991) and business process reengineering – BPR (Hammer 1990; Davenport 1993). Basically, this can be seen as an industrial view on business processes, where input (raw material) is transformed into output (finished products). As advocated by Keen and Knapp (1996), this is, however, not the only point of departure for the conception of business processes, e.g., the role of values (cf. vom Brocke et al. 2010) and the role of learning (cf. e.g., Leyking et al. 2007). These other dimensions do however require a foundational conception, a backbone, of business processes as a basis for contextualization.

This chapter relies on an ontological foundation by putting the action as the core of business processes. Such foundation has its root in American pragmatism (cf. e.g., Dewey 1922). In order to expand the scope beyond transformational dimensions of business processes, the notion of business act is conceived as the basic unit of analysis (cf. Lind and Goldkuhl 2003). A business act can be a speech act (communicative act) (cf. e.g., Searle 1969) or a material act. This notion of business act builds upon the notion of social action. An organization consists of humans, artifacts and other resources, and actions performed. Humans (often supported by artifacts) perform (internal and external) actions in the name of the organization (Ahrne 1994). Humans act in order to achieve ends (von Wright 1971). Human action often aims at making material changes. Humans, however, do not only act in the material world but they also act communicatively toward other humans. Human action is about making a difference, where such difference can have impact in the social world as well as in the material world. As described in Lind and Goldkuhl (2003), a business act is defined as the *performance of a communicative and/or material act by someone aimed towards someone else*. By using business act as the basic unit of business processes, transformative, co-coordinative, and interactive dimensions of business processes can be included (Goldkuhl and Lind 2008).

Transformative dimensions mean a focus on the transformation of deliverable products, in structured and sequenced ways, from base products (raw material). Coordinative dimensions mean that business processes involve important coordination mechanisms for the establishment, fulfillment, and assessment of *agreements* between involved stakeholders (e.g., suppliers and customers). Interactive dimensions are the special case of coordination in which the actors' performances of communicative and/or material exchanges are focused. As proposed by Goldkuhl and Lind (2008), these two viewpoints need to be combined to an integrative view where coordination (also including interaction) and transformation form an integrated texture of actions. In this sense, assignment processes become superior in relation to transformation processes.

3 Designing Business Processes in a Retail Chain

3.1 The Change Project at Intersport

In this action research project (cf. Lindgren et al. 2004), the main mission has been to identify and design Intersport's future business processes based on their new strategic business plan. Intersport is today a voluntary specialized retail chain for sports and recreation. This means that a majority of Intersport's stores are owned and run by individual merchants who cooperate under the common brand Intersport, a franchise concept. In addition to this, there are also a couple of stores in Stockholm and Gothenburg that are partly centrally owned by Intersport Sweden. The Intersport chain in Sweden is today constituted by 145 stores with a turnover of 3.3 billion SEK in 2007. Intersport Sweden is part of the Intersport International Corporation (IIC), which was founded in 1968 when ten independent European purchase organizations joined their forces. On the international arena, Intersport has over 4,900 stores in 32 countries. Intersport is the world's largest sports chain with stores in, for instance, Europe, Russia, Canada, and the Arabic Emirate. Intersport's total turnover is 8.37 billion Euros.

The background for this process design project is that Intersport Sweden has initiated an extensive change program where the goal is to meet the current and future need to create competitive advantage in retail for sports and recreation. In this change program, Intersport has made a major redesign of their strategic business model. The core of the change process for Intersport is to go from being a wholesale dealer with mostly independent stores to take an overall central responsibility over the value chain including the stores, i.e., to become both retailer and wholesaler in a structured and coherent value chain. In this sense, the scope of the business process design project covered activities arranged in a value chain spanning over several organizations. Intersport's change program goes under the name of Wholesaler – Business development – Retailer (WBR). In WBR, there are a number of business areas and change solutions suggested where the change process is spanning over the years 2007 to 201X. 201X means that Intersport's general plan is to have the new business strategy implemented to its full extent in 2013, but depending on the parts of the change program, the exact year can be 2012, 2013, or 2014. During this change process, there are a number of dimensions of the business that are planned to be (re-)designed and implemented.

Our way into this change program with process design was Intersport's evolving need to be able to address different change issues in WBR to different process contexts. They needed a solid ground for elaborating and dealing with different change dimensions that were expressed in WBR. One example of this is the ambition to develop a new IT strategy and new IS/IT architecture that were supposed to support the new strategic business plan. The business process design project has in this context meant to define the business practice for Intersport Sweden with respect to activities, results, prerequisites, work procedures, cooperation procedures, communication principles, roles, and responsibilities on different levels as descriptions of a future desired state. The focus of this project has been to describe how Intersport, in the future, wants to do business with their clients. For this purpose, business process models based on their new business strategy, which also included a new business model (The business plan 2007 "Towards future victories"), were derived. This was done through a high degree of involvement of people affected by the design. For Intersport, this covers everything in their business from strategic planning to products and services in use by their customers. Examples of new and important business principles covered by the new business plan for Intersport are:

- The responsibility for supplying and filling of the stores is moved from the stores to a central organization.
- A shift of focus from products to concepts.
- The coordination and distribution of Intersport's own and external brands should be done in the same way.
- Intersport should have control over 80% of the total collection in all stores (base collection and category collections).
- A shift from that stores initiate planning and ordering early in the process to a central unit that co-ordinate early planning and late distribution
- Implementation of a central retail function that should operate throughout the whole value chain, i.e. from strategic planning to customer.

Through these changes, Intersport expects to strengthen their position by adopting a retail focus with a centralized management and coordination. In combination with this, Intersport is also moving from a more narrow focus on products and purchase to a focus on concepts and sales. The external attraction should be increased in the value chain through development and clarification of Intersport's concepts, clarity in marketing, and placing the customer in focus. The aim is also to increase the internal efficiency through development of product logistics and cost programs. The mission is to take back the position as the strongest actor on the market of sports and recreation.

3.2 The Work Process in the Process Design Project at Intersport

The work process in this project has been tailored for the purpose of fulfilling the goals that are expressed in the new business plan. This means that the process design has been performed on different levels of abstraction but without going into too great details of the processes. By the recruitment of new competences and in-service training of existing personnel, the requirements in the new business plan is to be met. This has enabled us to invite and involve key competences at Intersport that were necessary in relation to the new business plan. The process design has mainly been focusing on two levels as the main result:

- Main process model (the one overall process model that covers the total business model, see Fig. 2 below).

- Detailed process models (detailed process models of all the parts in the main process model, see Fig. 3 below for an example).

These two levels are based on a concept for business process modeling where different levels of the practice need to be investigated and designed in order to create a coherent and functioning wholeness. This means that decisions that are made on a strategic or business level and expressed in models on these levels should be reflected and understood on more detailed levels of modeling, i.e., there is a need for traceability both upwards and downwards between models with different focus and different abstraction levels. This way of working, by shifting between details and wholeness, has strong resemblance with other approaches to process modeling (cf. e.g., Davis 2001). It has, therefore, been necessary to develop understanding of the present (AS-IS) and development of the future (TO-BE) of both wholeness and parts in parallel. The basic principles in the concepts that we have used on the levels (level 1 – 3) are:

- Level 1 – Business map: Shows the business in its context and how it interacts with the environment (this level has been manifested through the main process model).
- Level 2 – Main processes: Comprehensive process map based on level 1, which also express internal relations within the business (this level has been manifested through the main process model and the detailed process models).
- Level 3 – Sub processes: Coherent business activities, input/output with focus on customers/clients (this level has been manifested through the detailed process models).

When working with these three upper levels, there has continuously been an interaction around the evolving business process models (artifacts), the environment (local practice), and the knowledge base (external theoretical and methodological constructs). Throughout the design process, different people at Intersport have been actively involved together with the researchers. This process has continuously been shifting between design activities and validation activities. This means that different constellations of people at Intersport have been involved in both design and validation during different stages of the process. Examples of constellations of people that have been involved are CEO, management group, controller group, retail group, different functional units, and different individuals with specific knowledge within a specific area. During this process, it has also been necessary to let the design process be informed by theories and methods in order to develop clear and coherent business processes. An example of this was that we, for instance, elucidated transformation, coordination, and interaction dimensions as explicit generic aspects in the evolving process models. The instantiation of categories in theories has, therefore, explicitly influenced the design in the models and helped us to translate and visualize Intersport's new business plan into process models. The evolving process models served as an important vehicle (transaction medium) for successive operationalization and design of the business processes of 201X.

The project was divided into three phases: an Initial phase, an Intermediate phase, and a Final phase. During the initial phase, we have mainly worked with the so-called *scoping models*, i.e., through different models, based on the business plan, try to clearly define what to focus on and what to exclude. During this phase, we mainly worked with versions of the principle process model, but after a while, we also started to work with initial versions of the main process model and detailed process models. The models that were produced during this phase addressed both AS-IS and TO-BE and mostly on a principle level of the practice. During the intermediate phase, we worked with a division between *chiseling models* and *design models*. The chiseling models were mainly used to identify and describe guiding principles for design based on the scoping models. During this phase, we worked with the principle process model, the main process model, and the detailed process models. At this point, the principle process model also had served its purpose and was phased out from the project. These chiseling models were then used as a base to design the future practice expressed in the main process model and the detailed process models. In the final phase, we then worked with so-called *change models*, i.e., models and a final report that should be used for the implementation of the new business processes. This phase was mostly about packaging, presentation, and documentation of the design. The models and the final report will now serve as change guide for the implementation of the final solutions (design of 201X), which should be aligned with the new business plan.

3.3 Using Different Process Models

During the project, we have produced different artifacts in terms of models that have had different roles during different phases of the project. Based on the two levels of modeling that was described earlier, we have mentioned that we worked with an intermediate level during the first half of the project. This means that we have in total actually worked with three modeling levels with corresponding three types of models: Main process model, Principle process model, and Detailed process models (for model examples, see Figs. 2–4 below).

Based on the earlier described phases in the project and the three types of models that we have worked with, the design process can be described according to Fig. 1 below.

The "X" in Fig. 1 represents the status of the example models that are shown in the figures below. The blue whales in Fig. 1 above represent the content development of the three types of models.[1] We can also observe in Fig. 1 that the two types of models (main process model and detailed process models) that were supposed to be the final design result was not what we started to work with.

[1]Because of business secret reasons the exact content of the models have been blanked out. They do however reflect essential characteristics of 201X as expressed in the business plan.

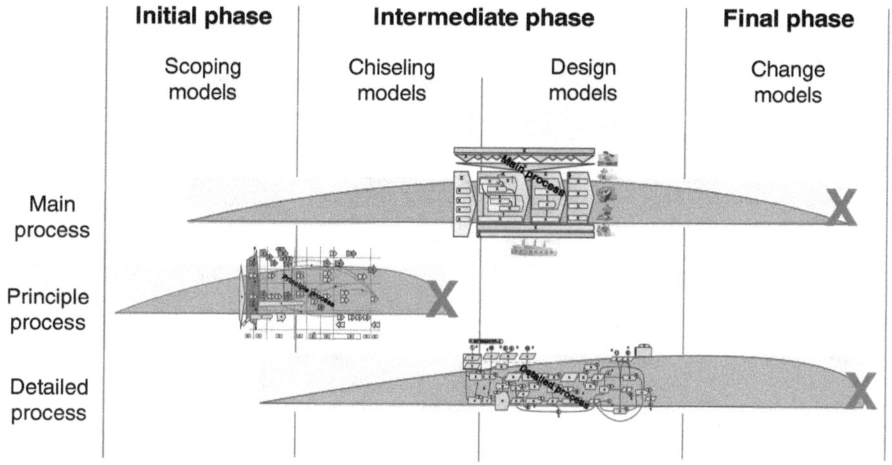

Fig. 1 The roles of different artifacts

The reason for this was that the initial versions of the main process model were regarded to be too abstract while the detailed process models got stuck in details. Therefore, we started to work with an intermediate level (principle process, see Fig. 4 below) that addressed principles in the new business model at the same time as we were able to understand the major consequences of these principles for further detailed design of the main process model and the detailed process models.

In Fig. 2 above, the main process model is depicted. The core of the model is a pattern of actions spanning from strategy development (left part) to sales and products in use by customers via generation and implementation of concepts to be supplied with and sold in stores. At the bottom of the model, relations to infrastructure are depicted, and on the top-layer, relations to governing and governing actors are expressed.

In Fig. 3, an example of a detailed process model is presented. This model shows relations between actions performed by actors, results, and conditions. At the top-part of the model, actions for governance are expressed.

In Fig. 4, the final version of the principle process is depicted. This model is more of a traditional swimlane model expressing relations within and between diverse organizational dimensions. This principle process served as a bridge between the main process model and the detailed process models for the first half of the project. As can be seen in Fig. 1, the principle model had served its purpose when the other two models had evolved to a state where the alignment between these two models had become clear. At this state, it started to be clear how the new business plan was instantiated and manifested on the main process level and how these principles were instantiated and manifested in the detailed process models. When the principle process model had been phased out, the main and detailed processes evolved together in parallel.

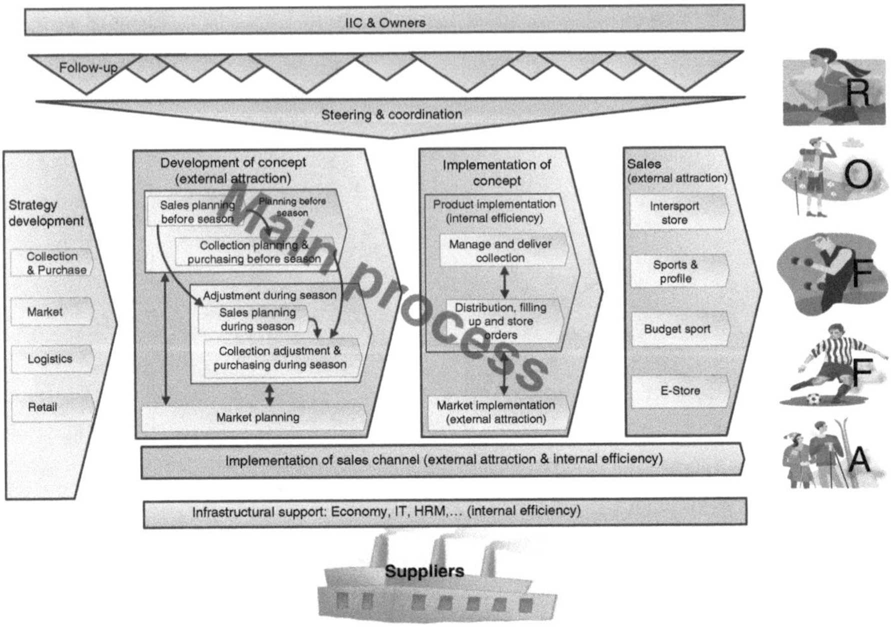

Fig. 2 The main process, final version

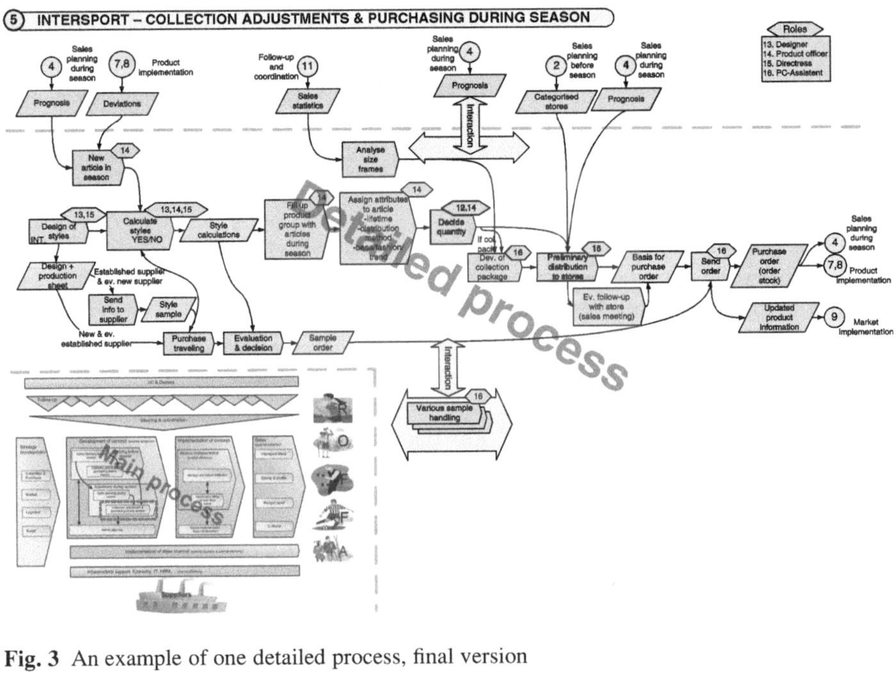

Fig. 3 An example of one detailed process, final version

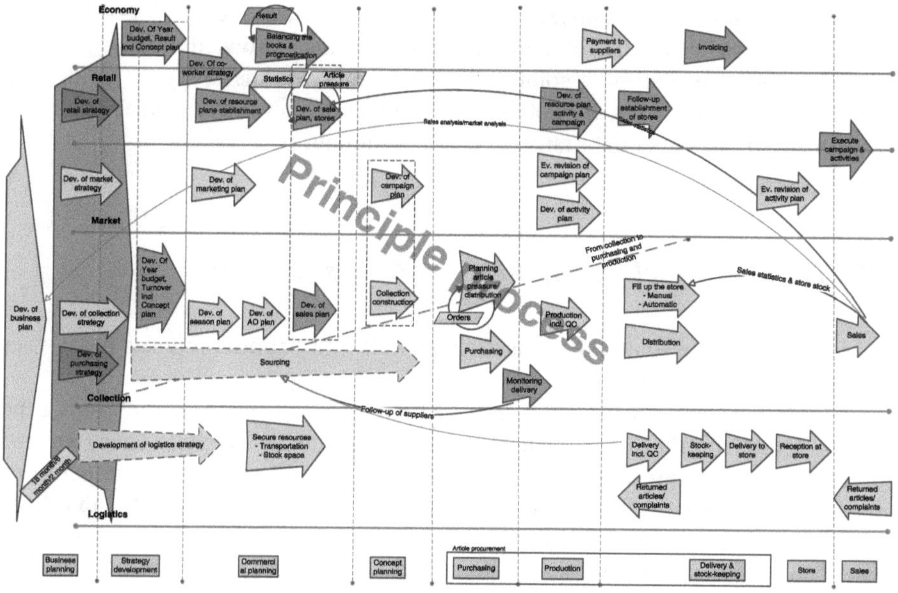

Fig. 4 Principle process, final version

4 Discussion: Designing Business Processes for the "Future" Through Collaborative Modeling

4.1 Process Modeling as a Design Process

During the design process performed at Intersport, a combination of action research and design research has been adopted. The process design has had as its focus to design and validate business models as artifacts, which has evolved based on an identification of business needs in the environment as well as the utilization of essential categories derived from the knowledge base.

Naturally, the practitioners have acted on behalf of the environment, and the researchers have taken responsibility to derive essential categories in the knowledge base. Even though the research performed and reported upon in this chapter has been performed in an action research setting, we still believe that, in the spirit of Walls et al. (1992), the principles and guidelines proposed by Hevner et al. (2004) give resonance to what has been going on in the process design project. This is also verified by other IS scholars (cf. Cole et al. 2005) and the establishment of the relationship between action research and design science is an emerging theme within IS research. We conceive the IS research as reported in this paper as an arena in which the artifacts are constructed, assessed, and refined. This means that actors being involved on this arena are both researchers as well as practitioners.

This puts attention towards different actors, their roles, and their actions related to the three dimensions (environment, IS research, and knowledge base). In the following parts, we will give some reflections related to the proposed guidelines as formulated by Hevner et al. (2004). These reflections serve as a base for bringing forward core issues in collaborative process modeling.

4.2 Design Guidelines Applied on Process Design

In Table 1, we make some reflections related to the guidelines proposed by Hevner et al. (2004).

In Table 1, some characteristics that we believe have been important during the design of Intersport's future business processes could be derived. These are the combination of action- and design research for elucidating procedural dimensions during a design process, the knowledge base as a driving force during both design and validation, and the close interaction between practitioners and researchers as a way to ensure useful results. These characteristics are elaborated in the following sections.

4.3 Strategic Alignment of Process Models

Throughout the project, different models have continuously been designed and refined. As claimed earlier, different process models were needed to capture different aspects in the business plan to pinpoint design results translated from the business plan on different levels of granularity. Building on pragmatic (Lind and Goldkuhl 2003) foundations for understanding, evaluating, and designing business processes that are aligned with the business plan, it is claimed that three essential process dimensions need to be elaborated on:

- Transformation, i.e., the refinement of basis to finished products.
- Coordination, i.e., the governance and management of the transformation.
- Interaction, i.e., the interaction between actors (organizational roles).

In the analysis, we have explored three types of models that have been designed in the project (main process model, principle process model, and detailed process model) in relation to their role during different phases in the project[2] (see Table 2). The table is horizontally divided into the phases that we have identified in the

[2]Coding; *Main* Main process model, *Princ* Principle process model, *Detail* Detailed process models. The influence is coded; *Dom* Dominant, *Part* Partial, *None* None and finally *N/A* Not applicable.

Table 1 Reflections of how the guidelines according to Hevner et al. (2004) have been applied in the process design project

Guideline according to Hevner et al. (2004)	Reflection (applied guideline in the process design project)
Guideline 1: Design as an artifact	Artifacts in terms of models, (main process model, principle process model, and detailed process models) as design of a future business state has been produced
Guideline 2: Problem relevance	The problem relevance is manifested through the new business plan and the desire to communicate the vision on a more concrete level
Guideline 3: Design evaluation	The real utility, quality, and efficacy of the designed artifacts (models) cannot be really evaluated until the business plan has been fully implemented. In this sense, we do not yet know the implications of the resulting (change) models. Will they be a support for action to reach the desired state? However, the artifacts have during the design process continuously been evaluated based on internal congruency, the knowledge base, and through the interaction (grounding) with the environment (the local practice)
Guideline 4: Research contributions	The research contribution is in the area of approaches for how to perform process design and process modeling
Guideline 5: Research rigor	Multi Grounded Theory (MGT) has been applied as research approach to ensure empirical, theoretical, and internal generative and validating dimensions of the artifacts (cf. Goldkuhl and Cronholm 2003). This also makes sense since both MGT and design science is rooted in pragmatism. The knowledge base has provided means for directing attention towards essential aspects during design. Evaluation has been performed based on different people's engagement in the artifact design
Guideline 6: Design as a search process	The goal has been to design and visualize a future business state through the search for "optimal" models, i.e., models that are as close as possible to the future desired state. Models have during the process been rejected and/or refined
Guideline 7: Communication of research	The final report that was delivered to Intersport was structured and presented for enabling the continuous and future implementation of business processes, on both detailed and on principal business level. The relation between detailed and more principle levels has also been kept clear

Table 2 Different models and the role of process dimensions during different phases in the project

Model type/aspect	Initial phase	Intermediate phase		Final phase
	Scoping models	Chiseling models	Design models	Change models
Transf.	Main: Part Princ: Dom Detail: Dom	Main: Dom Princ: Dom Detail: Dom	Main: Dom Princ: N/A Detail: Dom	Main: Dom Princ: N/A Detail: Dom
Coord.	Main: Part Princ: Part Detail: None	Main: Part Princ: Part Detail: Part	Main: Dom Princ: N/A Detail: Dom	Main: Dom Princ: N/A Detail: Dom
Interact.	Main: None Princ: None Detail: None	Main: Part Princ: None Detail: Part	Main: Part Princ: N/A Detail: Dom	Main: Part Princ: N/A Detail: Dom

project and vertically into the three core process dimensions that need to be elaborated in order to facilitate alignment between the process models and the business plan.

As can be seen in Table 2, the role of the three dimensions (i.e., transformative, coordinative, and interactive) in the models has evolved during the phases of the project. One can note that the transformative dimension has been important during all phases of the project while the interactive dimension of the models is suppressed until the latter phases. The reason for this is that we in the project needed to reach quite detailed descriptions of the business plan as process models before it was meaningful to really address which organizational roles that should be responsible and involved in different parts of the process. Similarly, the coordinative dimensions were only briefly addressed in the early phases and they were not fully developed until the latter phases of the project. The reason for this was also the need to translate the business plan into transformational process knowledge in order to know what to coordinate. It is also important to note that to be able to achieve a "usable" business aligned design, all three dimensions (i.e., transformation, coordination, and interaction) were needed to be elaborated and described in the process models. An important vehicle to develop the main process model and the detailed process models was the principle process model, which was a bridging facilitator during the first two phases. The principle process model had served its purposes after the first half of the intermediate phase (indicated as N/A during the two last phases in Table 2).

4.4 A Codesign Approach to Collaborative Process Modeling

The process design described in this chapter has been performed by collaborative modeling where different roles (stakeholders) have been involved in the design of a future state. The representation of people from Intersport in the project covered both new roles as a result of the business plan and "old" roles that had been preserved in the organization. The future design has been governed by joint creation of business process models on different levels. The involvement of stakeholders in the design conversation is one main core in codesign (Lind et al. 2008). Codesign as a design approach was originally coined by Forsgren (cf. Lind et al. 2008) who proposed a codesign framework as a multistakeholder model in which all stakeholders' concerns, related to a certain codesign situation, are taken into consideration by either inviting, or considering perspectives of, diverse stakeholders. Measurement scales and ideals are co-constructed by engaged stakeholders and perspectives driven by the hope for the future. In the design project at Intersport, most of the design work (process modeling) was performed in workshops where different people were involved based on their role in relation to the new business plan. The evolving process design was the common communication ground where different aspects of the new business logic could be elaborated. The workshops had a dual purpose where there continuously was a balance between generation and validation. Depending on the level of the design, there was a need to also have different hierarchical representations during the design, i.e., executive, management, and more operative levels. We as researchers also had an important role during this design process. Our main purpose was to serve as modeling facilitators in terms of modeling coordinator, method support, and to introduce useful theories and constructs into the design process.

By involving different stakeholders, the aim of the codesign process is to determine pros and cons, as well as determine new ideas and views in relation to the design (Lind et al. 2008). The resulting models of the process design (i.e., the change models) are to be regarded as agreements of future actions among the involved stakeholders in which different views of the stakeholders have been taken into consideration in the modeling process.

5 Conclusions

In this chapter, we have reported upon a process design project performed in a retail chain setting with the purpose of letting people become engaged in describing and become committed to a future state as a mean for the implementation of business strategies. In this setting, a business process design has been performed as a step to transform business plans into detailed and comprehensive business process models.

The knowledge endeavor reported in this chapter is to be seen as a step towards a practical theory (Cronen 1995) with the purpose to support people in performing process design. As a frame of reference, we have used the guidelines as provided by Hevner et al. (2004). Due to the fact that the process design has been performed as an action research project collaboration procedures and actor roles have been possible to reflect upon in relation to design science research. Among other things, the development of business process models as artifacts has been done by letting practitioners and researchers jointly codesign these models.

Framing this process design as design science has meant that the design science framework as proposed by Hevner et al. (2004) has been used as a base for reflection and bringing forward aspects that is worthwhile paying attention towards. In the project reported in this chapter, we have had success in combining a design science approach with an action research approach. In our knowledge endeavor, inspired by Markus et al. (2002) and experiences from this action research project, some tentative process design theory principles (guidelines), for aligning business process models with the business strategy in collaborative process modeling endeavors, are:

- Essential characteristics from business strategies and business plans should be derived as foundational structuring principles of the business processes.
- The modeling process should allow the inclusion of viewpoints from diverse stakeholders as a foundation for grounded descriptions and commitments of future actions for realizing business plans.

- The modeling process is a transformational process where models will have different roles during different phases of the project; scoping models, chiseling models, design models, and change models.
- One way to reach good design results is to ensure that the business process models in the end manage to express vital business dimensions such as transformation, coordination, and interaction.
- The involvement of different stakeholders, from practice and research, in a joint action arena is vital for the production of models that will be accepted, implemented, and executed as the new business practice.
- Different types of models serve as important transition vehicles and common design ground during the process to actually reach the desired design.

An important task of further research is to elaborate further on these tentative process design theory principles by giving them further meaning through more theoretical and empirical validation.

References

Ahrne G (1994) Social organizations. Interaction inside outside and between organization. Sage, London

Albinsson L, Lind M, Forsgren O (2007) Co-design: an approach to border crossing, network innovation. In: Cunningham P, Cunningham M (eds) Expanding the knowledge economy: issues, applications, case studies, Part 2, vol 4. IOS Press, Amsterdam, pp 977–983

Bandara W, Gable G, Rosemann M (2006) Business process modeling success: an empirically tested measurement model. 26th international conference on information systems, Milwaukee

Cole R, Purao S, Rossi M, Sein MK (2005) Being proactive: where action research meets design research. 26th international conference on information systems, Association of Information Systems, Las Vegas, Nevada

Cronen V (1995) Practical theory and the tasks ahead for social approaches to communication. In: Leeds-Hurwitz W (ed) Social approaches to communication. Guildford Press, New York

Davenport TH (1993) Process innovation. Reengineering work through information technology. Harvard Business School Press, Boston, MA

Davies I, Green P, Rosemann M, Indulska M, Gallo S (2006) How do practitioners use conceptual modeling in practice? Data Knowl Eng 58(3):358–380

Davis R (2001) Business process modelling with ARIS – a practical guide. Springer, London

Dewey J (1922) Human nature and conduct. Henry Holt, New York

Dorst K, Cross N (2001) Creativity in the design process: co-evolution of problem–solution. Des Stud 22(5):425–437

Goldkuhl G, Cronholm S (2003) Multi grounded theory adding theoretical grounding to grounded theory. 2nd European conference on research methods in business (2ECRM), Reading

Goldkuhl G, Lind M (2008) Coordination and transformation in business processes: towards an integrated view. Bus Process Manage J 14(6):761–777

Gottesdiener E (2002) Requirements by collaboration: workshops for defining needs. Addison-Wesley, Boston, USA

Günther C, Rinderle-Ma S, Reichert M, Van der Aalst WMP, Recker J (2008) Using process mining to learn from process changes in evolutionary systems. Int J Bus Process Integrat Manage 3(1):61–78

Hammer M (1990) Reengineering work: don't automate, obliterate. Harv Bus Rev 68(4):104–112

Harmon P (2009) The scope and evolution of business process management. In: vom Brocke J, Rosemann M (eds) Handbook on business process management. Springer, Heidelberg

Henderson JC, Venkatraman N (1999) Strategic alignment: leveraging information technology for transforming organisations. IBM Syst J 32(1): 4–16

Harrington HJ (1991) Business process improvement. The breakthrough strategy for total quality, productivity and competitiveness. McGraw-Hill, New York, NY

Hevner AR, March ST, Park J, Ram S (2004) Design science in information systems research. MISS Q 28(1):75–105

Keen PGW, Knapp EM (1996) Every manager's guide to business processes: a glossary of key terms and concepts for today's business leaders. Harvard Business School Press, Boston, MA

Langefors B (1973) Theoretical analysis of information systems, 4th edn. Studentlitteratur, Lund

Lankhorst M (ed) (2005) Enterprise architecture at work – modelling, communication, and analysis. Springer, Berlin Heidelberg

Leyking K, Chikova P, Martin G, Loos P (2007) Integrating learning and business process management. Proceedings of the 18th Australasian conference on information systems, Toowoomba, pp 981–990

Lind M (2006) Determination of business process types founded in transformation and coordination. Syst Signs Actions 2(1):60–81

Lind M, Albinsson L, Forsgren O, Hedman J (2007) Integrated development, use and learning in a co-design setting: experiences from the incremental deployment of e-Me, eChallenges e-2007. The Hague, The Netherlands

Lind M, Forsgren O (2008) Co-design and web 2.0: theoretical foundations and application. In: Cunningham P, Cunningham M (eds) Collaboration and the knowledge economy: issues, applications, case studies. Amsterdam, IOS Press, pp 1105–1112

Lind M, Goldkuhl G (2003) The constituents of business interaction – generic layered patterns. Data Knowl Eng 47(3):327–348

Lind M, Seigerroth U, Forsgren O, Hjalmarsson A (2008) Co-design as social constructive pragmatism, the inaugural meeting of The AIS Special Interest Group on pragmatist IS research (SIGPrag 2008) at international conference on information systems (ICIS2008), France

Lindgren R, Henfridsson O, Schultze U (2004) Design principles for competence management systems: a synthesis of An Action Research Study. MISS Q 28(3):435–472

Liu K, Sun L, Bennett K (2002) Co-design of business and IT systems. Inf Syst Front 4(3):251–256

March ST, Smith G (1995) Design and natural science research on information technologies. Decis Support Syst 15(4):251–266

Markus ML, Majchrzak A, Gasser L (2002) A design theory for systems that support emergent knowledge processes. MISS Q 26(3):179–212

Pearlson KE, Saunders CS (2006) Managing and using information systems – a strategic approach. Wiley, Hoboken

Rittgen P (2007) Co-designing models for enterprises and information systems – a case for language integration. In: Magyar G, Knapp G, Wojtkowski WG, Zupancic J (eds) Advances in information systems development: new methods and practice for the networked society, vol 1. Springer, Berlin, pp 73–83

Schuette R, Rotthowe T (1998) The guidelines of modeling – an approach to enhance the quality in information models. Proceedings of the international conference on conceptual modeling – ER '98, Springer, Berlin, pp 240–254

Searle JR (1969) Speech acts. An essay in the philosophy of language. Cambridge University Press, London

Stirna J, Kirikova M (2008) How to support agile development projects with enterprise modelling. In: Johannesson P, Söderström E (eds) Information system engineering – from data analysis to process networks. IGI Publishing, Hershey, PA. ISBN 978-1-59904-567-2

van Aaken JE (2007) Design science and organization development interventions – aligning business and humanistic values. J Appl Behav Sci 43:67–88

van der Aalst WMP, Rosemann M, Dumas M (2007) Deadline-based escalation in process-aware information systems. Decis Support Syst 43(2):492–511
von Wright GH (1971) Explanation and understanding. Rouledge & Kegan Paul, London
Vernadat FB (2002) Enterprise modeling and integration (EMI): current status and research perspectives. Annu Rev Control 26:15–25
vom Brocke J, Thomas O (2006) Reference modeling for organisational change: applying collaborative techniques for business engineering, Proceedings of the 12th American conference on information systems, Acapulco, Mexico, pp 680–688
vom Brocke J, Recker J, Mendling J (2010) Value-oriented Process Modeling: Integrating Financial Perspectives into Business Process Re-design. Business Process Management Journal (BPMJ), 16(2):333–356
Walls JG, Widmeyer GR, El Sawy OA (1992) Building an information system design theory for vigilant EIS. Inf Syst Res 3(1):36–59
Ward J, Peppard J (2003) Strategic planning for information systems, 3rd edn. Wiley, Chichester

Designing Business Processes with a Recommendation-Based Editor

Agnes Koschmider and Andreas Oberweis

Abstract Knowledge of modeling language syntax is usually not sufficient for building "good" process models. Profound modeling experience is required to apply a modeling language in practice. The productivity of users without any modeling experience is low and thus the quality of the modeling result may be unsatisfying if respective modeling tool support is missing. In this chapter, we present a recommendation-based editor for process modeling, which can help overcome this problem by reducing the need for the user to study the modeling notation and consequently direct her to focus on the model content. Early evaluations indicate the effectiveness of our approach, which goes beyond conventional modeling support for business processes.

1 Introduction

The increasing interest in Business Process Management (BPM) by academia and industry has resulted in a multitude of modeling languages and tools supporting business process modeling (Davies and Reeves 2010). Modelers, therefore, frequently have to adapt to new modeling tools and techniques. A shortcoming of today's modeling tools is that they usually do not support users in adopting these new modeling techniques. Instead, most of these tools merely focus on providing a repository of graphical symbols and advanced visualization techniques to facilitate understanding of the relationships between the various process elements. These tools may overwhelm those users inexperienced in process modeling due to a lack of features that really assist the user during the modeling process.

A. Koschmider (✉)
Institute of Applied Informatics and Formal Description Methods – AIFB, Technical University Karlsruhe, Karlsruhe, Germany
e-mail: agnes.koschmider@kit.edu

J. vom Brocke and M. Rosemann (eds.), *Handbook on Business Process Management 1*, International Handbooks on Information Systems,
DOI 10.1007/978-3-642-00416-2_14,

The recommendation-based modeling support system introduced in (Hornung et al. 2008) can help overcome this limitation by reducing the need for the user to study the modeling notations and instead direct her focus on the model content. Generally, recommender systems collect preferences or opinions from individual users, then aggregate and transfer those recommendations to other people to help individuals in a given community in more effectively identifying the content of interest from a potentially huge set of choices (Herlocker et al. 2004).

Translated to the field of business process modeling, the recommendation-based modeling support system takes the user's modeling context and the modeling history of a community of users into account and suggests process model parts to the user that may help her achieve an individual modeling goal. For this, the modeling support system works on top of a repository, which stores business process models (respectively parts) previously designed and stored by users from the same enterprise or from the same business branch. We define a process model part as a logically coherent group of process elements belonging together (e.g., approval, billing, or shipping).

We validated our support system with two experiments using real-life process models and a prototype implementation. The evaluation confirmed that users are willing to follow recommendations and the system contributes to a higher quality of the produced process models.

The ideas presented in this chapter have partially been presented in (Hornung et al. 2008; Koschmider et al. 2008a; Koschmider et al. 2008b).

The focus of this paper is guided by the following research question: *how can process modeling be supported by means of recommendations*? To answer this question, we subdivide it into the following questions: (1) *What kind of modeling support is to be offered by a recommendation system*? and (2) *What are the influence factors of process modeling to be incorporated within such a recommendation system*?

To provide answers for these questions, the remainder of the paper is structured as follows. The next section presents a brief survey on recommender systems. Sect. 3 then describes influence factors on process modeling, which need to be considered when implementing a recommendation-based modeling support system for the Business Process Management area. In this section, we will answer question 2. The relationship between traditional recommender systems and our modeling support system is discussed in Sect. 4. This section will provide an answer for question 1. Sect. 5 concludes the paper and gives a summary of the main results.

2 Survey of Recommender Systems

Recommender systems have emerged as a popular technique for helping members of a community in more effectively identifying content of interest from a potentially huge set of choices. The interest in this area still remains high because recommender systems help people facing the challenge of dealing with today's information overload (e.g., recommender systems of eBay or Amazon). Various types of such systems can be distinguished. A *content-based* recommender system (Basu et al. 1998) suggests an item to a user based upon a description of the item and the user's interests in the past. This kind of recommender system has its roots in the information retrieval (IR) community (Baeza-Yates and Ribeiro-Neto 1999) and suggests items containing text documents, web sites, or movies. To explain the functionalities of a content-based recommender system, Table 1 shows a book database with three entries. Each entry is described by a bookID, a title, the year of publication, and the two genres drama and action. The rating of the genres ranges from 0 (not at all) to 6 (absolutely). E.g., a ranking of five means a high dramatic movie. Assume, the user has already selected the book *Last Minutes*, thus the system predicts the following relevance order based on a comparison between the book's content and the user profile: (1) *The Absolute Truth*, (2) *The Fight*.

Shortcomings of a *pure* content-based recommender system are that they can only deal with text-based objects and do not consider a user's subjective opinions in the ratings.

These limitations are overcome by *collaborative recommender systems* (Claypool et al. 1999), which predict what a user wants based on what she and other users with similar preferences liked in the past. A popular example for a collaborative recommender system is the Amazon system. The focus of collaborative recommender systems is the similarity calculation of users rather than of items (like in content-based systems). Consequently, for each user, a set of "nearest neighbors" is calculated, which lays the foundation for the recommendations. The functionality of a collaborative-based recommender system is illustrated in Table 2, which shows a book data table with three users and four items. The preferences regarding an item user are somehow obtained for each user. The rating for the preference ranges from 1 (excellent) till 6 (insufficient).

With this table, we can calculate the similarity between users based on, e.g., the Euclidean distance (Breu et al. 1995). The result of this similarity calculation is the strongest correlation between user 2 and 3. Thus, the system recommends the same books for user 2 as for user 3.

Table 1 A book database

BookID	Title	Year	Drama	Action
001	The absolute truth	2006	5	4
002	The fight	2007	5	5
003	Last minutes	2006	4	4

Table 2 Data table for books

	The fight	The absolute truth	Last minutes	Action man
User 1	3	–	3	4
User 2	3	2	1	2
User 3	3	2	2	2

Pure collaborative recommender systems solve the shortcomings given for pure content-based systems (e.g., they can deal with any kind of content and recommend any items, even the ones that are dissimilar to those seen in the past (Adomavicius and Tuzhilin, 2005)). However, they have shortcomings as well. The amount of available information correlates positively with the number of users. Thus, a small number of users relatively to the amount of information results in sparse and unsatisfactory results. Therefore, several authors propose the combination of content-based and collaborative-based recommender systems, which are integrated to hybrid recommender systems (Burke 2002; Balabanovic 1997). Additionally, several extensions for content-based and collaborative-based systems have been proposed, e.g., such as the consideration user feedback (Klink 2004).

A specific system relevant in the BPM area is the recommendation-based modeling support system proposed in (Hornung et al. 2008). The system suggests process model parts to process builders taking into account their modeling intention as derived from the user's interest and patterns observed in other users' preferences. The influence factors on the modeling intension and on preferences of users will be explained in the next section. Based on these influence factors, we will give an answer to our research question 2 in the following Sections. Thus, the next two sections consider the investigation of influence factors on process modeling when implementing a recommendation-based process modeling support system.

3 Influence Factors on Process Modeling

Usually, when modeling business processes, users have in mind a life cycle model. This model may depend on several factors such as the organization where the user is working (e.g., the enterprise is using the Six Sigma DMAIC (Pyzdek 2003)) or the user's level of experiences (inexperienced, advanced, or expert).

Nevertheless, the life cycle model is influenced by the modeling intention of users, which is mainly driven by factors such as the modeling purpose (e.g., analysis vs. execution), the user's role (e.g., secretary vs. CIO), or the user's view (e.g., customer vs. software engineer) (Koschmider et al. 2008). For instance, the role *secretary* has a view limited to the options for which she is responsible and needs aggregated information of the process. Her modeling purpose may be rather documentation than computer-based execution, which deals with the actual enactment and thus lacks facilities allowing nontechnical users to easily comprehend the model. Her point of view may be rather customer-oriented than technical, because she is working on a nontechnical level and is not able to model technical processes. Consequently, her business process model differs from processes modeled for execution purpose from a technical point of view.

Additionally, users may follow specific process model properties, which should be satisfied by the model. For instance, a process should be a low cost process, a process with full exploitation of resources, or a standardized process.

Table 3 Influence factors on process modeling

Purpose	E.g., analysis, documentation, execution, reengineering.
View	User view in the modeling process: e.g., administrative-oriented, customer-oriented.
Role	User involvement in the modeling process: e.g., process owner, secretary, administrator.
Model properties	E.g., low cost, full exploitation of resources, minimal fault rate, standard process.
Complexity	E.g., high abstraction: limited number of elements granularity level: high number of process elements

A last influence factor on the business process model results from the complexity of the intended model, which reflects the amount of elements to be modeled. An abstract view on the model only presents an overview of process elements, without providing more detailed descriptions of process elements, and contains only a limited number of elements. When using several abstraction levels, users model more specific processes and significantly more elements (they complicate the model), which are, e.g., subsequently linked together to coarse-grained process models. Table 3 summarizes the main influence factors on process modeling to be incorporated within a recommendation-based process modeling support system.

Beside such "conventional" influence factors, users may be driven by modeling guidelines (Becker et al. 2000), which include, e.g., correct syntactical structuring or standardized process element names (Reijers et al. 2010). For instance, a Petri net-based business process model is considered as being structurally correct if it complies with the well-handledness respectively with the well-structuredness property (van der Aalst 1998). This structural property for business process models is violated if for example an alternative flow initiated by an OR-split is later to be synchronized by an AND-join. A correct syntactical structuring of process models is considered in our recommendation system, but this feature will not be explained in detail in this chapter.

One result of the evaluation of our tool was that the recommendation system is equally useful for all users, independently of their modeling expertise. Therefore, we disregard the user's modeling expertise as influence factor for the model recommendation process.

In the next section, we will explain how these influence factors are considered in the recommendation-based modeling support system.

4 Integration of Influence Factors into the Recommendation-Based Editor

The implementation of the recommendation-based modeling support system was inspired by traditional recommender systems as introduced before and the auto-completion function for words in mobile phones. Initially, we implemented the recommendation system as an autocompletion system for business process models. However, one of the bottlenecks of an autocompletion system is that a large set of business processes models is required in the repository to provide exact recommendations. Additionally, we found out in experiments that users are not searching for an exact match but rather for a less strict one. Therefore, we decided to provide a tool that recommends not only completely syntactically correct and semantically appropriate business process models. Recommended process model parts can be modified by users to perfectly fit.

To provide the user a close match between her modeling intention and the recommendation, the recommendation system embeds two concepts of modeling support:

1. A *query interface* allows users to request process models or process model parts that are of interest to them. The user can significantly save time in process modeling if a process model matches the user request.
2. A *recommender component* proposes appropriate process model parts, which fit to a business process model that is currently being edited. The user can invoke the recommender component by highlighting the corresponding element group to be completed by process reuse. This component of the modeling support should be used if the user is not sure how to complete the process model. In this case, the results from the query can be unsatisfying due to the user's vague intention of the process model.

The current implementation of our modeling support system is shown in Fig. 1. The user wants to model a process describing the handling of order requests.

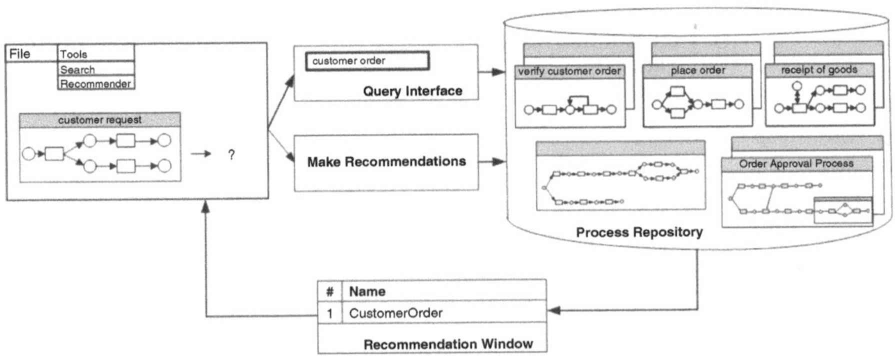

Fig. 1 Edited business process model and two types of modeling support

Her intention is to model this process from a customer perspective. Via a query interface she can search for process model parts concerning customer requests. The results of the query are displayed according to a ranking function and she can then insert the business process model part into the active workspace, which best matches her modeling intention.

Subsequently, she might not be sure how to complete her process model. In this case, she has two options: she can either search again via the query interface for fitting process model parts or she can invoke the recommender component, which automatically suggests appropriate process model parts for completing this model. If the user invoked the recommender component, the system would take as input for appropriate recommendations all labels of process elements (as explained below). Unlike the query component, the recommender component can only be invoked after the user has already started modeling the business process.

In our running example, she has opted for the recommender component, which suggests (among others) the *Customer Order* process model for completion. If the user decides to insert this recommendation in her workspace, she can configure this process model by inserting or deleting elements. Finally, she can save the modified process model version in a process repository for further process reuse.

In the initial development of our prototype for this system, we used Petri nets (Oberweis and Sander 1996) as the process modeling notation and populated a repository with 21 process models composed out of 15 process parts, all about order and shipment procedures. All models were derived either from real world projects or from academic literature.

Before making process models and process model parts searchable, we need to index them. Process model parts are handled in the same way as the complete models, but additionally we store a pointer to the business process model with which they are associated. For example, for a business process model that consists of three distinct process model parts, we would include four virtual documents in our index: the whole process and each of the three parts.

After indexing the process models, users can use the query interface, which uses Lucene's query parser syntax[1] and users can enter six query arguments:

1. Title: referring to names of process elements (e.g., *approved request*),
2. First element: searching for a specific first element in the process model,
3. Last element: searching for a specific last element in the process model,
4. Objective description: searching for process models fulfilling an objective (e.g., processes modeling handling of order request). The objective of a process is annotated by users before storing the process model in the repository,
5. Complexity: referring to the number of process elements. *Low* signifies a business process model with no refinement and less than 25 elements. *Medium* is a process model with up to two refinements and *high* is all above these limits,

[1]http://lucene.apache.org/java/docs/queryparsersyntax.html

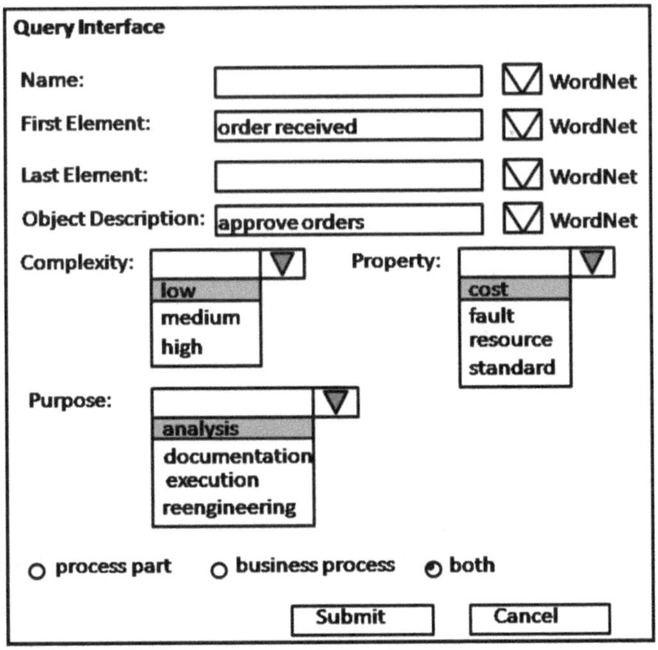

Fig. 2 Query interface

6. Property: referring to specific properties of a process model assigned by users before storing the process in the repository (e.g., *standard* signifies a standard process),
7. Purpose: referring to models fulfilling one of the four modeling purposes such as analysis, documentation, execution, and reengineering.

In Fig. 2, the user is searching for process models with the first element *order received* and the objective *approve orders*. Her modeling intention is driven by the analysis purpose, a low process complexity and cost-effective processes. Additionally, she is searching for both process model parts and entire business process models. To overcome a limitation caused by a controlled vocabulary, she activated WordNet[2] (a free English taxonomy). With standard Boolean operators, such as AND, OR, and NOT, she can express more complex queries.

This query interface fulfills three influence factors described in Fig. 1: *purpose*, *complexity*, and *property*. The last two influence factors (*view* and *role*) are achieved by analyzing the user's modeling vocabulary and incorporating the role-relevant process-views approach of (Shen and Liu 2004).

[2]http://wordnet.princeton.edu/

To analyze the user's modeling vocabulary, the system generates tags[3] from the labels of the edited process model elements. If the user starts modeling by invoking the query interface, then the input of the query after stop word removal is regarded as tags. Several inputs in the query interface are regarded as a concatenation of the tags. In case the user has already modeled several activities, then the labeled elements are regarded as tags.

After stop word removal, each keyword is assigned a tag score for a business process model based on a modified version of the value *term frequency* × *inverse document frequency* (Salton et al. 1975). This weight is often used in information retrieval or text mining and is a statistical measure to evaluate how important a word is to a document. Subsequently, this measure implies a ranking of recommendations. The process with the highest tag score is displayed first followed by recommendations with lower tag scores in a descending order. However, the tag score is not the exclusive criterion for ranking. Inspired by common recommender systems, the ranking depends on more factors as explained in the next section.

In an experiment, Heymann et al. 2008 found out that tags chosen by users seem to have considerable redundancy when compared to the text and domains of pages they annotate. This favors an automatic generation of tags, which is also confirmed by (Brooks and Montanez 2006) for blog entries.

Continuing the investigation, how influence factors have been incorporated in the modeling support, the current version of the recommendation system adheres only to the guideline of correct syntactical structuring. The verification of structural properties is performed once for all process models that match the automatically generated Lucene query mentioned before. Process elements, which cause (in case the edited business process model and a recommendation process are interconnected) structural problems, are highlighted with a gray rectangle.

In the next section, we will address research question 1 (What kind of modeling support is to be offered by a recommendation system?). We will discuss whether the recommendation-based modeling support, which incorporates all influences factors enumerated in Table 3, can be regarded as a specific type of a recommender system.

5 Reference of the Recommendation-Based Modeling Support System to Common Recommender Systems

Ranking of results in common recommender systems mainly depends on (1) user behavior or (2) similarities between a query and a (web) document. In our recommendation system, the ranking of process models (parts) depends on (1) similarity between a query and a process model, (2) patterns observed in other users' preferences, and (3) implicit user feedback. Thus, our recommendation system incorporates ranking criteria of common recommender systems.

[3] In the following, we regard keywords as tags.

Table 4 Table-based representation of recommendation results

#	Process name	Score	Freq.	Avg.Del.	Avg.Ins	Previous user
1	Approval of orders	96.58	7	5	10	A. Oberweis
⋮	⋮	⋮	⋮	⋮	⋮	⋮
7	Verify order	47.10	2	10	3	A. Koschmider

Based on Table 4, we will explain our ranking criteria. Initially, process models that meet users' requirements (being displayed as results of the query or the recommender component) are enumerated first in a table-based result.

This result list contains information that is affiliated in common recommender systems. For instance, the criterion *Frequency* describes how often a process model has been selected/reused by other users and refers to the criterion of implicit user feedback. The same can be applied for the criterion *Operation*, which indicates the average number of deletions or insertions made when selecting a recommendation. This criterion also describes implicit user feedback.

To control the average number of deleted and inserted elements for a specific recommendation, we first calculate the frequency score for this recommendation, then the number of newly inserted elements, and finally the number of deleted elements, which were initially available in the specific recommendation. To determine the number of deleted, newly inserted elements in a specific process model, we recursively retrieve all these elements.

To encourage user's trust and participation by those users who are unskilled in process modeling, the system provides the information about users who selected a recommendation, which is represented in Table 4 by the column *Previous User*. Trust mechanisms are very common in recommender systems (Massa and Bhattacharjee 2004).

By a right mouse click (in the previous user column in Table 4), the user can open network structures, which were generated from a process model repository, from a user history, and from the insertion history of recommendations (Koschmider et al. 2008b). The social network from a *process model repository* allows users to view and contact related persons regarding collaborations. This social network provides an organizational view of business processes. An example of the information that could be derived from such a network is the average distance between performers who belong to that part of a business process model that has already been edited and the parts which belong to a candidate process model. A user can apply this result to complete a process model in a way that is similar to earlier selected proposals. The social network from *user history* shows the relationships among modelers who use the recommendation system. From this social network's usage history, social networks can be generated that express the similarity between its nodes (users). The social network allows propagating changes across "clique" members and supports reusing modeling history of "neighborhoods" in order to complete an edited process model faster. The social network from *insertion history* shows the relationship among modelers who decided for equal recommendations.

This information about previous users refers to patterns observed in other users' preferences (like observing the preferences of users in the past in a collaborative recommender system).

The ranking criterion *similarity between a query and a process model* is coped by the *Score* criterion (see Table 4), which reflects the match between a query input and tags, which have been annotated for a process model. In several evaluations, we found out that a high match between the user's query and the recommendation is the greatest influence factor for selecting a recommendation. Therefore, when ranking all the criteria given in Table 4, we assign the greatest weight for the *Score* criterion.

Assume the user is interested in the first two recommendations suggested in Table 4. Then she can open a graphical view of the recommendations by selecting the corresponding rows in the table-based view. Fig. 3 shows a graphical-based visualization of the two processes.

If the user is not sure about which one of the two recommendations to select, she is supported in her decision process by two additional functionalities. When pushing the button *Show related process parts*, related process parts that were used in the user's current modeling domain (e.g., Manufacturing) and that follow or precede the respective model part are displayed. By pushing the button *Show related process models*, the user can preview all phases of the BPM life-cycle, from the early documentation of a process through subsequent phases of analysis and execution.

To realize the functionality of previewing related process models, we construct a user profile based on the respective search history. To define such a user session, the following information is used:

1. A sequence of accessed recommendations by a user
2. A sequence of queries typed by a user (after removing stop words)
3. A sequence of newly created models or models opened for editing by user

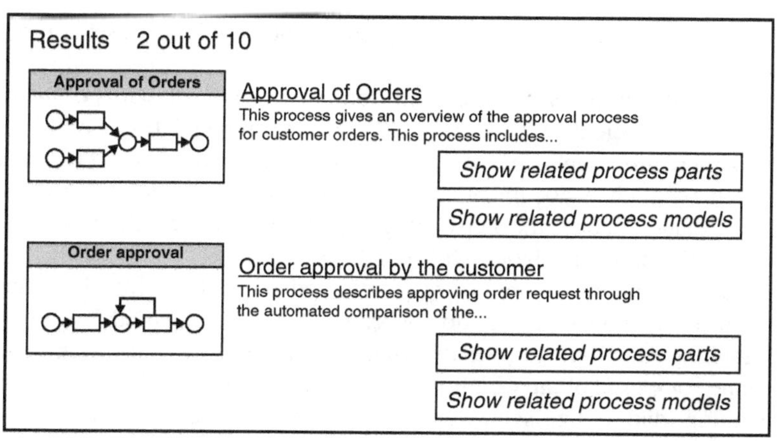

Fig. 3 Graphical-based representation of recommendations

Generally, in common recommender systems, user profiles are created by user feedback (Balabanovic 1997). In our system, we consider (implicit) user feedback through the frequency and the operation score. However, our user profiling mechanism has the same intention as in a common recommender system, which is to satisfy more accurately user searches.

To summarize, our recommendation-based modeling support system incorporates all influence factors on process modeling as enumerated in Table 3. If required, the modeling support system may be extended by more factors due to the simplification of the implementation of this support system.

The current version of the recommendation-based editor can be downloaded from www.sempet.org.

6 Conclusion

Recommender systems have emerged as a popular technique for helping members of a community in more effectively identifying content of interest from a potentially overwhelming set of choices. In this chapter, we sketched the functionalities of common recommender systems with a focus on content-based and collaboration-based systems. Inspired by these recommender systems, we described a specific recommendation system for application in the field of business process modeling. For this, we presented five influence factors on process modeling and explained their treatment in the proposed business process modeling support system. Upon this, we clarified the relationship between traditional recommender systems and our process modeling support system. The recommendation-based modeling support system can be regarded as a specific type of a hybrid recommender system, which incorporates some features of content-based and some features of collaborative-based systems.

Based on the promising results of our recommendation system, several research challenges remain.

Especially, it is important to provide information about the status of the modeling process when users decide to follow a specific recommendation. For this, we are standardizing requirements documents being used as a foundation for the modeling task. Based on such a document, we can calculate the modeling progress and provide information about the steps being required to complete the process design when a specific recommendation will be selected.

Additionally, more research work is required on ranking functions for such business process modeling support systems. One possible modification of the current ranking function could be the usage of a multilevel benchmark instead of a single one composed of the weight *term frequency* $\times$ *inverse document frequency* and reranking (due to e.g., syntactical structuring). One benefit would be a better consideration of user objectives.

References

Adomavicius G, Tuzhilin A (2005) Toward the next generation of recommender systems: a survey of the state-of-the-art and possible extensions. IEEE Trans Knowl Data Eng 17(6): 734–749

Baeza-Yates R, Ribeiro-Neto B (1999) Modern information retrieval. Addison-Wesley, Boston MA

Balabanovic M (1997) An adaptive web page recommendation service. In: Proceedings of the 1st international conference on autonomous agents, Marina del Rey, California, Feb 1997

Basu C, Hirsh H, Cohen W (1998) Recommendation as classification: using social and content-based information in recommendation. In: Proceedings of the fifteenth national/tenth conference on artificial intelligence/innovative applications of artificial intelligence, Madison, Wisconsin, United States, American association for artificial intelligence, Menlo Park, CA, pp 714–720

Becker J, Rosemann M, Uthmann CV (2000) Guidelines of business process modeling. In: Proceedings business process management, models, techniques, and empirical studies, lecture notes in computer science. vol 1806, Springer, London, pp 30–49

Breu H, Gil J, Kirkpatrick D, Werman M (1995) Linear time euclidean distance algorithms. IEEE Trans Pattern Anal Mach Intell 17(5):529–533

Brooks CH, Montanez N (2006) Improved annotation of the blogoshere via auto-tagging and hierarchical clustering. In: Proceedings of the 15th world wide web conference, Edinburgh, Scotland, ACM Press, pp 625–632

Burke R (2002) Hybrid recommender systems: survey and experiments. User Model User-Adapt Interact 12(4):331–370

Claypool M, Gokhale A, Miranda T, Murnikov P, Netes D, Sartin M (1999) Combining content-based and collaborative filters in an online newspaper. In: Proceedings ACM SIGIR '99 workshop recommender systems: algorithms and evaluation, ACM Press, Aug 1999

Davies I, Reeves M (2010) BPM tool selection. The case of the Queensland Court of Justice. In: vom Brocke J, Rosemann M (eds) Handbook on business process management, vol 1. Springer, Heidelberg

Herlocker JL, Konstan JA, Terveen LG, Riedl JT (2004) Evaluating collaborative filtering recommender systems. ACM Trans Inform Syst 22(1):5–53

Heymann P, Koutrika G, Garcia-Molina H (2008) Can social bookmarking improve web search? In: Proceedings of the international conference on web search and web data mining, ACM Press, New York, USA, pp 195–206

Hornung T, Koschmider A, Lausen G (2008) Recommendation based process modeling support: method and user experience. In: Proceeding of the 27th international conference on conceptual modeling, Barcelona, Spain, Lecture notes in computer science. vol 5231. Springer, Berlin, pp 265–278

Klink S (2004) Improving document transformation techniques with collaborative learned term-based concepts. In: Proceedings reading and learning, adaptive content recognition, lecture notes in computer science. vol 2956. Springer, pp 281–305

Koschmider A, Habryn F, Gottschalk F (2008) Real support for perspective-compliant business process design. In: BPM 2008 Workshops, Sept 2008, vol 17 of LNBIB. Springer, Milan, Italy, pp 30–41

Koschmider A, Song M, Reijers H (2008) Social software for modeling business processes. In: BPM 2008 workshops, Milan, Italy, Sept 2008, vol 17 of LNBIB. Springer, pp 642–653

Massa P, Bhattacharjee B (2004) Using trust in recommender systems: an experimental analysis. In: Proceedings of the second international conference iTrust, Oxford, 2004, pp 221–235

Oberweis A, Sander P (1996) Information system behavior specification by high level Petri nets. ACM Trans Inf Syst 14(4):380–420

Pyzdek T (2003) The six sigma handbook: a complete guide for green belts, black belts, and managers at all levels. McGraw-Hill, New York

Reijers HA et al. (2010) Business process quality management. In: vom Brocke J, Rosemann M (eds) Handbook on business process management, vol 1. Springer, Heidelberg

Salton G, Wong A, Yang CS (1975) A vector space model for automatic indexing. Commun ACM 18(11):613–620

Shen M, Liu DR (2004) Discovering role-relevant process-views for disseminating process knowledge. Expert Syst Appl 26:301–310

van der Aalst WM (1998) The application of Petri nets to workflow management. J Circ Syst Comput 1(8):21–66

Business Process Simulation

Wil M.P. van der Aalst, Joyce Nakatumba, Anne Rozinat, and Nick Russell

Abstract Although simulation is typically considered as relevant and highly applicable, the use of simulation is limited in reality. Many organizations have tried to use simulation to analyze their business processes at some stage. However, few are using simulation in a structured and effective manner. This may be caused by a lack of training and limitations of existing tools, but in this chapter, we argue that there are also several additional and more fundamental problems. First of all, the focus is mainly on design while managers would also like to use simulation for operational decision making (solving the concrete problem at hand rather than some abstract future problem). Second, there is limited support for using existing artifacts such as historical data and workflow schemas. Third, the behavior of resources is modeled in a rather naive manner. This chapter focuses on the last problem. It proposes a new way of characterizing resource availability. The ideas are described and analyzed using CPN Tools. Experiments show that it is indeed possible to capture human behavior in business processes in a much better way. By incorporating better resource characterizations in contemporary tools, business process simulation can finally deliver on its outstanding promise.

1 Introduction

The correctness, effectiveness, and efficiency of the business processes supported by a Process-Aware Information System (PAIS) (Dumas et al. 2005) are vital to the organization. Examples of PAISs are not only workflow management systems but also other "process-aware" systems such as enterprise resource planning systems (e.g., SAP R/3, Oracle, JD Edwards, etc.), call-center systems, product-data

W.M.P. van der Aalst (✉)
Eindhoven University of Technology, Eindhoven, The Netherlands
e-mail: w.m.p.v.d.aalst@tue.nl

J. vom Brocke and M. Rosemann (eds.), *Handbook on Business Process Management 1*, International Handbooks on Information Systems,
DOI 10.1007/978-3-642-00416-2_15,

management systems, and process-centric middleware (e.g., IBM's WebSphere, JBoss, etc.). If a PAIS is configured based on a process definition that contains errors, then the resulting process may lead to angry customers, back-log, damage claims, and loss of goodwill. Moreover, an inadequate design may also lead to processes that perform poorly, e.g., long response times, unbalanced utilization of resources, and low service levels. This is why it is important to *analyze* processes not only before they are put into production (to find design flaws) but also while they are running (for diagnosis and decision support). In this chapter, we focus on the role of *simulation* when analyzing business processes. The goal is to identify *limitations* of existing approaches and to discuss possible solutions. In particular, we focus on the *availability of resources*. It will be shown that many organizations have a limited view on the availability of their employees and that today's simulation tools do not support the more refined views that are needed. The goal is to transform simulation from a "toy for managers and consultants" into a truly useful and versatile tool.

To introduce the concept of business process simulation, let us consider Fig. 1. In the background, a workflow specification is shown using the YAWL notation (van der Aalst and ter Hofstede 2005). The process starts with task *order cable*. After this task is executed, task *pay deposit* is enabled. However, if payment does not follow within two weeks, task *time-out* is executed. The details of the process and the exact notation are not important. However, it is important to see that a workflow model defines the ordering of tasks, model (time) triggers, etc. The arrow above a task indicates that the task requires a resource of a particular type, e.g., using the role

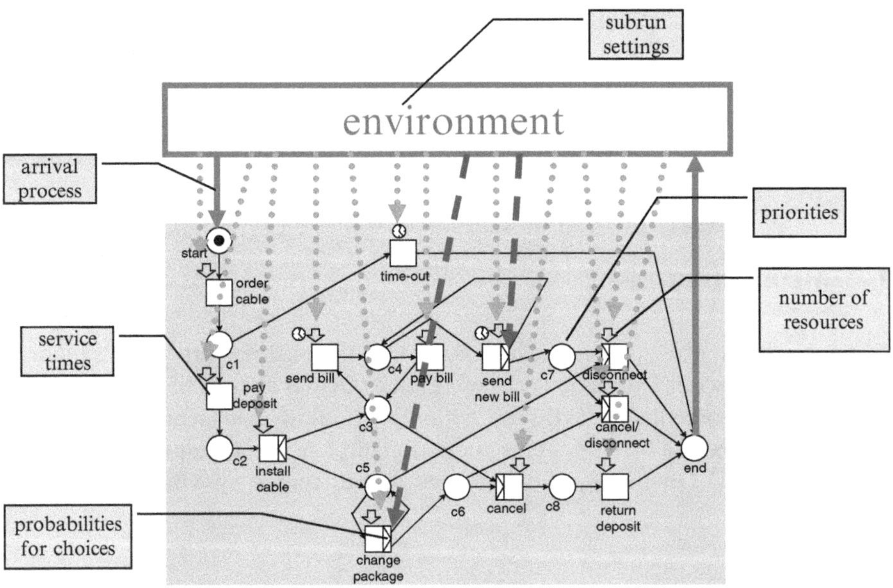

Fig. 1 Information required for a traditional simulation

concept resources is linked to tasks. When there are choices, conditions are added to specify when to take a particular route, etc. The YAWL model in Fig. 1 can be used to configure a PAIS (in this case, the workflow management system YAWL) and thus enact the corresponding business process. However, the YAWL model is not sufficient for simulation. The ordering of activities and information about roles, conditions, triggers, etc., are useful for simulation purposes, but as Fig. 1 shows, additional information is needed. First of all, an environment needs to be added. While in a PAIS the real environment interacts directly with the model, in a simulation tool, the behavioral characteristics of the environment need to be specified. For example, the arrival of new cases (i.e., process instances) needs to be specified (see box *arrival process* in Fig. 1). Typically, a Poisson arrival process is assumed and the analyst needs to indicate the average arrival rate. Second, the service time, also called the process time, of tasks needs to be specified. For example, one can assume that the service time is described by a Beta distribution with a minimum, a maximum, an average, and a mode. Note that the simulation model needs to abstract from the actual implementation of the task and replace the detailed behavior by stochastic distributions. Similarly, choices, priorities, etc., are replaced by probability distributions. Finally, the workflow model needs to be complemented by information about resources (e.g., number of people having a particular role). In order to conduct experiments, one also has to specify the number of subruns, the length of each subrun, etc. Based on all this information, simulation tools can provide information about, for example, expected flow times, service levels (e.g., percentage of cases handled within two weeks), and resource utilization.

Figure 1 presents a rather classical view on business process simulation. This is the type of simulation supported by hundreds, if not thousands, of commercial simulation packages. Some vendors provide a pure simulation tool (e.g., Arena, Extend, etc.) while others embed this in a workflow management system (e.g., FileNet, COSA, etc.) or a business process modeling tool (e.g., Protos, ARIS, etc.). All of these tools more or less use the information presented in Fig. 1 to calculate various performance indicators. In this paper, we will call this "traditional simulation." We will argue that this type of simulation is not very useful. Figure 2 shows the need to move beyond traditional simulation approaches.

The left-hand-side of Fig. 2 shows the role of a PAIS (e.g., a workflow engine as well as also other types of process-oriented information systems) in supporting operational business processes. The PAIS supports, controls, and monitors operational processes. The resources within the organization perform tasks in such processes and therefore also interact with the PAIS. The PAIS can do meaningful things only if it has knowledge of the process, the resources within the organization, and the current states of active cases. Moreover, a PAIS often records historical information for auditing and performance analysis. The four ellipses in the middle of Fig. 2 show these four types of data: (1) event log, (2) process state, (3) process model, and (4) resource model. The *event log* contains historical information about "When, How, and by Whom?" in the form of recorded events. The *process state* represents all information that is attached to cases, e.g., Customer order XYZ consists of 25 order lines and has been in the state "waiting for replenishment"

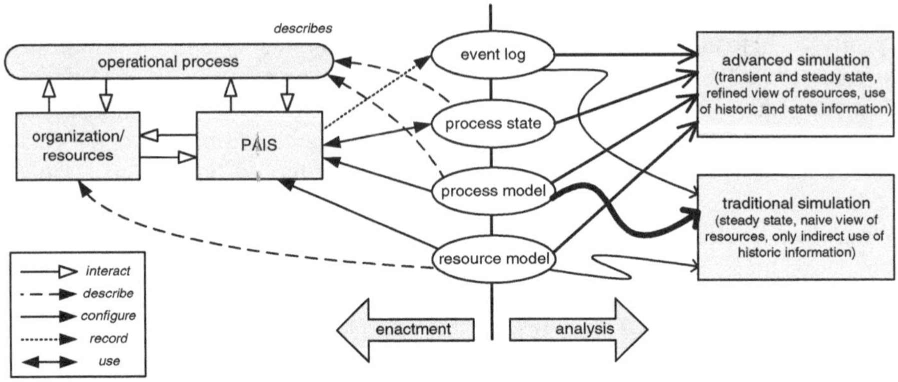

Fig. 2 Overview of the relationship between enactment and simulation and the different data sources

since Monday. The *process model* describes the ordering of tasks, routing conditions, etc. (cf. the YAWL model in Fig. 1). The *resource model* holds information about people, roles, departments, etc. Clearly, the process state, process model, and resource model are needed to enact the process using a PAIS. The event log merely records the process as it is actually enacted.

The right-hand-side of Fig. 2 links the four types of data to simulation. For traditional simulation (i.e., in the sense of Fig. 1), a process model is needed. This model can be derived from the model used by the PAIS. Moreover, information about resources, arrival processes, processing times, etc., is added. The arcs between the box *traditional simulation* and the three types of data (event log, process model, and resource model) are curved to illustrate that the relationship between the data used by the PAIS and the simulation tool is typically rather indirect. For example, the analyst cannot use the process model directly, but needs to transform it to another language or notation. The resource model used for simulation is typically very simple. Each activity has a single role and for each role there are a fixed number of resources available. Moreover, it is assumed that these resources are available on a full-time basis. The event logs are not used directly. At best, they are used to estimate the parameters for some of the probability distributions. Hence, traditional simulation can be characterized as having a weak link with the actual PAIS and historical data and a rather naive view of resources. Moreover, the current state is not used at all. As such, simulation focuses on steady-state behavior and cannot be used for operational decision making.

This paper advocates the use of more advanced notions of simulation. Key aspects of which include the establishment of a close coupling with the data used by the PAIS together with the extensive use of event log and process state information. Moreover, we will not only focus on steady-state behavior but also on transient behavior in order to also support operational decision making. This is illustrated by the box *advanced simulation* in Fig. 2. The contribution of this paper is twofold:

- First of all, we provide a *critical analysis of current simulation approaches and tools* as summarized by Fig. 2. We argue that there is too much focus on process design and that there should be more emphasis on operational decision making using transient analysis. We also advocate the use of existing artifacts such as workflow models, event logs, state information, etc. It is our belief that vital information remains unused in current approaches. In our analysis of current simulation approaches, we also address the problem that resources are modeled in a way that does not reflect the true behavior of people. For example, the working speed may depend on the utilization of people and people may prefer to work in batches.
- Second, we provide a *detailed analysis of the effect of resource availability* in simulation studies. We argue that resources are modeled inadequately because of incorrect assumptions (e.g., availability and processing speed are much more dynamic than often assumed). Using a concrete simulation model, we prove that such assumptions lead to incorrect predictions. As a result, the simulation model may indicate that the average flow time is around one hour while in reality the average flow time is actually more than one month.

The remainder of this paper is organized as follows. First, we provide an overview of the limitations of traditional simulation approaches. Then we look into the problem of describing resource availability. We develop a simple simulation model with which to do simulation experiments and use these results to show the effects of oversimplifying the availability of people. After providing concrete suggestions for improving the modeling of resources, we discuss related work and complementary approaches, and conclude the paper.

2 Pitfalls of Current Simulation Approaches

In the introduction, we used Fig. 2 to summarize some of the limitations of contemporary simulation approaches. In this section, we describe these pitfalls in more detail.

2.1 Focus on Design Rather than Operational Decision Making

Simulation is widely used as a tool for analyzing business processes but it mostly focuses on examining rather abstract steady-state situations. Such analyses are helpful for the initial design of a business process but are less suitable for operational decision making and continuous improvement. To explain this, we first elaborate on the difference between *transient analysis* and *steady-state analysis*.

The key idea of simulation is to execute a model repeatedly. The reason for doing the experiments repeatedly is not to come up with just a single value (e.g., "the

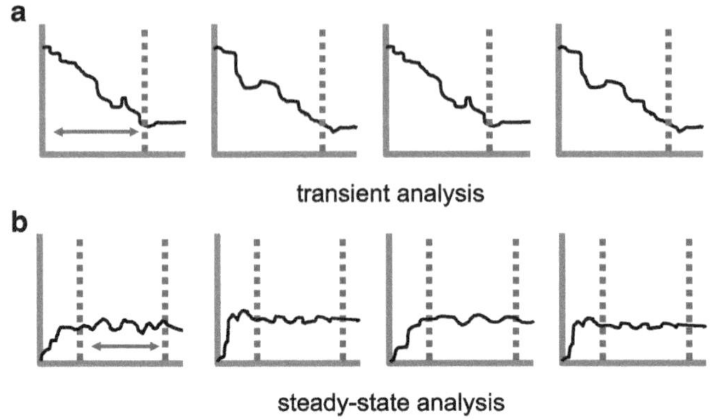

Fig. 3 For transient analysis, the initial state is vital. while for steady-state analysis, the choice of initial state should have no effect on the simulation result. Each graph shows one simulation run. The *X*-axis denotes time while the *Y*-axis represents the system state. The first four graphs (**a**) illustrate the importance of the initial state and the focus of transient simulation on the initial part. The other four graphs (**b**) show the focus on the steady-state behavior

average response time is 10.36 min") but to provide confidence intervals (e.g., "the average response time is with 90% certainty between 10 and 11 min"). This is why there is not a single simulation run, but several *subruns*. Figure 3 shows two sets of four subruns. (Typically, dozens of subruns are used to calculate confidence intervals and, in the case of steady-state analysis, subruns can be obtained by partitioning one long run into smaller runs (Kleijnen and van Groenendaal 1992; Ross 1990)). In the four subruns depicted in Fig. 3a, the focus is on the initial part of the process, i.e., starting from the initial state, the "near future" is explored. In the four subruns depicted in Fig. 3b, the initial part is discarded and only the later behavior is of interest. Note that for steady-state analysis, the initial state is irrelevant. Typically, the simulation is started "empty" (i.e., without any cases in progress) and only when the system is filled with cases, the measurements start. Figure 3a clearly shows that for transient analysis, the initial state is very important. If the simulation starts in a state with long queues of work, then in the near future flow times will be long and it may take some time to get rid of the backlog as shown in the diagram.

Despite the abundance of simulation tools, simulation is rarely used for operational decision making. One of the reasons is the inability of traditional tools to capture the real process (see above). However, another, perhaps more important, reason is that existing simulation tools aim at strategic or tactical decisions. Contemporary tools tend to support simulations that start in an arbitrary initial state (without any cases in the pipeline) and then simulate the process for a long period to make statements about the steady-state behavior. However, this steady-state behavior does not exist (the environment of the process changes continuously) and is thus considered irrelevant by the manager. Moreover, the really interesting questions are related to the near future. Therefore, it seems vital to also support transient analysis, often referred to as *short-term simulation* (Reijers and van der

Aalst 1999; Wynn et al. 2008; Rozinat et al. 2008b). The "fast-forward button" provided by short-term simulation is a useful option; however, it requires the use of the current state. Fortunately, when using a PAIS, it is relatively easy to obtain the current state and load this into the simulation model.

2.2 *Modeling from Scratch Rather Than Using Existing Artifacts*

In practice, it is time consuming to construct a good simulation model and to determine the input parameter. A pitfall of current simulation approaches is that existing artifacts (models, logs, data, etc.) are not used in a direct manner. If a PAIS is used, there are often models that are used to configure the system (e.g., workflow schemas). Today, these models are typically disconnected from the simulation models and created separately. Sometimes, a business process modeling tool is used to make an initial process design. This design can be used for simulation purposes when using a tool like Protos or ARIS. When the designed process is implemented, another system is used and the connection between the implementation model and the design model is lost. It may be that at a later stage, when the process needs to be analyzed, a simulation model is built from scratch. This is a pity as the PAIS contains most of the information required. As a result, the process is "reinvented" again and again, thus introducing errors and unnecessary work. The lack of reuse also applies to other sources of information. For example, the PAIS may provide detailed event logs. Therefore, there is no need to "invent" processing times, arrival times, and routing probabilities, etc. All of this information can be extracted from the logs. Note that all additional information shown in Fig. 1 can be derived from event logs. In fact, in Rozinat et al. (2008a), it is demonstrated that complete simulation models can be extracted from event logs.

As indicated in Fig. 2, simulation could use all four types of data provided by the PAIS, i.e., not just the event log and process model but also the process state and resource model. The process state can be used to enable short-term simulation (as described before) and the resource model may be used to more accurately describe resources. In most simulation tools, only the number of resources per class is given. However, a PAIS holds detailed information about authorizations, delegations, working times, etc. By using this information directly, more realistic models can be constructed.

It is interesting to note that today's data mining and business intelligence tools are completely disconnected from simulation. These tools are merely used to measure performance indicators and to discover correlations and trends. Yet, their objectives are similar, i.e., both simulation and data mining/business intelligence tools aim at improving operational business processes. Therefore, it seems good to combine things and exploit existing artifacts as much as possible.

2.3 Incorrect Modeling of Resources

Probably the biggest problem of current business simulation approaches is that human resources are modeled in a very naive manner. As a result, it is not uncommon that the simulated model predicts flow times of minutes or hours while in reality flow times are weeks or even months. Therefore, we list some of the main problems encountered when modeling resources in current simulation tools.

People are involved in multiple processes. In practice, there are few people that only perform activities for a single process. Often, people are involved in many different processes, e.g., a manager, doctor, or specialist may perform tasks in a wide range of processes. However, simulation often focuses on a single process. Suppose a manager is involved in ten different processes and spends about 20% of his time on the process that we want to analyze. In most simulation tools, it is impossible to model that a resource is only available 20% of the time. Hence, one needs to assume that the manager is there all the time and has a very low utilization. As a result, the simulation results are too optimistic. In the more advanced simulation tools, one can indicate that resources are there at certain times in the week (e.g., only on Monday). This is also an incorrect abstraction as the manager distributes his work over the various processes based on priorities and workload. Suppose that there are five managers, all working 20% of their time on the process of interest. One could think that these five managers could be replaced by a single manager ($5 \times 20\% = 1 \times 100\%$). However, from a simulation point of view, this is an incorrect abstraction. There may be times that all five managers are available and there may be times that none of them are available.

People do not work at a constant speed. Another problem is that people work at different speeds based on their workload, i.e., it is not only the distribution of attention over various processes but also their absolute working speed that determines their capacity for a particular process. There are various studies that suggest a relation between workload and performance of people. A well-known example is the so-called Yerkes–Dodson law (Wickens 1992). The Yerkes–Dodson law models the relationship between arousal and performance as an inverse U-shaped curve. This implies that for a given individual and a given type of task, there exists an optimal arousal level. This is the level where the performance has its maximal value. Thus work pressure is productive, up to a certain point, beyond which performance collapses. Although this phenomenon can be easily observed in daily life, today's business process simulation tools do not support the modeling of workload dependent processing times.

People tend to work part-time and in batches. As indicated earlier, people may be involved in different processes. Moreover, they may work part-time (e.g., only in the morning). In addition to their limited availabilities, people have a tendency to work in batches (cf. Resource Pattern 38: Piled Execution (Russell et al. 2005)). In any operational process, the same task typically needs to be executed for many different cases (process instances). Often, people prefer to let work-items related to the same task accumulate, and then process all of these in one batch. In most simulation tools, a resource is either available or not, i.e., it is assumed that a resource is eagerly waiting for work and immediately reacts to any work-item that arrives. Clearly, this does not do justice to the way people work in reality. For example, consider how and when people reply to e-mails. Some people handle e-mails one-by-one when they arrive while others process their e-mail at fixed times in batch.

Related is the fact that calendars and shifts are typically ignored in simulation tools. While holidays, lunch breaks, etc., can heavily impact the performance of a process, they are typically not incorporated in the simulation model.

Priorities are difficult to model. As indicated above, people are involved in multiple processes, and even within a single process, different activities and cases may compete for resources. One process may be more important than another and get priority. Another phenomenon is that in some processes, cases that are delayed get priority, while in other processes, late cases are "sacrificed" to finish other cases in time. People need to continuously choose between work-items and set priorities. Although important, this is typically not captured by simulation models.

Process may change depending on context. Another problem is that most simulation tools assume a stable process and organization and that neither of them change over time. If the flow times become too long and work is accumulating, resources may decide to skip certain activities or additional resources may be mobilized. Depending on the context, processes may be configured differently and resources may be deployed differently. In van der Aalst et al. (2007c), it is shown that such "second order dynamics" heavily influence performance.

The pitfalls mentioned above illustrate that simulation techniques and tools have a very naive view of business processes. As a result, the simulation results may deviate dramatically from the real-life process that is modeled. One response could be to make more detailed models. We think that this is not the best solution. The simulation model should have the right level of detail, and adding further detail does not always solve the problem. Therefore, we propose to use the data already present in a PAIS more effectively. Moreover, it is vital to characterize resources at a high abstraction level. Clearly, it is not wise to model a person as a full-time resource always available and eager to work, nor should we attempt to make a detailed model of human behavior. In the next section, we try to characterize resource availability using only a few parameters.

3 Resource Availability: How to Get It Right?

The previous section listed several pitfalls of contemporary simulation approaches. Some of these pitfalls have been addressed in other papers (van der Aalst et al. 2007c; Rozinat et al. 2008a; Rozinat et al. 2008b). Here, we focus on the *accurate modeling of resource availability*. This can be used to capture various phenomena, e.g., people working in multiple processes or working part-time, and the tendency of people to work in batches.

3.1 Approach

As already indicated in this paper, there are a number of issues that need to be considered when modeling resources. These issues deal with the way people actually carry out their work. The first issue is that people are not available to work all the time but for specific periods of time. In most cases, people are only part-time available (e.g., in the mornings, or only on the weekends). In this paper, this is described as the *availability* (denoted by a) of the resource, and it is the percentage of time over which a person is able to work. Secondly, when people are available to work, they divide up their work into portions, which are called *chunks*, and the size of a chunk is denoted by c. Chunk sizes may vary among different people, for example, a person that is available for 50% of his time may work whenever there is work and he did not exceed the 50% yet (i.e., small chunk size), or only in blocks of say half a day (i.e., large chunk size). Another case is that a person may save up work and then work for an extended period (large c) while another person prefers to regularly check for new work items and work on these for a shorter period of time (small c). The chunks of work to be done are distributed over particular *horizons* of length h. This is the time period over which constraints can be put in place.

Figure 4 shows the relationship between chunk size and horizon. The empty circles represent case arrivals, i.e., the points in time where a new work-item is offered. The filled circles represent case completions, i.e., the points in time where some work-item is completed. The chunks of work are divided over the horizon (see the double headed arcs labeled with c). The periods where the resource is actually working is denoted by the horizontal bars. A resource can have three states:

- *Inactive*, i.e., the resource is not allocated to the process because there is no work or because all available capacity has been used.
- *Ready*, i.e., the resource is allocated to the process but there is currently no work to be done.
- *Busy*, i.e., the resource is allocated to the process and is working on a case.

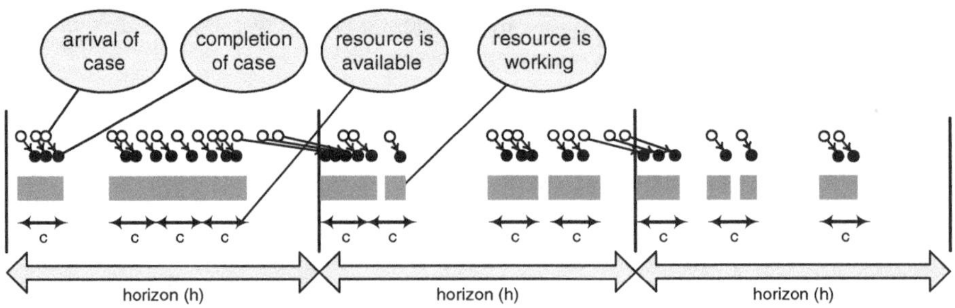

Fig. 4 Overview of the relation between horizon (h) and chunk size (c). Resources are made available in chunks of size c. In this example, not more than four chunks can be allocated per period of length h. If all four chunks are used and still work needs to be done, processing is delayed until the next period when new chunks are made available

When a case arrives and the resource is inactive and still has remaining chunks of time (given the current horizon), then a chunk of time is allocated and the resource starts working. If a case arrives and the resource is busy, the work is queued until the resource becomes available. Note that it may be the case that work cannot be completed in the current horizon and is postponed to the first chunk in the next period of length h, as illustrated in Fig. 4. Furthermore, if a chunk has been started, then it will be completed even though there might be no work left (in this case, the resource is in the ready state).

The main parameters of the model are as follows.

- *Arrival rate* λ, i.e., the average number of cases arriving per time unit. We assume a Poisson arrival process, i.e., the time between two subsequent arrivals is sampled from a negative exponential distribution with mean $1/\lambda$. Note that $\lambda > 0$.
- *Service rate* μ, i.e., the average number of cases that can be handled per time unit. The processing time is also sampled from a negative exponential distribution. The mean processing time is $1/\mu$ and $\mu > 0$.
- *Utilization* $\rho = \lambda/\mu$ is the expected fraction of time that the resource will be busy.
- *Chunk size* c is the smallest duration a resource is allocated to a process. When a resource leaves the inactive state, i.e., becomes active (state ready or busy), it will do so for at least a period c. In fact, the active period is always a multiple of c.
- *Horizon* h is the length of the period considered ($h > 0$).
- *Availability* a is the fraction of time that the resource is available for the process ($0 < a \leq 1$), i.e., the resource is inactive at least $1 - a$ percent of the time.

Not all combinations of these parameters makes sense, as is illustrated by the following requirements.

- $\rho = \frac{\lambda}{\mu} \leqslant a$, i.e., the utilization should be smaller than the availability.
- $c \leq h$, i.e., the chunk size cannot be larger than the horizon.
- $(a \times h) \bmod c = 0$, i.e., the maximum time a resource can be active each period should be a multiple of c, otherwise it would never be possible to actually use all of fraction a.

We use an example to explain the last requirement. Suppose that the horizon is 8 h, the availability is 0.5, and the chunk size is 3 h. In this case, $a \times h = 4$ h and $c = 3$ h. Now it is obvious that only one chunk can be allocated per period. Hence, the effective availability is not 4 h but just 3 h (i.e., effectively $\alpha = 3/8$). Therefore, we require that $a \times h$ is a multiple of c.

Figure 5 summarizes the parameters used in our basic model. Cases arrive with a particular arrival rate λ and are then placed in a queue. A resource, described by four main parameters (availability a, horizon h, chunk size c and service rate μ), is then made available to work on the case as shown in Fig. 5. A resource will work on the first case in the queue. If the case is not completed within a particular chunk, then it is sent back to the beginning of the queue to wait for the next chunk to be allocated.

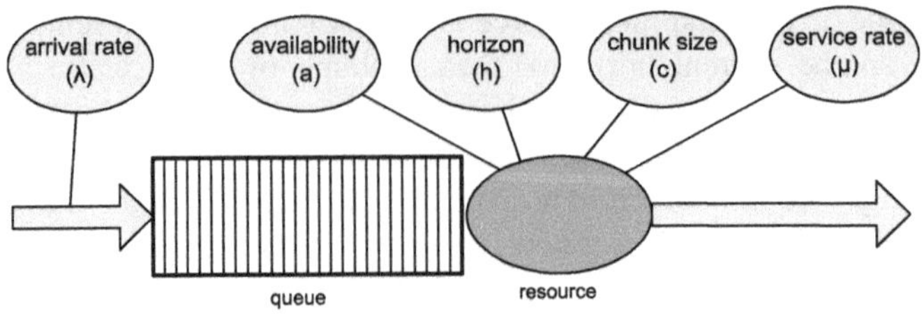

Fig. 5 Cases arrive with intensity λ and are placed in a queue and a resource with parameters a, c, h, and μ handles each case

3.2 Modeling in Terms of CPN Tools

We analyzed the effects of the various resource characteristics using a simulation model. Colored Petri Nets (CPNs) (Jensen 1992; Jensen et al. 2007) were used as a modeling language. CPNs allow for the modeling of complex processes. Using CPN Tools (Jensen et al. 2007), such models can be analyzed in various ways, i.e., simulation, state-space analysis, etc.

CPNs extend the classical Petri net with *data* (colored tokens), *time*, and *hierarchy*. Places are typed, i.e., all tokens on a place have a value of some common type. In CPN-terms, this means that all tokens in a given place should belong to the same color set. This implies that each place has a color set (i.e., type). Tokens also have *timestamps* indicating when they can be consumed. When producing a token, it may be given a *delay*. This delay may be sampled from some probability distribution. The CPN language, also referred to as CPN-ML, is based on the functional language (Standard) ML. Therefore, CPN inherits the basic types, type constructors, basic functions, operators, and expressions from ML. Inscriptions on the arcs specify the values of the tokens to be produced. Complex models can be structured in a hierarchical manner, i.e., nodes at one level may refer to subprocesses at a lower level. CPNs are distributed over the so-called *pages*. One page describes a network of places and transitions and may refer to other pages. For a more detailed introduction to CPNs and CPN Tools, we refer to (Jensen 1992; Jensen et al. 2007).

Our CPN model is a hierarchical model that is divided into three pages, which are the *generator* page (which creates cases for which a task needs to be performed), the *activation* page (which models the availability of resources), and the *main* page (which models the actual execution of tasks). This CPN model is used to clearly study the behavior of a single resource, but it can easily be extended to more realistic situations with different resources (see Sect. 3.4). In the following, we briefly describe each of the 3 pages of the CPN model.[1]

[1]The interested reader can look up the declarations that would initialize this model with $\lambda = 1/100$, $\mu = 1/15$, and one resource "r1" characterized by $h = 1{,}000$, $a = 0.2$, and $c = 200$ in Appendix 6.

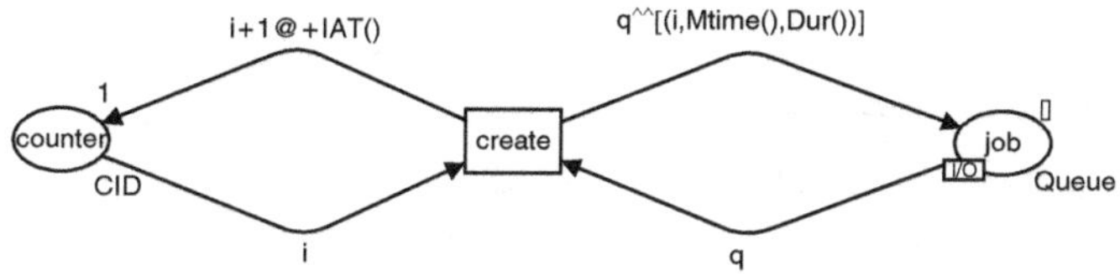

Fig. 6 The *generator* page. The time between two subsequent case arrivals is given by the function *IAT*(), the creation time of cases is recorded by the current model time function *Mtime*(), and the duration of the task is given by the function *Dur*(). Note that *Queue* is a list color set, i.e., a single token represents a queue of cases

Figure 6 shows the *generator* page of the CPN model. Cases arrive through this page and are put in a queue. We assume the arrival process to be Poisson with parameter λ (i.e., negative exponential interarrival times with mean $1/\lambda$). The cases themselves are represented by tokens with a value, which is a product of three parameters: *caseid*, *arrival time*, and *duration* (the processing time is sampled from a negative exponential distribution with mean $1/\mu$).

The modeling of the availability of resources is done in the activation page of the CPN model shown in Fig. 7. We consider the variables introduced earlier in this section, i.e., h, a, and c. The token in place *resource info* holds details about a resource with values related to its availability a, chunk size c, and horizon h. It is important at this point to determine the amount of work that a person can do. This is obtained by multiplying availability by horizon. The availability can be distributed over the period h in chunks of size c. Not more than $(a \times h)$ *div* c chunks can be allocated. Moreover, allocation is eager. i.e., as long that there is work to be done and available capacity, the resource is active. When transition *activate* fires, then a resource with the parameters r and $Mtime() + c$ becomes available to work. The resource will have a delay attached to it, which is equivalent to the current time plus the chunk size, i.e., the resource will be active for c time units, and this period ends at time $Mtime() + c$.

The actual processing of the cases is carried out in the main page shown in Fig. 8. This page uses the *generator* and *activation* pages described above. Cases come in from the generator page through the place *job* and a resource is made available from the activation page through the place *ready*. The token in place *busy* indicates the actual processing of a case by the resource. The length of the processing of a case is restricted by the task duration (already sampled during case creation) and the remaining chunk size. If cases leave place *busy* but are still incomplete, because the resource is no longer available for a time period sufficient to complete the case, then these cases are put back on the queue. When the processing of the case is completed, the resource is made available to work again, but this is only possible if there is still time left in the current chunk. Otherwise, the resource will be deactivated and is no longer available until the next chunk is allocated. The deactivation is controlled by the *activation* page shown in Fig. 7.

The CPN model just described specifies the resource behaviors considered. As indicated before, we assume a very basic setting and the model can easily be

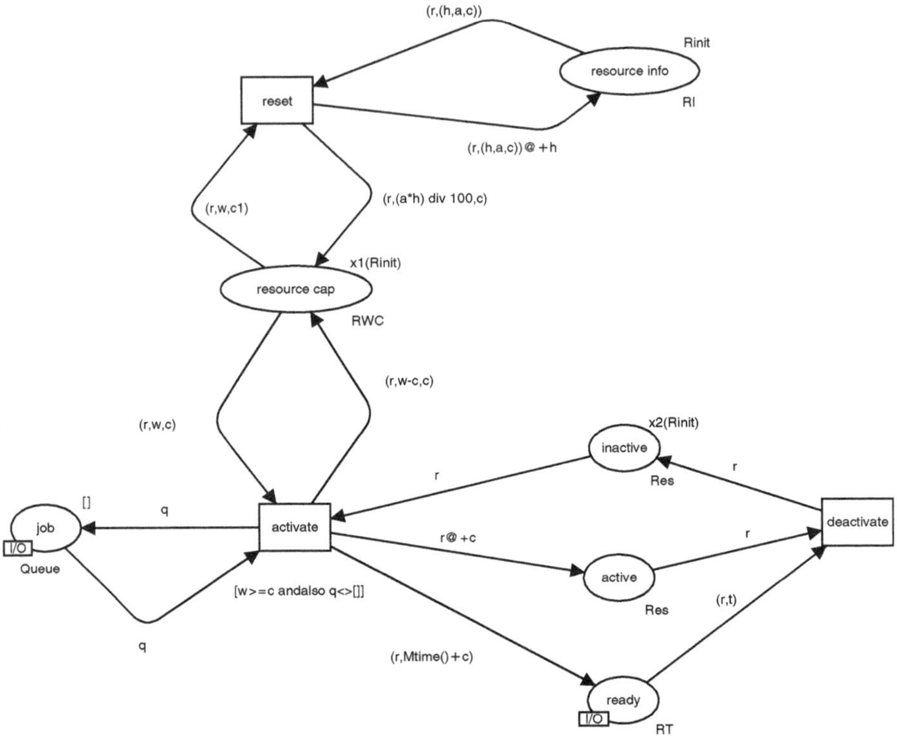

Fig. 7 The *activation* page. Transitions *activate* and *deactivate* control the actual availability of resources. Transition *reset* resets the "chunk capacity" at the start of each period of length h. A token in place *resource cap* is a three-tuple (r, w, c) where r is the resource id, w is the remaining availability, and c is the chuck size

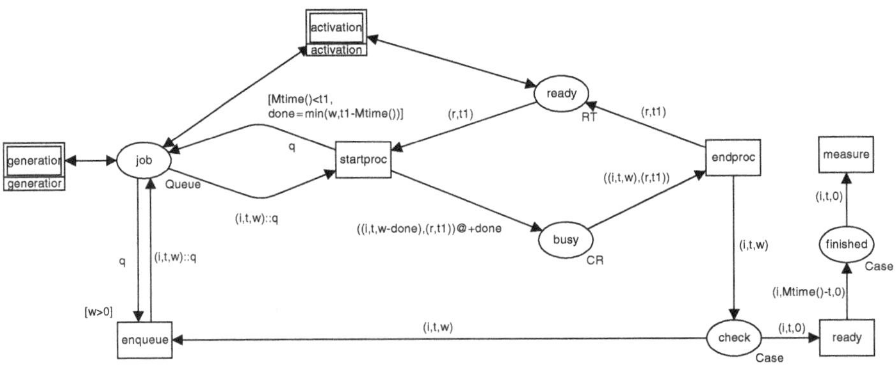

Fig. 8 The *main* page. Place *busy* shows the interaction between a resource and a case while *ready* shows that a resource is available to process a case

extended. However, our goal is to show that parameters such as availability a, chunk size c, and horizon h really matter. Most business simulation tools do not provide such parameters and assume $a = 1$ (always available), $c \rightarrow 0$ (resources are only active if they are actually busy working on a case), and $h \rightarrow \infty$ (infinite horizon). The next subsection shows that this may result in unrealistic simulations with huge deviations from reality.

3.3 Experiments

Using the CPN model, experiments were carried out to investigate the relationship between the flow time of cases and the main parameters related to resource availability. Monitors were used to extract numerical data during the simulation. The monitor concept of CPN Tools allows for the measurement of various performance indicators without changing or influencing the model (Cpn Group, http://wiki.daimi.au.dk/cpntools/). All experimental results reported here are based on a simulation with ten subruns, each subrun having 10,000 cases. For each performance indicator measured, we calculated the so-called 90% confidence interval. These are shown in the graphs but are typically too narrow to be observed (which is good as it confirms the validity of the trends observed).

As discussed already, the availability a of a resource is the percentage of time over which a person is able to work. In the CPN model, different availability values were investigated while keeping the chunk size and horizon constant. The results from the experiment are shown in Fig. 9. The graph was plotted to show the values of the averages with a 90% confidence interval and in the caption all fixed

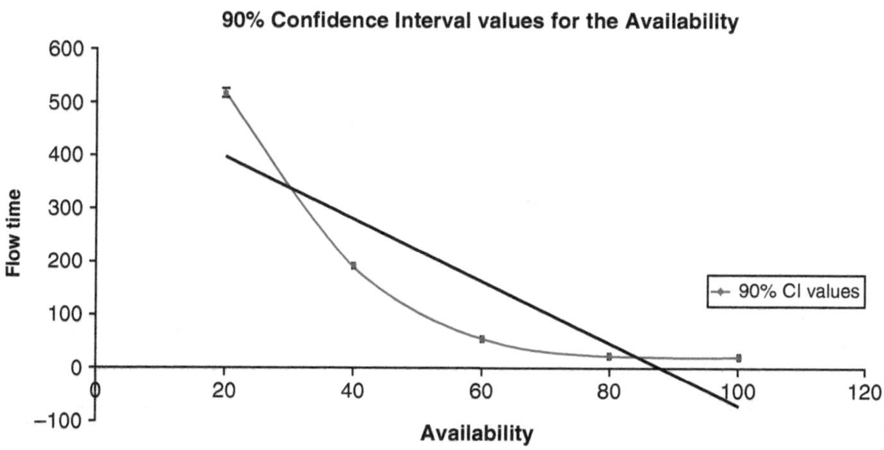

Fig. 9 Graph showing availability against flow time ($\lambda = 1/100$, $\mu = 1/15$, $\rho = 0.15$, $c = 200$, and $h = 1{,}000$). The flow time reduces as the availability increases. (The *straight line* shows the trend using linear regression.)

parameter values are shown. The idea behind this experiment was to determine whether one's availability has any effect on the flow time. The result is obvious: the more people are available, the more work they can do and the shorter is the flow time. However, one should realize that in most simulation tools, it is not possible to set the parameter a, i.e., a 100% availability ($a = 1$) is assumed. Figure 9 shows that this may lead to severe discrepancies.

While the effect of reduced availability may be obvious, the effect of the chunk size c on the flow time may be more surprising. People can divide up their work into chunks of varying sizes. When availability is distributed over chunks, the bigger the chunk, the larger the flow times of cases. This is because work is more likely to accumulate. The results obtained from the experiments carried out with different chunk sizes (while keeping all other parameters constant) are shown in Fig. 10. The graph shows the values of the average flow times and the 90% confidence intervals. Our findings indeed confirm that flow time increases as the chunk size increases. The reason is that the larger the chunk size, the longer the periods between chunks become. Figure 10 shows an important insight that people making simulation models often do not realize.

When a horizon is large, then the distribution of chunks is more flexible. If $a \times h = c$, then only one chunk per period is possible. This chunk will typically start in the beginning and if a is small, then for a large part of h, no resource is available. If $a \times h$ is much larger than c, then more chunks are possible and these can be more evenly distributed over the period h. Note that the effect of making the horizon longer is similar to making the chunk size smaller. Figure 11 shows the relation between flow time and horizon observed and clearly shows that shortening

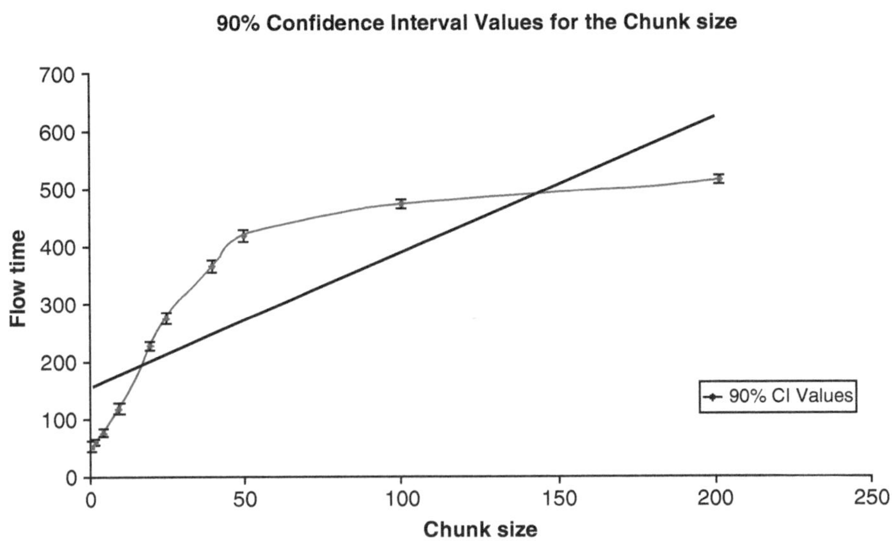

Fig. 10 Graph showing chunk size against flow time ($\lambda = 1/100$, $\mu = 1/15$, $\rho = 0.15$, $a = 0.2$, and $h = 1{,}000$). The flow time increases as the chunk size increases

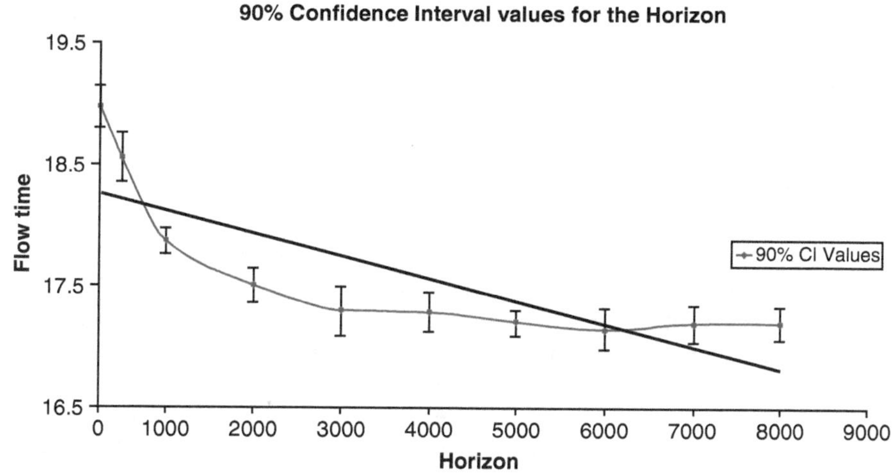

Fig. 11 Graph showing the horizon against the flow times ($\lambda = 1/100$, $\mu = 1/15$, $\rho = 0.15$, $c = 200$, and $a = 0.8$). The flow time decreases as the horizon increases

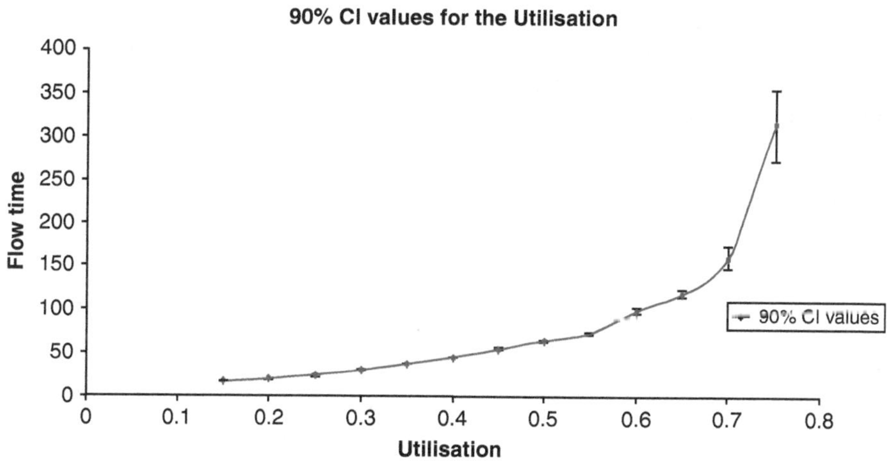

Fig. 12 Graph showing utilization against flow time ($\mu = 1/15$, $c = 200$, $a = 0.8$, and $h = 1{,}000$). The flow time increases as utilization increases

the horizon may lead to longer flow times. However, if the horizon is sufficiently large (in this case more than 3,000), it does not seem to matter anymore.

Finally, it is important to measure the effect of utilization on the flow times of cases. With a higher utilization, the flow times obviously increase as shown in Fig. 12. Typically, flow times dramatically increase when ρ get close to 1. However, with limited availability, the flow time dramatically increases when ρ gets close to a. Figure 12 shows the average flow times with 90% confidence intervals.

Note that ρ results from dividing λ by μ. In this graph, we keep μ constant and vary λ to get different utilization values. As expected, the confidence intervals get wider as ρ approaches a.

3.4 Example

This section describes a model that deals with the handling of claims in an insurance company (taken from (van der Aalst and van Hee 2002)). The insurance company processes claims that result from accidents with cars where the customers of the insurance company are involved. Figure 13 shows the workflow modeled in terms of a Petri net using the YAWL notation (van der Aalst and ter Hofstede 2005). A claim reported by a customer is registered by an employee of department Car Damages (CD). After registration, the insurance claim is classified by a claim handler of department CD. Based on this classification, either the claim is processed or a letter is sent to the customer explaining why the claim cannot be handled (50% is processed and 50% is not handled). If the claim can be handled, then two tasks are carried out, which are *check_insurance* and *phone_garage*. These tasks are executed in parallel and are handled by employees in department CD. After executing these tasks, the claim handler makes a decision, which has two possible outcomes: OK (positive) and NOK (negative). If the outcome is OK, then the claim is paid and a letter is sent to the customer. (Half of the decisions lead to a payment and the other half not.) Otherwise, just a letter is sent to the customer.

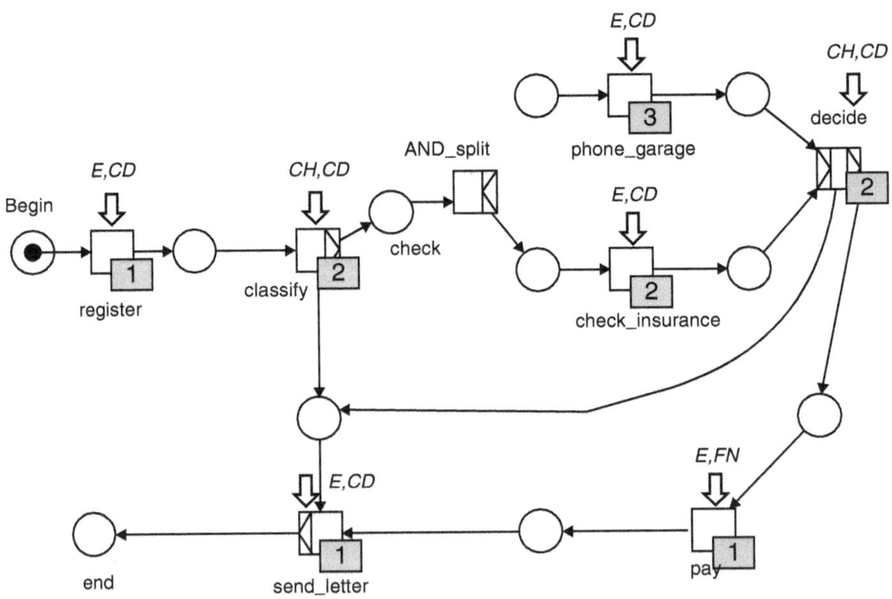

Fig. 13 Workflow model of the insurance company

Each of the tasks shown in Fig. 13 corresponds to an instance of the CPN model explained in Sect. 3.2. Each task shown in the workflow model has a number attached to it and this corresponds to the number of people (potentially) available to carry out that task. For example, there is one person able to execute task *register* and there are two persons able to execute task *classify*. The workflow model was implemented in CPN Tools and Fig. 14 shows the main page of the CPN model.

Initially, a base scenario was chosen with suitable values for the chunk size, horizon, availability, and utilization of the resources. Based on these values, experiments were carried out to determine the sensitivity of these parameters with respect to the flow time. For example, we were interested to see whether the flow time was affected by larger chunk sizes or not. Table 1 summarizes the values of the flow times obtained when experiments with different parameters were varied. Appendix 2 lists the parameters of the individual tasks, e.g., task *register* takes on average 18 min $\left(\mu_a = \frac{1}{18}\right)$ and the time between two subsequent arrivals is 50 min on average $\left(\lambda_a = \frac{1}{50}\right)$. Since the two choices in the model split the flow with equal

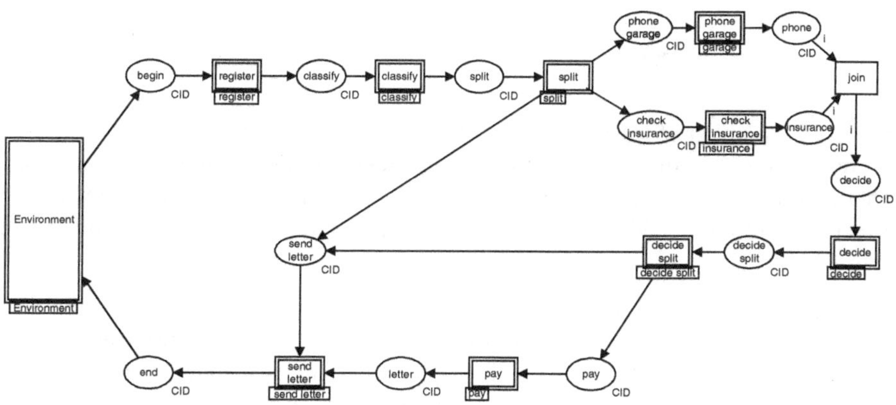

Fig. 14 The *Main* page. The sub page *Environment* creates cases. After completing all the steps in the process, cases are sent back to the environment to measure their flow times

Table 1 Results of experiments carried out to determine the effect of varying different parameters against the flow time

		Parameters	Flow time
(a)		Base case scenario ($c = 5$, $h = 2{,}000$, $\lambda = 1/50$ and $a = 0.4$, see Appendix 2 for all other parameters)	757.6 ± 65.0
(b)	(1)	Divide the horizon by 20 ($h = 100$)	1,218.9 ± 72.3
	(2)	Divide the horizon by 40 ($h = 50$)	1,247.8 ± 51.8
(c)	(1)	Multiply the chunk size by 5 ($c = 25$)	1,158.7 ± 47.2
	(2)	Multiply the chunk size by 20 ($c = 100$)	1,698 ± 139
	(3)	Multiply the chunk size by 80 ($c = 400$)	1,950 ± 83.7
	(4)	Multiply the chunk size by 160 ($c = 800$)	2,025 ± 99
(d)	(1)	Decrease availability and arrival rate by 2 ($a = 0.2$, $\lambda = 1/100$)	1,634 ± 105
	(2)	Decrease availability and arrival rate by 4 ($a = 0.1$, $\lambda = 1/200$)	3,420.32 ± 252

probabilities, only 25% of the cases that arrive are actually paid (i.e., 50% is classified as relevant, and of these 50% again 50% is rejected). Tasks have different processing times, but, for simplicity, all the tasks share the same value for chunk size (c), horizon (h), and availability (a). In the base scenario: $c = 5$, $h = 2{,}000$, and $a = 0.4$. The flow time is with 90% confidence within 757.6–65.0 and 757.6 + 65.0 min.

The results shown in Table 1 indeed confirm that the parameters for chunk size (c), horizon (h), and availability (a) have dramatic effects on the flow times. Based on the initial values, variations were made and different flow time values were obtained. For example, when the chunk size was increased from $c = 5$ to $c = 100$, the flow time more than doubled. When the availability and the horizon were varied, the effects were as expected. For example, when the availability and arrival rate decrease by a factor 4 (i.e., the relative utilization ρ/a remains unchanged), the flow time goes up from approx. 757 to approx. 3,420. Our experiments confirm that the parameters identified in this paper are relevant. In fact, it is easy to see that the effects accumulate when the workflow is larger.

3.5 Lesson Learnt

There are a number of lessons to be learnt from our experiments and CPN model. It is important to note that the modeling of resources is typically done in a naive way. There are issues characterized by parameters such as a, c, and h that dramatically affect performance, and these have to be considered to make simulations more realistic.

- First of all, it is important not to assume that people are always available and eager to work when cases arrive. In real-life situations, this is not true because people are available for only specific times and may let work accumulate before commencing it. This heavily impacts performance as shown in Fig. 9.
- Secondly, when people are available to work, they will do this work in chunks whose size may vary between different people. The bigger the chunk size, the longer the flow times of cases. So, even if the availability is the same, the flow time heavily depends on this parameter and it cannot be ignored as shown in Fig. 10.
- Chunks are divided over a particular horizon and so the larger the horizon, the shorter the flow times because of increased flexibility. Increasing the length of the horizon corresponds to making chunks (relatively) smaller.
- Utilization of people is also an important factor that greatly affects the flow times of cases. When it is high, the flow times increase.
- The example in Sect. 3.4 shows that these effects may accumulate in larger workflows. The typical assumptions made in today's simulation tools (i.e., $a = 1$, $c \rightarrow 0$, and $h \rightarrow \infty$) may result in flow times of minutes or hours, while with more realistic settings for a, c, and h, the flow time may go up to weeks or months and actually coincide with the actual flow times observed.

4 Complementary Approaches and Related Work

Simulation has been used for the analysis of business processes since the seventies (Shannon 1975). In fact, the simulation language SIMULA was developed in the sixties and influenced the development of general purpose programming languages (Dahl and Nygaard 1966). Hence, it is fair to say that simulation is one of the earliest and most established applications of computing. While the initial focus was on programming languages extended with simulation capabilities, gradually more and more simulation packages became available that offered some graphical environment to design business processes. These languages provide simulation building blocks that can be composed graphically (e.g., Arena). Today, most business process modeling tools provide some form of simulation (cf. Protos and ARIS). Moreover, the more mature workflow management systems also provide simulation capabilities (cf. FileNet, FLOWer, WebSphere, COSA, etc.). In parallel with the development of simulation tools and embedding of simulation capabilities in larger systems, the analysis of simulation data and the setting up of experiments was investigated in detail (Kleijnen and van Groenendaal 1992; Law and Kelton 1982; Pidd 1989; Ross 1990; Shannon 1975). In some cases, it is possible to use analytical models (Buzacott 1996); however, in most cases, one needs to resort to simulation.

The use of simulation was also stimulated by management approaches such as Business Process Reengineering (Hammer and Champy 1993; Davenport 1993), Business Process Improvement (Harrington 1991), Business Process Intelligence (Grigori et al. 2004), etc. (Hammer 2010). When reengineering a process from scratch or when improving an existing process design, simulation can be very valuable (Ardhaldjian and Fahner 1994). Despite the interest in simulation and the potential applicability of simulation, its actual use by end-users is limited.

In Sect. 2, we mentioned some of the main pitfalls of simulation. The core contribution of this paper is to provide an overview of these problems and to address one particular problem in detail (resource availability).

The results presented complement our earlier work on "short-term simulation," i.e., the analysis of transient behavior using the actual state as a starting point. The idea of doing short-term simulation was raised in (Reijers and van der Aalst 1999) using a setting involving Protos (modeling), ExSpect (simulation), and COSA (workflow management). This idea was revisited in (Wynn et al. 2008), but not implemented. Recently, the approach has been implemented using ProM (van der Aalst et al. 2007a), YAWL (van der Aalst et al. 2004), and CPN Tools (Jensen et al. 2007) (cf. Rozinat et al. 2008b). Processes are modeled and enacted using YAWL, and YAWL provides the four types of data mentioned in Fig. 2. This information is taken by ProM to create a refined simulation model that includes information about control-flow, data-flow, and resources. Moreover, temporal information is extracted from the log to fit probability distributions. ProM generates a colored Petri net that can be simulated by CPN Tools. Moreover, CPN Tools can load the current state to allow for transient analysis. Interestingly, both the real behavior and the simulated behavior can be analyzed and visualized using ProM. This means that decision makers view the real process and the simulated processes using the same type of dashboard. This further supports operational decision making (Rozinat et al. 2008b).

The approach presented in (Rozinat et al. 2008b) heavily relies on process mining techniques developed in the context of ProM (van der Aalst et al. 2007a). Of particular importance is the work presented in (Rozinat et al. 2008a) where simulation models are extracted from event logs. Process mining (van der Aalst et al. 2007b) is a tool to extract nontrivial and useful information from process execution logs. These event logs are the starting point for various discovery and analysis techniques that help to gain insight into certain characteristics of the process. In (Rozinat et al. 2008a) we use a combination of process mining techniques to discover multiple perspectives (namely, the control-flow, data, performance, and resource perspective) of the process from historical data, and we integrate them into a comprehensive simulation model that can be analyzed using CPN Tools.

When discussing the factors influencing the speed at which people work, we mentioned the Yerkes–Dodson law (Wickens 1992). Some authors have been trying to operationalize this "law" using mathematical models or simulation models. For example, in (Bertrand and van Ooijen 2002), both empirical data and simulation are used to explore the relationship between workload and shop performance. Also related is the work presented in (Sierhuis and Clancey 2002) where the authors present a different view on business processes, namely describing work as a practice, a collection of psychologically and socially situated collaborative activities of the members of a group. In this view, people are concurrently involved in multiple processes and activities. However, in this work, modeling aims at describing collaboration rather than focusing on performance analysis.

Finally, we would like to mention the work reported in (Reijers and van der Aalst 2005) where the effectiveness of workflow management technology is analyzed by comparing the process performance before and after introduction of a workflow management system. In this study, sixteen business processes from six Dutch organizations were investigated. Interestingly, the processes before and after were analyzed using both empirical data and simulated data. This study showed how difficult it is to calibrate business process simulation models such that they match reality. These and other real-life simulation studies motivated the work reported in this paper.

5 Conclusion

Although simulation is an established way of analyzing processes and one of the oldest applications of computing (cf. SIMULA), the practical relevance of business process simulation is limited. The reason is that it is time-consuming to construct and maintain simulation models and that often the simulation results do not match with reality. Hence, simulation is expensive and cannot be trusted. This paper summarizes the main pitfalls. Moreover, it addresses one particular problem in detail, namely the availability of resources. It is shown that resources are typically modeled in a naive manner and that this highly influences the simulation results. The fact that people may be involved in multiple processes, and that they tend to work in batches, has dramatic effects on the key performance indicators of a process.

In this paper, we provide a simple model to characterize resource availability. Using this model, important insights into the effectiveness of resources are provided. Moreover, it is shown that these characteristics can be embedded in existing simulation approaches.

Using Fig. 2, we discussed the role of different information sources and how information systems and simulation tools can be integrated. This enables new ways of process support. For example, we are working on predictions and recommendations in the context of a PAIS. Using simulation, we can predict when a running case is finished. Based on historical information, we calibrate the model and do transient analysis from the current state loaded from the PAIS. Similarly, we can provide recommendations. For example, by using simulation and historical data, we can predict the execution path that is most likely to lead to a fast result. Initial ideas with respect to prediction and recommendation have been implemented in ProM (van der Aalst et al. 2007a; Weber et al. 2007).

Appendix 1: Declarations for CPN Model in Sect. 3.2

The colset, variable, and function declarations of the CPN model have been listed in the ML language.

Colset Declarations

```
colset CID = int timed;
colset Tm = int;
colset Work= int;
colset Case = product CID * Tm * Work timed;
colset Queue = list Case;
colset Res= string timed;
colset Hor = int;
colset Av = int with 1..100;
colset Chunk = int;
colset Info = product Hor * Av * Chunk;
colset RWC = product Res * Work * Chunk timed;
colset RT = product Res * Tm timed;
colset RI = product Res * Info timed;
colset CR = product Case * RT timed;
```

Variable Declarations

```
var i: CID;
var t, t1, t2, done: Tm;
var w, w1, w2: Work;
var r: Res;
var h: Hor;
var a: Av;
var c, c1: Chunk;
var q: Queue;
var hac : Info;
val Rinit = [("r1", (1000, 20, 200))];
```

Function Declarations

```
fun x1([]) = [] | x1((x, (h, a, c))::r) = (x, 0, c)::x1(r);
fun x2([]) = [] | x2((x, y):: r) = x :: x2(r);
fun Mtime() = IntInf.toInt(time()):int;
fun Dur() = floor(exponential(1.0/15.0));
fun IAT() = floor(exponential(1.0/100.0));
fun min(x, y) = if x < y then x else y;
```

Appendix 2: Task Parameters for Base Scenario Described in Sect. 3.4

	Task	Parameters
(a)	Register	Resources $r_a = 1$ Arrival rate $\lambda_a = 1/50$ Service rate $\mu_a = 1/18$ Utilization $\rho_a = 0.36$
(b)	Classify	Resources $r_b = 2$ Arrival rate $\lambda_b = 1/50$ Service rate $\mu_b = 1/36$ Utilization $\rho_b = 0.36$
(c)	Phone garage	Resources $r_c = 3$ Arrival rate $\lambda_c = 1/100$ Service rate $\mu_c = 1/100$ Utilization $\rho_c = 0.33$
(d)	Check insurance	Resources $r_d = 2$ Arrival rate $\lambda_d = 1/100$ Service rate $\mu_d = 1/70$ Utilization $\rho_d = 0.35$

(*continued*)

	Task	Parameters
(e)	Decide	Resources $r_e = 2$ Arrival rate $\lambda_e = 1/100$ Service rate $\mu_e = 1/70$ Utilization $\rho_e = 0.35$
(f)	Pay	Resources $r_f = 1$ Arrival rate $\lambda_f = 1/200$ Service rate $\mu_f = 1/70$ Utilization $\rho_f = 0.35$
(g)	Send Letter	Resources $r_g = 2$ Arrival rate $\lambda_g = 1/50$ Service rate $\mu_g = 1/36$ Utilization $\rho_g = 0.36$

References

Ardhaldjian R, Fahner M (1994) Using simulation in the business process reengineering effort. Ind Eng 26:60–61

Bertrand JWM, van Ooijen HPG (2002) Workload based order release and productivity: a missing link. Prod Plan Control 13(7):665–678

Buzacott JA (1996) Commonalities in reengineerd business processes: models and issues. Manage Sci 42(5):768–782

CPN Group. University of Aarhus, Denmark. CPN tools home page. http://wiki.daimi.au.dk/cpntools/

Dahl OJ, Nygaard K (1966) SIMULA: an ALGOL based simulation language. Commun ACM 1:671–678

Davenport TH (1993) Process innovation: reengineering work through information technology. Harvard Business School Press, Boston

Dumas M, van der Aalst WMP, ter Hofstede AHM (2005) Process-aware information systems: bridging people and software through process technology. Wiley, Hoboken, New Jersey

Grigori D, Casati F, Castellanos M, Dayal U, Sayal M, Shan MC (2004) Business process intelligence. Comput Ind 53(3):321–343

Hammer M (2010) What is business process management? In: vom Brocke J, Rosemann M (eds) Handbook on business process management, vol 1. Springer, Heidelberg

Hammer M, Champy J (1993) Reengineering the corporation. Nicolas Brealey, London

Harrington J (1991) Business process improvement: the breakthrough strategy for total quality. McGraw-Hill, New York, NY

Jensen K (1992) Coloured petri nets. Basic concepts, analysis methods and practical use. EATCS monographs on theoretical computer science. Springer-Verlag, Berlin

Jensen K, Kristensen LM, Wells L (2007) Coloured petri nets and CPN tools for modelling and validation of concurrent systems. Int J Softw Tools Technol Transfer 9(3–4):213–254

Kleijnen J, van Groenendaal W (1992) Simulation: a statistical perspective. Wiley, New York

Law AM, Kelton DW (1982) Simulation modeling and analysis. McGraw-Hill, New York

Pidd M (1989) Computer modelling for discrete simulation. Wiley, New York

Reijers HA, van der Aalst WMP (1999) Short-term simulation: bridging the gap between operational control and strategic decision making. In: Hamza MH (ed) Proceedings of the IASTED international conference on modelling and simulation. IASTED/Acta Press, Anaheim, USA, pp 417–421

Reijers HA, van der Aalst WMP (2005) The effectiveness of workflow management systems: predictions and lessons learned. Int J Inform Manage 25(5):458–472

Ross SM (1990) A course in simulation. Macmillan, New York

Rozinat A, Mans RS, Song M, van der Aalst WMP (2008a) Discovering colored petri nets from event logs. Int J Softw Tools Technol Transfer 10(1):57–74

Rozinat A, Wynn M, van der Aalst WMP, ter Hofstede AHM, Fidge C (2008) Workflow simulation for operational decision support using YAWL and ProM. BPM Center Report BPM-08-04, BPMcenter.org

Russell N, van der Aalst WMP, ter Hofstede AHM, Edmond D (2005) Workflow resource patterns: identification, representation and tool support. In: Pastor O, Falcao e Cunha J (eds) Proceedings of the 17th conference on advanced information systems engineering (CAiSE'05), Vol. 3520 of lecture notes in computer science. Springer-Verlag, Berlin, pp 216–232

Shannon RE (1975) Systems simulation: the art and science. Prentice-Hall, Englewood Cliffs

Sierhuis M, Clancey WJ (2002) Modeling and simulating work practice: a method for work systems design. IEEE Intell Syst 17(5):32–41

van der Aalst WMP, ter Hofstede AHM (2005) YAWL: yet another workflow language. Inform Syst 30(4):245–275

van der Aalst WMP, van Hee KM (2002) Workflow management: models, methods, and systems. MIT press, Cambridge, MA

van der Aalst WMP, Aldred L, Dumas M, ter Hofstede AHM (2004) Design and implementation of the YAWL system. In: Persson A, Stirna J (eds) Advanced information systems engineering, Proceedings of the 16th international conference on advanced information systems engineering (CAiSE'04), vol 3084 of lecture notes in computer science. Springer-Verlag, Berlin, pp 142–159

van der Aalst WMP, van Dongen BF, Günther CW, Mans RS, Alves de Medeiros AK, Rozinat A, Rubin V, Song M, Verbeek HMW, Weijters AJMM (2007a) ProM 4.0: comprehensive support for real process analysis. In: Kleijn J, Yakovlev A (eds) Application and theory of petri nets and other models of concurrency (ICATPN 2007), vol 4546, Lecture notes in computer science. Springer-Verlag, Berlin, pp 484–494

van der Aalst WMP, Reijers HA, Weijters AJMM, van Dongen BF, Alves de Medeiros AK, Song M, Verbeek HMW (2007b) Business process mining: an industrial application. Inform Syst 32(5):713–732

van der Aalst WMP, Rosemann M, Dumas M (2007c) Deadline-based escalation in process-aware information systems. Decis Support Syst 43(2):492–511

Weber B, van Dongen BF, Pesic M, Günther CW, van der Aalst WMP (2007) Supporting flexible processes through recommendations based on history, BETA working paper series, WP 212, Eindhoven University of Technology, Eindhoven

Wickens CD (1992) Engineering psychology and human performance. Harper Collins, New York

Wynn MT, Dumas M, Fidge CJ, ter Hofstede AHM, van der Aalst WMP (2008) Business process simulation for operational decision support. In: ter Hofstede A, Benatallah B, Paik HY (eds) BPM 2007 international workshops (BPI, BPD, CBP, ProHealth, RefMod, Semantics4ws), vol 4928, Lecture notes in computer science. Springer-Verlag, Berlin, pp 66–77

BPM Tool Selection: The Case of the Queensland Court of Justice

Islay Davies and Micheal Reeves

Abstract This chapter reports on the experiences of an Australian government department in selecting a BPM tool to support its process modeling, analysis, and design activities. With the growing number of tools in the market that claim to support BPM, the variance in actual functionality supported by these tools, and the potentially significant cost of such a purchase, BPM tool selection has become an arduous task. While there is some independent guidance available on how various tools support different aspects of BPM initiatives, organizations still need to determine what their specific needs are and be able to establish how information gathered on tool functionality can be evaluated against these needs. The chapter presents the evaluation criteria that the Queensland Courts derived and used for their needs; the process followed to find and short-list candidate tools to evaluate; and a discussion on findings against the established criteria. While the requirements and evaluation criteria will differ for each organizational context, this chapter provides guidance for business managers on how they may structure and conduct a BPM tool evaluation from a business user perspective. In particular, it provides a score sheet tailored for a business process redesign initiative, which other organizations can use as a starting point and further refine to their specific needs. In addition, it provides suggestions on methods for identifying candidate tools for evaluation (i.e., via market research, on-site visits, gathering recommendations from experiences of others, etc.) from the multitude of BPM solutions currently available. The chapter also highlights the need for BPM tool vendors to invest more in understanding the varying needs of organizations across the BPM spectrum so as to provide accurate information to the right market in a way that potential business users/customers can understand.

I. Davies (✉)
Shared Service Agency, Queensland Government, Brisbane, Australia
e-mail: Islay.davies@ssa.qld.gov.au

J. vom Brocke and M. Rosemann (eds.), *Handbook on Business Process Management 1*, International Handbooks on Information Systems,
DOI 10.1007/978-3-642-00416-2_16,

1 Introduction and Background

Business Process Management consists of various activities, depending on the type of initiative; the phase within the BPM lifecycle (Rosemann 2004); and the level of BPM maturity of an organization (deBruin 2006; Rosemann et al. 2006) (Rosemann and vom Brocke 2010). These days, a range of technologies (software, hardware, and information management systems) exist to support many of these activities. Business process modeling is a core activity undertaken at various points in most BPM initiatives to discover, review, and specify improvements in a way an organization conducts its work; and there are many computerized tools that support this, with varying levels of sophistication.

1.1 Business Process Modeling

For the purpose of a business process review initiative, business process modeling is the act of representing both the current "As-Is" and future "To-Be" processes of an organization, so that the current process may be analyzed and improved. Essentially, it provides a graphical depiction of the process, enabling ease of communication and a common understanding with different stakeholder groups. Furthermore, this "documented knowledge" provides the means for structured analysis and discussion for improvement opportunities.

With the right tool, these models can be enriched with information regarding issues, risks, assumptions, opportunities, etc., and linked to information elements from other models, such as data models and organizational charts, to allow for deeper analysis and better enterprise-wide reporting.

There are a broad range of other purposes for process modeling such as simply providing documentation on an organization's work practices (without a view for improvement) at the one end to designing automated workflow solutions at the other extreme (Weske 2007). Therefore, it is critical to ensure that the correct tool has been selected to meet the process modeling needs and purpose.

Within the Department of Justice and Attorney-General, the Queensland Courts' Future Courts Program was established to deliver the business requirements for a new technological solution to support the core business process of court case management. As such, the program's purpose for modeling is to review, standardize, and streamline court processes and provide models that define the business requirements for the procurement of a new system. Therefore, the requirements that a BPM tool must provide in this context are primarily limited to the integrated conceptual documentation of processes, information, and organizational structures as well as sufficient support for analysis, consolidation, and redesign of these. In addition, the resulting process and information models, which define the Business Process and Information Architectures, provide an opportunity for a continued program of business process improvement and management. Therefore, these models should be easily accessible and maintainable by the business owners so as to provide an up-to-date description of processes as a basis for any future system implementations and for continual process improvement initiatives beyond the Future Courts Program.

A top-down approach to document the courts business processes was chosen to facilitate the effort toward standardization. This involves defining the courts business process architecture within a hierarchical framework (Davis and Brabander 2007) in which the core processes can be defined in relation to one another (vertically and horizontally). This approach saves time and resources by avoiding modeling all the existing variations of a process. It also makes it easy to define best "standardized" practices for carrying out processes, by deriving high level process patterns as a basis against which to compare and analyze multiple variations that exist within the business (i.e., different implementations of the process depending on location or case type etc.). The idea behind the pattern-based approach is further explained by Stephenson and Bandara (2007) as part of the work conducted in the Queensland Government Office of the CIO[1] toward a Whole-of-Government approach to business process review initiatives.

With this purpose, the Future Courts Program required a tool that supported the hierarchical approach to process design, as well as the needs of those charged with modeling (i.e., business expert process modelers, data modelers, process architects/designers, information architects/designers), and those requiring access to read and use the resulting models (i.e., process owners, operational staff, and management). The tool also needed to provide a central repository that was accessible (and restricted) to assigned modelers; ease of use and inbuilt semantic checks to aid in producing correct and complete models; a means to depict and relate process variant models for analysis and comparison; the ability to publish models to an intranet for the business to easily access for review and feedback; and the ability to customize and capture additional details (e.g., attributes) for models and model objects and to run customized reports on these. More details of the requirements and evaluation criteria are provided in a dedicated section later.

1.2 Tools That Support the Activity of Business Process Modeling

1.2.1 Modeling Notations

There are numerous business process modeling notations. The common aspect of these is that they contain a set of graphical symbols that depict different business system concepts, such as business activity/task, start and end events (i.e., the triggers and outcomes of a process), organizational units involved in the process/

[1]http://qgcio.govnet.qld.gov.au/02_infostand/downloads/BPMN%20Process%20Modelling%20Guidelines%20v1.0.0.pdf, (date accessed: Nov 2007).

activities/tasks (e.g., business units, roles), resources/documents and systems that support the process/activities/tasks, decision symbols that depict the splits and joins within a process, and arrows that depict connections between all these business concepts, including the sequence flow of the activities/tasks within a process.

BPMN (Business Process Modeling Notation) has been widely adopted as the "de-facto" standard for business process modeling, partly due to the OMG's (Object Modeling Group)[2] efforts to advocate this as a standard. As the notation recommended by the Queensland Government Office of the CIO, the Future Courts Program has adopted BPMN for business process modeling.

1.2.2 BPA (Business Process Analysis) Tools

Business process analysis tools (also known as business process modeling tools) are a type of BPM tools that are specifically used for modeling business processes and information related to the processes, in order to document an organization's work practices and/or provide business requirements for improvement, redesign, or automation. These tools provide a shared environment for the capture, design, and simulation of business processes by business analysts and managers. Some BPA tools work on a central repository, while others store model elements and their relationships in a flat file. BPA tools are modeling-only environments, not execution environments (Hill et al. 2006).

Because of the complexity of capturing end-to-end processes (particularly in a court environment), and maintaining and reusing these models for continual process improvement alongside their corresponding information elements, a dedicated business process analysis tool is essential, as opposed to simple drawing tools such as Visio or SmartDraw. BPA tools provide more flexibility for business users as well as adding extra dimensions to process models. In addition to depicting process information via the symbols within the modeling notation, information ranging from human and physical resources, legislative authorities (and restraints), and issues and risks can be linked to individual tasks and processes. Some tools provide reporting options that allow the various aspects of the captured information to be retrieved and published electronically, in Web format, and/or in hard copy form. This allows the information to be shared through a variety of media amongst managers, staff, and relevant internal and external stakeholders (Blechar and Sinur 2006).

1.2.3 BPMS (Business Process Management Suites)

Businesses Process Management Suites are intended for more than just business process modeling. While they may be used to model business requirements, the

[2]http://www.omg.org/

main use is to implement and monitor processes in, e.g., a workflow environment allowing for "real time" monitoring and management of processes (Hill et al. 2007). These tools have not been included in this evaluation as their complexity and cost goes beyond that required for process modeling within the Future Courts Program.

1.3 Issues Choosing an Appropriate BPM Tool

There is a vast range of BPM tools currently available on the market to cater for a wide variety of modeling objectives. For each objective, there are different modeling notations and approaches, and the various tools are adaptive to these. However, not all BPM tools support the same type of activities, or BPM purpose. In addition, some tools are more comprehensive and/or sophisticated in their offerings than others (Wolf 2007). In Fig. 1 above, Harmon (2008) has identified groupings based on core functionality of existing tools, highlighting the complexity and overlaps in the current BPM tool market. The circle named BP Modeling Tools is where the Queensland Courts requirements are focused. From this point on, the term "BPM tools" will be used to refer to this subset of tools that provide process modeling and analysis support.

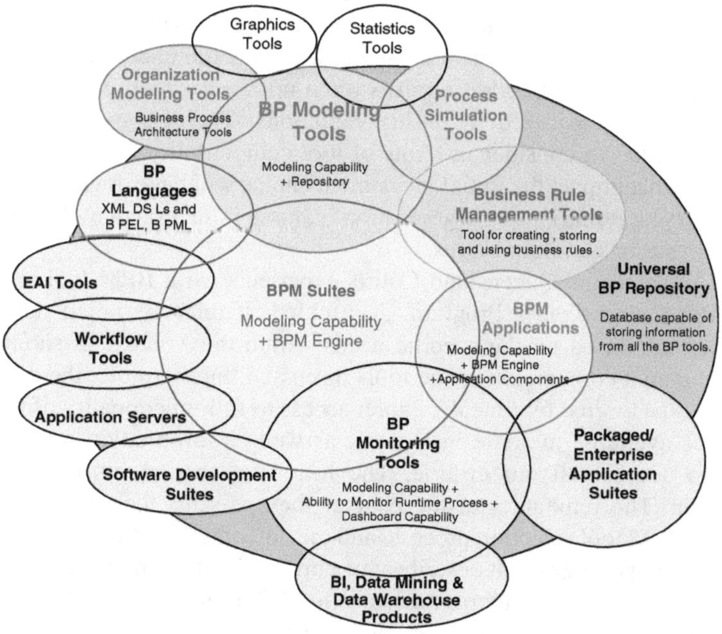

Fig. 1 An overview of the variety of software products being used by Business Process Management practitioners (Harmon 2008)

There is currently little business-oriented guidance on how to determine which tools are the best fit for a particular organization's needs. Indeed Harmon (2007) points out that "it is too early to propose a way of evaluating which business process modeling tool is best, [...] as companies are reevaluating their Business Process Management practices and exploring new, more comprehensive ways to employ process modeling tools". Simultaneously, BPM tool vendors are marketing their tools with exaggerated promises and baffling concepts to this wide audience on the back of the current BPM hype, without fully understanding what functionality is actually required to support the varying needs of these organizations (Hill et al. 2008). As a result, organizations, who have limited understanding of the many facets of BPM or the technical jargon delivered by tool vendors, are placed in a vulnerable position and face a difficult task to select a tool that will support their needs without unwanted additional functionality and wasted expense.

While independent reviews of BPM tools are conducted annually by Gartner Research (e.g., Blechar 2007, 2008a) and the Forrester Wave (e.g., Peyret and Tenbner 2006; Peyret 2009), these evaluations are also rather technical and do not go so far as to categorize the tools in terms of what specific functionality (and/or overall composition of specific functionality) supports different "types" of BPM initiatives. However, some recent articles are beginning to address this issue. Harmon (2007) attempts to describe the kind of BPM activities that different tools support. Likewise, Blechar (2008b) defines eight focus areas of BPA tool use, and in a subsequent article (2008c) highlights the need for organizations to understand their intended uses of a tool to ensure that the most appropriate tool can be chosen. But these articles are still quite technical and segmented to be of optimal use to "business-oriented" decision makers, who may not understand the technical implications discussed. In addition, it is often not clear which components of the tools have been considered in these evaluations. There is even less guidance available on what to consider in terms of tool compatibility, flexibility, and scalability; and what impact the initial investment choice will have down the track (e.g., in 1, 2 or 5 years time) as an organization matures in its practice of BPM toward longer term visions and objectives.

In this chapter, the Queensland Courts experience with BPM tool selection to support the Future Courts Program is unfolded. It must be noted that the tool evaluations are based on the specific needs within this context. It should not be viewed as a total comparison of the tools discussed. Furthermore, the depth of the evaluation was limited by time available; access to full functionality of tools (only trial demos available in some instances); as well as information requested from vendors to address all our criteria. The following section introduces the case organization. The remainder of the chapter then presents the strategies used for the overall BPM tool selection process, and the outcomes for the specific context of the Future Courts Program. It describes the current situation in the organization and how the need for a more appropriate tool for BPM emerged. Realizing the need for a BPA tool to satisfy a number of functional and technical requirements, a rating and weighting matrix was considered the best approach. Evaluation criteria were established, divided into categories, and assigned appropriate weightings of importance. Each tool was then evaluated against the criteria to establish recommendations for the procurement of the most suitable tool. The chapter ends with some lessons learnt and concluding comments on the BPM tool selection process.

2 Introducing the Case Organization

The Department of Justice and Attorney-General is the government agency responsible for administering justice in Queensland's community and marketplace.[3] One of the core services of the department is to support safe and secure communities through a court, tribunal, and prosecution system that hears and resolves civil and criminal matters.[4] The Queensland Courts was established as a single cohesive entity in 2007 in order to facilitate consistency of vision and practices between the three levels of court across the State, i.e., Supreme, District, and Magistrates courts, and their related registries.

In line with this, on 1 July 2007, the Future Courts Program was established to create a modern, innovative, and effective courts system for Queensland. The program will achieve this by developing relevant and easy to use online services for litigants, their legal representatives and the broader community, and improving registry operations through the more effective use of information, new technology, and process innovation. The business scope for the program incorporates the Supreme, District, and Magistrates Courts of Queensland and encompasses both the civil and criminal domain as well as the tribunals that are administered by these courts.

A core objective of the program is to design a standardized Business Process Architecture and an Information Architecture for court case management across all Queensland Courts and Tribunals, and to implement this using a common technology framework. To achieve this, a review of current court case management processes will be conducted, with the support of modeling software to:

- Document a shared understanding of current processes,
- Facilitate analysis of these to identify improvement opportunities, and
- Design a set of future state "to-be" models to document the new business requirements.

The external stakeholders of the program are the community, litigants, the legal profession, and partner agencies and departments (such as Police, Correctional Services, Department of Transport). Internal stakeholders include model users such as Courts Executive Management, Court Process Owners, Court Operational Staff; and the Future Courts Program Team, which consists of Process Architect/

[3]From Department of Justice and Attorney-General Annual Report 2007–08.

[4]From 2008–09 Queensland State Budget - Service Delivery Statements – Department of Justice and Attorney-General.

designers, Information Architect/designers, and Business Experts as modelers; as well as other model users such as Communications Officer, Legal Officers, and Program Management.

At the time of the tool evaluation, the department had no standard for business process modeling software. However, System Architect had been the existing option prior to the establishment of the Future Courts Program, as the Queensland Government's recommended tool for a Whole-of-Government "Enterprise Architecture" initiative. Unfortunately, numerous issues were experienced with the Queensland Courts' implementation of System Architect, ranging from limited IT support and organizational competence in using the tool for process analysis and process architecture design, to limited availability of training and mentoring services in these aspects from vendor consultants. In addition, the future direction and vendor support for System Architect was in question with Telelogic's[5] imminent acquisition by IBM and the Queensland Courts' supporting vendor Prologic's[6] decision to no longer onsell System Architect, but to go with another leading tool instead.

In light of the complex nature of this program of work and the inability of the existing implementation of System Architect (coupled with the limited availability of external support to assist in building internal capability), to meet the program's needs, an evaluation of available modeling tools was undertaken to ensure commitment to a product that meets both the business and information modeling needs of the Future Courts Program.

The final recommendations report outlined the approach undertaken to perform the evaluation of BPM tools, and presented findings and recommendations regarding the procurement of the most suitable tool. It provided:

- An overview of business process modeling generally and an explanation of how this relates to the Future Courts Program purpose,
- A summary of the importance of selecting the right tool to meet our requirements,
- An overview of the evaluation and short-listing criteria,
- Detailed analysis and comparison of candidate tools, and
- Final recommendations.

The recommended tool, ARIS Business Architect (from vendor IDS Scheer), was endorsed and implemented in April 2008. The Future Courts Program currently holds 14 Business Designer and two Business Architect licenses as well as Business Server and Business Publisher licenses. As of February 2009, the repository now has approximately 100 business process models, 30 data models, and a number of other model types to document and relate other organizational elements, such as organizational units and roles, organizational objectives, current systems, etc.

[5]http://www.telelogic.com/

[6]http://www.prologic.com.au/

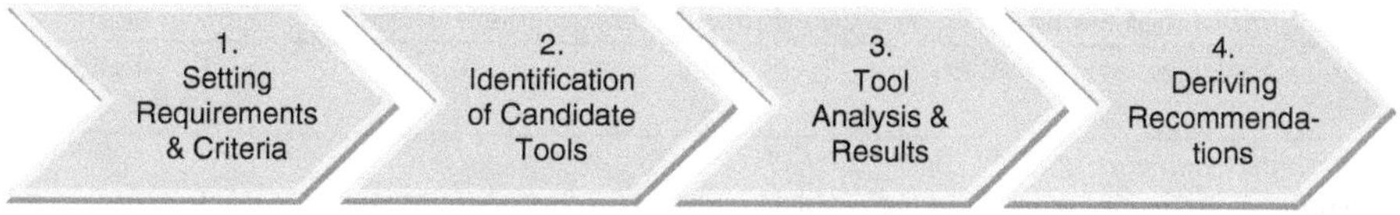

Fig. 2 Four step tool selection process followed

3 The Tool Selection Process

Having established the need for a tool to support the process modeling and analysis activities of the program, this section walks through the overall steps of the tool selection process followed (see Fig. 2), describing each step in detail. The approach is based on a commonly used weighted scoring model (Keeney and Raiffa 1976; Belton 1985). The essence of this approach is adaptable and has been applied across a multitude of disciplines from CASE Tool selection (e.g., Baram and Steinberg 1989), to ERP system selection (e.g., Shyur 2003), to construction industry procurement (e.g., Griffith and Headley 1997).

With the time constraints imposed on the evaluation process, the requirements and evaluation criteria were derived from a global perspective, considering the needs of all internal stakeholder groups as a whole, but in particular those required as a minimum to achieve the objectives of the program, stated earlier. In addition, limited resources meant that the bulk of the scoring was conducted by only one coder, a business process expert, and a primary process modeler from the Future Courts program team (wearing the hats of multiple stakeholder groups) and then reviewed and moderated by the team's Business Process Management advisor. These limitations in the overall governance of the evaluation process were unfortunately unavoidable.

A subsequent evaluation of Enterprise Architecture tools was recently conducted (but not yet published) by the Department of Justice and Attorney-General, which followed a more structured approach around consultation with the various stakeholder groups.[7] This was also to encompass a broader scope (seeking one tool that would support both BPA and Enterprise Architecture initiatives) and to evaluate the tradeoffs when multiple requirements cannot be met by one tool.

3.1 *Setting Requirements and Criteria*

The Future Courts Program management team defined a set of evaluation criteria that were considered necessary in a BPM tool to support the objectives of the program. These were grouped into Functional, Technical, and Nonfunctional

[7] This report is not yet published.

Table 1 BPM tool requirements and criteria for the future courts program

Requirements and evaluation criteria	Weighting (1–10)
Functional requirements	
Ability to import/export data (preferably in .xml/.xmi format)	9
Data dictionary/glossary capability	10
Ability to set up a list of data elements with definitions, attributes, relationships to other data elements. (e.g., ER diagram)	
Ability to make references to alternative terms (used in different contexts) for the same data concept. (thesaurus)	
Ability to classify/group data elements and provide a hierarchical decomposition of data elements.	
Flexible/easy to use report design capability (e.g., Ability to easily create customized MS Word reports, do matrices, etc.)	8
Easy to deliver to HTML for intranet/internet	8
BPMN (full support, decomposition, link to data elements, etc.)	10
UML support (to import /reuse small number of existing UML models created in Enterprise Architect)	6
Easy-to-Use and Understandability (intuitive)	7
Customizing views for ease of use by different user types	
Repository and symbols easy to find and use	
Navigation	
Flexibility to show different views and symbols for different stakeholders	
Drag and drop	
Customization to fit specific needs	10
Look and feel / set of model elements / attributes, etc.	
Create own model elements for our library	
Ease of customization, i.e., we can do ourselves	
Can apply Filters to hide irrelevant functionality and attributes	
Support for business rules, policies, and procedures (i.e., capture business rules, policies, and procedures during process analysis so that reports comprising these can be easily produced in line with registry management requirements).	10
Stability (i.e., stop auto reformatting of model connections, etc.)	8
Version Control	10
Semantic Checking (i.e., automatic checking of model semantic correctness)	8
Simulation (i.e., for process analysis and improvement measurements)	7
Technical requirements	
Able to be networked	10
SQL Server back end	9
DB is accessible independently	9
Consistent with Whole of Government requirements	9
Consistent with other related programs, platforms, and tools within the department	9
License Type (one off license fee can be capitalized)	9
Security (e.g., able to configure and manage user groups, etc.)	10
Support and maintenance	
Locally based contractors available to come to us?	10
Help Desk phone line available during Business hours?	8
On-line/real-time Help Desk availability, including guiding documentation within tool	8
Training	
Courses readily available in Queensland and aimed at assisting us to become self-sufficient with the tool, including future customization requirements?	10

(*continued*)

Table 1 (continued)

Requirements and evaluation criteria	Weighting (1–10)
Training materials available? (manuals etc)	10
Trainers readily accessible?	9
Reference sites	
Local, Queensland Government references checked (Query requirements 1–4)	6
Other reference sites using these tools	6
Costs	
Software (Licenses, Installation, and Customization) (against budget)	10
Ongoing Support and Maintenance (against budget and in-house skills for server)	10
Training (against budget)	8
Other considerations	
Team's current skills and knowledge of tools	7
Team's previous modeling experiences transferable to tool	7
Associations membership / accreditation status	8
Future Outlook of tool and support	10

Requirements and assigned appropriate weightings according to their importance, as shown below in Table 1:

The points below provide a further explanation of the criteria weighted as *most important*:

- Data dictionary/glossary capability to meet the requirement of developing the Information Architecture;
- Full support of BPMN, as this is our chosen modeling notation that supports decomposition of processes. Also, existing models created within CPIP (Continual Process Improvement Program) are in this notation;
- Ability to customize the tool according to our modeling guidelines and standards;
- Support for capturing and linking business rules to process tasks so that reports comprising these can be easily produced in line with registry management requirements;
- Necessity for version control and ability to network clients to a central repository, preferably on an SQL Sever backend, as our projects are large and complex with multiple concurrent model users;
- Necessity to allow different levels of access and views on repository elements for security and reduced complexity depending on the user type;
- Queensland based contractors who are readily available to come to us for assistance, courses and training materials, and who can provide the level of training that allows us to become self-sufficient in the use, and any further customization, of the tool as well as custom reports as our needs change;
- Consistent with Whole of Government requirements and other related programs, platforms, and tools within the department;
- Cost is within our budget;
- Future outlook of tool is strong, with a proven track record and an established plan and vision for the future.

3.2 Identification of Candidate Tools

Once we had established our evaluation criteria, we began identifying candidate tools for evaluation by researching case studies and market overviews including (but not limited to)

- Business Process Trends – Newsletters and Articles on BPM Tools
- Gartner Reports – on Magic Quadrant for Business Process Analysis Tools
- The Forrester Wave reports – on Business Process Modeling Tools

Information sourced from these studies included evaluation of vendors based on their ability to meet a broad range of modeling needs across multiple organizational roles as well as those that perform well in the areas of functional coverage, strategy, support, and marketing. Their analysis clearly identified a common group of vendors whose modeling tools were considered to be good performers under the established criteria. These findings became the foundation upon which potential candidates were short-listed for our evaluation.

At the same time, we approached members of the BPM Roundtable[8] (an Australian Community of Practice on Business Process Management), to request input from their experiences using BPA tools, based on our evaluation criteria. We received responses from approximately 10 different organizations (from both the private and public sectors).

Before a "short list" of tools was eventually selected for evaluation by the Future Courts Program, we conducted further research on sites such as BPMEnterprise.com for any published white papers regarding each vendor/tool. Information regarding each tool was also sourced from the vendor's website and trial/evaluation versions of the tools downloaded. We also accepted tool demonstrations from vendors who offered this, i.e., Lombardi, ARIS, and Mega.

The following ten tools were finally selected by the Future Courts Program for evaluation. Each tool has been assigned a letter code to assist with the discussion in the findings section. The tools are not listed in any particular order.

A – System Architect 10.8 (www.telelogic.com)
B – Enterprise Architect 7.0 Corporate Ed. (www.sparxsystems.com.au)
C – Casewise Corporate Modeler Suite 10.3E (www.casewise.com)
D – ARIS Business Architect 7.02 (www.ids-scheer.com)
E – Holocentric Modeler 5.1 (www.holocentric.com)
F – Metastorm Provision BPA (www.proformacorp.com)
G – iGrafx Process 2007 (www.igrafx.com)
H – Savvion Process Modeler (www.savvion.com)
I – Mega Modeling Suite (www.mega.com)
J – Lombardi Blueprint (www.lombardi.com)

[8]see: www.bpm-collaboration.com

3.3 Tool Analysis and Results

For each tool, each criterion was evaluated and given a score out of 10 (with 10 being completely satisfied and 0 being completely nonexistent). Each criterion score was then adjusted according to its weighting (as per Table 1). As there was only one primary coder, the criteria scores given for each tool were reviewed and adjusted iteratively to ensure they were relative to one another. This was necessary as the coder developed a greater understanding along the way of how well the criteria could be supported from the information obtained on the various tools. The scores for each criterion were then totaled to give an overall rating for each of the Functional, Technical, and Nontechnical Requirement groupings for each tool.

Overall, ARIS emerged as the most suitable tool for the needs of the Future Courts Program, as depicted below in Table 2. Following is a discussion on how ARIS measured up against each of the requirement criteria, in relation to the next two highest rating tools for each requirement grouping.

3.4 Discussion on Findings

3.4.1 Functional Requirements

(a) The tool that rated best on *import/export capability* was ARIS, which is able to import/export in the following formats: XML, XMI, WSDL, XSD, XPDL, CADM(DoDAF), BPEL, BPML. This also enables future integration with BPM suites and compatibility with Visio, txt, and Excel, as well as IBM Rational Rose and ERwin.
The Mega suite can generate BPEL from workflow models and XML schema from class models and also provides various APIs and import/export formats. It uses an SCCI interface for third party tool integration and the Mega Exchange module provides text-based import/export facility, XMI import/export facility for UML models, Rational Rose import/export facility for all UML models, BPEL export, and Erwin, Visio, and ARIS import.
System Architect also supports numerous industry standard interfaces including BPEL for integration with BPM suites, XMI for UML, IDL for IDEF and XML. However, third party products are required to enable metadata Integration to exchange data with ERwin, Oracle Designer, and other data modeling tools. System Architect also has a COM-enabled APL; however, we found this process cumbersome.

(b) For *data dictionary/glossary capability* ARIS and Mega rated the highest, with both driven by a central database repository containing all models and knowledge of business processes. This ensures maximum reusability of the data and models. In addition, each of these tools provides data modeling notations that can decompose and group data into data sets, and maintain

Table 2 Ratings of each tool against future courts' requirement groupings

Tool Code	A	B	C	D	E	F	G	H	I	J
Tool Name	System architect	Enterprise architect	Casewise corporate modeler	ARIS	Holocentric modeler	Metastorm provision	iGrafx process 2007	Savvion process modeler	Mega modeling suite	Lombardi blueprint
Requirements										
Functional	354	387	399	**507**	342	366	377	216	447	301
Technical	**406**	226	235	**406**	260	332	205	108	143	116
Support and Maint.	138	120	96	**228**	54	104	164	40	164	164
Training	232	50	149	**261**	118	70	175	70	175	175
Reference sites	96	0	0	**108**	0	0	0	0	0	0
Costs				Quote received			Quote received			Quote received

attributes and relationships to other data elements. ARIS has the additional capability of linking these data elements in a graphical way to process models. System Architect rated next as it also maintains a central repository of definitions that can be reused. However, to link these definitions to the process model is not straight forward and requires specific customization. It also does not support a graphical depiction of the relationship between the process and data views.

(c) ARIS Business Architect leads in *flexible/easy to use report design capability* and includes more than 100 predefined standard reports. A report wizard can be used to create a report (in MS Word/Excel, Adobe, PDF, HTML, etc.) by accessing report scripts within the package or that have been created (user defined) with the integrated ARIS Script Editor (IDE) or JavaScript. The latest version to be release in early 2008 has a new drag and drop feature to design layout. ARIS is also able to produce matrices for analysis of relationships between elements in tabular format.

Mega and Enterprise Architect rate second after ARIS. Mega comes with a set of easy-to-use document templates and can be customized to produce feature rich and graphically good reports. Enterprise Architect produces detailed and quality documentation in RTF and HTML formats. It can also produce Relationship Matrices.

It is important to note that the tool that rated lowest on this feature, where the feature could be identified, was System Architect. From our experience, we encountered extreme difficulty in developing customized MS word reports. In particular, System Architect restricts the order in which models can be extracted to reports.

(d) ARIS rated highest for the criteria of *easy to deliver to HTML for intranet/internet*. In addition to being able to publish models and reports in HTML format, ARIS has the unique ability to allow direct entry of feedback into the HTML interface. Furthermore, models can be easily navigated, including drill down capability, and attributes of model elements viewed.

Casewise Corporate Modeler and Mega also contain administration publishing modules that provide automated document generation in HTML to automate the generation of documents and Web Sites with hyperlinks and drill down capabilities.

Again, System Architect rated the lowest of the top three for this criterion. While the capability is present, we encountered extreme difficulty and high costs of developing HTML templates.

(e) ARIS and System Architect provide *full support for BPMN*. In addition, ARIS has the capability of extending BPMN with additional elements from its core process view, as well as bringing further elements and attributes from other views into the BPMN models, such as business rules, goals, and data elements, to provide richer graphical models.

Mega, iGrafx, Metastorm, and Casewise Corporate Modeler all also have strong support BPMN.

(f) Most of the evaluated tools provide *support for UML* with the exception of Lombardi and Savvion (unknown). However, this criterion was included primarily to ensure that our UML models, previously created in Enterprise Architect, could be brought into the selected modeling tool if required.
(g) ARIS, while a powerful and complex tool out of the box, rated well with *Ease of use and understandability (intuitive)* as it is easily customized to provide the limited set of functionality required by its users.
(h) ARIS provides *customization* to allow an individualized look and feel depending on the user by applying any number of standard filters or by creating your own customized filters. Furthermore, customized model elements can be easily added without the need for specialist consultants.
(i) Both ARIS and System Architect provide strong support *for capturing business rules, policies, and procedures.* In addition, ARIS Business Rule Designer available as "add-on" if required provides additional functionality in this area.
Casewise Business Rules Extension supports Corporate Modeler users to capture, define, and manage business rules within their natural context of business processes. Mega Modeling Suite also has the facility to store business data.
(j) It was difficult to rate *stability* (*i.e. stop auto reformatting of model connections etc.*) with only demo versions and limited time to use these.
However, this criterion was an issue with System Architect, which contained several bugs including moving message flows and throwing users out unexpectedly during modeling. As a result, information and work hours were lost.
(k) Version Control –
This was a difficult criterion to rate as we could not establish the extent of this feature for many tools without full demo versions. However, most of the leading tool vendors refer to a basic level of version control.
(l) Semantic Checking –
ARIS, System Architect and Holocentric Modeler rated highest for semantic-checking of models to comply with established modeling conventions. However, System Architect does not provide sufficient user feedback to be useful.
(m) Simulation –
This was a difficult criterion to rate as we could not establish the extent of this feature for many tools without full demo versions. However, most of the leading tool vendors refer to a basic degree of simulation capability. ARIS also has an extra "add-on" feature that allows for more sophisticated simulation.

3.4.2 Technical Requirements

System Architect, Enterprise Architecture Corporate Edition, Casewise Corporate Modeler, and ARIS can all *be networked* with an *MSQL server Backend.* They can all provide *security* to limit access privileges of different user groups.

A main problem encountered with System Architect, however, was its volatility and regular crashing while in use, which often caused hours of work to be lost.

3.4.3 Support and Maintenance

ARIS was the only tool that can provide all of the following: (a) Queensland based contractors available to come to us, (b) Help Desk phone line available during Queensland Business Hours, and (c) On line/real time Help Desk availability, including guiding documentation within tool. Furthermore, procurement of the tool from the local onseller of ARIS includes client and server implementation and a complete package covering initial customization from thorough needs analysis, training, and ongoing support.

System Architect has one consulting group that can provide local training in the use of the tool; however, specific customization requires further cost. The next closest consulting group we could find was in Tasmania. In addition to the cost of having customization designed by this group, there was very little support in the actual implementation of this. Furthermore, the online help center for System Architect is located in India.

3.4.4 Training

ARIS was the only tool where each of the following were available: (a) Courses readily available in Queensland, (b) Training materials available, (c) Trainers readily accessible and willing to train to enable self-sufficiency with the use of the tool. We discussed this service with other users of ARIS and were told that the consulting company "Leonardo," who are the onsellers of ARIS in Brisbane, provide excellent service in this area. Furthermore, they have a genuine interest in passing on the knowledge and tools required for tool users to become self-sufficient. Our reference contact added that they very rarely require additional assistance from these consultants.

3.4.5 Reference Sites

ARIS was favorably referred to us by three organizations from the BPM Roundtable. This tool is also used by the Queensland University of Technology and the Sydney University of Technology in their highly esteemed courses on Business Process Management.

System Architect has been adopted by some local government agencies, including some sections of JAG. However, it was not reported as a tool used by any of the respondents from the BPM Roundtable, which represent leading process-aware organizations in Australia.

We also received anecdotal evidence suggesting that System Architect is more suitable as an Enterprise Architecture tool, specifically for modeling the technical architecture. Whereas, ARIS Business Architect is more suitable for developing a Process Architecture and Information Architecture (collaboratively with the Business) and has better capability to graphically relate elements within these two architecture layers.

3.4.6 Cost

Throughout the evaluation process, two formal quotes were received from ARIS and iGrafx. While some vendors incorporated costing information into their marketing materials, the prices provided were both vague and challenging to comprehend without explanation.

The desire to capitalize the selected software modeling tool meant that the cost was limited to the capital budget and the license type limited to that of a one off fee. ARIS costing was the only product to fulfill both the budget and license type requirements. ARIS offers both a Sybase and SQL Server Solution. While the SQL Server was a more expensive option, it became apparent that it was the more appropriate choice when taking into consideration ongoing costs and general support available in-house.

3.5 Deriving Recommendations

Overall, ARIS Business Architect 7.02 rated the highest for all categories of criteria. In particular, ARIS satisfies our main requirements for data dictionary/glossary capability; BPMN full support; ability to customize the tool according to our modeling guidelines and standards; support for capturing and linking business rules to process tasks; necessity for version control and ability to network clients to a central repository; necessity to allow different levels of access and views on repository elements for security and reduced complexity; has Queensland based contractors who are readily available to come to us and assist us in becoming self-sufficient in the use and customization of the tool; and is consistent with Whole of Government requirements and other related programs, platforms, and tools within the department.

Furthermore, we evaluated that ARIS satisfied other important criteria, including: ability to import models previously created in System Architect; provide customized reports and web-published models; can be easily customized for an intuitive look and feel; is in line with the team's current knowledge and experience with process modeling tools; provides supplementary help documentation; is a well established tool with a proven track record and well positioned for the future.

It was therefore recommended that ARIS Business Architect be procured as the tool of use for the Future Courts Program.

4 Lessons Learnt

Even with extensive research into these tools, and in-depth discussions with vendors and fellow practitioners, it can still be difficult for business-oriented decision makers to know how well the tool will support their organization's needs until the tool is actually implemented. From such research, discussions, and tool demonstrations, the Future Courts Program believed that ARIS would support certain requirements that we are yet to see realized. For example, we have found support for the requirement to map complex data is not so simple and have needed to use Microsoft Excel and Microsoft Access to assist ARIS in meeting this requirement. Similarly, while vendors (and independent reports alike) allude to providing support for importing and exporting models in different formats for portability, we have since discovered that this is also not so practical or feasible. While there is compatibility between the many file types that can be exported and imported between the most sophisticated tools, e.g., System Architect and ARIS, reproducing the graphical structure of these models is not a straightforward task and requires extensive and costly bridging tools for this to be possible. The Future Courts Program team had hoped to import and reuse some BPMN models that had been created in System Architect in work preceding the commencement of the Future Courts Program, but to date this has not yet been accomplished. Future evaluations could look at ways of predicting/ anticipating these risks and evaluating their likely impact.

On the other hand, some additional considerations we have since found to be useful (and could be added to a future criteria list) are the capability to measure and automatically evaluate To-Be models against the As-Is models; flexibility in the way models can be presented and accessed for different model user groups; and ease of maintainability, reusability, and availability of the models that make up the Business Process Architecture to capitalize on the time and effort spent documenting these and as a basis for continual process improvement initiatives beyond the Future Courts Program.

Finally, we did not have access to the more recent information available to guide BPM tool selection (e.g. Harmon 2007; and Blechar 2008b, 2008c) at the time of our evaluation. These articles, as discussed in the earlier section on "Issues Choosing an Appropriate BPM Tool", confirm the potential for the difficulties we faced, and will remain a great resource for future BPM tool selection projects.

5 Conclusion

This chapter has described the Future Courts Program's experiences in selecting an appropriate BPM tool for their needs. Candidate tools were identified for evaluation by researching case studies and market overviews. Information sourced included evaluation of vendors based on their ability to meet a broad range of modeling needs and performance in the areas of functional coverage, strategy, support, and marketing. The vendors whose modeling tools were considered to be good performers under the established criteria were clearly identified. Ten Business Process Modeling Tools were evaluated to reveal ARIS as the most suitable tool for the purpose of the Future Courts Program within the Department of Justice and Attorney-General.

The selection process was constrained by time, and the findings should only be considered in the context of the Future Courts Program. However, the case study provides some guidance on how an organization might approach the task of evaluating BPM tools against their specific needs. In addition, the chapter provides useful references to various articles that provide detailed and relevant information on the current state of the BPM tool market, future directions, and the current pitfalls to be aware of and avoid.

However, the issue still remains as to how an organization can best determine what kind of investment it should make when embarking on a new BPM initiative without clearly understanding what their future needs will be, i.e., how might Business Process Managers weigh the costs and risks to make the best choice from the outset? For example, do they risk investing a significant amount of cost and time in a sophisticated tool at the beginning when they are just starting process mapping, knowing that their longer term vision is, for example, to implement workflow or a BPMS in three to five years time? Or do they start with a cheap drawing tool such as Visio as an easy, low cost option to start their mapping and then risk encountering problems converting their models into a more appropriate format/tool down the track when they may wish to make these models executable? There is a clear opportunity for future research to explore the correlation between tool maturity and organizational maturity to further guide organizational decision making when entering into the practice of BPM. The options to explore might fall under the following three situations:

- Buying a tool with significant higher maturity and the company slowly catches up (but unutilized functionality for a long time)
- Corresponding development of maturity (requiring scalable tool)
- Or tool migration with increased maturity levels

Additionally, it will be important for BPM-aware organizations to keep abreast of the rapid changes in the BPM tool market. And it is hoped that future information about BPM tool functionality will be framed around "What functionality is provided to support the various objectives and activities of organizations embracing BPM", in a format that business users can understand and relate to for better decision making and effective outcomes.

References

Baram G, Steinberg G (1989) Selection criteria for analysis and design CASE tools. ACM SIGSOFT Softw Eng Notes 14(6):73–80. ACM, New York. http://portal.acm.org/citation.cfm?doid=70739.70748. Accessed Feb 2009

Belton V (1985) The use of a simple multiple-criteria model to assist in selection from a shortlist. J Oper Res Soc 36(4):265–274. Palgrave Macmillan on behalf of the Operational Research Society. http://www.jstor.org/stable/2582412. Accessed Feb 2009

Blechar MJ, Sinur J (2006) Magic quadrant for business process analysis tools, 27 February 2006 ID Number: G00137850, Gartner Research

Blechar MJ (2007) Magic quadrant for business process analysis tools, 8 June 2007 ID Number: G00148777, Gartner Research

Blechar MJ (2008a). Magic quadrant for business process analysis tools, 23 September 2008 ID Number: G00161090, Gartner Research

Blechar MJ (2008b) Consider eight areas of focus when selecting a business process analysis tool, 7 August 2008 ID Number: G00160260, Gartner Research

Blechar MJ (2008c) Understanding vendor placement in the BPA tools magic quadrant, 23 September 2008 ID Number: G00161106, Gartner Research

Davis R, Brabander E (2007) ARIS designer platform: getting started with BPM. Springer, Heidelberg

de Bruin T (2006) Evaluating and advancing BPM using a BPM maturity model. In: Proceedings of IQPC's business process management conference, Sydney, May 29–30 2006

Griffith A, Headley JD (1997) Using a weighted score model as an aid to selecting procurement methods for small building works. Constr Manage Econ 15(4):341–348

Harmon P (2007) Intro-1. Why the current interest in business processes? BPTrends 2007 Enterprise Architecture, Process Modeling & Simulation Tools Report 2.1. http://www.bptrends.com/reports_toc_02.cfm. Accessed Nov 2007

Harmon P (2008) Software tools for BPM. BPTrends Spotlight 1(6). http://www.bptrends.com/publicationfiles/spotlight_062008.pdf. Accessed Nov 2008

Hill JB, Sinur J, Flint J, Melenovsky MJ (2006) Gartner's position on business process management, 16 February 2006 ID Number: G00136533, Gartner Research

Hill JB, Cantara M, Deitert E, Kerremans M (2007). Magic quadrant for business process management suites, 2007, 14 December 2007 ID Number: G00152906, Gartner Research

Hill JB, McCoy DW, Cantara M, Blechar M, Kerremans M, Lheureux BJ, Gilbert MR, Shegda KM, Schulte RW, Genovese Y, Olding E, Gassman B, Natis YV, Norton D (2008) Hype cycle for business process management, 2008, 9 July 2008 ID Number: G00159215, Gartner Research

Keeney RL, Raiffa H (1976) Decisions with multiple objectives: preferences and value tradeoffs. Wiley, New York

Peyret H, Tenbner C (2006) The forrester wave: business process modeling Tools, Q3 2006, 29 September 2006. www.proformacorp.com/Downloads/files/ForresterWaveQ3.pdf. Accessed Nov 2007

Peyret H (2009) The forrester wave: business process analysis, EA tools, and IT planning, Q1 2009, 7 January 2009. http://www.metastorm.com/news/analyst_archives.asp. Accessed Jan 2009

Rosemann M, de Bruin T, Power B (2006) Chapter 27 – a model to measure business process management maturity and improve performance. In: Jeston J, Nelis J (eds) Business process management. Butterworth-Heinemann, London

Rosemann M (2004) Business process lifecycle management. Whitepaper, Queensland University of Technology, Brisbane

Rosemann M, vom Brocke J (2010) The six core elements of business process management. In: vom Brocke J, Rosemann M (eds) Handbook on business process management, vol 1. Springer, Heidelberg

Shyur H-J (2003) A semi-structured process for ERP systems evaluation: applying analytic network process. J e-Bus 5(1):33–48

Stephenson C, Bandara W (2007) Enhancing best practice in public health: using process patterns for business process management. In: Proceedings of European conference of information systems, St. Gallen, Switzerland

Weske M (2007) Business process management: concepts, languages and architectures. Springer, Berlin

Wolf C (2007) Foreword. BPTrends 2007 enterprise architecture, process modeling & simulation Tools Report 2.1. http://www.bptrends.com/reports_toc_02.cfm

Additional Sources Used to Evaluate the Tools

DiToro L (n.d.) BPM Software Report: Lombardi TeamWorks Enterprise Edition. www.bpmenterprise.com/content/c060918a.asp. Accessed Nov 2007

DiToro L (n.d.) BPM software report: Savvion business manager. www.bpmenterprise.com/content/c060717a.asp. Accessed Nov 2007

DiToro L (n.d.) BPM software report: BPM simplicity with iGrafx. www.bpmenterprise.com/content/c070305a.asp. Accessed Nov 2007

Hall C, Harmon P (2007) Proforma corporation's provision, the 2007 Enterprise architecture, process modeling and simulation tools report – version 2.1 July 2007. www.bptrends.com/reports_toc_02.cfm. Accessed Dec 2007

Hall C, Harmon P (2007) IDS Scheer's ARIS, the 2007 Enterprise architecture, process modeling and simulation tools report – version 2.1 July 2007. www.bptrends.com/reports_toc_02.cfm. Accessed Dec 2007

Hall C, Harmon P (2007) iGrafx's iGrafx, the 2007 Enterprise architecture, process modeling and simulation tools report – version 2.1 July 2007. www.bptrends.com/reports_toc_02.cfm. Accessed Dec 2007

Hall C, Harmon P (2007) MEGA's mega suite, the 2007 Enterprise architecture, process modeling and simulation tools report – version 2.1 July 2007. www.bptrends.com/reports_toc_02.cfm. Accessed Dec 2007

Hall C, Harmon P (2007) Holocentric's Holocentric Modeler, the 2007 Enterprise architecture, process modeling and simulation tools report – version 2.1 July 2007. www.bptrends.com/reports_toc_02.cfm. Accessed Dec 2007

Hall C, Harmon P (2007) Popkin Software's System Architect, the 2007 Enterprise architecture, process modeling and simulation tools report – version 2.1 July 2007. www.bptrends.com/reports_toc_02.cfm. Accessed Dec 2007

Miers D, Harmon P, Hall C (2007) Metastorm Inc's Metastorm BPM, the 2007 BPM suites report – version 2.1, July 2007. www.bptrends.com/reports_toc_01.cfm. Accessed Dec 2007

Thompson M (2007) Technology audit, Metastorm BPM v7 November 2007 Ref Code: TA001330BPM. www.metastorm.com/library/reports/AR_Butler_Metastorm_BPM_V7.pdf. Accessed Dec 2007

Implementing Six Sigma for Improving Business Processes at an Automotive Bank

Florian Johannsen, Susanne Leist, and Gregor Zellner

Abstract Today, in the eyes of both customers and suppliers, product-related financial services take an eminent position. This does also apply to the automotive industry and its financial service providers (e.g., automotive banks). As a consequence, quality management and especially business process improvement methods (e.g. Six Sigma) attract growing attention in (the field of) financial services. Above all, the Six Sigma approach is being increasingly discussed in both literature and practice. This chapter is the result of the prototypical implementation of Six Sigma at an automotive bank; the focus is on the selection and the combination of quality techniques used at an automotive bank, the crucial points of the successful implementation.

1 Introduction

Over the last couple of years, financial services have increasingly been growing in importance. In the automotive industry, too, synergies between new car sales and financial products have been systematically exploited and advanced. Apart from increasing sales numbers, customer loyalty is in focus. Besides, product supporting financial services are more and more used to differentiate and strengthen the own position in the market. At the same time, a change of values on the part of the customers has been taking place, causing more severe customer service pressures than ever for the organizations (Smith et al. 1999). Evidently, the probability of customer desertions due to poor service is often rated higher than desertions due to defects in a physical product. Thus, quality management, which some years ago was still regarded as solely referring to manufacturing industries, does now take an

F. Johannsen (✉)
Department of Management Information Systems, University of Regensburg, Regensburg, Germany
e-mail: florian.johannsen@wiwi.uni-regensburg.de

J. vom Brocke and M. Rosemann (eds.), *Handbook on Business Process Management 1*, International Handbooks on Information Systems,
DOI 10.1007/978-3-642-00416-2_17, © Springer-Verlag Berlin Heidelberg 2010

eminent position in financial services, too. Many different approaches such as, for instance, KAIZEN, EFQM (European Foundation for Quality Management), or TQM (Total Quality Management) were developed. Especially for the finance industry, Six Sigma (see Sect. 2.1) has been paid considerable attention, both in literature and practice. Six Sigma is a specific concept because it combines different parts and techniques of the mentioned approaches (e.g., the Six Sigma cycle (DMAIC (Define, Measure, Analyze, Improve, Control)) and incorporates the main steps of the PDCA (Plan, Do, Check, Act) cycle of KAIZEN). A central problem, however, is the selection of adequate quality techniques in a project (Arneson et al. 1996; also Conger 2010). There are numerous criteria and individual approaches, but generally accepted guidelines do not exist, even though the application of appropriate techniques is a critical-to-success factor when implementing improvement measures: they have significant influence on whether the results originally intended are obtained or whether resources are wasted on suboptimal approaches (Okes 2002; Pande et al. 2000; Bunney and Dale 1997). Other difficulties (e.g., lack of valid data, ambiguous customer requirements, etc.) often occur only when applying the Six Sigma cycle (DMAIC) during an improvement project (Antony 2006). These difficulties are, therefore, not included in this investigation.

We aim at identifying an approach for the selection and subsequent combination of quality techniques within a Six Sigma initiative. Furthermore, results and experiences from the practical application at an automotive bank will be described.

This article contains the following sections: in Sect. 2, the basic principles of Six Sigma (definition, Six Sigma cycle) are explained; they define essential concepts (quality techniques and tools) and describe the lack of support to select quality techniques in Six Sigma. Section 3 concentrates on how to select and integrate quality techniques and presents the development of a 3-step approach. In Sect. 4, we refer to the enterprise-specific application of this approach as well as the practical implementation at an automotive bank. In the last section, the approach and results are discussed.

2 Six Sigma Quality Management and Quality Techniques

2.1 Six Sigma Basics

Quality management is not really a new issue in manufacturing. In the late nineteenth century, the inspection of finished goods was introduced by F.W. Taylor, and during the last half-century, the concept of quality changed from a pure product specification toward a method and evolved by contributions made by quality leaders like Crosby (1979), Deming (1982), Ishikawa (1985), Juran (1988), and Feigenbaum (1991). But after several decades of literature, quality management still does not have an accepted or agreed definition (Foley 2004). Following the ISO

9000:2005 definition, quality management includes all the activities that organizations use to direct, control, and coordinate quality. These activities include formulating a quality policy, setting quality objectives, planning quality, controlling quality, assuring quality, and improving quality.

The Six Sigma method has been influenced by previous quality management work and industrial engineering approaches and now comprises a well-defined set of techniques and methods that support each of the five phases of a process lifecycle (i.e., DMAIC) (Harry and Schroeder 2006; Conger 2010). In the context of quality management, the term "Six Sigma" refers to a method that aims at significantly increasing the value of the enterprise as well as the customer satisfaction. The parameter "Six Sigma" is taken from statistics indicating the "sixfold standard deviation". The standard deviation (σ) shows the deviation (rate of defects) from the statistical mean. Based on a standard deviation of 6σ, 99.99985% of all outcomes would be produced within acceptable limits. That equals 1.5 defect parts at a production of 1 million parts (Breyfogle 2003). As especially in financial services the output permanently fluctuates, a correction of 1.5σ is common sense (Breyfogle 2003). That means that a 6σ-level in the long run is equal to 4.5σ, which results in a 99.99966% quality level or 3.4 defects per 1 million opportunities (DPMO) (Pande et al. 2000).

Even though, for a couple of years now, Six Sigma has been applied in enterprises, the concept of the approach is not entirely confirmed. This fact is mirrored in numerous attempts at defining Six Sigma, which have to be investigated against the background of the individual application (Magnusson et al. 2004). In this context, the application as an enterprise-wide strategy (a management-driven top-down approach) (Harry and Schroeder 2000) as well as the implementation as an improvement method or purely as a set of techniques (Breyfogle et al. 2001) can be differentiated.

In most of the cases, Six Sigma (as in this chapter) is interpreted as an improvement method (Magnusson et al. 2004); here, a business process is systematically optimized by means of the DMAIC-cycle (Antony 2006). In each phase, specific results are worked out (see Table 1) using widely established techniques (Pande et al. 2000).

Table 1 Results of Six Sigma phases

Phase	Results
Define	Description of project/problem, identification of customer requirements (Voice of customer), customer-critical characteristics (critical to quality (CTQ)), business-critical characteristics (critical to business (CTB)), specification of performance standard.
Measure	Selection of values (process output, process input), data collection, data visualization, determination of current process performance.
Analyze	Data analysis, statistical determination of causes for the problems (correlations).
Improve	Generation of improvements, prioritization of solutions, and estimation of potential benefits
Control	Control of process performance, action plan for deviations.

As an improvement method, Six Sigma seeks to identify and eliminate defects, mistakes, or failures in business processes and therefore combines human elements (e.g., culture change) of improvement and process management (Snee 2004; Antony 2006) (Baumoel 2010; vom Brocke et al. 2010). The Six Sigma cycle (DMAIC) supports process lifecycle management in a structured way using a well-defined set of techniques and methods.

2.2 Definition of Concepts

Both in practice and literature, there are different notions of the concept of "quality technique" (Theden 1996). Apart from that, there are ambiguities as regards the definition of "quality tools" (Antony 2006). It therefore seems to be helpful to look for consistent definitions of the concepts of "technique" and "tool" in the context of quality management. *Quality technique* is understood as an instrument, which, on the basis of guidelines and by means of several quality tools, leads to one or more results on different conceptual levels. As an element of a method, techniques determine what is perceived and help to generate results during each phase of the method (Leist and Zellner 2006). A technique consists of certain steps that are performed in a defined order (Hellsten and Klefsjö 2000), for instance QFD, SPC, DOE, or FMEA. A *quality tool* is a means, which in a goal-oriented manner works out a result or supports the process of working out a result. The quality tool is set apart from the techniques by means of a limited application context with a clearly defined role (McQuater et al. 1995). Examples are cause–effect diagrams, histograms, or flow diagrams. Quality tools can occur independently or as an integral part of a technique (e.g., the House of Quality within the framework of QFD Akao 1990). Since tools could be part of a technique, the selection or integration of tools and techniques must focus both. But for selection and integration, the distinction (e.g., whether an instrument obtains only one or more results) is not relevant. Therefore, we use the notion *technique* only.

2.3 Related Work

Even though Six Sigma as well as most of the quality management approaches have a manufacturing background, the concept, originally inspired by the results achieved at enterprises such as Motorola (Pande et al. 2000), General Electric (Snee and Hoerl 2003), or Polaroid (Harry and Schroeder 2000), was more and more applied to service industries. This fact is mirrored in the growing number of publications that explicitly deal with the topic of Six Sigma in services. Breyfogle et al. (2001) and Hensley and Dobie (2005) published Six Sigma procedures for service processes, in a rather general way. In an empirical study, Antony (2004) investigates the application of Six Sigma at British service enterprises and identifies, e.g., success factors as well as the most frequently used quality techniques.

The works published by Pande et al. (2000), Harry and Schroeder (2000), or Magnusson et al. (2004) describe Six Sigma more from an industrial perspective, but emphasize fundamental differences for the service sector. Despite these numerous publications on Six Sigma, there is an obvious lack of works dealing explicitly with the selection and integration of adequate quality techniques for a successful implementation of Six Sigma (Kwok and Tummala 1998).

In literature, there is consensus concerning the steps to be followed in a Six Sigma initiative. In addition, the results to be achieved in each Six Sigma phase are described unambiguously. But it is also recognized that processes in the manufacturing industry differ from those in the service industry (Hensley and Dobie 2005). The lack of measurement systems for service processes for example is just one of several challenges Six Sigma initiatives face in the service industry (Chakrabarty and Tan 2007; Antony 2006). Therefore, many quality techniques cannot be used for production and service processes in the same way. Due to the difficulties in gathering data for service processes, techniques such as, for instance, Design of Experiments are quite uncommon in the service industry and are usually not used within Six Sigma initiatives. But also within enterprises, the project environment (regarding process documentation, customer interaction, or performance measurement for instance) may differ drastically favoring or opposing the use of certain quality techniques. Therefore, the selection of techniques has to be dealt with great care when starting a Six Sigma initiative. The missing standardization of Six Sigma (Harmon 2007) concerning the use of quality techniques makes their selection a central issue when implementing the concept in a certain company.

3 Development of the Approach for Selecting and Integrating Quality Techniques

In literature, it is often pointed out that Six Sigma combines or integrates established quality management methods and techniques (Pande et al. 2000). The choice among the many different quality techniques of Six Sigma raises the question of the specific characteristics of individual techniques, which allow making statements on the suitability of particular techniques as well as on the possibilities to combine different techniques. As a consequence, we introduce a 3-step approach. The 3-step approach helps to first classify the quality techniques, then select them, and it finally shows how to integrate them into a consistent "roadmap". Our 3-step approach uses the schema of method comparison (see comparisons in Olle et al. 1983) and complements it by the integration of techniques, which is the last phase of our 3-step approach.

1. *Identification of Appropriate Approaches and Classification of Quality Techniques (Classification)*
   The starting point of the investigation is a compilation of different quality techniques, which may (potentially) be used in a process improvement project.

To keep the scope of techniques manageable (a total number of 93 techniques were compiled), they are transferred into a standardized structure. This structure is based on a classification approach appropriate to deal with the problem in question and simplifies the subsequent steps of selection and integration. In doing so, not all techniques have to be examined at the same time, but the user can focus on clusters (see Sect. 4).

2. *Identification of Appropriate Criteria and Selection of Techniques (Selection)*
   Further down, starting points are identified, which are adequate to evaluate the techniques. In doing so, specific requirements of the particular enterprise have to be considered (e.g., it is required that techniques can be quickly explained and almost instantly used in workshops). To be able to consider these requirements, selection criteria (e.g., a technique must be easy to learn and it should be possible to use it after a short period of familiarization) must be derived and prioritized before they can serve as a basis for the selection of the techniques. At the same time, possible interactions and interdependencies have to be identified. For instance, the degree of complexity of individual techniques has to be adapted to the circle of users addressed in each case. To support a structured way of choosing the selection criteria, we used the approach of the technology acceptance model (TAM).
3. *Integration of Techniques into a Coordinated Approach (Integration)*
   Finally, the selected techniques are integrated to form a consistent approach or roadmap for an (quality) improvement initiative.

The 3-step approach supports the selection and integration of Six Sigma techniques. In doing so, it primarily offers criteria for the classification and selection as well as restrictions for the integration. The 3-step approach explicitly avoids the prioritization of the criteria and restrictions. Since a prioritization is only possible for a particular case of application, the 3-step approach contains nonweighted criteria and restrictions.

As a starting point and a basis for the 3-step approach, we collected Six Sigma techniques from theoretical and practical sources, mainly from literature. Due to the immense scope of quality techniques, they are not explicitly described in this chapter. The listing of techniques is made on the basis of an extensive literature research. Figure 1 shows some of the techniques found.

3.1 Classifying Approaches for Quality Techniques

Different approaches for classifying quality techniques can be found in literature:

- Gogoll and Theden (1994), who take a manufacturing view, classify according to "classical quality supporting tasks", "organizational measures", "quality techniques in the broader sense (auxiliary techniques)", and "quality techniques in the narrow sense".

Technique	About the technique				Technique supports the following milestone	Milestone applies to phase
	Goal	Description	Advantages	Disadvantages		
SIPOC diagram	- determine important process customers - determine customer-supplier-relationship by means of process inputs and outputs - ensure consistent understanding of process	- determine starting and end points of a process - rough description of the process in 5-7 process steps - put down which supplier has provided which process input and which customer has used up which output - show a maximum of 6-7 process steps	- simple list of all relevant substeps - identification of essential input and output values - intuitively comprehensible	- can only be used, if the detail in question is definite - exact beginning and end of the process in question is often hard to determine - often problematic for a huge number of different inputs/ outputs	*Clear process description as basis of communica-tion*	**DEFINE**
VOC & CTQ - Matrix	- specification of result requirments by means of customer inter-views - particularly critical points are high-lighted as CTQs - determine potential variables and target corri-dors for the result requirements	- identify customer requirements in inter-views or by means of questionnaires and summarise them to key messages - in case of external customers, first evaluate data of inhouse customer service division - derive 1-5 CTQs from key messages	- refine unstructured statements to a small number of key messages	- danger to concentrate on too many key messages thus neglecting the essen-tial statements - often unclear allocation to key messages	*Customer requirements*	
...	...	...	...	...	...	...

Fig. 1 Extract from list of compiled quality techniques

- According to that scheme, Okes (2002) considers only the last two of the above categories in his subcategorization. Here, the "seven elementary quality techniques" (7Q) according to Ishikawa (1980) and the "seven management techniques" (7M) according to Nayatani (1986) can be found again, which, according to Gogoll and Theden (1994), have to be allocated to the quality techniques in the narrow sense.[1] Correspondingly, (Okes 2002) creativity techniques, statistical techniques, design techniques, and measurement techniques have to be assigned to the "quality techniques in the broader sense".
- Apart from the "7Q" and "7M techniques" categories, Dale and McQuater (1998) allocate quality techniques to the generic classes "other techniques" and "techniques".
- Particularly in the context of Six Sigma, the 7 × 7 technique box has established itself, which subsumes common quality techniques under the categories management techniques, quality control techniques, customer techniques, lean techniques, project techniques, statistical techniques, and design techniques (Magnusson et al. 2004). The first two classes are congruent with the above so-called "7M" or "7Q" techniques, while the remaining categories comprise techniques that can be categorized as auxiliary techniques, according to Gogoll and Theden (1994).
- Furthermore, there are works that make classifications according to the steps of specific quality management approaches, e.g., the Six Sigma cycle (Roenpage et al. 2006) or the seven steps according to Juran and Gryna (1988).

[1]Basically in literature for "7Q" and "7M" the notion "tool" is established, speaking of "seven elementary quality tools" (7Q) and the "seven management tools" (7M). But we do not distinguish and use the term "technique" only.

In summary, it shows that the above classification approaches not only follow the proposed roles of the techniques, e.g., communication and illustration of information ("7M" and "management techniques") (Dale and Shaw 1999) or the individual character of the technique (i.e., whether it leads to an actual result or whether it helps to obtain it) but also follow the procedures of specific quality management concepts (Roenpage et al. 2006; Juran and Gryna 1988).

3.2 Selection Criteria for Quality Techniques

The next question is about the criteria, which support an adequate selection of the quality techniques. Even though Dale and McQuater (1998) argue that the techniques in quality management can principally be qualified as being equivalent (Dale and McQuater 1998), it may be objected that the adequacy of a technique as well as of their characteristics depends on the context of application. That being said, it is generally difficult to forecast which quality techniques can best be used for quality initiatives since it is very difficult to verify their actual influence on obtaining the intended performance level (Tari and Sabater 2003).

For classifying the criteria, we use the framework of TAM (technology acceptance model) by Davis (1986, 1989) and Davis et al. (1989). As the constructs of TAM are sufficiently general, they can also be translated to other domains (Moody 2003). TAM describes how users come to accept and use a technology. It suggests a number of factors that influence the acceptance and usage of technologies. All influence factors are classified into three main categories: external variables, perceived usefulness, and perceived ease of use. Transferred to the domain of selecting techniques, the *perceived usefulness* depends upon whether the user believes that the technique is adequate to support the goals or milestones of the Six Sigma initiative and enhances his or her job performance. The *perceived ease of use* depends on technique-specific criteria and expresses the user's belief that using a particular system would be free from effort. The *external variables* comprise all other criteria, which influence the perceived usefulness and ease of use of techniques used in the project.

To be able to select adequate techniques, the three main categories must be substantiated in more detailed criteria. TAM suggests criteria for the acceptance and usage of technologies, which should be used several times. Six Sigma techniques are selected for the use in only one project subsequent. Even though it is possible that subsequent Six Sigma initiatives (re)use the (same) techniques, users choose a suitable technique in accordance to the requirements of only the next initiative. Since the criteria for the ease of use and usefulness differ depending on whether a unique or repeated use is assumed, we were looking for detailed criteria in the Six Sigma literature.

Thia et al. (2005) identify 13 parameters to select techniques (when developing new products), which can be subdivided into external and internal parameters. Among the internal parameters count "user friendliness", the "(non)-tangible benefit of the application", the "aspect of time (application, learnability)", "monetary costs occurring (for the application)", the "flexibility (degree of freedom of the application)", and the "familiarity" with the technique. Among the external parameters count the "degree of novelty of the project", the "support of the management", the "cohesiveness", the "technical competence", the "size of the enterprise", the "line of business", and the "cultural background" (Thia et al. 2005). Thus the external parameters help to include characteristics of the project as well as the enterprise environment into the selection process. Apart from parameters that directly refer to techniques (such as restrictions, difficulties, expected benefit, training time (and effort), etc.), (Dale and McQuater 1998), too, list as well higher order parameters such as the organizational environment, the corporate culture, and the integration of further techniques (Dale and McQuater 1998). Authors like Harrington (1995) emphasize the importance of the level of maturity of an enterprise in quality management when looking at the selection of techniques; in doing so, parallels with the parameter "technical competence" according to Thia et al. (2005) become obvious. Bunney and Dale (1997) report similar experiences in their long-term study of the chemical industry. McQuater et al. (1995) propose the categories "tangibility", "importance for staff", "relevance", as well as "frequency of use" by means of which the application of quality techniques in practice can be evaluated.

Bamford and Greatbanks (2005) describe a generic procedure for the execution of quality initiatives in different lines of business, which is heavily based on the phases of the DMAIC cycle; depending on the partial results, which are supposed to be obtained as well as on the situation, the selection of techniques is made from "7Q" or "7M" techniques. Shamsuddin and Masjuki (2003) point out the necessity of a systematic application of techniques, depending on the intended aim of the individual operational phase. The following Table 2 gives a summary of the above mentioned criteria.

To sum up, the literature reviewed names criteria that directly address the characteristics of a technique (e.g., learnability, flexibility, etc.), which can represent the perceived ease of use and higher order parameters referring to the specific project periphery, correspond to the perceived usefulness and the enterprise reality (e.g., resources), and correspond to the external variables.

3.3 Requirements on the Integration of Quality Techniques

In quality management, techniques must not be regarded in an isolated manner (Hellsten and Klefsjö 2000) but must be integrated to fulfill given quality objectives (e.g., reducing waiting times or waste of money) (Shamsuddin and Masjuki 2003). It is thus necessary that the selected techniques, both in a specific phase of the cycle and across the phases, complement one another and are based on each other (Snee and Hoerl 2003). Similar considerations are addressed by Bruhn (2006) as well who describes the interdependencies between quality management differentiating between functional, temporal, and hierarchic interdependencies. The functional

Table 2 Selection criteria for techniques

Constructs of TAM	Selection criteria	Author(s)
External variables	Size of the enterprise	Thia et al. (2005)
	Line of business	
	Cultural background	
	Organizational environment	Dale and McQuater (1998)
	Corporate culture	
Usefulness	(Non)-tangible benefit of the application	Thia et al. (2005)
	Monetary costs occurring (for the application)	
	Flexibility (degree of freedom of the application)	
	Degree of novelty of the project	
	Support of the management	
	Cohesiveness	
	Integration of further techniques	Dale and McQuater (1998)
	Importance for staff	McQuater et al. (1995)
	Relevance	
	Frequency of use	
	Depending on the partial results which are supposed to be obtained as well as on the situation, the selection of techniques is made from "7Q" or "7M" techniques	Bamford and Greatbanks (2005)
	Systematic application of techniques and techniques, depending on the intended aim of the individual operational phase	Shamsuddin and Masjuki (2003)
Ease of use	Technical competence	Thia et al. (2005), Harrington (1995), Bunney and Dale (1997)
	User friendliness	Thia et al. (2005)
	Aspect of time (application, learnability)	
	Familiarity with the technique	
	Tangibility	McQuater et al. (1995)

interdependencies address contents synergies between techniques to obtain a common goal (Bruhn 2006). Techniques can compete with one another (for instance as regards their mode of action), complement each other, require the application of other techniques, achieve identical results for a problem, or work entirely independently of each other. As regards the parameter time, techniques can be applied successively, parallelly or intermittently. Furthermore, techniques can be classified according to their application, and focus on either strategic or operational problems (hierarchical interdependencies) (Bruhn 2006).

3.4 Summary of the 3-Step Approach

The 3-step approach is summarized in Fig. 2. Based on the description of the technique and the milestones and deliverables of the project, the techniques can

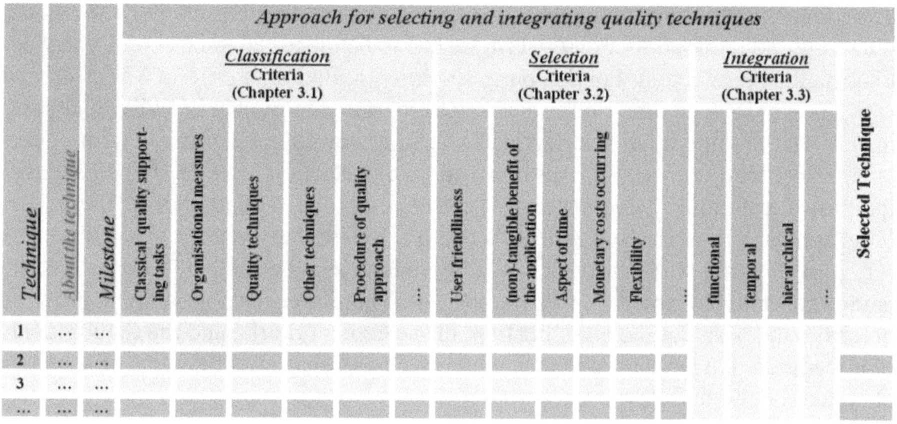

Fig. 2 Summary of the 3-step approach

be classified according to the classification criteria. This allows a quick selection of the technique according to a certain stage in the project.

To be able to select the adequate technique for a certain type of project members, it is useful to declare certain criteria for the application of the technique. Depending on the needs and milestones during the project, the appropriate technique can be selected then. Besides the integration criteria are a helpful mean to notice the dependencies between the techniques and to use the techniques in a useful order.

How this 3-step approach was adapted for the automotive bank will be described in the following chapter.

4 Application of the Developed Approach at an Automotive Bank

The 3-step-approach was applied in a cooperation project with an automotive bank. It is the affiliate of a German automotive group and is responsible for the activities of the group's division concentrating on financial services in Germany. Founded in 1971, it belongs to the leading automotive banks in Germany and was (at the time of the project) represented in 53 countries with 26 subsidiaries and 27 cooperations. From the central headquarters, about 760 employees took care of more than 800,000 customers. The automotive bank has no branch network. Its portfolio comprises individual solutions to ensure the mobility of private and business clients, as well as financing and leasing, car insurance, dealer financing, and fleet management. 62% of all buyers of new cars finance the purchase by means of credit or leasing contracts at the car manufacturer's in-house bank (automotive bank). In the long term, the automotive bank intended to implement Six Sigma as an integrated quality management approach. According to the introduced 3-step approach, the quality techniques were first classified to simplify the subsequent selection, and integration. Finally, criteria had to be identified to be able to carry out a substantiated selection. For this purpose, the compilation of criteria was discussed with the project team and questioned regarding the importance of individual parameters. At the same time, selected staff was interviewed to determine requirements on the techniques to enable the derivation of selection criteria. On this basis, individual techniques were evaluated, selected and, finally integrated. The underlying approach is generally applicable, being comparatively generic. Thus, the steps ((1) classification, (2) selection, (3) integration) can be adapted to the specific environment of the enterprise or the project. Therefore, the following subsection describes the basis for the classification, the selection criteria, and the requirements of integration that were used in the automotive bank project. Afterwards, the results obtained will be laid down.

4.1 Classification of Quality Techniques at the Automotive Bank

The project manager decided at the beginning that the systematic implementation of quality techniques had to adhere strictly to the phase results of the Six Sigma cycle. Therefore, a structuring approach based on the DMAIC-cycle was selected. Those quality techniques were allocated to each phase of the cycle that led directly to the intended phase results or supported their development (see Table 1). To keep the classification clear, clusters were supposed to be used to clarify the allocation of individual techniques to specific phases of the cycle (compare Fig. 3).

The classification results are shown in Table 3. Due to the tremendous number of techniques, the table comprises only a subset of the classified techniques (for a brief explanation of some of the listed techniques (Conger 2010).

When carrying out the selection later on, it was possible to regard each phase separately thus keeping the number of techniques to be evaluated manageable. In doing so, the basis was created for the subsequent integration (across the phases) of the selected techniques within the framework of the DMAIC-cycle.

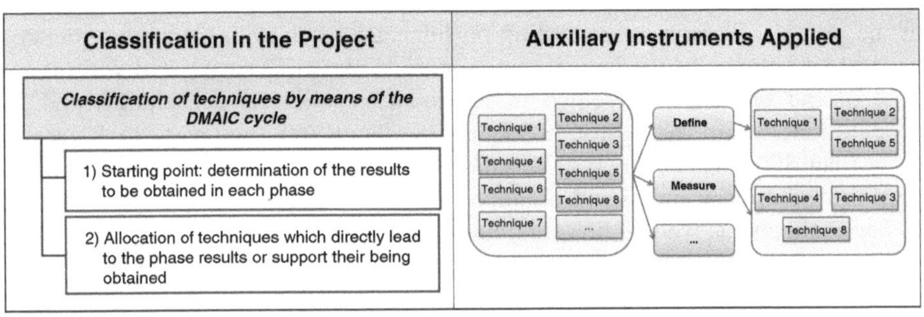

Fig. 3 Classification of techniques

Table 3 Classification results

Phase	Techniques
Define	Project charter, CTQ/CTB matrix, stakeholder analysis, SIPOC, process flow diagram/process map, customer segmentation, structured interviews, KANO …
Measure	Capability analysis, performance metrics (DPMO, DPU, …), check sheets, value matrix, data collection plan, trend/run chart, dot plot diagram, box plot diagram, gage repeatability and reproducibility, …
Analyze	Cause–effect diagram, histogram, FMEA, scatter diagram, regression analysis, hypothesis testing, correlation calculation, pareto diagram, multivariate charts,process flow diagram/process map, design of experiments, process simulation, 5S, value stream map, …
Improve	Brainstorming, affinity diagram, priority matrix, cost benefit analysis, network planning technique, brainwriting, anti-brainstorming, Poka Yoke, TOC, etc.
Control	Control charts, reaction/control plan, mistake proofing/automated control, etc.

4.2 Selection of the Classified Quality Techniques at the Automotive Bank

At the automotive bank, the "user friendliness" of the techniques as well as the technical, organizational, and temporal restrictions were identified as the most important parameters. Therefore, the selection criteria (see Sect. 3.2) were discussed within the project team. In addition, staff interviews were carried out to identify those criteria that employees at the automotive bank considered to be the most significant for selecting quality techniques. Based on the discussion and the interviews, the criteria were prioritized. In the following, only those criteria are focused on that considered to be the most important ones, namely "user friendliness" and the restrictions listed above.

At the automotive bank, *technical restrictions* referred to existing software packages that were used for purposes of analysis, documentation, and execution of techniques. It was not intended to buy additional software but to draw on existing applications. This had an influence on the mode of data evaluation, on the analysis as well as on the collection of the performance data of adequate measuring systems. *Organizational restrictions* mostly referred to the implementation of the improvement initiative. The phase results of the project were supposed to be worked out in workshops across the divisions, which were joined by staff in charge. To proceed in this way has the advantage of integrating all the staff involved in the exchange of experiences: this is one major factor of success when implementing quality techniques (McQuater et al. 1995; Bunney and Dale 1997). It is, however, only possible to tap the full potential if all project members cooperate. This requires that all participants, irrespective of their actual knowledge of techniques and quality management methods, understand the techniques applied in the workshop and are able to work with them. Thus the way the workshop works has an essential influence on the criterion "user friendliness" described later on in this chapter. Moreover, it must be pointed out that not all techniques can be used in project work.

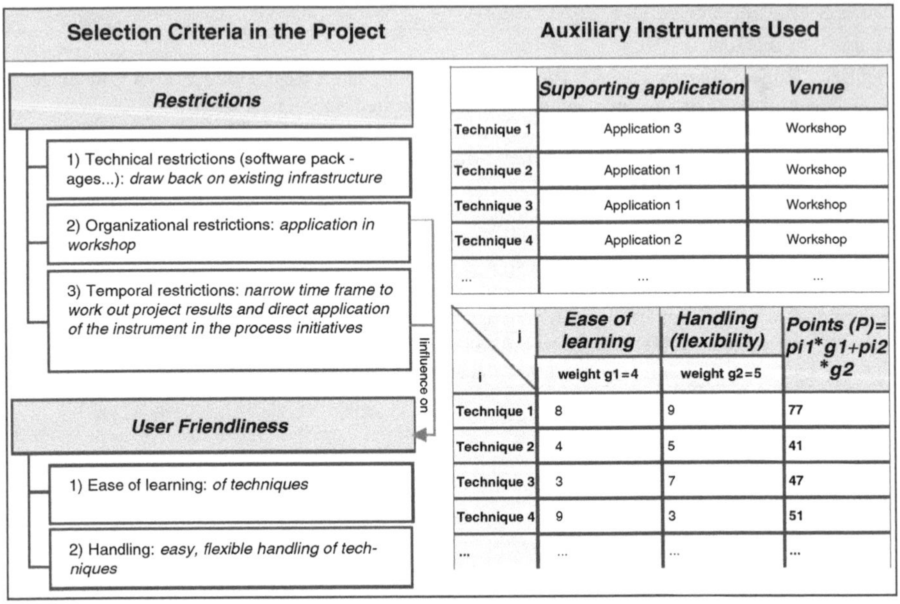

Fig. 4 Selection of techniques

For instance, the analysis of performance data should not be done in the workshop, since it may be necessary to provide further datasets, something that will only become obvious during the process of analysis. To evaluate the techniques against the background of *technical* and *organizational restrictions*, a matrix was used (see Fig. 4). Column 1 shows for each technique which supporting application was available for the implementation, the results documentation, as well as for the subsequent electronic processing of the results (verification of the technical restrictions). Techniques that did not have any software or system support were not considered. The second column shows the appropriate venue. The bulk of the techniques was supposed to be implemented in workshops across the divisions; only data collections and analyses were supposed to be done outside these workshops (mainly during the Analyze and Control phase). In doing so, details for the subsequent organization of the improvement initiative were obtained since it became obvious which steps had to be worked on together and which were to be dealt with separately (organizational restrictions).

Temporal restrictions are the third form of restrictions. On the one hand, they referred to the training period needed for learning specific techniques, on the other hand, they affected the tight schedule to produce presentable results. The techniques had to be easy to learn and it had to be possible to compile results in relatively short time. These requirements had an influence on the criterion "user friendliness" (see Fig. 4). To provide results fairly rapidly, it was decided to only use those techniques for the subsequent integration, which either led directly, or by combining them with as few as possible further techniques, to the intended phase results. To account for these interdependencies, the temporal restrictions will be considered under the criterion "user friendliness" and the subsequent integration (see Sect. 4.3).

The criterion "*user friendliness*" referred directly to the quality techniques to be applied. Two essential characteristics that add to the user friendliness of a technique were dealt with, namely *ease of learning* and *easy handling* (Thia et al. 2005). As has been mentioned above, the time needed to learn the techniques was supposed to be as short as possible. Easy handling was supposed to ensure that the techniques could be adapted to the needs of the users. To evaluate the techniques, they were compared with the criteria "*ease of learning*" and "*easy handling*" (see Fig. 4). Both criteria were weighted. At the automotive bank, the project team ranked the last point a little higher than the "ease of learning" of the technique. Afterward, the techniques were evaluated on the basis of the two above criteria. This evaluation resulted in differing expectations as regarded the line totals, which were calculated taking into account the weightings (depending on the intended venue). While techniques to be used in workshops were supposed to be easy and intuitive to learn, this was also intended for techniques to be used for data collection and analysis; however, for the final selection, the criterion data quality (which at the time could merely be estimated) was of higher importance.

Eventually, the following techniques were selected:

- *Define*: project charter, CTQ/CTB matrix, SIPOC.
- *Measure*: data collection plan, dot plot diagram, box plot diagram.
- *Analyze*: cause–effect diagram, histograms, scatter diagrams, correlation calculation.
- *Improve*: brainstorming, affinity diagram, priority matrix.
- *Control*: reaction/control plan, control charts.

4.3 Integration of the Selected Quality Techniques at the Automotive Bank

To obtain a consistent roadmap according to the Six Sigma cycle, the techniques were supposed to be combined expediently, both within a DMAIC phase and across the phases. Having said that, staff interviews were held to find out which interdependencies between the techniques were necessary. For the category of functional interdependencies, conditional and complementary relationships, in particular, were seen as being essential. On the one hand, the selected techniques were supposed to support each other as to their effects, and on the other, the number of techniques to be applied had to be manageable, which automatically leads to cause–effect interdependencies between techniques that make a combined application necessary. For instance, doing data analyses does not make sense if a data collection plan has not been worked out and if project-oriented performance data

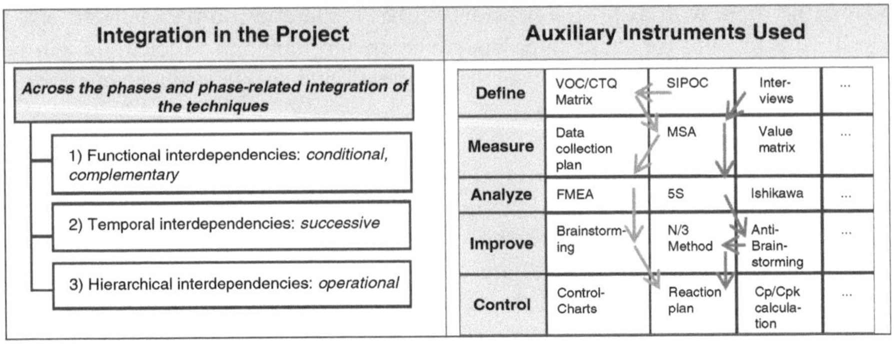

Fig. 5 Integration of techniques

have not been collected beforehand. In view of the temporal criterion, a successive application of the techniques had been intended. At the same time, merely one quality technique was supposed to be applied. In hierarchic terms (Bruhn 2006), the techniques applied were supposed to have a predominantly operational character. Strategic importance was only to be attributed to the previously made project selection. Alternative possibilities of combining the techniques across all phases of the Six Sigma cycle were supposed to be demonstrated by means of a morphological box with combinations also being allowed within a line (meaning within a cycle phase) (see Fig. 5). The main focus of attention was on the mutual support as well as on the operational sequence of the techniques.

The combination of the techniques, under consideration of the above written inter-dependencies, revealed several options that made a final decision necessary. The final decision was up to the project management. The project management constituted eventually the following sequence of tools for the initial Six Sigma initiative.

- *Define*: The Define-Phase started with the SIPOC diagram to get a visual representation of the business process. Afterward, the CTQ/CTB matrix was used to structure the requirements of internal and external customers. Furthermore, these requirements were transformed into measurable characteristics of the business process (CTQs and CTBs). Organizational matters (team members, milestones, etc.) were determined by means of a project charter.
- *Measure*: In the Measure-Phase, data collection plans were established first to get a clear picture of the data needed for determining the performance level of the business process. The data gathered was then visualized by the help of dot plot and box plot diagrams.
- *Analyze*: To identify root causes for failure, cause and effect diagrams were used. In addition, process data (when available) was analyzed in more detail by means of correlation calculation. The results were then communicated by histograms and scatter diagrams.

- *Improve*: To eliminate root causes for failures, brainstorming was performed to find solutions. The solutions proposed were structured by means of affinity diagrams and prioritized by using the priority matrix.
- *Control*: Control charts are used to control performance levels of the business process continuously. In the reaction plan (respectively control plan), arrangements are described if significant deviations in process performance occur.

For internal training purposes of the techniques, a global intranet portal was designed, which, apart from guidelines, descriptions, and general support, also offered templates for the application and documentation of results.

4.4 Benefits of the 3-Step Approach

The 3-step approach comprises a generic structure, which is applied only once at the beginning of a Six Sigma initiative and supports the selection and integration of appropriate techniques. The selection considered all individual requirements of the automotive bank. Since the users were integrated in the decision process, the acceptance of the techniques was given. Moreover, users fully understood the techniques and used its full potential.

The 3-step approach was completely adopted and subsequent projects were using the 3-step approach in order to select and integrate adequate techniques. All in all, five Six Sigma projects were conducted from April 2006 to November 2007. The investigation was carried out in each project by four experienced Six Sigma users working full-time. In addition, approximately 10–30 employees from the operating departments supported each project working part-time, mostly in workshops.

In addition, project improvements underline that users of the automotive bank selected and integrated based on the 3-step approach appropriate techniques. The five projects achieved multifold short-term as well as long-term improvements. Short-term improvements that could be implemented immediately included, for instance, the restructuring of forms and the simplification of sorting procedures. Long-term improvements focused on the reduction of media breaks and cycle times. Altogether, the projects achieved tremendous monetary benefits.

5 Lessons Learnt

Several lessons can be learnt from the project. On the one hand, these refer to the application of the 3-step approach for selecting and integrating quality techniques; on the other hand, a couple of insights can be derived from actually working on Six Sigma initiatives within the automotive bank.

Considering the application of the 3-step approach for the selection and integration of quality techniques, the following experiences have been made:

- During step 1 of our approach (classification), it became obvious that the exact allocation of individual techniques to a certain phase was not always possible. For instance, cause-and-effect diagrams (Ishikawa 1980) could both be applied in the Analyze phase – to collect potential causes for problems – and in the Measure phase – to restrict performance metrics. In these cases, techniques were allocated to all possible cycle phases.
- The selection of the techniques was done by the responsible project team. It is advisable that the selection process (step 2 of our approach) is done by the same persons for all techniques. Otherwise, the selection results may not be commensurable. As a supporting measure, short profiles were used, which for each technique listed advantages and disadvantages, functioning, and intended use. This proved to be very helpful in evaluating the techniques.
- The application of possible techniques for data analysis was intensively discussed. Since some of the operating departments did not have access to statistics software, the sample of usable techniques was restricted. It was necessary to find out which technique could be used with the existing applications and with which technique project members could work out the required results. In addition, possible quality losses had to be detected. The final decision was up to the project management.

Furthermore, several lessons can be learnt from the Six Sigma initiative themselves. These lessons can be divided into two groups: those which concern the *project progress and project preparation* and those which concern the phases of the *Six Sigma cycle.*

Regarding the project progress, it turned out to be useful to divide the project into four blocks (see Fig. 6):

- A workshop where the phases "define" and "measure" of the Six Sigma cycle were discussed forms the first block.
- The second block deals with gathering data and analyzing it.
- In the third block, a second workshop takes place where the results of the analysis are presented and suggestions are made for improvement.
- The last block then deals with controlling the improved process.

Regarding the project *preparation* and the different phases of the *Six Sigma cycle*, the following points in Fig. 7 may be helpful to keep in mind when performing a Six Sigma initiative.

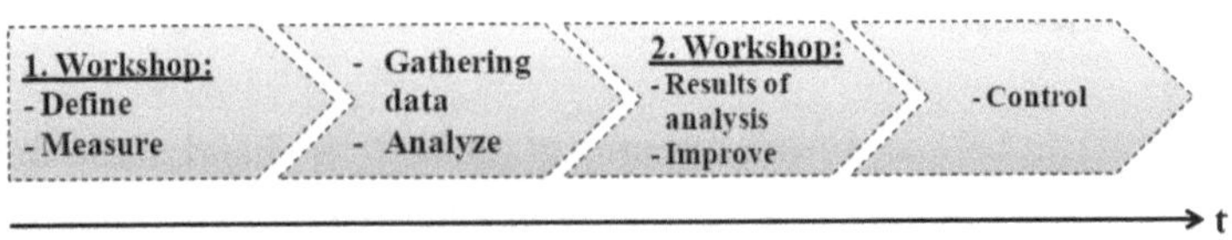

Fig. 6 Main blocks of project progress

Main points		Lessons learnt from the project
Project preparation		The inspection of existing process documentation should lead to the decision whether a whole process model or only parts of process chains should be modelled.
		The assembly of the project team is depending on the organisational units that are involved in the process. To find a holistic solution, it would be good to assemble an adequate team. Before starting the project possibilities for synergies with current projects could be checked in case of minimising the needed resources.
		Even if there is a huge data collection available, the use of it for later analysis might be not clear. The awareness for that circumstance should be derived.
Six Sigma Cycle	Define	Focussing only two or three CTQs, CTBs during having a workshop in the define phase might ease the start of the project.
	Measure	Most complexity will occur during building measurement systems and gathering data, so be aware that the use of existing data reports might not meet the demands of performance measurement in the Six Sigma context.
	Analyze	• In our case study the basic statistic techniques (histogram, run-charts) to visualise the data were sufficient at all. • Correlation calculations mostly were used for the analysis of the cycle time of certain process steps and their effect on the total cycle time.
	Improve	It is challenging to estimate the cost-use potential of developed solutions and their influence on possible output levels.
	Control	Continuous, automatically data gathering is needed, which is not easy to realise, because often measuring points are missing or cannot be established (e.g. customer satisfaction).

Fig. 7 Lessons learnt

6 Conclusions

This chapter starts with the problems of selecting and integrating adequate quality techniques from a great number of existing quality techniques. Each technique has its own advantages and can make its own contribution to the Six Sigma initiative. In addition, the integration of the selected techniques has to meet different requirements to avoid interdependencies and to obtain a consistent roadmap for the project. These problems were supposed to be solved when doing a prototypic implementation of Six Sigma at an Automotive Bank. For this purpose, a generic 3-step approach was developed, adapted to the needs of the automotive bank, and afterwards implemented. In doing so, the design of the second phase (selection) and the third phase (integration), in particular, was strongly shaped by the needs and demands of the staff. The technical restriction (draw back on existing infrastructure) and the organizational restriction (phase results should be worked out in workshops) in the second phase are examples for that. Having said that, it may well be expected that variations will occur where other enterprises are concerned, since, so far, there is a lack of generally valid guidelines and instructions; thus the adaptation to the individual environment will be necessary in any new case.

The 3-step approach was applied in a cooperation project with the automotive bank and has not yet been subjected to a broad evaluation at different service enterprises or financial service providers. For even though convincing results were obtained in this project (see Sect. 4.4) and substantiate not only the feasibility but also that the five Six Sigma projects could achieve several benefits. It is, at present, not possible to make any final statement as to whether the approach can be transferred to other projects. Nonetheless, the 3-step approach introduced in this chapter seems to be promising as a starting point for project-specific extensions and modifications.

Apart from the above, the relevant literature deals with further problems regarding the Six Sigma application and implementation in services, which often occur in similar process initiatives. These problems were not referred to in this chapter since the focus was explicitly on higher order aspects that have to be addressed at the beginning of any Six Sigma initiative.

References

Akao Y (1990) QFD: integrating customer requirements into product design. Productivity Press, Cambridge, MA

Antony J (2004) Six Sigma in the UK service organizations: results from a pilot survey. Manage Audit J 19(8):1006–1013

Antony J (2006) Six sigma for service processes. Bus Process Manage J 12(2):234–248

Arneson T, Rys M, McCahon C (1996) A guide to the selection of appropriate quality improvement tools. In: Chen J and Mital A (eds) Proceeding of the 1st annual international conference on industrial engineering applications and practice. Houston

Bamford D, Greatbanks R (2005) The use of quality management tools and techniques: a study of application in everyday situations. Int J Qual Reliab Manage 22(4):376–392

Baumoel V (2010) Cultural change in process management. In: vom Brocke J, Rosemann M (eds) Handbook on business process management, vol 2. Springer, Heidelberg

Breyfogle F (2003) Implementing Six Sigma. Smarter solutions using statistical methods. Wiley, Hoboken, NJ

Breyfogle F, Cupello J, Meadows B (2001) Managing Six Sigma. Wiley-Interscience, New York

Bruhn M (2006) Qualitätsmanagement für Dienstleistungen, 6th edn. Springer, Berlin

Bunney HS, Dale BG (1997) The implementation of quality management tools and techniques: a study. TQM Mag 9(3):183–189

Chakrabarty A, Tan KC (2007) The current state of six sigma application in services. Manag Serv Qual 17(2):194–208

Conger S (2010) Six Sigma and Business Process Management. In: vom Brocke J, Rosemann M (eds) Handbook on Business Process Management 1, Springer, Heidelberg, pp 129–150

Crosby PB (1979) Quality is free, the art of making quality certain. Hodder & Stoughton, New York

Dale BG, McQuater R (1998) Managing business improvement & quality: implementing key tools and techniques. Blackwell Business, Oxford

Dale BG, Shaw P (1999) Tools and techniques: an overview. In: Dale BG (ed) Managing quality. Blackwell Business, Malden, pp 280–314

Davis FD (1986) A technology acceptance model for empirically testing new end-user information systems: theory and results. Sloan School of Management, Massachusetts Institute of Technology, Cambridge, MA

Davis FD (1989) Perceived usefulness, perceived ease of use, and user acceptance of information technology. MIS Q 13(3):319–340

Davis FD, Bagozzi RP, Warshaw PR (1989) User acceptance of computer technology: a comparison of two theoretical models. Manage Sci 35(8):982–1003

Deming WE (1982) Quality, productivity and competitive position. MIT Center for Advanced Engineering, MIT Center for Advanced Engineering, Cambridge, MA
Feigenbaum AV (1991) Total quality control. McGraw-Hill, New York
Foley K (2004) Five essays on quality management – presented in honour of homer Sarasohn. Standards Australia International Ltd., Sydney, Australia
Gogoll A, Theden PH (1994) Techniken des quality engineering. In: Kamiske GF (ed) Die hohe Schule des total quality management. Springer, Berlin/Heidelberg, pp 329–369
Harmon P (2007) Business process change: a guide for business managers and BPM and Six Sigma professionals. Elsevier LTD, Oxford
Harrington HJ (1995) An international view of what works and what doesn't work. In: American Society of Quality Control (ed) Proceedings of the 49th annual quality congress, Cincinnati, OH
Harry M, Schroeder R (2000) Six Sigma: the breakthrough management strategy revolutionizing the World's top corporations. Currency, New York
Harry M, Schroeder R (2006) Six Sigma: the breakthrough management strategy revolutionizing the World's top corporations. Doubleday, New York, NY
Hellsten U, Klefsjö B (2000) TQM as a management system consisting of values, techniques and tools. TQM Mag 12(4):238–244
Hensley R, Dobie K (2005) Assessing readiness for six sigma in a service setting. Manag Serv Qual 15(1):82–101
Ishikawa K (1980) Guide to quality control. ASIAN PRODUCTIVITY ORGANIZATION, Tokyo
Ishikawa K (1985) What is total quality control? The Japanese way. Prentice-Hall, London
Juran JM (1988) On planning for quality. Collier Macmillan, London
Juran JM, Gryna FM (1988) Juran's quality control handbook. McGraw-Hill Education, New York
Kwok KY, Tummala VMR (1998) A quality control and improvement system based on the total control methodology (TCM). Int J Qual Reliab Manage 15(1):13–48
Leist S, Zellner G (2006) Evaluation of current architecture frameworks. In: Haddad HM, Chbeir R, Wainwright RL, Liebrock LM, Palakal M, Yetongnon K, Nicolle C (eds) 2006 ACM symposium on applied computing (SAC). Bourgogne University, Dijon, France, pp 1546–1553
Magnusson K, Kroslid D, Bergman B (2004) Six Sigma umsetzen. Hanser, München/Wien
McQuater RE, Scurr CH, Dale BG, Hillmann PG (1995) Using quality tools and techniques successfully. TQM Mag 7(6):37–42
Moody DL (2003) The method evaluation model: a theoretical model for validating information systems design methods. In: Ciborra C, Mercurio R, De Marco M, Martinez M, Carignani A (eds) Proceedings of the 11th European conference on information systems, ECIS 2003. Naples, Italy
Nayatani Y (1986) Seven Management Tools for QC. Rep Stat Appl Res JUSE 33(2):1–6
Okes D (2002) Organize your quality tool belt. Qual Prog 35(7):25–29
Olle TW, Sol HG, Tully CJ (1983) Information systems design methodologies: a feature analysis. In Olle TW, Sol HG, Tully CJ (eds): Proceedings of the IFIP WG 8.1 working conference on feature analysis of information systems design methodologies. York, UK
Pande P, Neumann R, Cavanagh R (2000) The Six Sigma way – how GE, Motorola and other top companies are honing their performance. Mc Graw Hill, New York
Roenpage O, Staudter C, Meran R, Johan A, Beernaert C (2006) Six Sigma + Lean Toolset. Springer, Berlin
Shamsuddin A, Masjuki H (2003) Survey and case investigations on application of quality management tools and techniques in SMIs. Int J Qual Reliab Manage 20(7):795–826
Smith AK, Bolton RN, Wagner J (1999) A model of customer satisfaction with service encounters involving failure and recovery. J Mark Res 36:356–372
Snee RD (2004) Six sigma: the evolution of 100 years of business improvement methodology. IJSSCA 1(1):4–20
Snee R, Hoerl R (2003) Leading Six Sigma. Prentice Hall, New York

Tari JJ, Sabater V (2003) Quality tools and techniques: are they necessary for quality management? Int J Prod Econ 92(3):267–280

Theden P (1996) Beschreibung ausgewählter Qualitätstechniken. In: Kamiske GF (ed) Digitale Fachbibliothek Qualitätsmanagement: Methoden – Praxisbeispiele – Hintergründe. Symposion Publishing, Düsseldorf, pp 1–13

Thia C, Chai KH, Bauly J, Xin Y (2005) An exploratory study of the use of quality tools and techniques in product development. TQM Mag 17(5):406–424

vom Brocke J, Petry M, Sinnl T, Østerberg Kristensen B, Sonnenberg C (2010) Global processes and data: the cultural journey at the Hilti Corporation. In: vom Brocke J, Rosemann M (eds) Handbook on business process management, vol 2. Springer, Heidelberg

Part III
Process-aware Information Systems

Information technology (IT) support for business processes has been a topic of interest as early as office automation, and the related vision of a paperless office has emerged approximately 40 years ago. IT has traditionally gained an important role in many BPM initiatives up to the point that not a small part of the wider BPM community actually believes that process automation equals Business Process Management. In alignment with the comprehensive BPM understanding that underlies this Handbook, we believe that there is much more to BPM than the automated process execution. That said, it cannot be negated, however, that Information Technology has been and will continue to be a main enabler for progression and innovation in the BPM discipline.

Software solutions displaying an explicit awareness for the execution of business process have recently been coined process-aware information systems (PAIS). The core set of principles and capabilities of PAIS has been informed by workflow management systems. Workflow management has traditionally been dedicated to the design, execution, and controlling of at least semi-automated business processes. In the opening chapter in this section, Chun Ouyang, Michael Adams, Moe Thandar Wynn, and Arthur ter Hofstede provide a contemporary overview about the field of workflow management covering, among others, workflow patterns, workflow languages, formal foundations, and the exemplary workflow system YAWL. An alternative to the control flow focused view of classical workflow management systems is presented in chapter two by Akhil Kumar and Jianrui Wang. Instead of the flow of activities, the authors present a resource-driven workflow approach. They outline resource dependencies, present a resource taxonomy, an architecture, and a prototype for resource-driven workflow management.

The already mature understanding of workflow management has received a significant inspiration by the emergence of the service paradigm that is postulated by means of Service-oriented Architectures (SOA). In four chapters, the mutual impact of process management and service management is unfolded. Marlon Dumas and Thomas Kohlborn describe how processes have to be designed to take full benefits of service-enabled infrastructures. They also outline related contemporary technology standards. Closely aligned with this chapter is the contribution by Fred Cummins who explains the interrelationships between BPM and SOA in the fourth chapter. Rather than concentrating on the technological challenges, he concentrates on the value proposition of this new unification under the headings of enterprise optimization and enterprise agility. These arguments are further strengthened by Thomas Gulledge who differentiates between "Business BPM" and "Technical BPM". He also presents an implementation plan from BPM to SOA considering currently available technologies. The fourth and final contribution in this cluster on integrated process and service management is the sixth chapter presented by Alexander Dreiling, who interlinks BPM and semantic interoperability. In this context, the author explains the ideas behind the Internet of Services and the Internet of Things and proposes a related research agenda.

Further issues characterize contemporary IT-enabled BPM: Business Process Management relies on well-defined and accepted standards so that the critical transformation from design and analysis to execution forms a smooth pathway. This evolution and the essence of Business Process Management standards is discussed in the seventh chapter by Frank Leymann, Dimka Karastoyanova, and Mike Papazoglou. The authors differentiate between graph-based and operator-based approaches. They showcase and compare influential standards with a focus on the role of BPEL and BPMN. A focus on the important field of B2B processes is taken on by Marco Zapletal, Rainer Schuster, Philipp Liegl, Christian Huemer, and Birgit Hofreiter. They present the UMM that has been developed within an UN/CEFACT initiative. In addition, another recent development is the integration of collaborative social networking solutions into the world of BPM solutions. Under the "Enterprise 2.0" heading, Sandy Kemsley discusses the drivers for collaborative BPM and speculates on the possible impact these fast growing applications might have on the future of BPM.

1. Workflow Management
   by Chun Ouyang, Michael Adams, Moe Thandar Wynn, and Arthur H.M. ter Hofstede
2. A Framework for Designing Resource-Driven Workflows
   by Akhil Kumar and Jianrui Wang
3. Service-Enabled Process Management
   by Marlon Dumas and Thomas Kohlborn
4. BPM Meets SOA
   by Fred Cummins
5. Integrated Business Process and Service Management
   by Thomas Gulledge
6. Business Process Management and Semantic Interoperability
   by Alexander Dreiling
7. Business Process Management Standards
   by Frank Leymann, Dimka Karastoyanova, and Mike Papazoglou

8. Modeling Interorganizational Processes with UMM
   by Marco Zapletal, Rainer Schuster, Philipp Liegl,
   Christian Huemer, and Birgit Hofreiter
9. Enterprise 2.0 Meets Business Process Management
   by Sandy Kemsley

Workflow Management

Chun Ouyang, Michael Adams, Moe Thandar Wynn, and Arthur H.M. ter Hofstede

Abstract Workflow management has its origin in the office automation systems of the seventies, but it is not until fairly recently that conceptual and technological breakthroughs have led to its widespread adoption. In fact, nowadays, process-awareness has become an accepted and integral part of various types of systems. Through the use of process-aware information systems, workflows can be specified and enacted, thus providing automated support for business processes. A workflow explicitly represents control-flow dependencies between the various tasks of the business process, the information that is required and that can be produced by them, and the link between these tasks and the resources, be they human or not, which can execute them. In this way, processes can be performed more efficiently and effectively, compliance with respect to standard procedures and practices can be monitored more closely, and rapid change in response to evolving market conditions can be achieved more easily. This chapter provides an overview of the field of workflow management.

1 Introduction

Workflow management is concerned with providing automated support for business processes. Typically, a workflow involves both people and software applications. Work is assigned to participants based on explicit resource allocation directives, which may link into an organizational model, and the timing is driven by an explicit representation of the temporal order of the various activities of the business process.

C. Ouyang (✉)
Business Process Management Group, Faculty of Science and Technology, Queensland University of Technology, Brisbane, Australia
e-mail: c.ouyang@qut.edu.au

J. vom Brocke and M. Rosemann (eds.), *Handbook on Business Process Management 1*, International Handbooks on Information Systems,
DOI 10.1007/978-3-642-00416-2_18,

Apart from the obvious fact that there is potential for savings in terms of time and money, there are other benefits in deploying workflow applications. By having explicit representations of these resource and control-flow dependencies, it can be claimed that changing workflows is easier and hence a business that has automated its processes by means of a workflow management system may be more responsive to changes in its environment, such as changing legislation or evolving market conditions. As workflow management systems log events that pertain to business processes (e.g., the fact that a certain resource has completed a certain task at a certain point in time), process logs may be used to demonstrate that a business complies with best practices or with existing legislation. Log files provide a valuable starting point for process analysis and for subsequent process improvement. The area of *process mining* (van der Aalst et al. 2004b) is concerned with process-related information that can be derived from log files.

The Workflow Management Coalition[1] has defined what the components of a workflow environment are and what interfaces these components should have to support interaction with each other and with external components (Fischer 2005). In a workflow management environment, there is typically a component that supports the specification of workflows and another that supports the execution of these workflows. There are also, usually, components that can deal with external applications or other workflow engines or that provide support for administration and monitoring.

A workflow can be examined from a number of perspectives (van der Aalst et al. 2003; Jablonski and Bussler 1996). The temporal order of the various tasks in a workflow can be referred to as the *control-flow perspective*. The way data is defined and passed between workflow elements and/or the external environment is captured in the *data perspective*. The *resource perspective* is concerned with controlling the way resources become involved in the execution of tasks. Naturally, these perspectives are related, e.g., a missing data item may hold up the execution of a certain task or the resource selected for the execution of a certain task may be determined on the basis of the number of times they have performed this task in the past. Understanding the role of these perspectives is vital to understand what workflow management is about.

In this chapter, we aim to provide the reader with an overview of concepts and technology that underlie modern workflow management. We will start by exploring the conceptual foundations of workflow management, which will inform the subsequent discussion of a number of approaches to workflow specification. More advanced topics follow, dealing with change and unexpected exceptions, simulation, verification, and configuration, after which we discuss an existing workflow management system that can be seen as a reference implementation for some state-of-the-art concepts. The aim of presenting this system is to reinforce the understanding of concepts discussed. The chapter ends with a case study in the domain of screen business, followed by a brief overall conclusion.

---

[1] http://www.wfmc.org

1.1 An Introductory Example

A workflow, sometimes used as a synonym for "a business process," comprises a series of tasks (activities) through which work is routed. Workflow management systems are a class of software that supports business processes by taking on their information logistics, i.e., they ensure that the right information reaches the right person at the right time (van der Aalst and van Hee 2002). The information logistics of business processes can be captured by a workflow or process modeling language. Different workflow management systems may be implemented supporting the use of different languages.

Consider an example of a process that models a credit card application. The process starts when an applicant submits a credit card application (Task 1). Upon receiving the application, a clerk examines if the requested loan amount is large (e.g., greater than $5000) or small (Task 2) and then performs different eligibility checks accordingly (Task 3 for large loan and Task 4 for small loan). Let us stop here for the moment (we will continue describing the process in the languages section). It can be observed that there are dependencies between the above tasks. Task 1 is (sequentially) followed by Task 2, and after Task 2, an exclusive choice is made, determining whether to perform Task 3 or Task 4. A workflow language can be used to capture these in a precise manner. However, many workflow languages exist due to lack of consensus. For example, as Fig. 1 illustrates, the flow comprising the above tasks in a credit card application process can be captured using five mainstream workflow or process modeling languages: BPMN (Business Process Modeling Notation) (Fig. 1a), EPC (Event-driven Process Chain) (Fig. 1b), BPEL (Business Process Execution Language for Web Services) (Fig. 1c), Petri nets (Fig. 1d), and YAWL (Yet Another Workflow Language) (Fig. 1e). We shall describe these in more detail in the languages section. For the moment, it is sufficient to observe that in Fig. 1, each of these languages models the same exclusive-choice behavior (i.e., XOR-split) in a different way.

The exclusive choice is just one of many recurring modules that may exist in business processes. So, is there a way to identify these modules in a language- and system-independent manner? In the next section, we answer this question by introducing the concept of workflow patterns.

2 Workflow Patterns

Workflow patterns are a specialized form of *design patterns* defined in the area of software engineering. They refer specifically to recurrent problems and proven solutions related to the development of process-oriented applications in both a language- and technology-independent manner. The Workflow Patterns Initiative[2]

[2]http://www.workflowpatterns.com

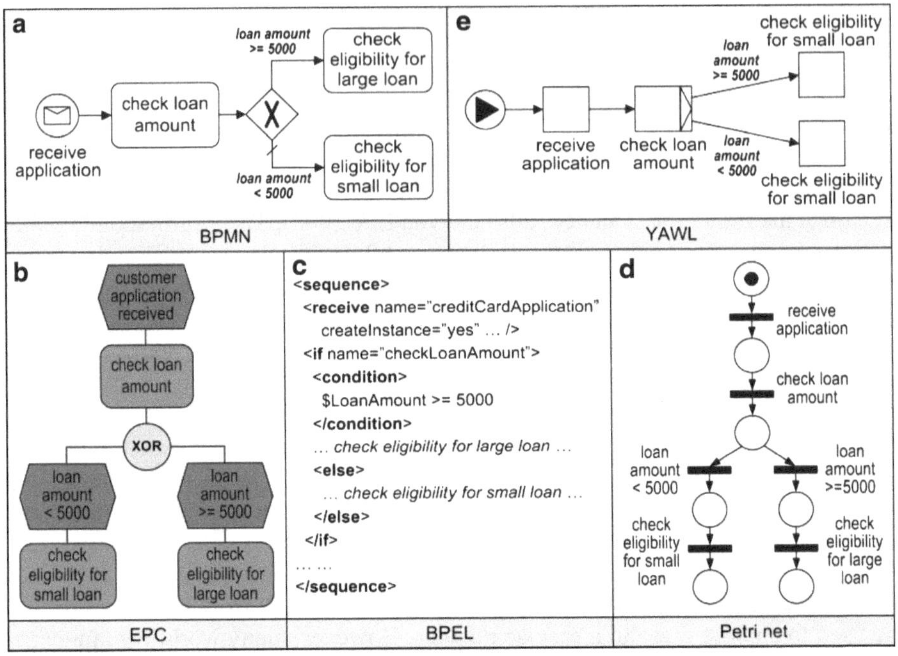

Fig. 1 Modelling the first four tasks in an example of a credit card application process using each of five mainstream workflow or process modeling languages

was established in the late 1990s with the aim of delineating the fundamental requirements that arise during business process modeling on a recurring basis and describing them in an imperative way.

Originally, a set of twenty patterns was identified describing the control-flow perspective of business processes (van der Aalst et al. 2003). These patterns capture structural characteristics of a business process and the manner in which the thread of execution flows through the process model. Since their release, they have been widely used by practitioners, vendors, academics alike in the selection, design and development of workflow systems, and standards. For example, they were used to evaluate 15 commercial workflow systems including such as IBM's WebSphere, Staffware Process Suite, and the case handling system FLOWer. Established process modeling languages such as Petri nets, EPCs, and UML Activity Diagrams (both versions 1.4 and 2.0) were also subjected to a pattern-based evaluation. In addition, vendors and organizations performed analysis of their tools or standards based on workflow patterns. Examples include White's report (White 2004) showing how BPMN supports the original control-flow patterns and TIBCO's report on how Staffware realizes these patterns, to name a few.[3]

[3]See an up-to-date list of vendors' evaluations of tools and standards in terms of the original twenty control-flow patterns at http://www.workflowpatterns.com/vendors.

Later, a detailed review of the original 20 patterns led to the identification of 23 new patterns (Russell et al. 2006b). In total, the 43 control-flow patterns can be classified into eight categories: basic control-flow, advanced branching and synchronization, multiple instances, state-based situations, iteration, external triggering, cancelation, and termination. For example, one of the advanced synchronization patterns is called the General Synchronizing Merge (or OR-join). The OR-join synchronizes only if necessary, i.e., it will synchronize only the active incoming branches and it is certain that the remaining incoming branches, which have not been enabled, will not be enabled at any future time. In general, this synchronization decision cannot be made *locally*. It requires awareness of both the current state and possible future states for the current process instance. Another example is the Deferred Choice, one of the state-based patterns. It captures the scenario when the choice among a set of alternative conditional branches is based on interaction with the operating environment. The decision is delayed until the first task in one of these branches is initiated, i.e., there is no explicit choice but rather a race between different branches.

In addition to the control-flow patterns, workflow patterns have also been extended to cover the data and resource perspectives. There are 40 data patterns (Russell et al. 2005b) capturing a series of data characteristics that occur repeatedly in business processes. These cover data visibility (e.g., scoping of data variables), data interactions within a business process (internal) or between the process and its operating environment (external), data transfer between one process component and another, and data-based routing that describes how data elements can interact with other perspective (particularly the control-flow perspective) and influence the overall operation of a process instance.

For the resource perspective, 43 patterns (Russell et al. 2005a) have been identified, capturing the various ways in which resources are represented and utilized in business processes. Based on the lifecycle of a work item (which include resourcing states such as *offered*, *allocated*, *started*, and *completed*), the resource patterns can be classified into seven categories: creation patterns for design-time work allocation, push patterns for system distributing work items to resources, pull patterns for resources identifying to executing work items, detour patterns for work item rerouting, auto-start patterns for automated commencement of work items based on criteria, visibility patterns for configuration of the visibility of work items for certain participants, and multiple resource patterns for work allocations involving multiple participants or resources. For example, one of the detour patterns is called the delegation pattern. It captures the scenario where a resource allocates an unstarted work item that was previously allocated to it to another resource. This provides a resource with a means of rerouting work items that it is unable to execute (e.g., the resource is going to be unavailable).

Finally, there are also patterns for exception handling, which deals with the various causes of exceptions and the various actions that need to be taken as a result of exceptions occurring. This will be described later in the chapter.

3 Languages

Workflow languages are used to design workflow models in order to capture processes at a level of detail that is sufficient to enable their execution (van der Aalst and van Hee 2002; Weske 2007). Examples include: dedicated workflow specification languages such as XPDL and YAWL; executable process definition languages based on Web services such as BPEL and XLANG; and workflow products such as Staffware and IBM's Websphere. It is also possible to use languages designed for business process modeling, such as BPMN and EPC, to specify workflows. However, for process execution, these models need to be transformed to models specified in an executable language such as BPEL or YAWL.

In this section, we firstly introduce BPMN and BPEL, which are considered as two mainstream languages for capturing business processes from a practitioner's point of view. We then move onto YAWL, which is developed in the academic domain and supports most workflow patterns identified so far. YAWL can be seen as state of the art in the domain of workflow languages. It is therefore used to illustrate the main concepts in the field of workflow management in this chapter.

3.1 BPMN and BPEL

BPMN is a business processing modeling notation intended to facilitate communication between domain analysts and to support decision making based on techniques such as cost analysis, scenario analysis, and simulation. Process models specified in BPMN are therefore not meant to be directly executable. On the other hand, BPEL is intended to support the definition of a class of business processes for Web service interactions. The logic of the interactions is described as a composition of communication actions that are interrelated by control-flow dependencies expressed through constructs corresponding to parallel, sequential, and conditional execution, event, and exception handling. BPEL allows for the specification of executable business processes, and therefore can be used to support the execution of BPMN models.

The use of BPMN (for process modeling) in conjunction with BPEL (for process execution) is a typical example of the approach where two different languages are used, respectively, for the modeling and execution stages and thus a transformation between these languages is required. There are obvious drawbacks to this separation of modeling and execution, especially when both languages are based on different paradigms or when the modeling language contains potentially complex concepts and little consideration was given to their precise meaning. For example, BPMN is graph-oriented, which means that a model captured in BPMN can have an arbitrary topology, while BPEL is block-structured; thus, if a segment of a BPEL model starts with a branching construct, it ends with the corresponding synchronization construct. A mapping from BPMN to BPEL, such as the one proposed in

Ouyang et al. (2009), needs to handle the above mismatches properly and may still result in BPEL code that is hard to understand.

3.2 YAWL and Its Formal Foundation

As mentioned in the previous section, the original 20 control-flow patterns were used to evaluate various workflow and process modeling languages, standards, and workflow products. The evaluation results showed that Petri nets have at least three distinct advantages for being used as a workflow language: formal semantics, state-based instead of (just) event-based, and abundance of analysis techniques (van der Aalst 2000). They are quite expressive compared to many process languages, e.g., they offer direct support to all state-based patterns. Nevertheless, there are serious limitations in Petri nets (as in other languages) when it comes to capturing three categories of patterns: (1) patterns involving multiple instances, (2) advanced synchronization patterns (e.g. OR-join), and (3) cancelation patterns. For example, patterns involving multiple instances capture scenarios where within the context of a single workflow instance (i.e., case), part of the process (e.g., a task or a sub-process) need to be instantiated multiple times, e.g., within the context of an academic paper review, multiple reviewers need to review the paper, and these review results will then be used to determine the final result. The number of multiple instantiations may be known a priori at design-time/runtime, or not be known at all until the process proceeds to the next part (at runtime). In high-level Petri nets, it is possible to use advanced constructs to capture multiple instances of a task or a subprocess. However, there is no specific support for *patterns involving multiple instances*, and the burden of keeping track of splitting and joining the various multiple instances is borne by the designer.

The observation of the limitations in Petri nets for capturing certain workflow patterns triggered the development of a new language – YAWL. YAWL took Petri nets as a starting point and introduced mechanisms that provide direct support for the control-flow patterns especially the above three categories of patterns.

3.2.1 Petri Nets

A Petri net (Murata 1989) is a directed graph composed of two types of nodes: *places* and *transitions*. Usually, places are represented as circles and transitions as rectangles. Petri nets are bipartite graphs, meaning that an arc in the net may connect a place to a transition or vice versa, but no arc may connect two nodes of the same type. A transition can have a number of immediately preceding places (called it *input places*) and a number of immediately succeeding places (called its *output places*).

Places may contain zero or more *tokens*, which model the thing(s) that flow through the system. The state, often referred to as *marking*, is the distribution of

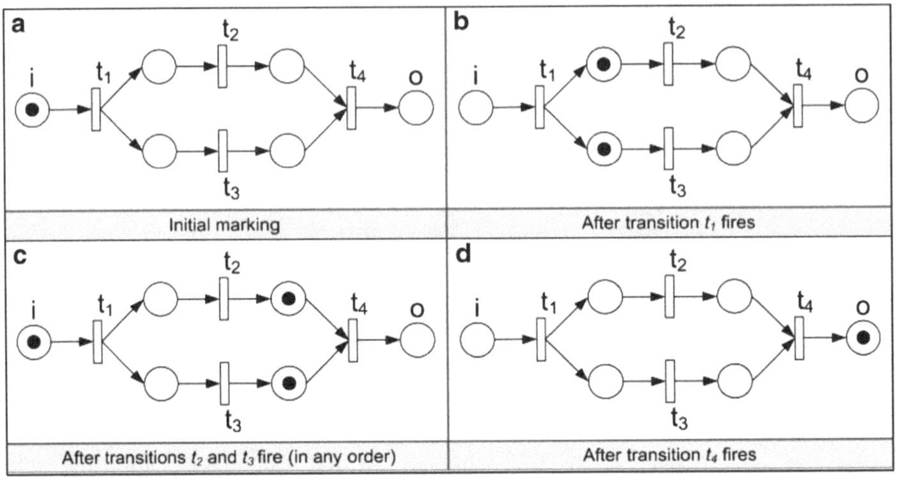

Fig. 2 A sample Petri-net in four different markings

tokens over places. For example, Fig. 2a depicts an initial marking of a Petri net where there is one token in the leftmost place i and no token in any other place. The state of a Petri net changes when one of its transitions fires. A transition may fire if there is at least one token in each of its input places. In this case, we say that the transition is *enabled*. For example, in Fig. 2a, the transition labeled t_1 is enabled since it has only one input place and this input place has one token. When a transition fires, it removes one token from each of its input places and adds one token to each of its output places. For example, Fig. 2b depicts the state obtained when transition t_1 fires starting from the initial marking in Fig. 2a. The token in place i has been removed, and a token has been added to each of the output places of transition t_1. In a given marking, there may be multiple enabled transitions simultaneously. In this situation, any of these transitions may fire at any time. For example, in Fig. 2b, two transitions t_2 and t_3 are enabled, and any of them may fire in the next execution step. After both t_2 and t_3 fire, transition t_4 is enabled (Fig. 2c), and after t_4 fires, the net reaches a final marking where only the rightmost place o holds a token and none of the transitions are enabled.

It can be observed that in the Petri net shown in Fig. 2, transition t_1 behaves like an AND-split, transition t_4 behaves like an AND-join, and transitions t_2 and t_3 capture concurrent executions of two parallel branches. In comparison to this, Fig. 3 depicts two examples of Petri nets modeling executions of conditional branches. In each net, the output place of transition t_1 is the input place of two transitions. When there is a token in this place, the two transitions sharing the place are both enabled, but only one of them may fire, i.e., firing of one of the two transitions will consume the token, thus disabling the other transition. In Fig. 3, the difference between the two Petri nets is with regard to how the choice is made among the conditional branches. In Fig. 3a, the choice can be made (explicitly) by the system upon evaluating the condition c. If c evaluates to true, transition c will fire; otherwise,

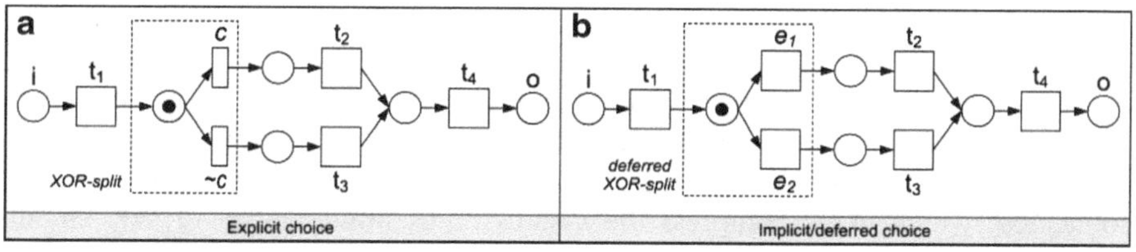

Fig. 3 The sample Petri-nets capturing two types of choices between conditional branches

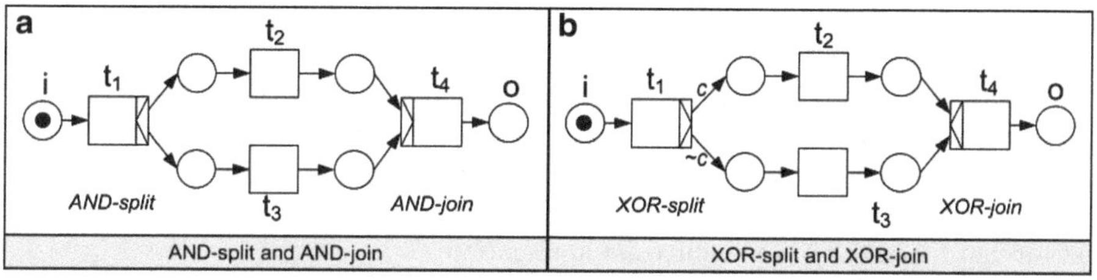

Fig. 4 WF-net notations for AND/XOR splits and joins

transition $\sim c$ will fire. In Fig. 3b, the choice is deferred until one of the events e_1 and e_2 occurs, e.g., e_1 may indicate the arrival of an external message, and e_2 may signal a timeout. Triggers of such events come from the environment.

3.2.2 Workflow Nets

Workflow nets (WF-nets) (van der Aalst 1997) are a subset of Petri nets used to model workflows. A WF-net satisfies the following requirements: there is a unique input place (i) and a unique output place (o), and every other place and transition are on a directed path from place i to place o. In other words, WF-nets have a distinct start place and a distinct end place. For example, the Petri nets in Figs. 2 and 3 are all WF-nets. Intuitively, a WF-net models the execution of one instance of a business process. The initial marking of a WF-net contains a single token in the start place, and in principle, at least one token should reach the end place.

In a WF-net, special notations are introduced to illustrate constructs such as AND-split, AND-join, XOR-split, and XOR-join due to their frequent occurrences in modeling workflows. Figure 4 depicts these notations using the WF-nets shown in the previous figures. In Fig. 4a, the WF-net in Fig. 1 is redrawn (without affecting the behavioral semantics of the net) by replacing transition t_1 with an AND-split and t_4 with an AND-join. In Fig. 4b, the WF-net in Fig. 3a is redrawn using XOR-split and XOR-join. The XOR-split (t_1) captures the fact that after t_1 occurs, a token must be produced for one of its output places (based on the evaluation result of condition c). The XOR-join (t_4) is enabled if one of its input places contains a token. Alternatively, an XOR-join can also be modeled by a place, e.g., the input place of transition t_4 in Fig. 3.

3.2.3 YAWL

YAWL (van der Aalst and ter Hofstede 2005) extends the class of WF-nets with three categories of patterns: multiple-instance, OR-join, and cancelation patterns. In contrast to Petri nets and WF-nets, the syntax of YAWL allows tasks to be directly connected, which helps compress the visual representation of a YAWL model. Figure 5 shows the modeling elements of YAWL. A process definition in YAWL consists of *tasks* (i.e., transition-like objects) and *conditions* (i.e., place-like objects). Each process definition starts with a unique *input condition* and a unique *output condition.*

A workflow specification in YAWL is a set of workflow nets which forms a directed rooted graph. There are *atomic tasks* and *composite tasks*. Both types of task can also be *multiple instance* tasks at the same time and thus have multiple concurrent instances at runtime. Each composite task refers to a net that contains its expansion. Atomic tasks correspond to atomic actions, i.e., actions that are either performed by a user or by a software application.

As shown in Fig. 5, YAWL adopts the notations of AND-splits/joins and XOR-splits/joins used in WF-nets. Moreover, it introduces *OR-splits* and *OR-joins*. As compared to XOR-splits, which support exclusive choice, OR-splits support multiple choices among conditional branches. Finally, YAWL provides a notation for *removing tokens* from a specified region upon completion of a certain task. This is denoted by associating a dashed lasso to that task that contains the conditions and tasks from which tokens need to be removed or that need to be canceled. This region is called a *cancelation region*, a notion that provides a generalization of the cancelation patterns.

A Running Example: Credit Card Application Process

Let's return to the example credit card application process described earlier in the chapter. To make it more interesting, we extend the process and describe it from the beginning. The process starts when an applicant submits an application (with the proposed amount). Upon receiving an application, a credit clerk checks whether it is complete. If not, the clerk requests additional information and waits until this information is received before proceeding. At the same time, a timer is set so that if

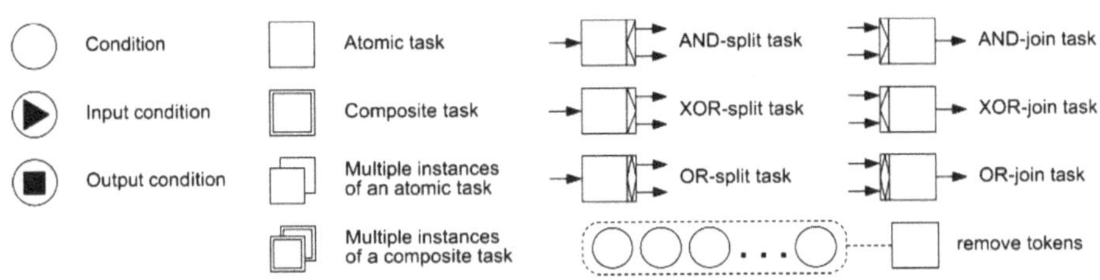

Fig. 5 Modelling elements in YAWL (taken from (van der Aalst & ter Hofstede 2005))

certain period elapses before any information is received, the request for additional information will be sent again. For a complete application, the clerk performs further checks to validate the applicant's income and credit history. Different checks are performed depending on whether the requested loan is large or small. The validated application is then passed on to a manager to decide whether to accept or reject the application. In the case of acceptance, the applicant is notified of the decision and at the same time is asked for his/her preference on any extra features before a credit card is produced and delivered. For a rejected application, the applicant is notified of the rejection and the process ends. Two more facts are to be mentioned in this process. Firstly, an application may be canceled at any time after it was received and before the manager makes the decision. Secondly, for an approved application, three features are offered including customized card, reward program, and secondary cardholders, and any number of them may be chosen.

Figure 6 depicts a YAWL model of the process. We will not go through every element of the model but select a number of typical examples for illustration. Firstly, the task *check for completeness* uses an XOR-split to capture the checking result and an XOR-join to capture further checks to be performed after additional information is received. Next, the place *waiting* models a deferred choice between tasks *receive more info* and *time out*. Thirdly, the selection of extra features is modeled by a subprocess related to the composite task *choose features*. In this subprocess, task *start features* uses an OR-split to capture the fact that a set of extra features can be added, possibly one, two, or all, and task *complete features* uses an OR-join to collect only the features that were actually selected. Note that the definition of a suitable semantics of the OR-join within the context of YAWL can be found in Wynn et al. (2005). Also, task *add secondary cardholders* can have multiple instances, which

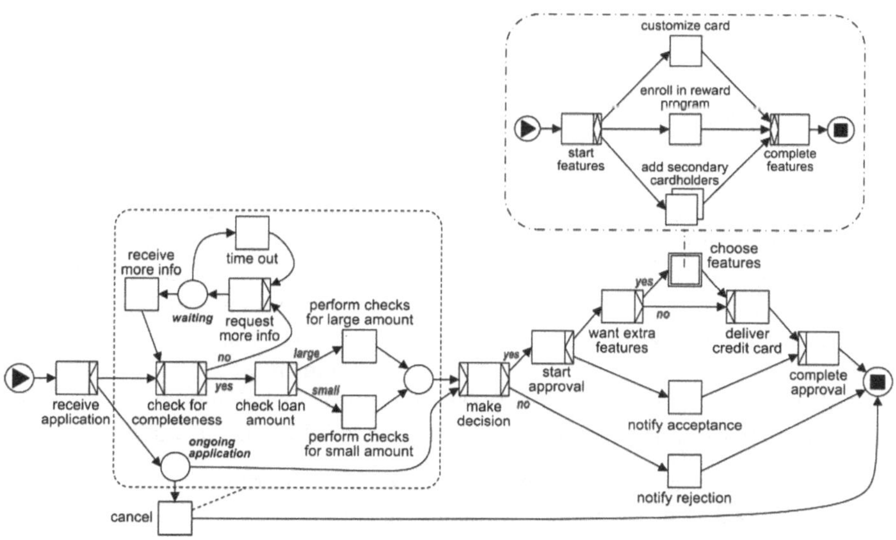

Fig. 6 A credit card application process in YAWL

allow the addition of more than one secondary cardholder in parallel. Finally, in the process model, task *cancel* with its associated cancelation region capture the withdrawal of an ongoing application before an approval/reject decision is made.

In addition to the control-flow definition depicted in Fig. 6, the YAWL model also allows for the specification of the data perspective and the resource perspective. The data specification defines data elements and their usage for exchanging information with the environment, for conditional routing, for creating and synchronizing multiple instances, and so on. Data are represented in XML and data manipulation relies on XML-based standards like XPath and XQuery. The resource perspective specifies task-resource allocation for each task within the process. Note that the term "resource" here refers to human resource, e.g., a role or a participant. Both the data and resource definitions of the process model shown in Fig. 6 will be described further in the section on the YAWL environment later in the chapter.

4 Before Deployment

The development of workflow specifications can be considered as an iterative process, whereby, the specifications are carefully checked and modified to ensure their correctness. In this section, we briefly describe the two techniques, verification and simulation, which can be used to analyze structural and behavioral properties of workflow specifications before deployment. This is followed by a brief description of process configuration, a technique whereby a reference workflow specification is customized based on specific requirements of an organization.

4.1 Verification

Workflow verification is concerned with determining, *in advance*, whether a workflow exhibits certain desirable behaviors. Although one would expect verification functionality to be present in any workflow management system, this is not the case. Typically, these systems at best do some basic syntactical checks but cannot detect the modeling of processes with deadlocks, livelocks, and other anomalies. There are several academic process verification tools. However, until recently, these tools could not verify realistic processes because they assume highly simplified models completely disconnected from real-life languages and systems.

There are established methods for the verification of workflow specifications using Petri nets (van der Aalst 1997). These analysis techniques enable a process designer to answer important questions about a workflow specification, including:

- Can the process model be completed without errors (termination)?
- Are there tasks that are never executed (dead tasks)?
- Are there tasks that are still executing when the process is supposed to be completed (proper completion)?

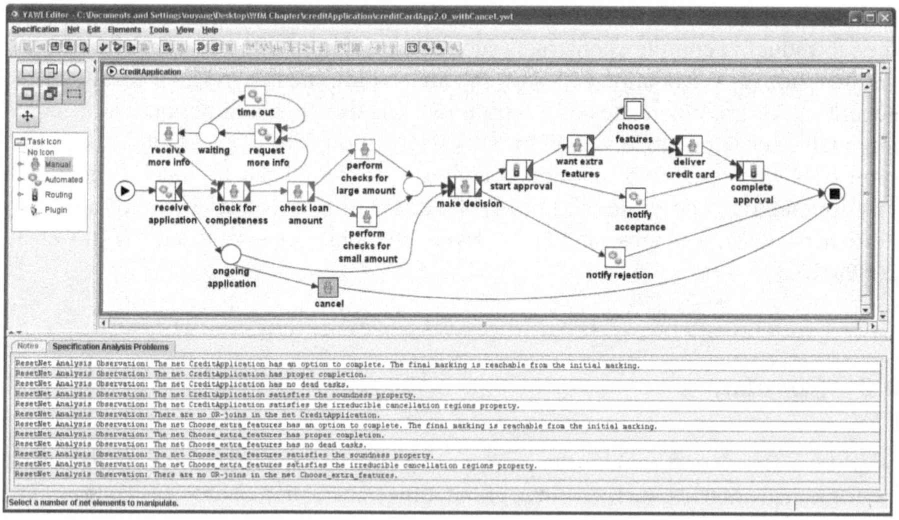

Fig. 7 A screenshot of the verification results for the credit card application process shown in Fig. 6

The answers to these questions are closely related to the soundness property of a workflow specification (van der Aalst 2000).

Three sophisticated verification techniques for workflow specifications with cancelation and OR-joins have been developed in the context of the workflow language YAWL (Verbeek et al. 2007; Wynn et al. 2009c). These techniques make use of Petri nets with reset arcs and Petri nets with inhibitor arcs to detect the soundness property and the relaxed soundness property. Reset arcs can remove tokens from its reset places when a transition fires and they are used to model cancelation regions in YAWL. Similarly, inhibitor arcs can check for empty tokens and they are used to approximate the behavior of OR-joins in YAWL. It is also possible to perform a behavior check of the model using semi-positive transition variants.

Figure 7 shows the verification analysis results for the credit card application example. As this example makes use of complex constructs, such as OR-join and cancelation, to accurately capture the business logic in the workflow specification, no other verification tool except the verification functionality in the YAWL Editor[4] can validate this model and provide information on whether the workflow is sound and whether there are unnecessary OR-joins and/or unnecessary cancelation regions in the specification. In addition to the verification of YAWL process models, Petri nets have also been used to analyze other process modeling languages such as BPMN (Dijkman et al. 2008) and BPEL (Ouyang et al. 2007).

[4]The YAWL editor is a graphical design environment for creating YAWL specifications.

However, there is a clear trade-off between the expressive power of a language (i.e., introducing complex constructs such as cancelation and OR-joins) and ease of verification. As verification relies on the state space analysis, which results in the generation of possible states of a workflow, it is time consuming and can become intractable for large models. Reducing a specification, while preserving its essential properties with respect to a particular analysis problem, is an approach to deal with this complexity. Therefore, a number of soundness preserving reduction rules for Petri nets with reset arcs, and for YAWL elements, are proposed (Wynn et al. 2009a, b).

4.2 Simulation

Workflow simulation enables the analysis of workflow specification with respect to performance metrics such as throughput time, cost, or resource utilization. The main steps in workflow simulation involves developing an accurate simulation model, which reflects the behavior of a process, including the data and resource perspectives, and then performing simulation experiments to better understand the effects of running that process. In general, a simulation model consists of three components: basic model building blocks (e.g., entities, resources, activities, and connectors); activity modeling constructs (e.g., branch, assemble, batch, gate, split, and join); and advanced modeling functions (e.g., attributes, expressions, resource schedules, interruptions, user defined distributions) (Tumay 1996). The interested readers can find more details in van der Aalst et al. (2010), which is dedicated to the topic of business process simulation.

Simulation is regarded as an invaluable tool for process modeling due to its ability to perform quantitative modeling (e.g., cost-benefit analysis and feasibility of alternative designs) as well as stochastic modeling (e.g., external factors and sensitivity analysis) (Giaglis et al. 1996). Simulation has been used for the analysis and design of systems in different application areas and for improving orchestration of supply chain business processes. Simulation can also be used as a decision support tool for business process reengineering to identify bottlenecks and to reduce wait-times between activities. For instance, a simulation model based on the credit card applications process with reliable input data can be used to answer questions about how long it takes on average to process a credit application, how many applications are processed per month, the number of human and nonhuman resources required, the cost of processing these applications, and so on.

Even though simulation is well-known for its ability to assist in long-term planning and strategic decision making, it has not been considered to date as a mainstream technique for operational decision making due to the difficulty of obtaining real-time data in the timely manner to set up the simulation experiments (Reijers 2003; Reijers and van der Aalst 1999). This can be achieved by making closer alignment between a workflow system and a simulation environment, and could involve making use of available case information from workflow system and historical data from process mining tools (Rozinat et al. 2008; Wynn et al. 2007; Russell et al. 2006a).

The state-of-the-art workflow simulation environment should be powerful enough to fully represent underlying business processes and their environment and should support strategic, as well as operational, decision making. One way to identify the requirements for such a simulation environment could be determined in terms of its support for the control flow patterns (van der Aalst et al. 2003), the data flow patterns (Russell et al. 2005b), and the resource patterns (Russell et al. 2005a). Business process simulation tools survey conducted by Jansen-Vullers and Netjes (Jansen-Vullers and Netjes 2006) highlights the fact that these simulation tools are lacking support for complex control flow patterns as well as many of the data and resource patterns. There is a need for simulation environment to support different resource allocation strategies and resource behaviors. In addition, the simulation environment should offer support for ease of integration of historical data into the experiments. The simulation environment also should provide an ability to add customized attributes. These requirements for a state-of-the-art simulation environment are currently being considered and researched, and there is a proposal to support this as part of the YAWL workflow framework.[5]

4.3 Configuration

A reference model represents a generic business process for a particular domain, which can be customized to realize the business process in an organization. More than one reference model may be available for a particular business domain (e.g., supply chain management), and model selection is a crucial task, which requires a good understanding of available reference models in that domain (Fettke and Loos 2003). Process configuration is concerned with the customization of a process specification based on the different variants of the model by allowing for the enabling or disabling of actions (Gottschalk et al. 2008). To this end, Rosemann and van der Aalst (2007) propose the notion of a *configurable reference modeling language* using Event-Driven Process Chains (EPCs). Although the notion of reference models and the advantage of reusing these models for process design are well known, current approaches for configuring reference process models are manual and thus error-prone (van der Aalst et al. 2008).

It is possible to integrate configuration choices into workflow models as runtime choices. However, the advantage of using the configuration approach is that it allows a clear distinction between configuration choices and runtime choices and results in a smaller and clearer workflow model. The approach proposed in Gottschalk et al. (2008) involves three phases: (1) the build time of the model

[5] www.yawlfoundation.org/theory/simulation.php

when all the variants of a configurable model is specified, (2) the configuration time when a particular workflow variant is selected based on some criteria, and (3) the run time when process instances executed based on the configured model. The authors describe their approach using hiding and blocking operators, and realize the approach in the context of the YAWL language, through Configurable YAWL (C-YAWL). The authors also show the applicability of the approach to other languages such as the workflow engine of SAP R/3 and to BPEL.

For large reference models, the designer can find it difficult to make all the configuration choices one by one. To make this configuration process easier, a questionnaire-based approach is proposed to identify the viability in the reference models and to assist the designer in making configuration decisions (La Rosa et al. 2007, 2009). To ensure the correctness of the resulting configured model, a framework for configuring reference process models in a correctness-preserving manner has been proposed (van der Aalst et al. 2008). The syntactic correctness and the semantic correctness can be checked at each intermediate step of the configuration procedure. If a configuration step violates the constraints, suggestions are provided to make the configuration step correctness-preserving.

5 Dealing with Change

With its roots in office automation and document routing, workflow management systems have traditionally followed an *assembly-line* metaphor, where rigidly structured business processes derive strongly prescriptive process models, which in turn produce invariant process instances. While organizational environments performing highly repetitive activities were early benefactors of workflow solutions, a much larger proportion of workplaces undertake activities that do not easily conform to such constricting representations of their work practices. Due to inflexible modeling frameworks, process models are said to be system-centric, meaning that processes are *straight-jacketed* (van der Aalst et al. 2005) into the paradigm supplied, rather than the paradigm reflecting the way work is actually performed, resulting in often substantial differences between real processes and the models designed to represent them (Rozinat and van der Aalst 2005).

Change is unavoidable in the modern workplace. To remain effective and competitive, organizations must continually adapt their business processes to manage the rapid changes demanded by the dynamic nature of the marketplace or service environment. It is also the case that, even in the most structured processes, deviations or unpredicted events will occur with almost every instantiation. Therefore, so that the benefits of workflow management system may be offered to the broader organizational spectrum, the ability to deal with change must be effectively addressed.

The types of change that workflow systems must deal with are generally categorized into two distinct but related groups: Dynamic Workflow and Exception Handling.

5.1 *Dynamic Workflow*

Dynamic (or adaptive) workflow refers to the extending of otherwise static workflow processes so that, when change occurs, the process model can be modified or augmented in some way, rather than defaulting to the construction of a completely new model. The change may be considered ad hoc (i.e., only affecting the current instance) or may need to be applied, either temporarily or permanently, to all (or a subset of) current and future instantiations.

Adaptation takes place on two levels. First, the process model is modified, which has associated issues regarding what kinds of changes are allowed and whether the changes maintain support for the objective of the activity. Second, any currently running instances have to be managed when the process model from which it was instantiated changes, which has its own issues, such as whether the instance should be aborted, restarted using the modified model, allowed to continue (so that there are several co-existing versions of the same business process), and other associated problems to do with migration, synchronization, version control, and syntactic and semantic correctness (van der Aalst 2004; Ly et al. 2006; Rinderle et al. 2004). For a closer look at the phenomenon of adaptation, please also refer Hallerbach et al. (2010).

So dynamic workflow provides support for *occasional* changes to the business process model, and assumes the model is basically correct, but incremental or ad hoc changes may be accommodated as required.

An example of a commercial system providing some support for dynamic adaptation is *Tibco iProcess Suite* (version 10.5),[6] which offers an *Orchestrator* component that provides dynamic allocation of subprocess variants at runtime. It requires a construct called a *dynamic event* to be explicitly modeled that contains a number of subprocesses listed as an "array". When execution reaches the dynamic event node, it will execute members of the array based on predefined conditionals, which, like the array, must be statically defined before the process is instantiated – that is, there is no scope for runtime modifications. Another commercial system, COSA (version 5.4),[7] allows *manual* ad hoc runtime adaptations such as reordering, skipping, repeating, postponing, or terminating tasks.

The *ADEPT2* prototype (Reichert et al. 2005) supports process modification during execution (i.e., add, delete, and change the sequence of tasks) both at the model (dynamic evolution) and instance levels (ad hoc changes). Such changes are made to a traditional monolithic model and must be achieved through the manual intervention of an administrator, abstracted to a high-level interaction. The system also supports forward and backward "jumps" through a process instance, but only by authorized staff who instigate the skips manually.

The YAWL system (cf. Sect. 7) provides support for flexibility and dynamic exception handling through the concept of *worklets*, an extensible repertoire of

---

[6] www.staffware.com/resources/software/bpm/tibco_iprocess_suite_whitepaper.pdf

[7] www.cosa-bpm.com/project/docs/COSA_BPM_5_Productdescription_eng.pdf

self-contained subprocesses and associated selection rules (Adams et al. 2006). This approach directly provides for dynamic change and process evolution without having to resort to off-system intervention and/or system downtime.

5.2 Exception Handling

If an event occurs that impacts on the execution of a process instance but is not explicitly catered for in the process model (such as a process abort, an unavailable resource, or a constraint violation), then certain strategies need to be undertaken to "handle" the event. Traditionally, exceptions are considered to be events that by definition occur rarely. But virtually, every process instance will experience some kind of exception during its execution. It may be that these events are known to occur in a small number of cases, but not often enough to warrant their inclusion in the process model (which implies an off-line, manual handling of such events); or they may be things that were never expected to occur (or maybe never even *imagined* could occur). In any case, when they do happen, since they are not included in the process model, they must be handled in some way before processing can continue. In some cases, the static process model will be modified to capture this unforeseen event, which often involves a large organizational cost (downtime, remodeling, testing, and so on), or in certain circumstances, the entire process must be aborted. However, since most processes are long and complex, neither manual intervention nor process termination is satisfactory solutions (Hagen and Alonso 2000).

Alternately, an attempt might be made to include every possible situation into the process model so that when such events occur, there is a branch in the process to take care of it. This approach often leads to very complex models where much of the original business logic is obscured by exception handling forks, and does not avoid the same problems arising when the next unexpected exception occurs.

Approaches to workflow exception handling generally rely on a high degree of runtime user interactivity, which directly impedes on the basic aim of workflow systems (to bring greater efficiencies to work practices) and distracts users from their primary work tasks into process support activities. For example, most systems support simple deadline expiries (timeouts), but in almost every case, unless an appropriate action is explicitly modeled, a deadline results in a message to an administrator for manual handling.

Russell et al. (2006a) present a framework for the classification of exception handling in process-aware information systems based on patterns. They point out that systems supporting some degree of exception handling may allow exceptions to occur during the execution of a process instance, then provide mechanisms called *exception-handlers* (external to, but linked to, the "parent" business process) to handle the exception and allow the process instance to continue unhindered. These handlers may be defined graphically, or as rules, or as a combination of the two. Thus, a distinction between static workflow systems and exception handling systems is that in the former, all business rules, conditions, and exception handling branches must be explicitly defined in the business process model itself, whereas for the latter, the exception handling parts of the process can be separated from the main business process. It is important to note that, typically, handlers can only be specified for exceptions that are expected (because the definition of exception-handlers must be completed before an instance is executed), although some recent developments in this field also provide the ability to capture and handle *unexpected* exceptions at runtime (for example, the YAWL *Worklet Service* (Adams et al. 2007)).

For any work process, it may be more productive to accept the fact that deviations to any plan will occur in practice and to implement support mechanisms, which allow for those behaviors to be *implicitly* incorporated into the model, rather than to develop a closed system that tries to anticipate all possible events, then fails to accommodate others that (inevitably) occur. This notion supports the idea of evolutionary workflow support systems, which over time and through experience *tune* themselves to the business process they are supporting.

6 Beyond Enactment

When an instance of a workflow specification is being executed, workflow participants can monitor its progress. Also, historical information about the execution of the various workflow instances is saved by the workflow system. This information can be used for several purposes, e.g., process mining and workflow recovery. In this section, we briefly discuss the topics of workflow monitoring and process mining.

6.1 Monitoring and Escalation

Active workflow monitoring enables workflow administrators to be aware of workflows, which are deadlocked, taking exceptionally long time to complete, etc. With workflow systems typically handling long-running business processes, the need to monitor these processes and to act quickly when changes are required is paramount. However, it is typically not possible or easy to change a deployed workflow. These situations become more and more unavoidable at runtime due to the nature of interorganization workflows. In such situations, there is a need to consider escalation strategies, which involve making decisions regarding alternative arrangements to achieve the goal of completing the workflow within a reasonable timeframe. Escalation may imply "performing a task in a different way, allowing less qualified people to do certain tasks, or making decisions based on incomplete data" (van der Aalst et al. 2007b). van der Aalst et al. (2007b) propose a set of escalation strategies by looking at the three perspectives of workflow. They include alternative path, escalation subprocess, task predispatching, overlapping and prioritization for the process perspective, resource redeployment and batching for the resource perspective, and deferred data gathering and data degradation for the data perspective.

6.2 Process Mining

Process mining is concerned with discovering, monitoring, and improving business process by extracting relevant information from the event logs produced by a wide variety of systems (van der Aalst et al. 2004b; Weijters et al. 2007). The basic idea behind process mining is to learn from observable execution behavior of a business process by analyzing event logs, audit trails, and transaction logs, which may contain detailed information about the activities of the business processes that have been executed (van der Aalst et al. 2007a).

A wide range of process mining techniques and algorithms exist to perform analysis on the control, the data, and the resourcing perspectives of a workflow specification. The research group headed by Prof. Wil van der Aalst has been actively researching in the area of process mining for a number of years (http://www.processmining.org). To support this research, the open-source Process Mining ProM framework has been developed. ProM supports a pluggable software architecture, which allows developers and analysts to add their own process mining techniques with ease. ProM currently offers almost 200 plug-ins. Over the last couple of years, ProM has been applied in a wide range of real-life case studies, and several ideas have been incorporated in the commercial tools such as ARIS and the BPM suite of Pallas Athena (van der Aalst et al. 2007a).

7 A Sample System: The YAWL Environment

Today, many workflow management systems are available, both commercial and open source. Firstly, let's have a brief look at a number of commercial products. *Staffware* is one of the leading workflow systems since 1998 and is now owned by TIBCO Software. *COSA* is a Petri-net-based workflow system developed by a German company called Ley GmbH. *SAP R/3 Workflow* is an integrated workflow component of SAP R/3 software suite and now runs over the platform of SAP NetWeaver. *Visual WorkFlo*, part of the FileNet's Panagon suite (Panagon WorkFlo Services), is one of the oldest and best established products on the market of the workflow industry. *WebSphere MQ Workflow* is developed by IBM for process automation and enables use with WebSphere Business Integration Modeler and Monitor for design, analysis, simulation, and monitoring of process improvements. *Oracle BPEL Process Manager*, now part of the Oracle SOA Suite, is a BPEL engine that enables enterprises to orchestrate disparate applications and Web services into business processes.

In the area of open source workflow systems, the four most downloaded systems (as at July 2008) are OpenWFE, jBPM, Enhydra Shark, and YAWL. OpenWFE (or more precisely, OpenWFEru or Ruote) is a workflow management system written in Ruby. It is aimed for developers and distributed under the BSD License. JBoss jBPM is abbreviation of Java for Business Process Management. It is JBoss' (RedHat's) workflow management system and is written in Java. The tool is distributed through SourceForge under the LGPL license. Enhydra Shark is a Java workflow engine offering from Together Teamlösungen and ObjectWeb. While it is an open source offering, its architecture allows for the use of closed-source or proprietary plug-ins to enhance it. The open-source version of Enhydra Shark is licensed according to the LGPL. Finally, the YAWL System (van der Aalst et al. 2004a) and its environment represent an implementation of a workflow management system supporting the YAWL language. Like jBPM, the YAWL system is distributed through SourceForge under the LGPL license. The YAWL environment is unique in its near-complete support for the workflow patterns. It is therefore used as a sample workflow management system for discussion in this section.

7.1 Architecture

The high-level architecture of the YAWL environment is depicted in Fig. 8. The most obvious feature of the environment is the separation of functionality between the core YAWL Workflow Engine and a number of so-called YAWL Custom

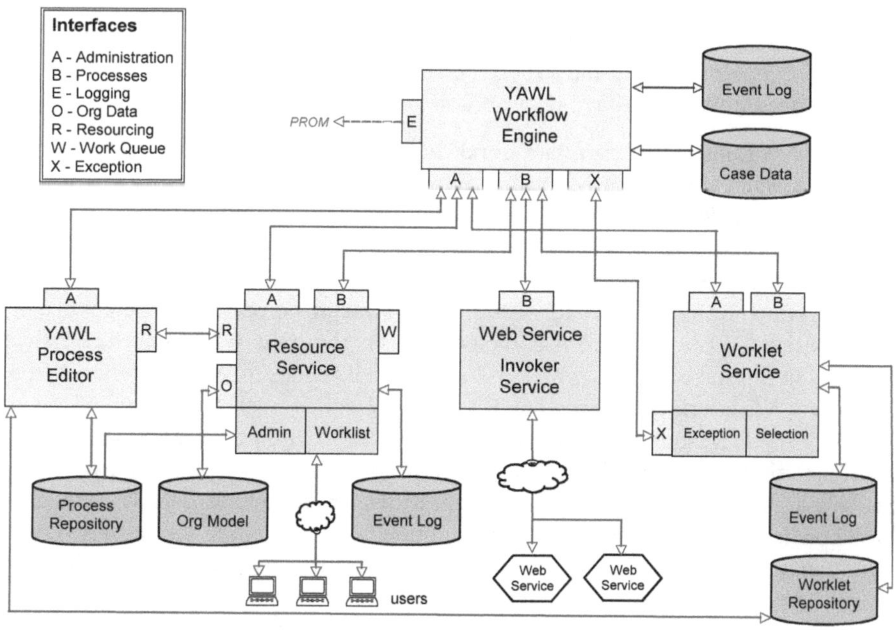

Fig. 8 YAWL system architecture

Services. Inspired by the "web services" paradigm, end-users, applications, and organizations are all abstracted as services in YAWL. Figure 8 shows the three major YAWL services: (1) the Resource Service, with integrated worklist handler and administration tool; (2) the Web Services Invoker; and (3) the Worklet Service, which provides dynamic flexibility and exception handling capabilities.

Workflow specifications are designed using the YAWL Process Editor and stored in the repository as XML. From there, they may be deployed into the YAWL Engine, which, after performing all necessary verifications and task registrations, makes the specifications available to the environment so that they can be instantiated through the Engine, leading to workflow instances. The Engine handles the execution of these cases, and based on the state of a case and its specification, the Engine determines which tasks and events it should offer to the environment.

YAWL Custom Services interact with the engine and each other via a number of interfaces, which provide methods for object and data passing via HTTP requests and responses. All data are passed as XML; objects are marshaled into XML representations on the server side of each interface and reconstructed back to objects on the client side. The YAWL Engine provides four interfaces:

- Interface A: which provides endpoints for process definition, administration, and monitoring;
- Interface B: which provides endpoints for client and invoked applications and workflow interoperability, and is used by services to connect to the engine, to start and cancel case instances, and to check workitems in and out of the engine;
- Interface E: which provides access to archival data in the engine's process logs; and
- Interface X: which allows the engine to notify custom services of certain events and checkpoints during the execution of each process instance where process exceptions either may have occurred or should be tested for.

The YAWL interfaces correlate somewhat loosely to those defined in the Workflow Reference Model (WRM) of the Workflow Management Coalition (WfMC) (Hollingsworth 1995). The WRM describes a core Workflow Enactment Service (or Engine) interacting with a number of generic components via a defined set of standardized interfaces and data interchange formats. In addition to the core Engine, the Workflow Reference Model identifies five major component types and their interfaces. YAWL's interface A corresponds strongly to the WRM interface 1 (and partially to interface 5), while YAWL's interface B relates to WRM interfaces 2, 3, and 4. YAWL interface E corresponds to parts of WRM interface 5 also.

The YAWL Resource Service incorporates a full-featured worklist handler and administration toolset, implemented as a series of web pages. The service automatically assigns tasks to resources and places them in the appropriate work queues based on design time specifications and runtime decisions, while the administration tools can be used to manually control workflow instances (e.g., loading or removing a workflow specification, launching, or canceling case instances), manage resources and allocate them to tasks, and provide information about the state of running workflow instances.

The Resource Service provides three additional interfaces that allow developers to implement other worklist handlers and administration tools while leveraging the full functionality of the service. Interface R provides organizational data to (authorized) external entities such as the YAWL Process Editor; Interface W provides access to the internal work queue routing functionalities; and Interface O allows organizational data to be provided to the service from any data source. In addition, the service's framework is fully extendible, allowing further constraints, filters, and allocation strategies to be "plugged in" by developers.

The worklist handler, incorporated into the Resource Service, corresponds to the classical worklist handler present in most workflow management systems. It is the component used to assign work to users of the system. Through the worklist handler, users are offered and allocated work items, and can start and signal their completion. In traditional workflow systems, the worklist handler is embedded in the workflow engine. In YAWL, however, it is considered to be a service completely decoupled from the engine so that the Engine has no knowledge of how work will be assigned.

The YAWL Web Services Invoker is the glue between the engine and other web services. Note that it is unlikely that web services will be able to directly connect to the YAWL engine, since they will typically be designed for more general purposes than just interacting with a workflow engine. Similarly, it is desirable not to adapt the interface of the engine to suit specific services; otherwise, this interface will need to cater for an undetermined number of message types. Accordingly, the YAWL web services broker acts as a mediator between the YAWL engine and external web services that may be invoked by the engine to delegate tasks (e.g., delegating a "payment" task to an online payment service).

The YAWL Worklet Service (Adams et al. 2006, 2007) comprises two discrete but complementary subservices: a Selection Service, which enables dynamic flexibility for otherwise static process instances, and an Exception Service, which provides facilities to handle both expected and unexpected process exceptions (i.e., events that may happen during the lifecycle of a process instance that affect the execution of the instance but were not explicitly modeled in the process specification) at runtime.

In addition to the three services shown in Fig. 8, any number of additional custom services can be implemented for particular interaction purposes with the YAWL Engine. For example, a custom YAWL service could offer communication with devices such as mobile phones, printers, and assembly robots. A custom service may be used to manipulate the data of certain tasks, or may be implemented to enhance the presentation of work to end-users (for example, via a graphical interface or as a component within a virtual environment). It is also possible that there are concurrent multiple services of the same type, e.g., multiple worklist handlers, web services brokers, and exception handling services. For example, there may exist multiple implementations of worklist handlers (for example, customized for a specific application domain or organization) and the same worklist handler may be instantiated multiple times (for example, one worklist handler per geographical region).

7.2 Design Time

A YAWL workflow with control, data, and resource perspectives can be created using the YAWL Process Editor, which is a standalone component of the YAWL workflow system. Figure 9 provides a screenshot of the credit card application process modeled in the YAWL Editor. The control flow perspective of the workflow is specified using the YAWL icons on the top-left side of the screen. The data perspective of the workflow such as input and output data as well as the data used for flow decisions (XOR-split and OR-splits) are modeled using XML data elements. The resource perspective specifies who should do a particular task from a set of available resources from the organizational database. This feature requires client-server access to an executing resource service via interface R (Fig. 8) so that information regarding resources can be retrieved, and can be configured in the YAWL Editor using a 5-step wizard. As an example, Fig. 10 shows a screenshot of the second step in specifying the resource perspective for task *make decision* in the credit card application process.

The YAWL specification can be checked using the "Validate Specification" feature to ensure the structural correctness of the workflow. Furthermore, the specification can be analyzed using the "Analyze Specification" feature to ensure the behavioral correctness of the workflow with regards to the control flow. A validated specification can then be exported to the YAWL engine for enactment.

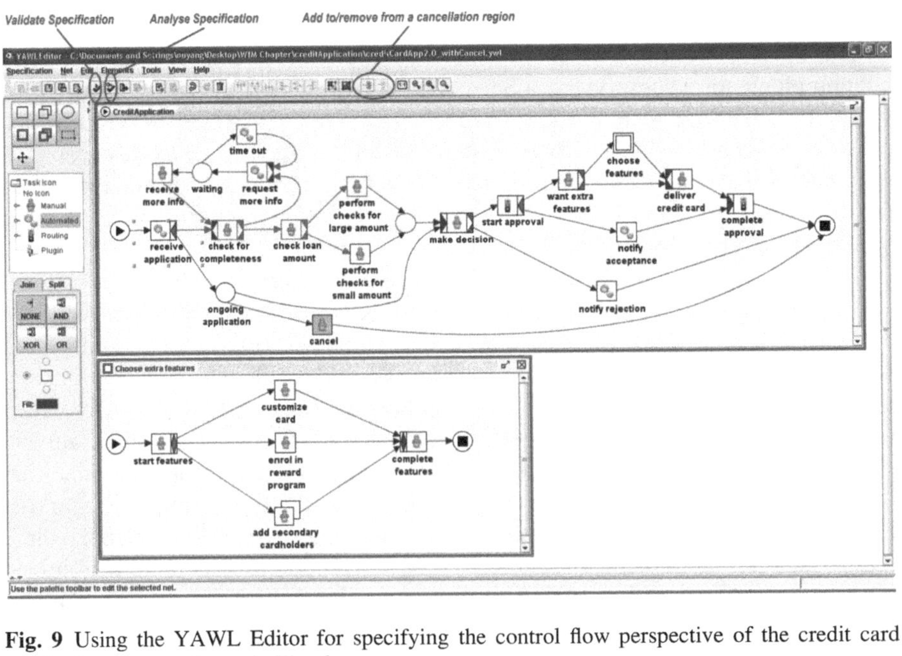

Fig. 9 Using the YAWL Editor for specifying the control flow perspective of the credit card application process shown in Fig. 6

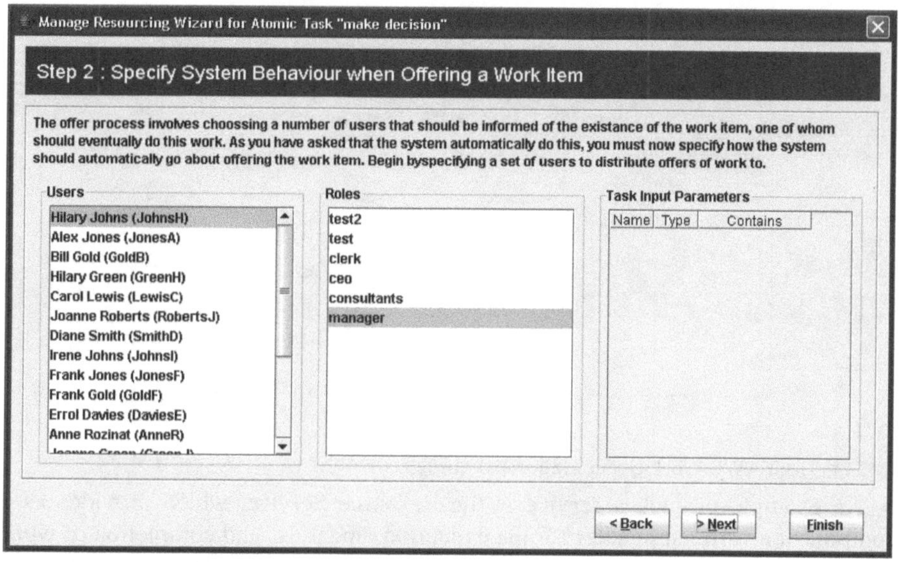

Fig. 10 Using the YAWL Editor for specifying the resource perspective (Task *make decision* should be performed by a user with a manager role)

Currently, version 2.0 of the YAWL Editor provides support for specifying extended attributes such as cost, priority, etc., integrated support for timeout tasks using timers, and the support for 38 out of 43 resource patterns. It can be downloaded from SourceForge.[8]

7.3 *Runtime*

At runtime, the YAWL Engine presents events and tasks to the environment as they occur during the lifecycle of process instantiations via the interfaces described earlier. Using those interfaces, custom services may elect to be notified of certain events (i.e., when a workitem becomes enabled, or is canceled, or when a case instance completes) or of changes in the status of existing workitems and case instances.

For example, on receiving notification from the Engine of an item-enabled event (i.e., when a work item becomes ready for execution), a custom service may elect to "check-out" the workitem from the Engine. On doing so, the Engine marks the work item as *executing* and effectively passes operational control for the work item to the custom service. When the service has finished processing the work item, it will check it back into the Engine, at which point the Engine will mark the work item as *completed* and proceed with process execution.

[8]http://sourceforge.net/projects/yawl/

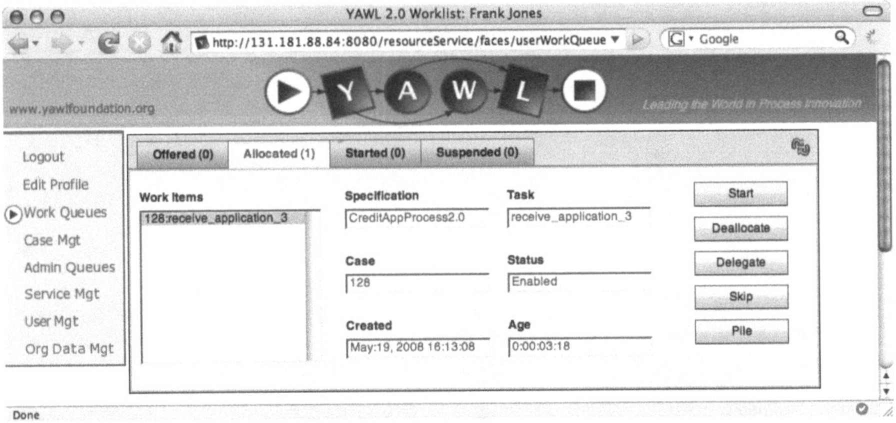

Fig. 11 The YAWL Work Queues (allocated queue active)

An example of such a service is the Resource Service, which provides as a component a worklist handler for the execution, updating, and completion of work items at runtime. The user interface is provided as a series of web pages. Each work item is presented to the appropriate user work queues based on four interaction points: offered, allocated, started, and suspended.

Figure 11 shows a screen of an allocated work queue in the YAWL runtime environment. The screen displays the information about a work item that has been allocated, including the process specification, the identifier of the process instance (i.e., case number), the task to which the work item belongs, and its creation time and age. There are also functionalities that support different operations with the work item, for example, to delegate the work item to another human resource. The types of functionality available vary relevant to each of the four work queues.

When a work item is started, its data may be viewed and edited via a dynamically generated form. Each completed work item is passed back to the Engine, allowing the case instance to progress. While the Resource Service offers a default worklist handler, custom services may be designed to handle the work and events offered by the YAWL Engine in a variety of ways. For example, the exception-handling component of the Worklet Service uses the same task and event notifications to determine if exceptions have occurred during a process instance's life cycle and take appropriate action as required.

8 A Case Study: YAWL4Film

As part of the Australian Research Council Centre of Excellence for Creative Industries and Innovation,[9] we move well beyond the traditional use of workflow management systems and investigate how they can deliver benefits to the field of

[9] http://www.cci.edu.au

screen business. The screen business comprises all creative and business related aspects and processes of film, television, and new media content, from concept to production and then distribution. A film production process includes daily shooting activities like acting, camera, and sound recording over a period varying from days to years. It involves handling large amounts of forms and reports on a daily basis and coordinating geographically distributed stakeholders. Traditionally, the forms and reports are purely paper-based and the production of these documents is a highly manual process. Not surprisingly, such a process is time-consuming and error-prone, and can easily increase the risk of delays in the schedule.

Within the above context, YAWL was applied to the automation of film production processes (Ouyang et al. 2008a, b). This led to the development of a prototype, namely YAWL4Film, which exploits the principles of workflow in order to coordinate work distribution with production teams, automate the daily document processing and report generation, ensure data synchronization across distributed nodes, archive and manage all shooting related documents systematically, and document experiences gained in a film production project for reuse in the future. The system was successfully deployed in two pilot projects at the Australian Film, Television, and Radio School in October 2007.

Below, we briefly describe YAWL4Film. It consists of a YAWL model capturing the control-flow, data, and resource perspectives of a film production process. It also extends the general YAWL system with customized user interface to support templates used in professional filmmaking.

8.1 Process Model

Figure 12 depicts the YAWL model of a film production process. An instance of the process model starts with the collection of specific production documents (e.g., *cast list*, *crew list*, *location notes*, and *shooting schedule*) generated during the preproduction phase. Next, the shooting starts and is carried out on a daily basis. Each day, tasks are performed along two main parallel streams. One stream focuses on the production of a *call sheet*. It starts from task *Begin Call Sheet* and ends with task *Finish Call Sheet*. A call sheet is a daily shooting schedule. It is usually maintained by the production office and is sent out to all cast and crew the day prior. A draft call sheet can be created from the shooting schedule. It may go through any number of revisions before it is finalized, and most of the revisions result from the changes to the shooting schedule. The other stream specifies the flow of onset shooting activities and supports the production of a *daily process report* (DPR). It starts with task *Kick Off on-set* and ends with task *Distribute DPR*. At first, tasks are executed to record the logs and technical notes about individual shooting activities into a number of documents. These are *continuity log* and *continuity daily*, which are filled by the Continuity person, *sound sheet* by a Sound Recordist, *camera sheet* by a Camera Assistant, and *2nd Assistant Director (AD) Report* by the 2nd AD. It is possible to interrupt filling in the continuity log and the 2nd AD report, e.g., for a

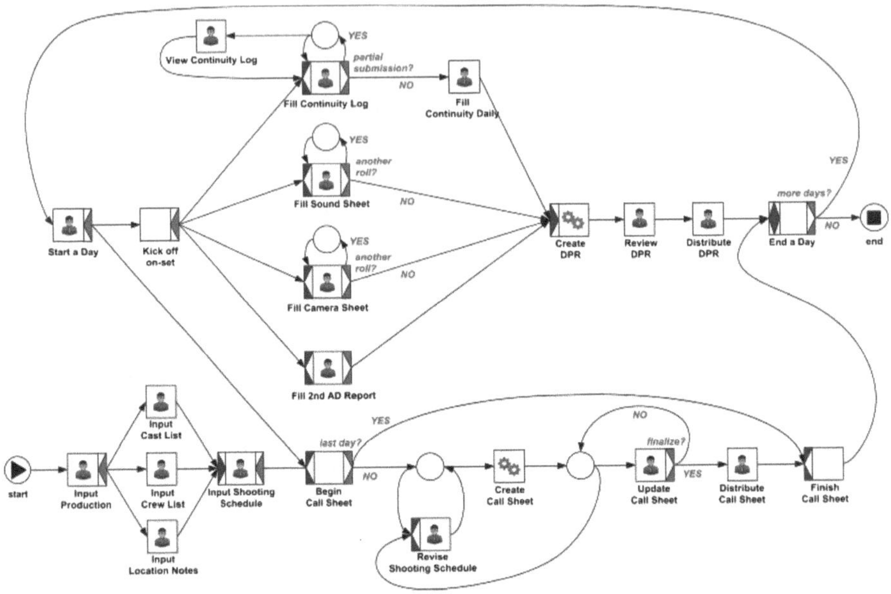

Fig. 12 A film production process model in YAWL

meal break, and then to resume the work after the break. Also, there can be many camera and sound sheets to be filled in during a shooting day. Upon completion of these on-set documents, a DPR can be generated and passed onto the Production Manager for review. After the review, the DPR is circulated to certain crew members, e.g., Producer and Executive Producer.

In this process model, it is interesting to see how the OR-join associated with task *End a Day* behaves. Before the first shooting day starts, an instance of the call sheet branch is executed for producing the first day's call sheet. Since it is the only active incoming branch to task *End a Day*, the task will be performed once the call sheet has completed, without waiting for the completion of a DPR. In this case, the OR-join behaves like an XOR-join. On the other hand, if both call sheet and DPR branches are active (which is the case for the rest of the shooting days), the OR-join behaves like an AND-join.

8.2 User Interface

Most tasks in the film production process are manual (annotated with an icon of a human) and require users to fill in forms. While the YAWL environment supports automatic generation of screens based on input/output parameters and their types, in order to support templates used in professional filmmaking, custom-made Web forms were created and linked to the worklist handler of YAWL. Figure 13 for

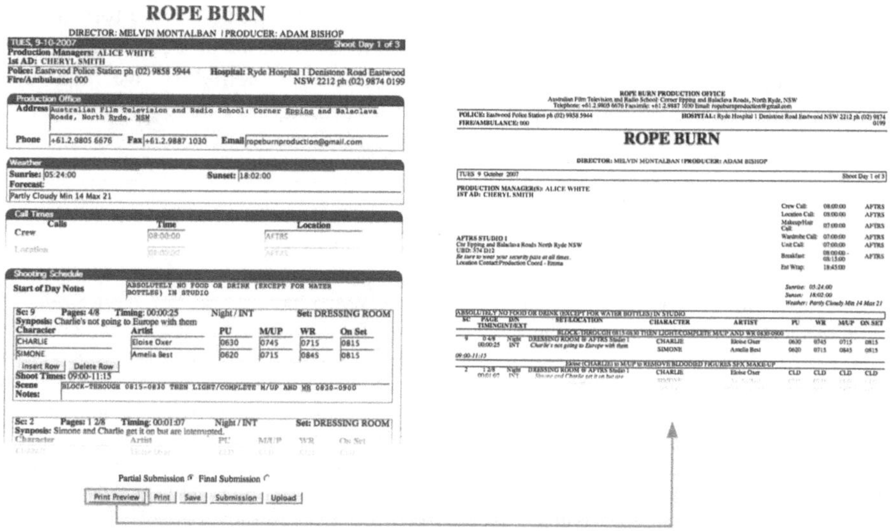

Fig. 13 An example of custom Web form – call sheet

example depicts the Web form for task *Update Call Sheet* (in Fig. 12) as seen by a production office crew member. The custom forms and their links to YAWL were developed using standard Java technology. Each form can load/save an XML file (complying with the schema of the work item), and submit the form back to the worklist handler once it has been completed by the user. Upon submission, a backup copy is stored on the server. Moreover, each form provides data validation upon save and submission to prevent the generation of invalid XML documents that would block the execution of the process. Finally, a print-preview function[10] allows the user to generate a printer-ready document from the Web form, which resembles the hard copy format used in practice in this business.

9 Outlook

This chapter covered many of the main areas that are of relevance in modern workflow management, and more broadly, modern Business Process Management. These included workflow patterns, which are part of the conceptual foundations of workflow management, a number of workflow languages, which exhibit different approaches to workflow specification, and more advanced topics such as handling changes and unexpected exceptions, simulation, verification, and configuration. An existing workflow management system was presented in order to demonstrate some state-of-the-art aspects of workflow management. However, space considerations

[10]This function relies on XSLT transformations to convert the XML of the form to HTML.

prevented in-depth treatment of the various topics covered, and some topics were not covered at all, e.g., support at the language level for interprocess communication (Aldred et al. 2007; Decker and Barros 2007). Nonetheless, we hope that enough pointers were provided to the reader for further study or exploration.

References

Adams M, ter Hofstede AHM, Edmond D, van der Aalst WMP (2006) Worklets: a service-oriented implementation of dynamic flexibility in workflows. In: Proceedings of the 14th international conference on cooperative information systems. LNCS, vol 4275. Springer, Berlin, pp 291–308

Adams M, ter Hofstede AHM, van der Aalst WMP, Edmond D (2007) Dynamic, extensible and context-aware exception handling for workflows. In: Proceedings of the 15th international conference on cooperative information systems. LNCS, vol 4803, pp 95–112

Aldred L, van der Aalst WMP, Dumas M, ter Hofstede AHM (2007) Communication abstractions for distributed business processes. In: Proceedings of the 19th international conference on advanced information systems engineering. LNCS, vol 4495. Springer, pp 409–423

Decker G, Barros AP (2007) Interaction modeling using BPMN. In: Proceedings of business process management workshops 2007. LNCS, vol 4928. Springer, Heidelberg, pp 208–219

Dijkman R, Dumas M, Ouyang C (2008) Semantics and analysis of business process models in BPMN. Inform Softw Tech 50(2):1281–1294

Fettke P, Loos P (2003) Classification of reference models – a methodology and its application. Inform Syst E Bus Manage 1(1):35–53

Fischer L (ed) (2005) Workflow handbook 2005. Workflow Management Coalition

Giaglis G, Paul R, Doukidis G (1996) Simulation for intra- and inter-organisational business process modeling. In: Proceedings of the 28th conference on winter simulation, pp 1297–1308

Gottschalk F, van der Aalst WMP, Jansen-Vullers M, La Rosa M (2008) Configurable workflow models. Int J Cooper Inform Syst 17(2):177–221

Hagen C, Alonso G (2000) Exception handling in workflow management systems. IEEE Trans Softw Eng 26(10):943–958

Hallerbach A, Bauer T, Reichert M (2010) Configuration and management of process variants. In: vom Brocke J, Rosemann M (eds) Handbook on business process management, vol 1. Springer, Heidelberg

Hollingsworth D (1995) The workflow reference model. http://www.wfmc.org/standards/docs/tc003v11.pdf. Accessed 4 Apr 2008

Jablonski S, Bussler C (1996) Workflow-management: modeling concepts, architecture and implementation. International Thomson Computer Press, London

Jansen-Vullers M, Netjes M (2006) Business process simulation – a tool survey. In: Proceedings of the 7th workshop and tutorial on practical use of coloured petri nets and the CPN tools, Aarhus, Denmark

La Rosa M, Lux J, Seidel S, Dumas M, ter Hofstede AHM (2007) Questionnaire-driven configuration of reference process models. In: Proceedings of the 19th international conference on advanced information systems engineering. LNCS, vol 4495. Springer, pp 424–438

La Rosa M, van der Aalst WMP, Dumas M, ter Hofstede AHM (2009) Questionnaire-based variability modeling for system configuration. Software Syst Model 8(2):251–274

Ly LT, Rinderle S, Dadam P (2006) Semantic correctness in adaptive process management systems. In: Proceedings of the 4th international conference on business process management. LNCS, vol 4102. Springer, pp 193–208

Murata T (1989) Petri nets: properties, analysis and applications. Proc IEEE 77(4):541–580

Ouyang C, Verbeek HMW, van der Aalst WMP, Breutel S, Dumas M, ter Hofstede AHM (2007) Formal semantics and analysis of control flow in WS-BPEL. Sci Comput Program 67(2–3):125–332

Ouyang C, ter Hofstede AHM, La Rosa M, Rosemann M, Shortland K, Court D (2008a) Camera, set, action: automating film production via business process management. In: Proceedings of the CCI conference on creating value: between commerce and commons, the ARC Centre of Excellence for the Creative Industries and Innovation, Brisbane, Australia

Ouyang C, La Rosa M, ter Hofstede AHM, Shortland K (2008b) Towards Web-scale workflows for film production. IEEE Internet Comput 12(5):53–61

Ouyang C, Dumas M, van der Aalst WMP, ter Hofstede AHM, Mendling J (2009) From business process models to process-oriented software systems. ACM Trans Softw Eng Meth 19(1): Article No. 2

Reichert M, Rinderle S, Kreher U, Dadam P (2005) Adaptive process management with ADEPT2. In: Proceedings of the 21st international conference on data engineering, Tokyo, Japan, pp 1113–1114

Reijers HA (2003) Design and control of workflow processes: business process management for the service industry. LNCS, vol 2617. Springer, Berlin

Reijers HA, van der Aalst WMP (1999) Short-term simulation: bridging the gap between operational control and strategic decision making. In: Proceedings of the IASTED conference on modeling and simulation, Philadelphia, USA, pp 417–421

Rinderle S, Reichert M, Dadam P (2004) On dealing with structural conflicts between process type and instance changes. In: Proceedings of the 2nd international conference on business process management. LNCS, vol 3080, pp 274–289

Rosemann M, van der Aalst WMP (2007) A configurable reference modeling language. Inf Syst 32(1):1–23

Rozinat A, van der Aalst WMP (2005) Conformance testing: measuring the fit and appropriateness of event logs and process models. In: Proceedings of BPM 2005 workshops (workshop on business process intelligence). LNCS, vol 3812. Springer, Berlin, pp 163–176

Rozinat A, Wynn MT, van der Aalst WMP, ter Hofstede AHM, Fidge CJ (2008) Workflow simulation for operational decision support using design, historic and state information. In: Proceedings of the 6th international conference on business process management. LNCS, vol 5240. Springer, Heidelberg, pp 196–211

Russell N, van der Aalst WMP, ter Hofstede AHM, Edmond D (2005a) Workflow resource patterns: Identification, representation and tool support. In: Proceedings of the 17th conference on advanced information systems engineering. LNCS, vol 3520. Springer, pp 216–232

Russell N, ter Hofstede AHM, Edmond D, van der Aalst WMP (2005b) Workflow data patterns: Identification, representation and tool support. In: Proceedings of the 24th international conference on conceptual modeling. LNCS, vol 3716. Springer, Berlin, pp 353–368

Russell N, van der Aalst WMP, ter Hofstede AHM (2006a) Workflow exception patterns. In: Proceedings of the 18th international conference on advanced information systems engineering. LNCS, vol 5074. Springer, Berlin, pp 288–302

Russell N, ter Hofstede AHM, van der Aalst WMP, Mulyar N (2006b) Workflow control-flow patterns: a revised view. BPM Center Report BPM-06-22, BPMcenter.org

Tumay K (1996) Business process simulation. In: Proceedings of the 28th conference on winter simulation, pp 93–98

van der Aalst WMP (1997) Verification of workflow nets. In: Proceedings of the 18th application and theory of Petri nets. LNCS, vol 1248. Springer, Heidelberg, pp 407–426

van der Aalst WMP (2000) Workflow verification: finding control-flow errors using Petri net-based techniques. In: Business process management: models, techniques and empirical studies. LNCS, vol 1806. Springer, pp 19–128

van der Aalst WMP (2004) Exterminating the dynamic change bug: a concrete approach to support workflow change. Inform Syst Front 3(3):297–317

van der Aalst WMP, ter Hofstede AHM (2005) YAWL: yet another workflow language. Inf Syst 30(4):245–275

van der Aalst WMP, van Hee KM (2002) Workflow management: models, methods, and systems. MIT press, Cambridge, MA van der Aalst WMP, ter Hofstede AHM, Kiepuszewski B, Barros AP (2003) Workflow patterns. Distrib Parallel Database 14(3):5–51

van der Aalst WMP, Aldred L, Dumas M, ter Hofstede AHM (2004a) Design and implementation of the YAWL system. In: Proceedings of the 16th international conference on ad-vanced information systems engineering. LNCS, vol 3084. Springer, Heidelberg, pp 142–159

van der Aalst WMP, Weijters AJMM, Maruster L (2004b) Workflow mining: discovering process models from event logs. IEEE Trans Knowl Data Eng 16(9):1128–1142

van der Aalst WMP, Weske M, Grünbauer D (2005) Case handling: a new paradigm for business process support. Data Knowl Eng 53(2):129–162

van der Aalst WMP, van den Brand PCW, van Dongen BF, Günther CW, Mans RS, Alves de Medeiros AK, Rozinat A, Song M, Verbeek HMW, Weijters AJMM (2007a) Business process analysis with ProM. In: Proceeding of the 17th annual workshop on information technologies and systems, pp 223–224

van der Aalst WMP, Rosemann M, Dumas M (2007b) Deadline-based escalation in process-aware information systems. Decis Support Syst 43(2):492–511

van der Aalst WMP, Dumas M, Gottschalk F, ter Hofstede AHM, La Rosa M, Mendling J (2008) Correctness-preserving configuration of business process models. In: Proceedings of fundamental approaches to software engineering. LNCS, vol 4961. Springer, pp 46–61

van der Aalst WMP, Nakatumba J, Rozinat A, Russell N (2010) Business process simulation. In: vom Brocke J, Rosemann M (eds) Handbook on business process management, vol 1. Springer, Heidelberg

Verbeek HMW, van der Aalst WMP, ter Hofstede AHM (2007) Verifying workflows with cancelation regions and OR-joins: an approach based on relaxed soundness and invariants. Comput J 50(3):294–314

Weijters AJMM, van der Aalst WMP, van Dongen B, Günther C, Mans R, Alves de Medeiros AK, Rozinat A, Song M, Verbeek HMW (2007) Process mining with ProM. In: Proceedings of the 19th Belgium–Netherlands conference on artificial intelligence, Utrecht, The Netherlands

Weske M (2007) Business process management: concepts, languages, architectures. Springer, Berlin

White S (2004) Process modeling notations and workflow patterns. BPTrends, pp 1–24

Wynn MT, Edmond D, van der Aalst WMP, ter Hofstede AHM (2005) Achieving a general, formal and decidable approach to the OR-join in workflow using reset nets. In: Proceedings of the 26th international conference on application and theory of petri nets and other models of concurrency. LNCS, vol 3536. Springer, Heidelberg, pp 423–443

Wynn MT, van der Aalst WMP, ter Hofstede AHM, Edmond D (2006) Verifying workflows with cancelation regions and OR-joins: an approach based on reset nets and reachability analysis. In: Proceedings of the 4th international conference on business process management. LNCS, vol 4102. Springer, Berlin, pp 389–394

Wynn MT, Dumas M, Fidge CJ, ter Hofstede AHM, van der Aalst WMP (2007) Business process simulation for operational decision support. In: Proceedings of the 3rd international workshop on business process intelligence. LNCS, vol 4928. Springer, Berlin, pp 66–77

Wynn MT, Verbeek HMW, van der Aalst WMP, ter Hofstede AHM, Edmond D (2009a) Reduction rules for reset workflow nets. Inf Sci 179(6):769–790

Wynn MT, Verbeek HMW, van der Aalst WMP, ter Hofstede AHM, Edmond D (2009b) Reduction rules for workflows with cancelation regions and OR-joins. Inform Softw Tech 51 (6):1010–1020

Wynn MT, Verbeek HMW, van der Aalst WMP, ter Hofstede AHM, Edmond D (2009c) Business process verification – finally a reality! Bus Process Manage J 15(1):74–92

A Framework for Designing Resource-Driven Workflows

Akhil Kumar and Jianrui Wang

Abstract This chapter presents a general framework of resource-driven workflows as an alternative to the more popular control flow-driven workflows approach. We argue that this approach is more holistic than control flow-driven approaches because it considers availability of resources such as data, people, equipment, space, etc. Control flow-driven approaches usually either disregard resource considerations or account for them only implicitly. In our approach, the control flow is a derivative of the resource needs of various tasks. Moreover, we make a clean separation between hard constraints that arise from resource considerations and soft constraints that result from business policy. The new methodology for process design is described at length, along with an architecture and a detailed discussion of implementation issues. This approach is more holistic and is particularly suited for ad hoc workflows as opposed to production workflows.

1 Introduction

There are many approaches and frameworks for designing business workflows (van der Aalst 1998; Dumas et al. 2005; Grefen et al. 1999; OASIS; Scheer 1998; Scheer et al. 2005; Workflow Management Coalition). Most of them are based on mapping a control flow that specifies the coordination of various activities. An overview is given in the previous chapter (Ouyang et al. 2010). Here, we discuss another approach, which differs from the control flow-driven workflow approach, called *resource-driven workflows*. The main idea is to design a process so that the tasks within it can be driven based on the availability of resources required to perform them without an explicit control flow. In general, a process contains several tasks,

A. Kumar (✉)
Department of Supply Chain and Information Systems, Smeal College of Business, Pennsylvania State University, University Park, PA, USA
e-mail: akhilkumar@psu.edu

J. vom Brocke and M. Rosemann (eds.), *Handbook on Business Process Management 1*, International Handbooks on Information Systems,
DOI 10.1007/978-3-642-00416-2_19,

and each task requires resources such as data, people performing roles, equipment, facilities, etc., for its completion. If any resource is not available, then the task cannot be performed. We argue that in some scenarios, particularly those involving frequent changes in the environment, as well as resource-intensive or ad hoc workflows, the control flow-driven approach to workflow design is less suitable. Instead, since exceptions and changes are more likely to occur in these cases, a resource-based approach may be more promising. From a management standpoint as well, in the recent years, the resource-based view of organizations is assuming greater importance as a basis for developing competitive business strategy (Collis and Montgomery 1995).

In a conventional control flow-based workflow, the coordination among various tasks is prespecified using constructs such as *sequence*, *choice*, *parallel*, and *loop*. More advanced constructs or patterns (van der Aalst et al. 2003) may also be used. Thus, a sequence construct between tasks A (e.g., "receive order") and B (e.g., "check order") creates a dependency between them, which means that B cannot start unless A is finished. Now, in general, such a dependency could be for a variety of reasons. It could be because B needs the data produced by A. It could also be because A and B are to be done by the same individual. It could be because A and B need the same facility or equipment. Finally, it could be because of a business policy in the organization. Thus, a process design based on a control flow creates dependencies between tasks, but it does not give a reason for them.

Similarly, consider another scenario where two tasks C (e.g., "check customer credit") and D (e.g., "check inventory") are in parallel in the control flow of a process. This means that they do not have a dependency between them. During execution of the process, it may turn out that, in general, both C and D might well need the same human resource, say, a manager, and since there is only one person available in that role, both C and D cannot be done in parallel. They might also need some equipment of which there is only one instance. Hence, this suggests that often because of resource conflicts, it is not possible to design a control flow without knowledge of the resource requirements of the various tasks and the available resources. Since the available resources change dynamically, there is some value in not "hard-coding" them into the process design. Thus, in this situation, we cannot really say whether C and D are in sequence or in parallel. Consequently, a resource-based approach to process design and execution may be more useful.

As an example to motivate the need for resource-based workflow modeling, consider the new product development process in a company. Such a process involves steps such as product planning, conceptual design, component design, overall assembly, prototype, performance test, etc. In each step, individuals from different departments (e.g., marketing, engineering, and development) performing various roles (such as designer, engineer, manager, etc.) are involved (see Table 1). The main features of this process are that the tasks have complex coordination and routing requirements and must be routed among individuals or teams, which may be geographically distributed. They may need to share documents and other resources. Finally, access to all documents must be carefully controlled based on permissions.

Table 1 An example of tasks and their resource needs in product design

Task	Data resource	Human resource	Physical resource	Equipment resource
Product planning	*In*: marketing report *Out*: design spec.	Marketing, Design manager	Conference room (capacity 10)	White board, PC, projector
Conceptual design	*In*: design spec. *Out*: detailed design	Design engineer	Design room	Design PC
Design review	*In*: detailed design *Out*: discussion transcript	Design team	Conference room (capacity 25)	White board, PC, projector
Component design	*In*: detailed design, transcript *Out*: drawings.	Manufacturing engineer	Office room	CAD workstation

In this table, there are four types of resources. The successful completion of a process requires coordination among all the resources. In a resource-driven workflow, the various tasks can be scheduled only when all their resource needs are satisfied. Thus, it is not necessary to specify a control flow before hand, but it is necessary to specify all the tasks that must be performed and the resource requirements for each task. Document- and entity-centric approaches for modeling business processes are discussed in Bhattacharya et al. (2007), Botha and Eloff (2001), Dourish et al. (2000), Krishnan et al. (2002), LaMarca et al. (1999), Mazumdar and AbuSafiya (2004), and Wang and Kumar (2005).

The objective of this chapter is to present an alternative way of designing workflows. The proposed resource-driven workflow framework is useful when multiple resources are involved in a process and resource conflicts are likely to arise. Therefore, it becomes necessary to look beyond a control flow-centric approach. In addition, this framework can also be used to generate a preliminary design for ad hoc workflows, which may be refined further to create a final process design. The organization of this chapter is as follows. We will first provide some background and contrast resource-driven workflows with control-driven ones in Sect. 2. Next, in Sect. 3, we will discuss the resource-driven approach in detail. Later, Sect. 4 gives a general framework for developing resource-driven workflows and an algorithm for handling exceptions, while in Sect. 5, a comparison between the two approaches is conducted. Section 6 provides a detailed discussion, and Sect. 7 concludes the paper.

2 Background

2.1 Resource Dependencies

Conventional workflow systems emphasize the control flow of a process, that is, the execution sequence of the various tasks. Control flow diagrams assume that the

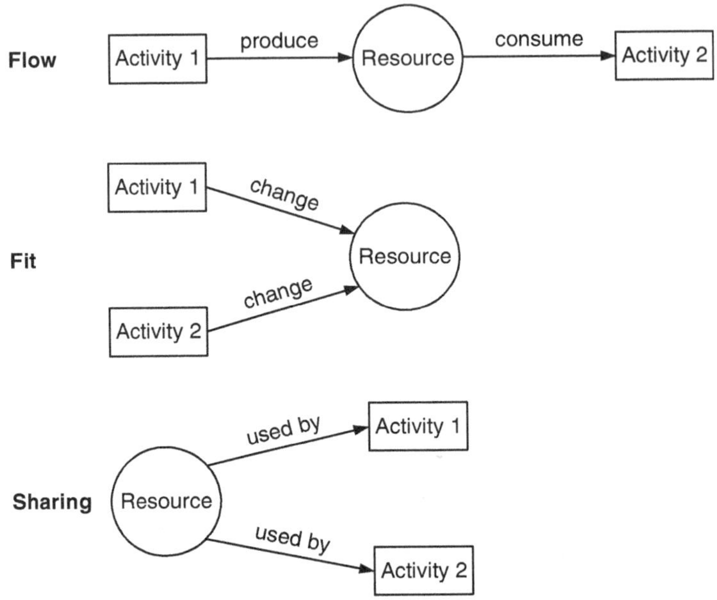

Fig. 1 Three basic types of dependencies in any collaboration environment

process designer possesses the business domain knowledge to layout the task sequence without addressing the resource requirements of each task. Task sequencing follows from the various kinds of dependencies that exist between them. Malone (Malone and Crowston 1994) summarizes three basic types of dependencies that arise in collaboration enterprises: *Flow*, *Fit*, and *Sharing*, as shown in Fig. 1. A *flow dependency* arises when one activity produces a resource that is used by another activity. *Fit dependencies* occur when multiple activities collectively produce a single resource. In such situations, these activities must be synchronized. For example, a series of activities are required to process a customer order such as the one shown in Fig. 2 (to be described shortly). These various activities must be synchronized. A *sharing dependency* arises when several tasks compete for the same resource, e.g., when two activities need to be done by the same person. It should be noted that current workflow systems are particularly weak in handling sharing dependencies.

Figure 2a shows the main steps in a simple workflow process for handling orders from customers. After an order is received, a *credit check* is performed to verify the payment information. Then, there is a *split fork* corresponding to a condition test: if the credit check passes, the order is *picked*, *shipped*, *invoiced*, and *closed*; otherwise, it is canceled. At an AND fork, both branches can be taken in parallel, while at an OR fork, only one branch can be chosen. Each fork has a matching join node where the branches meet. Each process also has a distinguished start and end node. The shortcomings of this method are that there is no information about resources required for each task such as:

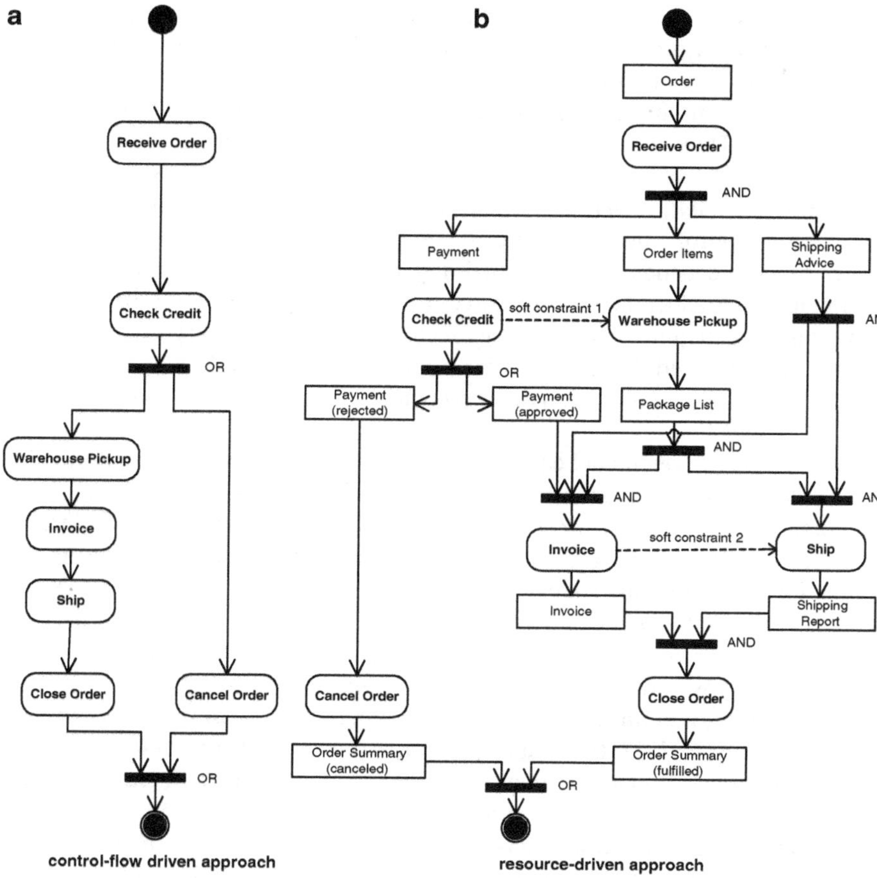

Fig. 2 An example order process modeled by control flow and resource-driven workflow

- *Data Resource*: What input documents are needed for the task?
- *Human Resource*: Who will perform the task (a generic role, a team, or individual person)?
- *Physical Resources*: physical space/facilities, etc.
- *Equipment Resource*: PC, video projector, workstation, etc.

In the absence of this additional information, the workflow description is incomplete. Perhaps, the additional information exists in different systems and if so, it will be hard to integrate with the workflow system. Moreover, any attempt at such integration will slow the performance of the system because of the need to exchange different formats and perform transformations. Ideally, a complete or more holistic description must capture such missing information in a common framework. Of course, additional modeling effort is required in the latter case.

Figure 2b shows an example to contrast the traditional approach for describing workflows and the resource-driven one. In this example, when we use the term resource, the focus is on the document resource. Both parts of the figure show a workflow for order processing. The approach in Fig. 2a is called the *control flow-driven approach* because the exact flow of control is specified precisely. In Fig. 2b, the various tasks are shown only with respect to the documents they need, and not as a control flow. Thus, the *receive order* task can only be performed when an order document is available as an input. Moreover, this task produces three output documents: *payment*, *order items*, and *shipping advice*. While this figure also looks like a control flow, yet, there is a subtle difference in that the ability to perform a task depends on the availability of the input documents required to perform it. Since a document is a resource, we call this a *resource-driven approach*. Also, a task may require other resources such as people, physical space, equipment, etc. It should be noted that one significant difference between Fig. 2a and b is that the former has only an implicit assumption on resource dependencies but the latter makes it explicit.

The resource-driven model can be developed by first conducting an information or data flow analysis as shown in Table 2. This analysis naturally leads to a derivation of the *data dependency constraints* (Sun et al. 2006). Such constraints are called *hard constraints* because they are dictated by the resource needs of various tasks. On the other hand, a second type of constraint is dictated by the business policy of the organization, such as the one shown by dotted lines between *check credit* and *warehouse pickup*, and also between *invoice* and *ship* tasks in Fig. 2b. Such constraints are called *soft constraints*.

Consequently, it is important to make a distinction between these two types of constraints: *hard and soft* (see Table 3). A *hard constraint* between tasks A and B arises when task A produces output that serves as input for task B. Hence, B must wait for A to finish (assuming each task is atomic). This gives rise to a strict data dependency between two tasks. Thus, *credit check* can only be done after an order is received. However, *soft constraints* reflect rules in the form of business policy, as

Table 2 Information flow analysis for tasks in an order process

Task	Input data	Output data
Receive order	Order information Payment information (i.e., name, customer ID, credit card) Order items (SKUs, unit price, quantity) Shipping information (i.e., Fedex)	The order information in the input document is split into three output documents: Payment, Order items, and Shipping advice
Check credit	Payment	Approved or rejected
Warehouse pickup	Order items	Package list
Invoice	Payment, Package list, and Shipping advice	Invoice
Ship	Package list; Shipping advice	Proof of shipment

Table 3 Scenarios to illustrate hard and soft constraints between two tasks, A and B

Constraint type	Description	Example (see Fig. 2b)
Hard	Output of Task A is input for Task B	The check credit step can only be done after the order is received
Soft constraint 1	There is a guard condition for Task B	check_credit. status == "done"
Soft constraint 2	There is a guard condition for Task B	invoice.status == "done"

opposed to a strict data dependency. So the control flow of a process (see Fig. 2a) may have a *check_credit* step to be followed by *warehouse pickup* and *invoice* (if *check_credit* succeeds). However, the *warehouse pickup* does not require any input data from the output of the *check_credit* step. Such a business rule can be expressed by a *guard constraint* of the form: *check_credit.status == "done"*, for the *warehouse pickup* step. This constraint states that the credit must be approved before *warehouse pickup* can start (even though warehouse pickup does not require any *specific* input data from the *credit check*). It is shown in Fig. 2b as *soft constraint 1*. Similarly, the control flow in Fig. 2a shows that the *invoice* step is followed by the *ship* step. Yet, this again is just a business rule because normally the *ship* step does not need any input from the *invoice* step. This is also represented by a guard constraint of the form: *Invoice.status == "done"*, for the *ship* step. Perhaps, the rationale for this constraint might be a company policy that goods cannot leave the company unless the invoice is prepared. It is shown in Fig. 2b as *soft constraint 2*.

As discussed above, documents that contain data are a resource. Similarly, there are other resources also. One can store resources and availabilities in a database. For doing so, the following data/characteristics should be stored for each type of resource.

- *Document* (doc_id, description, availability)
- *Human* (role_id, person_id, time_period_id, availability)
- *Space* (type, location_id, description, capacity, time_period_id, availability)
- *Equipment* (type, equip_id, description, location_id, time_slot_id, availability)

The document resource describes a doc_id, description and availability (yes/no) at the current time. For a human resource, each tuple contains a role, an id of a person that fills the role, and time periods and availability during those time periods. In the case of a space resource, we store the type of resource (conference room, office, lecture room, etc.) and its unique location id, along with attributes such as capacity, and availability during various time periods. For an equipment resource, the schema contains an equipment type and unique id along with attributes like description, location, and availability information. A workflow process consists of tasks. Each task is associated with the resources as follows:

Task(task_id, task name, doc_id, role_id/person_id, location_id, equip_id)

At runtime, a process is instantiated and tasks that are ready to run can be started. The database can be queried to determine if the resources required for a task are available. Thus, if the Warehouse Pickup task needs a Warehouse clerk, then a query on the *Human* resource table can determine if an individual in this role is available before this task can be performed. Similarly, the *Space* and *Equipment* tables can also be queried. As availability of resources changes, the data in these tables is updated dynamically. Incidentally, the assignment of human resources to tasks can be done either in *pull mode* where tasks are offered to individuals and they choose tasks they would like to perform, or *push mode* where tasks are automatically assigned to persons who are qualified for them.

In the next subsection, we will give a resource taxonomy and discuss the difference between instance level and process level resources.

2.2 Resource Taxonomy

It should be noted that the resources shown in Table 1 have different features. For example, data resources, such as marketing report and design specification, are tightly related to the process instance (or case), and are meaningful only in the context of a specific case because information in these data resources varies from case to case. On the contrary, human resources, such as engineer and manager, may be shared by many cases of a process and can also exist independently of any cases.

In general, resources used in workflow systems can be classified into two classes: (a) instance-level and (b) process-level (see Fig. 3). A document is an *instance-level resource* because it is specific to a case. On the other hand, a human role or

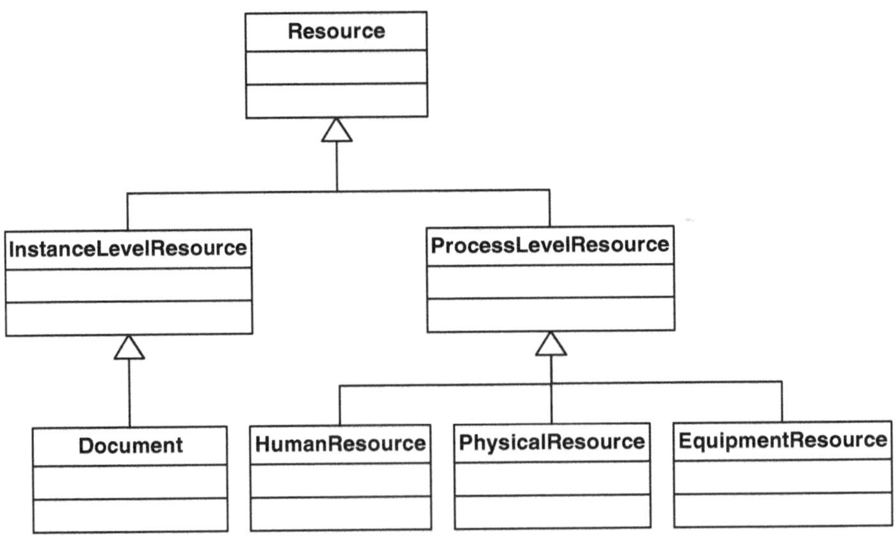

Fig. 3 A resource taxonomy

equipment is a *process-level (or organizational) resource* since it belongs to the organization and may apply to a variety of instances. A document or data resource triggers a *workitem*, which is an instance of a task that pertains to a specific case. A document is also updated by the case. Thus, a document resource is always "owned" by a case. A process-level resource is not owned by any case. Instead, it enables a workitem to become an activity that is ready for execution. The reason for making this distinction is that these two types of resources are very different. Process level or organizational resources are physical in nature and have implications for scheduling (a human can only do one task at a time), utilization, substitution, etc. There are also business policy considerations like separation of duties, i.e., the same person may not be allowed to perform two tasks in the same process (such as submit a purchase order and approve the purchase). On the other hand, an instance level resource like a document is nonphysical, and there are implications in terms of its ownership, privacy, sharing rules, etc.

This distinction between the two main classes of resources is reflected in the prototype design for a resource-driven workflow system discussed in Sect. 4.

3 Proposed Approach for Designing Resource-Driven Workflows

3.1 Task Analysis

As discussed above, the proposed resource-driven approach differs from the control flow-based approach, in that it relies upon understanding the prerequisite resources for each task. The underlying premise here is that by focusing on the requirements for each task, the process flow will emerge organically rather than being predetermined. The resource-driven approach can be modeled as shown in Table 4. This table can be normalized for storing in a database. Here, along with each task, we show the input document it requires, the output document produced by it, the human resource and role that performs the task, the input constraints that must be satisfied (guard-in), and the output conditions produced by the task (guard-out). Thus, row 2 shows that the *check credit* task is performed by the system automatically. The input for it is the payment information document and the output is the approval number (if credit is approved). The *guard-out* condition is: "*credit* == *pass*" or "*credit* == *fail*". The *guard-in* condition is essentially a soft constraint discussed in Sect. 2, while the *guard-out* condition acts as an integrity check on the output of a task. This example shows us that in this way it is possible to associate optional *entry* and *exit* constraints for each task based on resource dependencies. Additional columns can be added to the schema of Table 4 to capture needs for other resources. Once a *Schema* table like Table 4 is constructed, then a standard database engine can drive the process flow by running simple SQL queries that find the next task that is ready to run.

Table 4 Schema table to describe the order processing workflow

	Data resource		Human resource	Conditions (optional)	
Task	In_doc	Out_doc	Role	Guard-in	Guard-out
Receive order	Order		Order clerk		
Check credit	Payment	Approval number	System task		credit == "fail" credit == "pass"
Warehouse pickup	Order items	Package list	Warehouse clerk		
Ship	Package list Shipping advice	Shipping confirmation	Shipping assistant		
Invoice	Package list Shipping confirmation Payment	Invoice	Accounts officer	Ship. status == "done"; Credit == "pass"	
Close order	Invoice	Close confirmation	Accounts	Invoice. status == "done"	
Cancel order	Invoice	Cancel confirmation	Accounts	Credit == "fail"	

The query will basically return the task(s) for which resources are available. If multiple tasks are enabled, they may be executed simultaneously (or in parallel). Thus, the *parallel* control flow construct of a workflow system is automatically simulated. On the other hand, parallel execution of two enabled tasks can also be prevented by adding a soft constraint as in the example of Fig. 2b. Thus, the entry constraints are applied to these tasks (through guard-in) to determine which task(s) can be executed. Other related SQL queries can be written to find:

- Whether an individual is available in the role required to perform a task?
- What tasks can a role perform?

In general, additional tables would be added to this schema to define mappings between users and their roles (e.g., Jill is a vice-president, Joe is a manager), between teams and their members (e.g., a design review committee consists of a manager and three engineers), etc. The schemas for some of these tables are:

- *Role* (id, role, user_name)
- *Team* (id, name, member_role)

Hence, it is possible to assign a task to a team (van der Aalst and Kumar 2001) as well, although Table 4 only shows individual roles.

3.2 Data Dependencies

This section discusses at length the dependency analysis of one important resource type namely information or data. As noted above, if the input of task B is contained in the output of task A, then task B cannot start before task A finishes. This is the

Table 5 Possible data relationships between two tasks

Type	Relation	Description
1	$D_{IA} \cap D_{IB} = \varphi$	Task A and Task B have no common input data
2	$D_{IA} \cap D_{IB} \neq \varphi$	Task A and Task B have common input data
3	$D_{IA} \supseteq D_{IB}$	Task B uses no more input data than Task A
4	$D_{OA} \cap D_{OB} = \varphi$	Task A and Task B have no common output data
5	$D_{OA} \cap D_{OB} \neq \varphi$	Task A and Task B have common output data
6	$D_{OA} \subseteq D_{OB}$	Task A produces no more output data than Task B
7	$D_{OA} \cap D_{IB} = \varphi$	Task B does not use Task A's output
8	$D_{OA} \cap D_{IB} \neq \varphi$	Task B uses Task A's (partial) output as input
9	$D_{OA} \supseteq D_{IB}$	Task B only uses Task A's output data

most important kind of data dependency. However, there are other data dependencies as well that are more subtle and should be analyzed. Consequently, in this section, we discuss data dependencies in more detail since they play a crucial role in our framework.

We have identified nine types of data relationships between two tasks, say Task A and Task B, as shown in Table 5. D_{IA} and D_{IB} (D_{OA} and D_{OB}) are inputs (outputs) of tasks A and B, respectively. Type 1 and 2 dependencies are straightforward. Moreover, type 3 is a special case of type 2, while type 6 is a special case of type 5, and type 9 is a special case of type 8. Type 2 and 3 dependencies prevent two tasks from executing concurrently because they compete for the same input data. Types 5 and 6 indicate that only one of these tasks will be executed because their outputs overlap and cannot be written concurrently. Types 8 and 9 impose a sequential constraint on the two tasks because one needs the other's output to start. Furthermore, a combination of these relationships can decide the execution order of two tasks. For example, a combination of types 1 and 7 means two tasks can be executed simultaneously; a combination of types 4 and 9 defines a sequential ordering between two tasks, etc.

It is important to realize that dynamic changes made to a workflow process routing in order to handle exceptions may produce violations in the above data dependencies. The dependency analysis in Table 5 can also be used to improve the design of a process by determining suitable task boundaries. Intuitively, if a task (or activity) uses multiple input resources to produce multiple output resources, then it may suggest it can be divided into two separate tasks (see Fig. 4). On the other hand, if two tasks have a sharing dependency on the input side and a fit dependency on the output side (see Fig. 5), then we may consider combining them into one task. Detailed discussion of an algorithm to determine suitable boundaries is beyond the scope of this chapter. Further discussion of data dependencies appears in Sun et al. (2006) and Wang and Kumar (2005).

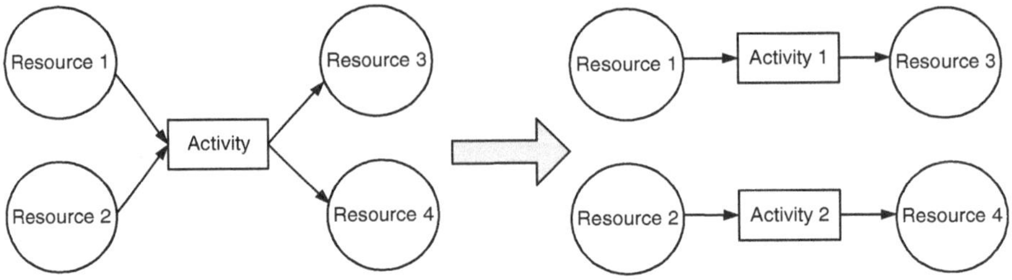

Fig. 4 Split a task based on the dependency analysis

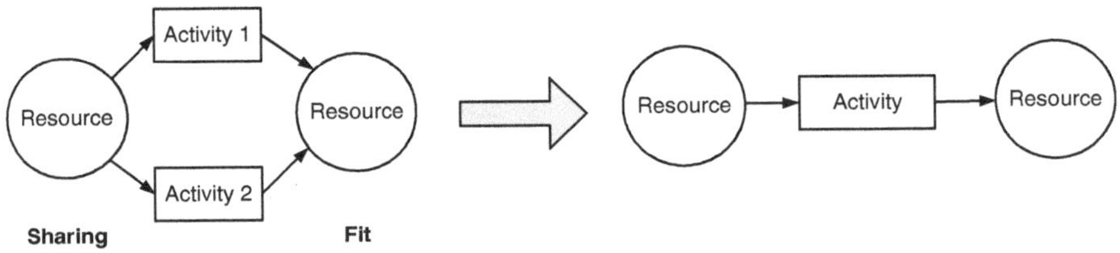

Fig. 5 Combine tasks based on the dependency analysis

In summary, the general procedure for creating and running resource-driven workflows is as follows:

- Create a database schema that describes the resource requirements for each task in a workflow.
- Create a schema for each resource to describe the resource and the availability of the resource.
- Run database queries to identify tasks for which all resources are available.
- Perform data dependency analysis and check if guard-in constraints are satisfied.
- Identify a subset of tasks that are executable.
- Execute the subset of tasks; check if guard-out constraints are satisfied; and update the database.
- Identify a new subset of executable tasks and execute it.
- When all the tasks are executed for the process or its exit conditions are satisfied, the workflow is completed.

More details about architecture and implementation are discussed in the next section. In particular, we shall describe a layered architecture and illustrate how it can be implemented in a database system.

4 A General Architecture for a Resource-Driven Workflow

We propose a four-layer architecture for modeling resource-driven workflow systems as shown in Fig. 6. The four layers are *schema*, *runtime*, *scheduling*, and *application layer*. The *schema layer* defines workflow processes, which consist of

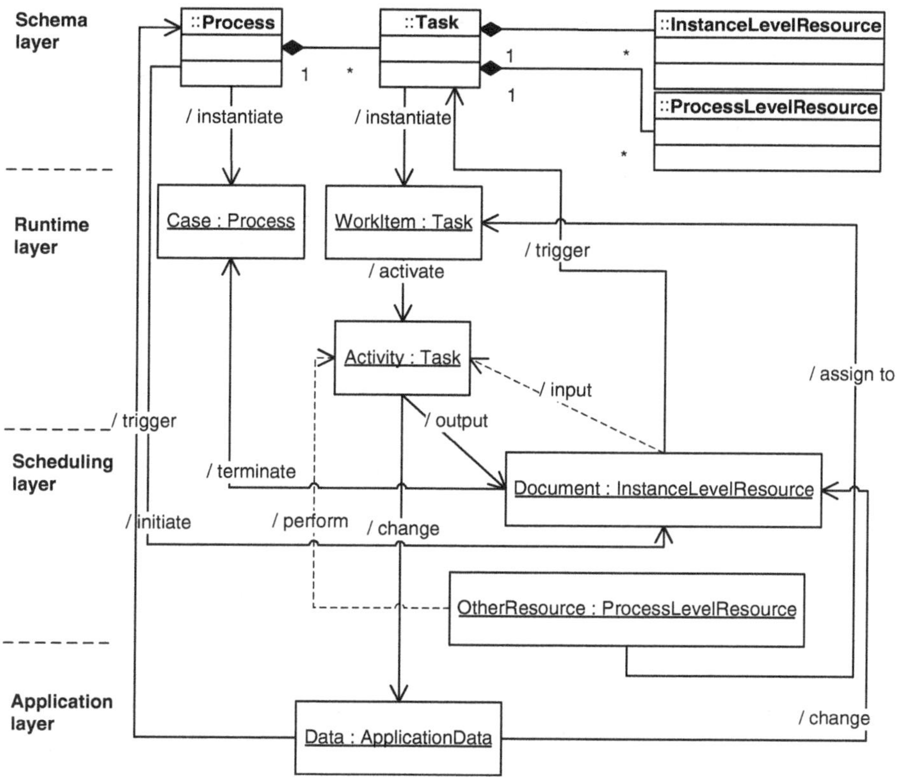

Fig. 6 A resource-driven workflow architecture

tasks, instance-level resources and process-level resources. The *runtime layer* specifies how processes and tasks are started and ended. The *scheduling layer* manages assignment of resources to a task so that they can be executed. This may entail use of suitable assignment algorithms that are outside the scope of the current paper. The *application layer* provides links between the workflow system and the applications. It defines how application data can be linked to the corresponding resources. Since there is a clear separation between workflow data and application data, the details of the application data are not important here in the context of the workflow architecture.

The significant differences between resource-driven workflow systems and conventional control flow-based workflow systems lie in the runtime and the application layers. In *resource-driven workflow systems*, a process is instantiated into a case when certain instance-level resources (i.e. documents) arrive. In Fig. 6, drawn in UML syntax with classes and associations, *Process* and *Task* are top-level classes, and *case* and *workitems* are their subclasses, respectively. A set of initial documents of the process instance (or *case*) are created as instances of the instance-level resources. Other resources are instantiated similarly from the *Process Level Resource* class. A *task* is instantiated into a *workitem* when its input documents exist. The input documents required by one task are usually the output documents from a previous task, except the initial documents for the first task, which are generated by the process repository when the process is instantiated. After a work-item gets its input documents and associated resources (at the scheduling layer), it becomes an *activity* that can be executed. An activity potentially changes the values in its input documents or produces new documents, thus making next tasks ready to run. The dotted lines in Fig. 6 show that an activity uses input document data and needs other resources to perform a task. A case terminates when documents satisfying its exit conditions are produced.

4.1 A Prototype for a Resource-Driven Workflow System

We have implemented an initial prototype system using Transact-SQL on a Microsoft SQL Server 2000. Triggers are used to enact the workflow system. The framework presented in Fig. 6 is mapped into a DBMS using the execution architecture described in Fig. 7. It shows that when a database table is changed (through an insert, update, or delete operation), a corresponding trigger is fired.

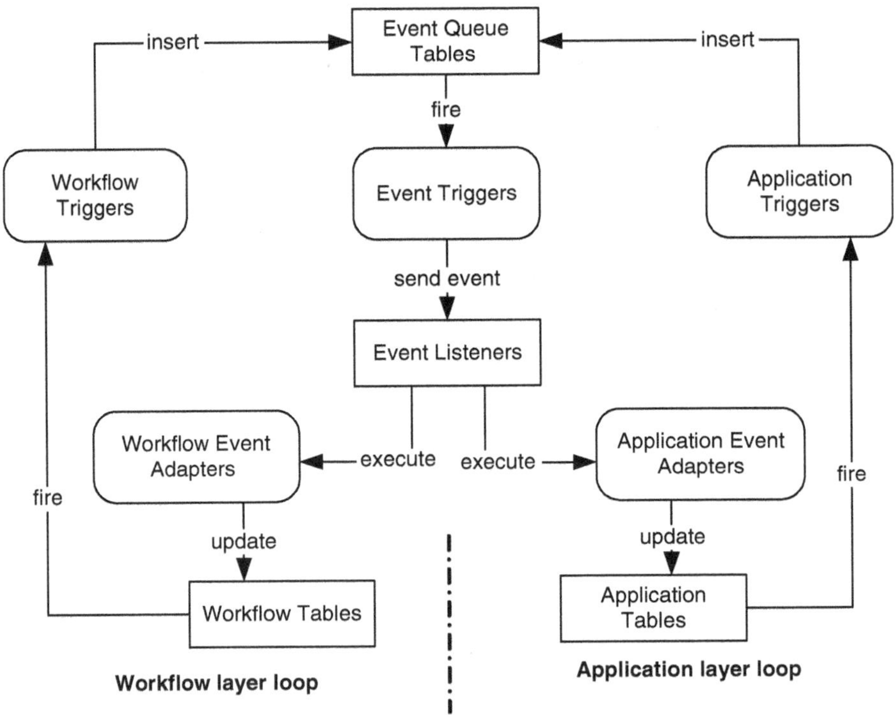

Fig. 7 Execution architecture for a resource-driven workflow system

This trigger generates appropriate events and puts them into the event queue table. Then the trigger associated with the event queue table sends new event messages to event listeners and the listeners execute all the event adapters who registered for these events. Finally, the event adapters update the associated tables and start the next iteration. The architecture shown in Fig. 7 consists of two loops: *workflow layer loop* and *application layer loop*. The workflow layer loop updates the workflow tables (through Workflow Event Adapters) and the application layer loop updates the application table (through Application Event Adapters). An event adapter propagates information about an event to the appropriate database tables. There are two types of triggers shown in Fig. 7, the system triggers (i.e., workflow and event triggers) and application triggers. Note that Figs. 6 and 7 offer two different perspectives, and the layers in the high level design architecture of Fig. 6 map only approximately into the execution architecture of Fig. 7. The top two layers in Fig. 6 are captured in the workflow and application tables in Fig. 7. The scheduling and application layers in Fig. 6 are incorporated into the workflow and application event adapters, respectively, in Fig. 7.

Another advantage of implementing a workflow system inside a database is that transaction management features, such as concurrency control and crash recovery, are already built into most database systems. In the next section, we show how exceptions are handled in a resource-driven workflow system using these features of the underlying database.

4.2 Handling Exceptions by Task Deferral

We show here how resource-driven workflows facilitate easier handling of exceptions. The main idea is that when a task throws an exception, it may be skipped or deferred. To skip a task, one can simply remove it from the list of required tasks and make sure that no other task depends on the output from this task. *Task deferral* is more sophisticated because several issues must be considered before deferring a task. First, a task should be deferred only if some alternate task can be started instead of it. If the output of the task is required by all the succeeding tasks, it cannot be deferred without redefining the subsequent tasks. Second, deferring a task changes the workflow execution path, which may cause complex process changes and even lead to an invalid process. Third, deferring a task increases compensation cost if the delayed task eventually fails.

Task deferral is achieved by relaxing soft constraints. Thus, we may relax soft constraint 1 of Fig. 2b if, say, the credit approval system is temporarily down, or soft constraint 2 if the invoicing system is unavailable. In such cases, an exception may be thrown, perhaps when a deadline for a task completion expires and a timeout occurs. Figure 8 gives a proposed algorithm for handling a task deferral. In this algorithm, the states of a task are: *ready (to run)*, *running*, *deferred* and, *finished*. A task (or workitem) is ready to run when all its input resources are available, and it becomes an activity at this point. When a task throws an exception,

```
1: Capture exception (by a timeout)
2: Find the task to be deferred
3: Assign a temporary result to the deferred task
4: Repeat{
5: Get remaining ready tasks
6: Add to promoted queue
7: Select a task to run
8: Run selected task with temporary result from deferred task
9: if (deferred task has finished)
     if (temporary result == actual result)
      {exit and resume normal processing}
    else
      {roll back promoted tasks}
          } until (no task is ready)
10: At end if deferred task is still running, then abort.
```

Fig. 8 Procedure for task deferral to handle exceptions

the workflow runtime environment first captures the exception (step 1), identifies the task to be deferred (step 2), and assigns a temporary value to its result such as "done"/"fail" or "true"/"false" (step 3). The temporary values may be assigned based on rules or past frequencies. Then, it identifies those that can be executed without completion of the deferred task (step 5) based on the temporary value assigned in step 3. This is done by searching all the tasks for which the input resources are already available. These tasks are called *promotable*, and in step 6, they are added to the *Promoted Queue*. Then in step 7, the workflow runtime environment performs a dependency analysis on the set P of promotable tasks and finds the one that does not depend upon any other task in P. This task is executed in step 8. Upon completion of this task, the workflow system will look for the next task to be executed based on the new state of documents. The deferred task may either have finished or it may still be running (step 9). If the deferred task is still running, steps 4 through 9 are repeated to find yet another promotable task. On the other hand, if the deferred task has finished, then the normal processing can resume. However, we need to compare the temporary result assigned to the deferred task (in step 3) with the actual result. If they are different, then the promoted tasks must be rolled back. The schema should specify whether a task can be rolled back. Finally, if a deferred task is still running at the end of the process or after a maximum time limit, then it must be aborted and the entire process is rolled back. Roll back can be done quite easily by treating the entire process as a transaction, and then the promoted tasks as a subtransaction within the outer transaction. Then it is possible to use the SQL Rollback statement with appropriate parameters to rescind all changes of the current transaction.

The above procedure can be easily implemented when there is a soft constraint between a deferred task and its successor. By assuming a temporary output from the deferred task, the workflow instance can proceed. The temporary output can be included as part of the workflow schema. Obviously, this is only possible for planned exceptions. In the case of unplanned exceptions, this approach would require that a

Table 6 Handling of hard and soft constraints between two tasks, A and B

Constraint type	Description	Example (see Fig. 2b)	Handling
Hard	Output of Task A is input for Task B	Check credit can only be done after order is received	Task B can start only after Task A is finished
Soft constraint 1	Guard condition for Task B	check_credit. status == "done"	Relax constraint and start Task B. Later, check actual status value

temporary value be provided by the user for the output of the deferred task. The major advantage of using temporary outputs for deferred tasks lies in the simplicity of the approach. It does not violate the dependencies, so the correctness is guaranteed. However, it may cause extra compensation cost if the actual output of the deferred task cannot be easily predicted. Therefore, this approach is suitable only when the output of the deferred task can be predicted with a high probability, e.g., an assumption that most credit card transactions are approved.

Table 6 summarizes the main scenarios for our approach. By relaxing certain soft constraints that serve as guard conditions for a task, it is possible to proceed past the delayed or deferred task temporarily. However, this does not mean that we are skipping this task altogether. As noted above, before the instance is completed, a check must be made to ensure that the task did finish, and the actual result was indeed the same as the one presumed; else, the subsequent tasks are rolled back. Finally, if the deferred task is still running when all other tasks have finished or after a certain time limit, then it is aborted and the other tasks are rolled back.

5 A Comparison of Two Approaches

A summary comparison between the resource-driven and control flow-driven approaches is given in Table 7. Flexibility is an important issue in a workflow management system. Different methods, such as structured processes (Kiepuszewski et al. 2000), workflow patterns (van der Aalst et al. 2003), and Petri-Nets (van der Aalst 1998), offer varying degrees of flexibility. These techniques are based on a control flow described using modeling constructs like splits, forks, joins, and other complex flow structures. On the one hand, some structures like forks enhance parallelism and thus flexibility. But, on the other hand, a predefined control flow also restricts flexibility by forcing a certain ordering of tasks. The resource-driven design can dynamically discover the process flow simply based on the resource dependencies. Thus, if a task generates multiple documents, a subsequent task that needs only the first one can proceed without waiting for the task to finish. Such situations of *partial dependencies* are quite common, and one can increase throughput by exploiting them. In fact, in a real-time workflow, the need for an input document may also be deferred in some situations to meet deadlines by presuming temporary default data values from it as explained in the previous section. This can

Table 7 Comparison between resource-driven workflow and control flow-based workflow

Resource-driven workflow	Control flow driven workflow
The process is driven by the resources	Process is driven by the predefined control flow
The process is very flexible and can be changed instantly by changing constraints	The process is less flexible because the limitations imposed by flow patterns are hard to change
More suited for ad hoc workflows	Better for production workflows with mature processes
Clear separation of hard/soft constraints	No such separation
Exceptions are easier to handle	Exceptions are not so easy to handle
Verification is relatively easy	Verification could be hard
More scalable as part of a DB system	Less scalable; workflow systems are usually small
Interoperability is easier because resource information is in standard SQL database	Interoperability is harder because different workflow systems use different representations
Difficult to visualize the process	Process can be visualized easily

be done easily by relaxing soft constraints (or business rules) and is much harder to do in a control flow-driven approach where it is difficult to distinguish between soft and hard constraints. This added flexibility makes the resource-driven approach especially suitable for *ad hoc* workflows. Lack of flexibility can hinder effective use of workflow systems because actual work practices often differ from predesigned processes and exceptions also arise. This may require changing the order in which certain tasks are done. Our approach can handle such operations relatively easily.

Our approach also relies on the use of database triggers. The use of triggers in workflow system has been discussed in the WIDE project (Grefen et al. 1999) as a way to capture events and handle exceptions in addition to the normal workflow, which is designed as a control flow. However, our study takes this approach one step further by using triggers as mechanisms to drive and enact the workflow system, thus obviating the need for a "workflow engine" module. As a result, the workflow system can be implemented entirely inside the database and is more scalable because database systems can handle thousands of transactions per second.

A user does not have to worry about the control flow design, and verification is also easier in our approach. In a control flow-driven workflow system, the structure of the control flow must be checked to ensure there are no deadlocks, live-locks, or other problems. In a resource-driven workflow, it is only necessary to analyze resource flows between tasks and ensure that each task will obtain its input resources. Such a workflow is also more scalable because database systems can handle thousands of transactions per second, whereas most workflow systems have throughput rates that are much slower. Moreover, resource-driven workflows can interoperate with one another more easily if they use common database schemas. In the case of control driven workflows, this is harder because there is no accepted standard yet for describing control flows. By far, the biggest disadvantage with our approach is that it is harder to visualize the process graphically. In a control flow based-workflow, this is much easier because the control flow is always depicted visually, and it shows the temporal relationships between various tasks. Of course, one could use the information in a resource-driven workflow description and convert it into a control flow, but algorithms for doing so are not discussed here.

6 Discussion

The main idea behind our proposal is that a *process* is driven by *resources* such as data, human or system roles, physical space, and equipment rather than an explicit, predefined *control flow*. A *task* is instantiated into a *workitem* when its input documents exist *and* any associated *guard* constraints are satisfied. After a workitem gets its input documents and other associated *resources* (at the scheduling layer), it becomes an *activity* that can be executed. An activity produces new documents and changes the database, which triggers the next task. The process completes when all tasks are executed. Moreover, soft constraints that reflect business policy can be added separately through guard conditions. This means that when business policy changes, only the soft constraints are modified without a need to change a control flow diagram. Constraints have been studied extensively in many database systems and they are usually represented as ECA (Event-Condition-Action) rules (McCarthy and Dayal 1989). A key aspect of our approach is that it can be executed inside a database, i.e., the database system becomes a workflow engine. Since databases are very fast and more scalable than workflow systems, they can handle larger numbers of workflow instances than workflow engines, thus leading to better performance.

Control flow-driven workflows are based on basic patterns such as sequence, choice, parallel, and loop and advanced patterns such as multichoice, interleaved parallel, etc. However, all workflow products do not support all the patterns and this can affect interoperability. In the resource-driven approach, the patterns are not specified explicitly; rather they arise as a result of resource dependencies. Thus, if there is an input–output dependency between two tasks, they are in sequence. If the guard-in conditions of two tasks are in conflict, then they are in choice, and if two tasks have mutually exclusive guard-in conditions and no data dependency between them, then they are run in parallel. A loop involving one or more tasks is created by changing the status of a running task in a workflow instance from "done" to "undone". This would force the tasks to be rerun as in a loop. Advanced patterns can also be simulated by using the guard conditions and locking features of a database. Guard-in conditions can help to select a subset of tasks to execute from a larger set that is potentially executable. A task, while running, may optionally lock a document if it needs exclusive access. If a document is locked by a task, then it must be unlocked before another parallel task can access it, thus creating the effect of interleaved parallel routing.

There are several current approaches based on the control flow perspective of workflow. Examples are Petri-nets (van der Aalst 1998), XPDL (Workflow Management Coalition 2010), BPEL (OASIS 2010), BPMN (Object Management Group), etc. These approaches are quite expressive for modeling the control flow, but they do not model resources very well. On the other hand, among approaches that focus on resources, the WIDE project (Grefen et al. 1999) and ADOME-WFMS (Chiu et al. 2001) use ECA rules in RDBMS and OODBMS respectively, which do not explicitly model the control flow. ADEPT takes a more comprehensive approach, which includes both data flow and control flow, and is promising for solving most dynamic change problems (Rinderle et al. 2004). There are other proposals such as Placeless documents project (Dourish et al. 2000), which adds action code into documents, so the coordination can be done within the documents and no explicit workflow system is required. An approach for entity-centric process models is described in Bhattacharya et al. (2007). In this approach, the main organizing principle for creating processes is entities, which can be treated as a kind of a resource. In the EPC (Scheer et al. 2005) approach, each activity has input events that trigger it and output events that it produces, which in turn trigger other activities. This approach has some similarity to our proposal; however, EPC diagrams are essentially control flow diagrams. In a broader sense, it is also noteworthy that despite a plethora of approaches for modeling workflows, there is as yet no established standard that is used widely and can serve as a means to exchange workflow schemas between organizations.

Research on exception handling in workflows is still quite limited. Some work on exceptions in workflows is discussed in Curbera et al. (2003), Hwang and Tang (2004), Klein and Dellarocas (2000), and Luo et al. (2000). A different perspective for handling exceptions based on deadlines is presented in van der Aalst et al. (2007). WIDE manages exceptions by first activating a local, process-specific exception handler, and then allowing propagation of the exception to the parent process. ADOME-WFMS uses Problem Solver Agent (PSA) to handle exceptions.

Another kind of exception can be handled through resource delegation. Thus, if a resource is not available to perform a task that has a tight deadline, then a substitute can be found. For a human resource, a subordinate or a superior substitute may be assigned. Similarly, for space and equipment resources, substitutes may be kept in the database and assigned in order to expedite a task if the desired resources are not available. We do not go into details here, but there is related work on delegation in the literature (Wainer et al. 2007).

7 Conclusions

This chapter provided a general framework for the design and implementation of resource-driven workflows in contrast to conventional control flow-driven workflows. In a resource-driven workflow, resources serve as an organizing principle. The tasks in a process are executed in the correct order based on the availability of *resources* such as data documents, human or system roles, physical space, and equipment rather than an explicit, predefined *control flow*. We argue that when multiple, dynamic, and possibly conflicting resources are involved, it is not possible to predesign a business process based on the control flow alone; rather it emerges from the interaction of resources that are a prerequisite for each task in the process. We showed how resource-driven workflows are especially promising for ad hoc workflow environments, and can be implemented within a database system, thus obviating the need for a workflow engine. A distinction was also made between hard constraints that depend on data dependencies and resource availability, and soft constraints that are determined by business rules. This distinction leads to a systematic way of designing business processes, and also enables relaxation of soft constraints to handle exceptions. Handling exceptions within a database becomes easier because most database systems provide rollback capability.

There are several avenues for more work in this area. First, there is a need for a language to describe resource-driven workflows. Second, the types of resources to be modeled, and the level of detail at which each resource is modeled, should be investigated further. Naturally, there is a tradeoff here between modeling complexity and the value gained from the model, and it should be explored further. Third, algorithms for converting resource-driven workflows into an equivalent control flow for visualization purposes should be developed. Finally, more detailed quantitative comparisons between the resource-based and control flow-based approaches, perhaps through simulations, would also be helpful.

References

Bhattacharya K et al. (2007) Towards formal analysis of artifact-centric business process models. Proceedings of business process management, 5th international conference (BPM 2007), Brisbane, Australia, pp 288–304

Botha RA, Eloff JHP (2001) Access control in document-centric workflow systems-an agent-based approach. Comput Secur 20(6):525–532

Chiu DKW, Li Q, Karlapalem K (2001) Web interface-driven cooperative exception handling in ADOME workflow management system. Web Inf Syst Eng 26(2):93–120

Collis DJ, Montgomery CA (1995) Competing on resources: strategy in the, 1990's. Harv Bus Rev 73:118–128

Curbera F et al. (2003) Exception handling in the BPEL4WS language. In: van der Aalst W, ter Hofstede A, Weske M (eds) BPM 2003. LNCS, vol 2678, pp 276–290

Dourish P et al. (2000) Extending document management systems with user-specific active properties. ACM Trans Inf Syst 18(2):140–170

Dumas M, van der Aalst WMP, ter Hofstede AHM (2005) Process aware information systems. Wiley, Hoboken, NJ, USA

Grefen P et al. (1999) Database support for workflow management – the wide project. Kluwer Academic Publishers, Norwell, MA

Hwang S-Y, Tang J (2004) Consulting past exceptions to facilitate workflow exception handling. Decis Support Syst 37(1):49–69

Kiepuszewski B, Hofstede AHM, Bussler C (2000) On structured workflow modeling. In: Proceedings CAiSE'2000. LNCS, vol 1797. Springer

Klein M, Dellarocas C (2000) A knowledge-based approach to handling exceptions in workflow systems. Comput Support Coop Work 9:399–412

Krishnan R, Munaga L, Karlapalem K (2002) XDoC-WFMS: a framework for document centric workflow management system. Lect Notes Comput Sci 2465:348–362

LaMarca A et al. (1999) Taking the work out of workflow: mechanisms for document-centered collaboration, ECSCW'99, pp 1–20

Luo Z et al. (2000) Exception handling in workflow systems, Applied Intelligence: the International Journal of AI. Neural Netw 13(2):125–147

Malone TW, Crowston K (1994) The interdisciplinary study of coordination. ACM Comput Surv 26(1):87–119

Mazumdar S, AbuSafiya M (2004) A document-centric approach to business process management. In: Proceedings of the international conference on information and knowledge engineering, pp 461–466

McCarthy DR, Dayal U (1989) The architecture of an active database system. In: Proceedings ACM SIGMOD conference on management of data, Portland, pp 215–224

Microsoft Corporation (2000) SQL Server books online: transact-SQL reference

OASIS (2010) Web Services Business Process Execution Language (WSBPEL). http://www.oasis- open.org

Object Management Group (OMG). Business process management notation. http://www.bpmn.org/

Ouyang C, Adams M, Wynn MT, ter Hofstede AHM (2010) Workflow management, In: vom Brocke J, Rosemann M (eds) Handbook on business process management, vol 1. Springer, Heidelberg

Rinderle S, Reichert M, Dadam P (2004) Correctness criteria for dynamic changes in workflow systems – a survey. IEEE Trans Knowl Data Eng 50(1):9–34

Scheer AW (1998) ARIS – business process frameworks, 2nd edn. Springer, Berlin

Scheer AW, Thomas O, Adam O (2005) Process modeling using event-driven process chains. In: Dumas M et al. (eds) Process aware information systems. Wiley, Chichester

Sun SX et al. (2006) Formulating the data-flow perspective for business process management. Inform Syst Res 17(4):374–391

van der Aalst WMP (1998) The application of Petri nets to workflow management. J Circ Syst Comput 8(1):21–66

van der Aalst WMP, Kumar A (2001) A reference model for team-enabled workflow management systems. IEEE Trans Knowl Data Eng 38:335–363

van der Aalst WMP et al. (2003) Workflow patterns. Distrib Parallel Databases 14(1):5–51

van der Aalst WM, Rosemann M, Dumas M (2007) Deadline-based escalation in process-aware information systems. Decis Support Syst 43(2):492–511

Wainer J, Kumar A, Barthelmess P (2007) DW-RBAC: a formal security model of delegation and revocation in workflow systems. Inf Syst 32(3):365–384

Wang J, Kumar A (2005) A framework for document-driven workflow systems. In: van der Aalst WMP et al. (eds) BPM 2005. LNCS, vol 3649, pp 285–301

Workflow Management Coalition (2010) (WFMC), XML Processing Description Language (XPDL). http://www.wfmc.org

Service-Enabled Process Management

Marlon Dumas and Thomas Kohlborn

Abstract This chapter discusses some relationships between service-oriented architecture and Business Process Management. In particular, the chapter presents a method for analyzing a business process to enable its execution on top of a service-oriented application landscape, thereby leading to the notion of service-enabled business process. The chapter also provides an overview of contemporary technology standards for implementing service-enabled processes.

1 Introduction

Service-Oriented Architecture (SOA) is a paradigm for structuring information and software systems based on capabilities that parts of a system provide to other parts. Compared to components, services have typically a higher level of abstraction as well as a different underlying philosophy, especially regarding the respective delivery mechanism (Elfatatry 2007). A widely used definition of SOA is provided by the Organization for the Advancement of Structured Information Standards (OASIS) in its SOA Reference Model (OASIS 2006):

> SOA is a paradigm for organising and utilising distributed capabilities that may be under the control of different ownership domains.

In this definition, the notion of capability refers to both capabilities that the business provides as well as capabilities provided by specific application systems. In this respect, this definition advocates the view that service-orientation is relevant both at a business level and at a technical level. In other words, SOA is meant to provide common abstractions and principles for structuring systems uniformly from

M. Dumas (✉)
Institute of Computer Science, University of Tartu, Tartu, Estonia
e-mail: marlon.dumas@ut.ee

J. vom Brocke and M. Rosemann (eds.), *Handbook on Business Process Management 1*, International Handbooks on Information Systems,
DOI 10.1007/978-3-642-00416-2_20,

the IT perspective and the business perspective. It is worth noting that the term "service" is above all a business concept. The fact that the term has been turned into an IT concept reflects a desire to close the gap between business and IT and to achieve higher degrees of business – IT alignment.

Another key element of the above definition is the notion of ownership. Services need to be continuously delivered to exist. This entails that the resources encapsulated by a service need to exist at a particular location and need to be maintained and managed by a service provider for the purpose of delivering a capability to one or multiple service consumers. Service providers and consumers operate independently and may be located in different ownership domains. These characteristics lead to a natural fit between Business Process Management (BPM) and SOA as discussed in more detail in the next chapter. Indeed, business processes often need to span multiple functional domains. For example, a typical order-to-cash process involves a customer, a sales department, a finance department and a logistics department. And precisely, SOA aims at structuring systems in a way that eases communication and handovers across such a plurality of domains.

Not surprisingly, SOA is often presented as an enabler of BPM (Brahe 2007). On the one hand, the execution of individual activities in a business process requires certain resources and capabilities. In this respect, services provide an abstraction to bridge activities with underlying resources and capabilities. On the other hand, entire business processes may be exposed as services so that they can be consumed by users or can be plugged into other business processes. In other words, a service may serve as an entry point to a business process (vom Brocke 2007). For example, an invoicing service may offer the capability to lodge an invoice, track its progress, withdraw or amend it, etc. Behind this invoicing service may lay one or multiple business processes. The relation between BPM and SOA is further discussed in the following chapter by Cummins (2010).

One key question when designing services and linking them with business processes is that of service granularity (Haesen et al. 2008). Should services be defined at the level of individual atomic activities (e.g., a service to cenceling invoices)? Or should they be defined at the level of long-running business processes (e.g., an invoicing service, which encapsulates the entire lifecycle of an invoice)? Several considerations need to be taken into account when making such design decisions. In this chapter, we discuss some of these considerations, in the form of a set of service-orientation principles, and we present a method for identifying and delimiting the scope of services in an SOA, with an emphasis on services that are either linked to activities in a business process or that encapsulate entire processes or parts thereof. We will also discuss different viewpoints and languages for modeling service-enabled business processes at different levels of abstraction.

The chapter is organized as follows. First, we provide an overview of some concepts and principles underpinning service-oriented architectures and foundations of service-enabled process management. Next, we introduce a method for identifying services from business process models. We then provide a brief overview of languages for modeling service-enabled processes, and finally we draw conclusions and outline open perspectives.

2 Service-Oriented Architectures

Below, we introduce general concepts of service-oriented architectures and provide modeling principles for service-enabled processes.

2.1 *Service-Oriented Architecture Principles*

Based on the definition of SOA quoted above and in alignment with the World Wide Web Consortium (W3C), we characterize a service as an abstract resource that represents a capability (W3C 2004). For example, a capability may be to "correlate invoices with purchase orders". This capability is offered by a service provider (an accounts payable unit within a financial department) who performs some action(s) on behalf of a service consumer at some time and place, and in doing so, it interacts with the consumer through some channel (Dumas et al. 2001).

Next to services, two other elements are of particular importance in the context of a SOA, namely a service bus and a service repository. The *service bus* is as a medium connecting the service provider and consumer, and consists of a number of technical infrastructure elements (e.g., Web application servers) (Bieberstein et al. 2005; Krafzig et al. 2006). Furthermore, the *service repository* facilitates the discovery of services and provides additional information about services, e.g., constraints and service levels (Krafzig et al. 2006).

According to (OASIS 2006), specific aspects of a SOA must be taken into account when analyzing and designing services for interaction, namely amongst others the visibility and interaction. One has to ensure that the service provider and consumer are able to interact with each other, regardless of whether these provider and consumer entities are humans or applications, for example. For a successful interaction, the service consumer needs to know the type of inputs and outputs of the service and the actions that can be performed against the service as part of the service description (OASIS 2006).

Since the core elements of any SOA are services, they have to be designed properly to leverage the proposed benefits of a SOA (Krafzig et al. 2006; Erl 2007). Five principles are applicable for the identification of services, namely contract orientation, cohesiveness, coupling, reusability and autonomy.

- *Contract orientation*: To allow services to interact with each other and to be invoked by their service consumers, they need to share a formal contract that defines the terms of information exchange and the commitments made by both parties to define a relationship (Legner and Vogel 2007; Erl 2005). The contract encompasses a description of the functional and non-functional characteristics of a service including a description of the exposed operations that can be invoked (O'Sullivan et al. 2002; Krafzig et al. 2006).
- *Cohesiveness*: Cohesiveness typically refers to the concept of grouping operations based on their functional relatedness to perform a certain task (Papazoglou

and van den Heuvel 2006). One indicator for the cohesiveness of operations is the analysis of the underlying business object. High relatedness of the operations regarding one common business object indicates high cohesiveness. If operations within two different services are highly related, one should consider merging the two services.

- *Coupling*: This service principle describes the strength of interdependency between multiple services and service compositions. Services that are not dependent on the other services have a high reusability and maintainability potential. Thus, the coupling between services should be as loose as possible (Gold-Bernstein and Ruh 2004; Legner and Vogel 2007). As the levels of dependency can be minimized by minimizing the number of interactions between two services, one can consider merging two services if the degree of coupling is too strong. In practice, a balance has to be found between the design principles of cohesion and coupling as explicated by Erradi et al. (2007). Coarse-grained interaction might be preferable compared to fine-grained interaction as transactions involving large chunks of data typically result in fewer interactions than transmitting multiple smaller data chunks (Erradi et al. 2007).
- *Reusability*: The principle of reusability has a basic underlying concept as it advocates making the service useful in multiple scenarios. Thus, services should be applicable in different situations and, under unforeseen circumstances, be used by different service consumers (Erl 2007).
- *Autonomy*: Autonomy refers to the level of independence of a service. This means a purely autonomous service has full control over its environment, which results in increased reliability and predictability, since external unpredictable influences are minimized (Erl 2007). Data normalization techniques might be utilized to design the operations in a non-redundant manner (Feuerlicht 2005).

The described design principles are applicable for multiple types of services. In the following, we will describe the different types of services that we distinguish in this chapter.

2.2 Types of Services

Services at the core of any SOA can be classified according to the underlying SOA concept and their distinctive meaning. A fundamental distinction has to be made between business and software services that relate to the SOA concept applicable on the business and technical levels of an organization.

The term *business service* is used to represent the outcome of "chunk of operation" in an organization (Sanz et al. 2006). Since the operations of an organization can be analyzed on different granularity levels, business services can represent these operations on different levels as well. Hereby, the business service can be aligned along the hierarchical structure of a company or they can be based on the actual business capabilities and domains (Bieberstein et al. 2005; Sehmi and

<table>
<tr><td>Service type</td><td colspan="3">Business-related service</td><td colspan="3">Technical-related service</td></tr>
<tr><td>Granularity</td><td>Business process</td><td colspan="2">Task</td><td colspan="2">Entity</td><td>Utility</td></tr>
<tr><td>Composition</td><td colspan="3">Composite service</td><td colspan="3">Elementary service</td></tr>
<tr><td>Interaction</td><td colspan="3">Synchronous (blocking)</td><td colspan="3">Asynchronous (non-blocking)</td></tr>
<tr><td>Exchange patterns</td><td colspan="2">Request/Response</td><td colspan="2">Notific ation (one-way)</td><td colspan="2">Conversational Interaction</td></tr>
<tr><td>State</td><td colspan="3">Stateless</td><td colspan="3">Stateful</td></tr>
<tr><td>Accessibility</td><td colspan="3">Intra-organizational</td><td colspan="3">Inter-organizational</td></tr>
</table>

Fig. 1 Software service typology [adapted from Legner and Vogel (2007)]

Schwegler 2006; Jones 2006). A business service may or may not leverage existing IT infrastructure and is therefore distinguishable from a software service.

A *software service* describes part of an application system, which can be consumed separately by several entities. A software service may enable a business service or it may provide a capability that contributes to delivering a business service, but it may also have a technical (non-business) purpose.

A typology of software services [inspired from Legner and Vogel (2007)] is shown in Fig. 1. This typology includes business-related services and technical services. Business-related services are identified and specified based on business requirements. These requirements may refer to business processes, tasks or business entities (documents, resources, etc.). Technical services on the other hand are business-logic agnostic and include utility services providing generic functions used by other software services.

A service can be elementary (atomic) or it may be composed of other services (composite service). Elementary services can be further classified into task services (logic-driven), entity services (data-driven) and utility services. Composite services in turn can be classified into data-aggregation services and process-driven composite services.

Services may additionally be differentiated according to the style of interaction, to the way of information exchange patterns and to the way state information is managed. The accessibility of a service can be used to classify services based on their intended service consumers. Thus, a service may be exposed to external or to internal service consumers or to both.

In the following, we will provide a short description of the types of services that will be discussed further in the course of this chapter.

- *Utility services* are typically business-logic agnostic as their main objective is to provide reusable, cross-cutting functionalities related to processing data within legacy application environments (e.g., event-logging) (Erl 2007).
- *Entity services* are responsible for the creation and management of business entities (also known as business objects). An entity service typically provides Create-Read-Update-Delete (CRUD) operations over the business objects it

manages and ensures that these operations comply with business rules (Legner and Vogel 2007). In accordance to Krafzig et al. (2006), entity services (or data-centric services) handle persistent data in a similar way to a traditional data access layer of traditional applications. However, "whereas a traditional data access layers manages data for the entire application, a data-centric service deals with one major business entity only" and thus enforces vertical layering of data (Krafzig et al. 2006). Any service that needs access to these data must use the respective entity service.
- *Task services* are directly related to business tasks of a process. They are modeled for specific processes to meet immediate requirements of the organization and therefore contain specific business logic (Erl 2005). Task services encompass business rules and functionality that can be provided centrally in a consistent manner throughout the organization, whereas traditionally, this information has been encapsulated in libraries and business frameworks (Krafzig et al. 2006).
- *Composite services* can act as the parent controller of a number of entity, task and utility services. Thus, they invoke their operations based on the process logic which they encapsulate (Erl 2005). Composite services control and maintain the state of the process for their clients and thus are stateful to a certain extent (Krafzig et al. 2006). As mentioned earlier, composite services include data aggregation services and process-driven services. In this chapter, we focus on process-driven composite services. Such services are typically implemented based on the concept of orchestration described in the following section.

2.3 Service-Enabled Process Models: Choreography Versus Orchestration

Service-enabled processes can be modeled from two distinct perspectives, namely choreography and orchestration.

A service choreography is a global model of the interactions that may or must occur between a set services in the context of a service-enabled business process (cf. Barros et al. (2010)). It captures a set of interactions as well as dependencies between these interactions, including control-flow dependencies (e.g., that a given interaction must occur before another one), data-flow dependencies (e.g., that the data produced by an interaction is used by another), time constraints and possibly also other quality-of-service constraints. A choreography is a high-level view of a service-enabled business process in the sense that:

1. It does not capture any internal action that occurs within a participating service that does not directly result in an externally visible effect. Internal actions include computational steps or data transformations.

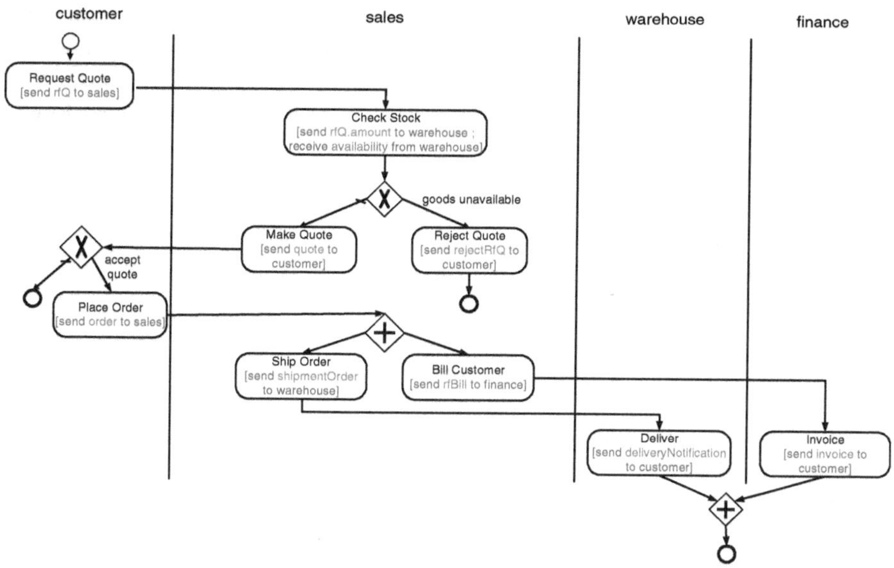

Fig. 2 Choreography view on a quote-to-delivery process

2. It provides a global perspective: interactions can be described from a viewpoint of an ideal observer as opposed to be described from one of the participants.
3. Services referred to in the choreography are abstract, meaning that they do not necessarily correspond to an actual service deployed at a particular endpoint. Instead, services are abstracted as "roles".

Figure 2 depicts a service choreography described using the Business Process Modeling Notation (BPMN). Four service roles are involved in this choreography: customer, supplier, warehouse and finance. The activities in the BPMN diagram represent business activities that result in interactions between services. For example, the activity "Place Order" undertaken by the customer results in a message being sent to the supplier (this is described as a textual note below the name of the action). Every "message send" action has a corresponding "message receive" action, but to avoid cluttering the diagram, only the send or the receive activity (not both) are shown for each message exchange.

In this BPMN diagram, we use swimlanes to represent each participant in the choreography. An alternative approach would be to use pools instead of swilanes (one pool per service role) and to represent interactions using message flows. However, in this particular example, this would result in a more cluttered diagram, defeating the purpose of choreographies, which is to provide a high-level view of a service-enabled process that can be readily understood by all stakeholders.

If we take a choreography and we restrict it to one particular role, we obtain a contract that the service(s) implementing this interface is expected to fulfill. This contract should include descriptions of messages that the service in question is expected to send/receive, and relations between these messages. These messages carry information about business entities, such as for example invoices, shipment orders or shipment notices. We use the term behavioral interface (also called a protocol by some authors) to refer to a view of a choreography restricted to one particular role. In the literature, the term interface is often used in a restrictive term: it generally refers exclusively to the operations offered by a service, and the inputs and outputs of these operations (which are captured as message types). But here, we use the term interface is a more inclusive way, in order to capture not only the types of messages and operations, but the way multiple service operations are related in the context of a process.

Figure 3 (excluding actions marked in dotted lines such as "prepare quote") depicts the behavioral interface process that is required from a "sales service" to participate in the choreography of Fig. 2. A behavioral interface encompasses both the structure of the interactions in which a service can engage and the ordering dependencies between these interactions.

A service orchestration is a refinement of the behavioral interface. In addition to interactions, an orchestration may include internal actions that a service is required to perform. For example, the dashed activities in Fig. 3, such as "prepare quote", represent internal actions that a "sales service" may need to perform. The figure also shows the point where these actions should be inserted. The entire diagram, including interactions and internal actions, represents an orchestration of a "sales

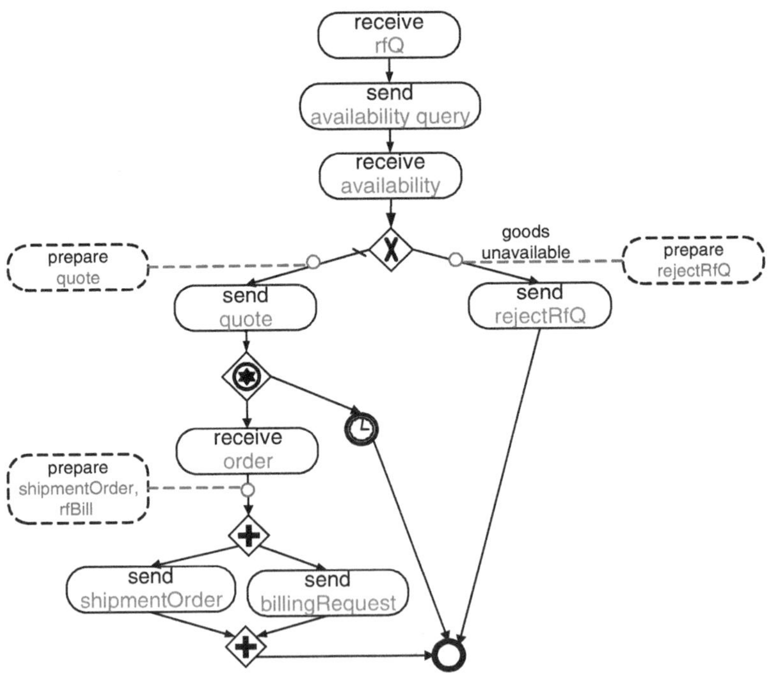

Fig. 3 Orchestration of the sales service

service". Compared to a choreography, an orchestration represents a lower-level and more focused view of a service-enabled process. With further refinements, an orchestration may give place to an executable service-enabled process, which can be described (for example) using the Web Services Business Process Execution Language (WS-BPEL) as discussed below.

Having identified the concepts of choreography and orchestration, we can define two approaches to service-enabled process design, namely: choreography-driven and orchestration-driven. The choreography-driven service design approach involves the following steps:

- Design a choreography covering all the service roles in an end-to-end collaborative process. In some cases, it may be possible to adopt standard choreographies such as those defined by the RosettaNet consortium in the form of Partner Interface Processes (PIPs);
- From the choreography, derive the behavioral interface of the services that need to be further refined in the context of the project at hand;
- Refine these interfaces in order to obtain orchestrations that can then be taken as blueprints for implementation.

Meanwhile, the orchestration-driven approach involves the following steps:

- Define an orchestration of a service-enabled process that would fulfill a given goal (e.g., an invoicing service).
- Find appropriate sub-services to plug into the orchestration – for example, an invoicing service may need to interact with a customer account management service;
- Derive an interface from the orchestration – that is, a view of the orchestration without internal actions – and expose the service and its interface for further composition into a broader system.

Choreography-driven service design is a top-down approach, while orchestration-driven design corresponds to a bottom-up approach. In reality, these are just two ends of a spectrum of possible approaches. When designing service-enabled processes, one is confronted with design tasks at the level of the choreography and others at the level of orchestrations, and these may need to be pursued in parallel.

Typically, methods are utilized as a guideline for service analysis and design that prescribe the sequence of actions to be undertaken in order to derive a sound set of services. In the following, we will give a short presentation of different types of methods that can be utilized, before we will present one specific method in more detail.

2.4 Methods for Service Identification

Based on different starting points that can be used for the identification of software services, different methods can be distinguished.

- *Domain-driven* methods utilize business models, enterprise architecture models or domain models to identify capabilities that should be exposed as services. The main focus lays on the identification of what the business of an organization is about and defines the boundaries of a service accordingly. Once these high-level services have been identified, they can be decomposed until elementary software services are derived (Jones 2006; Hess et al. 2007).
- *Process-driven* methods typically utilize business process models as a prerequisite for service identification. Based on the information provided by the models, e.g., the flow of information and objects, software service candidates can be derived that should be realized by IT (Erl 2005; Sewing et al. 2006).
- *Entity-driven* methods rely on models detailing the information entities within an organization. Thus, entity models, class diagrams, information models, taxonomies or simple brainstorming techniques about the main entities of an organization can be utilized to identify services that operate with/on these entities (Erl 2005).
- *Reference models* can also be used as an input for service identification. High-level reference models can provide first insights for the definition of appropriate service boundaries. As reference models are typically applicable in multiple scenarios and contexts, they do not reflect specific organizational requirements that need to be incorporated in the service identification phase (vom Brocke 2006; Rosemann and van der Aalst 2007). Thus, a mapping between reference models and organization-specific characteristics needs to take place if reference models are used for service identification (Sehmi and Schwegler 2006; APQC 2006; Supply-Chain Council 2008; Merrifield and Tobey 2006).
- *Hybrid methods* combine the aforementioned approaches. (Arsanjani 2004) proposes to combine business-driven approaches, such as domain decomposition or process analysis, with approaches that focus on the analysis of legacy systems for service identification (e.g., entity-driven methods). Additionally, goal-modeling should be integrated as well to identify and eliminate redundant services.

In this chapter, we will present a process-driven method for the identification software services, although parts of entity-driven approaches are included as well.

3 Process-Driven Identification of Services

In this section, we describe a foundation to understand how processes and services relate to one another. Based on this foundation, we describe a method for process-driven identification of services and we illustrate it using an example.

3.1 Processes and Services

Before services are derived from the process model, one should understand the relationships between services, processes, operations and messages. Figure 4 illustrates the relationships between these elements.

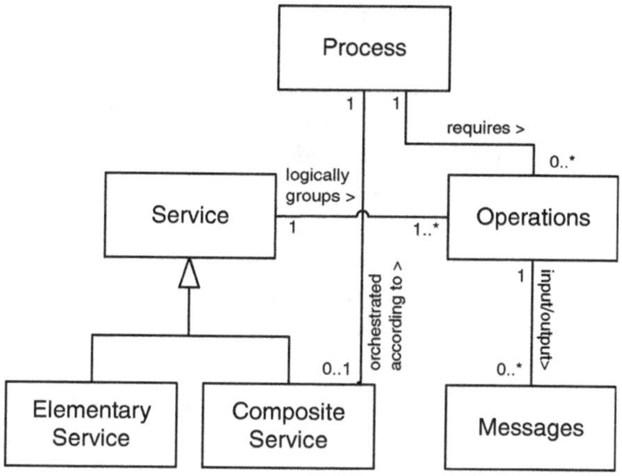

Fig. 4 Relationship between services and processes [adapted from Erl (2005)]

A process is a logical sequence of activities related to the accomplishment of a business goal. In the case of service-enabled processes, the performance of these activities requires that certain operations are invoked. Operations are invoked by means of message exchanges. Operations are logically grouped into services, which may be elementary services or composite services. The execution of composite services is driven by a process, which may require certain operations provided by other services.

In the next section, we will present a step-by-step method for identifying potential software services based on the analysis of business process models. For the identification of business services, other methods can be utilized (for example Jones 2006).

3.2 Service Identification Method

Below, we discuss a method for identifying services based on the analysis of business process models. This is not a completely new method, but rather a consolidation of other methods that have been developed and validated independently, mainly Erl (2005), Klose et al. (2007) and Sewing et al. (2006). This consolidation was undertaken by identifying commonalities and differences between these methods, and reconciling differences based on the SOA principles formulated above. The consolidated method was then tested using a quote-to-cash process of which we present several extracts below.

The method starts with the assumption that the scope for the service identification exercise has been defined beforehand, by means of an analysis aiming at pinpointing which processes and areas within an organization may benefit the most from service enablement. The identified processes and areas serve as input for the service identification method.

In the rest of this section, we consider a sample process similar to (Klose et al. 2007) that starts when a request for a product or a product variant is received from a customer. The data necessary for creating a quote is entered into the quotation system. Subsequently, two automatic activities are executed in parallel. On the one hand, the price for the product is calculated; on the other hand, the delivery date is determined. Afterwards, both results are verified and modified if required. As the last step, the quote is copied to a local network folder that is accessible by the top-management for controlling purposes. The customer is allowed to enter his or her own quote data into the system. However, since it has to be ensured that the data provided is accurate and detailed enough, the input data has to comply with the product specification. Customers are allowed to calculate the delivery dates and prices independently of the availability of any account manager or sales representative. Furthermore, customers have the possibility to gain insights into the details of their own quotes.

The method comprises seven steps described below.

3.2.1 Analyze Visibility and Handover of Process Steps

The process has to be decomposed into its most elementary process steps. Based on this decomposition, the process can then be analyzed regarding its visibility and interaction potential based on the following notions (Klose et al. 2007; Zeithaml and Bitner 2002):

- Line of interaction: specifies the parts or functions of the process that may be taken over by the service consumer. Especially with multiple channels facing the consumer, one has to decide what process functions may reside in the sphere of control of the service consumer.
- Line of visibility: defines how much of the process should be visible to the stakeholders. The stakeholders may comprise external business partners (e.g., customers, suppliers) and internal actors.

By analyzing functions based on their visibility and level of interaction with stakeholders, one can identify potential groupings of functionality that must/should be explicitly exposed to the organization's stakeholders by means of services.

Figure 5 shows the analysis of the sample process based on these considerations.

3.2.2 Identify Entity Services

Taking the process of the previous step as an input for the service identification, one should first identify entity services, since they are very generic and reusable in nature. They are not tightly coupled to processes, meaning that the provided interface of that service is not process-specific (Erl 2005). Since these services may not contain any process logic, they require a parent service or controller, which makes them dependent to a certain extent. To define the boundary of an entity

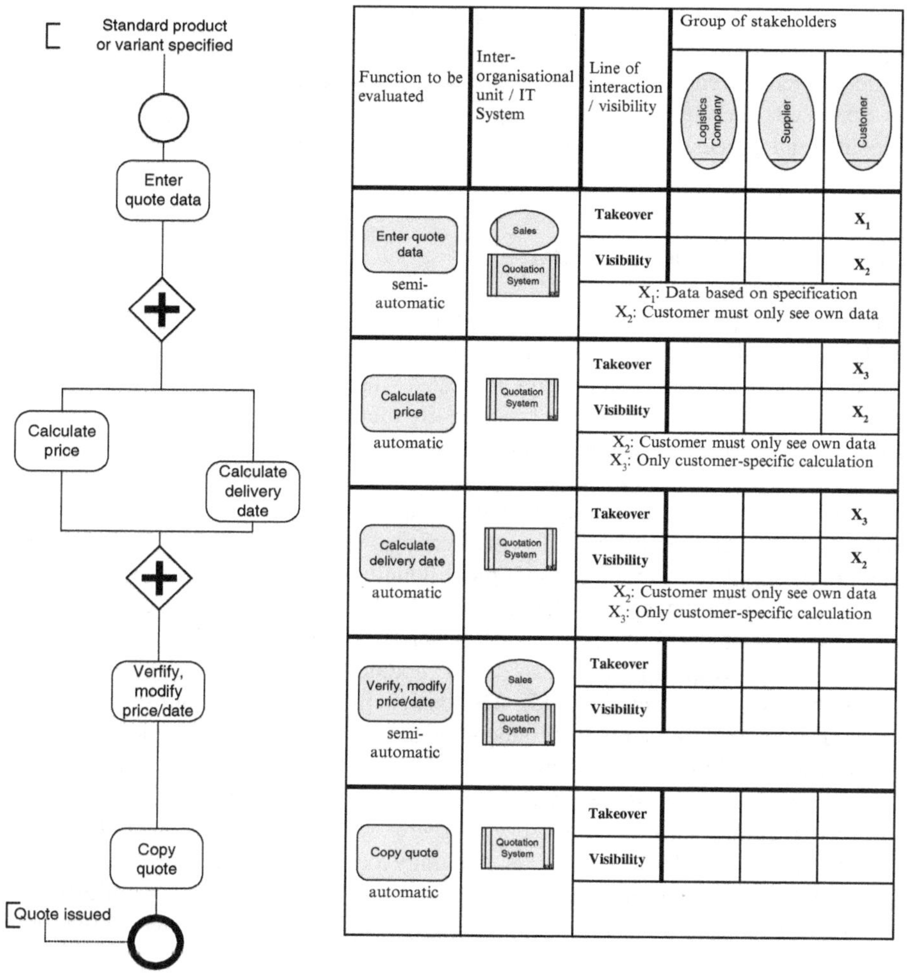

Fig. 5 Visibility and takeover analysis of sample process [adapted from Klose et al. (2007)]

service, one has to analyze the actual context of the service. This can be achieved by examining the selected process models. Processes might be analyzed to define the entities that are processed and the operations that are used for processing the entity.

In our case, the entity "Quote" can be identified as can preliminary entity service.

3.2.3 Identify Potential Service Operations

Once the process itself has been decomposed into its most granular process steps, one has to identify potential service operations. Each process step can be regarded as a potential service operation (Inaganti and Behara 2007). However, all process steps that represent solely manual tasks or process steps that are executed by a legacy system that cannot be service-enabled have to be excluded from the potential logic that can be encompassed by a service (Sewing et al. 2006).

Since all operations in our sample process are at least semi-automatically executed, all process steps are regarded as potential service operations.

3.2.4 Define Logical Context(s)

The remaining process steps should be grouped based on their logical context (Erl 2005). Thus, the identified context confines the service boundary. Hereby, the principle of service cohesion plays the most important role. The objective is to group operations together that are functionally related as this is seen as the strongest form of cohesion. The design principle of reusability can be applied to specify further operations within the boundary of a service. Depending on the scope of the service identification, one may define service operations that have the highest potential to be consumed in different scenarios (Erl 2007). However, the added operations should still relate to the logical boundary of the service. Especially, the entity services that have been identified during the second step should be analyzed regarding potential adjustments. As entity services represent business objects, they should include operations to create, read, update and delete (CRUD operations) these objects (Krafzig et al. 2006). The design principle of coupling can also be applied to identify sequential dependencies between operations. Sequential operations, which are only depended in one way, may be combined inside a service. One may also identify process steps that are recurring within that process, which can be grouped together into a single service. New services may be created as well depending on new logical contexts that may be identified. However, in Chang and Kim (2007), the authors propose to develop two different services, if different service consumers can invoke two different operations of a service in different time lines. Furthermore, one can identify services that are purely technology-related and business-logic agnostic. Thus, these services can be classified as utility services. At this stage, we have identified task, entity and utility services.

The first preliminary service candidate could be the entity service "quote" comprising all process steps. However, based on the principle of reusability, the operations "Calculate price" and "Calculate delivery date" are defined as two separate services. This way, both services can be utilized independently without invoking the complete entity service. Furthermore, both services are related to different underlying documents. For example, the "Calculate price" service is regarded as a task service that utilizes different documents about prices based on the specific customer. Given the two operations can be used independently of one another, the operations "Calculate price" and "Calculate delivery date" are split into two separate task services. The "Calculate price" operation is grouped together with the "Modify price" operation to form the "Price" task service. Similarly, the "Calculate delivery date" operation and the "Modify delivery date" are comprised by the "Delivery date" service. The "Copy quote" operation comprises purely business-agnostic logic. Hence, it is classified as a separate utility service.

3.2.5 Define Compositions

Once the services have been identified, they have to be "tested" to identify further potential for enhancements and adjustments. Scenarios have to be developed in order to identify any chances for composition and consolidation of services. This analysis allows one to evaluate the appropriateness of the service boundaries and to discover missing logic that can then be shifted to the task services or composite services (Erl 2005). Consequently, new services may be created. The main objective is to specify composite services that bring together the task, entity and utility services related to the underlying process. Based on the visibility and interaction analysis, one may create composite services that are exposed to a specific set of stakeholders (Klose et al. 2007).

Based on a close business and IT alignment, the process is represented by one composite service that coordinates the entity and utility services as well as the task services. Furthermore, the composite service invokes the operations of the composed services based on the process flow. The interaction and takeover analysis of the process steps identified that the operations "Enter quote data", "Calculate price" and "Calculate delivery date" are also executable by the customer. Thus, these operations are comprised in a second composite service that can be utilized by customers independently of any sales representatives or account managers.

3.2.6 Detail the Operations

Once the services have been identified, one should detail the operations in order to identify further potential for enhancements. Operations are detailed by specifying the input parameters and the output parameters. The following basic principle should be followed: The input data represented by the respective parameters should only be directly used by the operation in question (Feuerlicht 2005). Hereby, the aim is to maximize cohesiveness and to minimize coupling between operations. Another principle that needs to be followed is that of reusability. When the operations are too specific regarding their inputs, they need to be redesigned to provide more generic input parameters relative to the business requirements (Erl 2007). The decision about the generality of the interface of a service is a design choice that must be made with regards to the business requirements at hand.

Regarding our sample process, the utility service "Copy quote" should be made more reusable by extending the allowed parameters. Thus, the service should not only copy quotes, but different data types. The outcome of this step is a detailed description of each service. Tables 1 and 2 show the detailed service descriptions for the running example.

Table 1 Detailing elementary services [adapted from Klose et al. (2007)]

Elementary services	Operation	Input parameter	Output parameter	Service consumer
Quote (entity)	Create()	Quote data (payment and delivery conditions)	QuoteID	CU (customer)
	Update()	Quote data [payment and delivery conditions (delta)]	Notification	
	Read()	QuoteID	Quote data	CU
	Delete()	QuoteID	Notification	
Price (task)	CalculatePrice()	MaterialID, values	Price	CU
	ModifyPrice()	QuoteID, new Price	Notification	
Delivery date (task)	CalculateDeliveryDate()	MaterialID, values	Delivery date	CU
	ModifyDeliveryDate()	QuoteID, new delivery date	Notification	
Copy (utility)	Copy()	Data	Notification	

Table 2 Detailing of composite services [adapted from Klose et al. (2007)]

Composite service	Service consumer	Function	Service	Operation
Enter quote		Enter quote data	Quote	Create()
		Calculate price	Price	CalculatePrice()
		Calculate delivery date	Delivery date	CalculateDeliveryDate()
		Modify price, delivery date	Price delivery date	ModifyPrice() ModifyDeliveryDate()
		Copy	Copy	Copy()
Calculate quote	CU	Calculate price	Price	CalculatePrice()
		Calculate delivery date	Delivery date	CalculateDeliveryDate()
		Enter quote data	Quote	Create()

3.2.7 Perform Mapping

For each operation candidate within the identified software service, one has to analyze the underlying processing requirements, especially the application logic that needs to be executed for each operation candidate (Erl 2005). Subsequently, one has to identify which application logic already exists in order to make decisions about the development of the specific logic, and the sourcing of the functionality by a third party service provider (Inaganti and Behara 2007). One may also break down the application logic requirements into smaller steps in order to identify new operation candidates within a proposed service, which can then be clustered in accordance to the design principle of cohesion and autonomy by grouping steps together associated with a specific legacy system, for example Erl (2005). However, it may be possible that all the operation candidates identified in the previous phase are of sufficient granularity and supported by the application portfolio and do not need to be revised. If new services or operations have been identified, one needs to analyze the original service compositions and identify if any changes need to be made concerning the inclusion of new services or operations (Erl 2005).

All operations based on our sample process are already executable by the existing applications. Thus, no changes have to be made.

The presented method for service analysis provides a systematic basis to identify service operations from business process models and to link task and composite services to entity services. Note that despite the step-by-step nature of the method, different service designers may end up identifying a different set of services for the same business problem. Such differences arise most notably from the use of different ontologies, or from differences in the way SOA principles are prioritized in a given project (e.g., less emphasis on reuse versus more emphasis on loose coupling).

Having identified the different types of services, one needs to refine the descriptions into service implementations. The following section provides an overview of different technologies and platforms that can be used to implement service-enabled business processes.

4 Languages and Technology for Service-Enabled Processes

Several languages can be used to specify service interaction models at different levels of abstraction. On the standards front, these include BPMN (as illustrated above) and the Web Services Business Process Execution Language (BPEL).[1] BPMN can be used to capture choreographies and orchestrations at a high level of abstraction – mainly during the analysis and design phases of the development lifecycle. As an alternative to BPMN, one could use UML Activity Diagrams and Sequence Diagrams, which offer comparable features. At a lower level of abstraction, BPEL is a standard language for defining orchestrations down to the point where they can be executed by dedicated platforms. Also, BPEL can be used to specify process-oriented interfaces (called business protocols in BPEL).

WS-CDL (Web Service Choreography Description Language) was an attempt (now abandoned) to define a standard language for the specification of choreographies. One of the key issues with WS-CDL is that it treated choreographies as implementation artifacts, when in fact choreographies are design artifacts and higher-level languages are required to capture them. Another standardization proposal for a language for choreography and protocol modeling is OWL-S. OWL-S combines constructs from several sources, including logic-based languages (to capture preconditions and effects) and process algebra (to capture control-flow dependencies between operation invocations in a composite service).

Outside the standardization arena, an extension of BPEL, namely BPEL4Chor (Decker et al. 2007), has been proposed to support the specification of

[1]http://www.oasis-open.org/committees/wsbpel/.

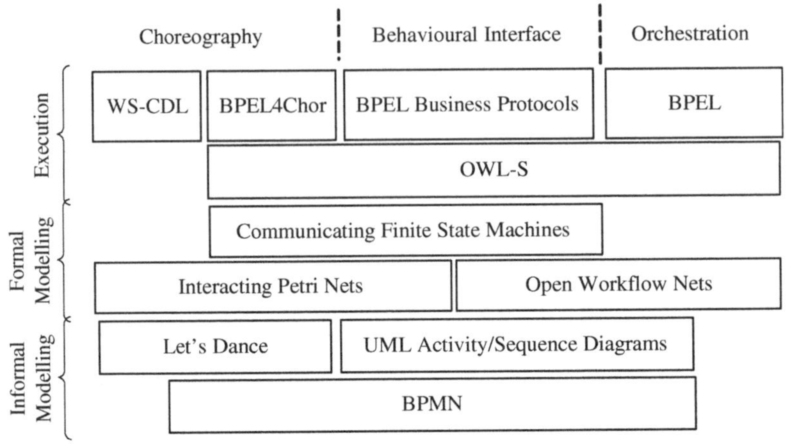

Fig. 6 Languages for service-enabled process definition

choreographies – since standard BPEL does not support the specification of choreographies. Another language proposed for specifying choreographies and service protocols is Let's Dance (Zaha et al. 2006). In Let's Dance, choreographies are described from a global perspective, while in BPEL4Chor, choreographies are described in the form of a collection of interconnected process-oriented interfaces.

In addition, researchers have studied choreographies, protocols and orchestrations on the basis of formalisms such as finite state machines, message sequence charts, process algebra and Petri nets, among others.

An overview of languages for specifying service interactions is depicted in Fig. 6. The languages plotted in this figure are classified according to two dimensions: (1) whether they are designed to capture choreographies, behavioral interfaces or orchestrations; and (2) whether they are intended for service implementation, formal analysis or high-level informal modeling of service interactions.

5 Conclusion

This chapter presented an overview of the principles of SOAs, as well as an operationalisation of these principles in the form of a method for designing SOAs on the basis of process models. A brief overview of modeling viewpoints (choreography, interface versus orchestration) and specification languages for service-enabled processes was also provided.

There is a need for further empirical studies to understand the interplay between SOA and BPM and the benefits of using these two paradigms in combination. Beyond a few case studies (see Suggested Readings below) showing the benefits of SOAs and service-enabled process management, mainly from a technical perspective, there is a lack of empirically grounded studies aimed at quantifying the long-term benefits that a service-enabled process management approach can generate in different types of organizations.

Another area that deserves further investigation is the applicability of combined SOA-BPM approaches in the context of wide-scale service ecosystems (Barros and Dumas 2006). In these environments, networks of services emerge in unpredictable manners based on ever-changing relationships between highly independent business stakeholders. In contrast, methods for service-enabled process management, such as the one outlined in this paper, assume rather stable business relationships driven by the need to streamline the execution of business processes with long-term benefits in mind. An open question is how to enable business processes in more agile ways by tapping into dynamic networks of services, while still ensuring high levels of business predictability and reliability.

Acknowledgements This research is supported by an ARC Linkage Project (LP0669244) involving SAP Research and Queensland Government, and by the Estonian Centre of Excellence in Computer Science.

References

APQC (2006) Process classification framework v4.0.0. http://www.apqc.org/pcf. Accessed 23 Nov 2007

Arsanjani A (2004) Service-oriented modeling and architecture. How to identify, specify, and realize services for your SOA. http://www.ibm.com/developerworks/library/ws-soa-design1/. Accessed 20 Jan 2009

Barros AP, Dumas M (2006) The rise of web service ecosystems. IT Prof 8(5):31–37

Barros A, Hettel T, Flender C (2010) Process choreography modeling. In: vom Brocke J, Rosemann M (eds) Handbook on business process management, vol 1. Springer, Heidelberg

Bieberstein N, Bose S, Walker L, Lynch A (2005) Impact of service-oriented architecture on enterprise systems, organizational structures, and individuals. IBM Syst J 44(4):691–708

Brahe S (2007) BPM on top of SOA: experiences from the financial industry. In: Alonso G, Dadam P, Rosemann M (eds) BPM 2007, vol 4714, LNCS. Springer, Berlin, Heidelberg, pp 96–111

Chang SH, Kim SD (2007) A systematic approach to service-oriented analysis and design. In: Proceedings of the 8th international conference on product-focused software process improvement (PROFES). pp 374–388

Cummins F (2010) BPM meets SOA. In: vom Brocke J, Rosemann M (eds) Handbook on business process management, vol 1. Springer, Heidelberg

Decker G, Kopp O, Leymann F, Weske M (2007) Extending BPEL for modeling choreographies. In: IEEE internation conference on web services (ICWS). IEEE Computer Society, Salt Lake City, Utah, USA, pp 296–303

Dumas M, O'Sullivan J, Heravizadeh M, Edmond D, ter Hofstede A (2001) Towards a semantic framework for service description. In: Meersman R, Aberer K, Dillon TS (eds) Proceedings of the IFIP TC2/WG2.6 9th working conference on database semantics: semantic issues in e-commerce systems, vol 239. Kluwer, B.V., Hong Kong, pp 277–291

Elfatatry A (2007) Dealing with change: components versus services. Commun ACM 50(8):35–39

Erl T (2005) Service-oriented architecture. Concepts, technology, and design, 4th edn. Prentice Hall, Upper Saddle River, NJ

Erl T (2007) SOA: principles of service design. Prentice Hall, Upper Saddle River, NJ

Erradi A, Kulkarni NN, Maheshwari P (2007) Service design process for reusable services: financial services case study. In: Proceedings of the 5th international conference on service-oriented computing (ICSOC). pp 606–617

Feuerlicht G (2005) Design of service interfaces for e-business applications using data normalization techniques. Inform Syst E Bus Manage 3(4):363–376

Gold-Bernstein B, Ruh W (2004) Enterprise integration: the essential guide to integration solutions. Addison Wesley Longman Publishing Co., Inc., Redwood City, CA

Haesen R, Snoek M, Lemahieu W, Poelmans S (2008) On the definition of service granularity and its architectural impact. In: 20th International conference on advanced information systems engineering (CAiSE). Springer, pp 375–389.

Hess A, Humm B, Voss M, Engels G (2007) Structuring software cities – a multidimensional approach. In: Proceedings of the 11th IEEE international enterprise distributed object computing conference (EDOC). IEEE Computer Society, Washington, DC, USA, p 122

Inaganti S, Behara GK (2007) Service identification: BPM and SOA handshake. BPTrends 3:1–12

Jones S (2006) Enterprise SOA adoption strategies. Using SOA to deliver IT to the business. C4Media, Lulu Enterprises, Raleigh, NC, USA

Klose K, Knackstedt R, Beverungen D (2007) Identification of services – a stakeholder-based approach to SOA development and its application in the area of production planning. In: Österle H, Schelp J, Winter R (eds) Proceedings of the 15th European conference on information systems (ECIS), St. Gallen, pp 1802–1814

Krafzig D, Banke K, Slama D (2006) Enterprise SOA. service-oriented architecture best practices, 5th edn. Prentice Hall PTR, Upper Saddle River, NJ

Legner C, Vogel T (2007) Design principles for B2B services – an evaluation of two alternative service designs. In: Proceedings of the IEEE international conference on services computing (SCC). pp 372–379

Merrifield R, Tobey J (2006) Motion lite: a rapid application of the business architecture techniques used by Microsoft Motion. http://msdn2.microsoft.com/en-us/library/bb736727.aspx. Accessed 08 Nov 2007

OASIS (2006) Reference model for service oriented architecture 1.0. http://docs.oasis-open.org/soa-rm/v1.0/soa-rm.pdf. Accessed 20 Jan 2009

O'Sullivan J, Edmond D, ter Hofstede A (2002) What's in a service? Distrib Parallel Databases 12 (2–3):117–133

Papazoglou MP, van den Heuvel W-J (2006) Service-oriented design and development methodology. Int J Web Eng Technol 2(4):412–442

Rosemann M, van der Aalst WMP (2007) A configurable reference modelling language. Inf Syst 32(1):1–23

Sanz J, Nayak N, Becker V (2006) Business services as a modeling approach for smart business networks. IBM Research Devision Almaden Research Center, Tech. Rep. RJ10381 (A0606-001)

Sehmi A, Schwegler B (2006) Service-oriented modeling for connected systems – part 1. Arch J 7:33–41

Sewing J-H, Rosemann M, Dumas M (2006) Process-oriented assessment of web services. Int J E Bus Res 2(1):19–44

Supply-Chain Council (2008) Supply-chain operations reference-model (SCOR)

vom Brocke J (2007) Service portfolio measurement. Evaluating financial performance of service-oriented business processes. Int J Web Serv Res 4:1–32

vom Brocke J (2006) Design principles for reference modelling. Reusing information models by means of aggregation, specialisation, instantiation, and analogy. In: Fettke P, Loos P (eds) Reference modelling for business systems analysis. Hershey, PA, USA, pp 47–75

W3C (2004) Web services glossary. http://www.w3.org/TR/ws-gloss/. Accessed 20 Jan 2009.

Zaha JM, Dumas M, ter Hofstede AHM, Barros AP, Decker G (2006) Service interaction modeling: bridging global and local views. In: 10th IEEE international enterprise distributed object computing conference (EDOC). IEEE Computer Society, pp 45–55

Zeithaml V, Bitner M (2002) Service marketing: integrating customer focus across the firm, 3rd edn. McGraw-Hill, Boston, MA

BPM Meets SOA

Fred A. Cummins

Abstract Service-Oriented Architecture (SOA) provides a framework for the design of business processes that manage shared capabilities. Shared capabilities can be engaged in multiple lines of business and achieve both economies of scale through consolidation and enterprise agility through the ability to configure new lines of business using existing capabilities. Capabilities are managed as service units that include the skills and resources to deliver well-defined services. In a transformed enterprise, service units engaged by each line of business become participants in a value chains that form the basis for optimization of operations and delivery of customer value.

1 Introduction

Service-Oriented Architecture (SOA) describes an approach to integration of systems where business capabilities are accessed across organizational boundaries. Though the development of SOA has been driven by the development of supporting technology, SOA should not be viewed as a technical discipline, but rather an approach to designing enterprises, including extended enterprises that involve multiple, collaborating companies, agencies, or institutions. SOA provides a framework for the design of business processes to promote consolidation of redundant operations and an improved ability to adapt to changing business needs. At the same time, it provides alignment of business processes with the organization structure, shared capabilities, and delivery of customer value.

SOA emerged from the ability to engage automated business services electronically, over the Internet. Technical standards and the Internet enable ad hoc interactions

---

F.A. Cummins
Hewlett-Packard, Pinckney, MI, USA
e-mail: fred.cummins@hp.com

J. vom Brocke and M. Rosemann (eds.), *Handbook on Business Process Management 1*,
International Handbooks on Information Systems,
DOI 10.1007/978-3-642-00416-2_21,

with systems implemented using diverse technologies. Loose coupling is achieved through message exchanges where the implementation of a service is hidden from the consumer and the service is designed to be used by a diverse community of consumers. The message exchanges are driven by the internal business processes of the service consumers and providers.

The full potential of SOA is realized when it is applied as an architecture for business design. The enterprise becomes a composition of capabilities that can be employed in a variety of business contexts. As such, SOA provides the basis for structuring and integrating business processes. The result of applying this architecture will be an enterprise that is more efficient and flexible – an agile enterprise. The agile enterprise is designed for change and optimization through specialization and sharing of capabilities.

Traditionally, the design of enterprises has been an art guided by experience, iterative improvements, and survival of the fittest. Conventional organization structures are a product of this evolution. Each line of business is typically developed as a separate organization, and business processes are optimized for each line of business. Optimization will depend on the current state of the ecosystem and technology, so the optimum will change over time. The entanglement of business processes and organizations delays needed changes as expensive and disruptive undertakings and results in suboptimal operations. Change is further encumbered by the embedding of business processes in computer applications. In today's rapidly changing world, an enterprise must be able to continuously adapt and optimize its operations.

This adaptation and optimization cannot be confined by traditional organizational silos, and optimization should be from an enterprise perspective to maximize economies of scale. SOA enables rapid reconfiguration and adaptation along with enterprise-level optimization.

In this chapter, we begin by examining the definition of SOA from a business perspective and its relationship to the design of business processes, including a case management business process model. Next, we consider value chain modeling as an important new perspective on enterprise design and optimization. Finally, we examine how SOA and BPM support additional enterprise optimization and agility, with a brief look at the challenge of enterprise transformation. The illustrations and many of the concepts presented here are from the book, Building the Agile Enterprise with SOA, BPM and MBM (Cummins 2009).

2 Definition of SOA

Based on the OASIS (Organization for Advancement of Structured Information Systems) SOA Reference Model (OASIS http://www.oasis-open.org/committees/tc_home.php?wg_abbrev=soa-rm), SOA involves the delivery of services from shared capabilities accessed across organizational boundaries. A simple example of such a service is access to information such as stock quotes from another organization through a request over the Internet. This is the typical web services model. However, the value delivered by a service may be more complex information or a tangible product, the interaction may be more complex than a simple request-response, and the requester may itself be an organization providing value as a service to yet another organization.

A SOA enterprise is designed as a composition of services. For example, a customer order is processed by an order processing service, which in turn uses an order fulfillment service to pack and package products and uses a transportation service to deliver the products to the original requester. Each service provider applies its capability in response to a request from another organization. Together, they satisfy the customer order. At the same time, because they provide services in a defined way, they may each respond to requests from a variety of service consumers. A service provider must have a well-defined interface to receive requests and provide results so that it can serve a variety of service consumers representing different business contexts.

The transportation carrier can deliver goods for a variety of suppliers. Because it provides its capability to multiple suppliers, it can achieve economies of scale in the utilization of its resources and thus provide the service at a lower cost than each supplier could achieve on its own. It can also maintain a capacity that enables it to respond more quickly than a dedicated transportation capability. And by specializing, it can develop and maintain special skills and equipment that improve the quality of the service. These are the fundamental benefits of SOA: speed, lower cost, and quality.

Figure 1 illustrates the impact of SOA on a typical, large enterprise. Different lines of business operate in separate organizational silos, each optimized for its particular line of business as depicted in Fig. 1a. The boxes represent different capabilities needed to perform the line of business. The capabilities are typically tightly integrated so that the boundaries and relationships are not nearly as clear as suggested by the diagram.

When SOA principles are applied, similar capabilities from the different lines of business are combined as depicted in Fig. 1b. Each of the consolidated capabilities has an opportunity to achieve economies of scale that can improve speed, cost, and

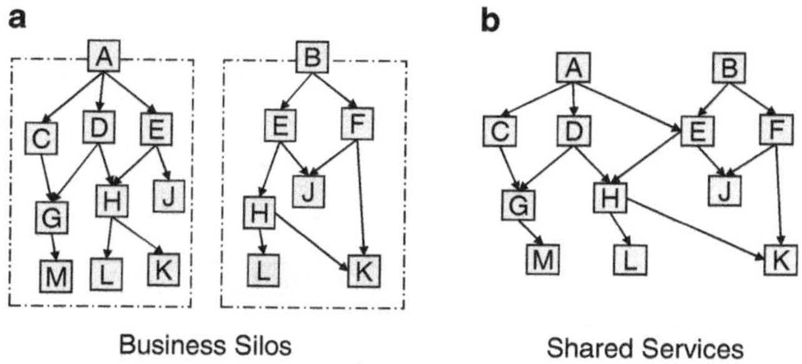

Fig. 1 From silos to services [figure originally published in Cummins (2009, p. 14 and p. 15)]

quality. I will refer to each of the organizations providing a shared capability as a *service unit*; this distinguishes it from its service, which is the thing of value it provides through application of its capability. In a fully transformed enterprise, all capabilities are implemented as service units that respond to requests from other service units or customers.

Of course, there is a trade-off. Each of the lines of business has less control over the shared service units. Each service unit potentially has multiple consumers to satisfy. The organization that owns a service unit must take responsibility for meeting the needs of all of its consumers. At the same time, economies of scale should enable the shared service unit to achieve better results than capabilities dedicated to each line of business.

Each line of business incorporates the services it needs to deliver value to its customers.

3 BPM in SOA

So where are the business processes in SOA? They are in the service units.

Many technical approaches to SOA position business processes above services, driving the use of services. While processes do use services, these approaches fail to comprehend that the business process that invokes a service is part of yet another service unit.

Figure 2 illustrates this relationship. Service unit A accepts two kinds of requests as indicated by the arrows entering from the top. Each of these invokes a business process – business processes X and Y, respectively. These business processes engage computer applications and people to apply the capability of the service unit. Business process X delegates some of its service responsibility to service unit B, which provides a different capability, potentially shared by other parts of the enterprise.

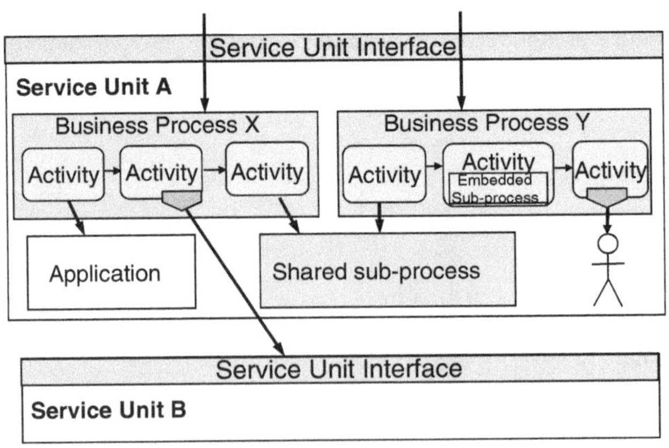

Fig. 2 Business processes within service units [figure originally published in Cummins (2009, p. 97)]

Each of these service units has capabilities provided by business processes, people, applications, facilities, intellectual capital, and other resources such as tools and materials. Each also has a responsibility to maintain, improve, and adapt the capability to changing business circumstances.

The business processes start and end within the scope of the associated service unit. Thus, the business processes are "owned" by the service unit and can be adapted and refined to improve the operation of the service unit without involving other organizations. The discretion of the service unit manager is restricted by the interface specifications of other services it uses as well as the interface specifications for the services it provides. There also may be resource constraints if some resources are shared with other service units to improve resource utilization. Later, we will discuss some of these optimization issues further.

Note that the business processes need not be automated, but there must be infrastructure that supports the integration with other service units. From the typical technology view of SOA, the rapid integration should be automated through web services technology, but integration could be through other forms of message exchange, including email or paper. Automation using XML (W3C http://www.w3.org/XML/) message structures (W3C http://www.w3.org/TR/2003/REC-soap12-part1-20030624/) and electronic message exchange protocols will be preferred for speed, reliability, and flexibility.

Conventional business applications have embedded business processes. These embedded business processes represent business needs and technical capabilities at a point in time when the applications were developed. They are obscured from view of the process owners, and they are difficult to adapt to changing business needs. While it is not essential for SOA, an agile enterprise should endeavor to remove its business processes from its applications, express them in a standard form such as BPMN (Business Process Modeling Notation)[1] and automate them with a BPMS (Business Process Management System). Note that BPMN 2.0 is currently under development and will define extended modeling capabilities, robust execution semantics, and model portability standards (OMG http://www.omg.org/spec/BPMN/2.0/).

As a result, the integration of business activities occurs through the integration of business processes rather than the integration of business applications. SOA essentially provides a business process architecture. This business process integration must be through well-defined service interfaces that make the associated services accessible to a variety of consumers. The information technology infrastructure of the enterprise, and the Internet, provide the vehicle for exchange of messages both between service units within the enterprise and with services provided to customers or by outside suppliers, which may include outsourcing of accounting, human resource, and information technology services.

---

[1]OMG http://www.omg.org/spec/BPMN/1.1/; White http://www.amazon.com/BPMN-Modeling-ReferenceGuide-ebook/dp/B002HJ3RH0/ref=dp_kinw_strp_1?ie=UTF8&m=AG56TWVU5XWC2.

The business processes may be automated with different Business Process Management systems (BPMS). Integration through a messaging infrastructure insulates service units from differences in the implementation technologies of their consumers and providers.

Standards are nevertheless required for the format and content of messages exchanged. It is desirable that the format of all message types represent agreements between participants, but integration facilities can be used to transform messages for compatibility if the content is equivalent. At the same time, the meanings of the data elements must be consistent to be properly interpreted even if they require conversion. In general, data exchanged between services within an enterprise should conform to an enterprise logical data model so that whether or not messages are translated, all services "speak" fundamentally the same language. If there is not a consistent enterprise logical data model, the ability to share and reconfigure the use of services will be significantly impaired.

There may be many different message types involved in a consumer–provider relationship. Interactions may involve more complex protocols than a simple request-response. These protocols must be specified with a *choreography*. BPMN 2.0 (currently under development) (OMG http://www.omg.org/techprocess/meetings/schedule/BPMN_2.0_RFP.html) presents choreography so that the exchanges between service units can be explicitly defined independent of the internal business processes by which services are performed and consumed. A choreography and the associated message types will generally be associated with a type of service. This enables consumers to easily engage alternative services of the same type.

More complex interactions will be required for services envisioned in *service science* (Lusch et al. 2008) where a service may be expected to adapt its resources to the needs of the consumer rather than simply responding to a request. This adaptation is more likely to require a negotiation of requirements and value exchange. A case management process is typically driven by such evolving consumer requirements.

4 Case Management

In many cases, the interchanges between consumers, providers, and potentially other participants extend over long periods of time, and the actions taken by participants depend on changing internal and environmental factors. In such relationships, the actions of a participant may not be described as a repeatable sequence of activities and decisions but rather as actions to be taken based on changing circumstances. Such processes have been described as *case management* (de Man http://www.bptrends.com/publicationfiles/01%2D09%2DART%2D%20Case%20Management%2D1%2DDeMan%2E%20doc%2D%2Dfinal%2Epdf). Case management processes complement SOA.

Case management generally revolves around management of services related to a particular entity, often a person. A case file is the focus of related actions, and various actions are taken as the status of the entity or surrounding circumstances change.

For example, a case is created for a hospital patient when admitted. As the patient is examined, tests may be performed and treatments administered. Various tests and treatments may be determined as the condition of the patient evolves, and the case file tracks the patient status and associated actions. The case file is likely retained by the hospital and reactivated if and when the patient returns.

In conventional business processes, the process performs a number of predefined activities to achieve a desired result. In case management, there may be many actions that could be performed, but the selection of actions and the sequence in which they are performed may be different for each case.

We may characterize the actions taken as services rendered. The case management service manages the case file and the performance of relevant services. The performance of services may be driven by an expert, by rules, by a schedule, or by a combination of rules, schedule, and expertise.

There are a variety of circumstances where a case management model may be appropriate. In addition to the hospital patient, an employee record could be viewed as a case file. The employee case may drive benefits, payroll, promotions, and other actions as the employee's status changes over time. Court cases or welfare cases are other well-known examples involving people.

Maintenance of a machine could be managed as a case. Preventive maintenance should occur on a schedule. Periodic examinations may reveal deterioration requiring repairs. A failure will require diagnosis and repair. As the machine ages and repair costs escalate, the repair history may provide a basis for replacement. An automobile repair history could be managed as a case, but more often, such a case begins when the automobile is brought in for repair and is completed when the automobile is returned to the owner. At the same time, there could be a lifetime case file maintained by the owner and individual cases for incidents of repair.

Case management processes tend to be long-running. An automobile repair case may endure for a few hours, days, or weeks, but a machinery maintenance case may go on for years, and a hospital or employment record may be maintained for decades.

Projects for development or construction could be viewed as case management processes. Regardless of how well the project plan is prepared, there will be changes in the sequence of actions and the scheduling of resources, and there will be rework. At the same time, many of the actions may be predictable sequences of activities that can be described with conventional process models.

In all these examples, the case file is the focus point for determination of actions to be taken. Similar actions may be taken for similar cases, but the set of actions taken and the sequence in which they occur will vary. The actions typically involve specialized capabilities that are provided as services in a SOA.

The case management process pattern is not a good fit for conventional business process modeling tools. An OMG (Object Management Group) initiative is being defined to develop modeling specifications for case management.

5 Value Chains

Conventional business process models as well as case management models define mechanisms of control over when work is performed, but the flow of control does not always correspond to the flow of work products that produces customer value. This flow of work products can be described as a value chain, and it provides the basis for understanding the impact of participating service units on a line of business.

SOA changes the structure and dynamics of the business processes and organization. A business process can no longer be designed to define a single stream of activities by different organizations as they contribute value toward an end product. In a SOA, organizations may contribute to many different lines of business at different points in the value creation process. A process for a line of business must engage a variety of services that are shared with other lines of business, and those services may engage other services to support their efforts. Business process improvement must comprehend the various ways services are engaged to produce customer value for all lines of business.

Organization structures must also change. Traditionally, a line of business could create an organization and control all the capabilities needed to deliver its value to its customers. With SOA, the line of business manager must give up control of shared services. Figure 1b, above, illustrated this. The shared services must not be optimized for the particular needs of one of its product-line consumers, but must optimize its operation for all of its consumers – essentially it must be optimized for the enterprise with an understanding of its impact on multiple lines of business.

Understanding the roles of service units in the creation of customer value requires a different perspective on the relationships between service units. A value chain provides this perspective.

The concept of a value chain was first introduced by Michael Porter in his 1985 book (Porter 1985). While the initial concept aligns most easily to manufacturing enterprises, it has also been applied to other sectors (Stabell and Fjeldstad 1998). The value chain enabled top management to focus on the delivery of value to the customer and evaluate the enterprise capabilities in that context. A primary value chain involves capabilities that are directly involved in the delivery of customer value. There are other support services that are involved in the management and effective operation of the enterprise such as accounting and human resource management.

The primary value chain typically focuses on a half-dozen high-level business functions and a hierarchical breakdown of the capabilities that contribute to producing customer value. Here, we expand that high-level executive management

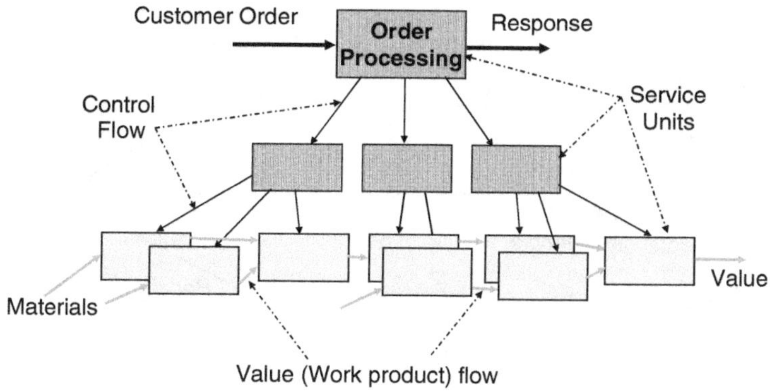

Fig. 3 Relationship of control flow and value flow

concept to a level of detail where the capabilities that contribute value are service units – capabilities that may be shared across multiple lines of business.

These value chain models are often described as process models, but there is an important difference between business processes and value chains, particularly in a SOA.

Figure 3 illustrates the relationship between the flow of control defined by business processes and the flow of value through the value chain. The business processes define how service units produce results, and the value chain defines the flow of value across service units and organizations to achieve customer value.

For example, in a manufacturing operation, business processes define production scheduling. Parts are produced in batches. The scheduling process optimizes the cost of setup against the cost of delayed production and inventory retention. The value chain describes the flow of parts and assemblies between production operations, i.e., capabilities, to produce customer value. The flow of control to request production and produce schedules is quite different from the flow of value between capabilities. A new schedule might be requested from a scheduling service on a daily basis, while the movement of parts between departments will likely occur as batches are completed. In the manufacturing operation, some batches of parts may meet the needs of multiple products and different customer orders, and multiple users of parts may draw on a single inventory. So the movement and consumption of parts, in other words, the value chain flow, is quite removed from requests for the daily production schedule.

The value chain is not directly concerned with orders and batching, but focuses on the capabilities needed to produce a product. The value chain will focus on the unit cost of production and time to deliver of each of the capabilities and thus the cost and timeliness for each product delivered to a customer. The scheduling process will have a significant impact on the production cost and time of each unit.

A value chain can be expressed as a capability dependency network. Figure 4 depicts such a dependency network. The value of the end product depends on production and delivery capabilities along with warranty repair and preventive

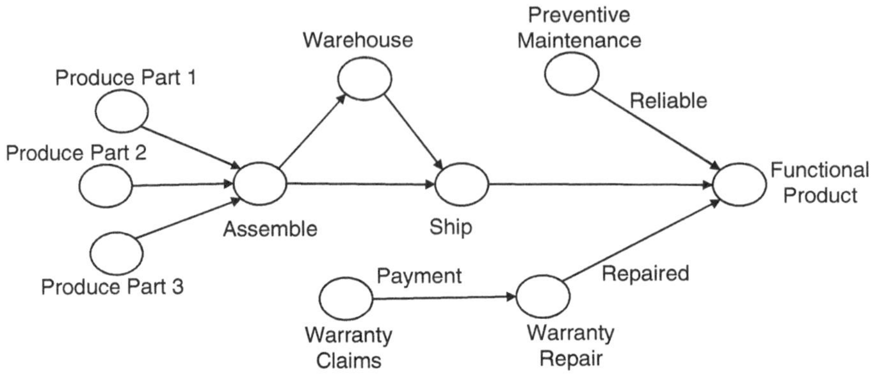

Fig. 4 A value chain dependency network [figure originally published in Cummins (2009, p. 66)]

maintenance. For delivery of the finished product, shipping depends on the availability of the product from a warehouse or the assembly operation, and the assembly operation depends on the production of parts.

A detailed value chain can be used to analyze a conventional business as well as a service-oriented business. In both cases, the analysis focuses on capabilities and their contributions to customer value. However, in an SOA, detailed value chain analysis is both more important and more meaningful. In a SOA, the service unit capabilities are shared by multiple lines of business. In order to understand the cost and timeliness of each line of business, it is necessary to consider the impact of the service units that contribute to that line of business. In a conventional organization, all the capabilities in that silo contribute to that line of business and only that line of business. In addition, the clear boundaries of service units clarify the costs and the contribution of each service unit.

Product development is typically included in the primary value chain. Unlike other value chain capabilities, its capability is not applied to each unit of production but defines how the production and delivery capabilities will produce customer value. For example, in a manufacturing enterprise, product development will define the design of parts and assemblies, special tools, and details of production processes typically utilizing existing general capabilities such as standard tools, machines, and personnel.

Product development has a value chain to produce a product delivery capability. The line of business is effectively an internal customer for the value produced by product development – the ability to produce the end customer product. The process by which product development delivers value can be characterized as a case management process as described above, where various actions are performed as various aspects of the product delivery capability are developed.

Costs of production capabilities can be allocated to individual units of production as discussed earlier. On the other hand, costs of product development are associated with the full product lifecycle. The full cost of a product includes development and production, so the line of business must allocate the cost of development to units of production based on a projected volume of business.

An enterprise includes other capabilities that are not directly involved in the delivery of value to a customer. These capabilities provide value to internal customers and are characterized as *support services*. Accounting, human resource management, procurement, and information technology services are high-level capabilities provided as support services. These general capabilities provide a number of services to their internal customers, and they also have value chains. The costs of these services are not incurred for each unit of production for end customers but are part of the overhead of the primary value chains that produce end customer value.

6 Enterprise Optimization

We have focused on optimization by consolidation of primary value chain capabilities across lines of business. The support services discussed above represent traditional consolidations of business activities to achieve efficiency and control of business operations. SOA also supports further optimization of enterprise operations.

Earlier, we observed that SOA supports consolidation of capabilities to achieve improved cost, quality, and timeliness of production. This consolidation removed capabilities from lines of business so that they could be shared, resulting in a loss of control of line of business managers over the capabilities they may have controlled directly to deliver customer value. This requires a change in thinking and approach to optimization and requires that optimization be considered from different perspectives: service unit optimization, line of business optimization, resource utilization optimization, and enterprise optimization.

The service unit boundary is key to the appropriate division of responsibility. The service interface, the specification of interactions, and performance requirements define what a service unit must do to meet the needs of its consumers. The interface should be designed to preserve flexibility in the design of how the service unit actually performs the service. Value chains define what the services contribute to customer value while the organizational hierarchy defines control over the management of service unit resources. Overall enterprise optimization is based on the specification of services and organizational groupings that meet the needs of multiple lines of business and enable optimization of resource utilization. Changes to service specifications and the scope of service units must be evaluated at an enterprise level to consider the impact on multiple lines of business.

Each service unit is responsible for optimization of its internal operations. In addition to its internal processes, this may include development of specialized techniques and skills, workload balancing and scheduling, and hiring and firing of personnel. This localized optimization enables innovation and initiative throughout the enterprise.

A line of business manager must optimize his or her value chain. This involves consideration of the roles and capabilities of shared services. This may involve analysis of the ways services are used as well as potential changes to the services.

For example, in a manufacturing enterprise, a customer order could initiate the production of each of the parts that go into a finished assembly. This could result in significant delay in response to customer orders. On the other hand, many parts and potentially final assemblies may be produced in anticipation of customer orders. The line of business should consider the trade-off between rapid response to customer orders and the cost of carrying inventory as well as the potential obsolescence of parts and assemblies that remain in inventory when new models enter production. Note that an enterprise should be able to accommodate different trade-offs for different lines of business.

A line of business manager has three alternatives to consider for improving needed capabilities: (1) advocate for changes to existing services, (2) establish and manage a duplicate capability optimized for the line of business, or (3) look for opportunities to outsource the capability to more accommodating service providers.

These options will be tempered at the enterprise level by consideration of the consequences to other lines of business. Changes to shared services may adversely affect the ability to meet the needs of other lines of business. A duplicate capability will reduce economies of scale, but that might be offset by economies of specialization. Outsourcing of the capability reduces enterprise control over the capability and will reduce economies of scale for other lines of business unless they also outsource. If the capability is a source of competitive advantage, the advantage may be lost if the capability is outsourced.

Economies of scale also may be achieved through better resource utilization across multiple service units. This is typically achieved by organizationally grouping similar capabilities. For example, Fig. 5 illustrates a grouping of similar capabilities in the value chain introduced in Fig. 4. These groupings enable the larger organizations to balance workloads, share expensive resources, and achieve

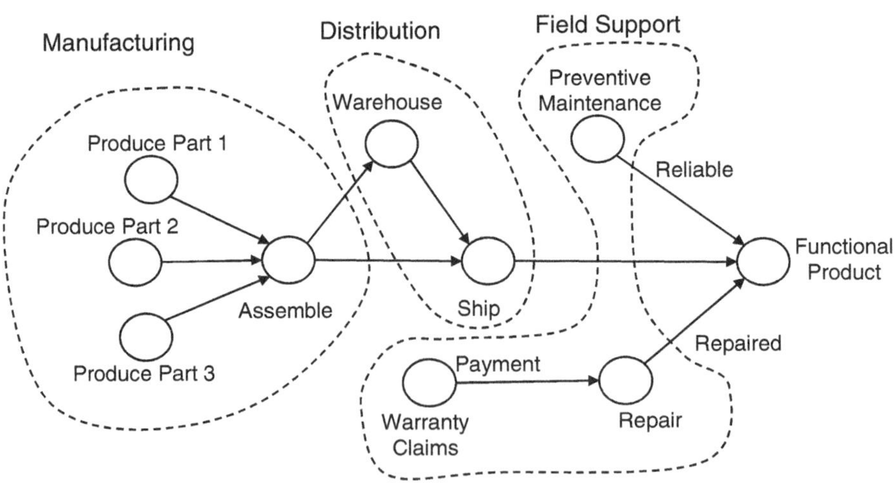

Fig. 5 Value chain abstraction for executive perspective [figure originally published in Cummins (2009, p. 67)]

other forms of synergy across the service units in their group. This grouping supports the value chain abstractions characteristic of the Michael Porter value chain models.

In the example, the manufacturing group has the opportunity to share personnel to balance workloads and schedule production in batches to reduce setup costs as discussed earlier. The distribution group has the opportunity to configure shipments for efficient delivery by holding some in the warehouse pending convenient load composition and routing. The field services group has the opportunity to share personnel and schedule repairs along with maintenance to reduce technician travel times.

Batching also affects customer value by delaying delivery, so line of business managers may play a role in determining the use of batching in a trade-off between cost and timeliness.

In addition, the larger organizations may be able to justify consolidation of capabilities at a finer level of granularity. So, in the manufacturing environment, there will be separate service units responsible for machinery maintenance and materials management (movement and storage of materials), rather than each service unit performing these operations on their own. Of course, there must then be consideration of the organizational placement of these consolidated capabilities to balance economies of scale vs. responsiveness to the needs of the service units they support.

At the enterprise level, the consolidation and grouping of capabilities and specification of services must be considered from an overall enterprise perspective. Top management leadership will be required to separate sharable capabilities from the lines of business or other organizations that depend on them. In addition to efficiency and timeliness, some consolidations may be implemented to improve consistency and control. These are important aspects of services provided by finance, human resource management, procurement, and information technology services.

Ultimately, top management must mediate trade-offs between lines of business and alternative sources of capabilities. The enterprise becomes a form of matrix management as depicted in Fig. 6. The groupings of similar service units form functional organizations. The line of business value chains cut across the functional organizations where the intersections of the matrix are the shared services. The functional organizations are primarily concerned with meeting service performance requirements and management of resources. The line of business managers are focused on optimization of their value chains to deliver customer value with competitive advantage. Service unit managers focus on meeting their service specification requirements, optimizing their internal operations to improve cost, timeliness, and quality.

An important component of optimization is the costing of services. The cost of each unit of service should be determined with reasonable accuracy and incorporated into the costs of its consumers. This cost includes both the direct cost of operations and materials consumed to produce a unit of service, and the indirect costs, the overhead, of supporting services.

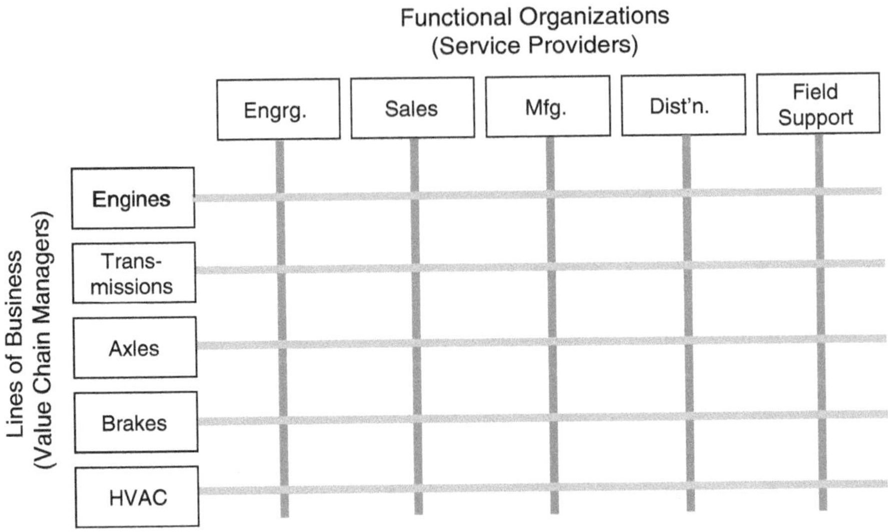

Fig. 6 SOA matrix management

When a service is shared by multiple lines of business, it is important that its costs be appropriately allocated so that the profitability of each product can be accurately determined. These costs will affect pricing and potentially decisions related to investments in growth or withdrawal from a market.

The cost and performance per unit of production of a service unit may depend on the specific service requirements. For example, the cost of shipping may depend on the size, weight, and potential hazards associated with the product, and it may also depend on the location of the customer. The cost of assembly will likely be significantly different for products of different designs, and there may be product differences between products of a single line of business. Furthermore, cost and performance will be affected by workload. An increase in the number of units produced will likely increase the time to respond to a customer order, but the fixed cost of overhead allocated to each unit of production will be reduced. These factors will affect decisions about the scope of service unit operations as well as product pricing and marketing.

Costs are also important in considering improvements in operations. Line of business managers should be able to compare the cost of a service with equivalent services from alternative sources. Alternatively, several operating units may have resources dedicated to activities that could be consolidated for economies of scale. If current costs are not well-understood, then it will be difficult to assess the business value of consolidation. Operations managers will be reluctant to relinquish control of capabilities that are important to their success. This applies, as well, where several different service units have a dedicated capability that might be consolidated into a shared service unit.

For example, a manufacturing department operates a group of presses and has a team of people that performs maintenance and repair on those presses. Other departments with different manufacturing capabilities also have their own maintenance and repair teams. Consolidation of the maintenance and repair capability could yield economies of scale that would reduce cost and improve response time for repairs. When a consolidated service unit is proposed, its costs must be computed on the same basis as current costs in order to support an objective evaluation. If some departments are using production personnel to perform maintenance, or some overhead costs are not included for current maintenance and repair activities, then the cost of the current, dedicated capabilities will appear inappropriately low.

Costing must be applied to support services as well as primary services so that overhead costs can be properly applied. Because these costs apply to multiple units of production and multiple service units, each unit of production should carry an appropriate allocation. In addition, some costs of production may be different based on product mix and volume. Consequently, effective costing is an art. Costs of units of service will be approximations, but should reasonably reflect actual costs in order to provide proper support for management decision-making.

Costing may also play a role in optimization by motivating changes of behavior of service consumers. The classic example is to charge more for a utility during peak hours so that consumers will make discretionary use of the utility during off-peak hours.

Such approaches are a topic of *service science* (Larson 2008) where the interaction of service characteristics and consumer behavior are studied to improve desired outcomes. For example, long lines at some voting facilities may alter the outcome of elections by discouraging some voters.

7 Enterprise Agility

SOA not only provides opportunities to improve cost, quality, and timeliness through consolidation, but the design of services for sharing by multiple lines of business improves enterprise agility (Cummins 2009). This benefit comes from (1) the ability to optimize processes within individual service units with minimal impact on the rest of the enterprise, (2) the ability to incorporate service units in new business processes as building blocks for new business endeavors, and (3) improved ability to adjust to changes in scale.

Since business processes begin and end within the scope of a service unit, and since service units are designed to function independent of the consumers they serve or the providers they use, the processes of a service unit can be changed locally as long as they conform to the defined service interfaces.

Top management should be able to consider a value chain for a new line of business that incorporates existing service unit capabilities and identifies capability gaps. The existing service units provide a jump-start in the ability to enter the new line of business and should provide reasonably reliable data on their contributions to cost, quality, and timeliness. The gaps then represent potential barriers to entry. This composition from existing capabilities will significantly reduce the time and cost to create a new line of business as compared to building a new organization, and the business case will be much more reliable.

Business changes often include changes in scale. An enterprise may need to scale up or down to adapt to changing market conditions. In a new market, the ability to scale with explosive growth may be the difference in maintaining market share in the long term. Consolidation of capabilities to serve multiple lines of business reduces the impact of changes in scale of individual lines of business.

In addition, SOA enhances the opportunity to outsource capabilities. Outsourcing may be used to off-load work in good times, and reduce costs in bad times. This is particularly true for commodity services such as accounting, human resource management, and information technology. A new enterprise may be unable to compete if the market for its product explodes because it cannot scale up its capacity to meet demand. An existing enterprise may be unable to scale down its capacity when market demand drops resulting in excessive product costs. An outsourcing service provider that realizes economies of scale across multiple clients, is impacted less by changes in workloads of individual clients, and accepts the burden of adjusting its capacity to the changing demands of its clients.

This strategy is not limited to dealing with changes in market demand but may be applied to transitional workloads such as significant transformation initiatives or new product development programs. It may also be applied where a needed capability can be immediately and more reliably obtained from an external provider.

Agility requires not only the ability to change, but the ability to recognize the need for change. The enterprise must incorporate business processes to sense threats and opportunities and take appropriate action. These threats and opportunities are signaled by changes in the enterprise ecosystem that have significance beyond the normal operation of the business. I characterize these as disruptive events.

Disruptive events may involve loss of personnel, supplier disruptions, inventions, changes in market demand, actions by competitors, new technology, natural disasters, cost of materials, and many other situations. At an enterprise level, these are the factors that are typically considered "influencers" that affect strengths, weaknesses, opportunities, or threats (SWOT). For the line of business manager, these events may affect the line of business sales or the ability to meet customer expectations for cost, quality, and timeliness. For the service unit manager, these events will affect the ability of the service unit to perform according to defined levels of service or to compete with alternative sources of its capability.

Facilities to respond to disruptive events have been described as an event driven architecture (EDA). This can be viewed as an extension to SOA that detects and filters events to determine their relevance and initiates appropriate actions. There is specialized technology to detect and filter events from monitoring business and market changes. In addition, personnel throughout the enterprise may become aware of disruptive events that cannot be detected electronically.

Event detection must be complemented by business processes that bring disruptive events to the attention of people who understand the implications. In some cases, there may be only operational impact to one or a few service units. In other cases, the disruptive event may affect the marketplace or the competitiveness of a product. Still other disruptive events may signal the need for strategic business change.

Business processes must support rapid resolution of the impact of disruptive events. This may be addressed by a service unit that receives events as inputs and properly directs them for appropriate action. This should probably be part of a broader enterprise intelligence capability. Over time, events that occur more frequently may be resolved automatically rather than requiring human judgment and planning. Case management automation will support the evolution from ad hoc to more predictable processes. This will further improve enterprise agility.

The full agility enabled by SOA requires a substantial transformation of the enterprise into a composition of service units.

8 Transformation to SOA

Transformation to SOA clearly has far-reaching effects on the operation of the enterprise. SOA essentially brings a new business paradigm – a new way of thinking about the organization and operation of the business. The associated changes cannot occur all at once but must be developed over a period of years.

HP Enterprise Services applies a SOA Maturity Model to guide this transformation. It provides assessment of the maturity of an enterprise in a number of dimensions, covering both business operations and information technology operations. The business must change to create and manage service units and implement new mechanisms of planning and governance. The information technology organization must change to provide appropriate infrastructure and supporting services for the integration of service units and the exploitation of technology in support of business operations.

The maturity model has five levels of maturity – level 1 is the status quo with minimal awareness of SOA. A transformation to level 2 brings a focus on specific opportunities for consolidation of capabilities with significant business value, primarily through economies of scale. These are approached as initial examples of service units that support multiple lines of business. The demonstration of value from these consolidations is the basis for development of a strategic plan for a more comprehensive development of services and supporting infrastructure described as level 3. Level 4 focuses on optimization with appropriate models, metrics, and management processes. Level 5 is the achievement of agility with formal processes for recognizing disruptive events, determining appropriate actions, and implementing the needed transformations. At level 5, change is an ongoing way of life.

9 Conclusion

SOA and BPM are complementary disciplines that, together, will yield valuable synergy and competitive advantage for those who exploit them. SOA provides an enterprise architecture discipline for organizing what is done, while BPM provides a design discipline for how it is done.

Like BPM, there have been aspects of SOA since the beginning of bureaucracies. The formation of accounting, human resource management, and procurement organizations represents the implementation of internal services, consolidating pervasive capabilities for economies of scale and control. The concept of a customer order is effectively a basic request for service as are many other internal business forms such as a purchase request, a material requisition, a personnel requisition, a payment order, and a work order.

The introduction of automated data processing led to the institutionalization of organization structures and business processes in the effort to achieve speed and reliability. In the early days of information systems, significant business changes occurred over decades. Information technology solutions optimized operations for the business and technology the way they were. They were not optimized for change. Today, significant business changes are under way all the time. Many of the principles of good enterprise design have been obscured by inflexible, technology-oriented business solutions. Information technology must not only be removed as a barrier to change but must also support change.

SOA brings a new business paradigm, a new way of thinking about the organization of the enterprise to achieve economies of scale and agility. Integration and modeling technologies now enable management of the complexity and consistent application of SOA principles both within an enterprise and in relationships with customers and suppliers.

Competition has become intense as the marketplace has become global. Enterprises cannot afford to overlook opportunities for economies of scale. The ability to change has become a major factor in the survival of enterprises. Business Process Management systems (BPMS) provide improved ability to change and optimize how work is done, and SOA provides a discipline for management of capabilities to achieve economies of scale and adapt to new business challenges and opportunities. The disciplines, processes, and organizational approaches to managing change are still evolving.

Several things are clear. Strategic planning must become a continuous process. The design and management of the enterprise has become more complex and can no longer be delegated to individual lines of business. Top management cannot comprehend nor direct all of the changes necessary to optimize the operation of the enterprise – optimization must be managed at different levels of scope and authority.[2] This

[2]These managerial issues are discussed in more detail in the second volume of the BPM handbook. Please refer to the chapters on Strategic Alignment, Government, People and Culture (vom Brocke and Rosemann 2010).

complexity must be managed through collaboration and the support of computer-based models. Models must help managers understand problems and trade-offs, evaluate alternatives, formalize the design of the enterprise, and drive implementation and automation. The models must support top management, line of business and service unit perspectives for optimization and rapid adaptation.

References

BPMN (Business Process Model and Notation) 2.0 RFP, Object Management Group (OMG). http://www.omg.org/spec/BPMN/2.0/

BPMN (Business Process Modeling Notation) specification, OMG (Object Management Group). http://www.omg.org/spec/BPMN/1.1/

Cummins FA (2009) Building the agile enterprise with SOA, BPM and MBM. Elsevier/Morgan Kaufman Publications, Amsterdam, Boston

de Man H. Case management: a review of modeling approaches. BPTrends. http://www.bptrends.com/publicationfiles/01%2D09%2DART%2D%20Case%20Management%2D1%2DDeMan%2E%20doc%2D%2Dfinal%2Epdf

Larson RC (2008) Service science: at the intersection of management, social and engineering sciences. IBM Syst J 47(1):41–51

Lusch RF, Vargo SL, Wessels G (2008) Toward a conceptual foundation for service science: contributions from service-dominant logic. IBM Syst J 47(1):5–14

Porter ME (1985) Competitive advantage: creating and sustaining superior performance. Free Press, New York

Stabell CB, Fjeldstad OD (1998) Configuring value for competitive advantage: on chains, shops and networks. Strat Manage J 19(5):413–417. http://www.agbuscenter.ifas.ufl.edu/5188/miscellaneous/configuring_value.pdf

SOA Reference Model, OASIS (Organization for the Advancement of Structured Information Systems). http://www.oasis-open.org/committees/tc_home.php?wg_abbrev=soa-rm

SOAP version 1.2 Part 1: messaging framework specification, WorldWide Web Consortium (W3C). http://www.w3.org/TR/2003/REC-soap12-part1-20030624/

vom Brocke J, Rosemann M (2010) Handbook on business process management. Strategic alignment, governance, people and culture, vol 2. Springer, Heidelberg

XML (eXtensible Markup Language) specification, WorldWide Web Consortium (W3C). http://www.w3.org/XML/

Integrated Business Process and Service Management

Thomas Gulledge

Abstract Service-oriented Architecture (SOA) is typically presented from a software development perspective, viewing the enterprise as an extension of the distributed network management model. The objective of this chapter is to demonstrate that the business value of SOA derives from aligning business services with business processes that are enabled as composite applications. This aligned approach to service-oriented implementation is called Business Process Management to SOA (BPM to SOA). This chapter describes BPM to SOA in some detail, including an implementation perspective that is based on successful project delivery. The business benefits of BPM to SOA are presented, and the chapter asserts that the business case for SOA cannot be completed without aligning business services to end-to-end business processes.

1 Introduction

Business Process Management (BPM) has received wide attention in the management and engineering literature. Managers, as part of their day-to-day activities, execute procedural logic that is embedded in business processes. Given this fact, it makes sense for managers to execute business process improvement initiatives, such as Lean Six Sigma, Continuous Process Improvement, Total Quality Management, and many others. However, process improvement projects do not always yield the results that were anticipated. The reasons are varied, and many of the critical success factors are documented by Bashein et al. (1994). However, as noted by Gulledge (2008), redesigned processes are only efficient if information flows are supported by systems that align with the redesigned processes. If system realignment does not occur, there is a tendency to revert to the old way of business.

T. Gulledge
Enterprise Integration, Inc., Alexandria, VA, USA
Prof. Emeritus George Mason University, Alexandria, VA, USA
e-mail: thomas.gulledge@eiisolutions.net

J. vom Brocke and M. Rosemann (eds.), *Handbook on Business Process Management 1*, International Handbooks on Information Systems,
DOI 10.1007/978-3-642-00416-2_22,

A current trend in the technology literature is Service-Oriented Architecture (SOA). SOA means different things to different audiences (Gulledge and Deller 2009), but SOA is only effective if it improves the quality of management information (Bugajski 2008). SOA as a technology concept is not very interesting, because managers are not keen to invest in "infrastructure refresh" projects with extended implementation time horizons (Manes 2008). SOA must add value to core business processes[1] or it will not be widely implemented.

The primary objective of this chapter is to demonstrate that the business value of SOA derives from aligning business services with business processes that are enabled as composite applications. Process innovation is widely accepted as an approach for enhancing business value (Davenport 1993). If SOA provides flexibility as argued in the literature, then the alignment with business processes should be a source of process innovation, and hence, directly correlate with the business value of SOA. This primary objective is accomplished by delineating the requisite foundational information on composite applications and linking BPM to SOA.

This chapter is not a case study, but we offer the following references for a project that was implemented using the advocated concepts. The project was implemented in a complex Product Lifecycle Management environment in the U.S. Army.[2] The general approach and the requirements definition layer are presented by Gulledge et al. (2008). An overview of the complete solution is provided by Gulledge et al. (2009). The details of the case study are not presented in this chapter, but these references are provided as supporting empirical evidence. Furthermore, many commercial software providers offer products for implementing the concepts that are described in this chapter, and contributions of some of the providers are described below.

2 The Basic Concept

A critical assertion is that BPM is a concept that must be understood in any discussions of service orientation. The term BPM is confusing, because it has one meaning for managers and another for technologists. It is necessary to separate the two definitions, and to add clarity, the two definitions are discussed in some detail. The term "Business BPM" is used to represent the manager's definition of BPM, and the term "Technical BPM" represents the technologist's definition of BPM. The concepts are discussed here, but they are covered in more detail in Gulledge (2008).

Managers must have a business process orientation. Since business processes define how work is executed, managers are constantly trying to improve business processes in an attempt to increase organizational performance. A typical approach involves interviewing subject matter experts and documenting the business processes for study and analyses. The concept is simple – you cannot improve what you

[1]Earl (1994) defines core processes as those business processes that add value directly to the customer.

[2]Iyer and Gulledge (2005) provide a general description of the environment.

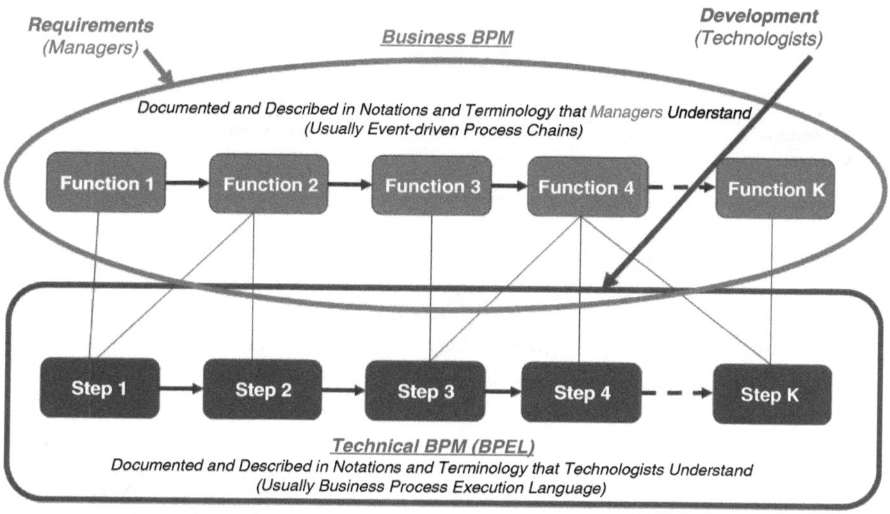

Fig. 1 Business and technical BPM

do not understand, so managers are constantly striving for improvement. These management-oriented processes are typically not documented using the technical notation of a system developer or integrator, but are documented in a notation that is comfortable to managers and using common business terminology (e.g., BPMN or EPCs). Since Business BPM describes how managers desire to execute their business, Business BPM represents the business process requirements of the organization. If the underlying systems do not support these requirements with pertinent information, an "organizational requirements gap" must be filled.[3]

Technical BPM is a software concept. It depicts the execution flow as objects (data and code) flow across systems. Technical BPM can be documented in a standard notation, and the most widely accepted standard is the Business Process Execution Language (BPEL). The processes that are documented in BPEL must perfectly align with the Business BPM processes, or business process requirements are not realized. The implication is that Business BPM dominates Technical BPM. Many information system projects are initiated at the Technical BPM level. While such an approach is practical from a technical point-of-view, there is no indication (much less guarantee) that business process requirements (defined by managers) will be realized if the requirements are defined from an IT point-of-view. Figure 1 depicts the relationship between Business and Technical BPM. Both concepts reflect processes, but their orientation is different. Business BPM is a management approach for documenting, analyzing, improving, and ultimately codifying a set of business process requirements. These requirements are often organized in an integrated repository, and in the form of a Business Process Management Framework.

[3]Gulledge (2006) for a discussion of business process oriented gap analysis.

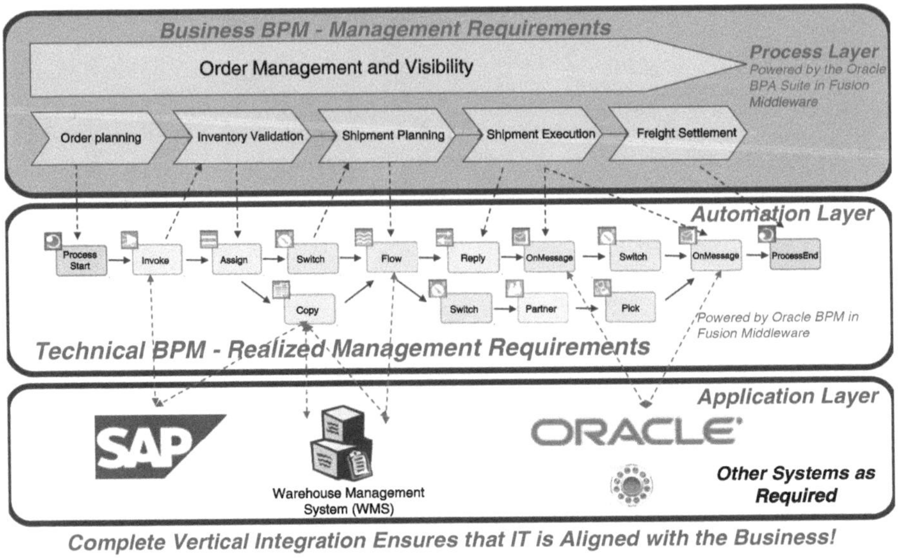

Fig. 2 Business and technical BPM in a logistics order-to-cash implementation project

As asserted, Technical BPM is a technology approach for documenting the flow of control within or across information systems. Technical BPM must align with Business BPM in order to realize business process requirements. Managers execute Business BPM, and system developers execute Technical BPM; however, the two concepts are tightly linked. Managers and technologists must work together while defining and realizing requirements.

Figure 2 presents the concept in an actual implementation that was completed in early 2008.

While the figure is conceptual, it describes the relationship that is more clearly delineated in the subsequent sections of the chapter. The organization has one set of desired business processes, and they are documented using a method that is useful for managers. The organization has many systems, and these systems provide information to support the business processes. The top layer of Fig. 2 represents the business process requirements and the lower level represents the supporting information systems. If the top and bottom are not aligned, the gap must be closed. Technical BPM (center section of Fig. 2) provides the linkage between Business BPM and the systems that provide the required information to automate the Business BPM processes.

3 The Link to Service Orientation

It is noted that Fig. 2 is only one view of SOA. Other views are discussed in detail by Gulledge and Deller (2009) and are not repeated here. We admit that these different views of SOA are confusing, and a common understanding is difficult, because managers and technologists usually have different views of the business. A complete understanding of SOA requires that all views be understood and reconciled.

However, we assert that the concept in Fig. 2 is the most practical for achieving successful service-oriented solutions that directly enable the value-adding processes of the business. This assertion has been noted by the superplatform vendors,[4] and they have responded with products that enable the model described in Fig. 2. The distinguishing characteristic of Fig. 2 is the business process-oriented view of service-orientation. That is, the major vendors are taking a business management approach to SOA implementation as opposed to the more technology-oriented view that has emerged in the software engineering community. This is an important point that requires reiteration. The elegance of the technology does not matter if the technology does not add business value. While the technology community may feel that they have made the appropriate business case for SOA, managers are still cautious.

It should also be noted that some of the smaller mid-tier vendors are providing service-oriented software products, but they are limited in scope and scale. This chapter does not describe the details of all the vendors, but we note without reference that all are adopting similar architectures for managing the layers in Fig. 2. To explain the architecture and specifically the linkage to business process, any of these vendors could be selected for a case study, but we use the Oracle solution as implemented in their Fusion Middleware product to show how BPM can be aligned with SOA and enabled through total business process integration. We select the Oracle solution because Oracle positioned a production solution in the summer of 2007, well ahead of the other vendors, and consequently there has been more time to understand the details of their solution. Other vendors are rapidly closing the gap, but for the purposes of this chapter, we selected a single vendor to delineate how a baseline architecture can actually be implemented.[5]

The Oracle-specific version of Fig. 2 is presented in Fig. 3, which is reproduced from Scharstein (2007).

The Oracle solution contains an integrated tool, within Fusion Middleware, for documenting Business BPM using notation that is useful and familiar to managers. Specifically, Oracle supports event-driven process chains (EPCs) or Business Process Modeling Notation (BPMN). These Business BPM models are automatically converted into a "first cut" Technical BPM layer that Oracle calls the Technical Blueprint. The Technical Blueprint is an automatically generated first draft BPEL model that represents the baseline for the Technical BPM layer. It is important to note that the Technical Blueprint is not executable BPEL or BPMN, but a "first cut" model that can be converted into executable BPEL or BPMN.

[4]The superplatform vendors are Oracle, SAP, IBM, Microsoft, and RedHat/JBOSS.

[5]An SAP version of the concept is presented by Stiehl (2007). An IBM view is provided by Ferguson and Stockton (2006).

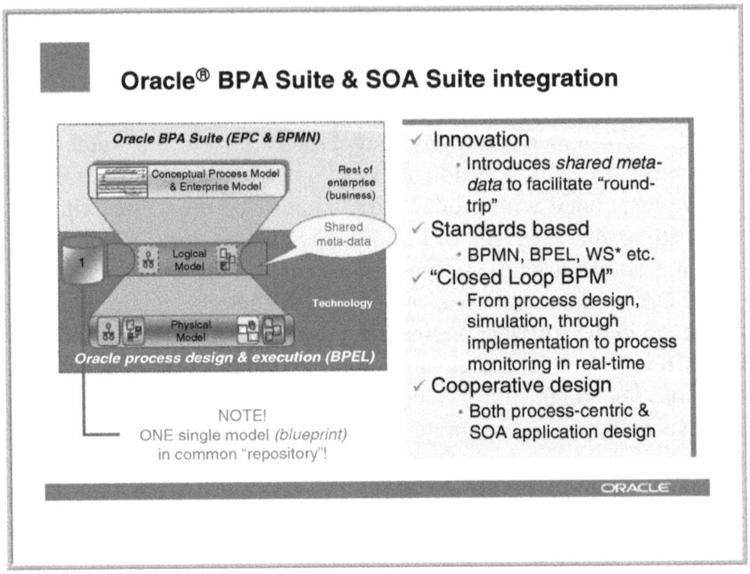

Fig. 3 BPM to SOA in oracle fusion middleware

The Blueprint can be revised and realigned with the Business BPM models, but a one-to-one relationship between the Blueprint and the Business BPM models is always preserved. In the SOA literature, this concept is known as the "round trip." Fusion Middleware manages the linkage between Business and Technical BPM in a single repository. Any number of iterations between business analysts and technical architects can occur before an "implementable" compromise is reached. The important concept is that the relationship between Business BPM and Technical BPM is maintained for each step in the iterative process. Some researchers call this interaction "Closed Loop BPM."

For the next step in the implementation process, the stabilized Blueprint is automatically passed into the Oracle development environment. In this environment, services may be developed or discovered for linking to the BPEL models for deployment on the Oracle application server. To create this executable BPEL model, development effort is required, but once again, the one-to-one relationship between Business and Technical BPM at each step of the iterative process is preserved, completing the "round trip." The process is described in detail by Oracle Corporation (2008).

The "round trip" implementation is not completely automated (i.e., iterations are required), but it is possible to visualize the early stages of how an executable architecture might be developed and deployed. At a minimum, there is a mechanism for ensuring that business requirements are actually implemented and the process is properly enabled by the systems that fall at a lower level. This is the technical link between service-orientation and Business BPM.

4 What Are the Services that Are Aligned with Business and Technical BPM Processes?

A service is conveniently described as a small application. Applications are comprised of code (logic), and they must have data in order to execute. For services to communicate with each other, the data must align and communicate through an interface. The situation is depicted in Fig. 4.

This definition (i.e., services as an application) is consistent with the definition of business services as opposed to technical services. Business services are aggregations of functionality that execute specific business tasks; e.g., process an order, check inventory, etc. A business service may be comprised as an aggregation of technical or infrastructure services, or even as wrapped transactions as with SAP Enterprise Services. The distinction used in this chapter is similar to that used by Werth et al. (2007).

Figure 4 also points out the critical role of data as an important characteristic of service interoperability. For the transfer of information in Fig. 4, the data must be complete, harmonized, and of high quality.[6] Organizations with fragmented and missing data should initiate a data readiness study prior to considering service-oriented implementation projects, or the implementation effort is likely to fail. That is, one could spend significant resources designing and developing a

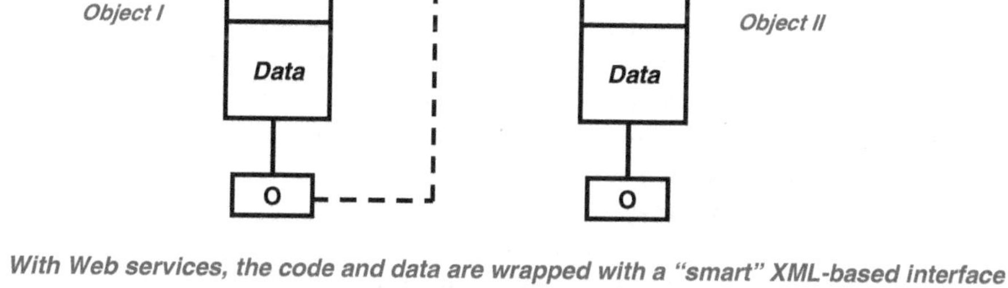

Fig. 4 Relationship between code and data in web services

[6]Data quality, as referenced in this chapter, is a practical concept that is focused on the ability of enterprise applications to have appropriate data to execute in accordance with business requirements. This definition is clarified by Xu et al. (2002).

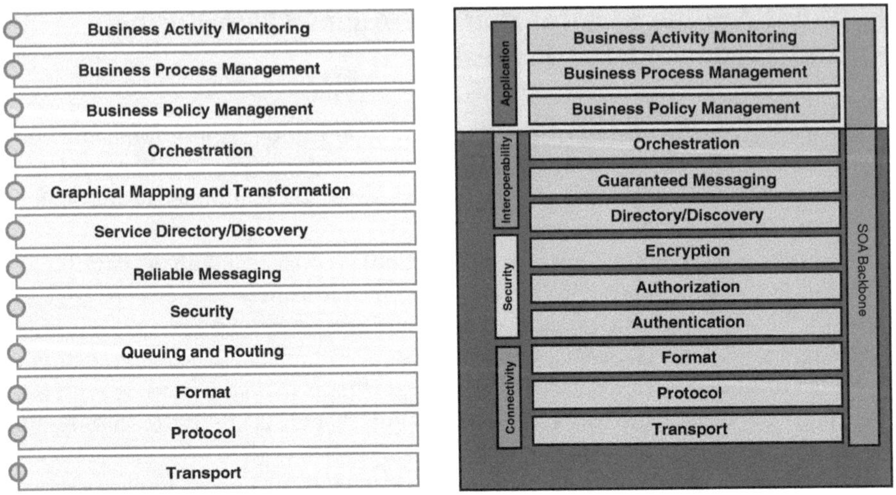

Linthicum, David S., Extending Your SOA Outside of Your Enterprise to Enable Service Provider Integration, Bridgewerx Technologies, 2007

McDowell, John, Long-Running Transactions: Mapping Conversations in the Asynchronous Enterprise, Grand Central Communications, 2006

Fig. 5 Two representations of service oriented architectures

service-oriented solution, only to discover that the detailed data required to support the application are not available.[7]

Service-Oriented Architecture (SOA) is an architecture built around a collection of reusable components (i.e., services) with well-defined interfaces. Services are groups of components that are executed within business processes; for example, verifying a credit card transaction or processing a purchase order. In other words, at the technical level a SOA is a collection of services that communicate with one another. The services are loosely coupled (meaning that an application does not have to know the technical details of another application in order to talk to it), have well-defined and platform-independent interfaces, and are reusable. SOA is a higher level of application development (also referred to as coarse granularity) that, by focusing on business processes and using standard interfaces, helps mask the underlying technical complexity of the IT environment. See the reference by Datz (2004). Figure 5 provides two similar views of Service-Oriented Architectures from a technical point-of-view.

The views in Fig. 5 are reproduced from Linthicum (2007) and McDowell (2006). While slightly different, the SOAs include all components and standards at a technical level that are necessary to "orchestrate" services into an application. There are a number of SOA reference architectures, and while one could argue

[7]It is noted that an enterprise wide data model is not required to implement composite applications; a canonical data model is sufficient. The canonical model can be expanded as additional processes are implemented.

about the components, one thing is certain. SOA, as presented in the trade literature, is not in the form of a business process architecture, nor is it presented from a business perspective. This is not a statement of right or wrong, but Fig. 5 presents two typical presentations of SOA. In both cases, the architecture is presented from a technical point-of-view. Technical BPM is the highest level in both architecture presentations. In Fact, Fig. 5 is a software developer's view of the enterprise that applies the basic concepts of distributed networking to the management of enterprise objects. By and large, the IT literature addresses the technical aspects of service orchestration, but not the business aspects. This lack of a business view is what distinguishes some interpretations of SOA from the business process-oriented approach that is presented in this chapter.

The considerations are paramount. Before the technology view of SOA will be widely accepted by management, SOA models similar to those in Fig. 5 must be aligned with management's orientation, which is the execution of end-to-end business processes that add value to the customer. Otherwise, SOA implementation will always be viewed as a costly technology project that is focused on infrastructure refresh, and such a "refresh model" cannot be easily reconciled with customer value-adding processes.

5 Implementing from the Technical Level

Many companies provide solutions for implementing Technical BPM. That is, the Business BPM requirements could be ignored and one could directly implement from a BPEL representation of the Technical BPM. This is certainly possible, and many implementation projects are initiated at this level. However, there is evidence that this implementation approach is not preferred. Table 1 contains data from a recent study reported by Ellis (2008).

A quick analysis of Table 1 indicates that none of the data are encouraging; a sure indication that a requirements gap does exist. If the IT organization or non-IT business owns the requirements, overruns are prevalent. The numbers are slightly better when the IT organization owns the requirements, which is logical. The IT organization knows the "easiest path to deployment," and the requirements are tailored to leverage this knowledge. The striking characteristic of Table 1, however,

Table 1 Diagnosing requirements failure (Ellis 2008)

Joint ownership of requirements is most effective

Who owned primary responsibility for requirements?	Budget % of target	Time % of target	Functionality % of target	Stakeholder time % of target
IT organization	162.9	172.0	91.4	172.9
Non-IT business	196.5	245.3	110.1	201.3
Jointly owned	143.4	159.3	103.7	163.4

$N = 109$

Source: IAG business analysis benchmark, 2008.

is that when the requirements are jointly owned, the numbers are improved in all categories.

One research study is insufficient to draw conclusions, but from a practical point of view, one would expect the outcome that is presented in Table 1. Furthermore, Joint Ownership is a requirement for aligning Business BPM with Technical BPM while preserving the "round trip."

6 The BPM to SOA Implementation Process

To formalize the theoretical relationships advanced in this chapter, an implementation roadmap that has been effectively developed, documented, and implemented at the project level is presented. This model has been refined over a 2-year period by researchers at Leonardo Consulting (Australia) and Enterprise Integration, Inc (USA). The roadmap combines an implementation methodology with a project planning structure to provide an approach to implementing Business BPM processes that are enabled by business services from multiple information systems. An overview of the roadmap is presented in Fig. 6.

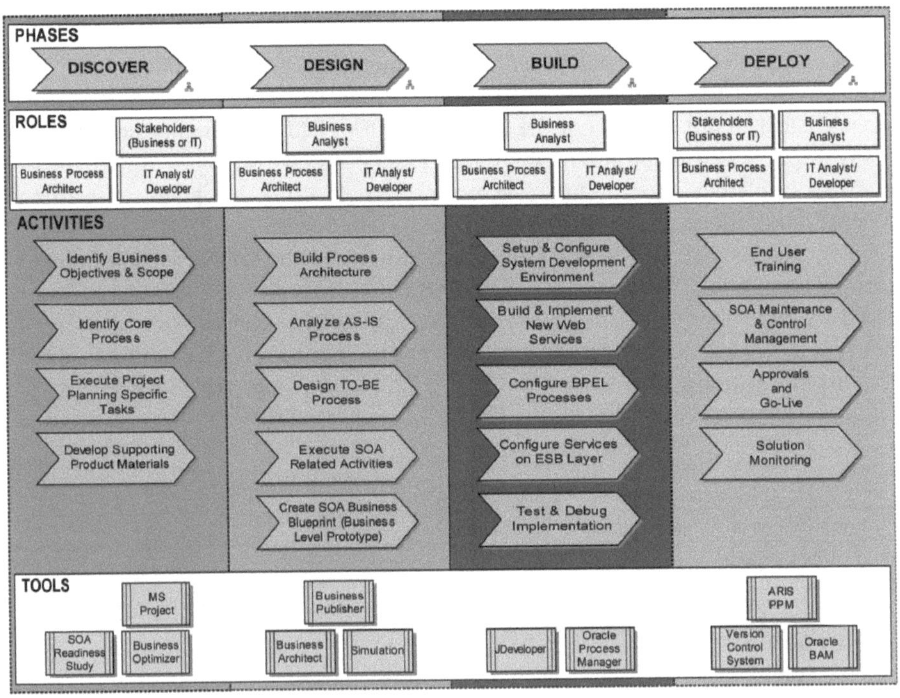

Fig. 6 Overview of BPM to SOA implementation roadmap

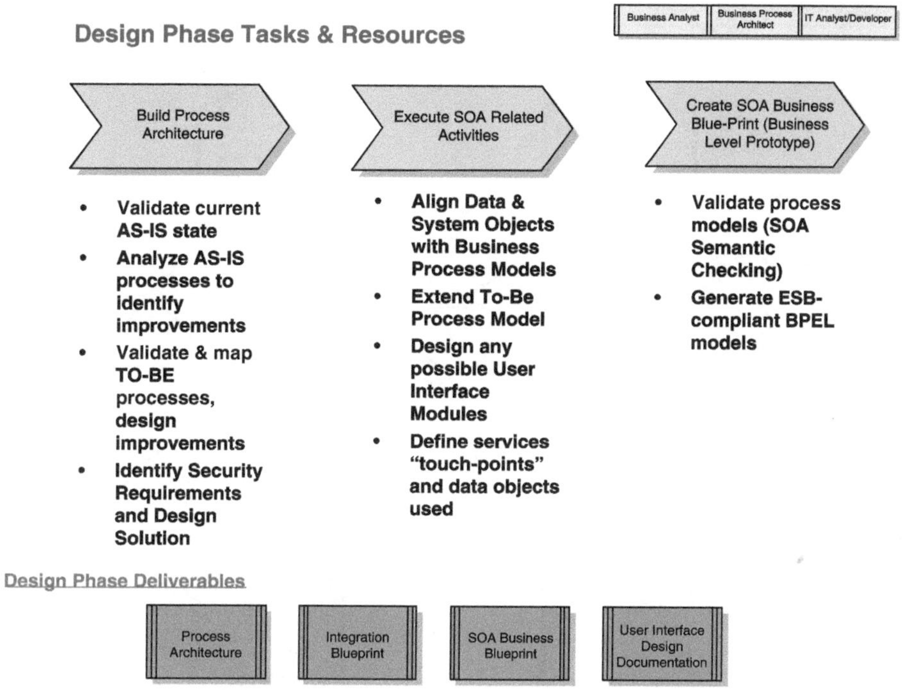

Fig. 7 Design phase decomposition for BPM to SOA roadmap

The roadmap is organized around a lifecycle model – discover, design, build, and deploy. Within this model, certain activities have to be performed, and the activities must be divided between technologists and managers. Each high level chevron in Fig. 6 is decomposable into more granular tasks. For example, Fig. 7 provides a decomposition of the design phase.

Space will not permit a detailed analysis of every step in every phase, but the point is that there is a well-defined roadmap that when properly followed does lead to successful implementation. An overview from a different perspective is presented in Fig. 8.

If the roadmap is followed, the implementation structure is hierarchical with Business BPM providing the requirements for the deployment at the implementation level. The linkage that aligns the business BPM requirements with the deployed solution is the Technical BPM layer. These linkages are from Business BPM to deployment as depicted in Fig. 9.

The relative positioning in the hierarchy can be described in a simple governance model as presented in Fig. 10.

The model requires business process governance at the business requirements level and business service governance and the execution level. The round trip is completely preserved by this model and business requirements are completely aligned with technology requirements.

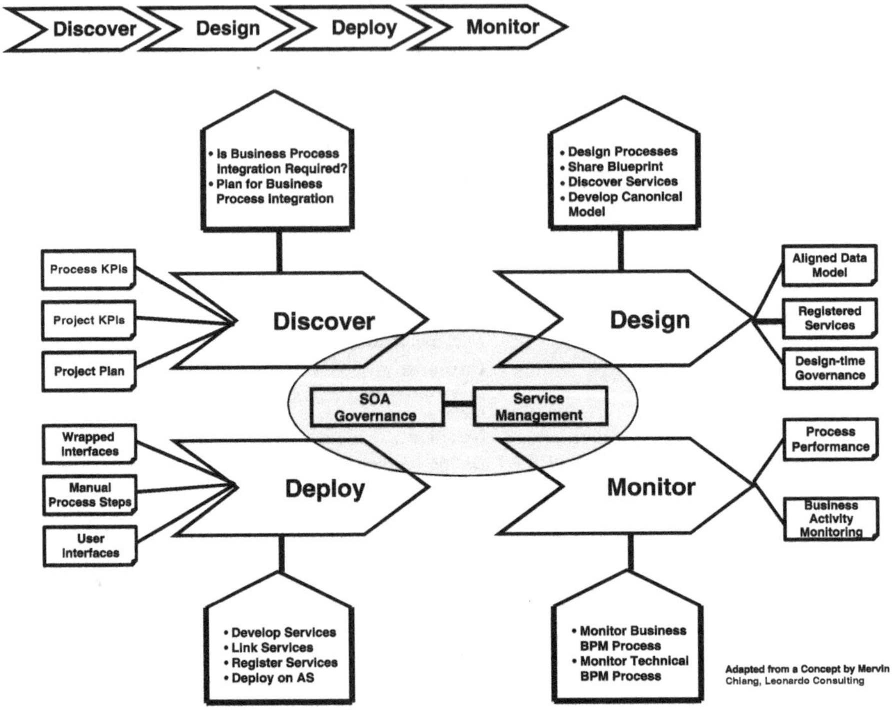

Fig. 8 BPM to SOA overview from a network perspective

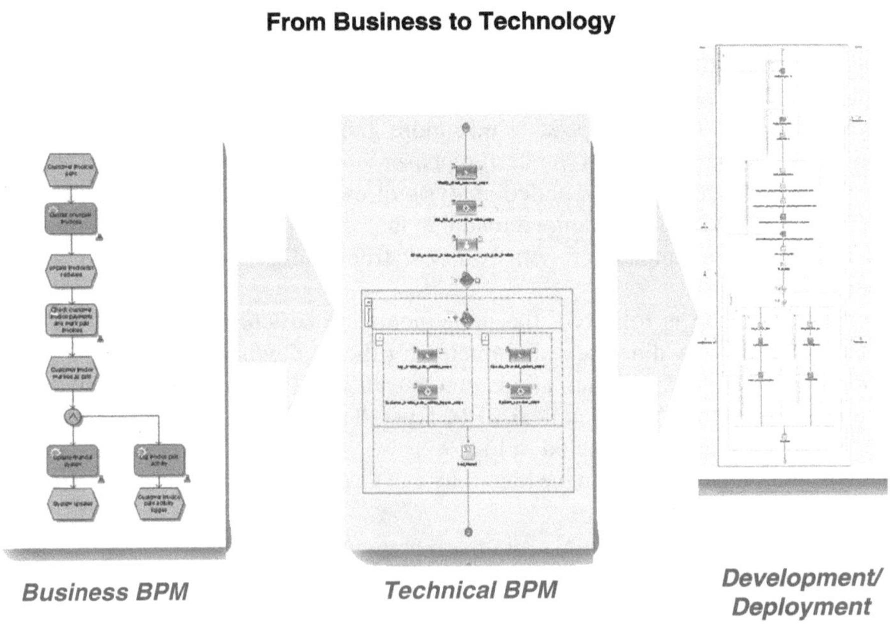

Fig. 9 Transition from business BPM to Service-oriented development and deployment

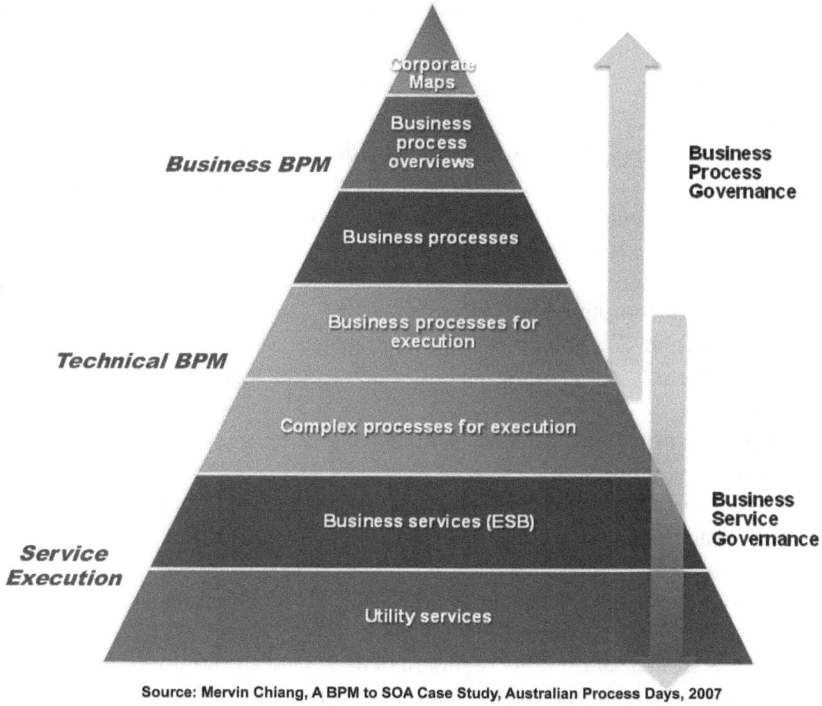

Fig. 10 Layered architecture that aligns BPM with service execution

7 Review and Analysis

As a review, it is noted that this model is only one view of SOA. Gulledge and Deller (2009) presented three possible views, and BPM to SOA represents only one of those views. Our assertion is that this view is more closely aligned with management activities than other views, but this assertion is biased by the strong belief that IT projects should support business outcomes.

BPM to SOA falls into a general class of solutions that is known as composite applications. We have extended the literature on composite applications through project implementation and the development of a top-to-bottom implementation roadmap. The assertion is that there is a successful path to business-value-adding SOA though composite applications as described in this chapter.

The key concept is the alignment of a three-layered model that is characterized by:

- Business process requirements as modeled in a Business BPM layer,
- Technical business process and flow control as modeled in a Technical BPM layer, and
- A service execution and deployment layer (as implemented in a modern SOA Suite such as the Oracle SOA Suite) that consumes services from multiple information systems.

The benefits of BPM to SOA are numerous. These are some of the most obvious benefits:

- Business process requirements are aligned with system implementation requirements.
- The composite application structure provides a framework for executing the SOA round trip to rapidly realign business processes to accommodate changing requirements, as indicated in Oracle Corporation (2007).
- The solution is deployed using state-of-the art SOA methodologies and technologies.
- The solution is complete and integrated.
  - Business and Technical BPM are managed in a single implementation environment without complex interfacing and synchronization across the layers.
- The business processes, defined in management terms, provide "control" over the technology landscape.
  - Since the middleware provides top-to-bottom integration, one can have confidence that end-to-end business processes are actually implemented in accordance with business requirements.
  - Technologists have confidence that they are developing and deploying in accordance with business requirements.
- All aspects of the solution are standards based, and the solution accommodates services provided by any vendor that adheres to the WS-* standards.
- The solution allows for the reuse of existing services or the development of new services.
- The solution allows for BPEL segmentation for reuse.
- The solution allows for canonical data model extensions that are reusable.
- The architecture leverages the investment in existing systems
- No one vendor dominates the technology landscape.
  - This is consistent with the technology landscape in most large organizations.
- Implementation does not require a "big bang" approach.
  - The deployment is on a process-by-process basis. This characteristic allows one to begin with smaller initiatives while moving to larger initiatives as experience matures.

The documentation and analyses of these derived benefits are the foci of our ongoing research efforts.

8 Conclusions

Service-orientation can be presented within a distributed network management framework, but at risk of overlooking the true value of SOA to the business. Managers are focused on the execution of end-to-end business processes that add customer value.[8] If SOA can enable these business processes with higher quality and more timely information, then the business value of SOA is defined.

This chapter presents a composite application approach for aligning a service-oriented model with value-adding business processes. The approach can be implemented using multiple vendor product suites, and the implementation roadmap is defined and documented in a procedural model.

BPM to SOA supports the complete alignment of business requirements to implemented processes in a round trip model. This structure generates many benefits over and above traditional approaches to aligning requirements with implementation projects. While manual intervention is still required, it is clear that the system implementation landscape is evolving to a new paradigm. The old paradigm was characterized by an enterprise architecture that is not formally connected with implemented systems. Therefore, plans that are documented in the architecture are seldom realized at the implementation level. With an executable architecture, the plan is directly linked to the implementation layer, ensuring that business requirements are realized.

References

Bashein BJ, Markus L, Riley P (1994) Preconditions for BPR success and how to prevent failures. Inform Syst Manage 11(2):7–13

Bugajski J (2008) Master data management: a pivotal process. The Burton Group, Midvale, Utah

Datz T (2004) What you need to know about service-oriented architectures. CIO Mag 17(7):78–85

Davenport TH (1993) Process innovation: reengineering work through information technology. Harvard Business School Press, Boston

Earl MJ (1994) The new and the old of business process redesign. J Strat Inform Syst 3(1):5–22

Ellis K (2008) Diagnosing requirements failure. IAG, New Castle, Delaware

Ferguson DF, Stockton M (2006) Enterprise business process management: architecture, technology, and standards. In: Dustdar S et al. (eds) BPM 2006. Springer-Verlag, Heidelberg

Gulledge T (2006) ERP Gap-fit analysis from a business process orientation. Int J Serv Stand 2(4):339–348

Gulledge T (2008) Architecture-driven enterprise integration. Int J Manage Enterp Dev 5(3):265–309

Gulledge T, Deller G (2009) Service-oriented concepts: bridging between managers and technologists. Ind Manage Data Syst 109(1):5–15

Gulledge T, Iyer R, Hiroshige S, Johansson M, Rosén J (2008) Modeling an enterprise services enabled product improvement process for military vehicles. In: Proceedings of the ASME 2008 international design engineering technical conferences & computers in engineering conference. American Society of Mechanical Engineers, New York

Gulledge T, Hiroshige S, Iyer R (2009) Conditioned-based maintenance and the product improvement process. Comput Ind (forthcoming)

Iyer R, Gulledge TR (2005) Product lifecycle management for U.S. army weapon system acquisition, In: Proceedings of the international conference on product lifecycle management PLM 05, Lyon, France

[8]Value considerations are focused on in more detail in the second volume of the BPM handbook. You may want to refer to the chapters on Strategic Alignment and Government (vom Brocke and Rosemann 2010).

Linthicum DS (2007) Extending your SOA outside of your enterprise to enable service provider integration (presentation). Bridgewerx Technologies
Manes AT (2008) SOA report card, presentation at the burton group catalyst conference
McDowell J (2006) Long-running transactions: mapping conversations in the asynchronous enterprise (presentation). Grand Central Communications
Oracle Corporation (2008) Composite application management: bridging the IT visibility gap in complex composite applications, an Oracle white paper. Redwood Shores, California
Scharstein P (2007) Oracle business process analysis suite, presentation at Nordic process days, Stockholm
Stiehl V (2007) Composite applications: NeueVerfahren für Flexible Geschäftsprozesse. Inform Spektrum 30(6):413–418
vom Brocke J, Rosemann M (2010) Handbook on business process management. Strategic alignment, governance, people and culture, vol 2. Springer, Berlin
Werth D, Leyking K, Dreifus F, Ziemann J, Martin A (2007) Managing SOA through business services: a business-oriented approach to service-oriented architectures. In: Georgakopoulos D et al. (eds) Proceedings, ICSOC 2006. Springer, Heidelberg
Xu H, Nord JH, Brown N, Nord GD (2002) Data quality issues in implementing and ERP. Ind Manage Data Syst 102(1):47–58

Business Process Management and Semantic Interoperability

Alexander Dreiling

Abstract Contemporary organizations are exposed to an environment that is changing at a continually increasing pace. Some of the external forces challenging organizations today are *Business Network Transformation, Business Process Outsourcing, Web 2.0*, the *Internet of Services, the Internet of Things* and the *Changing Needs of End Users* in organizations. In this environment, organizations must retain internal stability and focus on improving their core strengths to stay competitive and grow both their top and bottom lines. However, leveraging the full potential of each of these trends requires organizations to be agile, co-innovate within supply webs and continually redefine relationships. The major challenge that arises for Business Process Management and Semantic Interoperability (BPM&SI) research and future technology is the mitigation of risks arising from these conflicting themes. The purpose of this chapter is to motivate several research themes and technology research areas within the field of BPM&SI that will address this conflict in order to leverage the full potential of BPM in the future.

1 Introduction

Business Process Management and Semantic Interoperability (BPM&SI) research has its roots in three distinct areas: *Business Process Management, Semantics* and *Interoperability*. Each has a long tradition.[1] Today, we have a sophisticated

A. Dreiling (✉)
Business Process Management and Semantic Interoperability, SAP Research, SAP Australia Pty Ltd, Brisbane, Australia
e-mail: alexander.dreiling@sap.com

[1]Early examples of research emphasizing the notions of BPM are Taylor's Scientific Management (Taylor 1911) and Nordsieck's conceptualisation of an organization (Nordsieck 1934). In particular in the 1990's, business processes and their IT support gained increased attention (Davenport 1993; Hammer 1997). Research in semantics has its roots in linguistics and they are a tradition that

J. vom Brocke and M. Rosemann (eds.), *Handbook on Business Process Management 1*, International Handbooks on Information Systems,
DOI 10.1007/978-3-642-00416-2_23,

understanding of various aspects within these areas. While the term Business Process Management is rather established, Semantic Interoperability, despite past inflated expectations,[2] is a concept that has only recently emerged. In a recent research roadmap provided by the European Union,[3] the concept has been tangibly described within the domain of healthcare: All efforts at creating an electronic health record are pointless unless all relevant stakeholders can access these health records securely and meaning is transmitted correctly and without alteration between different systems, despite changing formats and languages, using different protocols, etc.

However, despite a lot of progress in recent years, the technical state-of-the-art in the area of BPM&SI is challenged through a range of trends in business and society. These trends include *Business Network Transformation, Business Process Outsourcing, Web 2.0* and the *Internet of Services and Things*. Together, they motivate a need for BPM Suites to the extent that the market for these suites will be among the fastest growing software markets at least until 2011.[4] But they also reveal a lack of emphasis on two general research themes in BPM&SI: the *end user* and *communities*. As of today, only with rare exceptions are products, tools, technologies, methods and languages in the area of BPM&SI usable for end users or specifically targeted at them. Similarly, they are not designed to facilitate a community or to be used by a large number of users within a community, whereby the use grows over-proportionally with a growing community. Pre-conditions for working end user or community approaches are usability and a solid value proposition. In turn, if these pre-conditions are not met, BPM tools and technologies will not achieve mass market readiness.

The lack of emphasis on end users and communities is not the only problem preventing BPM tools and technologies from broad adoption. Despite progress in the more technical space of Workflow Management, we are still not in a position to have a clear abstraction layer of processes within applications. Workflow management systems and business applications remain separate tool paradigms, burying application process logic within code and user interfaces. Moreover, current efforts in workflow technology do not target a paradigmatic shift in application development. That is, a shift towards describing process flows similarly to data structures in a dedicated abstraction layer is required. We continue to treat BPM as a tool, which allows us to package it for specific purposes, but prevents us from using related technology in an additional and very important way: as a means to ease application

---

dates back at least to the ancient Babylonians and later the ancient Greeks (Hymes 1974). In Computer Science, the notion of semantics became important within Artificial Intelligence, Expert Systems and later the Semantic Web.

[2]Rishel 2009.

[3]Stroetmann et al. 2009.

[4]Laurence and Carina (2008) The Business Process Outsourcing market alone (although currently BPM suites are not necessarily a technical enabler for BPO) is estimated by analyst firm IDC to be in excess of 120 Billion USD in 2009 (Dialani et al. 2008). Gartner estimates the same market to be sized around 172 Billion USD in 2009. Both analyst firms estimate the CAGR (compound annual growth rate) at around 10%.

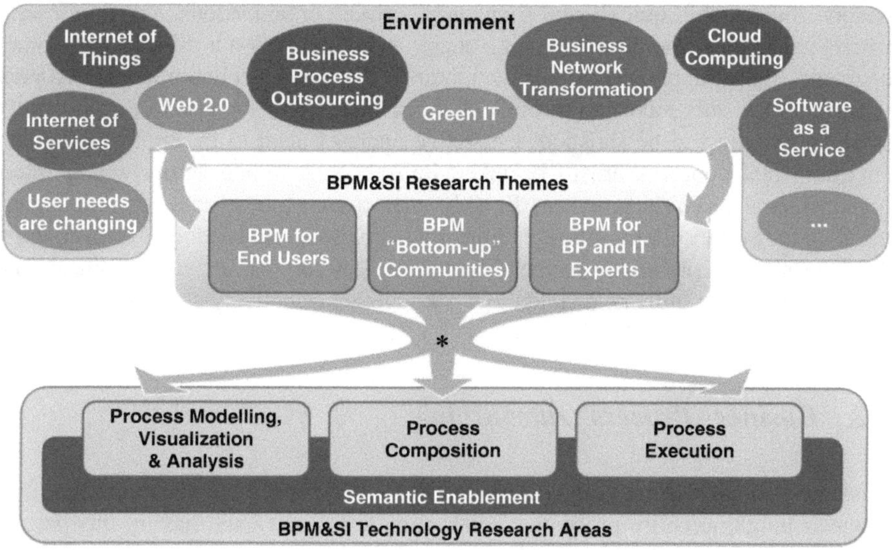

Fig. 1 Changing user needs

development, driving down total cost of development and introducing higher quality standards.

In order for BPM products, tools, technologies, methods and languages to become increasingly mainstream, BPM&SI research needs to focus on *end user and community enablement of BPM* as well as on significantly increasing capabilities in traditional research focussing primarily on business process (BP) and IT experts. In each of these three research themes, significant progress needs to be achieved in three technology research areas: *process modeling, visualization and analysis; process composition; and process execution.* Thereby, semantic *enablement* of these three technology research areas will be of paramount importance for achieving breakthrough results. The research themes and technology research areas mentioned as well as the business trends (introduced in the next section) that lead to a demand for these themes and areas are depicted in Fig. 1. It should be noted that the research challenges described here are of a technical nature. It is explicitly not the focus of this discussion to motivate non-technical challenges that would need to be addressed through sociological or economical research, for example.

2 Major Relevant Business Trends

2.1 Business Network Transformation

Business Network Transformation (BNT) enables contemporary organizations to leverage an entire network for innovation, top line growth and bottom line growth.

Responsibilities shift quickly and frequently between organizations in a supply web, whereby new tiers emerge and existing ones vanish. Innovation is driven by customer demands. Entire supply webs depend on their ability to react collaboratively in a very short time. Pressure increases through changes in the environment of a supply web: shareholders need to be satisfied, legislative changes need to be implemented and environmental concerns are to be taken into account. While actors within inter-organizational business processes flexibly enact upon quickly changing strategies, the technology they use must be enabling, not restricting. Furthermore, the technology they use must be tailored for business user profiles. Actors within inter-organizational business processes must be enabled to work together effectively as a community.

2.2 Business Process Outsourcing

Business Process Outsourcing (BPO) refers to a trend where an economic rationale suggests bundling entire processes, contracting a 3rd party and having this partner execute the process. On the provider-side, economies of scale are achieved through high volumes of transactions, driving down marginal cost for additional transactions, while having the ability to quickly ramp up new customers. On the demand-side, BPO requires similar technological capabilities to BNT. Economically, BPO's key success factor today is standardization. There is currently no market that targets more process flexibility, hence restricting the business case for BPO to a few scenarios such as human resources, procurement and payroll. In these scenarios, variations from standardized processes only rarely make sense from a business perspective or could be critical from a legal perspective. However, if the provider market is to be complemented with solutions where customers can subscribe to business processes that are tailored specifically for them, economies of scale must still be achieved through marginal cost, but the cost of flexibility must be significantly decreased.

2.3 Internet of Services

The vision of the Internet of Services (IoS) is to go beyond the short-tail focus of the current software-as-a-service marketplace and into the long tail of enterprise services, with shifting complexity for the supply and demand sides. Beyond present generation Web Services like ordering books, geographical mash-ups, and booking flights, more complex business transactions from mainstream industries are targeted for the next wave of consumable services; for example, from land search to property conveyance, from business directories to business formation and from disparate personal registrations to cohesive life event support (e.g., births, marriage, change of address). Complex challenges come into view when considering how these could be exposed as commoditised services. These are long-running, and interactions with backend applications from potentially several agencies need to be reliably mediated. Navigation of such services needs to be as seamless for consumers as linking to pages, facilitated by semantic descriptions of services and their interactions. On the demand-side, business processes, not just individuals, are expected to be consumers of "cloud" services. When harnessed through business processes, services are being drawn out of internal stovepipes and rigid B2B interactions. The demands of users and communities drive what business processes need to be composed out of services, whereby the detour through IT departments poses significant restrictions such as longer cycles, increased TCO, and problems associated with what is commonly called the business-IT divide. The single biggest challenge that arises for application providers is how to address the long tail imposed through the Internet of Services vision appropriately.

2.4 *Internet of Things*

The Internet of Things (IoT) fuses the digital world and the physical world by bringing different concepts and technical components together: pervasive networks, miniaturization of devices, mobile communication and new models for business processes. Applications, services, middleware components, networks, and end-points will be structurally connected in entirely new ways. Tangible business benefits will include high resolution management of assets and products, improved lifecycle management and better collaboration between enterprises. Improved sensor and device capabilities will also allow business logic to be executed on the "edges" of a network, enabling existing business processes to be decentralized for the benefit of performance, scalability and local decision making. Within supply webs, the IoT vision leads to increased transparency, shorter decision cycles and shorter exception handling cycles. It will be end users and communities that drive actual business processes leveraging the IoT, and therefore, supporting technologies must be tailored accordingly.

2.5 *Changing Needs of End Users*

The consequences of an ever increasing amount of technology surrounding us, particularly in the consumer space, are manifold in various areas such as society and business. Most importantly, with members of Generation Y now being the well-established young generation within contemporary organizations and members of Generation Z close to entering organizational life, there is an increasing amount of organizational actors that get quickly frustrated with cumbersome technology, restricting technology, the inability to do things themselves, interaction lengths that exceed their attention spans and the inability to share information and consume shared information. These highly connected young organizational actors live and act within various new digital networks in their private life, which becomes their mode of being. Unless these mechanisms are resembled in organizational IT, the full potential of Generation Y and Z members cannot be unleashed. Hence, there must be a specific emphasis on topics such as self-enablement, community enablement and information sharing within the area of BPM&SI.

3 Research Themes

All introduced business trends substantiate the claim made in the introduction: without an increased focus of BPM&SI research on *BPM for End users*, *BPM for BP* and *IT Experts* and *BPM "Bottom-Up" (for Communities)*, the resulting challenges cannot be addressed. Decisions to shift responsibilities between organizations (e.g., BNT and BPO) are not decisions made by IT departments. These decisions are made by senior executives within lines of business or by the executive board of organizations. Inefficient or ineffective software support for a certain business process is detected within the business not within IT departments. And finally, many organizational actors within business processes need to somehow interact with computers through traditional interfaces (keyboard, mouse and screen), whereby the gap between business applications and consumer applications has widened over the past few years. In particular, when innovation is introduced, the positive effects of increased efforts in end user consumption are undeniable.[5] Several BPMS vendors have recently started to target end users and communities in particular and were able to gain firsthand experience.[6]

In this section, we will introduce the three BPM&SI research themes, *BPM for End users*, *BPM for BP* and *IT Experts* and *BPM "Bottom-Up" (for Communities)* in more detail.

3.1 BPM for End Users

Today, most BPM&SI technologies, applications, methods, languages and products are primarily targeted at more technical users such as developers, process architects and technical consultants. Even though things are slowly changing, end users play virtually no role in BPM initiatives today. However, the knowledge on how business processes are executed in organizations resides in end users. This problem is commonly referred to as the business–IT gap and manifests in the space of BPM&SI in that the "business user is an untapped source of process operational expertise."[7] This is critical as the vast majority of IT users are non-technical users (Fig. 2).

---

[5]Phelan 2009.

[6]Kerremans et al. 2009.

[7]Rosser 2008.

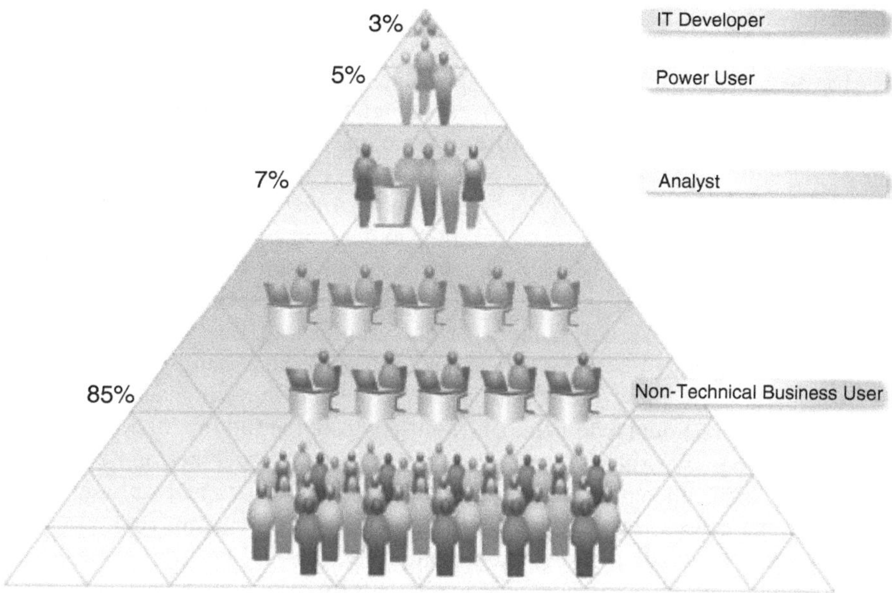

Fig. 2 Distribution of IT users in contemporary organizations (Quinn 2005)

Supporting the business user appropriately remains a major challenge from an application provision perspective if another fact, in particular, is considered: 82% of all decision makers consider the user interface a determining factor for a replacement of existing business applications; 86% of these decision makers see the user interface as the primary reason for productivity gains.[8] This shows how much the end user is emphasized in procurement decisions, not only in terms of functionality, but also in terms of experience. Unless the technological excellence of a BPM Suite is targeted at business or end users, applications with this target group will fail on the market.

3.2 BPM Bottom-Up ("BPM for Communities")

BPM Bottom-up focuses on leveraging two recent trends. The first is the *societal trend* of sharing information, consuming shared information, and relying on information that originated in a community (bazaar style[9]) rather than on information that originated in privileged groups (cathedral style). The second is a *technological* trend that makes end user devices and technologies increasingly usable so that more and more large-scale consumer platforms arise that depend purely on technology,

[8]Thornton 2007.

[9]For a discussion on the paradigms bazaar vs. cathedral in software engineering (Raymond 1999).

both hardware-based (e.g., mobile phones) and software-based (Internet platforms such as Facebook, LinkedIn, etc.). As of today, the community structure within BPM is such that a small amount of actors have knowledge on languages, tools, technologies, methods or products. Process modeling, implementation, analysis and re-engineering initiatives in organizations are executed by some of these few knowledgeable actors but often lack support and acceptance of a larger community within these organizations. Leveraging the societal and technological trends discussed above in the BPM&SI space will help to overcome the community structure that is unfavorable if BPM is to become increasingly mainstream.

As a result, a second major challenge from the perspective of application provisioning is the effective support of communities. A direct effect of better community enablement of BPM&SI technologies, methods, languages, tools and products is a value proposition that stretches beyond the top management and targets all organizational members. BPM initiatives of the future will be conducted bottom-up, whereby organizational actors expose their processes and share this knowledge with colleagues. Aggregations of such processes resemble an entire organizational process landscape whereby acceptance and support from the users who carry the knowledge on operations and procedures no longer pose a problem. Solutions of the future will be delivered as a platform, where users can subscribe to modeling and consuming processes, because they have an intrinsic motivation to do so. This motivation is manifold and consists of an interest in understanding organizational procedures beyond their reach, understanding best practices in other organizations and enabling more efficient and targeted interactions with colleagues.

3.3 BPM for BP and IT Experts

Research targeted at BP and IT experts has probably the longest tradition within the area of BPM&SI. Today, we have a sophisticated understanding of various aspects within these areas. In the area of BPM, examples include the knowledge of what patterns exist in business processes,[10] how to support business processes through workflow technology[11] or how to express business processes in models.[12] In the area of semantics, examples are ontologies and reasoners that help us to build representations of the real world and infer from sets of rules. Semantic interoperability in particular has been progressing with EDI over the past decades, which is nothing other than a taxonomy of business documents.

However, despite the progress made in these areas, many problems remain unsolved. The single biggest problem from an enterprise application provision perspective is the still prevalent separation of workflow management systems

[10]For a discussion on the paradigms bazaar vs. cathedral in software engineering (Raymond 1999).

[11]Aalst and Hee 2004.

[12]Weske 2007.

(WFMS) and business applications, or, to put it differently, an insufficient decoupling of a process perspective within business applications. Workflows, or more abstractly business processes, are hardcoded within applications (insufficient abstraction), and if they are explicit in WFMS, they are often decoupled from business applications (two different application paradigms). The consequences are higher total cost of application development, higher cost of process adaptation and insufficient transparency of how business processes are executed.

It has long been demanded to decouple a process layer within applications similarly to data that, in today's large-scale applications, is handled within database management systems. However, since we have clearly not yet arrived there, we must assert that such an abstraction has consequences beyond those originally anticipated. In fact, such an abstraction changes the current programming models fundamentally, leading to a new paradigm for application development. Developers in the future will describe processes within enterprise applications with a set of low-level technical patterns taking into account security, data access and integrity, constraints and business logic. Functionality will be invoked through fine-granular services. The paradigmatic shift will be to *describe* processes during application development rather than implementing them, similar to how data structures are described in SQL rather than implemented.

The third challenge from the perspective of application provisioning is thus not targeted at prospective users, but at the process of developing these applications. If successfully addressed, total cost of development will go down as developers do not have to implement business logic and constraints anymore. These aspects can be modeled and invoked. In the same instance, quality will be higher as the risk for errors decreases. Also, through the ability to change business processes more quickly, the business value associated with Business Process Outsourcing and Business Network Transformation can be realized. Furthermore, the visions of the Internet of Services and Things will be substantiated through a foundation for composing processes from fine-granular services invoking representations of objects in the real world.

4 Technology Research Areas

So far, we have discussed business trends and resulting research themes for the BPM&SI Research Program. This section is concerned with three technology research areas: *Process Modeling, Visualization and Analysis*; *Process Composition*; and *Process Execution*. Technological progress in these three areas will be used to facilitate the creation of a sufficient knowledge base within the three themes *BPM for End Users*, *BPM for BP* and *IT Experts and BPM Bottom-up*, which in turn aims at realizing the associated benefits.

Intersecting the three introduced research themes with the three technology research areas leads to nine different areas in which capabilities need to be built up. This relationship is depicted in Fig. 3.

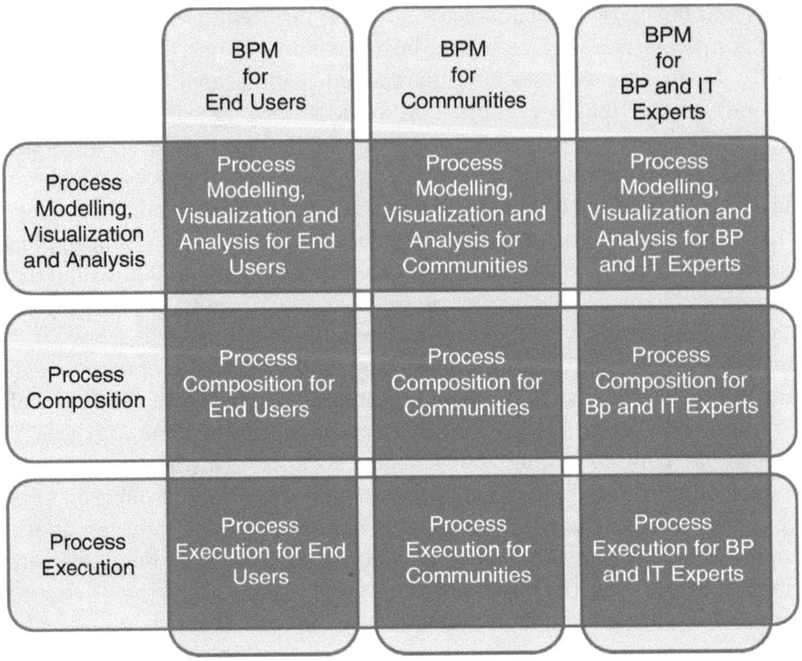

Fig. 3 BPM&SI research challenges as a result of research themes and technology research areas

4.1 Process Modeling, Visualization and Analysis

The first technology research area is concerned with expressing and analyzing business processes. In order to successfully target end users in particular, several research questions must be addressed. First and foremost, it must be understood what kind of modeling techniques and paradigms are most appropriate for end users. Research in this area will need to go beyond strip-down versions of BPMN. Good examples of mass consumable process description are cook books and they rarely come along as process models. A single end user nearly always works on tasks sequentially, hence if they are to express processes they work on, do we really need splits and joins or can we find alternative means to express conditions and their implications? Similarly, we need to understand how end users are most effectively enabled to analyze processes. How can process analysis information be embedded into applications familiar to end users such as MS Outlook, MS Excel or widgets and how can it be delivered through consumer appliances such as mobile phones? In many instances, the leading UI of end users follows a certain paradigm. For example, in GIS (Geo spatial Information System), users spend significant amounts of time looking at maps. How can process information be efficiently compiled, re-bundled and embedded into such environments? How can process analysis information be shared effectively amongst involved stakeholders? How can end users be enabled to define process KPIs that matter for them and analyze processes accordingly?

Enabling the end user is only the first step in order to transform the notion of BPM to be mass market ready. Understanding how communities can effectively collaborate on BPM initiatives is the next step and of paramount importance. How can a community of modelers overcome problems such as different levels of modeling abstraction? How can modelers work rather independently whereby the combination of all individual models not only makes sense but provides an organizational process landscape? With many of the problems being associated with stakeholders speaking different languages, what are the semantic prerequisites for working BPM community approaches? Also, can the viral models existing in other application domains work in BPM? This requires conditions in which single end users, or a single line of business profits from process modeling or analysis, and additional users increase the value for the entire user base. Quite possibly, a "cloud" infrastructure can help in this respect as public clouds can host a multitude of players and their users. So what does "cloud" BPM look like, in particular, for modeling, visualization and analysis? What is the benefit of a cloud solution over an on-premise solution other than common economic factors? Obviously, a successful BPM-related tool in this space must also be lightweight, interactive and to a certain extent entertaining so that a single user or a single line of business would want to subscribe to the corresponding service.

The third and final set of research challenges in the area of process modeling, visualization and analysis targets BP and IT experts. More traditional yet not fully addressed problems include mappings between flow-oriented (more native and understandable process description) and block-structured (machine-interpretable) BP languages in order to develop transformations from, e.g., BPMN to BPEL. While this problem targets WFMS (that are primarily decoupled from enterprise systems today), it needs to be examined in more detail which patterns (existing sets and news ones) allow application developers to declare processes similar to data structures in SQL so that a proper process abstraction layer in application development becomes reality. For both cases, significant research is necessary in order to bridge the gap between end user and community tools, and languages motivated above and the technical layers. With the envisaged progress in the end user and community spaces, particularly through using semantic mechanisms to describe process blocks, breakthrough in usability can be achieved. As constraint-based process languages get more popular, major challenges also remain in the area of bridging the gap between constraint-based languages and flow-based languages.

4.2 Process Composition

As with process modeling, visualization and analysis, three different research themes must be supported within the technology research area of process composition: end users, communities and BP and IT experts. Furthermore, there are two types of composition that need to be taken into account: core process composition and process context composition. The former refers to putting activities into a timely order to execute accordingly. The latter refers to putting an activity within a process into context to make informed decisions where necessary, also known as "mash-up". For information workers in particular, the borderline between both paradigms blurs.

For end users, important questions include from what they actually compose both processes and process context. In general, domain-independent modeling paradigms (e.g., "activity" or "event") seem to be too cumbersome to be handled by end users and too many problems remain, such as different levels of abstraction in modeling. Accordingly, how can domain-specific semantic building blocks (e.g., "print" or "file") be leveraged effectively for both types of composition? How can end users effectively contribute to the definition of such semantic building blocks? How can they change and configure them? What level of semantic commitment from end users is necessary for the adaptation of underlying domain ontologies?

Understanding what it is that end users can effectively compose processes and their context from is only the first step. What means of automatic process composition can be used to facilitate process composition for end users and what do they need to specify in order for a tool to automatically compose a process for them? What do composition tools look like or how can composition services be embedded in existing end user tools? What are good use cases for both process composition and process context composition, either defining processes from scratch or extend/configure/customize existing processes? How can collaboration between end users be facilitated most effectively? How can consumer space devices such as smart phones be systematically leveraged for collaboration within processes?

Enabling BPM community approaches is the next significant challenge along the way to mass market readiness. How can entire communities compose processes together while members specify their tasks independent of each other? What mechanisms are necessary in order to specify interfaces between users? What mechanisms must be in place in order to define processes along entire supply chains crossing organizational borders? If organizational borders are crossed, how can interoperability between different sets of semantic process building blocks be achieved? How can different sets of expertise in a community be leveraged in order to arrive at composed processes? What level of expertise is necessary in order to define business rules, conditions or possible combinations of process building blocks? Facilitating a community of modelers supposedly works best with a shared infrastructure. If so, how can a BPM-centric platform-as-a-service in the "cloud" be established that caters for the needs of a community? For instance, how can hosted processes be turned into services by their owners and offered for a charge? Use cases like this to highlight differences between on-premise and on-demand BPM solutions that go beyond mere technological distinctions or economic calculations.

Once end user and community enablement are sufficiently understood, the resulting mechanisms need to be tied back to a more technical layer. Here, it is necessary to make sense out of what end users have specified or documented.

Similarly, the task here is to abstract sufficiently from technical details within applications and to describe on a business level how processes are executed. At this stage, no sufficient integration between end user languages or tools and technical representations has been achieved within large-scale applications. A resulting question is how semantic process building blocks that make sense for end users are represented technically? The relationship between representations for end users and BP and IT experts is many-to-many. A technically identical concept can be translated into two different things for end users. Similarly, two things that are identical for an end user can have multiple technical representations. How can this many-to-many relationship be managed? How can it be guaranteed that there are no technical collisions from specifications of end users or communities? In addition to technical support for end user and community enablement, there is a range of technically hard problems that has not yet been sufficiently addressed. How do technical services need to be designed in order to qualify for the composition of a workflow? How does state-retaining information need to be specified in a workflow that is composed from services? How are exceptions handled, which exceptions are propagated back to end users, and how can this be done? How does all of this work in a "cloud" environment?

In the area of process context, we are far less mature than in the traditional technical workflow research. Here, the questions are centered around type systems for message exchange, suitability of bus concepts for event handling, architectural options of distributing workload between server and client with their security implications, development and delivery paradigms of mash-up components for technical experts, and their link to end user capabilities. In particular, the Internet of Services vision will be facilitated by addressing the research challenges in the process composition technology research area.

4.3 Process Execution

Important research challenges in the area of process execution remain for the end user. Most importantly, end users need to be able to take control of running workflows as they "own" the business processes behind the workflows. They need to be able to change or stop them, adapt them, adjust control flow and other activities. How can this be achieved without compromising the integrity of running processes? How can rollback mechanisms be added to points where end users can influence running processes? How can they systematically monitor a running process from a business perspective? How do compiler concepts look that translate high-level languages into kernel concepts? How can domain-specific semantic building blocks be translated to domain-independent kernel concepts? A recent trend in community ready applications is a blurred borderline between runtime and design time. Can this borderline be blurred in the area of BPM as well and, if yes, how? In particular for process context through mash-ups, it is of paramount importance that users can make changes that take immediate effect, ideally while they make these changes.

In the community context, process execution also faces a range of challenges. How does distributed workflow execution change through SOA across organizations? How can governance mechanisms be specified that retain various levels of integrity, such as legal integrity, integrity from a business perspective (such as constraints being in line with corporate goals) and integrity from a technical perspective (such as data integrity)? How can the semantic gaps be closed that inevitably exist in larger communities, in particular in communities that span across organizations? How can community approaches be integrated into legacy applications for seamlessly running larger processes and for analysis?

The single most important challenge that remains in the space of BP and IT experts is how to develop technologies that will aid application development by decoupling a process layer similarly to the separation of the data layer. In other words, how can the still existing distinction of WFMS and enterprise applications be overcome? How can business integrity mechanisms be manifested in a more technical process layer within applications so that a better segregation of duties can be achieved during development? If process technology is to be an integral part of applications, how can the corresponding technologies scale to throughputs of millions of daily transactions, particularly within larger communities? Furthermore, there are many challenges associated with defining workflows from services, which is the cornerstone for the Internet of Services vision. How can a workflow layer handle states if it is loosely coupled from services? How can rollbacks be achieved in such an environment? How can a workflow layer handle services if the services themselves impose activities that transcend the context of the workflow? How can rollbacks be achieved in such an environment?

5 Summary

In this chapter, we have motivated that research in BPM&SI needs to stretch beyond the directions currently taken. In order to achieve the benefits associated with systematically supporting business processes with technology, it is of paramount importance to specifically target additional user groups and scenarios.

Business or end users hold the expertise on procedures and operations in organizations. Systematically including them in BPM initiatives must go beyond involving them in interviews on how processes are executed. Unless they will be provided with tools and technologies, which they understand and from which they get value, they will never be part of a BPM initiative.

Understanding and supporting the needs of business or end users directly leads to a second research theme, that of communities. Human beings have formed communities for a long time, but it is an undeniable societal trend, enforced through technological progress that many of these communities become virtual. Examples within the consumer space show us that people see value in joining technology-enabled networks and building communities there. So far, there is no reason to believe that the mechanisms that work for Facebook, MySpace and others cannot work in an organizational setting for the sake of collaboration and for supporting business processes within and across organizations.

These two new research themes in the area of BPM&SI need to be complemented with breakthrough progress in the more traditional space of research, that of supporting BP and IT experts. After many years of research, business applications and workflow management systems remain separate paradigms. We have not yet fully understood what it means to replace application development with one of the prevalent paradigms (object-oriented, functional or imperative) by application development, whereby one part is the explicit description of processes. We also have not yet fully understood what it means to turn control of large-scale business applications to workflow engines at runtime to support this paradigm holistically.

Unless these three research themes are addressed appropriately, it is questionable as to whether BPM&SI tools, technologies, methods, languages and products will ever be broadly adopted. In this case, it is similarly questionable as to whether we will ever be able to overcome the current cathedral-style community structure in BPM&SI. In turn, it is our strong belief that the future will hold significant opportunities for those who will be able to provide answers to the questions outlined in this essay.

References

Aalst WM, Hee KM (2004) Workflow management: models, methods, and systems. The MIT Press, Cambridge, MA

Davenport TH (1993) Process innovation: reengineering work through information technology. Harvard Business School Press, Boston, MA, USA

Dialani M, Rowan L, Anderson C, Tapper D, Loynd S (2008) Economic crisis response: worldwide and US business process outsourcing services 2008–2012 forecast – market opportunities by key horizontal business process update. IDC, Framingham, MA

Hammer M (1997) Beyond reengineering: how the processed-centered organisation. HarperBusiness, New York, NY

Hymes D (ed) (1974) Studies in the history of linguistics. Traditions and paradigms. Indiana University Press, Bloomington, IN

Kerremans M, Cantara M, Plummer DC (2009) Cool vendors in business process management, 2009. Gartner, Inc., Stamford, CT

Laurence G, Carina F (2008) Business process management suites (BPMS) will be among the fastest growing software markets through 2011. Gartner, Inc. http://www.gartner.com/it/page.jsp?id=502645

Nordsieck F (1934) Grundlagen der Organisationslehre. Schäffer-Poeschel, Stuttgart, Germany

Phelan P (2009) Consuming innovation in ERP and other engineered application suites. Gartner, Inc., Stamford, CT

Quinn K (2005). Not everyone who drives a car fixes it themselves – strategic information infrastructure. DMReview.com. http://www.dmreview.com/news/1041222-1.html. Accessed Sept 2008

Raymond ES (1999) The cathedral and the bazaar. O'Reilly & Associates, Inc., Sebastopol, CA

Rishel W (2009) Semantic interoperability on the hype cycle for healthcare provider technologies and standards. Gartner, Inc., Stamford, CT

Rosser B (2008) Taking advantage of user-friendly business process modeling. Garnter, Inc., Stamford, CT

Stroetmann VN, Kalra D, Lewalle P, Rector A, Rodrigues JM, Stroetmann KA et al. (2009) Semantic interoperability for better health and safer healthcare. European Commission, Information Society and Media, Brussles, Belgium

Taylor FW (1911) The principles of scientific management. Harper and Row, New York, NY

Thornton J (2007) Well-designed user interface is critical in enterprise software buying decisions. Lawson Software. http://www.lawson.com/wcw.nsf/pub/new_3A0F0B. Accessed Sept 2008

Weske M (2007) Business process management: concepts, languages, architectures. Springer, Berlin, Heidelberg, New York

Business Process Management Standards

Frank Leymann, Dimka Karastoyanova, and Michael P. Papazoglou

Abstract This chapter discusses the evolution of standards for BPM. The focus is on technology-related standards, especially on standards for specifying process models. A discussion of the two fundamental approaches for modeling processes, graph-based and operator-based, supports a better understanding of the evolution of standards. For each standard discussed, we describe its core concepts and its impact on the evolution of standards. The corresponding influence on the overall architecture of BPM environments is worked out.

1 Introduction

There are a variety of reasons why standards in the area of Business Process Management is important today for both users of such systems as well as builders of such systems. We sketch the key reasons for this in what follows.

Users of Business Process Management suites are looking for investment protection by requiring the ability to port their process-based applications across different BPM environments. Portability includes both porting such applications across runtime environments as well as across build time environments (a.k.a. tool interoperability). This is needed because process-based applications support key business processes of a company, that is, the applications must be supported independent from the vendor environment chosen. The vendor providing the BPM environment actually in use may cease to exist or it may be decided to abandon the relation with that vendor. Thus, existing process-based applications

F. Leymann (✉)
Institute of Architecture of Application Systems (IAAS), University of Stuttgart, Stuttgart, Germany
e-mail: leymann@iaas.uni-stuttgart.de

J. vom Brocke and M. Rosemann (eds.), *Handbook on Business Process Management 1*, International Handbooks on Information Systems,
DOI 10.1007/978-3-642-00416-2_24, © Springer-Verlag Berlin Heidelberg 2010

must be able to be ported from one BPM environment to another with as less effort as possible.

A BPM environment itself is complex, consisting of many components: modeling tools, execution engine, monitoring tools, etc. These components must interoperate, that is, they must be able to be mixed resulting in an overall BPM environment. For example, companies using BPM technology often have a "best of breed" strategy, that is, components of the BPM environment from different vendors must be able to be mixed. Consequently, standards are needed to allow building a BPM environment out of components from different vendors in a "mix-and-match" mode.

Large companies often have a multivendor setup, that is, they run the same type of BPM component (or even complete BPM environments) from different vendors. For example, two different organizational units of a company may run two different execution engines from two different vendors, or they may run two different modeling tools from two different vendors. Thus, interoperability is a must because business processes often span organizational units within a company, and standards have to support this interoperability.

Major components of a BPM environment (e.g., a process engine) have become key ingredients of today's middleware stack. Process engines, especially, have importance comparable to application servers or even database management systems. Thus, many applications make use of BPM technology.

Standardization of BPM features will significantly contribute to skill reuse of the personnel involved in building process-based applications, running, and managing an overall BPM environment.

Also, accepted standards are a strong indicator of the maturity of a technology. When most vendors implement the standards covering a technology, this technology is typically established and proven. At that point in time, even companies not being early adopters of the technology begin to use the technology in their environments: the technology becomes an accepted element of the overall IT stack.

This chapter presents multiple standards, both standards of the past and standards that are actually implemented in products. Not all standards that have been proposed are presented but only a subset thereof. Note explicitly that this chapter is subjective, and it shows personal opinions: one of the authors is active in the field of Business Process Management and its standardization since more than two decades. The implication of this is that some background information is given in this chapter, but neutrality is not always ensured (although tried hard). Even the selection of standards covered may already be seen as subjective; note that the focus of the standards discussed will be on languages, not on the various APIs proposed. Because BPM standards are complex, this chapter cannot be a tutorial on any of the standards touched – for most of these standards, such a tutorial would fill a whole book. Instead, we sketch the main features of each standard discussed and its main contributions to the evolution of BPM standards as a whole. Evolution is a historic process, thus, we also discuss standards that are no longer pursued but that have a deep impact on today's accepted standards.

2 Workflow Management Coalition

The Workflow Management Coalition (WfMC) released a set of specifications, but the most influential of these specifications is the so-called "WfMC Reference Model" (Workflow Management Coalition 1995): This reference model describes the major components of a BPM environment and the interfaces between these components. The other standards published by the WfMC specify the details of these interfaces.

Figure 1 is an adapted variant of the architecture described by the reference model. The center of each BPM environment is the *execution engine*, which instantiates and executes models of business processes. Such models are created by a *process modeling tool* and are imported into the execution engine via a corresponding interface. Especially, a process model specifies whether an activity is to be performed by a human being (so-called "people activity") or directly by a program (so-called "automatic activity"). Correspondingly, when executing a process, the execution engine generates requests to human beings to perform a particular activity (so-called "workitems") or it ensures the immediate execution of the respective program. The component responsible for managing workitems is the *workitem manager*, while the *application invocation* component is in charge of dealing with all of the idiosyncrasies of communicating with a program performing an automatic activity. In cases where an activity is realized as another process (so-called "subprocess") performed by a second execution engine, a corresponding interface has to furnish this. Finally, the management of (actual and past) processes as well as artifacts related to process is performed via the *management tool*.

The importance of the reference model can be seen in having provided a clear mental model about the key ingredients of a process management environment.

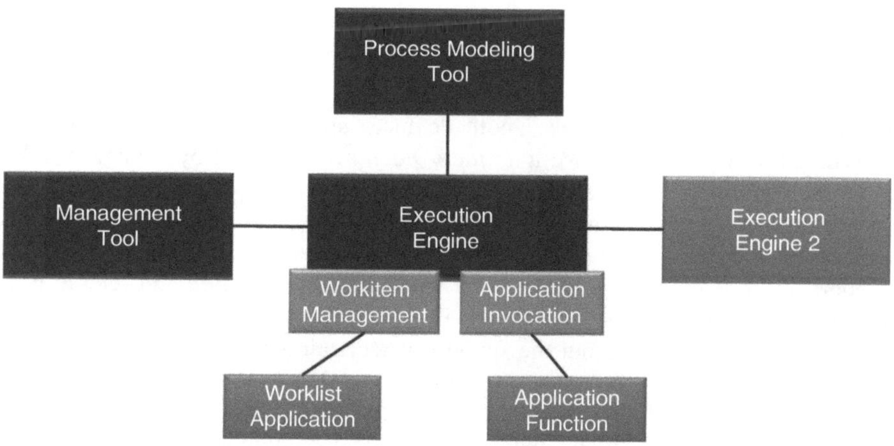

Fig. 1 BPM environment (adaptation of Workflow Management Coalition 1995)

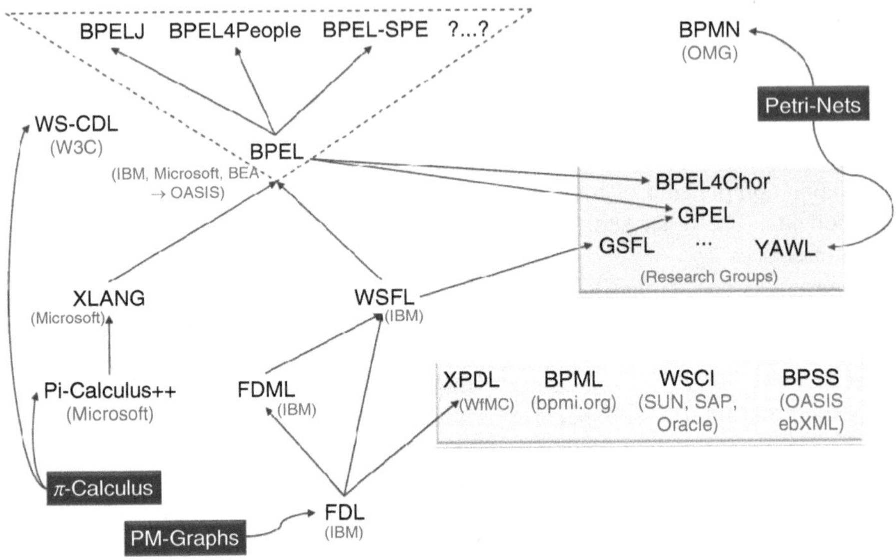

Fig. 2 Some relations between business process languages

This mental model is still applicable in today's service-oriented environment as we will show in Sect. 7.

Before discussing standards for specifying business processes in more detail in the rest of this chapter, we present the influence of one standard on other standards in the next section (see Fig. 2). We also introduce the two fundamental approaches to specify process models, namely the graph-based approach and the operator-based approach.

3 Some Influential Standards of the Past

When talking about "standards," both de facto and de jure standards must be considered in the area of BPM: a *de facto standard* is defined by a single vendor or a small group of vendors, and by the joint market share of these vendors, the specification becomes a standard within that market segment; a *de jure standard* is defined by a public (official) standardization body consisting of many different vendors and interest groups who jointly work on a specification and release it as standard based on majority agreement. But it must be noted that, in general, no conclusion can be made about the support of a certain standard in the industry in terms of its implementation or use based on the fact that a standard is de jure. Based on the motivation for BPM standards given in the introduction, a relevant standard should be supported by "many" vendors. The standard supported by most vendors today (i.e., at the time of publication of this book) is BPEL: it began as a de facto standard and transitioned into a de jure standard. This transition took place in order to enable to reflect input from as many parties as possible to cover requirements from many different areas.

Two main approaches are found in standards to specify process models: a graph-oriented approach (see Sect. 3.1) and an operator-based approach (see Sect. 3.2). Different vendors followed either of these approaches. End of the last century, this resulted in the jeopardy of splitting the BPM market into two different segments, since both approaches seemed to be very different. One very important aspect of BPEL (see Sect. 4) is that it combines both of these approaches, and by doing so, BPEL avoids this split resulting in a single BPM market.

The graph-based approach to process modeling is mostly influenced by PM-graphs and Petri-Nets: the flavor of graph-based approach described in Sect. 3.1 is the basis for languages such as FDL and WSFL (and thus, BPEL), and it has its origins in Process Model graphs (PM graphs for short) introduced in Leymann (1992) and refined in Leymann and Altenhuber (1994). Also, (high-level) Petri-Nets (Jensen and Rozenberg 1991) had a lot of influences on process modeling, mostly within the research community. Various calculi are the foundations of the operator- or calculus-based approach (see Sect. 3.2), the most influential one being the π-calculus (Milner 1999). Figure 2 depicts the relations between the most relevant process modeling languages and their origins; the arrows between two modeling languages indicate that the target of the arrow is based on the source of the arrow. FDL [described in more detail in Leymann and Roller (2000)] was the modeling language of former IBM workflow management products and this language is a textual rendering of PM graphs. This language was extended into FDML, which in turn evolved into WSFL (Leymann 2001), the latter of which supports both, what are today called orchestrations as well as choreographies (see Sect. 3.4). Many concepts of XPDL (Workflow Management Coalition 2005) (the process modeling language published by WfMC) are found in FDL before. π-calculus became the basis of a language developed by Microsoft, which is sometimes referred to a Pi-Calculus++ (Thatte 2008); this language was the predecessor of XLANG (Thatte 2001), which was implemented by Microsoft workflow products. Also, π-calculus is at the underpinnings of WS-CDL (W3C Candidate Recommendation 2005). BPEL resulted by combining WSFL (more precisely: its orchestration aspects) and XLANG. BPEL has been designed to be extensible from the outset; thus, it is the root of a series of specifications (like BPEL4People, for example) that might finally cover the complete space of BPM; we discuss some of these extensions below. In order to support workflow management in a Grid environment, WSFL was the basis for GSFL, which in turn got the foundation together with BPEL for GPEL. Petri-Nets have been exploited to propose process modeling languages out of research like YAWL, and BPMN has an operational semantics, which based on Petri-nets too. We will sketch the essentials of most of these languages below; readers interested in more details about these language but who do not want to read the original specification are referred to (Havey 2005).

3.1 Graph-Based Approach

In a graph-based approach, a process model is specified as an acyclic-directed graph. The *activities* of a process model are represented as nodes of the corresponding graph. The directed edges of the graph (*control connectors*) represent the potential flow of control between two different activities. The data consumed as input and produced as output (input and output *container*) of each of the activities of a process model is referred to as *process context*. To determine the actual control flow within an instance of the corresponding process model at runtime, the control connectors are weighted by *transition conditions*, that is, Boolean conditions in the "process context." Each of the activities is defined to be either a people activity or an automatic activity. A *people activity* is associated with a *staff query* that is used at runtime to find the human beings having the skills or duties to perform the work represented by the activity. An *automatic activity* is associated with a *locator*, which is a query to be used at runtime to find an appropriate program that will automatically complete the work of the activity. Note that because of these assignments to an activity, the graph is often referred to as *colored* graph. To specify how the input container of an activity is computed out of the process context, data connectors are used: a *data connector* is a directed edge (of another type than control connectors) between activities that indicate that the input container of its target activity gets some input data from the output container of its source activity. Like in Fig. 3, control connectors are drawn as solid lines, while data connectors are drawn as dotted lines. Not all approaches to process modeling have such an explicit means to specify the data flow between activities (like FDL or WSFL has); some approaches have no explicit data flow features at all, and some others support at least implicit data flow specifications, for example, by providing special types of activities that allow to define how input data for "regular" activities are materialized (like BPEL).

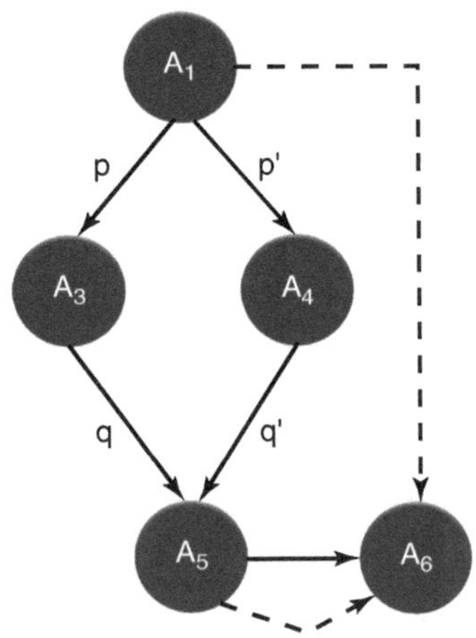

Fig. 3 A process model graph

A running process is created from a process model by *instantiating* the process model graph, which basically creates the (potentially empty) process context, determines the activities with no incoming control connectors (*start activities* – activity A1 in Fig. 3), and schedules them. *Scheduling* an activity means to evaluate its staff query or locator and to create either a work request (*workitem*) for the qualifying human beings (in case of a people activity) or to directly invoke one of the corresponding programs qualifying under the locator (in case of a program activity), respectively. The data connectors targeting at the activity are followed backwards and the data from the output containers of the sources of the data connectors are retrieved to compute the input of the activity. This input is then passed to the workitem or program, respectively. Once the workitem or the program completed, its output data will be copied into the process context; in such a way, the process context is highly dynamic and especially instance dependent. Next, the process engine will determine all outgoing control connectors of this activity, evaluate their transition conditions in the actual process context of the process instance, and will determine the activities being endpoints of those control connectors whose transition conditions evaluated to true. Those activities will be scheduled next. Because of the instance dependency of the process context, the subset of actual paths taken out of the set of potential paths defined by a process model may vary significantly from one instance to the other of a given process model.

When an activity has more than one outgoing control connector, it may be the cause of parallel work being performed in an instance of the process model, namely if more than one of the corresponding transition conditions evaluates to true in the actual process context. Such an activity is called a *fork* activity (A_1 in Fig. 3). In turn, an activity with more than one incoming control connector is referred to as a *join* activity (A_5 in Fig. 3). When the process engine reaches a join activity via a particular control connector, it waits until all other incoming control connectors are traversed and their transition conditions are evaluated before considering scheduling the join activity: thus, effectively, a join activity is a means to synchronize parallel work within a process model. "Considering" to schedule a join activity is based on a join condition associated with each join activity: a join condition is a Boolean condition in the truth values of the incoming transition conditions; the join condition must be true in order to schedule the join activity. The purpose of such a join condition is to define possible combinations of parallel paths at least one of which must have been successfully taken in order to properly perform the join activity. The actual truth value of the transition condition of a control connector targeted at the join activity is assumed to indicate the success of the whole path ending with the corresponding control connector. Thus, if the join condition is true, at least of these combinations of parallel paths has been successfully taken.

In case one of the incoming control connectors of a join activity is not traversed at all, the process engine waits forever blocking the execution of the join activity – a situation that must be avoided. For example, of p' in Fig. 3 evaluates to false, A_4 will never be scheduled and, thus, will never complete, which in turn means that the control connector (A_4, A_5) will never be traversed and A_5 will be blocked. The way how such blocking activities are avoided in the graph-based approach is referred to as *dead path elimination* (DPE): when the process engine detects that an activity will not be performed at all (such an activity is called *dead*), it determines all leaving control connectors of this activity and sets the transition condition of these control connectors to “false,” and this happens in a transitive manner. The reason why the transition condition is set to “false” instead of “true” is that a “true” transition condition would indicate that the corresponding path has been successfully taken, which is not the case. Performing DPE in a transitive manner ensures that all transition conditions of join activities will be evaluated, and the process engine can decide to schedule the activity or continue with dead path elimination. The behavior of dead path elimination is part of standards like FDL, WSFL, BPEL, etc. The above sketched way of how a process engine interprets a process model graph based on the actual process context of a process instance is referred to as *navigation*; navigation is an integral aspect of PM graphs and defines its operational semantics. For details of PM Graphs (Leymann and Roller 2000).

3.2 Operator- or Calculus-Based Approach

While the graph-based approach is very much related to the drawing style familiar to process modelers who are (business) domain experts, the operator- (or calculus-) based approach is much more geared towards a programming-like style of IT-level modelers.

Thus, the operator-based approach provides “constructs” (the operators – see below) that represent control flow mechanisms familiar to programmers to structure the control flow between activities like “sequence” or “loop.” Operators have activities as parameters. At runtime when a process engine applies an operator to its parameter activities, it schedules these activities in the order specified by the control flow semantics of the operator. At the modeling level, applying an operator to its argument activities results in a new activity, that is, the operator-based approach is recursive in nature.

More precisely: Let U be the set of all *activities*; activities act as parameters of operators and they represent the steps performed within a business process. An (*control flow*) operator ω (or operator for short) produces out of a set of parameter activities $\{A_1,\ldots,A_n\}$ a new activity ω $(A_1,\ldots,A_n)$, that is, an operator is a map $\omega:\wp(U) \rightarrow U$, where $\wp(U)$ denotes the powerset of a set U. For example:

- The sequence operator Σ produces out of the activities $A_1,\ldots,A_n$ the activity Σ $(A_1,\ldots,A_n)$, which results at runtime in the sequential unconditional execution of all of the activities $A_1,\ldots,A_n$.
- The parallel operator Π specifies an activity where its constituting parameter activities are performed concurrently, that is, at runtime Π $(A_1,\ldots,A_n)$ in an unconditional parallel execution of its parameter activities $A_1,\ldots,A_n$.
- The decision operator Δ represents an act of decision that chooses one of its parameter activities, that is, Δ $(A_1,\ldots,A_n)$ selects at runtime exactly one of the activities $A_1,\ldots,A_n$ for execution.

The decision as to which of the parameter activities of a Δ operator will be executed depends on conditions that guard each of the activities, and these conditions are further dependent on data produced by the activities that run before the Δ operator, that is, operators may have more complex parameters, but this is not relevant for our discussion. Also, there are more operators than the ones we listed above, that is, if Ω denotes the set of all operators, $\Omega \supseteq \{\Sigma, \Pi, \Delta\}$.

Since operators produce new activities from existing ones, operators can be applied to the result of operators. Especially, operators can be nested by providing an activity produced by an operator as one of the parameter activities of another operator. For example, $A = \Pi(\Sigma(A_1, \Delta(A_4, A_5)), \Sigma(A_2, A_3))$ is an activity that runs two activities in parallel, namely the activity $\Sigma(A_1, \Delta(A_4, A_5))$ and the activity $\Sigma(A_2, A_3)$. Activity $\Sigma(A_1, \Delta(A_4, A_5))$ executes activity A_1 first, followed by activity $\Delta(A_4, A_5)$. Activity $\Delta(A_4, A_5)$ chooses whether activity A_4 or activity A_5 will be performed; this depends on two conditions p and p′, which are not shown as parameters in the operator Δ. $\Sigma(A_2, A_3)$ will perform activity A_2 unconditionally followed by A_3. The control flow structure, that is, the potential flow of control within activity A is depicted in Fig. 4 as a graph.

The operator- or calculus-based approach has its origins in the various process calculi that have been developed since the early seventies of the last century. One of the distinguishing features that process calculi introduced is the ability to communicate via messages instead of communication based on shared variables considered before. Not assuming variables that are explicitly shared has several advantages, for example, contributing to information hiding because no internals of the communicating processes must be made visible to the outside, thus significantly increasing the dynamics of the set of communicating processes. Messages are exchanged via channels between (possibly concurrently executing) processes. The π-calculus even supports the exchange of channels (i.e., their names) between processes, which allows the description of highly dynamic process topologies; this feature of the π-calculus is referred to as *mobility*. Mobility becomes important in loosely coupled systems where the communicating participants do not know each other, thus having to exchange their communication channels amongst each other. Because systems based on SOA are loosely coupled by definition, mobility is important in SOA. Thus, the π-calculus had an impact on process modeling languages that have been proposed at the time SOA became dominant, that is, the early part of this century. For more details about the π-calculus (Milner 1999).

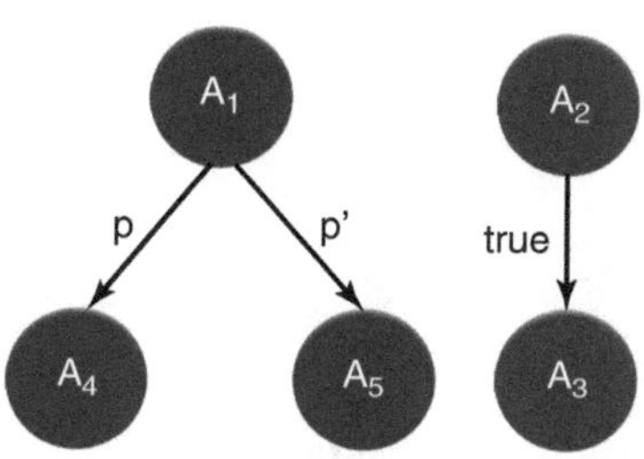

Fig. 4 Nested operators in graph representation

3.3 Running Sample

In the following sections, we describe some de facto or de jure standards, respectively, which had a broader impact on industry and academia. For this purpose, we show how some aspects of the following simple process model from Fig. 5 is represented in the corresponding standards. The sample process model is a simplified variant of the ubiquitous travel booking process. The process begins with an activity that receives the information about the itinerary the client wants to book; the fact that this activity has no incoming control connectors indicates that it is a start activity where each process instance begins. Once the itinerary has been received, the process continues with booking the corresponding flights and booking the hotel rooms required for trips staying overnight. Because not all trips are overnight trips, a corresponding transition condition that checks whether or not the trip is overnight is associated with the control connector between the Get Itinerary activity and the Book Hotel activity. Control flows from the Get Itinerary activity and the Book Flight activity unconditionally (assuming that travel is done by plane). Charge Credit Card is a join activity, that is, it is only scheduled once the Book Flight activity and the Book Hotel activity are completed (or handled by dead path elimination in case the trip does not require the booking of hotel rooms). The running example does not specify whether an activity is an automatic activity or a people activity because the standards we discuss differ in the support of specifying these kinds of activities. Also, the running example does not specify the data flow between the activities explicitly because of the significant differences in the corresponding support in the various standards.

3.4 FDL

Flow Definition Language (FDL) is a graph-based process modeling language that has been developed by IBM in the early nineties. It became a de facto standard

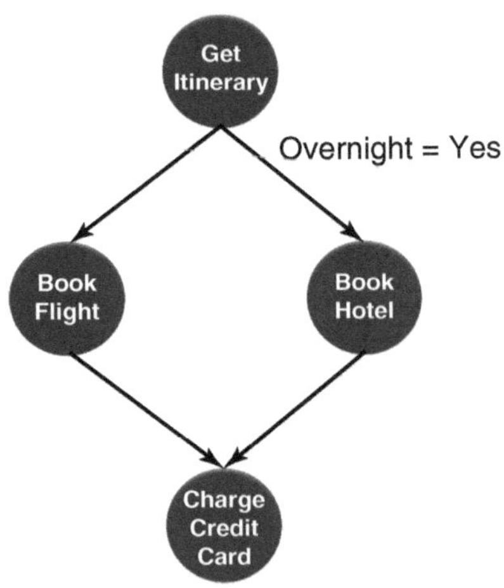

Fig. 5 Running example

supported by IBM Flowmark, IBM MQSeries Workflow, and other products of other vendors. It is a tag-based language that provides tags for all the elements of the modeling constructs of the metamodel behind the language (Leymann and Roller 2000 for a detailed discussion of this metamodel and FDL). It is one of the first (if not the first) language for modeling business processes implemented by a product and that has been supported by multiple vendors.

Listing 1 renders the running sample in FDL. Elements of the metamodel of FDL are specified enclosed by corresponding tags (e.g., by a STRUCTURE tag or a PROGRAM_ACTIVITY tag). Most tags require to name the element to be defined, and this name is used together with a preceding END tag to close the

```
STRUCTURE 'Order'
    ...
END 'Order'
...
PROGRAM_ACTIVITY 'Get Itinerary' ('Order', 'Confirmation')
    PROGRAM 'GetItin'
    DONE_BY MEMBER OF ROLE 'Customer Client'
    ...
END 'Get Itinerary'

PROGRAM_ACTIVITY 'Book Flight' (...)
    ...
END 'Book Flight'

PROGRAM_ACTIVITY 'Book Hotel' (...)
    ...
END 'Book Hotel'
PROGRAM_ACTIVITY 'Charge Credit Card' (...)
    START AUTOMATIC WHEN AT_LEAST_ONE_CONNECTOR TRUE
    ...
END 'Charge Credit Card'
CONTROL
    FROM 'Get Itinerary'
    TO 'Book Hotel'
    WHEN '"Overnight" = "Yes"'

CONTROL
    FROM 'Get Itinerary'
    TO 'Book Flight'

DATA
    FROM 'Get Itinerary'
    TO 'Book Flight'
    MAP 'FlightDate' TO 'DepartureDate'
...
```

Listing 1 Running sample in FDL rendering

corresponding element definition. Today, XML tags would be used instead (e.g., a <programActivity> tag) properly paired with a corresponding end tag.

Activities are specified via the PROGRAM_ACTIVITY element or a PROCESS_ACTIVITY element; while program activities are implemented (or supported) by a program, a process activity in turn is implemented by another process, that is, a subprocess. For example, lines 4–8 define the Get Itinerary activity as a program activity. In line 4, this activity is defined to get an Order container as input and to produce a Confirmation container as output. These containers are specified in FDL via corresponding STRUCTURE elements, for example, in lines 1–3 the Order container is defined (leaving out the details on how structures are actually defined in FDL). Line 5 points by name to the program that implements this activity via the PROGRAM clause. FDL provides a separate PROGRAM element (not shown in the listing) to specify the details about the program, for example, what kind of executable it is, the environment it runs in, etc.; the name of this element is used within the definition of a program activity to refer to the implementation of the program activity by name. The Get Itinerary activity is a people activity, which is specified by adding the DONE_BY clause in line 6: this clause allows to specify the staff query to determine the people who may work on the activity. Note that the DONE_BY clause is similar to a logical people link in BPEL4People (see Sect. 4.1). Line 9–14 add the definitions of the Book Flight and Book Hotel activity. The Charge Credit Card activity (defined in line 15–18) is a join activity having more one incoming control connector targeted at it (see next); for a join activity, a join condition can be specified by a Boolean condition in the transition conditions of the incoming control connectors. The join condition of the Charge Credit Card activity is specified in line 16 by the START clause, and the actual join condition defined requires that at least one transition condition must be true.

Control connectors are defined by using the CONTROL element. It has a FROM clause used to specify the source activity of the connector, a TO clause for defining its target activity, and a WHEN to specify the transition condition of the control connector; in case no WHEN clause is defined (as for the control connector in lines 23–25), the transition condition defaults to constant true. The control connector in lines 19–22 defines a transition condition that uses the Overnight field in the output container of the target activity of the connector. Finally, Listing 1 shows in lines 26–29 a sample data flow connector defined via a DATA element. Like for control connectors, its nested FROM and TO clauses define its source and target activity, respectively. Several MAP clauses may be nested in a data element that are used to specify fieldwise copy statements from a field from the output container of the source activity to a field of the input container of the target activity. Omitting MAP clauses assumes that the containers have identical structure and that all values are copied one-to-one. Note that MAP clauses are similar to BPEL <assign> activities (see Sect. 4).

It should be noted that FDL programs are bound to program activities in an early fashion. In BPEL, the PROGRAM clause of a program activity is substituted by a partner link (see Section 4). The program associated with an activity in BPEL is late bound and discovered at runtime based on information assigned to a partner link during deployment time. The middleware assumed to perform the discovery and binding is no longer the process engine itself but the so-called *enterprise service bus* (ESB). Thus, as expected, technological advancements have their impact on the evolution of standards (see Sect. 7 for more details).

3.5 WSFL

WSFL is a graph-based language proposed by IBM in 2001 (Leymann 2001). In contrast to FDL, WSFL is geared towards Web services, that is, implementations of activities are assumed to be defined via WSDL port types and provided via WSDL ports. Furthermore, WSFL binds implementation in a late manner, that is, activities specify the port types providing the functionality they expect at runtime, and implementations of these port types must be bound at runtime to a particular process instance. WSFL consists of two parts: an XML rendering of FDL (plus some extensions) defining business processes for a single partner side (called flow models) and a choreography language to wire together business processes of different partners (called a global model – not covered here). Listing 2 is the WSFL rendering of the running example; the similarities to the corresponding FDL definitions should be obvious.

Activities are specified via the <activity> element: an activity has a name, which is assigned via a corresponding attribute (line 1). Input and output data of an activity is defined by <input> and <output> elements nested in the corresponding activity specification (line 2 and line 3). Data is defined as messages consumed or produced, respectively, by an activity; the messages correspond to FDL containers. Data connectors correspond to WSFL data links that specify which activities contribute via their output message to the input message of the target activity of the data link (see lines 29–31) and how this input message is composed (line 30). Participants within a business process are referred to as *service providers* because participants have the obligation to provide an implementation of a service required as implementation of an activity. Communication between a business process and its partners is via exchanging messages through activities implemented by services consuming or providing the corresponding data. The type of implementation required by an activity is specified by the <implement> element nested within the activity (line 5). The type of partner obliged to provide this implementation is defined in the <performedBy> element of the activity. The concrete partner used by a particular instance of the process model can be bound both in an early manner or in a late manner; late and dynamic binding is supported in WSFL via a *locator* (e.g., line 14) that allows to specify a query that is evaluated at runtime to discover and select an implementation of the port type required by the activity (defined by the <target> element in line 14).

In Listing 2, the GetItinerary activity gets an Order message as input and produces a Confirmation message as output. It is performed by a service provider called TravelAgent, and the port type to be implemented by the TravelAgent and its

```
1 <activity name="GetItinerary">
2   <input message="Order"/>
3   <output message="Confirmation"/>
4   <performedBy serviceProvider="TravelAgent"/>
5   <implement>...</implement>
6 </activity>

7 <activity name="BookFlight">
8 ...
9 </activity>

10<activity name="BookHotel">
11 ...
12 <plugLink>
13    <target portType="HotelPT" operation="Book"/>
14    <locator .../>
15 </plugLink>
16</activity>

17<activity name="ChargeCreditCard">
18  ...
19  <join condition="flight_to_charge OR hotel_to_charge"/>
20</activity>

21<controlLink source="GetItinerary" target="BookFlight"/>
22
23<controlLink source="GetItinerary" target="BookHotel"
24  transitionCondition="Order/ReturnDate &gt;
     Order/DepartureDate"/>

25<controlLink name="flight_to_charge"
26  source="BookFlight" target="ChargeCreditCard"/>

27<controlLink name="hotel_to_charge"
28  source="BookHotel" target="ChargeCreditCard"/>

29<dataLink source="GetItinerary" target="BookFlight">
30  <map .../>
31</dataLink>
```

Listing 2 Running sample in WSFL rendering

operation used to realize the GetItinerary activity is defined in the corresponding <implement> element. The control link of line 21 specifies that once the GetItinerary activity is completed, the activity BookFlight (defined in lines 7–9) can be performed. The control link in lines 23 and 24 prescribes that after completion of GetItinerary, the activity BookHotel (defined in lines 10–16) is to be performed, but only if the transition condition associated with that control link (line 24) is evaluated to true (in the example, the transition condition checks whether the

ReturnDate field of the Order message is greater than the DepartureDate field of the same message). The definition of the BookHotel activity contains a <locator> element (line 14) used at runtime to determine the actual port to be used as implementation of the activity. While activities BookFlight and BookHotel run in parallel, the activity ChargeCreditCard (lines 17 to 20) can only be performed after these activities – as defined by control links pointing to it (lines 25–26 and lines 27–28). Furthermore, the join condition in line 19 specifies that one of these two control links must have a transition condition that evaluates to true; otherwise, the Charge Credit Card activity will not be performed at all. Since WSFL supports dead path elimination (see Sect. 3.1), the join condition ensures that the credit card will not be charged if neither a hotel nor a flight has been booked.

WSFL has been published in a single version only (like XLANG – see next), and this version has been abandoned by IBM in favor of BPEL (just like Microsoft abandoned XLANG in favor of BPEL). Like XLANG, WSFL ignores people as performer of activities, that is, it focuses on composing automatic interactions of services. Besides flow models, WSFL allows to specify global models that define which partner produces messages consumed by which other partner, independent of the fact whether or not the partners are specified transparently via process models or in an opaque manner by the port types participating in their joint interaction. Furthermore, WSFL global models allow to deploy the partner configuration making up an application: partners are represented in a WSFL global model at the type level and are bound to concrete partners during deployment. From this perspective, WSFL may be seen as a forerunner of SCA (OASIS Standard 2007a). Together, flow models and global models allow to specify choreographies.

3.6 XLANG

XLANG is an operator-based language that has been proposed by Microsoft in 2001 (Thatte 2001), and which is influenced by the π-calculus. It provides operators for sequential, parallel, and conditional execution of steps in a business process; operators can be nested to support more complex behaviors. Activities are referred to as actions and represent the basic steps to be performed within a business process. Like WSFL, XLANG is based on WSDL, which is the underlying language for defining the services used by actions that are composed into a process. XLANG provides XML tags to define processes based on operators and actions.

Sequential behavior is defined by the <sequence> tag (line 1): all actions or operators are performed sequentially in the order specified within this tag. Actions or operators directly included within an <all> tag (line 4) are executed concurrently. The <switch> tag (line 6) consists of branches (e.g., line 7) each of which is guarded by a condition (denoted by a QName in an enclosing <case> tag – line 9 and line 8, respectively); the conditions of the branches are evaluated in order and the first branch evaluated to true will be performed (all other true branches will be

```
1 <sequence>
2   <action operation="SubmitItinerary" port="pTravelAgent"
3           activation="true"/>
4   <all>
5     <action operation="Book" port="pAirline" .../>
6     <switch>
7       <branch>
8         <case>
9           fl:OvernightTrip
10        </case>
11        <sequence>
12         <action operation="Book" port="pHotel" .../>
13        </sequence>
14       </branch>
15     </switch>
16    </all>
17    <action operation="Charge" port="pCardCompany" .../>
18 </sequence>
```

Listing 3 Running sample in XLANG rendering

ignored). If no branch evaluates to true, no action of the corresponding <switch> will be performed at all.

While the approaches discussed until now assume a single kind of activity (namely one that represents work to be performed by a program or a human being), XLANG introduces different kinds of activities: the operation action (in lines 2–3, and lines 5, 12, 17) refers to the operation of a port that provides the proper service performing the activity. Other kinds of actions delay the execution along a path in the process for a certain time, or signal exceptions, for example.

The process in Listing 3 is at its outmost level a sequential execution. The first activity performed is the operation action in line 2: this action expects that the SubmitItinerary operation of the pTravelAgent port is used to send a message to the process. The attribute activation (line3) – when set to true – indicates that by using this action, a new instance of the process model is to be created. The next activity performed in the outmost sequence is an <all> operator: this operator performs the operation action of line 5 (which use the Book operation of the pAirline port) and concurrently the <switch> operator of line 6–15. This operator consists of a single branch only (line 7–14), which is guarded by the fl:OvernightTrip condition (line 9) referred to by the <case> tag in line 8–10. Note that it is expected that an engine executing the XLANG process understands which concrete predicate is denoted by the corresponding QName in line 9. The single branch of the <switch> is a structured as a <sequence> (line 11–13) consisting of the single operation actions (line 12) invoking the Book operation of the pHotel port. Effectively, the hotel is booked if and only if the OvernightTrip condition is true. Once the <all> operator is finished, the operation action in line 17 is performed, which invokes the Charge operation of the pCardCompany port. After that, the whole process is finished.

XLANG has been published in a single version only (like WSFL), and this version has been abandoned by Microsoft in favor of BPEL (just like IBM abandoned WSFL in favor of BPEL). While WSFL supports dynamic binding, XLANG is binding the services used by a process model statically by referencing the concrete port to be used in an operation action. XLANG ignores people activities, that is, it allows composing automatic interactions between services only. Besides providing the ability to specify the business process of a single partner, XLANG also defines language constructs used to wire single-side business processes into a choreography.

3.7 XPDL

XPDL is a graph-based language published by the WfMC in 2005 (Workflow Management Coalition 2005). It defines activities as the basic steps to be performed within a business process. Activities are connected by so-called transitions that define the control flow between activities. Activities may be realized by programs and even by people and by other processes (in contrast to WSFL and XLANG that only support programs/services as implementation of activities). From that perspective, XPDL is close to FDL, that is, XPDL can be easily understood based on an understanding of FDL or WSFL flow models – thus, we are not providing an XPDL rendering of the running example.

While XPDL provides a process modeling language, it is positioned in the specification as an exchange format for BPMN (see Sect. 6): BPMN 1.1 does not specify a dedicated exchange format for process models defined in BPMN, but such an exchange format is required for export from or import into BPMN tools. Because of this, XPDL contains XML renderings of BPMN constructs not found in FDL or WSFL or XLANG. The rational of the WfMS to relate XPDL close to BPMN may be based on the ubiquitous support of BPEL by all major vendors: it seems to be unlikely that vendors supporting BPEL would support a second (competing) standard. But there is the danger that BPMN will finally provide its own exchange format, in which case XPDL would lose its justification.

4 BPEL

BPEL has been published by IBM and Microsoft in 2001 (Curbera et al. 2002). A refined version of BPEL has been submitted to OASIS and got finally published in 2007 (OASIS Standard 2007b). From a language perspective, the most important aspect of BPEL is its existence: BPEL combines the graph-based approach and operator-based approach, thus getting rid of the need to chose between one or the other of the two different modeling approaches – within one and the same process model language elements of the two approaches can even be combined (and are in fact combined in practice). From a standard perspective, the most important aspect of BPEL is unanimous vendor support: BPEL enables portability of process models between different modeling tools as well as runtime environments – based on its well-defined operational semantics, a process model is performed the same way even in process engines of different vendors. Note that the latter requires some discipline avoiding vendor-specific extensions of BPEL (discussed below). Together, BPEL merged otherwise diverging markets and satisfied the hard requirements discussed in the introduction.

Like XLANG, BPEL distinguishes different kinds of activities: <receive> activities consume messages from the outside. <reply> activities send messages to the outside as "synchronous" responses to requests that have been received before. <invoke> activities are used to call operations by sending a message to the operation of a corresponding service and receiving a response from the same operation and service "synchronously." A variant of <invoke> simply sends a message to the outside; this message may be an asynchronous response to a formerly received message, or it may just be the submission of an unsolicited message. There are other kinds of basic activities that are not communicating with the outside, the most important of which is the <assign> activity. An assign activity is used to construct data within a process; it takes data stored within the process as input and produces data stored within the process as output. Typically, such data is stored in the so-called variables; a variable typically contains a message received or a message to be sent out, and such a latter message has to be constructed via an assign activity. Other basic kinds of activities allow to signal faults that occurred within a process (<throw>), to delay processing along a certain path of control (<wait>), or to immediately end the processing of the complete process (<exit>), for example.

The running sample is represented in BPEL in Listing 4. The <flow> element (line 1 and corresponding closing tag in line 44) specifies that a graph is used to structure the encompassed activities; a graph is simply referred to as a *flow* in BPEL. A flow starts with listing all control connectors required by the modeled graph; because only control flow connectors and no data flow connectors are supported, control connectors are simply called *links* and are specified by corresponding <link> elements (lines 2–7). Each link has a name that is used within activities to specify whether an activity is a start node (source) or an end node (target) of the edge represented by the link (e.g., based on line 13, the GetItinerary activity is the start node of the itin_to_flight link); effectively, one activity is connected with another activity in a flow by specifying one activity as source and one activity as target of the same link. Link names are also used to retrieve the actual truth value of an associated transition condition via a BPEL-provided function (getLinkStatus() in line 40, for example).

The first activity specified in the flow is the GetItinerary activity (lines 8–17): it is the source of the itin_to_flight and the itin_to_hotel link (lines 13–15). The itin_to_hotel link has a transition condition (lines 15 and 16) that compares the

```
flow>

<links>
  <link name="itin_to_hotel"/>
  <link name="itin_to_flight"/>
  <link name="flight_to_charge"/>
  <link name="hotel_to_charge"/>
</links>

<receive name="GetItinerary"
  partnerLink="Customer"
  portType="TravelAgentPT"
  operation="SubmitItinerary"
  variable="Order">
  <source linkName="itin_to_flight"/>
  <source linkName="itin_to_hotel"
   transitionCondition=
   "$Order/ReturnDate &gt; $Order/DepartureDate"/>
</receive>

<invoke name="BookHotel"
  partnerLink="Hotel"
  portType="HotelPT"
  operation="Book"
  inputVariable="Hotel">
  <target linkName="itin_to_hotel"/>
  <source linkName="hotel_to_charge"/>
</invoke>

<invoke name="BookFlight"
  partnerLink="Airline"
  portType="AirlinePT"
  operation="Book"
  inputVariable="Flight">
  <target linkName="itin_to_flight"/>
  <source linkName="flight_to_charge"/>
</invoke>

<invoke name="ChargeCreditCard"
  partnerLink="Billing"
  portType="CardCompanyPT"
  operation="Charge"
  inputVariable="Payment"
  joinCondition="getLinkStatus('hotel_to_charge')
                 or getLinkStatus('flight_to_charge')">
  <target linkName="hotel_to_charge"/>
  <target linkName="flight_to_charge"/>
</invoke>

</flow>
```

Listing 4 Running sample in BPEL rendering

Return Date and the Departure Date from the Order message received (line 16) to identify overnight trips. The partner Link attribute in line 9 defines the "channel" through which the Order message is received. In general, a *partner link* is defined by a pair of port types, one of which is provided by the process and the other is provided by an external partner communicating with the process; the operations of these port types effectively define the messages that may be exchanged between the process and its corresponding partner. The port type (line 10) and operation (line 11) define which service the external partner has to use to submit the message to be received by the process. The variable attribute in line 12 specifies where the message received will be stored persistently (and become part of the process context). The Book Hotel activity (lines 18–25) is an invoke activity, sending a message to an external Hotel partner (define in line 19); the variable containing the message to be sent in defined in line 22. The port type expected to be provided by the partner is defined in line 20 and the operation to be used by the process to send the message to the partner is defined in line 21. BookHotel is the target of the itin_to_hotel link (line 23), that is, it is the end node of the corresponding link starting at the GetItinerary activity. The hotel_to_charge link starts at the Book-Hotel activity (line 24). The definition of the BookFlight activity (lines 26–33) should now be obvious. The ChargeCreditCard activity (lines 34–43) is a join activity being the target of more than one incoming link (lines 41 and 42); thus, a join condition is specified (lines 39 and 40) that makes sure that the activity is only performed if the hotel_to_charge link or the flight_to_charge link is true.

Note that BPEL supports to specify the port type (not the actual port) used to exchange messages, but not the actual port (like in XLANG). It is assumed that during deployment time of a BPEL process model, enough information is associated with each partner link that at runtime the infrastructure can determine the actual port of the communication partner. This deployment information can be a static address of the corresponding port or a locator (see above) that allows dynamic discovery of the corresponding port. Thus, BPEL supports both early binding as well as late binding of services to processes.

The operator-based approach is supported in BPEL by providing operators for sequential execution (<sequence>), conditional execution (<if>), looping (<while> and <repeatUntil>), and multiple concurrent instantiation of activities of identical type (<forEach>). Operators can be nested, that is, they can be used again as parameters of operators. Note especially that <flow> is considered an operator too: without any links (that is, discrete graphs), this is the operator that corresponds to XLANG's <all> operator. But even with links (i.e. "regular" graphs), a <flow> can be nested in any of the other operators and vice versa, and it can be used to build graphs of operators (mixed with atomic activities). Thus, BPEL supports a hybrid approach to model business processes – and this is in fact often used on practice.

Transactional boundaries can be defined in BPEL via scopes based on the <scope> operator: the activities and operators within a scope share a joint exception handling. When a fault happens within a scope, all work in this scope stops and its corresponding fault handler gets control. The fault handler attempts to repair the faulty situation such that the work meant to be performed within the scope can be continued as determined by the fault handler. If the fault handler cannot repair the fault, the already performed work within the scope is undone by running compensation actions. This concept is based on the notion of compensation spheres (Leymann and Roller 2000); a variant of spheres support regular (i.e., ACID) distributed transactions and has been proposed as an extension of scopes in BPELJ (Blow et al. 2004).

As another important feature, mobility (as introduced by the π-calculus) is supported in BPEL too. This is achieved as follows: References to services are represented by so-called endpoint references (Weerawarana et al. 2005). An endpoint reference can be sent within a message to a process instance. An <assign> can then be used to copy the endpoint reference to a partner link. The partner link will then refer to the specified service: this is a very dynamic variant of late binding allowing partners of a process to specify at runtime which service to use.

Finally, BPEL is specified to be extensible. Various elements of the language can be extended. New types of activities may even be defined by means of the <extensionActivity> element that functions as container for newly defined activity types – BPEL4People, for example, makes use of the extensibility capabilities of BPEL (see next section). BPEL itself covers only a subset of the whole BPM spectrum, for example, it does not support monitoring of business processes; to support a phased roll-out of additional standards that together may finally cover all of BPM, extensibility of BPEL is key. The extensibility feature of BPEL is also the basis for vendor-specific extensions; but it must be noted that vendor-specific extensions are obstructions to portability. To be able to avoid such obstructions, BPEL allows to specify specific extensions used in defining a process model as "optional": all extensions used must be listed in the <extension> element, and extensions can be marked via the mustUnderstand attribute as optional. For more details about BPEL (Weerawarana et al. 2005).

4.1 BPEL4People

BPEL4People has been published by BEA, IBM, Oracle, and SAP in 2007 (Kloppmann et al. 2005a, b). Since 2008, OASIS is working on a corresponding de jure standard (OASIS WS-BPEL). The specification consists of two specifications, namely WS-HumanTask and BPEL4People proper. This split is based on the guiding principle that most Web service standards adhere to: modularity and composability. "Modularity" here means that a standard should carefully identify technologies that have a broader area of applicability, that is, technologies that can be used outside of the domain of the standard originally addressed, and that technologies should be split into a separate specification. That happened to the concept of a task: a *task* is a work request to a human being and such a request may originate not only from a process engine but also from other sources. Thus, task technology was specified independent from process technology (as WS-HumanTask) and in a "composable" manner, that is, in a way that it can be composed with the other standards of the Web service stacks (Weerawarana et al. 2005). BPEL4People makes immediate use of WS-HumanTask to specify how activities to be performed by human beings are realized by tasks.

As a consequence, BPEL4People has an impact on the overall architecture of the Web service stack in general and on process engines in particular. Via WS-HumanTask, services that are realized by human beings having the ability to impact the real world enter the domain of Web services as a new kind of service (namely tasks) managed by an infrastructure for such tasks also specified by WS-HumanTask (namely the *Task Manager*). Via BPEL4People, tasks become the representation of activities performed by human beings and the special component (a.k.a. workitem manager) provided by process engines to manage the corresponding work requests are now substituted by the task manager and by corresponding proper interactions between the (reduced) process engine and the task manager. Figure 6 depicts this situation: the left part of the figure shows the core components of the process execution engine, namely the navigator and the workitem manager. The workitem manager provides a workitem interface to be used by applications that render workitems for human beings, for example, work list clients. The right side of the figure shows that the process execution engine no longer contains a specific workitem manager; instead, it communicates with a new component, i.e. that is, the task manager. While earlier the navigator communicated with the workitem manager to create a workitem, it now uses a

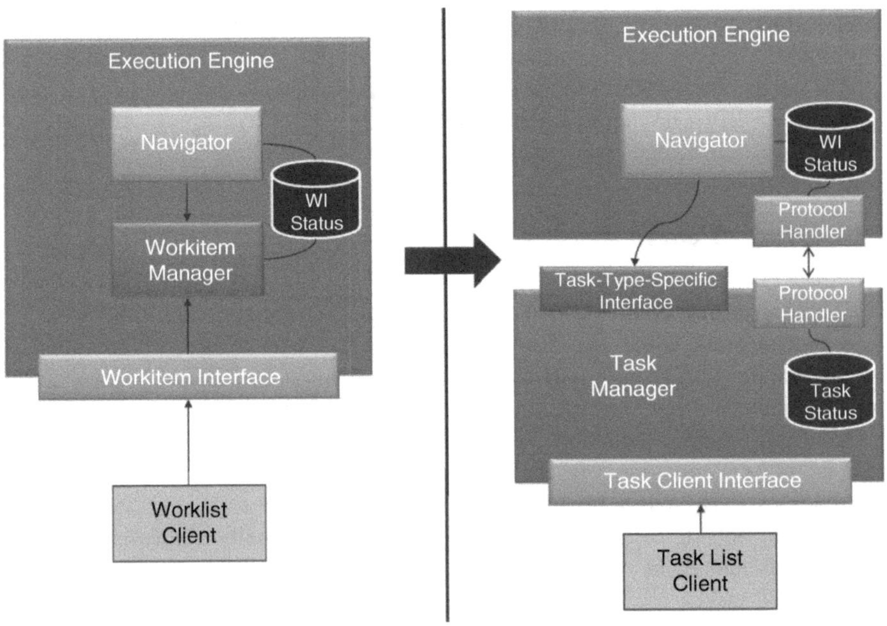

Fig. 6 Workitem manager becomes separate task manager

```
1 <logicalPeopleGroup name="FlightAgent">
2   <parameter name="Company" type="xsd:string" />
3 </logicalPeopleGroup>

4 <task name="BookFligt">
5   <interface portType="AirlinePT"
6    operation="Book".../>
7   <potentialOwners>
8     <from logicalPeopleGroup="FlightAgent">
9       <argument name="Company">
10       getInput("Flight")/Company
11      </argument>
12    </from>
13  <potentialOwners>
14</task>
```

Listing 5 Sample human task

task type-specific interface to create an instance of the task, that is, tasks are represented by task specific port types one of the operations of which is used by the navigator to create an instance of the corresponding task. The task manager now provides a standardized task client interface that can be used by applications to make task lists accessible to human beings. Because tasks are artifacts that are tightly coupled to particular process instances, WS-HumanTask specifies an agreement protocol between the process execution engine and the task manager; this agreement protocol is run to make sure that the lifecycle of a task is dependent on the lifecycle of the associated process instance (the figure of protocol handler component indicates this).

A sample task definition is given in Listing 5. We assume that the airline partner from the running example reserves flights by assigning an incoming order to a human being, the flight agent. The corresponding task named BookFlight is defined in lines 4–14. The task-specific interface to be used to create an instance of the task is defined in lines 5–6; as before the port type AirlinePT in the operation Book is used for that purpose. In lines 1–3, the logical people group named FlightAgent is defined: a *logical people group* represents a role (or an organizational entity, in general), that is, a declaratively defined set of employees at the airline partner in charge of making flight reservations. The Company parameter defined in line 2 is used to narrow down the appropriate employees. Logical people groups are deployment artifacts: at deployment time, they are associated with proper queries on organizational databases that are to be used at runtime to determine the actual employees playing the corresponding role; possible parameters defined for the logical people group are passed as actual arguments to those queries. For example, the Company parameter of the FlightAgent logical people group will be used at runtime to determine the flight agents that are making reservations for a specific company. The <potentialOwners> element in line 7–13 of the task definition connects the task with the people who may actually perform the task: the people represented by the logical people group FlightAgent. Lines 9–11 specify where the

Listing 6 Sample people activity

```
1 <extensionActivity>
2   <peopleActivity name="BookFlight"
3     inputVariable="Flight"...>
4     <remoteTask
5       partnerLink="Airline"
6       portType="AirlinePT"
7       operation="Book"...>
8     </remoteTask>
9   </peopleActivity>
10 </extensionActivity>
```

actual value of the Company parameter required by FlightAgent comes from; in this case, it is a field in the input message of the operation creating the task.

Listing 6 shows how the task defined before is used for defining a people activity. Since people activities are new kinds of activities not defined by BPEL itself, the <extensionActivity> element (line 1) must be used within a BPEL model to wrapper the <peopleActivity> element (lines 2–9) that used to define people activities within BPEL. Here, it is assumed that the BookFlight activity from the running sample is a people activity. The task representing the work to be performed by a human being is specified in line 4–8 via the <remoteTask> element: A *remote task* assumes that the details of a corresponding task has been defined somewhere (in a separate file); thus, the <remoteTask> element simply specifies the task specific interface to be used for creating the task (lines 6 and 7) and the partner link used to find the corresponding port at run time (line 5). The message to be sent to the creating operation is defined in line 3; note that according to BPEL mechanics, this message is derived from the context of the process instance, that is, from the variables (possibly by means of additional <assign> activities). Besides remote tasks, BPEL4People supports the definition of tasks directly within a people activity (*inline task*) or within a process model in the same environment of the referencing people activity (*local task*). Note that remote task supports interoperability at runtime, that is, the process engine hosting a particular process instance and the task manager hosting a remote task may in different environments, especially from different vendors.

5 Choreography

What we discussed until now have been process models that describe the behavior of a single partner only. Such a process model is referred to as *orchestration*. But business processes typically involve multiple partners and often, it is not sufficient to understand the behavior of a single partner only. Instead, an understanding of the behavior of all partners as a whole is needed as well as how they interact to achieve a common goal. Such an overarching process model is referred to as *choreography*. Figure 7 depicts a choreography between three partners: the process models P_1, P_2,

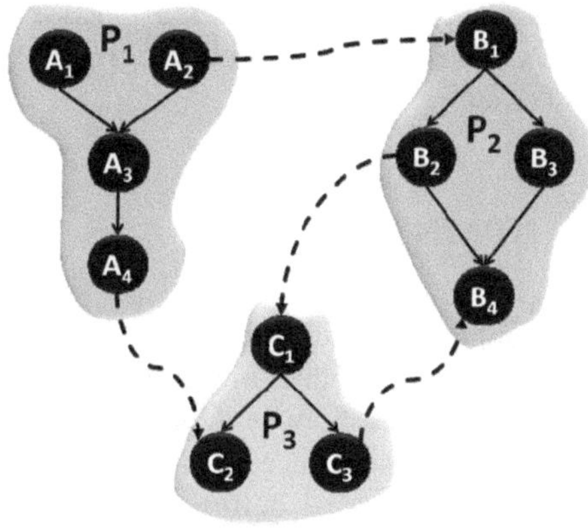

Fig. 7 Choreography and orchestrations

and P_3 show how each individual partner performs in the overarching business process (each of the individual process model is an orchestration). The *local* process models P_1, P_2, and P_3 are connected by a new kind of link (dashed arrows in the figure) resulting in the *global* process model. Note that no accepted term has been introduced for that kind of link, so here we simply call it *wire*. In a nutshell, a choreography results from wiring orchestrations. For example, activity A_4 of process model P_1 is wired with activity C_2 in process model P_3. The meaning of the wire (A_4, C_2) is that A_4 produces data that are required by C_2 before it can start. Thus, wires introduce a new kind dependency between activities of process models of different partners: from one point of view, a wire can be interpreted as a data flow connector; from another point of view, a wire can be interpreted as a control connector used to synchronize work.

Although W3C has published a standard called WS-CDL (W3C Candidate Recommendation 2005) for choreographies, this standard has no real acceptance in the industry: none of the major vendors has implemented WS-CDL in a product. The reason for this nonacceptance seems manifold (e.g., the current focus of users is on realizing their own internal processes). But one reason is the dominance of BPEL in the area of BPM, and WS-CDL has no clear positioning to BPEL. Amongst many other things, WS-CDL defines constructs like <sequence> that compete with corresponding BPEL constructs, thus making a positioning of BPEL and WS-CDL even more difficult. Especially, this overlap is in conflict with the modularity and composability principle guiding the creation of Web service standards. From that perspective, a choreography standard that is based on BPEL (may be an extension of BPEL itself) would be desirable.

The local processes being wired into a choreography are not necessarily full-fledged business processes. Often, models of the behavior of the individual partner suffice that allow to understand how the partner interacts with the other partners: other internal processing can be hidden. Thus, only those parts of the "real" internal business processes need to be specified for a choreography that is required for that understanding. In that sense, for each partner of a choreography, the *public view* on the corresponding internal process is defined. BPEL defines the concept of an *abstract process* that is intended for defining such public views. Thus, a potential choreography standard may be based on BPEL abstract processes.

6 BPMN

The languages discussed above make no assumptions at all about the graphical representations of the language elements they specify. For example, a <receive> activity in BPEL may be depicted as a simple rectangle or as a socket or somehow else. As a consequence, a graphical tool supporting one of the process modeling languages discussed before has its own proprietary graphical rendering for the elements of the supported language, but none of these graphical representations had been standardized, that is, the process modeling languages discussed before are not including standardized graphical representations of the elements making up the language proper. This is understandable, since these languages define virtual machines representing the execution engines for the languages, especially defining their operational behavior. As a consequence, those languages are "low level" and lack high-level features demanded by business modelers. Especially, it turned out over the last few years that the process modeling languages discussed before are too technical for business-oriented modelers.

As a consequence, process modeling is "moving up the stack" towards non-IT users. This happened earlier, for example, in the area of data modeling. The right part of Fig. 8 shows that data modeling takes place at (at least) two different layers:

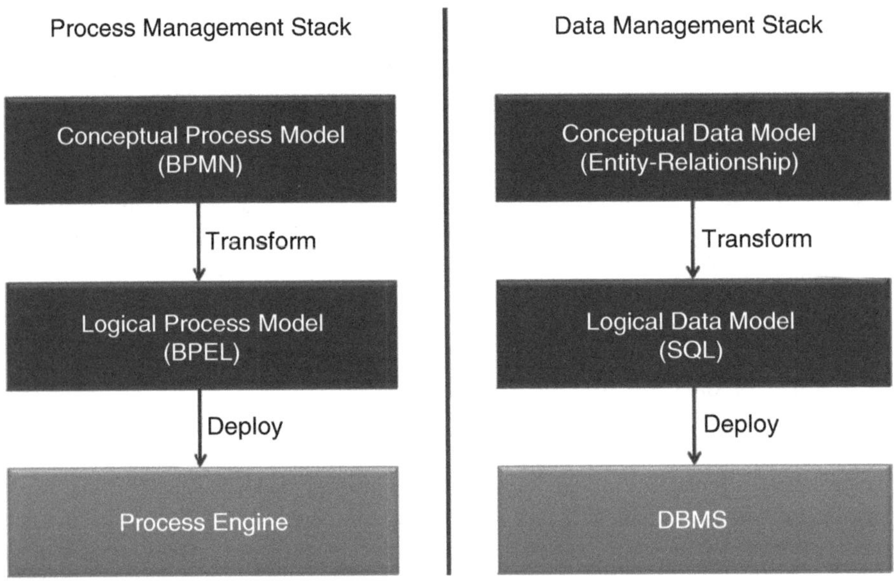

Fig. 8 Analogy process management and data management

the conceptual layer addressing the needs of nondatabase specialist by providing graphical languages like Entity-Relationship diagrams or UML diagrams, for example; the logical layer offering features and precision for database specialist to define data models based on SQL, for example. The same layering is occurring in process modeling, as shown in the left part of the figure: the logical layer offers all the capabilities discussed before addressing process modelers with a certain degree of IT skills; above that, a conceptual layer provides graphical languages offering the high-level constructs required by process models with none of the (or at least just a few) IT skills. The most prominent language at the layer is BPMN sketched next.

BPMN is a standard defining a graphical notation (the "N" in BPMN) for modeling business processes. Activities are represented as rectangles with rounded edges. Control flow is modeled by drawing directed edges between activities. Often recurring control flow patterns are supported by *gateways* that allow to define the special split- or convergence behavior of the control flow. For example, Fig. 9 is a rendering of the running example in BPMN. Control flows from the Get Itinerary activity to the Book Flight and Book Hotel activities; a gateway (the diamond) specifies that control can flow to one or both of the activities (as indicated by the circle within the diamond); this kind of gateway is called an inclusive gateway. Gateways with other behavior are defined in BPMN like exclusive gateways (where control can flow only through one of the outgoing edges), for example. Many other graphical elements exist, making BPMN a powerful notation for drawing diagrams of business processes.

BPMN allows a lot of flexibility in combing the graphical elements. As a consequence, it is very easy to model processes that have a faulty runtime behavior: Deadlocks may easily occur and lack of synchronization is easily introduced. Well-behaved models, that is, such without deadlocks and without lack of synchronization are called *sound* models. Sound models can often be transformed into BPEL. Thus, the state of practice is to use BPMN to graphically model business processes by business users. These graphical models are then transformed into fragments of BPEL process models that are then refined by process modelers with more IT skills in order to turn to BPEL fragments into executable BPEL process models.

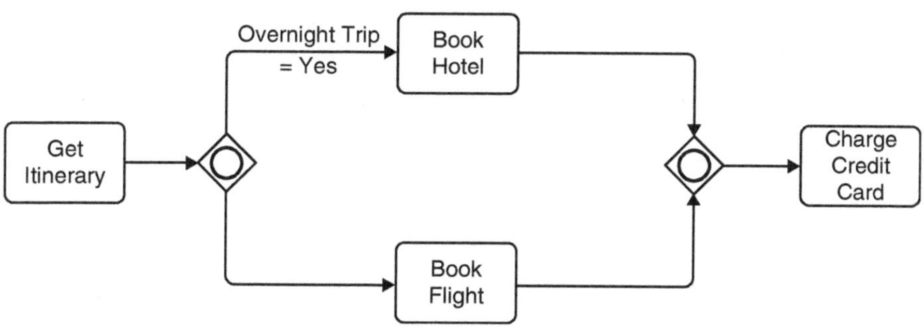

Fig. 9 Running sample in BPMN rendering

While writing this text, work is going on at OMG to create version 2 of BPMN. Significant changes are expected, but details are not publicly available yet. It is expected that BPMN will precisely define its metamodel and a corresponding operational semantics. As a consequence, reliable predictions of the behavior of process models will be possible (especially facilitating the detection of faults in models, for example) and misinterpretations of the meaning of a process model are reduced. Also, the definition of an operational semantics enables implementations of special BPMN-based process engines, that is, a positioning to BPEL becomes an interesting issue. Furthermore, it is expected that BPMN will define its own exchange format facilitating tool interoperability; the positioning of XPDL as exchange format for BPMN will be a challenge. Many clarifications or extensions are expected too, for example, the mapping of BPMN to BPEL, choreography features and so on.

7 Refined View on the WfMC Reference Model

SOA in general and Web services in particular resulted in a refined view on the WfMC reference model (Fig. 10). First, process modeling is seen to be a multistep endeavor in which business experts create a process model with their own notation (conceptual process model), which is then transformed into an executable format (logical process model) that can be performed by a process engine. Note that topologies different from that shown in Fig. 10 are possible, for example, the Logical Process Model layer could be part of the execution engine. Workitem

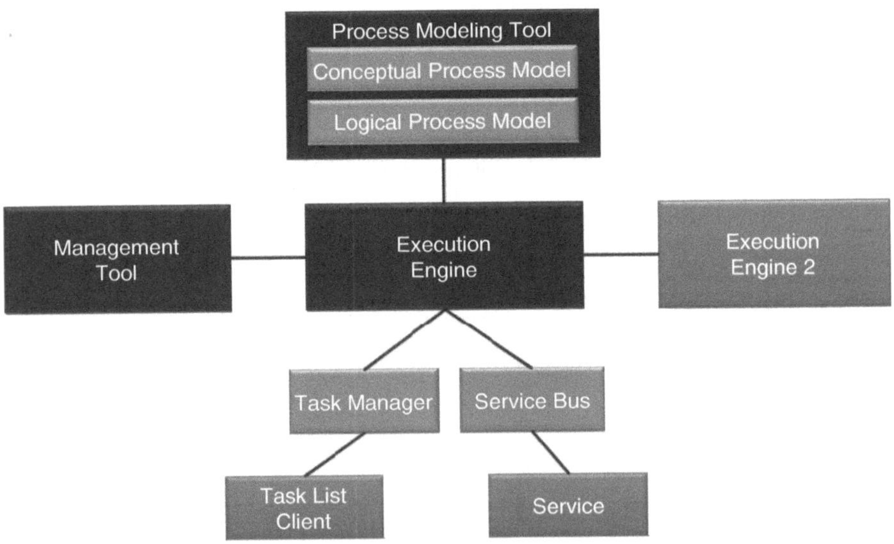

Fig. 10 The reference model in today's environment

Management in the original reference model (Fig. 1) is substituted by generic Task Management. Application Invocation is the duty of a generic Service Bus [based on the various Web Service standards (Weerawarana et al. 2005)]. The communication between execution engines for the purpose of subprocess execution is proposed to be based on BPEL extensions (Kloppmann et al. 2005b).

8 Conclusion

BPM technology is a key technology used in most enterprises today. This requires standards allowing interoperability and portability of BPM solutions. We sketched to evolution of those standards and provided an overview of standards that have been influential in the development of BPM technology. Besides giving selective details for some of the standards, we judged also their impact on BPM architecture and markets.

The pressure on vendors of BPM technology increased to jointly build and support a coherent stack of BPM standards covering the complete BPM lifecycle. Thus, it is likely that in a few years, all major features of BPM are specified by corresponding standards, just like database management is basically standardized via SQL. Since BPM shifts the focus of IT towards business (i.e., away from technology), modeling standards supporting non-IT professionals will likely be supported by most major vendors. Furthermore, domain specific business process models will be standardized that describe best practices in all major areas of business activities.

References

Blow M, Goland Y, Kloppmann M, Leymann F, Pfau G, Roller D, Rowley M (2004) BPELJ: BPEL for Java. BEA & IBM

Curbera F, Klein J, Leymann F, Roller D, Thatte S, Weerawarana S (2002) Business process execution language for web services Version 1.0. IBM & Microsoft

Havey M (2005) Essential business process modeling. O'Reilly, Hoboken, New Jersey, USA

Jensen K, Rozenberg G (eds) (1991) High-level petri nets: theory and applications. Springer, Berlin; Heidelberg [u.a.], Germany

Kloppmann M, Koenig D, Leymann F, Pfau G, Rickayzen A, von Riegen C, Schmidt P, Trickovic I (2005a) WS-BPEL extension for people (BPEL4People). IBM & SAP

Kloppmann M, Koenig D, Leymann F, Pfau G, Rickayzen A, von Riegen C, Schmidt P, Trickovic I (2005b) WS-BPEL extension for subprocesses (BPEL-SPE). IBM & SAP

Leymann F (1992) A meta model to support the modelling and execution of processes. In: Proceedings of the 11th European meeting on cybernetics and systems research Vienna, Austria, April 1992

Leymann F (2001) Web services flow language WSFL. IBM Corporation, New York, USA

Leymann F, Altenhuber W (1994) Managing business processes as information resources. IBM Syst J 33(2):326–348

Leymann F, Roller D (2000) Production workflow. Prentice Hall, Upper Saddle River, New Jersey, USA
Milner R (1999) Communication and mobile systems: the π-calculus. Cambridge University Press, Cambridge, UK
OASIS WS-BPEL extension for people (BPEL4People) TC. http://www.oasis-open.org/committees/tc_home.php?wg_abbrev=bpel4people. Accessed 10 Sept 2008
OASIS Standard (2007a) Service component architecture – assembly model specification, SCA Version 1.00
OASIS Standard (2007b) Web services business process execution language Version 2.0
Thatte S (2001) XLANG – web services for business process design. Microsoft Corporation
Thatte S (2008) Private communication
W3C Candidate Recommendation (2005) Web services choreography description language
Weerawarana S, Curbera F, Leymann F, Storey T, Ferguson DF (2005) Web services platform architecture. Prentice Hall, Upper Saddle River, New Jersey, USA; Munich [u.a.], Germany
Workflow Management Coalition (1995) The workflow reference model. Document number TC00-1003
Workflow Management Coalition (2005) Process definition interface – XML process definition language. Document number WFMC-TC-1025

Modeling Interorganizational Business Processes

Marco Zapletal, Rainer Schuster, Philipp Liegl, Christian Huemer, and Birgit Hofreiter

Abstract United Nation's Centre for Trade Facilitation and Electronic Business (UN/CEFACT) is an e-business standardization body known for its work on UN/EDIFACT and ebXML. One of its ongoing work items is the UN/CEFACT Modeling Methodology (UMM) for modeling global choreographies of B2B scenarios. The work on UMM started in 1998 and has improved since then by contributions from participating organizations, such as RosettaNet, SWIFT, and GS 1. Today, all new UN/CEFACT standards for data exchange scenarios must be backed up by a corresponding UMM model. In this paper, we revisit the UMM version 1.0 that is defined as a UML 1.4 profile. We introduce the main concepts of UMM and elaborate on the strengths and weaknesses of UMM 1.0. Being the editorial team of UMM, we have made improvements to UMM, which will be released shortly as a new standard version. Thus, we elaborate on the new concepts of UMM 2.0 that are further illustrated by means of a simple example.

1 Introduction

The concept of automating the exchange of business information between business partners has existed for a while. In the early days of electronic data interchange (EDI), the focus was limited to standardizing the business document types (Hill and Ferguson 1989). However, the business documents must also be exchanged in an agreed order to realize an agreed business goal. The interorganizational business processes between two organizations must be defined. Choreography languages describe protocols for the interactions in interorganizational business processes in which the partners interact in a peer-to-peer manner.

M. Zapletal (✉)
Institute of Software Technology and Interactive Systems, Vienna University of Technology, Vienna, Austria
e-mail: marco@ec.tuwien.ac.at

J. vom Brocke and M. Rosemann (eds.), *Handbook on Business Process Management 1*, International Handbooks on Information Systems,
DOI 10.1007/978-3-642-00416-2_25,

Developing an interorganizational system is a complex task. One cannot start simply by drafting a choreography and a schema for the business documents being exchanged. It requires a well-defined development process considering the requirements of the information systems of the participating partners, performing an analysis of the interorganizational system, coming up with a design for the choreography and the document schemes, and transforming those to machine-interpretable code.

The United Nation's Centre for Trade Facilitation and Electronic Business (UN/CEFACT), known for its standardization work in the field of UN/EDIFACT and ebXML (OASIS, UN/CEFACT 2001), took up the endeavor and started research for such a development process for interorganizational systems. This ongoing work resulted in UN/CEFACT's Modeling Methodology (UMM). UMM enables the capture of business knowledge independent of the underlying implementation technology, such as Web Services or ebXML. The goal is developing the design of an interorganizational system that serves as an "agreement" between the participating business partners in the respective collaboration. Each business partner derives in turn the code of its local choreography, enabling the configuration of the business partner's system.

In order to guarantee user acceptance of the UMM, it must be both effective and easy to understand for business process modelers and software architects. Due to the growing tool support of the Unified Modeling Language (UML), the decision in favor of UML as notation of UMM was already made in 1998. In the first years, UMM specified its own conceptual meta model and provided guidelines on creating compliant artifacts using the UML. The resulting guidelines were significantly influenced by other similar methodologies that were in place by member organizations of UN/CEFACT, such as SWIFT, Telemanagement Forum, EAN*UCC (now GS1), and RosettaNet.

In late 2004, it was decided to define UMM as a UML profile (UN/CEFACT 2006), that is, a set of stereotypes, tagged values, and constraints – customizing the UML meta model for the special purpose of modeling global B2B choreographies. At this time, the UML version of choice was UML 1.4 (OMG 2005). Our team was leading the editing of the UMM foundation module 1.0, which became a UN/CEFACT standard in October 2006. First experiences in applying the UMM 1.0 profile in real world projects have shown some shortcomings in the methodology. Our team has addressed these issues and we came up with new concepts for UMM 2.0, which is currently in the implementation verification phase of the standardization process. In this Chapter, we introduce the basic concepts of the UMM and highlight the new features of UMM to model interorganizational systems.

2 Related Work

See also Barros et al. (2010) introduce the notion of choreography in the area of business process modeling. Thereby, they highlight the need to specify a choreography from a global perspective, which is independent of the perspective of individual partners. In this Chapter, we elaborate on the UMM – a UML-based description technique for specifying global choreographies. Being a UN/CEFACT standard, UMM has a business-driven focus on describing B2B choreographies. Unlike other choreography approaches such as WS-CDL (W3C 2005), UMM is not bound to a specific implementation platform. In fact, a UMM model may be deployed to different platforms. In the past, bindings to popular deployment platforms such as BPEL (Hofreiter et al. 2007), ebXML BPSS (Hofreiter et al. 2006a), and Windows Workflow (Zapletal 2008) have already been defined.

Barros et al. (2010) identify three requirements for extending choreography languages in their chapter: (1) functional scoping; (2) stepwise refinement; (3) conversation semantics. As we will see in the remainder of this Chapter, UMM satisfies these requirements: (1) functional scoping may be conducted during requirements elicitation in the business domain view (BDV). (2) Stepwise refinement is supported by nesting *business collaborations* and *business transactions* (as well as by nesting *business collaborations* recursively). Requirement (3) – conversation semantics – is addressed by the concept of a *business transaction*.

In the field of choreography modeling, two major styles have evolved: interconnection models and interaction models. According to (Decker et al. 2008), the former modeling style describes the control-flow per each participant together with the information exchanges between them. On the contrary, models following the latter style are composed of so-called interactions, whereby an interaction defines request-response relationships between exactly two participants. The Business Process Modeling Notation (BPMN) (OMG 2009) as well as approaches such as BPEL4Chor (Decker et al. 2007) follow the interconnection modeling style. UMM as well as other modeling approaches like WS-CDL (W3C 2005), ebXML BPSS (UN/CEFACT 2003), iBPMN (Decker and Barros 2008), and Let's Dance (Zaha et al. 2006) go into the category of interactions models. In (Decker et al. 2009), the authors propose a requirements framework for assessing choreography languages and evaluate the aforementioned languages against it.

3 UN/CEFACT's Modeling Methodology 1.0

3.1 UMM 1.0 Concepts

The goal of this Section is to highlight the concepts of UMM as they are defined in version 1.0. We first start with the theoretical foundation, which is followed by an illustrating example. UMM 1.0 comprises three main steps to build a UMM-compliant *business collaboration model*. The top-level packages of a *business collaboration model* correspond to these three steps: the BDV, the business requirements view (BRV), and the business transaction view (BTV).

The BDV is used to gather existing knowledge from stakeholders and business domain experts. During interviews, the business process analyst tries to get a basic understanding of the business processes in the domain. Consequently, the BDV collects use cases of *business processes*. These *business process use cases* are classified into *business areas* and *process areas*.

The BRV is composed of five subpackages. The first subpackage is the *business process view*. It is used to further detail those *business processes* discovered in the business domain view that provide a chance for collaboration. A detailed *business process activity model* is developed for these *business processes*. By creating the corresponding activity graph, the business process analyst tries to discover interface tasks involved in creating/changing *business entities*.

A business entity is a real world thing having business significance that is shared among two or more business partner in a collaborative business process (e.g., order, account, article, etc.). Changing business entities require communication between business partners. Resulting state changes of *business entities* are modeled as *object flow states* in the *business process activity model*. These *business entities* are defined in the second subpackage called *business entity view*. Each *business entity* is further defined by a *business entity lifecycle* that is composed of *business entity states* occurring during this lifecycle.

The remaining three types of subpackages of the BRV are used to transform the previously gathered requirements into a solution for a future business collaboration. A *collaboration requirements view* subpackage covers exactly one *business collaboration use case* and its participating roles. Similarly, a *transaction requirements view* covers exactly one *business transaction use case* and its two participating roles. A business collaboration use case is an assembly of business transaction use cases, which is denoted by include relationships. The subpackage of a *collaboration realization view* is only used if the same business collaboration is executed between different sets of authorized roles – which is out of scope for this Chapter.

The third main view – the BTV – builds upon the *collaboration requirements view* and the *transaction requirements view* in order to define a global choreography of information exchanges and their document structure. It is composed of three subpackages. A *business choreography view* subpackage includes a *business collaboration protocol*. The *business collaboration protocol* is an activity graph modeling the choreography of a previously described *business collaboration use case*. The *business collaboration protocol* is composed of so-called *business transaction activities*. A *business transaction activity* maps to exactly one *business transaction*, which is considered as a subactivity graph. For the sake of reuse, a *business transaction* may refine multiple *business transaction activities*.

A *business transaction* itself is contained in a *business interaction view* subpackage. A *business transaction* follows always the same pattern: It is performed between two *authorized roles* that are already known from the *business transaction use case*. One authorized role performs the *requesting business activity* and the other one the *responding business activity*. The *requesting information envelope* is mandatory and is denoted by an object flow state from the *requesting* to the *responding business activity*. The object flow of a *responding information envelope* in the reverse direction is optional. Note that the activity graph of a *business transaction* shows only the exchange of business information in the corresponding envelopes. It does not show any business signals for acknowledgments. These are defined in tagged values, which are out of scope for this paper.

Each *requesting* and each *responding information envelope* is an object flow state that refers to an *information envelope*. An *information envelope* itself is a class contained in the *business information view* subpackage. An *information envelope* recursively aggregates structured *information entities* that are also contained in the *business information view*.

3.2 UMM 1.0 Example

For a better understanding, we illustrate the most important UMM artifacts – the business collaboration protocol, the business transaction, and their use cases – by means of a rather simple but still realistic example. This example is akin to a project in the European `waste management` domain. A waste transport must be announced and the receipt of the waste as well as the disposal of the waste must be notified. Exporter, importer, and the competent authorities in their countries and in transit interchange this information. For reasons of simplicity, we do not consider the information about the waste disposal. Figure 1 depicts the resulting artifacts. A more complete description of this example is given in (Hofreiter et al. 2006b).

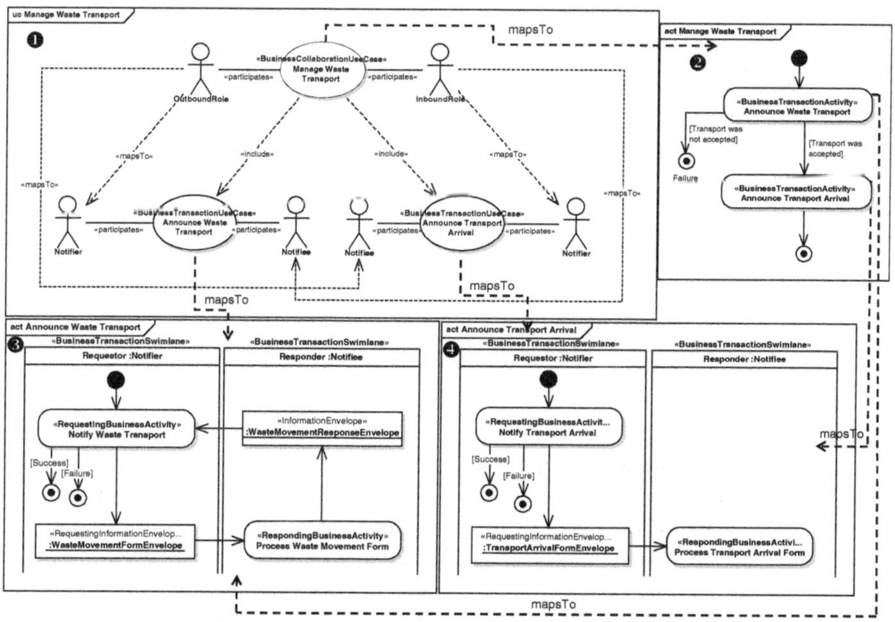

Fig. 1 Example using UMM 1.0: waste management

The *business collaboration use case* manage waste transport (1) involves an outbound role and an inbound role. It includes two *business transaction use cases*, announce waste transport and announce transport arrival. The participants in each of these *business transaction use cases* are a notifier and a notifiee. The outbound role maps to the notifier in announce waste transport and to the notifiee in announce transport arrival. In case of the inbound role, the mapping is vice versa. In order to enable these mappings, there exist two different *authorized roles* named notifier (and another two for notifiee), each defined in the namespace of the corresponding *business transaction use case*.

The behavior of the *business collaboration use case* manage waste transport is modeled using the corresponding *business collaboration protocol* (2). This activity graph is built by two *business transaction activities*. The first *business transaction activity* is announce waste transport. If the transport is not accepted, the collaboration ends immediately. Otherwise, the protocol continues with announce transport arrival, which is the final activity.

The *business transaction activity* announce waste transport maps to the corresponding *business transaction* (3), which models the behavior of the homonymously named *business transaction use case*. In the *business transaction* announce waste transport, the notifier performs the *requesting business activity* notify waste transport, which outputs the waste movement form envelope. This envelope is input to the notifee's *responding business activity* process waste movement form. This activity outputs the waste movement response envelope, which is returned to the notifier. Evidently, it is a two-way business transaction in contrary to the one of announce transport arrival (4), which does not return an *information envelope*. In announce transport arrival, the notifier sends a transport arrival form envelope to the nofifiee. However, the *responding business activity* process transport arrival form does not output an *information envelope*.

4 Business Documents

4.1 Limitations of UMM 1.0 and Suggested Improvement

UMM 1.0 is rather vague on its guidelines on modeling business documents. Currently, an *information envelope* being exchanged in a *business transaction* is (recursively) composed of *information entities*. UMM suggests that these *information entities* are based on UN/CEFACT's Core Components Technical Specification (CCTS) (UN/CEFACT 2009b), which provides an ontological base of reusable building blocks for interoperable business documents. However, the Core Components Technical Specification defines its own, very specific MOF-like meta model that is entirely independent from the UML meta model. As a matter of fact, core components must be represented as (a collection of) classes and their attributes to be used in a UMM business document model. If every modeler defines his own style of mapping core components to equivalent UML classes, business documents from different projects will differ significantly, even when based on the same concepts. This prohibits reuse and is in contradiction to UN/CEFACT's goal of cross-industry alignment.

It follows that UMM requires unambiguous rules for modeling business documents based on core components. For this purpose, the concepts of the proprietary core component meta model must be transformed to a semantically equivalent UML profile. We submitted such a UML profile for core components for standardization to UN/CEFACT (UN/CEFACT 2009c).

4.2 Detailed Solution

The UML Profile for Core Components (UPCC) introduces UML class diagrams as the method of choice for modeling business documents based on core components. By using a set of stereotypes, tagged values, and OCL constraints, the UML Profile for Core Components restricts the UML meta model to the specific needs of core component modeling. Figure 2 gives an overview of the UML profile's stereotypes. Since the full names of the core component concepts are rather long in many cases, the stereotype names are based on their abbreviations. Again the stereotypes

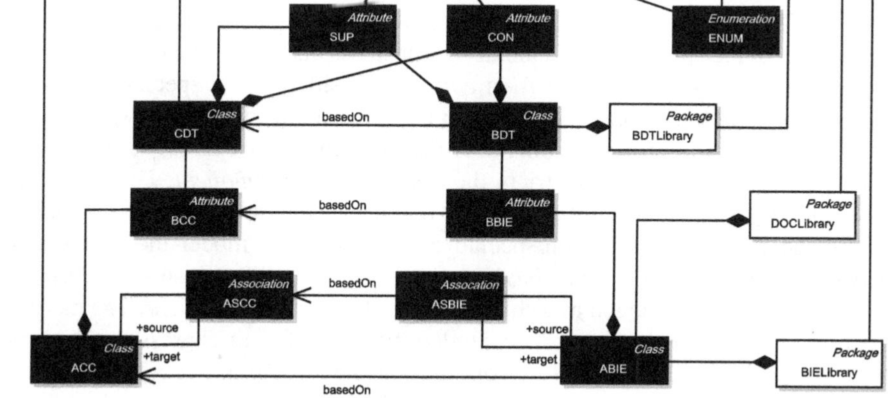

Fig. 2 Core components in UML: a conceptual overview

representing modeling artifacts are shown with a black background, whereas the stereotypes used to structure these artifacts into packages are denoted using a white background.

The *primitive* (PRIM) stereotype is used for the representation of primitive types such as String, Integer, etc. This concept is very similar to the UML concept of a type. Hence, *primitive* (PRIM) is based on the UML *type*. The core component standard defines a list of eleven primitive types defined in the Core Component Data Type Catalog (UN/CEFACT 2009a), which are partially overlapping with the types defined in UML. In addition, the modeler may create *enumerations* (ENUM) restricting *primitives* (PRIM) to a certain set of values, e.g., restrict a String value to a well-defined set of values such as ISO 3166 (ISO 2007) country codes. The concept of an *enumeration* (ENUM) is identical to the one defined by UML.

In contrary, a core data type (CDT) is more expressive than a UML data type. It is based on a UML class and includes a number of attributes. Exactly one of these attributes is stereotyped as content component (CON). The other ones are stereotyped as supplementary components (SUP). A CON represents an atomic value such as the number 32. SUP provide additional information about the CON, e.g., measurement (temperature) and unit of measurement (Fahrenheit). In UML, an attribute must be of a certain type. Both the CON and the SUP refer to a *primitive* (PRIM) or to an *enumeration* (ENUM), respectively.

An aggregate core component (ACC) is equivalent to a UML class and includes a number of attributes, which are basic core components (BCC). The type assigned to a BCC must be a CDT. It is possible to specify a composition between ACC in order to build a hierarchical document structure. This composition is stereotyped as association core component (ASCC). Each ASCC has a source and a target ACC.

So far, we discussed the concepts of *core components*, which may be reused in different business documents, or, in other words, in different business contexts. Hence, a *core component* is independent of a business context. It must represent all business semantics that may be required in any business context. However, the core component standard also covers the concept of so-called *business information entities*. A *business information entity* sets a *core component* into a certain business context. This means, that a *business information entity* qualifies and refines a *core component* to the specific requirements of a business document in a certain domain.

In general, a *business information entity* is considered as a specialization of a *core component*. It uses only those parts of the general-purpose *core component* that are relevant for the business context in the domain under consideration. Consequently, this specialization restricts the general *core component*. Unfortunately, derivation by restriction is not a native UML concept. Accordingly, we are not able to use the UML generalization/specialization concept to model the relationship between *core components* and *business information entities*. Instead, a *business information entity* is created as a shallow copy of the *core component*. The name of the *business information entity* is extended by a qualifier to express the business context. Qualifiers are attached in front of a business information entity name and are separated by underscores (e.g., `waste_`). A *based on* association is established between the *business information entity* and the original *core component* in order to allow traceability and consistency checks.

Following this concept, an aggregate business information entity (ABIE) is based on an ACC. A basic business information entity (BBIE) is based on a BCC and an association business information entity (ASBIE) is based on an ASCC. A business data type (BDT) is based on a CDT. Likewise to a CDT, a BDT is used to set the value domain of a BBIE. The relationships between these different kinds of business information entities are in analogy to the relationships between the different kinds of core components.

The libraries shown with a white background aggregate the different modeling artifacts for business documents into self-contained packages. A *DOCLibrary* as shown on the lower right hand side of Fig. 2 has a particular role – it is used to aggregate different ABIE to a specific business document, hence allowing the modeler to structure the business information view into subviews of different business documents.

The presented UML Profile for Core Components provides a solid basis for transforming business documents into a consistent XML presentation. We have implemented a first prototype of this transformation as described in (Liegl 2009).

4.3 Example

In the following, we show how to create a business document for a `waste movement form`, which is exchanged in the *announce waste transport* `business transaction` (see Fig. 1 (3)). We assume the existence of a generic `movement form` built by core components. The core components are shown in (B) in Fig. 3. The root core component `movement form` is an ACC with two BCC: `transport number` and `identification number`. In addition, the ACC has four ASCC namely `transport means`, `period`, `party`, and `transport mode`. These composites are ACC as well. It follows that each of them has its own BCC. The ACC `Party` in (B) has a BCC `identification` among others. The assigned type for `identification` is the CDT `identifier`. `Identifier` is defined in the CDT library depicted in (D).

In a next step, the general `movement form` is set into the business context of the waste management domain. Accordingly, a shallow copy of the `movement form` is created. The resulting ABIE is qualified by the keyword `waste`. Furthermore, the substructure of the `waste movement form` is created in analogy to the general `movement form`. However, the substructure is restricted to the elements relevant in the waste management domain. By comparing the *core components* in (B) with the *business information entities* in (E), the derivation-by-restriction mechanism becomes apparent. For example, the ACC `transport mode` has been omitted. The `waste party` is restricted to include only the *basic information entities* `description` and `identification`.

Furthermore, the example demonstrates the restriction of a CDT to a BDT. The BDT `identifier number` is derived from the CDT `identifier` (D). First of all, the `identifier number` includes only two SUP: `idf schema agency identifier` and `idf scheme name`. Furthermore, the `idf schema agency identifier` is a *primitive* `string` in the general case, but it is a `party identifier` in the business case. This is allowed, since `party identifier` (C) is an *enumeration* created on the basis of the *primitive* `string` (F).

A BBIE may replace a CDT by a BDT that is derived from this CDT. Whereas the `identification` of a general `party` is of type `identifier`, the `identification` of the `waste party` is of type `identifier number`.

In Fig. 3, the packages embracing the different UML classes are the different libraries as defined in the meta model. For example, package (A) depicts a *DOC-Library* covering the business documents exchanged in a *business transaction*. In this package, the ABIE `waste movement form envelope` is bound to the `waste movement form envelope`, which is exchanged in the *business transaction* `announce waste transport`.

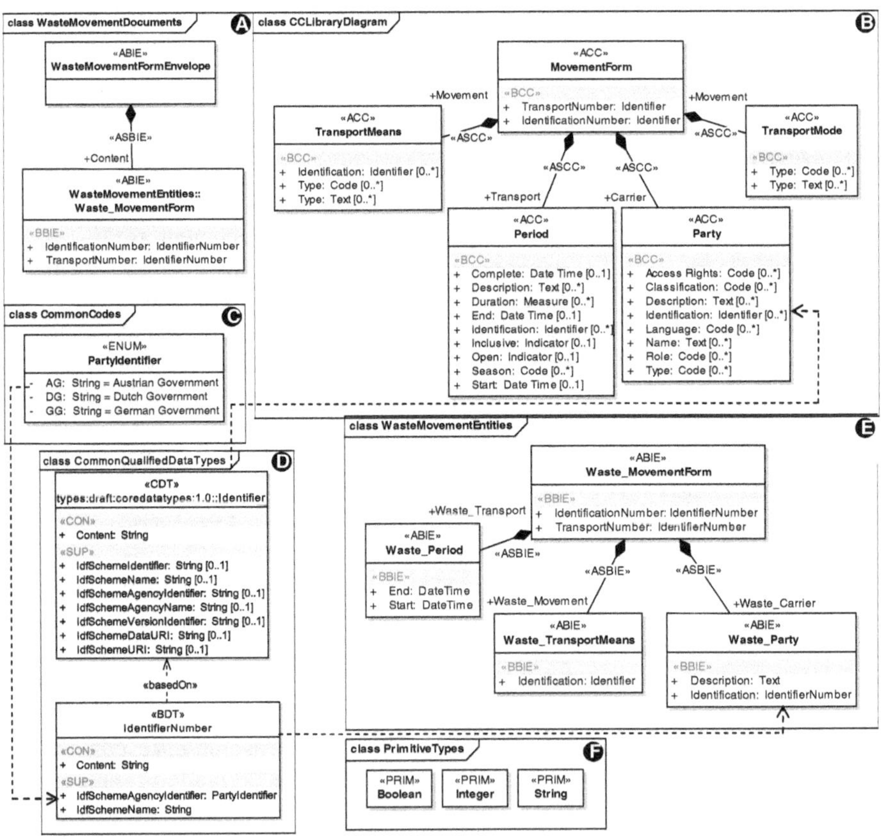

Fig. 3 Example: core components

5 Modeling Alternative Responses for a Single Request

5.1 Limitations of UMM 1.0 and Suggested Improvement

The main purpose of a *business transaction* is to change the state of a business entity. A positive response sent in a business transaction means that the response is aligned with the business goal and the preferred state change takes place. A negative response contradicts to the transaction goal and sets the state of a business entity into another state. This differentiation is currently not well supported by the strict pattern in UMM 1.0. In case of a two-way *business transaction*, the pattern requires that exactly one *responding information envelope* is sent in return. Usually, the type of response differs significantly in case of a positive and in case of a negative response. Today, the *information envelope* must foresee data structures to cover both positive and negative responses. Distinguishing positive and negative responses may only be achieved in UMM 1.0 by a work-around that is not explained in the standard's documentation: A positive response and a negative response are modeled as subclasses of a common abstract *information envelope* superclass. This work-around is not immediately recognized when just having a brief look on the *business transaction*, which only shows an object flow state that refers to the abstract superclass.

Thus, it is preferred to model different alternative responses in a *business transaction*. Accordingly, we must specify multiple *responding information envelopes* exchanged between the *responding* and the *requesting business action*. The exchange of *information envelopes* is no longer modeled by object flow states, but by action pins that are new in UML 2. Placing each action pin, representing a *responding information envelope*, into its own parameter set denotes an XOR-relationship between the different responses in order to model alternatives.

5.2 Detailed Solution

The suggested approach using action pins for alternative responses requires changes in the UMM meta model relating to *business transactions* as outlined in Fig. 4. In UMM 1.0, a *business transaction* was based on an activity graph that does not exist anymore in UML 2.1. Instead, UML 2.1 uses structured activities that are detailed in an activity diagram. Consequently, a *business transaction* is now based on an activity. The internal structure of this activity follows again the slightly adapted pattern.

A *business transaction* is still composed of a *requesting* and a *responding business action*. In the old version, they were based on action states resulting from the UML 1.4 dependency of activity graphs on state machines. Since this dependency has been resolved in UML 2.1, the *requesting* and the *responding business action*

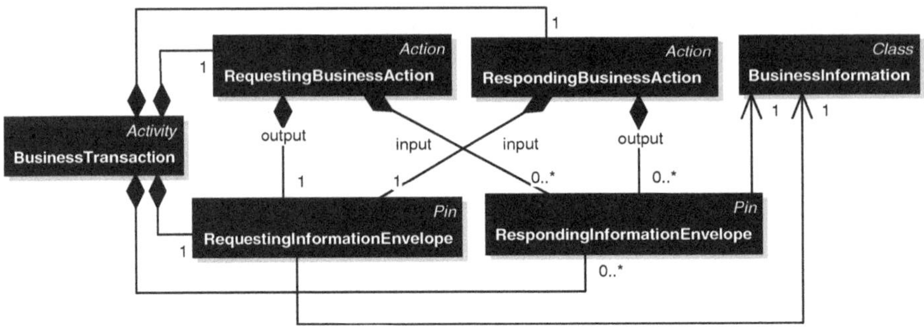

Fig. 4 Condensed UMM 2.0 meta model for business transactions

become opaque actions. This indicates that the "semantics of the action are determined by each partner's implementation" (OMG 2007).

Furthermore, an action may embed pins for receiving input and creating output. We use these pins to model the exchange of *information envelopes* between the *requesting business action* and the *responding business action*. The *requesting information envelope* and the *responding information envelope* are now pins instead of object flow states. The *business information* that is actually exchanged is assigned to the pins and usually modeled by core components as described in the previous section.

The output pin of a *requesting business action* and the input pin of a *responding business action* form the flow of the request. Both pins are stereotyped as *requesting information envelope*. Since a *business transaction* includes exactly one *requesting information envelope*, the *requesting business action* embeds one output pin and the *responding business action* embeds one input pin.

Analogical to the request, the combination of an output pin of a *responding business action* and an input pin of a *requesting business action* reflect a response. Accordingly, those pins are stereotyped as *responding information envelope*. Since a *business transaction* may include no response, one *responding information envelope* or even alternative *responding information envelopes*, the *responding business action* embeds zero to multiple output pins and the *requesting business action* embeds zero to many input pins. In UML, alternatives are modeled by parameter sets, which have an XOR relationship with each other according to the UML 2 specification. Thus, each alternative *responding business envelope* is located in its own parameter set.

5.3 Example

Figure 5 shows the activity diagram of the *business transaction* `announce waste transport`. It replaces the representation of the same *business transaction* (3) in

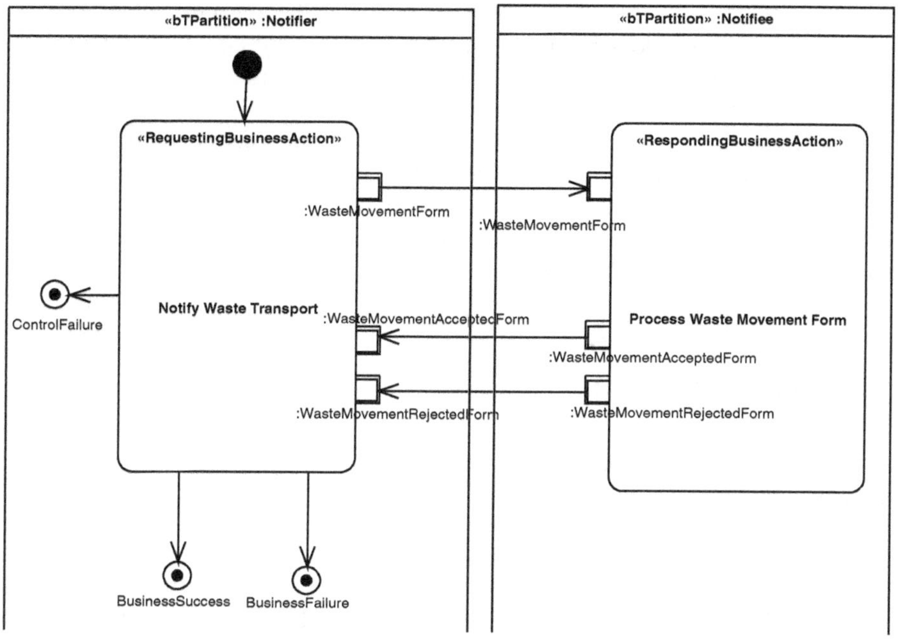

Fig. 5 Example: business transaction with alternative responses

Fig. 1. The *requesting business action* `notify transport` has one output pin and the *responding business transaction* `process waste movement form` has one input pin to exchange the `waste movement form envelope`. Note that we omit the stereotype *requesting business envelope* for these pins. There are two output pins for the *responding business action* and two input pins for *requesting business action* in order to alternatively exchange a `waste movement acceptance envelope` or a `waste movement rejection envelope`. Each of the pins is surrounded by another square to denote the corresponding parameter set.

6 Business Entity State Changes by Business Transactions

6.1 Limitations of UMM 1.0 and Suggested Improvement

UMM uses the concept of a *business entity lifecycle* showing the order of possible states of a *business entity* during its lifetime. However, the *business entity lifecycle* is currently only used for discovering possible business collaborations in the BRV. In fact, the intended purpose of *business transactions* is changing *business entity states*. By exchanging information, both partners involved reach a mutually understood business entity state change. Unfortunately, the current notation of *business transactions* does not make these *business entity state* changes explicit. The default states `business success` and `business failure` are up to human interpretation.

It is desired to explicitly define the characteristics of a response that lead to a success or failure. For this purpose, we introduce OCL constraints checking the response for certain characteristics that decide upon a positive or negative response. These OCL constraints guard the transitions to explicit *business entity states* leading to a success or failure, respectively.

6.2 Detailed Solution

In a two-way *business transaction*, the *requesting business action* receives the response by a *responding information envelope*. According to the previous section, the *responding information envelope* may be one out of several alternatives. It depends on the characteristics of the response whether a *business transaction* ends with a *business success* or a *business failure*. In case of multiple alternative responses, the success or failure is usually determined by the fact which alternative is actually received. In case of a fixed type of *responding information envelope*, the success or failure usually depends on whether certain elements of the response are instantiated or not, or on the actual values of certain elements.

A machine-interpretable solution requires a formal check of the response. We propose to specify this formal check by means of OCL, which enables the specification of invariants. An invariant is used to describe the characteristics of a response. It defines the type of the response, which elements have to be instantiated, and, if so, by which range of values. Usually, there will be an invariant for a positive response and another one for a negative response. In theory, one may think of more than the two basic kinds of invariants.

The invariants are used to guard the transitions to the final states of a *business transaction*. The *requesting business action* receives the response and checks which of the mutually exclusive invariants holds for this response. This triggers the transition guarded by the respective invariant.

Currently, these transitions immediately lead to the final end states *business success* and *business failure*. Thereby, we do not capture the business effect of a *business transaction*. The business effect of a *business transaction* is the change of state of one or more *business entities*. *Business entities* and their lifecycle of *business entity states* are modeled in the BRV. In UMM 1.0, the concept of *business entities* and their states is isolated from the concepts in *business transactions*, although there exists an evident dependency between them. Hence, we propose to explicitly denote the resulting *business entity states* in a *business transaction* before it reaches its final state. This means, the transitions guarded by the invariants do not immediately lead to an end state but result in a new *business entity state* triggered by the received invariant.

6.3 Example

We demonstrate the concepts of invariants and *business entity state* changes by means of the *business transaction* `announce waste transport`. This *business transaction* was first introduced in Fig. 1 and later refined by the concept of alternative responses in Fig. 5. The concepts introduced in this Section result in its final presentation in Fig. 6. The *business transaction* `announce waste transport` is successful if a waste movement acceptance envelope is received, and it fails by receiving a waste movement rejection envelope. Consequently, we specify two OCL invariants that constrain the type of the received response:

Listing 1 OCL constraint (a)

```
context NotifyWasteTransport
inv PositiveResponse:
self.input->one(x | x.isTypeOf (WasteMovementAcceptance-
Envelope) and x <> null)
```

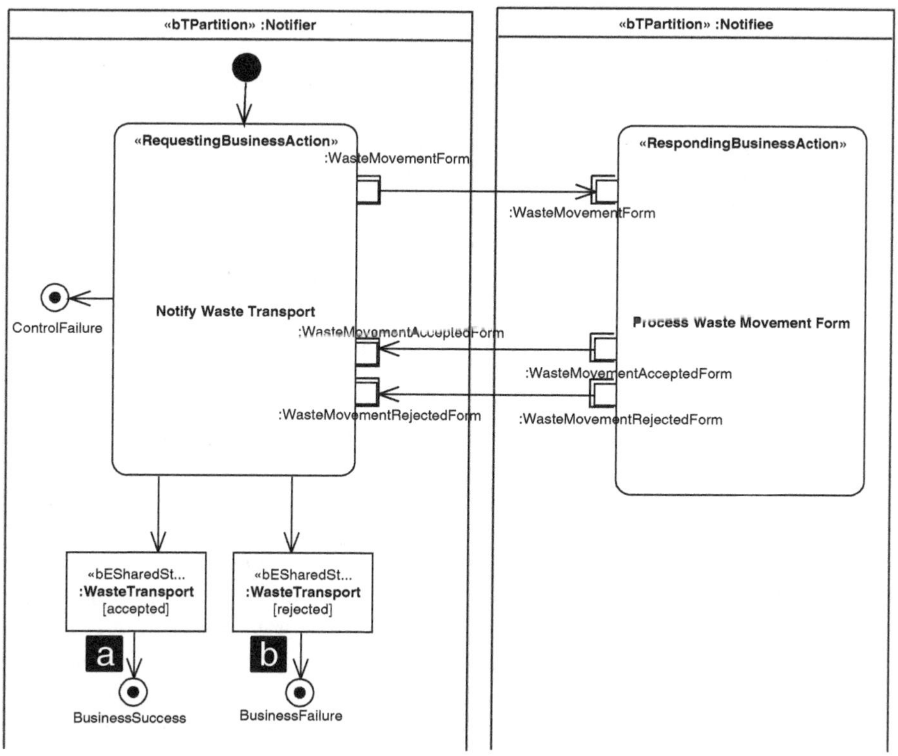

Fig. 6 Example: business transaction with business entity states

Listing 2 OCL constraint (b)

```
Context NotifyWasteTransport
inv NegativeResponse:
self.input->one(x | x.isTypeOf (WasteMovementAcceptance-
Envelope) and x <> null)
```

The two OCL constraints are placed on the transitions starting from the *requesting business action* `notify waste transport` (denoted by (a) and (b) in Fig. 6). If a waste movement acceptance envelope is received, the first invariant (a) holds. This changes the *business entity* `waste transport` to the state `accepted` and ends with a *business success*. On the contrary, receiving a waste movement rejection envelops fulfills the second invariant (b). It changes the *business entity* `waste transport` to the state `rejected` and ends with a *business failure*.

7 Machine Interpretable Business Collaboration Protocols

7.1 Limitations of UMM 1.0 and Suggested Improvement

Currently, *business collaboration protocols* suffer from three major limitations. The first limitation concerns the relationship between *business transaction activities* and *business transactions*. A *business transaction activity* must be refined by a *business transaction*. In addition, a *business transaction* may be called by multiple *business transaction activities*. The UML 1.4 meta model defines a 1:n relationship between an activity and refining activity graphs. Whereas an activity may be refined by different graphs, one and the same activity graph cannot refine different activities. In order to simulate reusable subactivity graphs, we have introduced the *maps to* dependency from a *business transaction activity* to the refining *business transaction*. This work-around leads to a proper model but is not natively supported by UML tools and thus provides rather poor usability. In UMM 2, a *call behavior action* has been introduced for exactly this purpose. Inasmuch, we base the *business transaction activities* on *call behavior actions* to eliminate the *maps to* dependencies.

The second limitation is the fact that a *business collaboration protocol* may be well interpreted by a human but fails to give an unambiguous machine-processable definition to further derive software artifacts. In fact, the states of a *business entity* determine the flow of *business transaction activities* within a *business collaboration protocol*. However, the guards in a *business collaboration protocol* do not formally reflect the *business entity states* but rather use plain text descriptions. Having explicitly introduced the `business entity state` changes at the *business transaction* level in the previous section, we are able to use the resulting states on the guards between *business transaction activities* at the *business collaboration protocol* level.

The third limitation addresses the quite complex role mapping mechanism in UMM 1.0 as introduced in the description of Fig. 1. For a more lightweight definition of role mappings, we propose a new modeling approach for business collaboration protocols in UMM 2.0. It is inspired by the modeling of participants in collaborative business processes in BPMN (OMG 2009).

7.2 Detailed Solution

A *business collaboration protocol* consists of *business transaction activities*, each calling a certain *business transaction*. UML 2 introduces the concept of a *call behavior action*. A *call behavior action* is used to call the control flow specified in another activity. We use this concept as the new base class for the stereotype *business transaction action*. In order to reflect the change of the base class, we also changed the name of the stereotype *business transaction activity* to *business transaction action*. A *business transaction action* calls the control flow specified in a *business transaction*. Therefore, the corresponding *maps to* dependency of UMM 1.0 is eliminated. Now, a *business transaction action* carries a little rake symbol in the lower right corner that denotes a *call behavior action*.

Furthermore, *business collaboration protocols* are improved by using a formal notation for transition guards. UMM 1.0 does not mandate any formal notation for the guards. Accordingly, transitions may be guarded by plain text descriptions (cf. Fig.1 (2)). Plain text helps a human to understand the *business collaboration protocol*, but it inhibits the generation of executable artifacts, such as BPEL code. Usually, the control flow is guarded by the states of *business entities*. Therefore, a formal notation for checking *business entity states* in the guard conditions is proposed.

In the previous section, a concept to bind the result of *business transactions* to *business entity states* was provided. Since *business transaction actions* represent a call of a *business transaction*, the resulting state may be checked in order to decide on the next activity. OCL provides the function `<Object>.oclInState(theState)` for checking the state of an object in general and of a *business entity* in specific. This function returns `true` if the *business entity* currently is in the specified state. Accordingly, we mandate this function on the guards of the transitions in a *business collaboration protocol*.

In order to depict the *authorized roles* participating in a *business collaboration*, we use the concept of partitions. Exactly one partition is created for each *authorized role*. The concepts of *initFlows* and *reFlows* are used to describe which role of the business collaboration initiates and responds in an underlying business transaction, respectively. Therefore, an *initFlow* connects a partition representing an *authorized role* with a *business transaction action*/*business collaboration action*. The same applies to *reFlows*.

7.3 Example

Figure 7 depicts the *business collaboration protocol* manage waste transport following the new approach. It consists of two *business transaction actions*. The first one calls the announce wastetransport *business transaction* and the second one calls the announce transport arrival *business transaction*.

As outlined in the Section before, the announce waste transport *business transaction* sets the *business entity* waste transport either to state accepted or rejected. In Fig. 7, the two outgoing transitions from the announce waste transport activity carry mutually exclusive OCL functions, checking whether waste transport has been set to one or the other state. The *business collaboration protocol* ends if waste transport is in state rejected, and continues with *announce transport arrival* if waste transport is in state accepted. Announce transport arrival is a one-way *business transaction* that is executed to inform about the arrival of the waste transport. The state change communicated by a one-way transaction is irreversible. Consequently, the state accepted of the business entity lifecycle waste transport has only one subsequent state – named arrived. Since there is no decision about the outcome of announce transport arrival, there is only one outgoing transition leading to the successful end state.

Using the concept of two *business collaboration partitions (bCPartition)*, the two *authorized roles* notifier and notifiee participating in the business collaboration are shown. The *business collaboration protocol* starts with the *business transaction* announce waste transport. The *initFlow* dependency from the

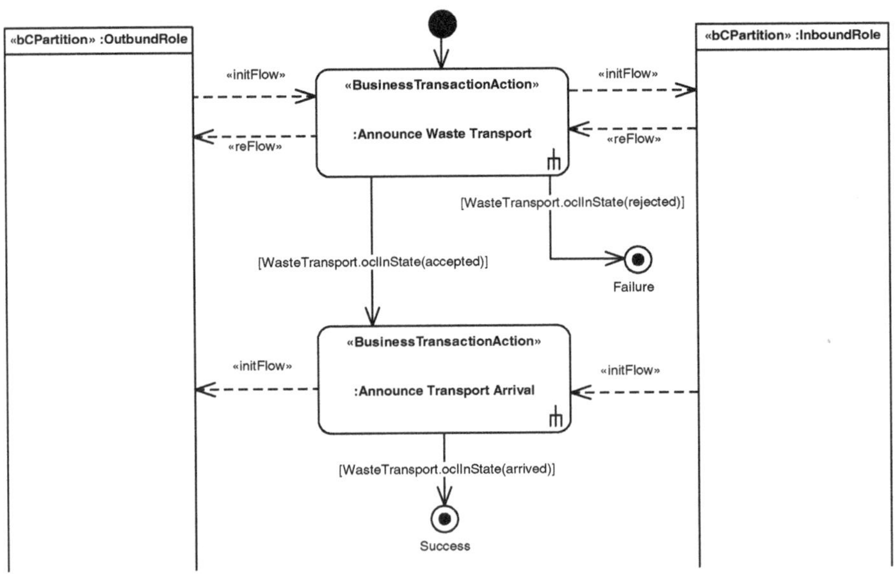

Fig. 7 Example: business collaboration protocol with OCL guards

`notifier` to the *business transaction action* `announce waste transport` indicates that the `notifier` initiates the *business transaction*. Consequently, the `notifier` of the *business collaboration protocol* plays the `notifier` in the *business transaction* `announce waste transport`. The other *initFlow* leads from the *business transaction action* `announce waste transport` to the partition of the notifiee. This declares that he plays the `notifiee` in the `announce waste transport` *business transaction*. The *reFlow* dependencies are not required for the unambiguous mapping between collaboration roles and transaction roles. However, they are used to visualize already on the *business collaboration protocol* that an underlying *business transaction* is a two-way transaction (which was a request by stakeholders). Correspondingly, the second *business transaction action* – `announce transport arrival` – has no *reFlows* connected since it is a one-way transaction.

8 Conclusion

In this article, we have presented UN/CEFACT's Modeling Methodology – an approach for unambiguously describing interorganizational business processes. We have elaborated on our contribution we made to the development of the standard's version 1.0 and have given an example from the waste transport domain. However, it has been shown that the current version 1.0 of UMM has some shortcomings. Due to these shortcomings, we have started to develop concepts overcoming the current limitations. The following concepts will improve UMM in the future version 2.0, which is currently in implementation verification:

- The UML Profile for Core Components (UPCC) gives precise guidelines for modeling the business documents exchanged in a choreography
- Alternative, that is, mutually exclusive, responses in a business transaction.
- A formal definition for guarding the control flow of business collaboration protocols that reflects the business entity state changes realized by business transactions.
- A call behavior function for business collaboration protocols to call business transactions and nested business collaboration protocols
- An efficient role mapping

Having introduced all new concepts, it also turned out that the UMM 1.0 package structure is inefficient. In order to avoid an unnecessary complex and overwhelming package structure, it is desired to group artifacts that belong together into the same package. As a consequence, we propose a repackaging in UMM 2.0. The new package structure is depicted in Fig. 8.

The new UMM package structure again includes three top level packages: the BRV, the *business choreography view*, and the *business information view*. The BRV captures *business process use cases*, their activity models, all *business partners* being involved, and the *business entity life cycle*.

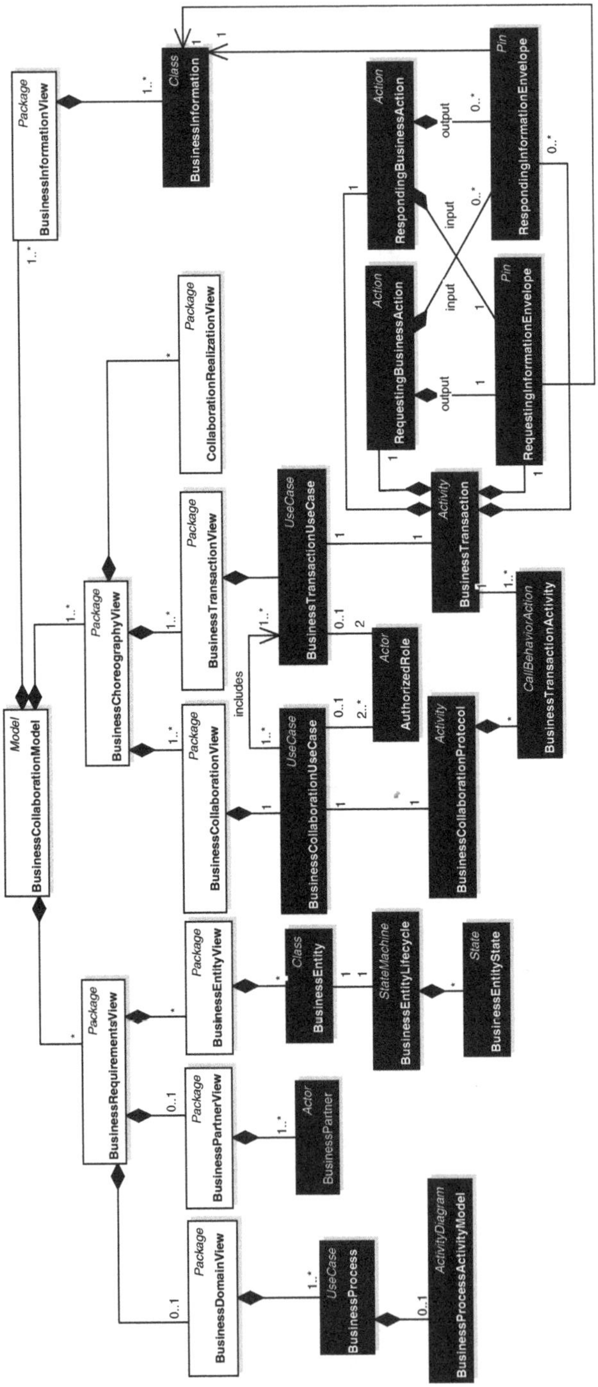

Fig. 8 Condensed UMM 2.0 conceptual meta model

The *business choreography view* is built by a structure to capture *business collaboration protocols*, *business transactions* together with their corresponding use case descriptions. The *business information view* covers the business information modeled according to the UML profile for core components. The suggested structure makes UMM easier to understand and simpler to use. Together, the suggested features and the repackaging result in a major improvement of the UMM. In order to create UMM-compliant models, one may use any UML tool. We provide special features such as worksheet support, model validation, and the generation of deployment artifacts by out VIENNA Add-In,[1] which extends the UML modeling tool Enterprise Architect.

References

Barros A, Hettel T, Flender C (2010) Process choreography modeling. In: vom Brocke J, Rosemann M (eds) Handbook on business process management, vol 1. Springer, Heidelberg

Decker G, Barros A (2008) Interaction modeling using BPMN. In: Business process management workshops. Lecture notes in computer science, vol 4928. Springer, Berlin, Heidelberg, pp 208–219

Decker G, Kopp O, Alistair B (2008) An introduction to service choreographies. Inf Technol 50 (2):122–127

Decker G, Kopp O, Leymann F, Weske M (2007) BPEL4Chor: extending BPEL for modeling choreographies. In: Proceedings of the IEEE international conference on web services ICWS 2007. pp 296–303

Decker G, Kopp O, Leymann F, Weske M (2009) Interacting services: from specification to execution. Data Knowl Eng 68(10):946–972

Hill NC, Ferguson DM (1989) Electronic data interchange: a definition and perspective. EDI Forum J Electron Data Interchange 1(1):5–12

Hofreiter B, Huemer C, Kim J-H (2006a) Choreography of ebXML business collaborations. Inf Syst E Bus Manage 4(3):221–243

Hofreiter B, Huemer C, Liegl P, Schuster R, Zapletal M (2006b) UN/CEFACT'S modeling methodology (UMM): a UML profile for B2B e-commerce. In: Advances in conceptual modeling – theory and practice, ER 2006 workshops. LNCS, vol 4231. Springer, Berlin, pp 19–31

Hofreiter B, Huemer C, Liegl P, Schuster R, Zapletal M (2007) Deriving executable BPEL from UMM business transactions. In: Proceedings of the IEEE international conference on services computing SCC 2007. pp 178–186

ISO (2007) ISO 3166 List of country names and code elements

Liegl P (2009) Conceptual business document modeling using UN/CEFACT's core components. In: Proceedings sixth Asia-Pacific conference on conceptual modelling (APCCM), Wellington, New Zealand, January 20–23. pp 59–69

OASIS, UN/CEFACT (2001) ebXML – technical architecture specification. Version 1.4

OMG (2005) Unified modeling language specification. Version 1.4.2

OMG (2007) Unified modeling language: superstructure. Version 2.1.1

OMG (2009) Business process modeling notation specification (BPMN). Version 1.2

UN/CEFACT (2003) UN/CEFACT – ebXML business process specification schema. Version 1.10

[1]http://vienna-add-in.googlecode.com.

UN/CEFACT (2006) UN/CEFACT's modeling methodology (UMM), UMM meta model – foundation module. Technical specification V1.0
UN/CEFACT (2009a) Core component data type catalogue 3.0
UN/CEFACT (2009b) Core components technical specification 3.0
UN/CEFACT (2009c) UML profile for core components technical specification 3.0
W3C (2005) Web services choreography description language. Version 1.0, W3C candidate recommendation
Zaha JM, Barros A, Dumas M, ter Hofstede A (2006) Let's dance: a language for service behavior modeling. In: On the move to meaningful internet systems 2006: CoopIS, DOA, GADA, and ODBASE. Lecture notes in computer science, vol 4275. Springer, Berlin, Heidelberg, pp 145–162
Zapletal M (2008) Deriving business service interfaces in windows workflow from UMM transactions. In: ICSOC '08: proceedings of the 6th international conference on service-oriented computing. Springer, pp 498–504

Enterprise 2.0 Meets Business Process Management

Sandy Kemsley

Abstract This chapter discusses the main aspects of Enterprise 2.0, how they are already impacting BPM, and how BPM is likely to evolve into a more social environment in the future. In particular, the impacts include cultural effects of collaboration during process modeling and process execution, as well as technological impacts of newer user interface models, development techniques, and delivery mechanisms. In turn, these have economic impacts for both development and delivery models that become more relevant during the current economic recession.

1 Introduction

As the spread of social software increases, expectations for how software systems should behave are changing, and Business Process Management Systems (BPMS) are no exception. Consumer social software – Web 2.0 – is changing what people will accept with respect to software capabilities and usability both in personal and business domains, leading to the rise of enterprise social software – Enterprise 2.0.

Web 2.0, the consumer-facing side of social software, was described by O'Reilly (2005) as having several key characteristics:

- Uses the web as a platform, with a browser-based rich user interface that provides equivalent functionality to a desktop application. In addition to requiring no local installation, thereby lowering costs and providing greater desktop platform support, this allows for a constantly refreshing software upgrade cycle. This is supported by software-as-a-service providers that offer everything from

S. Kemsley
Kemsley Design Ltd., Toronto, Canada
e-mail: sandy@kemsleydesign.com

J. vom Brocke and M. Rosemann (eds.), *Handbook on Business Process Management 1*, International Handbooks on Information Systems,
DOI 10.1007/978-3-642-00416-2_26,

email to document production to sales force automation via a monthly subscription, or even for free, rather than requiring the purchase and installation of software on a person's (or company's) own computers. Carr (2008) describes the emerging utility model of computing, comparing it to the shift from private electricity production to centralized power plants that sell electricity on a usage-metered basis.
- Harnesses collective intelligence by allowing user-directed and user-created content and collaboration. Although only a small percentage of users will contribute, their contributions are available to all users.
- Enables lightweight development models for assembling loosely-coupled composite applications or "mashups." This allows information from disparate sources to be easily assembled to facilitate collaboration, and provides a highly configurable user experience.

Many examples of Web 2.0 applications are available that illustrate these principles: Google's Gmail with its constantly upgraded feature set and rich email interface; Wikipedia with content contributed by a wide variety of authors; and Google Maps with its lightweight API allowing it to be easily integrated as the mapping function within other websites.

By 2006, McAfee (2006) had defined the enterprise equivalent, Enterprise 2.0, as "platforms that companies can buy or build in order to make visible the practices and outputs of their knowledge workers." Like Web 2.0 consumer applications, Enterprise 2.0 applications allow for emergent structure and processes rather than imposing predetermined taxonomies and procedures. Unlike Web 2.0, however, Enterprise 2.0 applications usually have a business-related purpose rather than a purely social function. These break down into two main categories:

- Applications focused on social interaction that strengthen weak ties within a large and/or geographically diverse organization. An example of this is Beehive (IBM Watson Research Center), IBM's internal social network, which allows their 300,000 employees to create profile pages about themselves and their interests, similar to the popular public social network, Facebook. Although it is not used directly to create IBM's work product, it is used for locating others with specific skills and interests for research and project collaboration.
- Applications focused on goal-oriented social production. An example is Intellipedia (Central Intelligence Agency news archive 2008), the US intelligence community's library of intelligence-related information. Built using the same wiki software that powers the public Wikipedia site, MediaWiki, articles in Intellipedia can be created, edited, and discussed by authenticated users across multiple intelligence and government agencies.

Concurrent with the emergence of Enterprise 2.0, commercial BPMS products were beginning to incorporate some of the characteristics of Web 2.0, particularly in the areas of browser-based rich user interfaces and lightweight development models (Kemsley 2006). The following sections discuss the drivers for this emergence, as well as the impacts on BPMS.

2 Drivers for Collaborative BPM

The motivation for including Enterprise 2.0 concepts and technology in BPM contains many facets: the expectations of individual users, the push toward greater collaboration within organizations, and the mismatch between the vision of BPMS agility and the reality of implementation.

2.1 The Change in User Expectations

Tapscott (2008) describes the impact of the under-30 "Net Generation" joining the workforce, expecting to use their social networking tools for collaboration and creation, only to find an antiquated state of technology in most organizations. Furthermore, the culture around creating and processing information in many organizations restricts them to a rigid set of rules and processes – often enforced by enterprise technology such as BPM systems (BPMS) – with no way to collaborate while remaining within the corporate standards (see also the Hilti case in vom Brocke et al. 2010).

This new generation of workers has vastly different expectations for corporate technology than previous generations: they expect to be able to configure their own environment to suit their working style, to collaborate with others at any point in a business process where they see fit, and to combine information from multiple internal and external sources in order to accomplish their tasks.

Most current BPMS implementations, with predefined processes and static user interfaces, do not meet those expectations; at some point, organizations must implement more flexible computing environments as part of wooing the younger generation into their workforce.

2.2 The Trend Towards Collaboration

Of the eight business technology trends that McKinsey (Manyika et al. 2007) advises tracking, three are focused on new forms of collaboration within enterprises: distributing cocreation across the value chain, using consumers as innovators, and using the internet to tap into talent wherever it exists. Organizations are beginning to understand the benefits of incorporating collaboration into their business processes, and the value of capturing the collaborative process and its results in an auditable environment; many are turning to Enterprise 2.0 tools for this collaboration when their BPMS cannot provide the functionality.

2.3 Lack of Agility in BPMS Implementations

Although most BPMS vendors design and market their products to be used as model-driven development environments, where processes can be modeled graphically by a business analyst, enhanced with technical underpinnings such as web services calls by a developer, then immediately deployed into production, the reality is far different. In many BPM implementations, a BPMS is used merely as a graphical development tool in a classic waterfall software development lifecycle rather than allowing the full model-driven development capabilities to be used in an agile development methodology. This typically manifests as highly customized user task interfaces that cannot be easily changed, and are "hard-wired" to a specific underlying process map and the disabling of some of the core BPMS capabilities such as collaboration.

This type of rigid design pattern has the effect of relegating the BPMS – a technology that is fully capable of delivering agile, model-driven solutions – to the realm of legacy enterprise software, with many innate collaborative capabilities unavailable to end users. Dissatisfaction with this outcome is encouraging many organizations to consider collaborative and user-driven design and development methods in order to achieve the degree of process agility required.

3 The Impact of Enterprise 2.0 on BPM

Enterprise 2.0 is impacting BPM – both the technology and the management practice – in a variety of ways: social/cultural, technological, and economic. It is important to note that these changes are observed primarily in the most technologically advanced vendors' products and the most forward-thinking end-user organizations at this time.

3.1 Social and Cultural Impacts

A significant cultural change in how BPM is used in organizations is due to the increase in collaboration, occurring in two key areas: collaborative process modeling and collaboration during the execution of a process.

Collaborative process modeling and analysis tools permit multiple people, both technical and nontechnical, to participate in the discovery, modeling, design, implementation, and optimization of a business process. This requires an easy-to-use wiki-like process modeler that maintains the process models in a shared repository: any participant can modify the model and the results are visible to all. As seen in text-based wikis, the network effect of multiple authors can increase productivity and generate innovative, emergent ideas. vom Brocke and Thomas (2006) examine the use of collaborative techniques for reference process models, and how sharing models with a greater range of stakeholders can result in a division of labor as well as an increase in model quality. In other areas of system modeling, it is recognized that having domain experts participate in modeling is essential (Martin 1997); collaborative process modeling tools are now allowing this to occur in BPM.

One example of a collaborative process modeling tool is Lombardi's Blue-print, which is delivered via a software-as-a-service monthly subscription. It offers an easy-to-use web-based interface for process modeling and documentation, but more importantly, provides a shared modeling environment that allows multiple geographically dispersed team members to create and edit a process model collaboratively in real time. Forrester Research's recent coverage of Blueprint (Richardson et al. 2009) highlights its use in customer organizations, including Tillamook County Creamery, a food and beverage manufacturer, which used Blueprint to turn 100 years of "tribal knowledge" into documented and validated business processes. More than 150 people across multiple business units – including farmer-owned dairies as well as the two manufacturing plants – were involved in collaboratively modeling, detailing, and reviewing processes, and capturing information that had previously been passed from one worker to another. Other case studies include Morphis Software, a supply chain management provider, which uses Blueprint to collaborate with their customers to capture their supply chain processes, remotely but in real time, significantly reducing travel costs.

A detailed case study of collaborative process modeling at Intersport (Lind and Seigerroth 2010) shows how participants from different parts and levels of the organization are involved in process design and validation. This codesign framework allowed for all stakeholder concerns to be addressed and for a common understanding of the business processes to be created.

Collaboration during the execution of a structured process in a BPMS allows a user at any step to choose to "step outside" the structured process and initiate an ad hoc collaboration with users of their choice in order to accomplish the task at hand. The collaboration participants, flow, artifacts, and results are captured in the audit history of the process in the BPMS, maintaining visibility into the ad hoc processes as well as gathering information on how the processes are executed, allowing them to be considered for future standardization and modeling as structured processes. Providing a dynamic BPMS environment, which can include ad hoc and collaboration scenarios in the context of a more structured business process, allows participants to use their own best practices and tools, particularly in processes that rely heavily on subjective human knowledge. Without this type of collaboration, process participants will use email, paper documents, and telephone calls to resolve an issue that cannot be handled in the structured process model within the BPMS; these conversations and their outcome will not be explicitly captured in the BPMS, creating a gap in the knowledge and audit history of the process. Although an organization's management may consider allowing ad hoc process definition and collaboration within a structured process to be a business risk due to loss of control over business processes, they should consider that the risk already exists due to the current methods of resolving issues that cannot be managed in the context of the structured process.

In-process collaboration is taking a number of different forms in commercial BPMS products. Several products, including those from smaller vendors HandySoft and ActionBase, build BPMS functionality on the Microsoft Exchange platform, which allows for email-based collaboration during the course of a process while still tracking all activities in the process by managing email requests and responses. Fujitsu is allowing for the integration of ad hoc, email-based collaboration into structured processes in upcoming releases of their Interstage BPMS product, which will allow process participants to create new tasks and subprocesses dynamically during process execution.

Other forms of in-process collaboration include notes or threaded discussions attached to a process instance: these do not change the structure or path of the process but capture conversations and status updates that occur about a task or process. One BPMS vendor providing this type of collaboration is Appian, which includes threaded discussions and collaboration dashboards as part of its standard product offering.

Collaboration in process modeling or process execution requires a shift to a more participatory organizational culture. Business management must be willing to commit time and resources to process modeling – a task that they may consider to be a technical responsibility – and the technical team must be willing to accept the business people as equal participants in process design. End users must feel sufficiently comfortable with deviating from the structured process during execution in order to take advantage of the process execution collaboration capabilities.

Johannesson et al. (2008) contrasted the differences in work organization between social software and BPM, noting differences such as the external authority that guides a process within a BPMS versus the voluntary participation in social software. Although many of their points are not valid for Enterprise 2.0, where participation may not be voluntary and specific endpoints and results are part of the process, they present some valuable guidelines for bringing social software concepts into a BPMS that will facilitate the necessary cultural changes. They present the metaphor of a process implemented in a BPMS as an assembly line, where each worker performs their specialized task on an artifact with little knowledge of the tasks before and after that point, whereas a process in social software is more of a workstation approach, where an artifact stays in one position while a variety of workers collaborate in order to perform the tasks necessary to accomplish a goal. These two approaches require different corporate cultures and management styles; making a BPMS assembly line process more collaborative requires more than just adding collaboration functionality to the software.

Collaboration is also not suited to every business process, particularly those governed by strict regulations, or those performed by inexperienced workers or outsourced participants. The decision to include collaboration in a process – or even in a single step within a process – must consider process governance requirements, the experience of the participant, and the nature of the work.

3.2 Technological Impacts

Enterprise 2.0 technology features, such as RSS feeds, browser-based rich user interfaces, and lightweight development models are now being provided in many BPMS products.

Standardized feeds (e.g., RSS, Atom) allow users to subscribe to new and changed data in their BPMS inbox or shared work queues. The use of a standardized feed mechanism not only allows a user to monitor work items of interest in the feed reader of their choice, it also allows them to easily manipulate, filter, and repurpose that data to create customized dashboards for data visualization, send threshold alerts via instant messaging (IM) or mobile text messaging, or post milestones to a microblogging site, all without programming or any deep technical knowledge. A rarity as little as two years ago, RSS feeds of queue contents are now available as standard features on several commercial BPMS products.

Rich user interfaces using technologies such as Asynchronous JavaScript and XML (AJAX) provide a desktop-grade user experience from within a web browser. This eliminates the need for the installation of any desktop software, except a standard web browser, and allows process participants at any location to have the same user experience. All mainstream BPMS products provide their end-user interfaces through a rich browser interface, and some also provide their process modeling and administration interfaces via a browser as well.

Lightweight development models allow semitechnical business users to combine BPMS functionality with corporate and external data and services into composite applications. Although feeds provide one mechanism for this, some BPMS' also provide functional units as widgets that can be combined into a standardized portal environment by a nontechnical user, similar to adding widgets to a consumer home page such as My Yahoo or iGoogle. These widgets can be connected to third-party widgets, for example, by displaying a Google Map corresponding to street address information that is held in a BPMS process instance.

All of these technological changes to BPMS products have the effect of empowering business users to configure their own work environment with less technical support.

3.3 Economic Impacts

BPMS' have gained a reputation as being expensive to buy and even more expensive to customize for use. As Enterprise 2.0 technology and functionality is integrated with BPMS, economic factors shift toward less costly alternatives in development and delivery models.

The lightweight development models that allow business users to create their own simple composite applications, or mashups, also provide robust high-level capabilities for developers, allowing them to create complex user interfaces in a fraction of the time required for traditional coding techniques. Automated interfaces between a BPMS and other systems use standards such as SOAP, eliminating the coding required to integrate calls to other systems into a process. This combination of high-level integration tools and standards significantly reduces the development efforts for a BPMS implementation, and often requires less-skilled (therefore, less costly) developers due to the reduction or elimination of programming in languages such as Java.

Many traditionally structured organizations struggle with the concept of allowing business users to create their own applications, although the users are currently doing so with tools such as spreadsheets and desktop databases. The demands of the business users and managers for greater agility in processes and functionality will drive the creation of composite applications within the business areas, primarily through the use of vendor-provided widgets in a configurable portal environment.

Software-as-a-service BPMS offerings are emerging in the marketplace, where the BPMS software is hosted by a third party and licensed using a monthly subscription model. This reduces the total cost of ownership by eliminating the large up-front hardware and software capital expenditures, and the associated ongoing staffing and maintenance costs, in exchange for a monthly per-user subscription fee.

The software-as-a-service BPMS market has met with resistance due to security concerns of hosting critical corporate data outside the enterprise. This attitude is changing as software-as-a-service in other technology areas shows successes, and will be further motivated as capital budgets are cut in the current economic downturn.

3.4 Barriers to Adoption

The inclusion of Enterprise 2.0 functionality into BPM – primarily collaboration, but also lightweight development models and software-as-a-service delivery mechanisms – has many barriers to adoption, particularly by large enterprises. As described within this section, these include:

- Loss of management control over processes by allowing increased collaboration. In reality, workers are already collaborating in an ad hoc in order to complete their work; providing collaboration within a BPMS would capture the results of that collaboration, which may currently be lost.
- Lack of understanding about, or lack of trust in, lightweight development models by information technology departments.
- Risk of data loss or security breach if processes are hosted on a software-as-a-service BPMS.

These barriers may be overcome through a better understanding of the underlying issues, as organizations see better results through collaboration, shorter development times due to lightweight development tools, and lower costs with manageable risks of software-as-a-service solutions.

4 Expectations of Future Innovations and Impacts

The more advanced commercial BPMS offerings are rapidly incorporating Enterprise 2.0 functionality: rich browser-based user interfaces configurable by the end-user, lightweight integration methods, feeds, process design collaboration, runtime collaboration, and software-as-a-service offerings. This, in turn, is facilitating sweeping change in how business processes are designed, implemented, executed, and monitored. In addition to greater acceptance and usage of the technologies previously discussed, there is the potential for other technology aspects of social software to be incorporated in BPMS:

- User tagging (bookmarking) of process instances allows a user to mark a process for easy retrieval at a later time, or to share knowledge with other users about the specifics of that process.
- IM and other synchronous communications integrated into structured processes for lightweight real-time collaboration, allowing a user to detect if a specific user is online and conduct a conversation by IM in order to resolve an issue and complete their current task, while capturing the IM conversation as part of the process history.

The largest future impacts, however, will be cultural. In the face of technology that allows for collaboration and user-created content, organizational management must cede some control to the end users in terms of how work is done, and the workers must accept that level of responsibility and participate in ways that are new to them. Provided with a goal plus a flexible set of tools, knowledge workers will create more effective work practices than if every step is dictated in advance; furthermore, since they are working within the tools in order to achieve the goal, their work practices and outputs are captured in the work environment.

5 Conclusion

Enterprise 2.0 has had, and continues to have, a significant impact on the technology of BPMS. The integration of social software technology and features into commercial BPMS has been occurring at variable rates: rich browser-based user interfaces for process participants are the accepted standard, but feeds and collaboration are just beginning to gain acceptance and are not widely used. Although not every BPMS could be categorized as Enterprise 2.0 today, any human-centric BPMS will need to incorporate significant Enterprise 2.0 features in order to remain competitive.

More important, however, are the cultural changes that are enabled by – and required by – the adoption of Enterprise 2.0 in the very structured world of BPM. As the technology advances to allow business users to take greater control over their work environment, the users must adapt to a participatory culture. Instead of being passive consumers of business processes designed by management and codified in enterprise software, they are expected to help design their own business processes, configure their working environment to fit their own needs, and collaborate with others in order to achieve business goals.

These cultural changes represent both the largest obstacle and the greatest potential benefit of Enterprise 2.0 and BPM.

References

Carr N (2008) The Big Switch, W. W. Norton & Company, New York, USA

Central Intelligence Agency news archive (2008) Intellipedia marks second anniversary. https://www.cia.gov/news-information/featured-story-archive/intellipedia-marks-second-anniversary.html. Accessed 20 Mar 2008

Johannesson P, Andersson B, Wohed P (2008) Business process management with social software systems – a new paradigm for work organisation

Kemsley S (2006) Web 2.0 and BPM, a presentation given at BPMG's process 2006 conference, London. http://www.slideshare.net/skemsley/web-20-and-bpm

Lind M, Seigerroth U (2010) Collaborative process modeling: the intersport case study, BPM handbook

Manyika J, Roberts R, Sprague K (2007) Eight business technology trends to watch. McKinsey Q

Martin F (1997) Analysis patterns

McAfee A (2006) Enterprise 2.0: the dawn of emergent collaboration. MIT Sloan Manage Rev 47 (3):21–28

O'Reilly T (2005) What is web 2.0: design patterns and business models for the next generation of software. http://www.oreillynet.com/pub/a/oreilly/tim/news/2005/09/30/what-is-web-20.html. Accessed 30 September 2005

Richardson C, Moore C, Nicolson N (2009) Vendor snapshot: Lombardi blueprint bridges gap between process discovery and execution

Tapscott D (2008) Grown up digital: how the net generation is changing your world. McGraw-Hill, New York

vom Brocke J, Thomas O (2006) Reference modeling for organizational change: applying collaborative techniques for business engineering, Proceedings of the Twelfth Americas conference on information systems, Acapulco, Mexico, pp 680–688

vom Brocke J, Petry M, Sinnl T, Østerberg Kristensen B, Sonnenberg C (2010) Global process and data: the cultural journey at the Hilti Corporation. In: vom Brocke J, Rosemann M (eds) Handbook on business process management, vol 2. Springer, Heidelberg

Who Is Who

Gustav Aagesen

Norwegian University of Science and Technology
Trondheim, Norway
gustav.aagesen@idi.ntnu.no

Gustav Aagesen is currently working on a PhD degree in Information Systems within the field of e-government. He has an M.Sc. in Telematics from the Norwegian University of Science and Technology and spent part of his studies at the Asian Institute of Technology. He has experience from the software and consulting industry as a system architect, programmer, and project manager for government and nongovernment organizations.

Dr. Michael Adams

Senior Lecturer/Senior Researcher
Business Process Management Group
Faculty of Science and Information Technology
Queensland University of Technology
Brisbane, Australia
mj.adams@qut.edu.au

Michael Adams is a senior researcher within the BPM group at the Queensland University of Technology in Brisbane, Australia, and was awarded his PhD in 2007. He is currently directly responsible for the ongoing development and maintenance of the YAWL project. He designed, developed, and implemented two core YAWL services: the Worklet Service, which provides support for dynamic flexibility and exception handling; and the Resource Service, which provides for resource allocation and task routing, integrating a built-in worklist handler, dynamic forms generation, and administration tools. He is additionally responsible for various improvements to the YAWL Engine and Process Editor and is the primary developer of YAWL Release 2.0.

Dr. Alistair Barros

Global Research Leader
SAP Research
Brisbane, Australia
alistair.barros@sap.com

Alistair Barros is Global Research Leader of the Internet of Services research field at SAP Research and Adjunct Professor of Queensland University of Technology. His areas of interests are in Business Process Management, service sciences, business networks, and software architectures. He has a PhD in Computer Science from the University of Queensland, and 23 years experience of working in the industry at the Centre for Information Technology and Communications and the Australian Collaborative Research Centre for Distributed Systems Technology Centre before joining SAP in 2004. Alistair's research has contributed to a number of international standards (including WS-CDL and BPMN) and references (notably the workflow and service interaction patterns in the BPM field). His research has also contributed to SAP product transfers including the recently released NetWeaver Galaxy BPM platform, patents, and commercial consultancies. He has also contributed to the acquisition of research funding for Australian Research Council projects, the Australian Collaborative Research Centre on Smart Services and European Union projects including SUPER. At SAP Research, he is currently steering efforts towards a next-generation Global Service Delivery Framework and contributes to the SAP, IBM, and Oracle submission to the OMG for BPMN 2.0.

Dr. Thomas Bauer

Group Research and Advanced Engineering
Daimler AG
Process Management
Ulm, Germany
tb.bauer@daimler.com

Thomas Bauer is a researcher at the Daimler Research Center in Ulm, where he is working in the area of process management. Earlier, he was a member of the Department Databases and Information Systems at the University of Ulm where he finished his PhD thesis on the efficient management of enterprise-wide workflows in 2001. Current research areas include, in addition to the management of process variants: engineering processes, user-specific visualization of business processes, workflow execution with BPEL engines (especially the integration of human tasks), continuous modeling from business processes up to executable workflows, and the combination of process management with service-oriented architectures.

Prof. Dr. Jörg Becker

Professor of Information Systems
Managing Director
European Research Center for Information Systems
University of Münster
Münster, Germany
becker@ercis.uni-muenster.de

Jörg Becker is Professor for Information Systems and Information Management and head of the Department of Information Systems at the University of Münster. Since 2004, he has been Managing Director of the European Research Center for Information Systems, and since 2008, he has been Prorector for Structure, Planning, and Quality of the University of Münster. He is Editor-in-Chief of the journal ISEB – Information Systems and E-Business Management and member of the North Rhine-Westphalian Academy of Sciences. His research and teaching fields encompass process management, information modeling, reference modeling, management information systems, retail – IS, IS for manufacturing industries, and e-Government. Jörg has published his work in more than 350 refereed papers at international conferences and in scientific journals. In addition, he is author/editor of several books, in particular, project management, and he regularly serves in the editorial board of internationally perceived conferences and journals.

Jim Champy

Chairman
Perot Systems Corporation's
Boston, MA, USA
Jim.Champy@ps.net

Jim Champy, Chairman of Perot Systems' consulting practice, is recognized throughout the world for his work on leadership and management issues and on organizational change and business reengineering. He is the co-author with Michael Hammer of REENGINEERING THE CORPORATION: A Manifesto for Business Revolution, the book that introduced the world to the concept of reengineering. That book sold more than 3 million copies and spent more than a year on The New York Times best seller list. Champy was also a founder and CEO of Index Systems, later CSC/Index. Much of the original research and practice of reengineering was developed at Index, in collaboration with Hammer. Champy's latest writing is a series of books for the Financial Times Press. The fist volume – OUTSMART! – was published in April 2008 and shows how to achieve breakthrough growth by consistently outsmarting your competition. The second volume in the series, INSPIRE!, Why Customers Come Back, was published in April 2009. Champy earned his BS in 1963 and his MS in Civil Engineering in 1965 from M.I.T., and a JD degree from Boston College Law School in 1968. Champy is a life member of the MIT Corporation, Massachusetts Institute of Technology's Board of Trustees, and serves on the Board of Overseers of the Boston College Law School. He is also a member of the Board of Directors of Analog Devices, Inc.

Dr. Sue Conger

Director, IT and IT Service Management Programs
University of Dallas
Graduate School of Management
Irving, TX, USA
sconger@gsm.udallas.edu

Sue Conger has a Ph.D. in Computer Information Systems from the Stern School of Management at New York University. She is the author of The *New Software Engineering* and Planning and *Designing Effective Web Sites*, and she is publishing *Process Mapping and Management* while beginning IT Service Management. She is currently on the faculty of University of Dallas where she manages both Information Technology and IT Service Management (ITSM) programs. Professor Conger is the Vice President of Special Interest Groups and Chapters for the Association of Information Systems (AIS), President of special interest group on IT Services (AIS SIGSVC), serves on the national Academic Executive Committee for the ITSMF-USA (a practitioner organization), manages the ITSMF-USA Research Subcommittee, and hosts the ITSMF-USA Academic Forum. She is on five editorial boards and the program and planning committees for several conferences.

Fred A. Cummins

Co-chair OMG Business Modeling and
Integration Task Force
HP Fellow
Hewlett-Packard Company
Pinckney, MI, USA
fred.cummins@hp.com

Fred Cummins is an HP Fellow with a long career in the development of information systems and information systems consulting. Throughout his career, Fred has worked in the fields of distributed systems architecture and integration, object-oriented systems, knowledge-based systems, and strategic planning. He has developed systems or functioned as a technical advisor across multiple industries including manufacturing and distribution, financial services, transportation, insurance, healthcare, and government. Fred continually utilized leading edge technologies and has had significant influence on application development and business modeling technology through representation of Hewlett-Packard and co-chair of the Business Modeling and Integration task force at OMG (Object Management Group). Fred has authored three books, most recently *Building the Agile Enterprise with SOA, BPM and MBM* (Elsevier, 2009).

Prof. Dr. Thomas H. Davenport

President's Distinguished Professor of IT and Management
Babson College
Wellesley, MA, USA
tdavenport@babson.edu

Tom Davenport holds the President's Chair in Information Technology and Management at Babson College. He has published widely on the topics of analytics in business, process management, information and knowledge management, and enterprise systems. His most recent book is *Competing on Analytics: The New Science of Winning*. On process management topics, he wrote *Process Innovation* in 1993, and *Thinking for a Living* in 2005. He wrote or edited ten other books and has written over 100 articles for such publications as *Harvard Business Review, Sloan Management Review*, the *Financial Times*, and many other publications. Tom has also been a columnist for *CIO*, *InformationWeek*, and *Darwin* magazines. In 2003, he was named one of the world's "Top 25 Consultants" by *Consulting* magazine. In 2005, *Optimize* magazine's readers named him among the top 3 business and technology analysts in the world. In 2007 and 2008, he was named one of the most 100 influential people in the information technology industry by Ziff-Davis magazines.

Islay Davies

Business Process Management Advisor
Future Courts Program
Queensland Courts
Department of Justice and Attorney-General
Brisbane, Australia
Islay.davies@ssa.qld.gov.au

Islay Davies worked as the BPM Advisor for the Future Courts Program at the Department of Justice and Attorney-General (JAG), Brisbane, Australia, from 2007 until June 2010. She then moved into the role of Manager of Business Process Management at Shared Service Agency, also within Queensland Government, to progress their journey in becoming a process-centric organization. Islay has taught tertiary level courses on Systems Analysis and

Design and conducted research in the area of Business Process Modeling, towards a PhD with the Business Process Management Group at Queensland University of Technology. Her work has been published in a number of international journals, conference proceedings and a book chapter. She received a Highly Commended Reviewer award from the Australasian Conference on Information Systems in 2005. Islay is an active member of the Australian BPM Community of Practice (http://bpm-collaboration.com) as well as a number of other BPM-related associations and forums.

Dr. Alexander Dreiling

Research Program Manager
Business Process Management and Semantic Interoperability
SAP Research/SAP Australia Pty Ltd
Brisbane, Australia
alexander.dreiling@sap.com

Alexander Dreiling is a Program Manager at SAP Research, currently based in Brisbane, Australia. He received his MSc and PhD in Information Systems from the University of Münster in Germany. Prior to joining SAP Research, he worked for the European Research Center for Information Systems in Münster and Queensland University of Technology in Brisbane, Australia. His research so far led to approximately 40 journal papers (amongst them EJIS and DSS), conference papers, book chapters, books, panel sessions, and interviews (amongst them IEEE). His work at SAP was included several times in demos given by executive board members and advisory board members of SAP in keynotes or other occasions. His primary interest is in BPM, analytics, and Web 2.0.

Prof. Dr. Marlon Dumas

Institute of Computer Science
University of Tartu
Tartu, Estonia
marlon.dumas@ut.ee

Marlon Dumas is Professor of Software Engineering at University of Tartu, Estonia. From 2000 to 2008, he held various academic appointments at Queensland University of Technology in Brisbane, Australia. He has also been visiting professor at University of Grenoble (France) and visiting researcher at SAP Research, Australia. He conducts research in the fields of Enterprise Systems and Business Process Management and has co-authored numerous refereed research papers, industry papers, and patent applications in these fields. He is also co-editor of a textbook on Process-Aware Information Systems (John Wiley and Sons 2005).

Dr. Thorsten Falk

CEO, PICTURE GmbH
E-Government Research-Group
European Research Center for Information Systems
University of Münster
Münster, Germany
falk@picture-gmbh.de

Thorsten Falk is co-founder and CEO of the PICTURE GmbH, based in Münster, Germany. The company provides consultancy services in the areas of BPM, IT-service design, and implementation for public administrations. Clients include governmental agencies from the municipal to the federal level. Thorsten holds a doctorate from the University of Münster and has a background in BPM research, teaching, and consultancy. With his colleague, and co-founder, Dr. Lars Algermissen, Thorsten has been the creative force behind the development of the PICTURE methodology. The approach supports the analysis and design of business processes in public administration and has been successfully applied for more than 5 years. Thorsten has published more than 30 peer-reviewed papers on domain-specific BPM for public administrations at major international conferences as well as in journals and books.

Christian Flender

Faculty of Science and Technology
Queensland University of Technology
Brisbane, Australia
christian.flender@qut.edu.au

Mr Christian Flender is a PhD candidate at the Faculty of Science and Technology, Queensland University of Technology, Brisbane, Australia. He received his M.Sc. from the University of Bamberg, Germany, in 2006. Since then, he has been conducting research in the area of information systems analysis and design. His main interests comprise conceptual modeling, quantum information, and cognition.

Dr. Thomas Gulledge

President
Enterprise Integration, Inc.
Alexandria, VA, USA
Prof. Emeritus George Mason University
Alexandria, VA, USA
thomas.gulledge@eiisolutions.net

Thomas Gulledge is the President of Enterprise Integration, Inc. and Enterprise Integration Pte Ltd. He is also Professor Emeritus of Public

Policy and Engineering at George Mason University. For over 30 years, he has worked on the management and technical aspects of Enterprise Integration. Through his university research laboratory, he managed an extensive research program in Extended Enterprise Integration, with a special emphasis on Back-Office Integration, Product Lifecycle Management, and Supply Chain Integration and Management. Through Enterprise Integration, Inc., he has transferred many of these research concepts into reality with many projects in the USA, Europe, and the Asia-Pacific region. He is the developer of the Architecture-driven Enterprise Integration methodology, and he has published extensively on that subject. EII is currently designing and implementing executable architecture solutions in the USA and Asia.

Dr. Alena Hallerbach

Group Research and Advanced Engineering
Daimler AG
Ulm, Germany
alena.hallerbach@daimler.com

Alena Hallerbach has studied Computer Science at the University of Ulm from 2001 to 2006. Since 2004, she works at the Daimler AG at the Department of Data and Process Management. Her research areas were the modularization of development processes and the optimization of processes for product quality. She is currently developing new approaches for the management of process variants.

Dr. Michael Hammer

President
Hammer and Company, Inc.
Cambridge, MA, USA

Dr. Michael Hammer has been the driving force behind the business process revolution. He was the originator of both reengineering and the process enterprise, concepts that have changed how businesses around the world do business. Thousands of companies have turned his ideas into practice and profit. Dr. Hammer was the author of four books, including the international best-seller Reengineering the Corporation, which Forbes ranked as one of the three most important business books of the past twenty years. His articles have appeared in periodicals from *Harvard Business Review* to *The Economist*, and his work has been featured in every major business publication. An engineer by training, Dr. Hammer's research and teachings focused on how to transform business operations; his work was relentlessly pragmatic and immediately applicable. Dr. Hammer was, for many years, a Professor of Computer Science at the Massachusetts Institute of Technology and has been a visiting Professor at MIT and a Fellow at Oxford University. He was a founder of several high-technology companies, and he was named by Time as one of America's twenty-five most influential individuals. Dr. Hammer passed away in September 2008.

Paul Harmon

Executive Editor
Business Process Trends
Co-Founder and Chief Methodologist
BPTrends Associates
San Francisco, CA, USA
pharmon@bptrends.com

Paul Harmon is a Co-Founder, the Executive Editor, and Senior Market Analyst at Business Process Trends – http://www.bptrends.com – a popular Web site that provides free information on trends, directions, and best practices in Business Process Management. He is also a Co-Founder and Chief Methodologist of BPTrends Associates, a professional services company providing executive education, training, and consulting services for organizations interested in understanding and implementing Business Process Management. Paul is the author of some 15 books, including *Business Process Change: A Guide for Business Managers and BPM and Six Sigma Professionals*. Paul's business process activities began in the late 60's when he worked with Geary Rummler, managing the overall development and delivery of performance improvement programs. He has worked on major process change programs at Bank of America, Wells Fargo, Prudential, and Citibank, to name a few. He is a widely respected keynote speaker and has delivered executive seminars, workshops, briefings, and keynote addresses to conferences and organizations throughout the world.

Thomas Hettel

SAP Research
Brisbane, Australia
Faculty of Science and Technology
Queensland University of Technology
Brisbane, Australia
thomas.hettel@qut.edu.au

Mr Thomas Hettel is a Research Associate at SAP Research in Brisbane and a PhD candidate at the Faculty of Science and Technology, Queensland University of Technology, Brisbane, Australia. As part of his PhD research, he is interested in applications of abductive reasoning to achieve round-trip engineering between models. He is also interested in logic reasoning and execution semantics of workflow languages. He received his M.Sc. in Computer Science from the University of Karlsruhe, Germany, and was awarded "best student at SAP Research" in 2006 for his final year project on the impact analysis of meta-model constraints. At SAP Research, Thomas has contributed to the recently released NetWeaver Galaxy BPM platform and the SAP, IBM, and Oracle submission to the OMG for BPMN 2.0.

Dr. Birgit Hofreiter

Assistant Professor
Martin Hilti Chair of Business Process Management
Institute of Information Systems
University of Liechtenstein
Vaduz, Principality of Liechtenstein
birgit.hofreiter@uni.li

Birgit Hofreiter is assistant professor at the Institute of Information Systems of the University of Liechtenstein. In addition, she acts as the head of the Competence Center for Enterprise Content Management (CC ECM) and she is Vice-President, Special Interest Group, of the Liechtenstein Chapter of the Association for Information Systems (AIS). Before her employment at University of Liechtenstein, she was granted an Erwin-Schrödinger scholarship for a postdoc research fellowship position at University of Technology Sydney (UTS) from November 2006 until July 2008. Her research interests focus on electronic data interchange (EDI), interorganizational business process modeling, and service-oriented architectures. Since 2003, Birgit is actively involved in the standardization efforts of the United Nations Center for Trade Facilitation and Electronic Business (UN/CEFACT) and, since 2009, she has been teaching in the international Master Program in Business Process Management at the University of Liechtenstein (www.bpm-master.com). She co-edited UN/CEFACT's Modeling Methodology (UMM).

Dr. Christian Huemer

Business Informatics Group
Institute of Software Technology and Interactive Systems
Vienna University of Technology
Vienna, Austria
huemer@big.tuwien.ac.at

Christian Huemer is an associate professor at the Institute for Software Technology and Interactive Systems of the Vienna University of Technology. In addition, he acts as the director of the Studio Interorganizational Systems of Research Studios Austria, a national research agency. Currently, he is Chair of UN/CEFACT's Techniques and Methodologies Group (TMG) and member of UN/CEFACT's Forum Management. Furthermore, he is also leading its efforts on the UN/CEFACT's Modeling Methodology (UMM). He is the Chief Standards Officer (CSO) of Austria Pro/Austrian Chamber of

Commerce and serves on its board of directors. In addition, he is leading the section on e-Commerce of the German computer society, Gesellschaft für Informatik (GI).

Florian Johannsen

Department of Management Information Systems
Chair of Business Engineering
University of Regensburg
Regensburg, Germany
florian.johannsen@wiwi.uni-regensburg.de

Florian Johannsen graduated from the University of Regensburg in March 2006. He received his Diploma in Business Informatics focusing on the disciplines Business Engineering, Supply Chain Management, IT-Security, Information Systems, and E-Business. His diploma thesis was awarded by the BDVB (Bundesverband Deutscher Volks- und Betriebswirte e. V.). Since April 2006, he is a research assistant at the chair of Business Engineering at the University of Regensburg. During his work, he participates in several cooperation projects with industry in the field of quality management.

Dr. Dimka Karastoyanova

Junior Professor
Institute of Architecture of Application Systems
University of Stuttgart
Stuttgart, Germany
dimka.karastoyanova@iaas.uni-stuttgart.de

Dimka Karastoyanova is a staff junior professor at the Cluster of Excellence "Simulation Technology" and the Institute of Architecture of Application Systems (IAAS) at the University of Stuttgart, Germany. She holds a PhD in Computer Science from the Technical University Darmstadt, Germany and a M.Sc. degree in Computational Engineering from the University of Erlangen-Nuernberg, Germany. Her research focus is on applying workflow technology for business applications and scientific simulations in a service-oriented environment and on the Grid. Additionally, she is interested in extending service-based middleware and the workflow technology to enable flexible service compositions. Her current research work is in the area of service-based scientific workflows. She is a member of several European projects involving industry and academia that deal with open issues in service middleware, Business Process Management, semantics, and fundamental research in SOC (Service-Oriented Computing) driven by the BPM, SOC, Grid, and Software Engineering communities.

Sandy Kemsley

BPM Analyst
Kemsley Design Ltd.
Toronto, Canada
sandy@kemsleydesign.com

Sandy Kemsley is an independent analyst, systems architect, and blogger, specializing in Business Process Management and Enterprise 2.0. During her career of more than 20 years, she has started and run successful product and service companies, including a desktop workflow and document management product company and a 40-person services firm specializing in BPM and e-commerce. She was FileNet's (now IBM) Director of eBusiness Evangelism during the launch of their eProcess BPM product and has been a featured speaker on BPM and its impact on business at conferences and customer sites in several countries. Currently, she practices as a BPM analyst and architect, performing engagements for end-user organizations and BPM vendors; she also writes the popular "Column 2" BPM blog at http://www.column2.com and is a contributing author on several social media-related blogs.

Thomas Kohlborn

BPM Group
Faculty of Science and Technology
Queensland University of Technology
Brisbane, Australia
t.kohlborn@qut.edu.au

Thomas Kohlborn received his Master degree in Information Systems at the University of Münster, Germany, in 2008. The major subjects were Information Systems, Business Studies, and Controlling. He wrote his Master's Thesis at the Queensland University of Technology in cooperation with SAP Research, Australia and Queensland Government, Department of Public Works. Currently, he is enrolled at the Queensland University of Technology as a PhD student working on service portfolio management and aggregation.

Dr. Agnes Koschmider

Institute of Applied Informatics and Formal
Description Methods – AIFB
Karlsruhe Institute of Technology
Karlsruhe, Germany
agnes.koschmider@kit.edu

Agnes Koschmider is a senior researcher (PostDoc) at the Institute of Applied Informatics and Formal Description

Methods at Karlsruhe Institute of Technology (KIT). Her current research concentrates on mashup engineering and methods that assist users during business process modeling. After her PhD in 2007, she joined the group of Wil van der Aalst at TU Eindhoven and the group of Oscar Pastor at TU Valencia for research visits. From May 2010 until April 2011 Agnes received a PostDoctoral Fellowship from the University of Pretoria (South Africa). Agnes Koschmider has served as a reviewer in many international conferences and journals and co-organized national and international conferences. She is an elected member of the GI (German Society for Informatics) presidium since 2006.

Prof. Dr. John Krogstie

Norwegian University of Science and Technology
Trondheim, Norway
krogstie@idi.ntnu.no

John Krogstie holds a PhD (1995) and an MSc (1991) in information systems from the Norwegian University of Science and Technology (NTNU), where he is currently a full professor in information systems. He also serves as a senior advisor at SINTEF. John Krogstie is the Norwegian representative for IFIP TC8 and vice-chair of IFIP WG 8.1 on information system design and evaluations. He has published around 100 refereed papers in journals, books, and archival proceedings since 1991.

Prof. Dr. Akhil Kumar

Department of Supply Chain and Information Systems
Smeal College of Business
Penn State University
University Park, PA, USA
akhilkumar@psu.edu

Akhil Kumar is a professor of information systems at the Smeal College of Business at Penn State University. He received his PhD from the University of California, Berkeley, and has previously been on the faculties at Cornell University and the University of Colorado, and also spent one year at Bell Labs, Murray Hill, NJ. His research interests are in workflow systems, Web services, distributed information systems, and intelligent systems. He has published more than 70 papers in academic journals and international conferences. His work has appeared in *Information Systems Research*, *Journal of MIS*, *Management Science*, *ACM Transactions on Database Management*, *IEEE Transactions*, *Decision Support Systems*, and *INFORMS Journal on Computing*. He also serves on several editorial boards and program committees.

Prof. Dr. Susanne Leist

Professor of Information Systems
Department of Management Information Systems
Chair of Business Engineering
University of Regensburg
Regensburg, Germany
susanne.leist@wiwi.uni-regensburg.de

Susanne Leist took over the chair of Business Engineering at the Department of Management Information Systems at the University of Regensburg in December 2004. Prior to this role, she worked in several research and business projects and was teaching at several Universities in Germany and Switzerland. Her main research and teaching fields contain methods and techniques in Business Engineering, especially Process and Quality Management, Method Engineering, and Enterprise Architecture. She is the spokeswoman of the section information systems in the Financial Management of the Gesellschaft für Informatik, a partner of the Virtual Global University, sits in the Editorial Board of the journal "Banking and Information Technology," and acts as a reviewer in several international committees.

Prof. Dr. Frank Leymann

Institute of Architecture of Application Systems (IAAS)
University of Stuttgart
Stuttgart, Germany
leymann@iaas.uni-stuttgart.de

Frank Leymann is a full professor of computer science and director of the Institute of Architecture of Application Systems at the University of Stuttgart, Germany. His research interests include service-oriented computing and middleware, workflow- and business process management, programming in the large, transaction processing, integration technology, and architecture patterns. Before accepting his professor position in 2004, he worked for two decades for IBM Software Group building database and middleware products. Especially, since the late eighties, he worked continuously on workflow technology and became the father of IBM's workflow product set. Also, he is co-author of many standard specification, including WSFL, the BPEL family, and BPMN 2.0. His third party-funded research projects are all in the area of SOA and workflow/process technology.

Philipp Liegl

Business Informatics Group
Institute of Software Technology and Interactive Systems
Vienna University of Technology
Vienna, Austria
liegl@big.tuwien.ac.at

Philipp Liegl works as a research assistant at the Business Informatics group at the Vienna University of Technology, where he earned his master's degree in business informatics in 2006. In his PhD thesis, Philipp examines different approaches for the definition of business documents and their integration into service-oriented systems. Philipp has published over 20 publications in international journals and conferences on the topic of interorganizational business processes and business document modeling. Since 2005, Philipp is also actively involved in the standardization efforts of the United Nations Center for Trade Facilitation and Electronic Business (UN/CEFACT). He co-edited UN/CEFACT's Modeling Methodology (UMM) and currently serves as the lead editor for the UML Profile for Core Components (UPCC).

Dr. Mikael Lind

Associate Professor of Informatics
University of Borås
Viktoria Institute
Linköping University
Gothenburg, Sweden
Mikael.Lind@hb.se

Associate professor Mikael Lind is with the University of Borås, Viktoria Institute, and Linköping University, Sweden. He is the director of the informatics department and the founder of the Innovation Lab at the school of Business and Informatics in Borås. He is also the co-founder of the Swedish GSI (Graduate School of Informatics) and is active in different international communities such as Language/action and Pragmatic Web. He is also part of the management board for the AIS special interest group SIGPrag (http://www.sigprag.org). His research focus is on Pragmatist IS research on Co-design of Business and IT accommodating four research areas; Business Process Management, e-Service Innovation, Method Engineering, and Research Methods for Information Systems Development. He is also the project manager of the citizen-centric e-service project, e-Me (http://www.e-me.se), as well as associate editor for the open journal Systems, Signs, and Actions (http://www.sysiac.org).

Prof. Dr. Jan Mendling

Institute of Information Systems
School of Business and Economics
Humboldt-Universität zu Berlin
Berlin, Germany
jan.mendling@wiwi.hu-berlin.de

Jan Mendling is a Professor for Information Systems at Humboldt-Universität zu Berlin, Germany. His research areas include Business Process Management, Conceptual Modeling, and Enterprise Systems. He has published more than 100 research papers and articles among others in *ACM Transactions on Software Engineering and Methodology, Information Systems, Data and Knowledge Engineering, Formal Aspects of Computing*, and *Enterprise Information Systems*. He is member of the editorial board of two international journals. His PhD thesis has won the Heinz-Zemanek-Award of the Austrian Computer Society and the German Targion-Award for dissertations in the area of strategic information management. He is one of the founders and chair of the Berlin BPM Community of Practice (http://www.bpmb.de) and organizer of several academic events on process management.

Joyce Nakatumba

Architecture of Information Systems Group
Eindhoven University of Technology
Eindhoven, The Netherlands
jnakatum@tue.nl

Joyce Nakatumba studied Computer Science at Makerere University Kampala Uganda, where she received a Masters Degree in Computer Science in 2006. Currently, she is a PhD candidate in the Architecture of Information Systems group at the Department of Mathematics and Computer Science, Eindhoven University of Technology. Her research interests include Business Process Management, simulation, and process mining.

Prof. Dr. Andreas Oberweis

Institute of Applied Informatics and Formal
Description Methods – AIFB
Karlsruhe Institute of Technology
Karlsruhe, Germany
andreas.oberweis@kit.edu

Andreas Oberweis received a Diploma Degree in Industrial Engineering from the University of Karlsruhe in 1984 and a

Doctoral Degree in Computer Science from the University of Mannheim in 1990. From 1985 to 1995, he was Research Assistant at the Universities of Darmstadt, Mannheim, and Karlsruhe. In 1995, he received a Habilitation Degree in Applied Computer Science from the University of Karlsruhe. From 1995 to 2003, he was a Full Professor for Information Systems at Goethe-University in Frankfurt/Main. Since 2003, he is a Professor for Applied Informatics at the University of Karlsruhe. Since 2004, he is also a Director at the Research Center for Information Technologies (FZI) Karlsruhe. His research and teaching interests include Business Process Engineering and Software Engineering, Distributed Information Systems, Digital Libraries, and eCollaboration.

Dr. Chun Ouyang

Senior Lecturer/Researcher
Business Process Management Group
Faculty of Science and Technology
Queensland University of Technology
Brisbane, Australia
c.ouyang@qut.edu.au

Chun Ouyang is a researcher within the BPM Group at the Queensland University of Technology, Australia. She is also a member of the Australian Research Council Centre of Excellence for Creative Industries and Innovation. She received her PhD in Computer Systems Engineering from the University of South Australia in 2004. Her research interests are in the areas of workflow management and its application, process modeling and analysis, workflow languages and formalization. Since 2006, she has actively undertaken research in application of YAWL to screen business.

Prof. Dr. Michael P. Papazoglou

European Research Institute in Service Science
Tilburg University
Tilburg, The Netherlands
mikep@uvt.nl

Michael P. Papazoglou is a Professor at Tilburg University where he is the Director of the European Research Institute in Service Science (ERISS) and the Scientific Director of the European Network of Excellence in Software Services and Systems (S-Cube). He is also an honorary professor at the University of Trento in Italy, and professorial fellow at the Universities Lyon (France), University of New South Wales (Australia) and Rey Juan Carlos, Madrid (Spain). Prior to this, he was full Professor and head of School of Information Systems at the Queensland University of Technology in Brisbane, Australia. His research interests lie in the areas of service-oriented computing, Web services, large-scale data sharing, business processes, and federated and distributed information systems. He has published 18 books in these topics and has authored well over 150 journal and conference papers. Most of his papers appeared in very selective and reputable conferences and journals. He is a golden core member and a distinguished visitor of the IEEE Computer Science section.

Dr. Daniel Pfeiffer

European Research Center for Information Systems
University of Münster
Münster, Germany
mail@daniel-pfeiffer.de

Daniel Pfeiffer holds a PhD in Information Systems from Westfälische Wilhelms-Universität Münster and Master's degree in Information Systems from Dresden University of Technology. Daniel's main research interests are in the area of business process modeling and analysis as well as in the field of method engineering. He has written more than 50 refereed papers that have been published in major IS-journals and at leading IS-conferences. Daniel was awarded with the Lohrmann medal in 2004, and he received a scholarship from the German National Academic Foundation. He has worked as visiting assistant in research at Yale University, as research associate at the European Research Center for Information Systems (ERCIS), and as freelance consultant in the public sector and the retail industry. Since March 2009, Daniel is a consultant in the Münster office of the Boston Consulting Group.

Artem Polyvyanyy

Business Process Technology Group
Hasso Plattner Institute of IT Systems Engineering at the University of Potsdam
Potsdam, Germany
artem.polyvyanyy@hpi.uni-potsdam.de

Artem Polyvyanyy is a research assistant and a PhD student at Business Process Technology research group at Hasso Plattner Institute of IT Systems Engineering at the University of Potsdam, Germany. He is a member of the Research School on Service-Oriented Systems Engineering at Hasso Plattner Institute. His research areas are Business Process Management and service-oriented computing. In particular, his topics of interest are process abstraction, modeling of ad-hoc processes, and service science. Artem has published his research results at international conferences on Business Process Management. He has a strong background in computer science, software engineering, and Business Process Management from the National University of Kyiv-Mohyla Academy in Ukraine and Hasso Plattner Institute in Germany. His industry experience includes internships at Wincor-Nixdorf GmbH in Hamburg, Germany, and SAP Labs in Palo Alto, USA.

Dr. Michael Räckers

European Research Center for Information Systems
University of Münster
Münster, Germany
michael.raeckers@ercis.uni-muenster.de

Michael Räckers holds a PhD in Information Systems from University of Münster. Since 2010 he works as Assistant Professor at the Chair of Information Systems and Information Management at the University of Münster. Before starting his PhD, he worked 5 years as assistant in a project on the process-oriented implementation and monitoring of a quality management system based on ISO 9000:2000. His current research activities focus on Business Process Management, Distributed Process Modeling, and E-Government. Michael has published more than 25 peer-reviewed papers on domain-specific BPM for public administrations at major international conferences as well as in journals and books.

Alan J. Ramias

Performance Design Lab
Chandler, AZ, USA
Aramias@ThePDLab.c

Alan Ramias is a Partner of the Performance Design Lab (PDL). PDL is a consulting and training organization with decades of experience in applying BPM and performance improvement. The founder of PDL was the late Dr. Geary Rummler. PDL continues to evolve and expand the theory base and methodologies introduced in Rummler's book, "Improving Performance." Alan started Motorola, where he worked for ten years as an internal consultant. He was a member of the team that founded Motorola University and was the first person to introduce Geary Rummler's pioneering concepts in process improvement and management to business units within Motorola. Alan joined The Rummler–Brache Group in 1991 and was a project leader at companies like Shell, Hewlett-Packard, 3M, Citibank, Motorola, Steelcase, Citgo, Hermann Miller, Louisiana-Pacific, and Bank One. He became a partner and Managing Director of Consulting Services at RBG and was responsible for selecting, training and overseeing RBG's consultant teams.

Dr. Jan Recker

Senior Lecturer
BPM Group
Faculty of Science and Technology
Queensland University of Technology
Brisbane, Australia
j.recker@qut.edu.au

Jan Recker is Senior Lecturer in the Business Process Management Group at the Information Systems Program at Queensland University of Technology Brisbane, Australia. He received a BScIS and MScIS from the University of Münster, Germany, and a PhD in Information Systems from Queensland University of Technology. His research interests include BPM Standards, User-centered Systems Analysis and Design, Process Flexibility and Post-Adoptive Usage. He is the author or co-author of more than 60 refereed articles, chapters, and proceedings. Findings from his research have been published in journals such as the *Journal of the Association for Information Systems, Information Systems, the Communications of the Association for Information Systems, the Australasian Journal of Information Systems, the Business Process Management Journal*, and others. He also manages QUT's Continuing Professional Education offerings on Business Process Management (http://www.bpm-training.com).

Micheal Reeves

Queensland Courts
Department of Justice and Attorney-General
Brisbane, Australia
Micheal.Reeves@justice.qld.gov.au

Micheal Reeves is a Business Process Expert with the Future Courts Program at the Department of Justice and Attorney-General, Brisbane, Australia. His 28 year career has encompassed all levels of the Queensland Courts system resulting in a wide range of experience and skills. He currently utilizes those skills in the analysis, modeling, and design/redesign of business processes, rules, and workflows to develop improved operational processes.

Prof. Dr. Manfred Reichert

Institute of Databases and Information Systems
University of Ulm
Ulm, Germany
manfred.reichert@uni-ulm.de

Manfred Reichert has been a full professor for Computer Science and Co-leader of the Institute of Databases and

Information Systems at the University of Ulm since 2008. From 2005 to 2007, he worked as Associate Professor at the University of Twente (UT) where he was coordinator of the strategic research initiatives on E-health (2005–2006) and Service-oriented Computing (2007). At UT, he was also member of the Management Board of the Centre for Telematics and Information Technology, which is the largest ICT research institute in the Netherlands. Manfred has worked on advanced issues related to process management technology and service-oriented computing for ten years, and he has published more than 150 refereed papers in these areas. Together with Peter Dadam, he pioneered the work on the ADEPT process management system, which currently provides the most advanced technology for realizing flexible process-aware information systems. Manfred was PC Co-chair of the BPM'08 conference in Milan and will be General Co-chair of the BPM'09 conference in Ulm.

Dr. Ir. Hajo A. Reijers

Associate Professor of Information Systems
School of Industrial Engineering
Eindhoven University of Technology
Eindhoven, The Netherlands
h.a.reijers@tue.nl

Hajo Reijers is an Associate Professor in the Information Systems group at Eindhoven University of Technology and an Affiliated Professor with the TIAS/Nimbas Business School of Tilburg University. His research interests are Business Process Management topics in general, and more specifically, business process redesign, business process modeling, workflow management technology, and simulation. He is the author/editor of a book on Business Process Management and more than 70 refereed papers (including *JMIS, Information systems, Data and Knowledge Engineering*, and *Organization Studies*) as well as a member of the editorial board member of two international journals. He is one of the founders of the Dutch BPM-Forum (http://www.bpm-forum.org) and is the co-chair of the 2009 edition of the International Conference on Business Process Management (http://www.bpm2009.org).

Prof. Dr. Michael Rosemann

Professor of Information Systems
Co-Leader of the BPM Group
Faculty of Science and Technology
Queensland University of Technology
Brisbane, Australia
m.rosemann@qut.edu.au

Michael Rosemann is a Professor and Co-Leader of the Business Process Management Group at Queensland University of Technology, Brisbane, Australia. His research areas are Business Process Management, Enterprise Systems, and conceptual modeling. He is the author/editor of seven books and more than 140 refereed papers (incl. *MISQ, IEEE TKDE, JAIS, DSS, Information Systems*) and Editorial Board member of seven international journals. His publications have been translated into German, Russian, Portuguese, and Mandarin. Dr Rosemann's PhD students have won the Australian award for the best PhD thesis in Information Systems in 2007 and in 2008. He is the founder and chair of the Australian BPM Community of Practice (http://bpm-collaboration.com) and has been the Chair of the 5th International Business Process Management Conference in 2007. He regularly conducts executive training in BPM (http://www.bpm-training.com) and provides BPM-related advice to organizations from various industries including telecommunications, banking, insurance, utility, retail, public sector, logistics, and film industry.

Anne Rozinat

Information Systems Group
Eindhoven University of Technology
Eindhoven, The Netherlands
a.rozinat@tue.nl

Anne Rozinat received her BSc and MSc degrees in Software Engineering from the Hasso Plattner-Institute (HPI), University of Potsdam, Germany. She is currently a PhD candidate in the Information Systems Group at the Department of Industrial Engineering and Innovation Sciences of the Eindhoven University of Technology. Her research interests include process mining, data mining, Business Process Management, process model evaluation techniques, and simulation.

Geary A. Rummler

Performance Design Lab
Tucson, AZ, USA

Dr. Geary A. Rummler was the founding Partner of the Performance Design Lab (PDL), where he was continuing his lifelong work on organizational performance improvement in complex systems until his death in October 2008. Prior to founding the Performance Design Lab, Geary was the founding partner of The Rummler–Brache Group, an organization that became a leader in the business process improvement and management business in the 1980s and 1990s. Prior to that, Geary was President of the Kepner–Tregoe Strategy Group, specialists in strategic decision making; co-founder and president of Praxis Corporation, an innovator in the analysis and improvement of human performance; co-founder and director of the University of Michigan's Center for Programmed

Learning for Business. In addition to consulting and teaching, Geary published a steady stream of articles and a variety of books. In 1988, he co-authored Training and Development: A Guide for Professionals, with George S. Odiorne. In 1990, he co-authored Improving Performance, How to Manage the White Space on the Organization Chart with Alan P. Brache. Geary received his MBA and Ph.D. from the University of Michigan.

Dr. Nick Russell

Eindhoven University of Technology
Eindhoven, The Netherlands
n.c.russell@tue.nl

Nick Russell has 20 years' experience in the IT industry in a variety of technical and senior management roles. During this time, he has led a number of high-profile systems integration, commercial research, and product development initiatives for organizations in the financial services and retail sectors. He is currently conducting research into Business Process Management and process-aware information systems at Eindhoven University of Technology in the Netherlands. Over the past 5 years, he has been the driving force for the extension of the workflow patterns to the data, resource, and exception handling perspectives and the development of the newYAWL business process modeling reference language.

Rainer Schuster

Vienna University of Technology
Vienna, Austria
Schuster@ec.tuwien.ac.at

Rainer Schuster received his MSc in Business Informatics at the Vienna University of Technology in 2006. His master thesis focuses on his work within the UN/CEFACT (United Nations Centre for Trade Facilitation and Electronic Business) standardization group and is located in the field of B2B. It was supervised at the Department of Distributed and Multimedia Systems at the University of Vienna and was awarded with the 1st prize of the INITS award 2006. Currently, he is working on his PhD thesis and employed as a researcher at the Institute for Software Technology and Interactive Systems (Electronic Commerce Group) at the Vienna University of Technology. His research interest focuses on business modeling and business process modeling methodologies within the field of inter-organizational data exchange between information systems.

Dr. Ulf Seigerroth

Assistant Professor of Informatics
Co-director of CenIT
Jönköping University
Jönköping, Sweden
ulf.seigerroth@jth.hj.se

Assistant Professor Ulf Seigerroth is with Jönköping International Business School, School of Engineering, Sweden. Seigerroth is the co-director and co-founder of CenIT (Centre of Evolving IT in Networked organizations) (http://www.hj.se/cenit). From 2004 to 2007, Seigerroth was Head of Department of Informatics. Seigerroth is one of the co-founders of GSI (Graduate School of Informatics) that was launched in April 2008. He is also part of the AIS special interest group SIGPrag (http://www.sigprag.org). Seigerroth's current research direction is towards issues concerning business and IT-alignment and transformation. Within this area, more specific issues of interest are enterprise modeling, enterprise architecture, information logistics, method engineering, co-design, and IT economics. His research is characterized by empirically driven and theory- and method informed development (action research). He is involved in different action research projects focusing on alignment of business processes and information systems and information logistics.

Sergey Smirnov

Business Process Technology Group
Hasso Plattner Institute of IT Systems Engineering at the University of Potsdam
Potsdam, Germany
sergey.smirnov@hpi.uni-potsdam.de

Sergey Smirnov is a PhD student at Business Process Technology research group at Hasso Plattner Institute of IT Systems Engineering at the University of Potsdam, Germany. His research interests include Business Process Management and process modeling methodologies with a focus on abstraction of business process models, customized business process views, and labeling of model elements. Sergey is an author of several conference and workshop papers. He gave a number of talks at international conferences on Business Process Management. Sergey graduated with honors from Saratov State University, Russia. Afterwards, he continued the education at Hasso Plattner Institute, where he earned a master of science degree in software engineering. During his studies, Sergey won fellowships of DAAD and Potanin Foundation Federal Program. His industry experience includes working for Russian software companies and an internship at SAP Labs in Palo Alto, USA.

Prof. Dr. Arthur H.M. ter Hofstede

Professor of Information Systems
Co-Leader of the BPM Group
Queensland University of Technology
Brisbane, Australia
arthur@yawlfoundation.org

Arthur ter Hofstede received his PhD in Computer Science from the University of Nijmegen in the Netherlands in 1993. Currently, he works as a Professor in the Information Systems Discipline of Queensland University of Technology in Brisbane, Australia, where he is co-leader of the BPM group. His main research interests are in the conceptual and formal foundations of workflow. He is involved in both the Workflow Patterns Initiative (http://www.workflowpatterns.com) and the YAWL (Yet Another Workflow Language) Initiative (http://www.yawl-system.com).

Prof. Dr. Ir. Wil van der Aalst

Professor of Information Systems
Leader of the AIS Group
Eindhoven University of Technology
Eindhoven, The Netherlands
w.m.p.v.d.aalst@tue.nl

Prof. Dr. Ir. Wil van der Aalst is a full professor of Information Systems at the Technische Universiteit Eindhoven (TU/e) having a position in both the Department of Mathematics and Computer Science and the Department of Technology Management. Currently, he is also an adjunct professor at Queensland University of Technology (QUT) working within the BPM group there. His research interests include workflow management, process mining, Petri nets, Business Process Management, process modeling, and process analysis. Wil van der Aalst has published more than 100 journal papers, 13 books (as author or editor), 200 refereed conference/workshop publications, and 30 book chapters. Many of his papers are highly cited (he has an H-index of more than 73 according to Google Scholar) and his ideas have influenced researchers, software developers, and standardization committees working on process support. He has been a co-chair of many conferences including the Business Process Management conference, the International Conference on Cooperative Information Systems, the International conference on the Application and Theory of Petri Nets, and the IEEE International Conference on Services Computing. He is also editor/member of the editorial board of several journals.

Prof. Dr. Jan vom Brocke

Martin Hilti Chair of Business Process Management
Director, Institute of Information Systems
University of Liechtenstein
Vaduz, Principality of Liechtenstein
jan.vom.brocke@uni.li

Jan vom Brocke holds the Martin Hilti Chair in Business Process Management (BPM) at the University of Liechtenstein. He is Director of the Institute of Information Systems and President of the Liechtenstein Chapter of the Association of Information Systems (AIS). Jan has more than ten years of experience in BPM projects and serves as an advisor to a wide range of institutions. He has published his work in more than 150 refereed papers at internationally perceived conferences and journals and is an invited speaker on BPM at a number of universities, such as the University of St. Gallen in Switzerland, the LUISS University in Italy, or the University of California at Berkeley. In Liechtenstein, Jan is initiator and academic director of Europe's first international university Master Program in Business Process Management (www.bpm-master.com). His PhD students regularly take part in doctoral consortia, just recently two of which have been awarded junior research fellows of the 3rd Lindau Nobel Prize Laureates Meeting in Economic Sciences.

Jianrui Wang

Department of Industrial and Manufacturing Engineering
Pennsylvania State University
University Park, PA, USA
JerryWang@psu.edu

Jianrui Wang is a PhD student at Department of Industrial and Manufacturing Engineering at Pennsylvania State University at University Park. His research areas are Business Process Management, Supply Chain Management, and Systems Modeling and Simulation.

Prof. Dr. Mathias Weske

Business Process Technology Group
Hasso Plattner Institute of IT Systems Engineering at the University of Potsdam
Potsdam, Germany
mathias.weske@hpi.uni-potsdam.de

Professor Dr. Mathias Weske is chair of the Business Process Technology research group at Hasso Plattner Institute of IT Systems Engineering at the University of Potsdam, Germany. His research interests include Business Process Management, process choreographies, process modeling methodologies, and service-oriented computing. He leads Oryx, an open source Business Process Management framework on the Web. Dr. Weske has published twelve books and over 70 scientific papers in journals and conferences. He is on the steering committee of the BPM conference series. He is the chairperson of EMISA, the German Computer Science Society Special Interest Group on Development Methods for Information Systems and their Application. Dr. Weske has published a textbook on Business Process Management. He is also the co-author of The Process, a narrative on using the Business Process Modeling Notation BPMN.

Dr. Moe Thandar Wynn

Lecturer/Researcher
Business Process Management Group
Faculty of Science and Technology
Queensland University of Technology
Brisbane, Australia
m.wynn@qut.edu.au

Moe Thandar Wynn is a researcher within the BPM Group at Queensland University of Technology, Brisbane, Australia. She received her PhD degree in the area of workflows with cancellation regions and OR-joins in 2007. She has been actively involved in the Yet Another Workflow Language (YAWL) research initiative (http://www.yawlfoundation.org) since 2004. Her main research interests include process automation, process verification, process simulation, process mining, Petri nets and Reset nets, service-oriented architectures, workflow patterns, and YAWL. She has published more than 20 referred papers on the topics of advanced synchronization (OR-join), reduction rules, workflow verification, and process simulation. She also conducts executive training on Business Process Modelling Notation (BPMN) for a number of Queensland government agencies.

Marco Zapletal

Electronic Commerce Group
Institute of Software Technology and Interactive Systems
Vienna University of Technology
Vienna, Austria
marco@ec.tuwien.ac.at

Marco Zapletal received his PhD in "business informatics" from the Vienna University of Technology in 2009. There, he is currently employed as a university assistant at the Electronic Commerce Group.

Furthermore, during his first PhD year, he was working as an Enterprise Architect at T-Mobile Austria. He was granted a Siemens scholarship for visiting TU Eindhoven in 2009. His research interests focus on electronic data interchange (EDI) and business-to-business electronic commerce (B2B), business process modeling, service-oriented architectures, and the derivation of deployment artifacts (e.g., Web service choreographies) from business process models. Marco has published over 20 publications in international journals and conferences. He chairs the Business Process Working Group (BPWG) within the United Nations Center for Trade Facilitation and Electronic Business (UN/CEFACT) and co-authors the UN/CEFACT's Modeling Methodology (UMM).

Dr. Gregor Zellner

Department of Management Information Systems
Chair of Business Engineering
University of Regensburg
Regensburg, Germany
gregor.zellner@wiwi.uni-regensburg.de

Gregor Zellner is senior research associate at the Department of Management Information Systems, particularly Business Engineering at the University of Regensburg, Germany. He has earned his doctorate from the University of St. Gallen in 2003 and is now working on his habilitation. His research areas are within the field of Business Engineering with a focus on quality management (especially Six Sigma), Business Process Management, and enterprise architecture. He has international contacts with the BPM Group at Queensland University of Technology, Brisbane, Australia, and cooperates with the Dublin City University in the field of Business Process Management. His research is internationally published and presented at conferences (e.g., ICIS, ACM (SAC), HICSS), where he regularly serves as associate editor.

Index

Note: Page numbers in Roman represent Volume 1. Those in italics are in Volume 2.

V

W

X

Y

Z

Kolibri 360 GmbH
Ferdinand-Jühlke-Straße 7
99095 Erfurt, Deutschland
produktsicherheit@kolibri360.de